Macedonia and Greece

To my beautiful Lillian

Macedonia and Greece

*The Struggle to Define
a New Balkan Nation*

JOHN SHEA

McFarland & Company, Inc., Publishers
Jefferson, North Carolina, and London

British Library Cataloguing-in-Publication data are available

Library of Congress Cataloguing-in-Publication Data

Shea, John
    Macedonia and Greece : the struggle to define a new Balkan nation /
John Shea.
        p.   cm.
    Includes index.
    ISBN 0-7864-0228-8 (library binding : 50# alkaline paper)   ∞
    1. Greece — Foreign relations — Macedonia (Republic)   2. Macedonia
(Republic) — Foreign relations — Greece.   3. Macedonia (Republic) —
International status.   4. Greece — Foreign relations — 1974–
5. Greece — Ethnic relations.   6. Macedonia (Republic) — Ethnic
relations.   7. Macedonia — Name.   I. Title.
DF787.M275S4   1997
327.49560495 — dc20   96-32035
                                                          CIP

Manufactured in the United States of America

*McFarland & Company, Inc., Publishers
Box 611, Jefferson, North Carolina 28640*

Table of Contents

LIST OF MAPS

Introduction

This book was produced as a response to a relatively recent argument between Greeks and Macedonians. Although an examination of that argument remains central to this discussion, ultimately the ideas covered go far beyond this specific issue. The dispute between Greeks and Macedonians has a special significance in world affairs today because of the importance of Macedonia in the Balkans. This tiny country, the new Republic of Macedonia, has a history of entanglement with small and large powers within the Balkans, with western Europe, with Russia and with Turkey. Macedonia is seen as a potential flash point for a war of major international proportions. Its affairs have a much greater potential to draw nations into conflict than any other part of the Balkans, including Bosnia-Herzegovina. This is not because it is intrinsically important in the overall scheme of things, but because so many nations believe their national interests are at stake there. For the first time in its history the United Nations has placed troops in a country, in Macedonia, as a preventive measure, to discourage external aggression. Half of these troops are American. This gives an indication of how important Macedonia is in the eyes of the international community in general and of the United States in particular.

Greece is one of the important Balkan powers in the late twentieth century. It has had a special relationship with western Europe since the time of its independence in the early part of the nineteenth century. Although it has a relatively small population, its position at the southern edge of the Balkans, a bulwark against the communist alliance to the north, gave it a special role in the North Atlantic Treaty Organization. The United States provided billions of dollars in military aid to Greece to help it fulfill this role. Greece has tried, also, to become a vital political and economic part of Europe. While the ending of the cold war has taken away specific factors that could lead to an active war in the region, some of the same processes that led to the breakup of the communist monolith have allowed the appearance of what Greece perceives as a new threat, the new Macedonian nation. This perceived threat provoked Greece into actions that other nations, including the United States, saw as a threat to peace in the Balkans. The argument between Greece and Macedonia, while less heated than previously, is still unresolved. More importantly, the factors that created Greek sensitivity remain, and are unlikely to be improved by any negotiation between Greece and Macedonia. These matters have to do with the continuing importance of nationalist feelings within Greece, its exiling of Greek citizens of Macedonian ethnicity in the recent past, and its ongoing refusal to acknowledge the human rights, and even the existence, of a Slavic-speaking minority, despite repeated rebukes on the issue from the United States State Department and various international human rights groups.

Of course, Greece, although important in the Balkans, is but one of the parties interested in the outcome of events in Macedonia. Other nations with which it has alliances, such as rump Yugoslavia and even Bulgaria, and those with which it has traditional enmities, such as Albania and Turkey, have become actively involved in Macedonian affairs. In many cases the involvements are sometimes subtle rather than obvious. Things are not always what they appear to be on the surface. The intrigues that characterized the "Macedonian question" at the end of the nineteenth century seem to be playing out again today. The Greek argument with Macedonia is seen by many commentators as one instance of such intrigues. The case that has presented explicitly to the world often seems inadequate to account for the level of emotion that Greeks have expressed, and for the vigor of the political action they have taken. This book attempts to evaluate the Greek position and to present explanations for the conflict that go beyond what Greek spokespersons have presented to the world.

Most of the arguments presented to the world have come from the Greek side. When I first began to investigate the conflict I was curious to know about the other side of the case, or at least to discover if there was any case for the Macedonian side. This book is a discussion of that case as it gradually unfolded for me, and a consideration of some of the broader issues within Greece, Macedonia and the rest of Macedonia's neighbors in the Balkans.

The picture is a complex one, and I first need to clarify some of my terminology. By Greeks, I mean those people who come from or feel ties with the nation that we recognize as modern Greece. By Macedonians, I mean those people who live in or feel ties with the former Yugoslav Republic of Macedonia. This is not a very precise way of speaking about them since there is quite a mixture of ethnic groups in the new Republic of Macedonia. I believe it is reasonable to use this label when speaking of Macedonia in an international context. When speaking of groups within the country, finer distinctions must be made. Sometimes the major ethnic group in Macedonia is called "Vardar Macedonians," after the river that runs through their land, and they call Slavic-speaking Macedonians who live in Northern Greece "Aegean Macedonians." Some of the Aegean Macedonians may see themselves as both "Greek," in terms of their state of citizenship, and "Macedonian" in terms of ethnicity.

A particular focus of attack by the Greeks is the use of the name Macedonia by the former Southern Republic of Yugoslavia. In international forums, such as the United Nations, the Greeks alone tried to prevent the establishment of an independent country called Macedonia. At the beginning of the Greek campaign against Macedonia the international media were filled with images of emotional demonstrations by Greeks in various parts of the world. There were huge and very expensive advertisements taken out in national newspapers in the United States, Canada, Australia, and other countries, by Greeks presenting their own particular concerns on the issue. The Greek government sponsored cultural exhibitions and academic seminars in these countries aiming to convey the same message. Much of this persuasive effort has occurred only in the last seven or eight years, an interesting point by itself.

Probably everyone has heard the idea that the use of the name Macedonia by the Macedonians is a threat to Greece because it shows the expansionist ambitions of the Macedonians. Usually this idea is presented alongside the view that the name Macedonia is Greek in any case and should be reserved for Greek use. However, the Greek claims go far beyond these assertions. This book presents ideas that contradict the Greek claims. In essence this book presents the counter-charge that the (formerly Yugoslav) Macedonians have a better claim to the name and the history of Macedonia than the Greeks in general, and even the northern Greeks who live in the lands that more than two thousand years ago formed the heartlands of the great Macedonian Empire. This might seem like an extraordinary position to take, given public perceptions about the issues. Such public perceptions stand as testimony to the effectiveness of the Greek presentation of their argument. However, it is now my view that an alternative argument can be made convincingly. At the very least this indicates that the issues are not black and white. It also tells us some very important things about Greek nationalism and its possible role in shaping Balkan affairs.

We need to be aware that the understandings, emotions and reactions of peoples must be considered separately from the aims of governments. It would be surprising if the mass of Greeks and Macedonians had any real knowledge of the historical matters that underlie the political claims. Their opinions will have been shaped by ideas available in the media, or presented by their governments. For the most part only those who have personally lived through significant events will have reliable first-hand knowledge of what really happened, and that confines us to very recent history. It would be naive in the extreme to believe that the publicly stated positions of any government that gets involved in the dispute between Greeks and Macedonians, including the Greek and Macedonian governments, will necessarily reflect any concern for historical truth. Indeed it would be realistic to expect a hidden agenda. The political purpose of modern Greeks, those who have been most actively bringing Macedonian issues to the world public, can only be surmised. Some analysts, whose views will be presented in some detail later in this book, suggest that it is all about ensuring stability within northern Greece, where strong sympathy with the Macedonian cause is said to be causing concern for the central government. Some Macedonians believe that it is about Greek intentions to take over some of their territory and strengthen Greek borders. Suffice it to say at this point that territorial strength and security has been of great concern to all the relatively powerful Balkan states, Serbia, Bulgaria and Greece, during this century, and it would be surprising if it were not very much a part of their present agenda.

It would probably be best to begin with a presentation of the Greek argument. This argument has been disseminated in various ways in America, including full-page political advertisements in leading newspapers, travel advertisements inviting people to visit "Macedonia" (meaning northern Greece), English-language materials published in Athens and distributed by the Greek embassy, and pamphlets distributed in Greek Orthodox churches. Recent statements by the Greek government have not deviated from these sources, so they remain a fair means of discovering what the Greeks appear to be concerned about. On the 26th of April 1992 and the 10th of May 1992, an organization called "Americans for the Just Resolution of the Macedonian Issue" placed full-page advertisements in the *New York Times*. The first of these was headlined, "Macedonia, what's in a name"; the second, "The name "Macedonia" is a time bomb! Mr President, you can defuse it." In both cases the appeal was directed at then president George Bush. The first of these advertisements focuses on the idea of a threat to Greece from a state called Macedonia. While the text says, "Recognize the Republic of Skopje, yes!" it adds, "With the name 'Republic of Macedonia,' why?" Thus, on the face of, it the problem is not so much the existence of the new state, but the possible consequences of it bearing the name Macedonia. The implication is that this name will somehow rekindle past territorial ambitions that would not be so easily stirred with a different name.

The advertisement gives a lot of attention to the involvement of Tito and Yugoslavia in the Greek civil war, referring for instance to "former communist designs on sovereign Greece." It informs the reader that

"in 1946, Tito and Stalin armed insurgents to trigger a bloody Civil war and unimaginable years of suffering for the Greek nation.... Today, Skopje's government aims to perpetuate the nightmare."

The advertisement goes on to say that the "Skopje's government":

• claims that Macedonians exist "under occupation" in Greece;

• calls for the "liberation" of all Macedonians, even those who regard themselves as free Greeks;

• issues currency depicting landmarks of sovereign Greek territory;

• publishes maps incorporating fully one-third of mainland Greece;

• has a constitution proclaiming Tito's expansionist goals, calling for the "unification of Greek provinces under a fabricated 'Macedonian' nation."

According to this ad, recognition of an independent republic called

Macedonia would encourage aggression, increase tensions, destabilize the Balkans, and validate a "shameless fraud."

In this last statement we have a reference to the wider issue concerning the name Macedonia. The Greeks say that they have the sole right to use the name, for various historical reasons. The rest of the advertisement contains statements from American and world leaders (including American senators, the president of the European Parliament, the prime minister of Australia and the Greek prime minister), opposing recognition of the state of Macedonia up to the time the ad was placed, and an open letter to President Bush appealing in particular to historic concerns about "communist expansionism" in the area, the bitter experience of the Greek civil war, and previous American support of anti-communist forces in Greece. In this latter connection it is worth considering the quoted statement by a former United States Secretary of State on December 26, 1944: "This government considers any talk of a Macedonian 'nation,' Macedonian 'Fatherland' or Macedonian 'national consciousness' to be unjustified demagoguery representing no ethnic or political reality ... a possible cloak for aggressive intentions against Greece."

The May 10 ad is much less detailed. It quotes a *New York Times* story (datelined May 2, 1992) on the European community's willingness to recognize the "breakaway republic of Macedonia" only if it changed its name, and once again appeals to past American concern about instability in the Balkans in general and about Macedonia in particular. "Since the break-up of Yugoslavia," reads the ad, "its people have suffered the relentless gunfire of hostilities: one tragedy after another — all stemming from ethnic violence and border disputes. The single stable border in the Balkans is provided by Greece. Now the breakaway southernmost Yugoslavian republic of Skopje insists on being recognized as 'Macedonia.'" The advertisement goes on to say that in 1944, the Roosevelt administration recognized Greek ethnic, cultural and historical rights to the name and condemned any reference to a so-called Macedonian "nation." Describing the same issue today as a "dangerous ticking time bomb," the ad says that recognition of what it calls "Skopje" as the "Republic of Macedonia" would legitimize and encourage extremist and false claims upon sovereign Greek territory. Furthermore, the advertisement suggests a threat of war in the Balkans in which the United States could become involved.

Any thoughtful reader of these advertisements not versed in the history of Macedonia and Greece could not help being concerned about the issues raised. To a large degree I will allow other international commentators to pass judgment on the strength of these Greek fears at a later point in the book, giving here only a brief indication of an alternative viewpoint. Before that comment, however, I will present the rest of the Greek position, expanding on the question of the "Greek ethnic, cultural and historical rights to the name." I will use, in particular, quotations from pamphlets distributed from Greek Orthodox churches, apparently deriving from Greek government publications available in the Greek embassy during 1992. I do this so that the Greek position is accurately represented. Here are some of the important claims that are made.

1. The *New York Times* advertisement of 4/26/92 says, "4000 years of Greek History, 4000 years of Greek Culture, 4000 years of Greek Heritage... Skopje's government seeking recognition as the 'Republic of Macedonia' perpetuates a fraud." Pamphlets distributed in churches stated, "Macedonia has been Greek for 3,000 years. In ancient times Macedonians spoke Greek, worshipped Greek gods, expressed their creativity through Greek art and maintained a refined Greek culture ... all archaeological discoveries continue to unearth more information attesting to the indisputable Greekness of Macedonia."

2. "Out of the blue, in 1944, the Yugoslav communist leader, Tito, wishing to weaken Serbia on the one hand, and set the footing for future territorial claims against Greece on the other, schemingly gave South Serbia the Greek name 'Macedonia' and re-wrote the 'history' books to declare that ancient Macedonia was Slavic and that these people were descendants of Alexander the Great."

3. "The existence of a 'Slav' Macedonia could never be, and indeed, has never been supported either by historical data, or by ethnographic maps, or by statistics, or by some census, or by archaeological finds, or by even an obscure mention of such a nation from antiquity till today."

4. "Macedonia has been the name of Northern Greece for more than 3000 years. The Greek region ... has one of the most homogeneous populations in the world (98.5% Greek). Its population speaks Greek, feels Greek, is Greek."

5. "An independent 'Macedonia' would monopolize the name at the expense of the real Macedonians who are twice the number of the Slavs. The use and abuse of the name would cause widespread confusion as is already apparent."

6. "Macedonia is an indispensable part of Greece's historical heritage — it cannot identify, in an ethnic sense another nation."

7. "The Skopje 'language' is undeniably Slavic."

8. "The Slavs did not set foot in the Balkans until 1000 years after Alexander the Great."

9. "The name 'Macedonia' (which is etymologically Greek) was in use at least 1500 years before the arrival of the first Slavs."

10. "Every known Macedonian town, river, and person had a Greek name — Philip (lover of horse), Alexander (protector of men), Archelaus (leader of people), Amyntas (defender), Ptolemy (warlike), Bucephalus (ox-head)."

11. "The Old Testament (Daniel Ch. 8) and the New Testament (Acts Ch. 17) confirm the Greekness of Alexander and the Macedonians."

12. "It was the Greek language that was taken to Asia (Bible written in Greek) and cities with Greek names and institutions that were founded."

13. "There are 60,000 archaeological finds that confirm that the Macedonians were Greek in language, culture and religion."

14. "The home of the Greek gods was in Macedonia. Is it feasible that a people would worship its national gods in a foreign country?"

15. " Yugoslav Macedonia is not even geographically in the territory occupied by ancient Macedonia."

16. "Independent sources in this century (Turkish Census of 1904 when the region was part of the Ottoman Empire, League of Nations Census of 1926 and declassified British Archives 1934) make no mention of any ethnic Macedonians whatsoever until the Communists came along with their preposterous concoction to dominate the Balkans."

17. "By appropriating and maintaining the name 'Macedonia' the Slavs are laying the foundations for future territorial claims against the region of the same name in Greece. They have clearly expressed this intention by:- (a) plagiarizing and blatantly falsifying history (b)... continuously using maps and emblems that include northern Greece as part of 'Macedonia' and (c) refusing to comply with the directive of the European Community in its declaration of 16th December 1991 to (i) cease hostile propaganda; (ii) commit itself to guarantees that it has no territorial claims and (iii) not use a denomination (Macedonia) which implies expansionist intentions."

This set of statements was widely circulated, with minor changes made for particular locations, in different parts of the English-speaking world. Copies of the main points were distributed through Greek churches, and were frequently published in the "letters to the editor" sections of local newspapers. Clearly the Greek communities were very keen to see the message spread and went to great organizational effort and expense to see that this happened. I have no doubt that most of those engaged in this effort hold these beliefs very sincerely. Indeed the mass demonstrations by Greeks in various parts of the world suggest deep emotional commitment to these ideas. All the more reason, of course, to examine the claims more closely.

In this book I will examine the Greek claims as fully as possible and present the views of historians, linguists, and other experts who will paint a different picture for us. While there are histories and anthropological analyses of the Greek and Macedonian positions emerging at the present time, to my knowledge there has been no significant presentation of the other side of the argument outlined above, nor any analysis of how it fits into broader Balkan politics centered on Macedonia at the present time. Macedonian interest groups in various parts of the world have taken to the streets themselves, indicating their distress at what they say is a one-sided airing of the Macedonian question in the media. Like the Greeks, the Macedonians express a strong emotional commitment to their interpretation of the situation.

I do not claim to be unbiased, though in my examination of the evidence available to me I have tried to be as objective as possible. When I began my own inquiry about the topic, I wanted to know the truth. I began the process of discovery from a state of quite profound ignorance. I had talked with elderly

Macedonian people about their lives, and about stories they remembered from the old days in Macedonia, and the things they told me often conflicted with the arguments of modern-day Greeks. I knew that these Macedonians, at least, thought of themselves as Macedonian long before the time of Tito. They told stories of Macedonian revolutionaries who, at the turn of the century, wanted a state separate from Bulgaria. They described how Bulgarian agents infiltrated the revolutionary movement and assassinated Macedonian leaders, and voiced a prevailing belief that Aegean Slavic Macedonians had been persecuted by successive Greek governments. But they told me little about the broader facts of the history of the Macedonians over the past two and a half thousand years.

My readings have established to my satisfaction the weakness of the Greek historical argument. It is also clear to me that national aspirations were alive and well in Macedonia long before Tito arrived on the scene. But by and large the Macedonians have had a pretty miserable time of it, dominated by one greater power or another for much of their history, a domination most recently perpetrated by the same European nations who were slow to support the Macedonians in the 1990s. As the Irish patriot Roger Casement (executed by the British after the 1916 uprising in Ireland) put it: "I know of two tragic histories in the world — that of Ireland, and that of Macedonia. Both of them have been deprived and tormented."

Casement was speaking primarily of the Macedonians who then inhabited the lands that fell within the borders of the ancient Macedonian homeland. A majority of them were Slavic speakers when Greece conquered a large part of Macedonia, taking it from the Turks, just before the First World War. Casement's rather eloquent lines by themselves must cause us to ponder Greek claims that a non–Greek Macedonia was merely a Communist invention.

Before I present my argument, I need to make a few introductory statements to establish the context of the discussion.

First, it should be noted that the Greek claims are a new political development. Just a few years ago the Greeks preferred not to use the name Macedonia at all. The *Macedonian* news magazine (Skopje, February 15, 1992, pp. 20-21) claims that "there were periods in Greece when use of the name 'Macedonia' was avoided with administrative measures. After the Balkan wars (1912-13) the area of Macedonia under Greek rule was called…the 'New territory' while the Ministry in Salonika was called the Ministry of Northern Greece. Whence such zeal to pre-empt the names 'Macedonia' and 'Macedonian' today when so recently they avoided them as the devil avoids church?"

Peter Hill, professor of Slavonic studies at the University of Hamburg in Germany, makes a similar point:[1]

> Funnily enough, northern Greece was for many years called just that, "Northern Greece"… and the name Macedonia was considered somehow suspect…. But three years ago that all changed. Now that name, Macedonia, is at the

heart of a dispute that has paralyzed the foreign policy of the European Community and brought thousands of people on to the streets of Melbourne, Sydney, Canberra and Brussels.

Second, I have tried to present ideas that can be critically examined. I have tried to avoid insupportable claims, and have cited the sources from which I have drawn my conclusions. It seems reasonable to me to read the views of people who are experts in the field, and to adjust my own conclusions on the basis of some aggregation of what they have said. You might think that this matter could be dealt with quite simply by referring to such historical experts. But one of the problems is that the Greek "experts" often do not agree with the "experts" from other parts of the world. Not surprisingly, the Greek experts almost invariably take a nationalistic line. The ancient Greeks are said to have been imbued with a "mythic imagination." They tended to interpret historical events in the light of their understanding of the role of supernatural powers in their lives, and of course they were often inclined to present stories that showed Greeks in the best possible light. What could be more natural? It is hardly surprising that writers throughout the world do exactly the same kind of thing these days. Bulgarians and Serbians tend to favor views that support their own nations' historical perspectives about Macedonia. Sometimes, though, Greek writers have gone to such extremes that other historians have actually ridiculed their conclusions. I will give some examples later on. Thus it is necessary to tread very carefully amongst the expert opinions. For this reason when discussing historical issues I have tended to give preference to writers from Britain, France, Germany, and the United States. When dealing with contemporary matters I have given much greater emphasis to news sources and interpretations from within Macedonia. Generally these are about uncontroversial matters of recorded fact.

Third, in some ways this kind of analysis is little more than an empty academic game, since we have to talk in part about ancient history. It is not a very convincing exercise to justify the boundaries of modern states on the basis of things that happened more than two thousand years ago. Ancient historical claims seem of trivial importance beside the realities of the present day. To people who live in former English colonies, such as Americans, Canadians and Australians, a lot of these ideas seem very strange. After all, at the very least the Slavic speakers have lived for around 1500 years in the territory that has been called Macedonia. (Some historians present a more extreme position, claiming that the invading Slavs were really just the returning Paeones who had inhabited northern and western parts of Macedonia before the Macedonian kingdom existed.) They would not have had to wait 1500 years to be entitled to call themselves Americans, Canadians or Australians. They have been there at least as long as the Germanic tribes, the Angles, Saxons and Jutes have been in Britain. No one seems to think it a problem that the English use a Celtic name, "Britain," for their land. So we have clear examples of this sort of thing happening elsewhere in the world without any necessary belittling of the original peoples and their historic achievements. However, we have to recognize that rationality may have little influence in matters of national pride. Nonetheless it can be argued that the Macedonians, by virtue of 1500 years of occupation, have a pre-eminent claim to the place and to the name, regardless of who lived there 3000 years ago. And that is precisely the case for recognizing the right of Macedonians everywhere to call themselves by that name today. Of course I will make the longer historical case too.

Greek advertising throughout the world has made a great play of using what are said to be historical facts to support the attack on the Macedonians. So I will discuss some of these ideas first before turning to the more recent past and to contemporary events. It is worth noting that after Macedonians voted to become independent from the Yugoslav state, the only resistance to their international recognition came from Greece. The other eleven members of the European Community accepted the Republic of Macedonia's claims to independence and to the use of a name which the population of these lands has used for thousands of years. Greece was able to block this recognition for a considerable time because of an EC requirement for consensus in its decision-making. The same requirement for consensus kept Macedonia out of some European organizations up until the end of 1995. It is something of a paradox that throughout its attack on Macedonia, Greece, claiming a threat from Macedonia, has been seen by its European allies and America as a greater threat to peace in the Balkans.

The issue of the Slavic minority in northern Greece is one that deserves attention in its own right. It has some bearing on our understanding of certain issues in areas bordering the state of Macedonia. In its annual reports from 1991 through 1994, the United States State Department complained about the Greek government's denial of civil rights to minority groups, including Slavic speakers in Aegean Macedonia and Turkish speakers in Thrace. This leads us into a fascinating exploration of the redistribution of populations in northern Greece earlier this century, and the repeated efforts by strong central government in Greece to create the impression of a tightly knit and coherent Greek-speaking community. At first blush one might think that northern Greeks have a legitimate claim to at least share the name Macedonia with the Vardar Macedonians. However, it turns out that the immediate forbears of a majority of the Greek population of northern Greece originate from outside of the Balkans, in Western Turkey. These northern Greeks are not indigenous to the area, a fact to be taken into consideration when seeking to discover who has a legitimate claim on the name Macedonia. We might also wonder at the unwillingness of Greece to use the name Macedonia when it conquered the southern part of Macedonia in the first Balkan war, and the apparent rehabilitation of the name in recent years.

Several analysts, who will be referred to later, suggest that Greek actions should not be seen in isolation, but must be viewed in the light of a strong alliance with Serbia. As we view Balkan events now, and see Serbians attempting to expand Serbian territory, first in one former Yugoslav state and then another, with very modest success up to the present time, we might wonder whether Serbia has designs on Macedonia. Certainly some Macedonians believe this to be the case. Skopje was the capital of the great fourteenth-century Serbian Empire, and just a few decades ago the Serbs ruled this territory by conquest. They have engaged in provocative border actions that have drawn in United Nations troops with a major United States contingent. It is not disputed that the Greeks are the strongest allies of the Serbs in the Balkans, and that they have reached some kind of accord with the Serbian leader Milosevic. What we cannot know yet is whether some master plan guides both the Greeks and the Serbians.

By way of introduction to some of the content that follows, here are some of the conclusions that seem to me arguable after my examination of historical literature. These points briefly deal with the list of Greek claims above, both those published in national newspaper advertisements and those distributed throughout Greek communities.

Firstly, regarding the appeals to the American people based on concerns arising from the Greek civil war and the involvement of Yugoslavia and the U.S.S.R. in support of that conflict: The Macedonia under discussion by Edward Stettinius, United States Secretary of State, in 1944, was the "Greater Macedonia" that had been dismembered by Greece, Bulgaria, Serbia and Albania after the Balkan wars some thirty years earlier. The nation under discussion today encompasses less than 38 percent of that Greater Macedonia. Furthermore, Greece acknowledges this new nation's right of existence. Can we believe that the use of the name Macedonia by the new state somehow constitutes a threat to Greek borders? It should be remembered that Slavic-speaking Macedonian partisans fought against the Nazis on the side of the allies (and in alliance with Tito) during the Second World War. They were among the most reliable and successful of the resistance fighters against the German and Bulgarian invaders. Their language of command was Macedonian. Their motivation to resist the Bulgarian and German occupation came partly from being forced to use Bulgarian language and customs in their schools. Since Tito himself was Croatian, and Croatians traditionally have been more sympathetic to Macedonians than Serbians, it is perhaps not surprising that he took advantage of this motivating force within the Macedonian community and harnessed it to the new socialist state he forged out of the diverse groups that became the new Yugoslavia.

There is little doubt that Tito saw the possibility of expanding his sphere of interest into parts of Greek territory. At one point the new socialist Bulgarian government, fired with ideological righteousness, expressed its concern at the repression of the Macedonian language wherever it existed, including Western Bulgaria (Pirin Macedonia), and seemed on the verge of forming a Balkan federation with the Yugoslav states. At the time of this activity, the issue of a greater Macedonian state was being proposed; both the U.S.S.R. and Yugoslavia were supporting insurgent forces in the Greek civil war; and Macedonian nationalists who had fought with the partisans had joined in an alliance with the Greek Communists in an effort to achieve a freedom which had been denied them previously. A Balkan federation incorporating a Greater Macedonia and other Yugoslav states and Bulgaria would have presented a very strong barrier to Russian influence. Stalin soon applied pressure to Bulgaria to change its tune and stopped support for the Greek Communists and Macedonian partisans. Thus it was not just the United States that was concerned about the development of a Greater Macedonia. On this issue the United States saw eye-to-eye with the U.S.S.R. This was the turning point in the Greek civil war. The statements made by American political figures must be understood in the context of those times. With changes in the political situation, American political figures changed their analyses of Balkan history.

The small Macedonian state has publicly, formally, and repeatedly disavowed any territorial claim on Greek lands since the Greeks first made their accusations. None of the surrounding states has expressed any support for the idea of a greater Macedonia, since it would threaten their own borders. It is simply not a live issue. Furthermore, it is unrealistic to think that a tiny nation of little more than two million people, with no heavy arms, no air force and no navy, could be a threat to the Greeks, who have been supplied and supported in their armed forces by NATO and the United States to the tune of billions of dollars in past years. No political analysts in the United States believes that this could happen.

I will now respond to the broader historical issues, dealing with these in the order listed above. My responses are a summary of ideas that will be expanded elsewhere in this book. For the moment they lay the groundwork for the more detailed arguments that follow.

1. Three thousand years ago the lands that came to be called Macedonia were inhabited mainly by Illyrians and Phrygians. The Macedonians who appeared around 700 to 800 B.C. were for centuries a small group confined to a very small area of land. This area of land is a tiny portion of what is now Greek Macedonia. The language of these Macedonians was not Greek, nor were their gods; nor were they recognized by the Greeks. In time their leaders aspired to be as culturally refined and politically powerful as the Greeks, and used Greek teachers for their children. By about the fourth century B.C. the Macedonian nobles often used Greek for official purposes, but they and the common people spoke the Macedonian vernacular at home. A version of the Greek language had become an important trade language in the area and was widely used for such purposes. This variety of Greek was from the southern Greek states, and

its use proves nothing at all about the native tongue of the Macedonians, which, if it had been Greek, would likely have been a different dialect. In any case, there are no inscriptions in any form of Greek from before about 400 B.C. found in material excavated in any part of Macedonia. Of course there were small Greek settlements in coastal areas of Macedonia, and until the Macedonians conquered the area, the Chalcidice peninsula was Greek.

2. It is certainly true that the Yugoslav leader Tito gave the Macedonians a degree of recognition as a unique nationality with their own language. No doubt there were various reasons for doing so. The Macedonian partisans were of great significance in the Yugoslav resistance to the Nazis, and the respect they earned at this time probably helped. It should be noted too that Tito adopted the same policy throughout Yugoslavia. All regions had a degree of autonomy, including the use of their own language. The success of Tito's policies in maintaining unity has become increasingly clear as we witness the bloody conflicts that erupted in Yugoslavia after his death. However, getting back to the point about the existence of Macedonia, even in the very long rule of the Turks Macedonia was recognized as a separate entity. It was this Greater Macedonia that was divided by the Greeks, Bulgarians and Serbians after the Balkan wars of 1912-13. No historian, Greek or otherwise, uses any name but Macedonia to describe the territories that were partitioned. After the division, none of the controlling powers permitted the use of the name in the portions of Macedonia that they had taken. The kingdom of the Serbs, Croatians and Slovenians used the name "South Serbia"; Greece referred to the "Northern Provinces"; and Bulgaria used the name "Western Bulgaria." Of relevance to the Greek claim is the interesting point that the people in the Yugoslav part of Macedonia were permitted to use the name Macedonia in this century long before the people in the Greek part.

The Greek assertion that Yugoslav history books claim the ancient Macedonians were Slavic seems not to be true. I have examined secondary school texts written in Macedonian and interpreted for me by Macedonian speakers. I am confident that these books do not present such a view of history. However, that view does exist; it is promulgated by historians who have sympathies with the "Illyrian" movement. (The Albanian language is thought by some linguists to be related to ancient Illyrian, and Albanians believe that they are the rightful heirs of the ancient Macedonians.) Their argument states that the ethnic predecessors of the Slavs were the Paeones, who inhabited significant portions of Macedonian lands before and during the time of the great Macedonian kingdom. They say that the Paeones returned to their Macedonian homelands in the fifth and sixth centuries A.D. and that these peoples have been called Slavs.

Whether or not these claims are verifiable, it should be noted that both Macedonia and Greece have changed dramatically in ethnic mix over the past 2000 years. Neither shows any close match to the ethnic nature of the area at the time of Alexander the Great. Over the past 2300 years or so, the Balkan peninsula has been invaded by hordes of newcomers, including Celts (third to first century B.C.), Germanic tribes (third century A.D.), Slavs (fifth and sixth century A.D.), and Turks (fourteenth century A.D.). The original peoples may not have been wiped out, or pushed out of Macedonia or Greece by these new peoples. What happened often was that after a time the new peoples merged with the existing peoples. Throughout the Balkans, in both Macedonia and Greece, the ethnic mix is profoundly complex. However, there is no evidence to suggest that the people of Macedonia are any less ethnically "pure" and representative of the ancient peoples than the Greeks. If it is argued that the Slavic ethnic influence predominates in Macedonia, precisely the same case can be made for most of Greece. Quite simply, in Macedonia we have a majority of people of mixed ethnic stock who speak a Slavic language and have a predominantly Slavic culture, and in Greece we have a majority of people of mixed ethnic stock who speak Greek and have a Greek culture.

3. Has there ever been a "Slav Macedonia"? By most people's standards, it would be very hard to make a case that there has not. A great Slavic Empire in the tenth century A.D. incorporated most of the territory that historians recognize as ancient Macedonia as well as Bulgaria. This empire was ruled by Samuil, a Macedonian Slav, who governed from Ohrid, in the Southwest of modern-day Macedonia. Although the Byzantine Emperor Basil II ("the Macedonian") vanquished this empire, he and subsequent conquerors always acknowledged the Slavic language, culture and ethnicity of the people that they ruled. They generally recognized the territory of Macedonia, although administrative boundaries changed from time to time. The fact that the Macedonian Slavs were ruled by others is no grounds for speaking as though they did not exist, or for saying that their territories should not retain the old name of Macedonia. In the chapters that follow, historical, ethnographic, statistical and census material demonstrates clearly the existence of a Slavic Macedonia.

There is evidence that the Slavs of Macedonia called themselves "Macedonian" as early as the tenth century A.D. At the same time, the Byzantine emperors came to call the Macedonian Slavs "the Macedonians" since they made up the politically most significant population of the area. Written evidence and surviving crests from the sixteenth century proclaim Macedonia's distinction from other Balkan territories. When other Balkan states began to assert themselves against the Turks between the seventeenth and the twentieth centuries, similar feelings of nationalism were seen in Macedonia, and recognized by the leading powers of Europe. During the twentieth century the Serbians, Bulgarians and Greeks tried to eliminate the influence of the Slavic Macedonian language, and to suppress the customs of Macedonian people in territories they conquered. The United Nations recognizes the Macedonian (Slavic) language.

4. While it is true to say that the name Macedonia has been applied to

Aegean Macedonia for a long time, "more than 3000 years" is pushing things just a little. Twenty-three hundred to twenty-six hundred years would be closer to the mark. However, most of the territory of the present Republic of Macedonia has also had that name for the same period of time. Although the boundaries of that land called Macedonia have changed from time to time under the rule of the Romans (this includes the period of Byzantium), the Bulgarians, the Serbians, the Turks and the Greeks, all historical analyses, even those emanating from Greeks, show certain territories to have been part of Macedonia since the time of Alexander the Great. Included in these territories are Skopje, Stobi, and Herakleia (later Monastir/Bitola). These towns come close to the northern and western boundaries of the present Republic of Macedonia. They have been Macedonian since before the great empire. The territory that is now northern Greece has also been an important part of Macedonia since ancient times, though most of this territory was not a part of the first Macedonian kingdom, but was gradually incorporated into that kingdom as Macedonian power grew.

Macedonia was split apart in 1912 when the Bulgarians, the Greeks and the Serbs united to push the Turks out of the Balkans. Succeeding in that, they split Macedonia among themselves. Aegean Macedonia, some 52 percent of Greater Macedonia, was taken by Greece by conquest, never by any act of self-determination. It could be argued that Greece created the very problem about which it now complains since Greece participated in the initial division of Macedonia earlier this century. Given this division of territories it is hardly surprising that some Macedonians hope for a restoration of older borders. Nationalist forces throughout the Balkans have very similar ambitions.

The Slavic-language Macedonian people who come from Aegean Macedonia, including those who left the country before and during the Second World War and the Greek civil war (many are now in the United States, Canada, and Australia), still call themselves Macedonian. Even Greek government publications admit that the different peoples of Macedonia, such as the Slavs, Greeks, and Vlachs, called themselves Macedonians in earlier times and during the last century. Only in the last few years have the Greeks publicly attempted to reclaim for themselves the name that they abandoned and actually tried to suppress for so many years.

The statement that the Greek region called Macedonia "has one of the most homogeneous populations in the world" (98.5 percent Greek) is very much without substance. For a start the number is probably a considerable exaggeration, according to United Nations and United States State Department estimates. But given that there is a high proportion of Greek speakers in this area, a more important question is how did northern Greece became so "ethnically pure"? There is no dispute that this happened through a process of exiling tens of thousand of Slav-speaking Macedonians, both Christian and Moslem, and resettling hundreds of thousands of Greek speakers from Asia

Minor and Armenia. By this process the Greeks accomplished a great change in the ethnic mix in Aegean Macedonia. Today, after the term was coined during the war in Bosnia, we would call this "ethnic cleansing." It is not a new phenomenon, and was not uncommon in Europe around and after the First World War. After this process in Aegean Macedonia, the Greeks made it illegal to speak the Slavic language and imprisoned and in other ways severely punished people who did so. Naturally enough, members of the minority Slavic population that remained after this social engineering were also forbidden to teach their children in their own language. The Greeks changed place names and forced people to use Greek names in place of their Slavic names. Given all of this extraordinary government intervention, it is hardly surprising to find a high proportion of Greek speakers in Aegean Macedonia. But clearly this does not tell us anything useful about historic rights to the name or the lands of Macedonia or the people who inhabited the area for fifteen hundred years. Brief reflection will show that the Greek speakers brought into northern Greece had no historic association with the land at all.

5. The idea that an independent Macedonia will somehow monopolize the name seems an overreaction to the situation. Many places in the world have the same names as other places, but human beings can deal with this. For instance, people can get used to the idea that a place in Greece and a place in the United States might have the same name and still be different places. This point also implies that since there are twice as many "real Macedonians" in Aegean Macedonia as there are in Vardar Macedonia, those with the numerical superiority should get the name. However, if we consistently appeal to the older historical justifications noted above, most of this Greek population would not count, since they are relative newcomers to Aegean Macedonia.

6. It is fine to say that Macedonia, meaning the history of ancient Macedonia, is an indispensable part of Greece's heritage. Given that the Greeks occupy a major part of ancient Macedonian territory, this seems fair enough. The fact that the ancient Macedonians and Greeks despised each other, and that the Macedonians conquered the Greeks, need not be relevant to this aspect of modern political life. However, it does seem quite paradoxical for Greeks to choose as a national symbol a recently discovered emblem used by the hated overlords of ancient times (the Macedonians). The implication that there is a coherent ethnic group existing today, living only in northern Greece, that we could recognize as "Macedonian"—people who have a strong line of descent from the ancient Macedonians—simply cannot be substantiated.

7. There is no dispute that the language of Vardar Macedonia is predominantly Slavic, though in modern times there are increasing demands to allow the official use (in schools for instance) of the languages of minority groups such as Albanians and Turks. If it can be demonstrated that the ancient Macedonians were neither Slavic speakers nor Greek speakers—and such a case is

presented in this book — the Greek position does not gain any advantage by pointing to the current language of the occupants of Vardar Macedonia.

8. The Slavs set foot in the Balkans about 900 years after the time of Alexander the Great. They, and some other "new" peoples, spread widely throughout the Balkans, but particularly into those lands that we have called Greece and Yugoslavia. The Slavs eventually mixed with the remaining peoples, but in Vardar Macedonia the language and culture that lasted was Slavic Macedonian, and in the south, in Greece, the language and culture that survived was Greek. In both cases it was necessary to have a very strong government support for the stabilization and establishment of an official modern form of the language. In Greece this happened a little more than a hundred years earlier than it did in Macedonia. The Greek language was not imposed on Aegean Macedonia until the mid–1920s. Until that time Slavic Macedonian was the "lingua franca" of the area.

9. The name Macedonia was not used until the second century B.C., and it was applied to the country by the Macedonian king, not by a Greek. The term "Macedon" and the expression "land of the Macedons" were used long before that time, though there is debate about the origins of the word "Macedon." Philologists are not certain of its derivation, though Greeks prefer to think that the word comes from Greek. In any case, neither the ancient Macedonians nor the ancient Greeks thought that the Macedonians were Greek; thus the name the Macedonians used for their land must surely belong to them alone. The weight of this issue does not seem to be substantial.

10. It is quite true that many Macedonian places and people were given Greek names. This was especially the case after the Macedonian rulers started to use a Greek dialect that came from the south (they were not using a dialect similar to that of their nearest Greek neighbors, but one borrowed from much farther away) and ostentatious features of Greek culture. However, we do not know the names that were given to many places and people because we have no written records. The contemporary records we have come from Greek writers, or others writing in the Greek language, for Greek-speaking readers. It would be surprising if they did not use Greek names.

11. Generally the Old Testament is not accepted as being very good history, at least as we understand history. As far as New Testament writings are concerned, we must be careful about what has really been said. Differences in interpretation have led to the establishment of different religious groups, so it can hardly be said that the New Testament writings are always subject to the same interpretation. It should be noted that several ancient writers acknowledged the close association of the Macedonians and the Greeks, once the Greeks had been conquered by the Macedonians. Often the Macedonian rulers wanted the Greeks to be working in concert with them, though the Greeks were less enthusiastic about this idea. As already noted, the Macedonian leaders, from about the fourth century B.C., moved increasingly to adopt the use of the Greek

language for official affairs, and were attracted by facets of Greek culture. Greek culture was spread widely throughout the world by Macedonians rulers in their Macedonian Empire, and then by Romans in the Byzantine Empire. To be consistent one might just as well argue that since the Romans maintained and spread Greek culture they must have been Greek. Of course this is obviously wrong, but it points to the weakness of this argument when applied to the Macedonians.

12. It is quite true that Alexander took the Greek language and some aspects of Greek culture to Asia. This was a period of flowering for the Greek language, and for Greek trading influence in the world. The time of Alexander marks a period in Greek history called the Hellenic period for this very reason. However, Alexander did not take that mainstay of Greek culture, democracy, to his new Asian empire, and in time he even abandoned most of the things he had started with, turning to a new blend of Asian, Macedonian and Greek ways. It became more important to appease Asians than to appease Greeks.

The fact that Philip and Alexander used the Greek language for administration and were supposedly "Hellenistic" in orientation has more to do with political manipulation and administrative convenience than any appreciation for the Greeks. This observation is not disputed by historians. Thus the use of the Greek language does not tell us anything about the ethnic or cultural origins of the Macedonians. The English language has had a similar role in recent international history. The third largest English-speaking country in the world today (at least in population terms) is the Philippines, according to that country's own claims. Yet no one would seriously suggest that the people of the Philippines are English, or even American, by race or by culture.

The evidence discussed in this book indicates that Alexander's mother tongue was not Greek, his mother was probably not Greek and his father was not Greek. Eventually Alexander himself became an "internationalist" rather than a Hellenophile, even to the extent of arranging marriages between thousands of Persian women and his own troops in a strange effort to merge the peoples and cultural extremes of his empire.

13. There are no archaeological finds that confirm the racial origins of the Macedonians. In a later section I discuss the writings of R. A. Crossland, who contributed to the Cambridge volumes on ancient history. Crossland thoroughly deals with this question and dismisses as worthless the supposed archaeological evidence about the alleged Greek origins of the Macedonians.

14. To say that the home of the Greek gods was in Macedonia is to embellish the truth. However, the real issue here is not whether a people (the Greeks) would worship its national gods in a foreign country, but whether Greeks believed Macedonians to be foreigners. If the latter is true, and if Greeks worshiped gods from Macedonia, then by definition they worshiped gods from a foreign country. Thus the argument fails if it can be shown that Greek people of ancient times believed that the Macedonians were foreigners. There is no

debate among historians about the fact that in historical times the Macedonians and the Greeks saw themselves as separate peoples. The Macedonians were always named separately from the Greeks, even when the two groups were in closest connection under the rule of Philip II, Alexander the Great, and later the Turks. Historians say that the two peoples were held together in ancient times only by force of arms, and as soon as the empire of Alexander collapsed, they split apart once again. So whatever linguistic analysis might be argued these days to suggest similarity of ethnic background for the ancient Greeks and Macedonians (and there is no such analysis that is widely accepted), those ancient peoples knew nothing of it. The Greeks explicitly classified the Macedonians as foreigners. That is what the word "barbaroi," frequently given to the Macedonians and other non–Greek groups, means. Since the ancient Greeks thought of the Macedonians as foreigners, if modern Greeks wish to argue that the home of Greek gods was Macedon, it is evident that the ancient Greeks must have worshipped gods from the lands of foreigners.

15. As noted above, even modern Greek texts show that the areas of modern-day Skopje, Stobi, and Bitola were included in the boundaries of the Macedonian homelands. These cities are close to the northern and western borders of the modern-day state of Macedonia. Although some texts show slight variations in the position of the northern borders, historians agree that virtually the whole of the territory of the modern-day Republic of Macedonia was a part of ancient Macedonia.

16. Most of the census figures cited here are of questionable relevance. A crucial date is the 1912-13 Balkan wars which resulted in the partitioning of Macedonia. Since Greece took about 52 percent of the territory of Macedonia it is not helpful to talk about census figures taken after that date. It might be noted again that by the late 1920s the Greeks had completed a major social engineering program in Aegean Macedonia, having exiled tens of thousands of Slavic speaking Macedonians, and imported perhaps ten times as many non-Macedonian Greek speakers from Turkey and Armenia. Figures taken after that date really do not help in this debate.

Another interesting issue contained in this Greek comment is worth mentioning briefly here, and that is the labeling of Slavic-speaking Macedonians as Bulgarian. The major powers that were fighting over Macedonia in the Balkan wars were Turkey, Serbia, Bulgaria, and Greece. The occupying power, the Turks, identified their Slavic subject peoples in the Balkans in terms of their religious affiliation. The usual possibility was for them to be Moslem, Jewish, Greek Orthodox, or Bulgarian Orthodox (although there were some other numerically insignificant classifications such as Roman Catholic). The Greek Church had been successful in pleading with the Turkish authorities to have the Macedonian Orthodox Church banned in favor of the Greek Orthodox Church towards the end of the eighteenth century; thus Macedonians had no Slavic-speaking church to attend. However, after about 1870 the Bulgarian

Orthodox Church was permitted in Bulgaria and began to attract Slav speakers in Macedonia. Orthodox Christian Macedonians were called Bulgarian if they had affiliated with the Slavic-speaking Bulgarian church, or Greek if they still attended a Greek Orthodox church. So, at the beginning of the twentieth century, the Turkish rulers of Macedonia used a classification of its Balkan peoples that spoke as if Macedonians did not exist. The competing powers, Bulgaria, Serbia and Greece, also wished to extend their territory, and it did not suit them to recognize a nationalistic group that might reduce their acquisition. The Serbians spoke of "South Serbians" when referring to Macedonians, and the Bulgarians simply spoke of "Bulgarians." This kind of classification suited the Greek political purpose also. Nevertheless, as you will see later in this book, European powers recognized the Macedonians, as did some newspaper accounts of the early part of the twentieth century. Even today the Greeks deny that they have any ethnic minorities, and their treatment of the Turkish and Macedonian speakers in Greece has brought international condemnation.

17. The politics of the use of the name Macedonia are rather more complex than the Greek writers suggest. I have no doubt that Macedonians throughout the world would like to see a reunification of Macedonia. However, the government of Macedonia seems to appreciate the political reality that it is beyond their power to achieve this. Some more radical groups in Macedonia still hope for such a development through armed struggle, but given the military might of Greece, this is undoubtedly a futile hope. The political group that takes this extreme nationalist position is a minority in the modern state of Macedonia. It is curious that the Greeks seem not to recognize that the politicians in power in Macedonia are moderate and that continued Greek agitation may actually strengthen the position of the radicals. One can only speculate about the intentions of the Greek government in this issue. As with any elected government there must be an acute sensitivity to the attitudes of the electorate. However, there may be a greater political game being played here, one that is suggested by some modern analysts and described in later chapters of this book. While only extremists in Macedonia speak about going to war, if we are to judge by the banners that have been waved in Salonika in mass demonstrations about the issue, Greeks in general seem to be prepared for war with the Macedonians. With luck, increased awareness of alternative analyses of history may serve to reduce the vigor of warlike thinking.

It is the intention of this book to clarify and present the conclusions of significant historians about the origins of the modern-day Macedonians. From time to time I will again compare those conclusions with the various points of the Greek position. For instance, it is appropriate to explain the complex ethnic mix that characterizes modern Greece. A major issue of international concern is the treatment of minority ethnic groups in Greece — Albanians, Turks, and Macedonians. Greece continues to deny the existence of all except a "Muslim minority," meaning Turkish speakers, and seems willing to acknowledge them only because they are specified in international treaties. There are some who argue that potential unrest from its Macedonian minority, or pressures for the return of exiled Macedonians to Greece (and resumption of confiscated lands), may be behind Greece's aggressive posture against Macedonia. The matter is well worth exploration.

By examining the particular dispute between Macedonia and Greece we can gain some understanding about other significant questions in the Balkans centered around Macedonia. Accordingly, this book examines the contemporary position of Macedonia. This has relevance to the Greek arguments, but introduces us also to broader questions about Macedonia's stability and ability to survive as an independent nation. A consideration of the new nation's international experiences gives us a context for examining the aims of its immediate neighbors and the attitudes of the United Nations and the United States. The American involvement is of particular interest, since the United States was unwilling to send men to participate in the peacekeeping force in Bosnia, but shared in the ground-breaking move of sending a contingent of troops as part of the first ever United Nations "war-prevention" effort. This seems to have come about because of the American recognition that forces within and around Macedonia could provoke a European war much greater in scale than the present war in Bosnia. The issues that have provoked Greek reactions seem unlikely to go away in the near future. The Macedonians are quite unlikely to agree to abandon the name, though they may be prepared to accept the use of a longer name, such as "New Macedonia." However, at the present time Greece insists that no name involving "Macedonia" is acceptable. But this is only one dispute among many. Like the Greek arguments, what is visible on the surface may reveal only a part of the overall agenda. The strength of many old ambitions is there to be seen. There are larger stories being played out, and it is very likely that Greece is a part of many of them. That is what makes the present case so fascinating.

1. Two Ancient and Separate Nations

To get to the real Macedonians we need to start a little before the time of Alexander the Great. If we go too far back, say to the seventh century B.C., we find that Macedon was a tiny little piece of land that no one today would really be interested in. It was an area that could be covered on horseback in a day's ride. Macedon at first included the area immediately east of Lake Kastoria and east and north of the Haliakmon River. Certainly there is little glory to claim from this period of Macedonian history. By the fifth century B.C. the kingdom had been extended eastward to what is now the Struma River, and a century later the Macedonian homeland was extended to include all of the territory west of the Nestos River.[1] In the time of Philip II and his son, Alexander the Great, the Macedonian homeland was at its largest, and Macedonian power was at its peak. This seems the obvious era in which to begin our enquiry.

Modern Greeks prefer to think of the ancient Macedonians as Greeks. This was part of their justification for taking a part of Macedonia by conquest earlier in this century, and is still used to justify their present international position. Greek arguments frequently focus on the time of Alexander because of his undoubted influence in spreading Hellenic culture to distant parts of the known world. It is clear, too, that they gain some satisfaction from imagining some family connection with that extraordinary figure. However, the modern Greek ideas would have been rejected by both the ancient Macedonians and the ancient Greeks.

If we start by looking at modern Greek discussions of these ideas we can then consider what historians have to say about their arguments, point by point. We get some of the flavor of Greek attitudes in the Greek publication *Macedonia, History and Politics* (published by George Christopoulos, John Bastias, printed by Ekdotike Athenon S.A. for the Center for Macedonians Abroad, and the Society for Macedonian Studies, 1991). This is a publication available in Greek embassies and distributed to Greek communities and multi-cultural organizations throughout the English-speaking world. The author of this book considers that the use of the Greek language by Macedonians is proof of their

THE ANCIENT MACEDONIAN KINGDOM

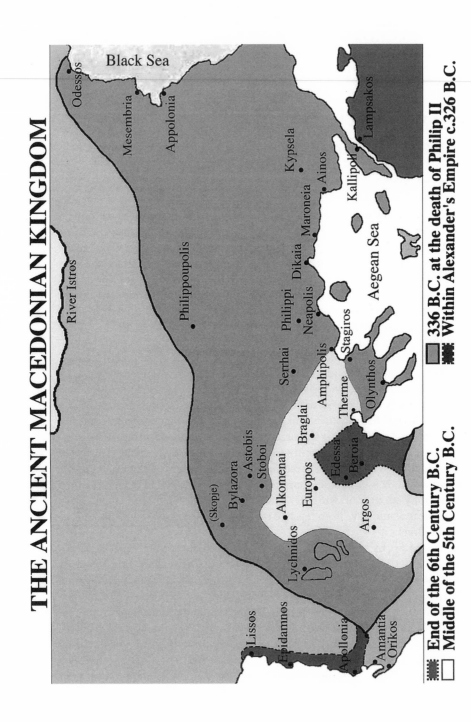

Black Sea

Odessos

Mesembria

Appolonia

River Istros

Philippoupolis

Kypsela

Ainos

Maroneia

Lampsakos

Kallipoli

Dikaia

Aegean Sea

Serrhai

Philippi

Neapolis

Amphipolis

Stagiros

Therme

Olynthos

(Skopje)

Bylazora

Astobis

Stoboi

Alkomenai

Braglai

Europos

Edessa

Beroia

Argos

Lychnidos

Lissos

Epidammos

Apollonia

Amantia

Orikos

Key:
- End of the 6th Century B.C.
- Middle of the 5th Century B.C.
- 336 B.C. at the death of Philip II
- Within Alexander's Empire c.326 B.C.

Renew books – Ask questions – Library hours

www.ksg.harvard.edu/library

The KSG Library
Your gateway to information resources

Library of Congress Call Number Schedule

A-AZ	General works (Directories, Almanacs, Encyclopedias, etc.)
B-BD	Philosophy
BL-BX	Religion
C-CT	Biography (Collective)
D-DX	General history; History outside the Americas
E	U.S. History
F	Local U.S. History; History of the Americas
G-GV	Geography; Environmental Sciences; Human Ecology
H-HB	Social Sciences (General); Statistics; Micro/Macroeconomics; Demography; Economic Theory
HC	Economic History and Conditions
HD	Industries; Labor; Economic Development
HE	Transportation; Communication
HF-HG	Commerce; Trade; Finance; Banking
HJ	Public Finance
HM-HN	Sociology (General); Social History; Social Problems; Social Reform
HQ-HV	Family; Women; Lifestyle; Social Pathology; Public Welfare; Criminology
HX	Socialism; Communism
J-JA	Political Science (General)
JC	Political Theory
JF	Political Institutions and Public Administration (General)
JK-JQ	Political Institutions and Public Administration (U.S. and International)
JS	Local Government; Municipal Government
JX-JZ	Foreign Relations; International Relations; Diplomacy
K-KJ	Law (General); Comparative Law; International Law
KF	U.S. Law
L	Education
P-PN	Philology; Linguistics; Literature; Mass Media; Broadcasting; Language Dictionaries; Journalism
Q-QE	Science (General); Mathematics, calculus, etc.; Climatology, climate change, etc.; Geology
R-RS	Medicine (General); Medical Care; Medical Economics; Public Health; Health policy
S	Agriculture
T-TX	Technology
U	Military Science
V	Naval Science
Z	Library Science

Greekness. In passing we might reflect on the modern use of English by many countries as a convenience for trade or war, and note that this usage proves nothing at all about the ethnicity or culture of the users. However, the author of *Macedonia, History and Politics* claims that the dissemination of the "Greek language and Greek culture throughout the known world by Alexander the Great and his Macedonians provides the most irrefutable confirmation" of the unity of the Macedonians with the other Greeks.

To explore thoroughly this issue of the proposed Greekness of the Macedonians, we need to consider evidence from a number of quarters. If the early Macedonians were Greek you would expect that (a) there might be clear evidence that the language of the Macedonians was a dialect of Greek, rather than a separate branch of the Indo-European language group; (b) writers of the time would have recognized Macedonians as Greek rather than as foreigners and would have spoken about Macedonia as though it was a part of Hellenism; and (c) historians today would speak of the ancient Macedonians as though they were Greek in ancient times. As we will see, none of these ideas is unequivocally supported.

Linguistic Evidence

In questioning the significance of the use of Greek by the ancient Macedonians we need to sort out some of the linguistic history of the Macedonians. Firstly, the language of the original Macedonians, whatever it was, existed long before Macedonia became a powerful state. This is before the time of the great kings Philip II and Alexander the Great. The name "Macedones" originated many centuries earlier, and probably came from the "real" Macedonian language. If the Macedonian language was recognized as Greek, and understood by Greeks, you would expect that this was the language used by the great Macedonian kings in a formal or legal context. But it was not.

We know with some certainty that Attic Greek, which came from much farther south (around the Athens area) and was being used in other parts of the world as a trade language, was used more and more as the language of state and used also in Alexander's multi-cultural army. No linguist accepts that this language was the original Macedonian. So we have clear evidence that the Greek used by the Macedonians was a new language. Therefore one cannot argue that the use of this language proves any linguistic associations between the original Macedonians and Greeks.

Many scholars have concluded that the ancient Macedonian language was not a Greek dialect and that it was more or less related to the languages of Macedonia's northern neighbors, the Illyrians and the Thracians. These scholars include Muller and Mayer, writing in the nineteenth century, and Thumb,

Thumb-Kieckers, Vasmer, Kacarov, Beshevljev, Budimir, Pisani, Russu, Baric, Poghirc, Chantraine, Katicic, and Nerosnak, writing in the twentieth. Here attention will be given to sources more readily accessible to those who want to inquire further.

The problem for modern-day linguists is that not a single sentence of the original Macedonian language has been retained. All that is left are records of proper names and isolated words — which, as historian E. Badian of Harvard University points out, is hardly sufficient basis for judgments about linguistic affinities.[2] We do know that the Macedonians increasingly came to use a southern form of Greek in their formal dealings. Traian Stoijanovich tells us[3] that in the fifth century B.C., the Macedonian rulers abandoned Macedonian and began using Attic Greek for public administration. This did not change the attitudes of the Greeks, who still regarded the Macedonians as barbarians.

However, Stoijanovich says it is not known whether the ancient Macedonian language was an independent language or a Greek dialect into which a non–Hellenic vocabulary and certain other non–Hellenic traits were introduced. Like other historians, he considers it quite possible that Macedonian was the language of the ruling class and that a considerable proportion of the subjects of the Macedonian chiefs spoke other languages.

Peter Hill, author of the section "Macedonians" in the official Australian bicentennial encyclopedia, *The Australian People* (perhaps 200,000 Macedonians live in Australia), writes:[4]

> What is certain is that Alexander's mother tongue was not Greek. Alexander enjoyed a Greek education and adopted Greek as the language of his empire — but to claim that that made him Greek is to suggest that the Irish and the Indians are really British because they have adopted English for administrative purposes.

Like Hill, E. Badian refutes the assumptions that a nation is essentially defined by a language and that a common language implies a common nationhood. He argues that this latter idea is patently untrue for the greater part of human history and to a large extent even today. The formal written language of ancient Macedonians was inevitably Greek, as was the case for various other ancient peoples. There was really no alternative. However, this in no way assures good relations between peoples, nor does it necessarily show any consciousness of a common interest. What is of greater historical interest, Badian says, is the documented evidence that Greeks and Macedonians regarded each other as foreign.

The use of the Macedonian language by Alexander's infantry. The Macedonian kings, Philip and Alexander, favored Hellenization and encouraged the use of Attic Greek in their administrations, but the use of this foreign tongue was not foisted upon ordinary Macedonians. Although at least some of Alexander's Greek companions knew the Macedonian language, having come to

Macedonia at an early age, Alexander never tried to impose Greek on his Macedonian infantry or to integrate this infantry with Greek units or Greek "foreign" individuals. Alexander's infantry continued to use the Macedonian tongue even late into his Asian expeditions. Badian describes some convincing cases in which Macedonian troops could not follow commands in Greek. For instance, during his argument with Clitus, which led to his good friend's death, at the end Alexander is said to have called for his guards in Macedonian when he felt his life threatened. Badian rejects the idea that this was a reversion to a more primitive part of his psyche, under stress. He prefers the simpler explanation that Alexander used the only language in which his guards could be addressed.

To establish his case, Badian quotes a surviving papyrus fragment that seems to be the only good source to reveal the facts of the infantry use of Macedonian. This fragment tells of a battle, early in 321 B.C., in which the Greek commander Ambiance faced the Macedonian Neoptolemus with his Macedonian phalanx. Wanting to have the Macedonians join him rather than fight him, Ambiance needed to convince them of his superior position. The story continues:

> When Eumenues saw the close-locked formation of the Macedonian phalanx … he sent Xennias once more, a man whose speech was Macedonian, bidding him declare that he would not fight them frontally but would follow them with his cavalry and units of light troops and bar them from provisions.

Badian tells us that Xennias' name reveals him to be a Macedonian. Since he was with Ambiance he was probably a Macedonian of superior status who spoke both standard Greek and his native language. Ambiance needed this interpreter to transmit his message. This means that the phalanx had to be addressed in Macedonian if they were going to understand. Ambiance did not address them himself, although this was the common way for leaders of the time, nor did he send a Greek. Badian concludes that Greek was a foreign tongue to the Macedonians. Similarly, Alexander used Macedonian to address his guards because it was their normal language, and he had to be sure he would be understood. It also seems clear that educated Greeks did not speak the Macedonian language unless (presumably) they had grown up with Macedonians and learned it from their childhood friends, as some of Alexander's Greek companions must have.

Other facts are consistent with this argument. Philip II seems not to have used any Greek commanders for his Macedonian troops. Presumably, the first-generation Greek immigrants into his cities had not learned the language. It is also a fact that Ambiance, the commander in the story above, was notorious for the trouble he repeatedly had in getting Macedonian infantry to fight for him, even though he was an able leader. His problem was probably not simply his troops' antagonism to the fact that he was Greek. His problem was that he could not directly communicate with Macedonian soldiers. In the end this defect cost him his life.

Political reasons for the use of the Greek language. Considering the use of Greek as the language of command in Alexander's armies, R.A. Crossland[5] concludes that this development was a matter of administrative efficiency. Although it was the Macedonians who had to learn Greek at first, the same requirement was made of at least some of his Persian troops after many conquests. For a long while Alexander thought that Greek was the best language to use as the common medium of communication among the peoples of his empire, "and not because Macedonian was similar to it."[6] Nevertheless, as we have already noted, even by the latter part of his Asian campaigns, Alexander's infantry still did not speak a Greek language.

In other words, a very important reason for Hellenization of the Macedonians was their new role of political power-broker. The Greek language was available in written form and was widely used throughout the Macedonian sphere of influence. It was a very convenient vehicle for use in creating an international empire, something that both Philip and Alexander hoped to do. Its use may have also have led to some appeasement of Greek hostility towards the dominating Macedonians. All of these are sound reasons for choosing to use the Greek language as the tongue of administration throughout the expanding empire. However, after a time the value of Greek culture to the Macedonians' cause began to fade. Eventually Alexander began to think in terms of a blending of the diverse cultures of his great empire. Perhaps in order to appease his new Persian subjects, it was now the blending of Macedonian and Persian that mattered, rather than the blending of Macedonian and Greek.

Macedonian attitudes to the Greek language. For the most part we have little information on Macedonian attitudes to the Greeks or their language. Badian reminds us that no Macedonian oratory survives, since the language was never a literary one. However, he concludes that the existence on both sides of a feeling that they were "peoples of non-kindred race" is very probable. The language barrier would keep this awareness alive, even though the literary language of educated Macedonians could only be Greek. That fact was as irrelevant to ordinary people, and perhaps even to those of higher status, as was the Hellenization of the Macedonian upper class. Badian gives a more recent example of a similar phenomenon. In eighteenth-century Europe, French language and culture prevailed amongst people of education. In fact, during the early part of the eighteenth century the language and culture of the German royal courts, including that of Frederick the Great in Prussia, were French. Most of the books published in Germany in the first half of the century were in Latin and French.[7] Thus upper-class German ladies might write only in French, yet this did not mean that they were French or even Francophile. Badian suggests that Clitus' anger toward Alexander was representative of a persisting antagonism to Greeks and their ways seen among all classes of Macedonians. He says that these feelings are most clearly evident where the historical record deals with ordinary people, like the Macedonian infantrymen referred to above.

The linguistic character of ancient Macedonia. Arnold Toynbee asserts that the Macedonians of all ancient historical periods spoke Greek. He argues firstly that "they (the Makedones) were already Greek speaking 150 years to 200 years earlier than Augustus' time."[8] This observation would seem to be of little weight in the present discussion since we have already noted the increasing, and deliberately chosen, use of Attic Greek by the Macedonian nobility. The use of a language from a distant location by a limited number of noble families tells us nothing about the native tongue of the Macedonians of the fourth century B.C., the Anglo-Saxons of thirteenth century England, or the Prussians of early eighteenth century Germany.

Nevertheless it is worth looking at Toynbee's point a little further to uncover its internal inconsistencies. Toynbee describes an occasion in 167 B.C. when L. Aemilius Paulus announced in a public speech at Amphipolis the Roman government's decisions for the settlement of continental European Greece. This speech was delivered in Latin, but there was a Greek translation of the speech "for the benefit of Paulus' audience which was drawn from all parts of Greece." From this Toynbee concludes that at this stage the Macedonians were Greek-speaking, since in the public meeting place at Amphipolis, the majority of the listeners must have been Macedonians. Yet Toynbee himself states that the Greek translation was provided because the audience "was drawn from all parts of Greece." However, if we follow Toynbee's line that we are dealing with a diverse group of native Greek speakers, many of whom were Macedonian and who, according to Toynbee, spoke a dialect of Greek that no other Greeks could understand, it is asking a bit much to expect us to believe that these representatives suddenly all understood the same "Greek"— that is, unless the "Greek" that was used was the *koine*, the international version of Greek developed from Attic, that was widely spoken in this area of the empire at the time. The audience was made up largely of leaders of one kind or another, people who were most likely to speak such a language. It is likely that virtually any trader, businessman, administrator, or political leader of the time would have spoken this language (or would have been in the company of an interpreter who could), as well as his own vernacular and perhaps other trade or administrative languages as well. Thus the translation of Paulus' speech into Greek tells us absolutely nothing about the native language of the Macedonians or of anyone else.

Toynbee presents other arguments based on linguistic analysis to support his contention that the Macedonians were native Greek speakers. He asserts that Macedonian is Greek based on the "Greekness" of the word "Makedones" and its variant "Makednoi," Macedonian place names, the names of the members of the Argead house, all recorded Macedonian personal names, the names of Macedonian from Upper Macedonia, the names of the Upper Macedonian cantons, the names of the Macedonian months, the majority of which he claims as Greek. Though at first glance this kind of analysis seems weighty, the counter-arguments are at least as powerful.

An issue that we have to deal with here is what constitutes a "Greek name." It is generally accepted that Indo-European Greeks, Illyrians, Thracians and others settled in the Balkan Peninsula in the fourth, third, and second millennium B.C. As we will see later in more detail, it has been argued that only 40 to 50 percent of the vocabulary of Greek is Indo-European in origin and that 80 percent of its proper names cannot be explained as Indo-European.[9] At least two possibilities might explain the presence of such linguistic forms in ancient Greek. One is that pre–Hellenic cultures were non–Indo-European and that the Greek newcomers adopted many proper names and other words from those peoples. Alternatively, the words might have been introduced by conquerors and settlers from the Levant and from Egypt in the second millennium B.C. In either case it is quite possible that such words came into Macedonian and other Balkan languages in the very same way. Thus both languages might have borrowed from others. If we favor the modern view that the pre–Hellenic influences in Greek are non–Indo-European, and we take into account the observed fact that place names often tend to last through conquest and assimilation, its would be reasonable to assume that some of the supposed "Greek" place names found in the "Macedonian" language are in fact pre–Hellenic names.

It is easy to find modern examples of the same phenomenon. Both France and Germany have many Celtic place names yet do not speak a Celtic language, or even the same language. The people of England are "British," a name based on a Latin word formerly applied to a Celtic-speaking people and now referring to an Anglo-Saxon people. A study of the word "British" does not help us to determine what language the British speak. It is certainly not Latin, yet there is historical evidence about the use of Latin in Britain, the same kind of evidence that is trotted out to prove that the Macedonians were Greek. For instance, since English coins have Latin on them, we might conclude that the British speak Latin, following the argument that it would not make sense to use a language no one could read on such common items. Similarly, many English parish churches have collections of epitaphs in Latin, dating from the Middle Ages. Classicist Andy Fear points out that most of the population of medieval England could not even read English, let alone Latin. Obviously, the significance of surviving Greek texts from Macedonia must be treated with caution. Fear notes, too, that Greek inscriptions from ancient Macedonia are in a mixture of Greek dialects. It is much easier to believe that this could occur if Greek was alien to Macedonia, instead of the common language. If the latter were the case, we might expect to see a consistent form employed.

If we study the month names used in England and France, we can see that they resemble each other. This is not a basis for concluding that French and

English are the same language. All one can reasonably conclude is that there has been similar heavy influence across these two languages. To say, for such superficial reasons, that Greek and Macedonian are the same language is to make far too much of a little thing. We must remember also that much of the history about ancient Macedonians that is passed on to us comes through Greek sources, and names are likely to have been shaped into Greek forms for a myriad of reasons, including the likelihood that Greek writers may not have been able to pronounce other tongues. A modern analogy would be to think that France is a German-speaking country because when reading a German textbook one comes across the name "Frankreich" ruled by, say, Karl rather than Charles. It is easy enough to find English forms of foreign place names that look far removed from their native form; Florence for Firenze, and so on.

In his essay "Linguistic Problems of the Balkan Area in Late Prehistoric and Early Classical Periods,"[10] R.A. Crossland directly addresses the issue of the linguistic character of ancient Macedonian. Crossland points out that the principal languages of the Balkan region in question* appear to have been Illyrian or an Illyrian language group; Thracian or Thraco-Dacian; and Macedonian. When it comes to the language of the Macedonians, Crossland takes a position very different from modern Greek writers. He rejects the idea that the Macedonians and their language were of Mycenaean origin. Then he goes on to consider linguistic and archeological evidence about the possible origins of Macedonian and in so doing directly contradicts Toynbee.

Crossland points out that the territory of the Macedones at the beginning of the fifth century B.C. seems to have lain between Tymphaea in the west, Pelagonia in the north and the river Axius in the east, but so far no category of place-names that we can identify as "Macedonian" has been identified in this area, and no inscription in Greek earlier than the late fourth century B.C. has been found in any part of Macedonia. Thus we have no substantial evidence about the nature of the Macedonian language in the time that it was most exclusively used (before the fifth century B.C.), but neither do we have evidence of any Greek language being in use at that point in history. The use of Greek came later.

Crossland says that the names of Macedonians mentioned in fifth- and fourth-century sources are almost all either certainly or possibly Greek, but he argues that this is not significant, since members of one people often borrow names from another whom they regard as culturally superior. Certainly the Macedonian craze for things Greek, including Greek education for the children of the upper classes, suggests such an attitude.

Next, Crossland points out that the ancient writers of the time gave impre-

*Crossland defined the region under consideration as lying between the Adriatic from northern Epirus northwards in the west, the Julian Alps to the northwest, the Carpathian mountains to the north, the western coasts of the Black Sea to the east, and the Greek-speaking parts of the Greek peninsula and the Aegean region to the south.

cise information about the language of the Macedonians. None of the ancient Greek writers gives a detailed statement about the language that the Macedones spoke. The limited evidence that remains consists of words preserved by Greek lexicographers, especially Hesychius, from about the fifth century A.D. According to Crossland, these words were listed as "used by the Macedonians" or "used in Macedonia" without any indication of the origins of the words. Crossland also cites several other authorities who confirm his conclusions.

Regarding the ancient writers' capacity to recognize significant linguistic features, Crossland agrees with Toynbee in pointing out that when language and speech seemed very different the ancient writers might have had difficulty in making correct classifications. We do not have an understanding of the details of their systems for classifying language. However, we need to remember that only in very recent times have linguists recognized the many languages that make up the Indo-European group. Crossland says that it is difficult to know whether one group of Greek speakers, say the Athenians, would have been able to recognize really different dialects of Greek, or whether they would have been influenced by differences of culture to classify such dialects as barbarian.

Crossland says that the evidence available is too sparse and unsatisfactory to tell us conclusively whether Macedonian was a dialect of Greek or a distinct language. He notes that another authority, N. Hammond, has actually concluded that Macedonian was a dialect of Greek, based on interpretations of information in ancient sources about the status and use of Macedonian under Alexander the Great and his successors. However, Crossland is skeptical of Hammond's reasoning and says that better evidence would come from comparative linguistic study.

Crossland says that two kinds of evidence would help us to conclude that Macedonian was a dialect of Greek. Firstly, we would have to be able to observe or reconstruct its sound system and morphology in a way that would reveal any similarities to recognized ancient Greek dialects, and any contrasts to other Indo-European languages. Secondly, we would have to know whether speakers of most of those Greek dialects could understand and be understood by Macedonians. But none of the necessary evidence is available. The lexical items thought to be Macedonian are too few and uncertain for any useful reconstructions of the language's sound system or morphology, and no Greek writer of the fifth or fourth century B.C. states explicitly whether Greek speakers such as the Athenians could understand the native speech of the Macedonians. Crossland says that these Greeks seemed to have had no difficulty in communicating with the Macedonian court, but this is probably because the royal family of Macedonia, and perhaps most of the nobility, spoke Attic Greek fluently. At home with their families or with their own clansmen they probably used their native tongue, Crossland believes.

We do not know either what form of "international" Greek speech might have been used in Macedonia since there are no substantial inscriptions in Greek from Macedonia earlier than the third century. The Greek speech used might have been Attic or an early form of the *koine* deriving from it that was already spoken even more widely in the Balkans before Alexander's conquest of the Persian Empire.

The information about supposedly Macedonian words given by ancient lexicographers may not be very reliable. Along with words that were a part of the real Macedonian tongue in the fourth century B.C., they might have listed words and usages typical of the variety of Greek that was used in Macedonia from the third century onwards. They may also have included words that were special to the Macedonian armies. Some Greeks in the early Hellenistic period may even have regarded as Macedonian words that belonged to the *koine* as a whole, but not to Attic. We have no way of knowing the underlying basis for classifying words as belonging to one language or another.

Crossland is very critical of Kalleris, a Greek writer who tries to make a case from a linguistics standpoint for Macedonian being a Greek dialect. It is worth looking at this material in detail because of its apparent thoroughness, and because of its relevance to Toynbee's arguments.

In an examination of the 153 words that are described as Macedonian in ancient sources, Kalleris considers that well over three-quarters of these words are Greek. Crossland finds this quite unconvincing. First, he says, a third of these words have no satisfactory etymology. Second, he says that a further 44 items should be disregarded as being false forms in the sources from which they came. They are simply adjectives of Greek formation based on place-names. Although these words seem to be Indo-European, they could belong to an Indo-European language other than Greek. Some of them might be military or technical terms which are Attic in form and were borrowed from Attic Greek in the fifth or fourth century.

Third, Crossland argues, if Macedonian was a dialect of Greek it is extremely unlikely that it would have been similar to Attic Greek. The original Macedonians did not come from the area of Athens and share no history with the Athenians. This means that the Attic words are a false lead, just late borrowings from Greek. It would be much more convincing, perhaps crucial, to find Macedonian words that were not specifically Attic but which occurred either in a considerable number of Greek dialects or in some of the dialects that were spoken in areas adjacent to Macedonia. Kalleris gives fifty-one words of this kind. Many of these words occur in Doric or other West Greek dialects or resemble words in these dialects. However, it is quite possible that these words were borrowed from West Greek dialects or from Thessalian, particularly since all except eighteen of them are the sort of words which the Macedonians might well have borrowed from their neighbors. They include titles of gods, names of festivals and months of the year, military terms, and names of objects that they might have learnt from neighbors to make and use. Such words are often borrowed from neighboring groups, so their existence in Macedonia is not convincing evidence that they were originally Macedonian.

Fourth, the remaining eighteen words, none of which corresponds exactly in meaning or form with Greek words, seem insufficient to make a case for classifying Macedonian as Greek. Once again there is the possibility that the words were borrowed from neighbors. At the western and southern borders of Macedonia were tribes speaking different Greek dialects, and we know that the Macedonians were in contact with these peoples. The Thessalians to the south are particularly likely to have been influential since they were culturally and politically more advanced than the Macedonians before the fifth century. They are likely to have influenced the Macedonians particularly strongly until the growth of Athenian influence. Herodotus reports on traditions in the same period of close contact between the Macedonians and the Dorians before the latter were supposed to have migrated southward.

Finally, though again it is hardly sufficient basis for any conclusion, there is one language feature evident in the surviving "Macedonian" words that points to the idea of a separate language. Macedonian seems to have had a phonological feature that marks it as different from Greek dialects. This is the correspondence of a sound written with B, to Ph in Greek. For instance, this would appear as something like *Bilippos* in Macedonian, and *Philippos* in Greek. Crossland says that this change puts Macedonian closer in phonology to Illyrian and Thracian than to Greek, but it does not mean that Macedonian was a dialect of either language.

Crossland is not convinced by claims that comments from writers such as Arrian and Plutarch in the first to second centuries A.D. (e.g. Plutarch, *Ant.* 27) show that Macedonians spoke a dialect of Greek as their native tongue. He says they are inconclusive since the expressions used are vague and might be referring to a "Macedonian style" rather than a "Macedonian language" or "dialect." These descriptions would be just as likely if Macedonian was a distinct language as they would be if it was a dialect of Greek. Crossland points out that it is possible that Macedonian kings and their courts, soldiers and colonists might have continued to speak a second language in their homes and among themselves for some generations even though they spoke Greek for most practical purposes. After all, it is easy to think of examples of this kind of thing in more modern times. Crossland notes that Gaelic was used alongside English for generations by Scots who emigrated to America. It is still used in this way in some small communities in North America. Similarly, although English was used as the language of command and administration in British army regiments recruited predominantly in Wales, the Welsh language was still used privately.

Like historians who have examined this question, Crossland suggests that Alexander may have required Macedonians in his armies to use Greek as the language of command, just as he required many Persians to learn it (Plut. *Alex.*

43.7), because it was efficient, and because he thought it the language best suited to serve as the common medium of communication among the peoples of his empire. This kind of strategic decision does not require that Macedonian should have been similar to the new "international" language.

In summing up, Crossland says again that the evidence does not indicate convincingly that Macedonian was a dialect of Greek rather than a separate Indo-European language. Even Toynbee, who is persuaded in the opposite direction by the very flimsy evidence we have considered above emphasizes that the evidence is "fragmentary, ... confused and self-contradictory."[11] In practical terms this suggests that modern Greeks may have to look elsewhere for convincing evidence that ancient Macedonians were Greek.

Ancient Greek Attitudes Toward Macedonians

Throughout antiquity, the Chasia and Kamvounia Mountains, Mount Olympus, and the Vale of Tempe were recognized as separating Macedonia from Greece. To the north, Macedonia extended as far as the Vardar watershed and along the Struma and Mesta valleys, past the city of Blagoevgrad to the sources of the Bistrica River in the Rila Mountains in today's Bulgaria. Macedonia covered a land area of c. 26,000 square miles. The northern boundary of ancient Macedonia ran either from the modern city of Preveza (a Macedonian name, meaning "ferrytown") or from Korfu to the Vale of Tempe south of Mount Olympus.[12] In antiquity, Macedonia was a northern neighbor of Greece, never a province of Greece. The ancients knew where Greece ended and where Macedonia began. They believed that Mount Olympus was in Macedonia, Mount Parnassus in Greece. Thus the geographer Strabo called Olympus the highest mountain in Macedonia. It still is today. Various ancient Greek geographers and historians in the classical and post-classical periods, such as Ephoros, Pseudo-Skylax, Dionysios son of Kalliphon, and Dionysios Periegetes, put the northern border of Greece at the line from the Ambrakian Gulf to the Peneios, therefore excluding Macedonia. Medeios of Larisa in Thessaly (which borders Macedonia), who accompanied Alexander on his campaign in Asia, called the Thessalians "the most northerly of the Greeks." Herodotus spoke of the Thessalians as the first Greeks to fall under Persian rule in 480 B.C. Thus, there was a clear distinction between Macedonian and Greek lands and peoples.

After the Persian wars, in the classical period of ancient Greece, there developed a consciousness of a common Hellenism that transcended the territorial divisions and mutual hostility of the Greek states. There was a general recognition of a bond that linked those who were "Hellenes" as opposed to those who were "barbarians," and certain standards of behavior were expected to apply amongst Hellenes that were not expected when dealing with foreigners.

The modern word "barbarian" comes from the Greek word *barbaroi,* meaning "foreigner." This is the word Greeks applied to Macedonians and other peoples they thought were different from themselves. Given that Greek scholars were very sophisticated — indeed we still recognize the ancient Greek teachers as among the greatest thinkers of all time — it hardly seems plausible that they were not clever enough to perceive obvious similarities. For example, Crossland points out that the ancient Greek writers Herodotus and Thucydides considered ancestry, language and culture to be the basis for Greek community, and says we can probably take as reasonably accurate their judgments about the ethnicity and language of major groups of people.[13]

The ancient Greeks recognized other peoples throughout the Balkans, in Asia minor, and in other colonies as Greek because they saw similarities of language, culture and religion. They thought in terms of a Greek identity that was established throughout the known civilized world. They did not see such similarities when it came to the Macedonians.

Cultural differences might have been the determining factor in making these classifications if there were no obvious similarities of language. This is an important point since some modern historians argue that Greekness is evident historically through culture rather than simply through race or language. Yet the great ancient Greek teachers could not see enough similarities in Macedonian culture to believe that it was Greek.

Other historians have drawn attention to the idea that cultural differences between the Macedonians and Greeks are the more important factors to be considered. In discussing the way that Greeks and Macedonians viewed each other, Pierre Jouguet, a French historian, comments that like the Greeks, the enemies of the Macedonians, called them "barbarians."[14] Jouguet goes on to remind us of the bitter language used by the great Athenian orator and leader Demosthenes, who spoke contemptuously of the Macedonian "barbarians" as he tried to rally support for an armed force to try and stop Macedonian expansion:

> Truly Philip calls himself a hellenophile, that is a friend of Greece... That is more than a lie. The king cannot be a Hellenophile because of his barbarian origin. He is not a Hellene and is not in any way connected by kin with the Hellenes. He is not even a foreigner with a decent origin. He is only a miserable Macedon; and in Macedonia, as is well known, one cannot even buy a decent slave.[15]

In this speech before the great defeat by the Macedonians, Demosthenes did not recognize the Macedonians as Greek. Some say that he spoke this way because it was politically necessary; he wanted the Greek states to join together to fight the Macedonians, so he painted the Macedonians as outsiders. This is a plausible argument. However, Demosthenes' public speeches after the Macedonian triumph still fail to show any recognition of the Macedonians as Hellene.

If we consider Demosthenes' epitaph to the Athenians who fell at Chaeronea, we still see the very clear belief that Macedonians were outsiders.[16] While it is fair enough to suggest that the great orator would have used every manipulative trick he could think of to get the Greeks to unify against the Macedonians, including scorning them as foreigners, it just does not make any sense that he would use the same kind of terminology after the Greeks had been defeated. Demosthenes had fled the battlefield. He had been humiliated individually and as an Athenian. He had been part of a delegation that pleaded with the Macedonians to permit the return of the dead Athenian soldiers to their homeland. It seems most unlikely that he would offer the Macedonians gratuitous abuse at this very sensitive time. More likely he was describing things as people generally believed them to be.

> Time, whose o'erseeing eye records all human actions,
> Bear word to mankind what fate we suffered, how
> Striving to safeguard the holy soil of Hellas
> Upon Boeotia's famous plain we died.

This is not a statement aimed at encouraging opposition to the Macedonians. It is a statement made while arranging the terms of the Macedonian takeover of the Greek states. It was a sad acknowledgment of the Athenians who had died while "striving to safeguard the holy soil of Hellas" from the invading Macedonian foreigners. For this reason we might take it as being an accurate reflection of Greek attitudes to the Macedonians.

The American historian E. Badian reflects on the fact that Greek opponents of the Macedonians still called the Macedonian king "barbarian" half a generation after Philip's revival of the Macedonian king's claim to eminent Greek descent had been accepted at the Olympic Games.[17] Badian tells us of another occasion that Demosthenes called Philip a barbarian.[18] Demosthenes claimed that a century before, "the king then in power in the country was the subject [of our ancestors], as a barbarian ought to be to Greeks." Badian acknowledges that Demosthenes' abusive statements may have had nothing to do with historical fact, but finds it curious that claims to Hellenic ancestry were rejected not only for the Macedonian people, but even for the king. The rejection is taken as a matter of course. Badian argues that Demosthenes could not speak in these terms if his audience was likely to regard his claim as plain nonsense. For instance, "barbarian" could not have been applied to a Theban, or even a Thessalian. This indicates that the notion of the Macedonian kings as Hellenes ruling a barbarian nation was still not totally accepted. There was still considerable division of opinion about the matter.

When it came to the Macedonian people, as distinct from the king, there was no division at all. They were regarded as clearly barbarian, despite the various myths that the Macedonian court had issued.

A speech by Isocrates provides good support for this assertion. Isocrates, the apostle of panhellenism, had become one of Philip's main supporters. He had tried to persuade each of the Greek states in turn to lead a holy war against the Persians, and all had turned him down. With the emergence of Macedonia as a Balkan power, Isocrates tried again to find support for his pet project. When visiting the court of Philip II, soon after the Peace of Philocrates, he made a speech of flattery to the Macedonian leader. The orator congratulated Philip on the fact that his ancestor had not attempted to become a tyrant in his native city (Argos), but "leaving the area of Greece entirely," had decided to seize the kingship over Macedon. This, explained Isocrates, showed that he understood that essential difference between Greeks and non–Greeks: that Greeks cannot submit to the rule of a monarch. It was this insight that enabled Philip's ancestor to found a dynasty over a "people of non-kindred race."[19]

As further evidence of this point, Jouguet notes that after the Sacred War, when Philip's successes allowed him to claim a voice in the Delphic Amphictyony, that privilege was given not to the people of Macedonia, which one might expect if the people were seen as Greek victors in battle, but to the king alone. Badian agrees that Philip had not tried to pass off his Macedonians as Greek and had accepted membership of the Delphic Amphictyony as a personal gift, not as something concerning his people.

In his book *In the Shadow of Olympus*, Borza points out that there are differences between Greek and Macedonian towns. In a collection of essays titled *Hellenistic Culture* (edited by Gruen), N.G.L. Hammond makes a similar point. One major difference is the lack of temples in Macedonian towns. This implies a difference in religious practices, confirming what we already know about the exclusion of Macedonians from the Delphic Amphictyony. Badian tells us also that the Macedonians had their own sacred city, Dion, while the Greeks focused their religious attention on Delphi. This religious communality of the Greeks was one of the defining characteristics of the Hellenes. Since the Macedonians were not a part of this grouping, they fail one of the most important tests for being members of the Hellenic community. Their inadequacies in this regard were widely understood by the ancient Greeks.

It seems that the Macedonian style of burial was different from that found in Greece.[20] Furthermore, excavations of ancient sites have often provided information that is open to different interpretations. For instance, the excavations at Kutles have revealed a group of tombs with Greek artifacts, but there are also artifacts which look Thracian and Scythian rather than Greek. The excavations in no way tell us that the occupants of these tombs were "Greek." We need to keep in mind, too, that ancient Macedonian tombs discovered in modern times are the tombs of the wealthy, the class which Hellenized its language for reasons of social snobbery and political gain. We must be as cautious regarding Macedonian use of Greek customs as we are about their adoption of one form of Greek language.

Similarly, we need to exercise reserve in interpreting the fact that Greek inscriptions have been found in Macedonia. Such inscriptions have been found all over the Mediterranean world because of the widespread use of Greek. We know that some of these inscriptions were made by non–Greek peoples. There is evidence from Judea as early as the seventh century B.C. of Jews, especially rich ones, from the towns of Seleucia and Gadara using Greek instead of Hebrew in business and government. Thracian burial sites from the fifth and fourth centuries B.C. yielded vessels with Greek inscriptions. From time to time, wandering Celts left messages behind in Greek.[21]

When speaking of Philip's war with the Persians, Jouguet notes the strength of Greek antagonism to the institution of kingship.[22] He says that those Greeks who were most attached to the ideal of Greek liberties felt that these were threatened by the prospect of rule by a Macedonian king. As a passing comment in connection with this observation, Jouguet says that the Macedonian people "stood outside of Hellenism." When he talks of the ethnic background of the Macedonians, Jouguet acknowledges claims that they were Illyrians or Epeirots, or a mixture of Greek, Albanian and Thraco-Illyrian elements. He says that this is beside the point. What really matters, he suggests, is that "the Hellenes and the Macedonians regarded themselves as different nations, and this feeling did not cease to be the source of great difficulties for the union of Greece under Macedonian rule."

Even by the time of the empire of Alexander the Great, Macedonians did not consider themselves to be Greek. For instance, in 319 B.C., a few years after Alexander's death, Polysperhon, heir to the Macedonian throne, was sent to the Greek city-states. His statement to his hosts confirms that the Macedonians did not think of themselves as Hellenes: "As our ancestors always did good to Hellenes, we also would like to continue that tradition; and to give proof of our friendliness towards Greek people."[23]

Peter Green, a Classics professor and the author of highly respected books and articles about the ancient Greeks and Macedonians, gives us some insights into the attitudes of the ancient Greeks towards the Macedonians.[24] He says that the Greek city-states regarded the Macedonians with "genial and sophisticated contempt." The Greeks saw the Macedonians as little better than savages, uncouth louts with uncivilized speech and politics, inadequate fighters, and habitual oath-breakers. They were men who dressed in bear-pelts, consumed barbaric alcoholic drinks, and regularly engaged in assassination and incest.

There are many reasons for the ancient Greek contempt for everything Macedonian. Green notes some of these, including the collaboration of Alexander I with the Persians, the ancient enemy of the Greeks, and the opportunistic way that Alexander switched sides to his own advantage when the time was right. There was the similarly duplicitous behavior of his son Perdiccas II, and the treacherous means used by Archelaus to reach the Macedonian throne by murdering his uncle, cousin and half-brother and marrying his father's widow.

As if all that were not outrageous enough, Archelaus was himself murdered as a result of his homosexual intrigues.

In the second half of the fifth century B.C., Thrasymacus of Chalcedon referred to Archelaus, king of Macedonia, explicitly describing him as a barbarian, and contrasting him with the Hellenes of Thessaly. He also indicated that the border on the Peneois River between Macedonia and Thessaly was an ethnic and a linguistic point of demarcation. In other words, Thrasymacus thought that the Greeks spoke a different language from the foreign Macedonians.

Philip II and the Macedonian army. British historian David G. Hogarth says that Philip II evolved the first European power in the modern sense of the word, and he did this by establishing the first national standing army to be seen in Europe. This army created new and special bonds between its own members as well as between the diverse peoples of Macedonia. Hogarth says that in setting up his standing army, Philip eliminated distinctions between Macedonians from different areas and tribes but at the same time increased the distinctions between Macedonians and Greeks. All who were joined in the army were called Macedonians. The only distinctions made from that time on were between Macedonians and other ethnic groups who lived outside Macedonian lands: Greeks, Thracians or Illyrians.

When Philip promoted his subjects to his heavy cavalry, the "Companions," all of these men who joined this group took on the name "Macedones," regardless of their ethnic origins. Similarly, his foot-soldiers were labeled "Kings' Followers" regardless of the clan or ethnic group they came from within Macedonia. In this way, Hogarth says, Philip distinguished the new nation from the Greeks, just as the original Macedonian clans had once distinguished themselves from the peoples they ruled within Macedonia.[25]

Hogarth says that Philip sought to make military service the main object of his soldiers' existence. Having a professional army with a national spirit was the new idea that Philip was to exploit with great success. Upper-class boys were trained from a young age, developing a passion and commitment to the army and its task. Hogarth believes that Philip must have foreseen that this training would be a powerful unifying force so that the small race divisions among his people would gradually fade. Indeed, it was so successful that "the Macedonians became one people, and their common military pride and exclusiveness barred even Alexander's way when he dreamed of a wider union... His first attempts to expand the great Macedonian union provoked open mutiny."

The View of Modern Historians

Modern historians, like the ancient peoples, continue to distinguish between the Greeks and the Macedonians and the lands that they inhabited. They do not speak as though these are the same peoples, as they might do when comparing different Greek city-states such as Sparta and Athens. They speak of them as though they were different, culturally and ethnically. This is a recognition of the way these ancient peoples viewed each other. Historians such as Donald Kagan, professor of history and classics at Cornell University and author of *The Great Dialogue: A History of Greek Political Thought*, generally describe ancient Greece as geographically divided from Macedonia and note that Philip brought Greece into union with Macedonia — obviously regarding the nations as distinct. In *The New Illustrated History of the World, The Triumph of the Greeks 800 B.C.–321 B.C.*,[26] we find references to Macedonia as a distinct entity:

> The man who finally welded the Macedonians into a cohesive nation was Philip II the father of Alexander the Great who was probably as great a man as his more famous son... Both in diplomacy and in open warfare Philip easily surpassed the Greeks.

Note that the author doesn't say "the other Greeks"; he says "the Greeks," and this form of description continues throughout the book. He talks of Demosthenes' contempt for the Macedonian foreigners, and the generally unreasonable sense of superiority that the Greeks had with regard to the Macedonians.

The view of the Macedonians as separate from the Greeks is still present when historians speak about the later period when the Greeks were under Macedonian dominance. For instance, in writing about the settlement of Alexandria in Egypt by the conquering Macedonian forces, C.A. Kincaid[27] makes a distinction between Macedonians and Hellenes. He says that the city of Alexandria, the capital of a Macedonian kingdom, required an infusion of Macedonian mercenaries in the surrounding countryside to provide a peasant stock from which the fighting men would come, and a civilian Hellenic population for the city itself.

In another example, *The New Illustrated History of the World* refers to Athens and Thebes joining against Philip in their "hope of saving Greece from the Macedonian threat."[28]

Some of those who speak of the Greeks and Macedonians as though they were separate peoples, such as N.G.L. Hammond, undoubtedly believe that the Macedonians were a Greek tribe; yet these historians are guided by historic custom to make clear distinction between the Macedonians on the one hand and the Greek states on the other. This necessary distinction reflects the reality of the ancient times. The ancient Macedonians and Greeks knew they were different peoples.

The Name of Macedonia

Michael A. Dimitri, a modern-day Macedonian (despite the Greek-sounding name), provides his own theory about the derivation of the name of the ancient Macedonians. He considers firstly the Greek claim that the early Makedones' name meant "tall ones" or "highlanders" who came down from the mountains to conquer the plains, or "tall mountains," a reference again to their original location. He dismisses support for these claims that comes from the manufactured genealogies of the Macedonian Argeadae dynasty given by the ancient historians, Herodotus and Thucydides, during the fifth century B.C. He echoes the point made by Badian that such genealogies were inventions for a political purpose. He proposes "a more defendable and likely derivation for the name of Macedonia" that "lies in prehistory." Dimitri argues that

> during this period in many parts of the world, the chief deity worshipped by early civilizations as they learned to cultivate, settle, and tame the lands they inhabited was the earth which they personified as a goddess. It was this Earth goddess who, like a mother, provided them with the abundant crops, herds, and shelters which they needed for survival. In return for her blessings, many of these cultures named their land for their own particular version of this Earth Mother. A well-known example is Italy whose name derives from Italia, an ancient Earth mother of that peninsula. In Macedonia's name also there is evidence of the early goddess. In the Indo-European languages of which Macedonian is a part, the word base "Ma" is associated with "female, woman, and mother." Examples would include "mater" in Latin, "madre" in Spanish, "mama" in English, and "majka" in Macedonian. Additionally, the word base "don" means "gift." Examples would include the verb "do, dare" in Latin, "dar" in Spanish, "donate" in English, and "donese" in Macedonian. If we add, then, the word "majka" to the base for gift, "don," with the typical Indo-European noun ending "-ia," we get "majkadonia" or Makedonia/Macedonia. The name Macedonia, therefore, dates to prehistory and its meaning is "The Mother's Gift." There is further evidence to support this theory such as the inscriptions found to a Macedonian Earth Mother named "Ma." There are also historical references to the name "Macedonia" in association with a people called "Macedonians" dating back millennia.[29]

Whether or not we choose to believe this theory about the origins of the name Macedonia, there is little doubt about the main theme presented in this chapter: The Macedonians and Greeks thought that they were different peoples. They could see no similarities of language or culture. The Greeks were contemptuous of the barbarian Macedonians. Furthermore there is insufficient linguistic evidence available today to allow modern scholars to come to a different opinion. While it is clear that the ruling class of the Macedonians began to use a form of Greek, and began to follow some Greek customs, especially after the fourth century B.C., historians do not see this as evidence that the Macedonians and Greeks were the same peoples. The use of a Greek written script was necessary for the Macedonians, as it was for other peoples of the time without their own written language, to further their trade and political ambitions. The cultural differences between the ancient Macedonians and Greeks are more evident than the language differences. Since culture became increasingly important in the definition of Hellenism, the weakness of claims regarding the "Greekness of Macedonia" is all the more apparent.

2. Origins of the Macedonian Population

Part of the Greek claim to Macedonian ethnic continuity with the ancient Greeks — a claim that embraces the Greek speakers of present-day Aegean Macedonia — is the idea that the original Macedonians were an ethnically and culturally homogeneous group. If they were not a homogeneous group, then any argument about ethnic continuity must refer to only a portion of these peoples. If it turns out that a majority of the population of ancient Macedon in the time of the great Macedonian kingdom was not ethnically Macedonian, then even the best case for a Greek connection with ancient Macedonia is seriously weakened.

The alternative idea of some kind of relationship by descent between modern-day Macedonians and ancient Macedonians, an idea that has not been put forth by the government of the Republic of Macedonia, can be argued from two different positions. First there is the possibility, proposed by at least one mainstream historian, that the Paeones, a major constituent group of ancient Macedonia, were Slavic speakers. It does not require great ingenuity to claim a connection between these peoples and the Slavs who were to occupy the same lands in the sixth century A.D. Second, there is the important but neglected question about what happened to the ancient Macedonians when the Slavs occupied their lands. As we shall see in a later chapter, it has been argued that this incursion in the south of the Balkan peninsula, in the area that is now Greece, though equally comprehensive, did not lead to the destruction of the local people, but to an extended assimilation process. There is no compelling reason to believe that such assimilation was restricted to the south. In other words, the invaders in Macedonia mixed with the existing peoples, and the descendants of these peoples could reasonably claim a direct connection with the ancient Macedonians.

Apart from these main themes about development in Macedonia, there are other historic ethnic contributions of interest, from the Celts and Germans in particular. In medieval times, cultural changes, including the conversion of the Macedonian Slavs to Christianity and the development of a written form of the

Slavic language, paved the way for the appearance of several Balkan nation-states in modern times. The pathway to this state of affairs was often tortuous, as Macedonian Slavs struggled first with the great Eastern Roman Empire, then endured Turkish occupation for five centuries. However, this process leads inevitably to the appearance of a modern Macedonian state. This chapter will sketch some of this background before the issue of a Macedonian national consciousness is considered in more detail.

The Coming of the Indo-Europeans

Indo-Europeans began to arrive in the Balkans about 3000 B.C.,[1] apparently emerging from an area to the north of the Black Sea. With their language they brought their culture. Archaeological evidence suggests the common source of the Indo-Europeans as the part of southern Russia lying between the Danube Basin and the Urals. As they moved west, the closely related dialects of the Indo-Europeans were mixed with the existing, older languages of eastern and central Europe. Over the last two thousand years B.C., these new dialects spread to every part of Europe, overwhelming, but not eliminating completely, the existing languages. The new languages created by this process, called the Indo-European languages, include almost all the living languages of Europe as well as many of the languages of the Middle East and northwest India.

Immediately we are presented with an idea relevant to this question about racial origins. All of the Indo-Europeans came from the same general area. Differences that arose between them sometimes were influenced by the natures of the original inhabitants of the lands they invaded, and sometimes by accidents of history. An instance of the latter development concerns a distinction that came about between one group of Indo-European dialects and another, the *kentum/satem* split. The dialects from which Illyrian, Greek, Italic, Celtic and Gothonic languages were to emerge retained the original *k* sound, while another group, from which arose the later Baltic, Slavic, Indo-Iranian, Albanian and Armenian, "palatalized" the *k*, making it a sibilant *s* or *sh*. Early philologists called these two groups *kentum* and *satem* (respectively) from the Latin and Avestan words for 100. This split probably resulted from a relatively long separation between the two different groups of dialects. Other differences are likely to have developed as peoples became separated from each other, inhabited different lands whose environments demanded different words, and established vital and novel culture in their own communities.

John Geipel explains that in pre–Roman times, Indo-European languages such as Thracian, Phrygian, Dacian, Getic and Bithynian were widely spoken throughout modern-day Hungary, Romania, Bulgaria, the former Yugoslavia, and Albania. By about the sixth century A.D. all of these were extinct, and there is little evidence of them today except perhaps for some traces of Thracian in modern Albanian. Geipel considers that Illyrian was a *kentum* language, which would make it different from Slavic dialects.

At the beginning of the second millennium B.C., the area later known as Macedonia was inhabited principally by Illyrians in the west and Thracians in the east.[2] During the second millennium B.C., the ancient Greeks descended in several waves of migration from the interior of the Balkans into what is now Greece. Some passed through the Morava-Vardar Valley and across the plain of Thessaly on their way south. Others traveled through Epirus. Some scholars recently suggested that Asia Minor was the original Greek homeland.[3]

The Bronze Age Mycenaean civilization, named after the city of Mycenae on the Peloponnesus, was at its height from about 1400 to 1100 B.C. in mainland Greece and on the Aegean islands. Some authorities cite archaeological evidence in arguing that the Mycenaeans, a people closely resembling the Vlachs, came down into the Balkans from South Russia in about 2200 B.C. Remnants of their burial pits (*tumuli*) have been found spreading from Albania to western Macedonia, and down the Haliacamon valley into Aegean Macedonia.[4] These people brought Greek and Illyrian into the Balkans. There have been few such archaeological finds from Macedonia, leading some scholars to believe that ancient Macedonia lay beyond the cultural and ethnic borders of Mycenaean culture.[5] In any case, the Mycenaeans had little if any long-term influence on Macedonia.

A little later, around 1250–1150 B.C., the Dorians, speakers of a Greek dialect, arrived in the Balkans. Hammond claims archaeological evidence for their presence in the pastoral areas of Albania, Macedonia, and North Epirus, but their visible impact was in the south. These people were called the "descendants of Hercules," or the Heracleidae. There is no evidence of contact between the Dorians and the Illyrians and Macedonians who occupied Macedonia soon after.

The Known Original Inhabitants of Macedonia

At the beginning of the last millennium B.C., the inhabitants of Macedonia were probably the Brygi. These people had a rich culture around Vergina, which ended about 800 B.C. Double axes that have been held to represent this culture have been found throughout Macedonia and Thrace, at Voynik near Kumanovo and in central Bulgaria.[6] Greek and other historians frequently mention the Brygians. Their name derives from the Macedonian word *breg*, "hill/mountain." Thus the Brygians were the "hillsmen" of Macedonia. The Brygians of Macedonia were believed to be the European branch of the people who in Asia Minor were known as the Phrygians.[7]

From about 800 B.C., in the east and west of Macedonia, including Pelagonia and Eordaea, new people appeared. These people were likely to have been

Illyrians who came from what was recently central Yugoslavia, an area that had acted as a reservoir of Illyrian peoples. There was a great expansion of the Illyrians, south to Thessaly, east to the middle Vardar valley, to places that were the forerunners of modern day Kumanovo, Skopje, Stip and Titov Veles, western Bulgaria and Romania, and west to northern Epirus. Most of upper and lower Macedonia were taken over. Thus Phrygian influence was replaced by Illyrian. The centers of Illyrian power in lower Macedonia were at Vergina by the Haliacamon and on both sides of the Vardar by Gevgheli. Other Illyrians took control of the middle Strymon valley and the coastal plain, including the site of Amphipolis. The Illyrians did not combine to form a centralized power, but remained nomadic or semi-nomadic pastoralists.[8]

To the east of the Illyrians were Thracians, with whom borders were often disputed. Around the time of the birth of Christ, Thracian speakers inhabited land that is now part of modern Bulgaria and the Greek provinces of Thrace and Turkey in Europe, except for the coastal districts.[9] It is also likely that Thracian and Phrygian dialects, bearing some resemblance to modern Albanian, lingered on in the less accessible northern parts of (modern) Greece until after the expansion of the Hellenes.[10]

The Coming of the Macedonians

In the first millennium B.C., the mountainous area of Orestis, near present-day Kastoria, and the valley of the Haliacmon River were settled by a people called the Macedons. About 700 B.C., this clan had migrated eastward from Orestis in the Pindus mountains, looking for arable land for their cattle. Lower Macedonia was ruled by Macedonian chiefs who subjugated or expelled the earlier Illyrian or Thracian inhabitants, while upper Macedonia was inhabited by semi-autonomous tribes.[11] The royal dynasty of the Argeads, to which Philip II himself belonged, was the leading family among the Macedonians. The Macedonians first occupied Pieria, the coastal plain running northward from Mt. Olympus, and afterwards extended their conquests to include the alluvial plain of Bottiaea, named Emathia by Homer, which lay west of the Thermaic gulf. The city of Edessa was a part of their territory, and nearby they established Aegae, which was to become a significant center of Macedonian administration.

The original Macedonian kingdom. While it is reasonable to argue that the original Macedones who emerged in Emathia in the eighth century were a homogeneous group, this is not true of the great Macedon kingdom at the time of Alexander the Great. A majority of the population of that kingdom was not Macedonian, but Illyrian and Thracian. There were many different tribes that Philip II welded together to form the Macedon nation. This mixture of peoples, few of whom were unequivocally Greek, makes suspect any claim of Greek ethnic continuity in Aegean Macedonia.

The Illyrians were first to became a part of the Macedonian people, not merely through assimilation, but in particular as the main element in the "out-kingdoms" which were to become firmly identified with the Macedonian nation under Philip II. The British historian Hogarth points out that at the beginning of Philip's reign, the Pindus ranges were controlled by the hill tribes (proba-bly Illyrian), Chalcidice was Greek territory, and the plain of Monastir was in the hands of the Paeonians.[12] As ancient history tells us:

> All these lands, indeed, except Chalcidice, as Thucydides bears witness, were to be called later by the common name Macedonia, and Lyncestians, and Elimiotes and other upland peoples were included eventually among Mace-donians, but as a result of conquest.

The point here is that whatever the ethnic and language character of the small group of original Macedones, there was a complicated mixture of peo-ples at the time of Macedonia's greatness.

A similar conclusion is made by F. W. Wallbank, Rathbone Professor of Ancient History and Classical Archaeology at the University of Liverpool, who refers to the writings of the Roman historian Livy to make the point that in Philip's time there was a *strategos* for Paeonia, which includes the area where Skopje is today, and some of modern Serbia. But these outlying areas maintained their tra-ditional culture, despite having a governor from Pella.[13] Wallbank says that although it is true that by the time of Alexander the absorption of the outlying districts into Macedonia was almost complete, there is evidence of a strong regional sense in these parts. Thus Illyrian culture and language were maintained.

The Greek towns showed an even stronger resistance to being ethnically and culturally absorbed by the Macedonians. Wallbank says that the Greeks liv-ing in Macedonia only sometimes called themselves Macedonian. These towns had once been independent, but had been forcibly absorbed into Macedon. However, ever since the fifth century when the Macedonian kings invented a family connection with Greek mythical figures and adopted a philhellenic pol-icy, towns such as Beroea, Pella and Edessa, on the Hellenic model, had existed in Macedonia. In general they were loyal to the rulers of Macedon, and on some special occasions they even called themselves Macedonians. Nevertheless, the essentially Greek nature of these towns persisted. It is worth noting this dis-tinction Wallbank makes between Greek culture within the borders of Mace-donia and Macedonian culture. Clearly they were different. Hellenes were rec-ognized as different from Macedonians.

Badian tells us that the annexed Greek cities counted as parts of the Mace-donian kingdom, not as allies. This was why they had not become members of the Hellenic League after the conquest of the Greeks. However, while counted as Macedonian subjects of the king, they still retained some sort of civic iden-tity that put them on a level with the districts of Orestis or Eordaea within old Macedonia. The Macedonian kingdom was thus formed of many parts.

The mixed nature resulting from this combination was evident in local interests and cultures. The original, non–Macedonian languages were still spoken in many areas. Historian Tom Winnifrith says it is very likely that even at the time of the Roman conquest, nearly two hundred years after Alexander the Great, quite a high proportion of the wilder districts of both Macedonia and Epirus were still speaking a non–Greek language.[14] This was less likely in Epirus, Winnifrith says, but more than likely in the north of territory which the Roman writer Strabo called "free Macedonia." In describing the people of these areas, Strabo talked of bilingual barbarians, and his use of the present tense suggests he was talking of his own time. An important point to understand is that before the Romans conquered Macedonia, Greek was the language of government and administration in Macedonia and in the Greek states. After the Roman conquest, the longer-established Greek language was gradually replaced by Latin in the Northern Balkans. In fact, the progress of Latin slowed and stopped after a time.

In the northwest of Macedonia, the second language for these "barbarians" was Latin, and in the southeast it was Greek. The presence of the official language says nothing at all about what language was used in private, in the family context for example. People tended to be at least bilingual, speaking both the official language (Greek or Latin) as well as their own language. The first language was their own vernacular, probably Illyrian in the north and west and Thracian in the east. This kind of bilingualism continued throughout the next two thousand years as one ruling power was replaced by another.

Many of these same issues are raised and explained in just the same way by other writers. On the matter of the ethnic character of ancient Macedonia, R. A. Crossland writes that the river Axius (Vardar), in the southwest of Macedonia, was the ethnic boundary between Thracians and Macedonians except where the Macedonians made conquests to the east of it in the fifth and fourth centuries. Crossland explains that the Paeones were probably Illyrian, and the Dardanoi are described as Illyrian by Strabo.

Furthermore, Strabo spoke about the hill tribes in the west of Macedonia as Illyrian tribes ruled by Greek dynasties. This is consistent with two ideas raised earlier: first, that the provinces retained their local culture and language, and second, that the use of Greek customs and language may well have been confined to a ruling elite.

Tom Winnifrith explains[15] that most of the people of the Macedonian kingdom spoke a rough-and-ready kind of Greek, but that Philip and Alexander and some other strong Macedonian kings also ruled over some peoples who never spoke Greek at all. He suggests that an important factor in determining the persistence of local languages in this area was the changing boundaries of Macedonia as Macedonian military strength waxed and waned. For instance, at times of Macedonian weakness, as with the invasion of the Celts in 279 B.C., the boundary receded much further south. He points out also that the fact that

Greek and later Latin were the language of the literati, and therefore the only languages likely to be recorded on written inscriptions, has tended to obscure the importance of Thracian and Illyrian. Nowadays, philologists have come to recognize the importance of these languages in explaining underlying common features in various Balkan languages.

Peter Green tells us more about the divisions between peoples in Macedonia.[16] He says that the country was divided, both geographically and ethnically, into two quite distinct regions: lowlands and highlands. Lower Macedonia comprised the flat, fertile plain around the Thermaic Gulf. This plain is watered by two great rivers, the Axius (Vardar) and the Haliacamon (Vistritza). On all sides except the east there are hills, and in the east the first natural frontier is provided by the Strymon (Struma) River. Green says that lower Macedonia was the old central kingdom, founded by the original Macedon migrants. Upper Macedonia and Paeonia formed a single geographical unit. The highlands lay mostly to the west and southwest of the central plain and were divided into three areas that were at first autonomous kingdoms. These were Elimiotis in the south, Orestis to the west, and Lyncestis to the northwest. The northern frontier of Lyncestis met with Paeonia. All three highland kingdoms shared frontiers with Illyria and Epirus. According to Green, in many ways their inhabitants had more in common with Illyrians, Paeonians or Thracians than with the lowland Macedonians. We should note that Orestis, the place from which the Macedonians came to their new lowlands home, remained essentially Illyrian in culture and language. We might wonder if this is a clue to the ethnicity of the Macedonians themselves.

In describing the religious preferences of the highlanders, Green notes that they were "much addicted to Thracian deities, Sabazius, the Clodones and Mimallones." Green concedes that the highlanders were at least partly of Illyrian stock, and that they intermarried with Thracians or Epirots more often than they did with the lowland Macedonians.

Towards the end of the fifth century B.C., the Macedonian king Archelaus increased his control over the highland "outkingdoms," as they have been called, by forming a contract with nobles of various origins in which they served the king from time to time in a special infantry group called the Companions, and in return were granted large tracts of land in the conquered territories. These grants served to increase the prestige of Archelaus' kingship and helped to assure the loyalty of these Macedonian nobles to himself and his family. In this way, a more or less permanent unification between Upper and Lower Macedonia was achieved. Partly by such means, and by the use of force when necessary, Archelaus established a much more stable relationship with his outkingdoms so that it became possible for him to think of expanding his conquests elsewhere.

Hogarth notes that the origin of the peoples who inhabited Macedonia is an obscure and perhaps insoluble question.[17] He points out that any inquiry based on philological or archaeological evidence must fail because there is not nearly enough evidence available to lead to any useful result. Hogarth was writing nearly one hundred years ago, and since his time there have been many fascinating excavations in Aegean Macedonia. Despite the wealth of knowledge that we have gained since Hogarth's time, the conclusions we come to today are essentially the same as Hogarth's. A quick look at Crossland's observations, described earlier, will confirm this idea.

According to Hogarth, ancient tradition held that the population of Macedonia had at least two different sources and histories. The Hellenic influence had become so strong amongst the ruling gentry and the lowlanders in general by the fourth century, that they were sometimes described as Hellene. He explains that the other group were sometimes labeled barbarian. This barbarian group was called *Pelasgic,* meaning "the old folk." Hogarth says it is certain that this group was largely Illyrian, the same peoples as the Bryges. These people, from Phrygia, brought us the myths of Gordius and Midas.

The lowland Macedonians pushed the older peoples into the western and northern highlands. These peoples were called Orestians, Lyncestians, Elimiotes, Paeonians, and so on. Hogarth says the belief that the Macedonians of the coastal plains and the highlands were distinct peoples with distinct traditions was held not only in Greece, but in Macedonia as well. However, Hogarth suggests, "probably much intermixture took place."

Hogarth says, perhaps in some contradiction to Green's comments, that until the time of Philip II there was, between the Macedonians of the coastal plain and the free men of the highlands, little of that "community of tradition and hope which alone consummates the identity of a nation." There had been an unsatisfactory kind of compromise between two forces that were very nearly equal in power and significance. It was only in Philip's time that these two very different parts of the Macedonian kingdom were truly bound together as one nation.

In explaining the ethnic nature of the peoples from the Macedonian out-kingdoms, Hogarth says that Greek historians did not clearly distinguish between the hill tribes and their Illyrian neighbors, who were at times their allies. He argues that in nine out of ten cases, when Macedonian kings went out to battle with "Illyrians," they were at war first and foremost with their own great feudatories of Lyncestis, Orestis, Elimiotis, or Paeonia. Thus, until the accession of Philip II, Macedonia was "a group of discordant units, without community of race, religion, speech, or sentiment."

An Ancient Slavic Kingdom?

Arnold Toynbee offers the suggestion that the Paeones, a numerous and powerful group spread widely in Macedonia, were Slavic or Illyrian peoples.[18]

He notes that there were Paeones in the Axios basin, but says that the majority of the Paeonian peoples were to be found in the Strymon Basin. Toynbee says also that place names acknowledged in various Greek states indicate that "bands of Paiones had once reached southern continental European Greece, but they are not evidence that the Paiones were a Greek-speaking people."

At least some Paeonian groups were in Macedonia before the Macedonians achieved political significance, and were still there more than a thousand years later when the new wave of Slavic peoples arrived. Toynbee says "the headwaters of the Strymon were held by the Agrianes — a Paeonian people according to all our authorities — at the time of Megabazos' campaign *circa* 511 B.C., at the time of Sitalkes' campaign in 429 B.C., and at the time of Alexander's campaign in 335 B.C., and both they and their neighbors and kinsmen, the Dentheletai, seem to have held their ground in this region until they were swamped, at last, by the Slav Volkerwanderung in the sixth and seventh centuries of the Christian era." Accordingly, it is of some interest to the present debate to ask whether these people might have been Slavic.

Toynbee explores the issue of the ancestral language and the nationality of the Paeones. He uses the study of geographical names, ethnika and personal names. After analysis of this material, Toynbee finds that these words are a combination of Greek, Illyrian, Thracian and either Slavonic or Slavonic-influenced Illyrian/Thracian and unspecified non–Greek elements.

With regard to specifically Slavonic elements, Toynbee notes a number of non–Greek sounding names, including Domerus and Doberos and "a set of names ending in -azoros or -azora: Azoros in the Perrhaebian Tripolis; Gazoros in Edonike; Hypsizorus, a mountain on or near the Pallene Peninsula; Bylazora on the upper Axios." He notes that some of these names have a distinctly Slavonic flavor: "'Astraios' calls to mind 'Ostrov' and 'Ostrva'; 'Doberos' calls to mind 'Dobro'; '-azor" calls to mind both 'izvor' and 'gora'; the 'Byl-' in Bylazora calls to mind the Slavonic word for 'white.'" These Slavonic-like sounds do not prove that the language was something other than Illyrian or Thracian since they might have appeared in Paionian through borrowings from neighboring peoples. Toynbee says that the Illyrian, Thracian and Slavonic speakers are likely to have been each other's next-door neighbors at some stages in the differentiation and diffusion of the Indo-European languages. However, he says, "It is also conceivable that the Paeones may actually have been a Slavonic-speaking people that had been caught up in the Thracian and Illyrian Völkerwanderung into south-eastern Europe some 1,700 or 1,800 years before the massive Völkerwanderung of the Slavs in the sixth and seventh centuries of the Christian Era." Toynbee concludes that, on the whole, the evidence seems to point to the Paeones' ancestral language having been Illyrian, or possibly Slavonic, rather than Greek, though he acknowledges that the evidence is not very clear.

Some of the Paeones tribes were deported by Megabazos to Phyrygia around 511 B.C. However, this does not seem to have had a major impact on Paeonian numbers. Before being conquered by King Antigonus II of Macedonia in the third century B.C., the territory of the present Republic of Macedonia was occupied by a Paeonian kingdom centered around Bylazora (Titov Veles) and nearby Stobi. There was a major depopulation of Paeonia in 182 B.C. when Philip V of Macedon deported a large mass of the original population and filled the area with "Thracians and other barbarians."[19] Some modern historians with Illyrian sympathies have taken the view that the Slavs who captured most of Macedonia from the East Romans in the sixth and seventh centuries B.C. were Paeonians returning to their ancestral homelands.[20]

Alexander's Ancestors

It is often said that Alexander the Great was at least half Greek because whatever ethnicity characterized his father, his mother, Olympia, was Greek. She was a Molossian from Epirus, a group that some historians have believed was Greek by language and culture. However, authoritative writers have explained the ethnic make-up of the Molossians as they do that of the Macedonians: the upper classes adopted Greek ways and the Greek language, but were not Greek by birth. Relying on the writings of Strabo from Roman times to form this judgment, R.A. Crossland[21] raises doubts about this supposed Greek ethnicity, noting the strong presence of Illyrians in Epirus. Although Greek was well established in the region, he says it may simply have been used by the leading families. Crossland says that even the existence of inscriptions in Greek around 370 B.C. does not prove that Greek was the original native language of the Molossians since the concept "Epirotic" may go back only to the fourth century B.C. and be basically geographic.

Furthermore, Crossland points out that the Greek writer Thucydides described a neighboring group, the Chaones, as *barbaroi* though their leaders from the ruling family had Greek names. Similarly, he classed the Thesproti, the Molossi, the Parauaei and the Atintanes as barbarian by associating them with the Chaones and not listing them among the Hellenes. If the Molossi and other Epirotic groups were not really of Greek ethnicity, then Alexander's mother, a Molossian, was probably not of Greek ancestry. Thus, neither Alexander's mother nor his father was Greek.

The idea that there were many different ethnic and cultural groups in Macedonia is not a novel one if we are talking about the Macedonian kingdom that was so greatly expanded in the times of Philip II and Alexander the Great. At first the Macedonians used to simply kill or expel tribes that they defeated in their struggle for new land. After a time this was no longer a useful policy, and the Macedonians learned how to rule over other peoples. It is these peoples who came to make up the new European power of Macedonia. The original Macedonians were a minority ethnic group in this new nation.

Celtic and German Influences

Apart from those bordering peoples already named, the first significant outside group to make an impact on the Macedonians were the Celts. Archaeological evidence indicates that during the fifth and fourth centuries B.C. the Celts had started to settle in the Balkan peninsula. The ancient historian Justin reported that the Celts "had various wars with their neighbors which lasted for a long time, and at last reached Greece and Macedonia, overthrowing everything before them."[22] It is often not recognized that the Celts had an enduring relationship with Macedonia before the invasions. The Illyrian tribe, the Antariatae, had been in conflict with the Macedonians for a long period, forcing Amyntas II to pay tribute in 393 B.C., and defeating the army of Perdiccas II in 359 B.C. It has been suggested that Philip II of Macedonia might have formed some alliance with the Celtic tribes settling in Illyria as a means of keeping the Antariatae under control. Evidence for this comes from the large number of his coins that have been located among the Celtic archaeological discoveries in the Danube Valley. Similarly, the Celts kept Alexander's northern borders safe from the Antariatae while Alexander was subduing the Thracians soon after he came to power.[23] The alliance with the Celts seems to have lasted during the rest of Alexander's reign.

During the political instability following the death of Alexander, rule of Macedonia passed from one leader to another. During this period the Celts were moving south. As a great Celtic army led by a chieftain named Molistomos moved into Antariatae territory, the Antariatae fled before them. Cassander defeated the Celts in the area of modern Bulgaria, but after Cassander's death in 297 B.C., the Celtic leader Cambaules led his people to the conquest of Thrace, which remained under Celtic dominance for a hundred years.

In 282–280 B.C., three separate Celtic armies moved on Macedonia and Greece. First, an army led by Bolgios came to Epiros and Macedonia. Bolgios entered Macedonia near Monastir (Bitola). He sent envoys to the king, Ptolemy Ceraunnos, who was consolidating his position in order to take control over Alexander's empire. Ptolemy Ceraunnos made the mistake of killing the Celtic envoys. Soon after, the Celtic army led by Bolgios came seeking vengeance. The famed Macedonian army, which had so recently conquered much of the known world, "was scattered like chaff." Ptolemy Ceraunnos was killed in the battle, and, following Celtic custom, his head was placed on the point of a spear. The Celts moved through Macedonia, pillaging and burning.

After sweeping unchecked through Greece and sacking the Temple at Delphi, the Celts returned north, apparently finding little room to settle in Greece and Macedonia. Most went further north and east. The Celts remained in Thrace, though they were Hellenized. Most of the Celts moved on, some even settling in Asia Minor, in Galatia. Thus, the cultural and ethnic impact of these Celts on the Macedonian peoples was relatively small.

Late in the second century B.C. the Romans tried to fight off the Celtic Scordisci, but about 90 B.C. Macedonia was devastated by them.[24] Thracians also invaded. These invaders adopted the language of the country they had invaded. In Macedonia, after the Roman conquests, this was usually Latin.

The next invading group, significant in terms of the size of their invasion, was the Germans (Goths). Gothic invaders came first in the third century A.D. Late in the fourth century, the Goths, pushed south by the Huns, moved south of the Danube and into the Balkan peninsula. During this period all sorts of brigands robbed Macedonia. German tribes were settled in the Balkans in the early fifth century, and there were serious raids by the Huns. More Germans came later that century. But in all of these cases the lasting effect of these invaders was small. The main incursions in the sixth century were by Avars, Slavs, and Bulgars.[25] It has been claimed that the invasions of the Goths, Vandals, and Huns during the fourth and fifth centuries did not significantly alter the ethnic character of the province.[26]

The Macedonian Slavs

The Slavs had a much greater impact than any other invading group. They came in greater numbers, and stayed, from one end of the Balkans to the other. One group of Slavs, the Macedonian Slavs, as they were called at first by the Byzantines, was to have a profound linguistic and cultural impact on Europe of the Middle Ages, giving the world its first written Slavic language, providing a center of Orthodox religion that guided the whole Slavic world, and creating an empire that was briefly to challenge even the great Byzantine Empire itself. The tenth-century emperor Constantine Porphyrgenitus mentioned Macedonians ("Makedones") in speaking of the Macedonian Slavs.[27] In the first half of the tenth century Constantine noted, "From a kingdom Macedonia turned into a province and now it has reached the position of a theme and strategy."[28]

Slavic expansion began about 150 A.D. In their southward movement the Slavs spread across the Hungarian plain to the eastern Adriatic and then through the Balkan valleys as far south as (modern) Greece. They reached these lands early in the seventh century A.D. In the Balkans, their own dialects, "ancestral forms of Slovene, Croat, Serbian, Macedonian, and Bulgarian," replaced the earlier Illyrian, Thracian, and Phrygian speech of the inhabitants.[29]

Slavs in the Byzantine empire. In the fourth century A. D., the Romans had divided Macedonia into three parts: New Epirus (present-day southern Albania), Macedonia Salutaris (the former Dardania and the present Republic of Macedonia), and Macedonia proper (the present Aegean Macedonia). Under the Romans, Stobi became the chief city of Vardar Macedonia. After the division of the Roman Empire in A.D. 395, Macedonia was incorporated into the

Eastern or Byzantine Empire. Thus the Slav invaders came into lands that were more or less under the control of the Eastern Roman Empire.

The Slav Macedonians, both before and after they adopted Christianity, had a profound influence on Byzantium. Ostrogost and Ostuj became commanders of the troops that stayed in Thrace in 469 A.D. Justinian's commanders in the Persian war in 555 A.D. included the Macedonian Slavs Dobogost, Sveugad, Svarum, and Velisarius. In the years 758-759 A.D., "in the eighteenth year of his reign, Constantine enslaved the Sclavinii of Macedonia and he subjugated the rest."[30] This gives us some indication of the extent of influence of just one Slavic tribe and reveals how they came to be recognized by the name of the land they inhabited. The Constantinople patriarch Nikita (766-782) was a Macedonian Slav.[31]

When in 855 A.D. the Byzantine emperor Michael, on the request of the Moravian prince Ratislav, decided to send Slav priests as educators, he chose the Salonika brothers Cyril and Methodius. The father of Cyril and Methodius, Lev, was a Macedonian Slav in the Byzantine service, occupying the post of assistant to the Salonika military commander. Lev himself had been born in Salonika.[32]

In 867, the first European dynasty assumed power in the Eastern Roman Empire. The dynasty, which lasted for almost two centuries, is called Macedonian because the parents of its founder, Basil I, the Macedonian, originated from the Byzantine province of Macedonia. There is some uncertainty about the ethnicity of Basil and his parents. One theory proposes that he was part of a colony of Armenians captured by the Bulgarians and then saved by troops of the empire. According to this view, Basil and his parents took the name "Macedonian" in memory of their birthplace, since this was the name given by the Byzantines to the theme (administrative district) which had Adrianople as its capital.[33] A.A. Vasiliev has a somewhat different explanation.[34] Agreeing that Basil was born in Macedonia — he says that in recent years scholars have succeeded in determining that Basil was born in the Macedonian city of Charioupolis — Vasiliev notes that historical sources vary greatly about the matter of his ethnicity. While Greek sources speak of the Armenian or Macedonian extraction of Basil I, and Armenian sources assert that he was of pure Armenian blood, Arabic sources call him a Slav. Vasiliev says that the majority of scholars consider Basil an Armenian who had settled in Macedonia, but in view of the fact that there were many Armenians and Slavs among the population of Macedonia, he says it might be correct to assume that Basil was of mixed Armeno-Slavic origin. Thus his family might have been very much Slavonized. Consistent with this idea are claims that the Macedonian rulers in Byzantium spoke a Slavic Macedonian dialect and Greek and thought of themselves as Macedonians and *Rhomaioi* (Romans).[35]

The Macedonian Slavic peoples were a constant problem for the Eastern Roman Empire. To weaken Slavs who rebelled on several occasions, the

Byzantine emperors forcibly transported some of the Slavs from Macedonia to Asia Minor and replaced them with Scythians (tribes from the Ukraine and Russia), who were settled along the lower portion of the Struma River, and Christian Turks (Vardariotes), who were settled near the Vardar River.[36] A critical incident for the Slavs of Macedonia was their defeat by the Eastern Roman emperor Basil II, the Macedonian. This is truly a remarkable irony since this Byzantine dynasty with a Macedonian Slavic background was responsible for the defeat of the other great Balkan empire of the early eleventh century, Samuilo's Macedonian Slavic empire.

The Bulgars, Christianity, and Slavic text. The Proto-Bulgarians or Bulgars, a Turco-Tatar people, crossed the Danube under their leader Khan Isperikh (or Asparukh) and moved into the area of present-day northern Bulgaria in the late seventh century. They conquered the pastoral Slavs already there, but since the Slavs were more numerous the Bulgars gradually merged with them, adopting their language and customs. The Bulgarian state was recognized by the Byzantine emperor in 681, and this year is generally taken as the beginning of what historians have called the First Bulgarian Empire. The Bulgarians expanded their empire and by the eighth century controlled Zagorie, the area to the south of the Balkan range. A hundred years later they were masters of the Rhodope Mountains and all of Macedonia except Salonika. To cope with the Bulgar threat, Byzantium settled Armenians in western Thrace. For a full century, however, the Slavs of Macedonia remained under the domination of the Bulgars.[37]

In the seventh century, the papacy attempted to convert the Slavs with little success. In the eighth century, the Constantinople patriarchate attempted this task. By the middle of the ninth century, however, only the Slavs of southern Macedonia had been Christianized. The Christianization of northern Macedonia occurred after the conquest of the province by the Bulgars, who had accepted Christianity. In 865 the Bulgarian emperor Boris had become a Christian. Baptized by the Byzantine emperor, he took the name of Michael.

In 855 A.D., the Byzantine emperor Michael sent the Salonikan brothers Cyril and Methodius as Christian missionaries to Moravia. In 885, Michael of Bulgaria and his son Simeon welcomed Cyril's and Methodius' disciples when they fled from Moravia. The first bishop of the "Bulgarian" people, according to his own description of events,[38] was Clement, who was appointed by the Bulgarian emperor Simeon to be Bishop of Drevenitza. Clement and Naum simplified the Glagolitic script devised by Cyril and Methodius, using the dialect of the Slavs of southern Macedonia, and created the Cyrillic script. It now became possible to translate Christian scripture into a written Slavic tongue. The Slavic text the missionaries had created became the official language of the so-called Bulgarian Empire.

In 886, Kliment Simeon sent Clement, who became known as "Clement of Ohrid" *(Kliment Ohridski)*, to spread Christianity and foster literacy in the southwest of the Bulgarian empire, in the area between the River Vardar and the Adriatic coast. The Macedonian archbishopric of Ohrid became the ecclesiastic center from which the Cyrillic script and the eastern Orthodox faith were spread throughout Serbia, Bulgaria, and Kievan Russia.[39] Both modern Bulgarians and Macedonians claim this development with pride as a part of their national heritage.

Tsar Simeon (893-927), the son of Michael, who had received a Greek education at Constantinople, developed an ambition to take control of the Byzantine Empire, and to become sovereign of a new Bulgarian-Roman empire. He fought battles against Byzantium from 913 to 924, but although he had dramatic success against several Byzantine field armies, his forces were never able to threaten Constantinople itself.[40] Eventually there was a treaty between the Bulgarian Empire and the Eastern Roman Empire, though in time Byzantium became the stronger force.

A Macedo-Slavonic empire. The Macedonian Slavs were responsible for creating a great empire, as well as giving the world an important language. When the Bulgarian empire collapsed, partly as a result of Macedonian Slav rebellions, a new empire in about the same territories arose, lasting from 976 to 1018 A.D. This empire was created by these Macedonian Slavs and other dissident ethnic elements. Its ruler was Samuil, who made his capital at Ohrid and promoted the archbishopric in Macedonia to the level of patriarchate.

Vasiliev calls the empire of Samuil "Bulgarian," but he acknowledges that others see things differently. He says that the status of eastern and western Bulgaria at the time is debatable and presents a very complicated question. He acknowledges the hypothesis[41] that John Tzimisces conquered the whole of the Bulgarian Empire, both west and east, and that it was only after his death, during the internal troubles in Byzantium, that Samuil revolted in the west and succeed in establishing his "Sloveno-Macedonian Empire."

The Macedonian revolt was made possible by the confusion that followed the death of the emperor in 976. Byzantine domination was never secure in the far western reaches of the empire, and in the high lakes and valleys of Macedonia seems not to have been felt at all.[42] Here, the sons of a provincial Macedonian governor, the four Comitopuli, began their revolt. The rebellion became a war of liberation. By 987, Samuil, the youngest of the four, was the sole ruler of a powerful kingdom, whose capital was first Prespa and later Ohrid. By the end of the century this empire included most of the former Bulgarian lands between the Black Sea and the Adriatic, with the addition of Thessaly and Epirus, as well as Serbia. Samuil's efforts to expand his own empire brought him into frequent conflict with the Roman Empire. However, he was defeated by forces of the emperor Basil II in 1014 at the battle of Kleidion. Basil ordered that the 14,000 captured Macedonian troops were to be blinded, leaving one man in a hundred with sight in one eye to lead these vanquished soldiers back over the mountains to their Macedonian homeland. It is said that Samuil, faced with the shock of defeat and the horror of this mutilation of his men, collapsed and died a few days after their return. After his death his empire quickly collapsed. Macedonia was annexed to Basil's East Roman state but retained its language, customs, and church organization.

Following this period Macedonia was partly controlled by a resurgent Bulgarian state, then by Boniface of Montserrat, then by the empire again. In the thirteenth century came the Serbians, who briefly established Skopje as their capital. Then in the fourteenth century the Ottoman Turks descended on the Balkans, conquering all before them. The town of Salonika surrendered to Sultan Murad II in 1430. This event marks the final incorporation of Macedonia into the Ottoman Empire. The Turks remained in control of Macedonia for five hundred years. However, despite these changes in political control, the land of Macedonia was still recognized as such by its own people and by the rest of Europe, and its people we still regard as Macedonians.

The Name Used for Macedonia and Its People in the Middle Ages

The use of the name Macedonians to describe the people of the Macedonian territories, most of whom were Slavs, is shown in archival documents of the Middle Ages. Most of the Byzantine chronicles, including those of Georgios Monahos, Lav Djakon, Ivan Geometer, Ana Kunmena, and Georgios Kedrions, make reference to "Macedonian Slavs."[43] Consistent with this, the name Macedonian was used by the Macedonian Slavs from the early Middle Ages in folk song and in folklore in general. Writing about the capture of Salonika, in 904 A. D. John Cametinae said, "I introduce you to the same, the great and the first city of the Macedonians."[44]

In 1041 A. D. the historian Bari wrote of "Sicily from where the unfortunate Macedonians, Paulicians and Calbrians arrived."[45] At the beginning of the twelfth century (about 1106 A. D.), the Byzantine satirist Timarion wrote about a special feast of the Macedonians. Those who celebrated the feast were the Christian Slav inhabitants of the city, and the events they celebrated concerned an occasion in the sixth century when Saint Demetrius saved the city from the invading heathen Slavs. "The day of Saint Demetrius in (Salonika) is as great a festival as the Panathinei in Athens or Panionii in Miletus; it is a grand Macedonian celebration in which not only the Macedonian people gather, but people of all sorts and from all directions: Greeks from different regions of Hellada, the Mizian tribes...."[46] Near the end of the twelfth century (around 1185 A.D.), the capital city of the Macedonians was under attack again. "Woe, woe, the city of Salonika is captured, I say, the metropolis of the Macedonians."[47]

The synod records of the Ohrid archbishopric at the beginning of the thirteenth century contain the words, "Ivan Ierakar by birth Macedonian."[48] In the middle of the thirteenth century (around 1246 A. D.), it was noted that "Ser was once a large city, but the Bulgarian Ivan had demolished it when besieging it and other Macedonian cities."[49]

In the fifteenth century Bertrand de la Brocuiere reflected on the lot of the peoples of the Balkans, saying, "I remember the great subordination under which the Turk holds the emperor in Constantinople and all the Greeks, Macedonians and Bulgarians.... As I said earlier, there are many Christians who are forced to serve the Turk, such as Greeks, Bulgarians, Macedonians, Albanians, Esclavinians, Rasians and Serbians."[50] The distinction between Bulgarians and Macedonians here is noteworthy. There were commentators of the time who believed that the Turks would not be able to maintain control over their subject peoples if these various peoples were given the opportunity to resist their control. Around 1461–1462 Jovan Radonic claimed, "When the enemy forces are battered, no one doubts that the whole of Serbia, Bosnia, Macedonia, Epirus, Thessaly, Greece or Attica and the Peloponnese will return to the faithful.... Inspired by this example the Thessalians, the Greeks, the Peloponnesians, the Epirans and the Macedonians will all rebel and will win."[51] On August 8, 1470 A. D., "the Sultan stopped and spent the night ... in a field that represented the Macedonian border.... The River Vardar is nearby, which flows through Macedonia ... of which some are Greeks, others Macedonians, Wallachs and even Italians, as well as other nations.... Greeks and Macedonians live there."[52]

On April 26, 1690, Leopold I sent a letter of protection:

> This is to inform you that two Macedonians, Marko Kraida born in Kosana, and Dimitri Georgi Popovic, born in Macedonian Salonika, have told us that the Macedonian people, with respect for our most righteous task, with devotion and zeal towards our service ... we graciously accept them under our imperial and royal mercy and in any case and way the above mentioned Macedonian people, cordially recommending to each and all of our willing commanders not to attack the Macedonian people....[53]

At the end of the eighteenth century, reports by the French consul in Salonika, Felix de Beaujour, about Macedonia describe the Turkish administrative district in terms of ancient Macedonian borders: "The pashalik of Salonika includes the whole of Lower Macedonia and covers 700 sq. miles ... it must be noted that here I am speaking only about the most populated part of Macedonia; since Upper Macedonia and Epirus are less populated.... In Macedonia, as in Poland, the peasants die from hunger, while the masters live in abundance of gold."[54]

Physical Characteristics of South Balkan Peoples

The Greeks have argued that the Slavic peoples of Macedonia have no real claim to the land in which they live, despite the fact that they have been there for more than fifteen hundred years, because (they say) they have no demonstrable ethnic connection with the ancient Macedonians. In this chapter we have examined evidence suggesting that this idea is not well supported. John Geipel applies a different kind of argument in examining the question of the people who live in (former) Yugoslavia and Greece. He suggests that despite the apparent lack of connections between ancient and modern peoples in the Balkans, the genes that have survived throughout Yugoslavia and Greece are the same as those that characterized the ancient peoples. In other words, the present populations of these parts are the same physical types as those who were there thousands of years ago. He says, "It seems likely that most of the Yugoslavs, despite their Slavic speech, which is of historically recent introduction, owe their physical characteristics to peoples who were established in the western Balkans at least three millennia before the Slavic infiltration." He says much the same about the Greeks: "Considering the number of incursions of Phoenicians, Romans, Kelts, Goths, Slavs, Vlachs, Turks, and others that have penetrated Greece during the past two thousand years, it is remarkable that the most conspicuous physical traits displayed by the living population of this exposed and accessible little country are probably those that were ancient hereabouts at the time of the Trojan Wars, let alone in Alexander's days."[55]

Whichever argument we consider — the one that describes the ethnic mix throughout the Balkans, or the one that maintains the physical character of the people to be the same today as in ancient times — the Greek position that the modern-day Macedonians have a lesser claim than their own is not supported.

3. The Hellenization of the Macedonians

One of the issues we can look at to evaluate the likelihood that the real Macedonians were ethnically distinct from the Greeks is the process of Hellenization that occurred in ancient times. The fact that this process was necessary implies that the Macedonian rulers, nobles, and peoples were not Hellenes to begin with. Historians who deal with the issue make the explicit point that the Macedonians may have become more Hellenic during certain time periods, but showed no evidence of Greekness at first. Even after centuries of a deliberate Hellenization policy, the common people, including the minority within Macedonia who were ethnically Macedonian, still did not speak Greek and were never accepted by Greeks as a part of the Hellenic fold.

Tom Winnifrith confronts the claims and counterclaims about the racial origins of the Macedonians, noting that some quite fantastic theories have been proposed. For instance, some have suggested that Aristotle was a Bulgarian, while an equally outrageous opposing view has sought to prove that the Macedonians were Greeker than the Greeks. Winnifrith presents a more moderate approach, suggesting that by the end of the classical period the influence of Greek language and culture had spread to the aristocracy of most of the semi-barbarian tribes of Macedonia.[1] In his book *The Medes and Persians*, Robert Collins is emphatic about the distinction between the Greeks and the Macedonians. He speaks of Macedon in the fourth century B.C. as "a land of vigorous people, not of Greek descent but much influenced by Greek culture."[2]

Henri Berr writes that Macedonia, though "originally alien to Hellenism," became more or less Hellenized by about the fourth century B.C.[3] Berr also noted that Isocrates had accepted Alexander as Hellene since he had argued that what made a person "Greek" was not his origins, but his education. Accordingly, every man cultivated in Greek letters and manners could be considered Greek. Isocrates was looking for political allies when he offered this particular argument, but it is interesting to note that a similar proposition has been offered in the twentieth century to argue that the modern Greeks are the heirs to Hellenism despite their mixed ethnic background.

In *Chronology of World History, A Calendar of Principal Events from 3000 BC to AD 1973*,[4] G.S.P. Freeman-Grenville says that during the fourth century B.C. the Macedonian state was "gradually influenced by Hellenic culture."

Pierre Jouguet, too, maintains that the Macedonians gradually came to Hellenism rather than originally belonging to it.[5] He says that when Macedon accepted Greek culture, the upper classes, at least, abandoned their own language in favor of Attic Greek, which was soon to be spoken by the whole of the Hellenic world. This sphere of influence was, of course, extended enormously by Alexander's conquests.

R. A. Crossland writes about the gradually increasing influence of Greek language and culture amongst the Macedonians. Like other writers, Crossland is not sure if the increasing Hellenization is something that happened just to the noble families or was more widespread. Crossland notes that at the same time that Macedonians were being Hellenized, negative Greek attitudes towards the Macedonians were being softened.[6] There were indications as early as the end of the eighth century that some Greeks thought that Macedonians, or at least their aristocracy, were in some way more related to Hellenes than other foreigners were. There was some confusion about this, since the genealogies given by prominent Greek writers (genealogies that concern figures from Greek myths) differ to some extent. Crossland reports that one genealogy described Macedon as the son of Zeus and Thyia, daughter of Deucalio. This made him the brother of Magnes and cousin of Dorus, Xuthus and Aeolus. In another genealogy, he was described as the son of Aeolus. Crossland questions whether such descriptions indicate any real knowledge of the customs and language of the Macedonians, or whether they simply indicate recognition that some Macedonians, probably the nobility, had become Hellenized to the point where a true Greek might wonder whether they were really of Greek origin.

Traian Stoijanovich says that by the time of the Roman conquest, the Macedonian and Thraco-Illyrian elements of Macedonia had been largely Hellenized,[7] but the other information we have considered suggests that this was certainly not the case at the time of Alexander the Great. That period was still one of suspicion and hostility towards the Greek language and Greek ways. Hellenization was followed by a more enduring process of Romanization, which lasted throughout the eight centuries of Roman rule.

Though Hellenization reached its peak in the fourth century B.C., it had been a deliberate policy of several Macedonian kings. Alexander I had first tried to have Macedonia accepted as a member of the Hellenic family. He had encouraged Greeks to establish themselves on Macedonian soil. Peter Green tells us that as a part of this process he offered patronage to distinguished artists such as Pindar and Bacchlides.[8] But he had moved towards Hellenization mainly by gaining admission to the Olympic games. This required that he establish a fictitious link between the Macedonian Argead dynasty and the Argos of mythology.

Some friends and supporters of Alexander I had regarded the decision to admit Alexander to competition in the Olympics as politically motivated — a reward for services to the Hellenic cause rather than an indication of genuine belief in the evidence he provided concerning his ancestry.[9] He is described by lexicographers, as far back as the fourth-century, as "Philhellene" or friend of the Greeks. Badian believes that such an appellation could not be given to an actual Greek. After all, it would not make sense. One would not call a Greek a friend of the Greeks. Badian says that no king recognized as Greek was ever referred to by the epithet "Philhellene." If we knew the precise timing of the events, we would be better able to decide the Greek motivation for Alexander's admission to the Olympics. One problem is that Herodotus does not date the story, which has led some commentators to think it was just made up anyway. If it was true, it would have happened just before or just after the Persian invasions. At both points in time the Greeks would have had good reason to try and win over Alexander as an ally. The Argead myth could salvage Greek pride by recognizing one family as Greek while preserving racial pride.[10]

This claim to a Greek ancestry had not been seen before from any of the Macedonian leaders, including Alexander himself. There is no evidence of any Macedonian claim to be Greek before the Persian War of 480–479 B.C. Before this, Amyntas I had recognized the overlordship of Darius I, the Persian king; his daughter had married an Iranian nobleman, and his son Alexander I loyally served his Persian master.[11] It seems that during this period Alexander I was careful to maintain friendly relationships with Greeks when the opportunity arose. When the Greeks defeated the Persians, good relationships with the Greek states became a central issue of his reign.

It may have been after this Greek victory, in about 476 B.C., that Alexander I presented himself at the Olympic Games and demanded admission as a competitor. To support his demand, he claimed descent from the Temenids of Argos. If true, this connection would have made him a Greek of the highest nobility. Alexander presented a royal genealogy going back for six generations, which, as Badian points out, is the first time this particular proof appeared. Alexander side-stepped the problem of the common belief that the Macedonians were *barbaroi* rather than Hellene, not by trying to prove that the Macedonians were Greeks, but by claiming that his own family, the Argeads, were not merely Hellene, but of the highest nobility — in other words, were not really Macedonians at all.[12] Thus the claim applies only to the ruling family and not the Macedonians in general. The appearance of such a story implies that the ancient Macedonians could not be convincingly presented as Greek, even by their own king.

It seems that the decision to admit Alexander to the Olympic Games was controversial. Other competitors complained bitterly, rejecting the story and describing Alexander I as a barbarian. At the very least, this indicates that his claim was a novel one as far as most Greeks were concerned. For whatever reasons, including political motivations, the Hellanodikai decided to accept Alexander's claim. Modern scholars tend to believe that the case presented by Alexander was largely built on a fortuitous resemblance of the name of the Argead clan to the name of the original city of Argos. Starting from this supposed connection, any descent from the heroes of Argos could only be royal. Appian in the Syriaca (63) notes that there is an Argos in Orestis and it was from there that the Argeads actually came.

Alexander's admission to the games is recorded by Herodotus as proof of the Macedonian king's Argive descent, and Thucydides accepts the word of Herodotus as final. However, other versions of the genealogy appeared. By the fourth century the royal line had been extended by several generations, as far as King Midas, a recognized historical figure, and had become generally accepted, perhaps even official.[13] Nevertheless, Peter Green points out that all the Greeks knew Alexander I had been prevented from competing in the Olympic Games until he manufactured a pedigree connecting his ancestors with a line of ancient Greek kings. Green quotes the ancient historians Herodotus and Justin to demonstrate that people of the time knew of this fabricated lineage.[14] He also says that the use "the Philhellene" to describe Alexander I was an ironic joke.

Jouguet also comments on the admission of the Macedonian leaders to the Olympic Games. He makes the point that their initial exclusion demonstrates that they were not considered part of the Hellenic community, and they were finally admitted to the Games after a suitable lineage was invented — "when the Kings of Macedon were admitted to them it was not as Macedonians, but as Heraclids."[15]

The Heraclids were descendants of the mythical figure Hercules. This makes it very clear that the reasons for letting the Macedonians into the Greek games had nothing to do with their real ancestry. For political reasons, the Greeks were prepared to make the Macedonian royals into honorary Greeks, adopting the pretense that the Macedonian kings came from a Greek line. But it was just a pretense, and both Greeks and Macedonians knew it.

Jouguet does not find anything unusual about the invention of a suitable ancestry for the Macedonian leaders or the Macedonian people. He says that this sort of creative thinking was commonplace at the time: "The mythic imagination was always fertile in Greece, and it would have found Greek ancestors for the Macedonian people as easily as it had done for the royal line."[16]

Despite Alexander's example, there is no reliable evidence that his successors, Perdiccass and Archelaus, continued to be involved in the Olympic Games, although they were certainly closely involved in relations with the Greek states and patronized Greek culture. No Macedonian king between Alexander I and Philip II shows any connection with the Olympic Games or with any other Greek games. Conversely, Archelaus seems to have founded a special Macedonian Olympics at Dium. Badian calls them counter–Olympics, since everyone knew where the real Olympic Games were held. It is possible that Archelaus tried to gain acceptance at the Olympics, was not accepted, and set up his own athletic contest. Badian points out that Greek approval might change according to the politics of the time, and that some Greeks were bound to challenge Alexander I's credentials.[17] The subsiding of the Persian threat after the death of Alexander I may have been an appropriate opportunity, since it was at this time that the Greeks refused his successor access to the Olympic games.

Euripides manufactured an older and convincing Temenid descent for the Argead line, but his story did not convince all of the Greeks. When Archelaus attacked Larisa, in Thessaly, Thrasymachus wrote an oration on behalf of the Larisaeans that became widely known. Badian reports that only one sentence of this oration survives, but it is a telling one. Thrasymachus wrote, *"Shall we be slaves to Archelaus, we, being Greeks, to a barbarian?"* It shows that, as late as about 400 B.C., the official myth of the Temenid descent of the Argead kings could be publicly brought into question. This is particularly interesting given the great efforts Archelaus made to attract Greek artists and writers and to gain their willing cooperation. Euripides was one of those Greek writers who worked for Archelaus, producing the myth of immediate descent from Temenos. Other poets of note also came to the court of Archelaus, as did the painter Zeuxis. Despite this immersion in Hellenism, Archelaus was still called a barbarian. Badian speculates that opposition to the earlier judgment about Alexander I may have increased since earlier times.

If the decision to accept Alexander I into the Olympic games was indeed attributable to his important Greek friends, this would explain why Perdiccass did not try for the same recognition, and why Archelaus ran into trouble when he did. Alexander I's claim is the first of many such claims among peoples associated with the Greeks, but it is the only one to have been validated by the Hellanodikai, the most competent authority in all the Greek lands.

Many other leaders, and sometimes their peoples, also claimed descent from mythical Greek figures for their own political purposes. This creative mythology was used by King Cleomenes of Sparta when he claimed to be an Achaean, not a Dorian, at Athens.[18] By the fourth century B.C., the rulers of Macedonian Lyncestis claimed descent from the Corinthian Bacchiads — a royal dynasty at least as significant as the Temenids claimed by their Argead rivals. The kings of the Molossi, another people regarded as barbarian, claimed descent from Achilles himself via Pyrrhus, son of Neoptolemus, and carried the names of these mythical figures to prove it. The Enchelei in Illyria, far to the north, were ruled by a royal house claiming to be descendants of the Thebans Cadmus and Harmonia. Long before the fifth century, Sicilian and Italian tribes and peoples had come to claim links with Greeks or Trojans as a way of claiming a connection with Hellenism. It seems probable that the ruling families of these peoples traced their own descent back to the mythical Homeric ancestor as a way of legitimating their rule, and of course this all happened generations before Alexander I tried the same strategy.[19]

Ancient writers do report some claims of a connection by descent between the Macedonian people and Greeks, but generally this idea was not accepted by the Hellenic world. Herodotus describes such a claim identifying the original Macedonians with the original Dorians. Badian believes that the claim probably emerged after the claims about the Macedonian royal lineage, perhaps in support of them. However, it was never submitted to the judgment of the Hellanodikai, presumably because supporting material could not be found. As Macedonian influence among the Greeks waned, the occasion for presenting such a claim did not arise. In any case, no Macedonian name appears on the lists of Olympic victors until well into the reign of Alexander the Great, despite the fact that Macedonian barons thought highly of physical prowess and would almost certainly have been capable of winning one of the personal contests, or at least a chariot race.[20] Presumably this accounts in some part for the establishment of the counter–Olympics.

Although the claim to Greek descent of the Macedonian people was never adjudicated by the Hellanodikai, it seems to have developed further. A story appeared describing an actual migration of Peloponnesians. Badian thinks that this kind of argument was produced because it was a more concrete, and therefore more plausible, idea than identity with the Dorians. Thus the claim to Greek origin of the Macedonians as a people appeared and developed within the fifth and possibly early fourth centuries, at a time when similar claims were familiar and even commonplace.

Macedonian Claims to Hellenism in the Changing Political Scene

Macedonia's political fortunes faded in the first half of the fourth century. After the assassination of Archelaus about 400 B.C. and the accession of Philip II, previous gains were largely lost. Macedon faced civil war and foreign invasion, and by 359 was in a desperate state. Even when Philip took control, first as protector of the young son of Perdiccass III after the latter was killed in Illyria, there were several claimants to the throne, each with powerful foreign support. During this long period of decline and difficulty, the Macedonian claim to Hellenism must have receded into the background. Affairs and arrangements conducted with Greek states were carried out in the name of the kings, but never the Macedonian people. In this respect, the Macedonians were dealt with in the same way as the Persians or the Thracians, other nations under monarchical rule. It was not until the time of Antigonus Doson that the Macedonians were acknowledged as a people in the political sense.[21] The issue of kingship may have been a large part of the problem. We have already noted the

Greek antipathy to the idea of kingship, and to the rejection of the idea that kingship could occur over Greek peoples. As we have already seen, when Philip II was given a seat on the on the Amphictyonic Council after winning the Sacred War, the seats went to him personally. He was not acting as the empowered ruler of his people, but on his own behalf. Badian suggests that a claim for admission of the Macedonian people to the Amphictyony would have been much harder to enforce, and Philip was far too good a diplomat to pursue this course of action.[22]

At the end of the fifth century, Archelaus had tried to encourage the use of Greek throughout his territories and had made considerable progress. We have already noted the degree to which Archelaus brought the lowland and highland kingdoms more firmly together. Hellenization was a deliberate part of his policy in both parts of his territories. However, after Archelaus was murdered, the whole administrative structure that he had established collapsed. The outkingdom princes, who had faced a reduction in status under Archelaus, had also "viewed the late king's Hellenization policy with fierce distaste."[23] With the king's death, the Hellenization policy suffered a major setback.

The continued contact with Greek culture, in the form of paintings by Zeuxis for instance, may have affected Macedonian tradition over a period of time, though this influence probably declined as Macedonian political power declined. With Perdiccass III, there is evidence of a genuine attachment to Greek philosophy. Perdiccass seems to have expected his nobles to share his fascination, and to have excluded those who did not give evidence of this. He had links with the Academy in Athens and appointed Euphraeus of Oreos to his court. The outcome of this process was the development of an abiding hatred among Macedonian nobles for Euphraeus and his influence. When Philip became king, he faced a problem of persisting antagonism to Greek culture, and he did not himself show overt interest in all things Greek, although he was quick to reinstate his family's claim to Temenid descent.

The greatest influence in the move towards Hellenization is attributed to the efforts of Philip II. Isocrates, the Greek teacher, had tried to interest Greek states in revenge on Persia. When no one else was interested, finally he turned to Philip of Macedon. In the address to Philip, he drew parallels between Philip's expeditions and the war conducted by Heracles against Troy. He proposed that Heracles (a mythical figure) was Philip's direct ancestor. Peter Green reports that Philip was pleased at such descriptions since it was politically advantageous to have his supposed descent from the Heraclids validated by such a revered Athenian teacher.[24] Green goes on to spell out very clearly the exclusively political motivation of Philip in this business. He says that "Philip did not give a fig for Panhellenism as an idea," but it gave him an admirable propaganda line that could help to camouflage his ambitions for conquest as actions in defense of the Greek cause. While attempting to serve Greek interests, Isocrates had unwittingly helped Philip to the likely disadvantage if the Greeks: "From now on he (Philip) merely had to clothe his Macedonian ambitions in a suitably Panhellenic dress."

It is generally recognized that as an organizer and as a politician, Philip was perhaps more capable than his son Alexander. It seems to have been Philip's planning that led to the dramatic increase in Hellenization in Macedonia. According to Peter Green, Philip saw that a great deal more Hellenization, involving quite deliberate cultural propaganda, was essential if the more advanced Greek states were going to begin to treat Macedonia on equal terms. One of his moves was to gain acceptance at the Olympic games, just as his ancestor Alexander I had done. In 356 B.C. Philip achieved the first recorded Macedonian victory at Olympia since Alexander I, and he did it at the first games after his accession to power.

Philip considered the image of the Macedonian monarchy in Greece a matter of urgent importance. His actions suggest that he had ambitious plans for his relations with the Greek international community, and that recognition of his standing as a Temenid and an Olympic victor would help in this. Philip recognized the value of propaganda and the importance of his image.[25]

The extent to which Philip's Hellenization policy was deliberate is indicated by David Hogarth, who writes, "The kings of Macedon bid for Greek support by being more Hellenic than the Hellenes."[26] Hogarth says that Philip wanted "unconditional supremacy over the Hellenes," and in order to achieve this he put into action a complex plan. First, he had to gain secure control over the land route into central Greece. Next, he wanted to be recognized as one of the Hellenes, or as Hogarth puts it, "to obtain a recognized position in the inner communion of the Hellenes." Finally, he set in motion a process in which the Greek states would be equal but relatively weak partners in a forced alliance with each other. Macedonia was not a member of this alliance, but retained control over this grouping of Greek states. This control was the purpose of Philip's panhellenism.

There is no serious debate about the extent to which Philip adopted a philhellenic policy as a political strategy. Peter Green uses almost exactly the same kind of terminology as Hogarth when talking about the issue. He notes that shortly after defeating the Greeks, Persia's leadership was weakened, and Philip wanted to take advantage of Isocrates' formula to bring the Greek states into line behind Macedonia. "Panhellenism now became Philip's watchword," and the Persian war was portrayed as a religious crusade, a war of Greek vengeance for the invasion by Xerces more than a century before.[27]

Philip's panhellenism was just a ploy, a device to keep the Greeks quiet while the Macedonians went about their task of building a great Asian empire. It was, Jouguet explains, simply "a cloak for further Macedonian aggrandizement."[28]

A forced union. Partly through Demosthenes' efforts, in 338 B.C. the Greek states Athens and Thebes overcame their traditional suspicion of each other to join in an alliance against Philip II of Macedonia. However, at the Battle of Chaeronea, Philip crushed the allied army. He then formed the Greek states into the League of Corinth. This league was responsible for the control of Greek internal affairs. It was supposed to be independent of Macedonia, but in reality was forced to do as Philip required since he was the commander-in-chief of its army.

Jouguet explains[29] that Philip required the Greek states to make a common peace and alliance with one another, and then to form themselves into a Federal Hellenic League. Macedonia was not a part of this league, but had a separate alliance with it. Though there was some equality between the Greek states in this alliance, there was no equality between the Greek League and Macedonia. When the two areas were united, it was under Macedonian domination.

Philip's plans for an Asian campaign seem to have been ready by the time of his victory in the Sacred War. By 342, he took the first step toward the military goal by invading Thrace, making the invasion of Asia strategically possible. At about the same time, he invited Aristotle to become the teacher for his son Alexander. Badian describes the invitation as a political master stroke, since it secured for Philip an alliance with the philosopher-tyrant Hermias of Atarneus, Aristotle's patron and relative by marriage, providing both a bridgehead to Asia and the possibility of communication with potential supporters amongst the Persian king's disaffected subjects. This move also restored Philip's connection with the Academy in Athens. While Greeks who mattered might be impressed by this development, Philip had to be cautious about the possible antagonism of the Macedonian barons. In his favor was the fact that Aristotle's father had been court physician to Philip's father, and Aristotle had been a boyhood friend of Philip himself, and presumably other nobles as well. This helped ensure personal loyalty, as did Philip's generous restoration of Aristotle's birth place. Aristotle also knew the Macedonian court and understood the cautions he would have to take. Finally he was given a place apart from the court at Mieza, which must have soothed the Macedonian nobles.[30]

The war against the Persians. The Greeks of today like to argue that the Macedonian war against the Persians is proof of the Hellenic nature of the Macedonians. This is not the view that historians hold. The war on the Persians was aimed at enhancing the glory and power of the Macedonian kings. Having the Greek states under control or even as allies would help this cause. Typically, historians speak of the need for the pacification of Greece and explain the Macedonian appeals to Greek patriotism in the Persian wars as a means rather than an end. Its purpose was to make the Macedonian kingdom greater than all others. This helps explain Philip's favorable response to the pleas of Isocrates. However, Jouguet argues that a war of revenge against the Persians for past humilities did not reduce the Greek anger at having the Macedonians in power over them.[31] Indeed, successes in such a war could lead to such an increase in Macedonian power that the Greek states and their way of life might be totally crushed. The Greeks were not at all happy with the secondary role they were being required to play in world affairs.

According to Hogarth, both Philip and Alexander recognized that the Greeks could be of enormous value in their plans to forge an Asian empire. They both believed that the Greeks and Macedonians could collaborate best in newly conquered territories, and that the Hellenes would prove to be much more valuable in holding on to an empire than in conquering one in the first place.[32] Thus it was important to continue the Hellenization policy, despite having conquered the Greek states. In time, when Alexander was the greatest emperor of all, the Hellenization plans would become less important, and Alexander would look instead to a fusion of Macedonian and Asian interests.

Alexander's Hellenization policy. For the time being, however, Alexander followed the tradition of manipulation of the Greeks that his father had begun. He probably had more feeling for Greek culture because of the influence of his teacher, Aristotle. He seemed also to believe that he was descended from mythical Greek heroes. However, in the final analysis, he was most driven by other motives, in particular personal ambition, i.e., the desire to create and to lead a great empire in Asia. Jouguet says that Alexander also had a wider conception of the greatness of Macedonia.[33]

Badian suggests we look at Alexander as the living symbol of the integration of Greeks and Macedonians, a tribute to the long-term planning of his father, Philip. Although Alexander's birth at the time of Philip's Olympic victory may have been a lucky coincidence, his preparation by Aristotle was hardly accidental. Probably Aristotle helped inspire the young prince with a love of Greek literature, especially poetry, and with the ideal of emulating the Homeric heroes. According to Harold Lamb,[34] his mother, Olympia, seemed to play a role in this regard also. She impressed upon her son the inferiority of his father's people, the Macedonians. She told young Alexander that the Macedonians had lived too long in the mountains, keeping to the old ways of clan life. They had no true nobility. Even the Companions, the king's personal cavalry who accompanied and advised Philip, were no more than the owners of the biggest horse herds. Olympia's view was that Macedonians were primitives who sang herder's chants, were still afraid of omens, and had a superstitious fear of drought and pestilence among the animals. She argued that there never had been one orator, philosopher, general or monarch equal in stature to even second-rate Athenians.

On the other hand, Thomas W. Africa tells us that Olympia taught young Alexander that Achilles was his ancestor, and that his father was descended from Hercules.[35] It seems that Alexander learned by heart the stories of the heroic deeds of Achilles. Aristotle, or Aristotle's relative Callisthenes, presented him with a text of Homer, which he treasured. Thomas Africa says Alexander carried a copy of the *Iliad* with him, and that Achilles became Alexander's model.

Alexander is said to have kept his copy of the Illiad under his pillow at night, next to his dagger.

Africa says that the young Alexander came to know and like Greek ways of living and was impressed by the ideals of Greek civilization. We can see from such ideas that Philip's own son was a leading instance of Philip's policy of Hellenization. Despite this indoctrination, Alexander himself made deliberate use of the associations with Greek culture to stake his own claim on the world, and when it came to political reality, sentiment did not protect recalcitrant Greek states from his dominance. When the Thebans revolted against Macedonian rule immediately on the assassination of his father, Alexander marched his troops at incredible pace, surprised Thebes, and then destroyed the city and sold its citizens into slavery. That was the iron fist. The velvet glove included a pro–Greek public attitude. He needed the Greeks, not so much as troops to help his ambitions for conquest, but as the traders, settlers and administrators who would run his new empire.

Although Philip made no social distinction between Greeks and Macedonians among his hetairai, Greeks never commanded his armies. This probably related to language differences between potential Greek commanders and the diverse Macedonians they might command, and to the lingering irritation of Macedonians towards Greek influence. However, Alexander, right from the start, entrusted commands to his Greek friends. Alexander grew up in a circle that included Greek and Macedonian friends. Some of the Greeks among them seem to have been loyal and close in their relationship with Alexander. Accordingly he had less reason for cautious bias against Greeks, and Greeks of talent were more likely to emerge.

When Alexander the Great landed in Asia Minor, he cast his spear on the ground in a grand gesture. He also set up altars to Zeus, to Athene, and to Heracle (his supposed ancestor), and made other dramatic gestures, such as laying a wreath on the tomb of Achilles, that Jouguet says were "skillfully calculated to strike the imagination of men, and to convince the world that a new Achilles was arming for the traditional feud of the Greeks."[36] He proclaimed himself the avenger of Greece.

Nevertheless, it seems clear that Alexander's prime concern in fighting the Persians was to gain glory for himself and for Macedonia. Thus although Alexander began the war in the capacity of commander-in-chief of all the Hellenes, there were very few Greeks in the army. Most of Alexander's force was Macedonian. Jouguet argues that the Macedonians alone were sufficiently attached to the royal house of their country to follow Alexander.[37] "The Empire to which he (Alexander) aspired was to be made chiefly by Macedonians, and for the King of Macedon."[38]

This assertion, of course, contradicts the modern Greek argument that Greeks participated in a major way in the empire-building that characterized Alexander's reign. They seem to want to share in the glory of this warlike personality. However, as noted above, Greeks were scarce amongst Alexander's troops, and they participated for only a portion of the conflict. Thomas W. Africa[39] explains that after the capture and burning of Persepolis, the Greek interest in the war ended, and Alexander sent their troops home. What is more, Greek troops in very large numbers often fought on the other side. For instance, in 334 B.C. when Alexander marched against the Persian emperor Darius, the Hellenes, led by the Satrap Menon, were on the side of Darius. In the first battle with the Persians at Granicus, Alexander captured 15,000 Greek prisoners. In the second battle at Issus in 333 B.C., 30,000 Greek soldiers took part and were annihilated. In describing the Macedonian success at Issus, Africa tells us that the Macedonians routed the "Greek and Persian heavy infantry." It is not recorded how many Greeks took part in the biggest battle at Gaugamela, in 331 B.C., but it is well established that Greeks were on the war council of Darius as advisers, and that they recommended that everything be burnt in front of Alexander's march to deprive the Macedonian soldiers of food.

Alexander, like his father before him, tried to portray war against the Persians as a holy obligation of the Greeks, and the Macedonian leaders presented themselves as those who would bring this Greek cause to fruition. It is clear that the Greeks often did not believe this story. Badian explains that at the beginning of his campaign, Alexander had very few Greek mercenaries; he could not afford many and, at that point, did not need many. The Persian king, on the other hand, seems to have had a large number. Alexander's first contact with them was at the Granicus, where Alexander won a great success. The Greek mercenaries who were captured were sent to forced labor in the Macedonian mines, as traitors to the cause of Hellas. Badian describes this action as a piece of terrorism, comparable with the destruction of Thebes, intended to make an example of the so-called traitors to deter others from the same actions.[40] It turned out to be a mistake. Firstly, the Greek cities asked for their citizens back, apparently not at all intimidated by the implication that they were betraying the Greek cause. Second, the effect on the Greek mercenaries fighting for the Persian king was the opposite of what had been intended. Since surrender led to such a terrible fate, they prepared to fight to the death. Once Alexander realized this, he quietly abandoned his former policy, promising safety to Greeks who surrendered.

That surrender, however, was generally not forthcoming. Many Greeks continued to fight on the other side. After the battle of Issus, eight thousand of them refused to surrender, made their way down to the coast, and escaped by sea.[41] They all fought against Macedon again when they had the chance. The small number of mercenaries who fought in the Persian ranks at Gaugamela escaped and remained loyal to the Persian king almost to the end.

Badian reminds us that not all Greek mercenaries hated Alexander, and that as his Asian campaign progressed, he himself enrolled far more Greek mercenaries than were fighting against him. However, the loyalty of those

Greeks to Darius is nonetheless striking, since it shows the continuing division of opinion among Greeks about the Macedonian conquest and the fact that some preferred the traditional and long-hated enemy to the new Macedonian overlords.

Not surprisingly, the Greeks in general did not like Macedonian dominance over them, and took any opportunity to throw off the Macedonian yoke. The Greek bitterness is indicated in the reaction to Alexander's death. When the news was announced in Athens, one politician remarked: "If it were true the whole world would stink of his corpse."[42] In the Greek states even before Alexander's death there were constant plots to be rid of Macedonian rule imposed by General Antipater. When Alexander the Great died in 323 B.C., the Greek cities revolted and fought for almost three months against Antipater's authority. Later, in 316 B.C., Antipater's son Cassander defeated the Hellenes and then proclaimed himself king of Macedon. It was he who first used the name Macedonia.[43]

In the argument that preceded the killing of Alexander's close friend, the Macedonian Clitus, Alexander made unfavorable comparisons of Macedonians with Greeks. Not surprisingly, Clitus became angry at these criticisms, given the already strong resentment of Macedonian nobles to the encroachments of the Greeks in Alexander's court.

Badian says that Alexander had shown tact reminiscent of his father in refraining from forcing military integration on his Greeks and Macedonians.[44] Both were useful to him as they were. Eventually Alexander gained a monopoly in the market in Greek mercenaries, and he forced them to settle in the northeastern frontier region of his empire, in a ring of colonies designed to guard its security. However, once rumors began to circulate that he would never return when he went into India, some of these mercenaries began a long journey home, and some were successful. Once Alexander was dead, many thousands more banded together for the long march back. They had to travel through territory held by hostile Macedonians and inhabited by natives often hostile to both Greeks and Macedonians. Although in a final battle with a Macedonian army led by Pithon, a large contingent of these Greeks betrayed their comrades and deserted to the Macedonians, showing that national antagonism was of limited power in motivating the Greeks, a subsequent slaughter of seventeen thousand surrendering Greeks by Macedonian troops indicates an irrational hatred for their Greek enemies that was not stemmed by the Macedonian commander's guarantee of their safety.

After Alexander's disappearance, there was a Greek rebellion at the other end of his empire. Once more Athens rallied the Greeks to freedom, and once more she found many followers. The war has come to be known as the Lamian War, but was described by its protagonists as a war for freedom "from the barbarian Macedonians by Greeks who saw Macedonian domination as an abrogation of Greek freedom and despotism as synonymous with barbarian rule."[45]

These two rebellions at opposite ends of the empire were the only ones for a long time. Badian feels it is significant that of all the subjugated peoples of Alexander's empire, only Greeks were sufficiently moved to challenge "what they felt to be the foreign domination." This shows that even after centuries of effort by the Macedonian kings to bridge the gap between Greeks and Macedonians, at this time there was no true integration of the two. The gap was not to be fully bridged for another hundred years.

Alexander Abandons Hellenism

As his Asian empire grew and his own conceptions of the nature of his empire changed, Alexander came to abandon some Macedonian and Greek cultural prescriptions. He adopted Asian ideas, and even dreamed of a fusion of races in a world empire. Hogarth notes that he "dreamed of effacing the distinctions of Macedonian, Hellene, and Asiatic, by making all march shoulder to shoulder to the conquest of Africa and Europe."[46]

Apparently this dream of a blended world was not simply driven by the desire to achieve administrative convenience. It was an idealistic notion, as Henri Berr says, "to unite nations and races ... to establish concord and peace."[47] Perhaps inevitably, the eastern world was more and more influenced by Hellenism, while the Hellenic world was increasingly exposed to Asian influences.

The policy of integrating Greeks and Macedonians, revived by Philip and continued by Alexander the Great, may have been consistent with Alexander's own later policy of attempting a limited integration of Greeks and Macedonians with Iranians, which came to be called the "policy of fusion." It aroused anger and resistance among the Macedonian forces near the end of Alexander's life, yet even after he calmed some of this opposition he kept on with this policy, and at the very end of his life he initiated a military reform that combined Macedonians and Persians in small tactical units on a permanent basis. Badian points out that he had never attempted such an integration of Greeks with Macedonians. But for tactical and political reasons, integration of Macedonians and Iranians became important, while integration of Greeks with either was not.[48] Evidently, Alexander had accomplished a shift in his priorities. The Hellenization program had achieved most of its objectives. In the military area, as well as others, the need now was for a different kind of fusion.

Thomas W. Africa tells us that Alexander planned to reorganize his government in order to make Asia and Europe one country and combine the best of the East with the West.[49] For his new capital city he selected Babylon; he encouraged intermarriages, at one time arranging for the marriage of 10,000 Macedonians and Greeks to Asian women, and marrying a Persian princess (Roxanne) himself; and he demanded that his subject peoples worship him as a god. These policies strained Alexander's relationships with both Greeks and Macedonians.

To sum up, the beginning of an era of international importance for the Greek language and culture was the reign of Philip II. His strategies were carried on in great measure by his son Alexander, whose reign is recognized as the period of the greatest flowering of Hellenic culture in ancient times. Greek culture and language achieved this significance not because the Macedonians were Greek, but because the Macedonians saw unity of purpose with the Greeks as crucial support for their own ambitions; they used Greek settler-soldiers and traders to consolidate their territorial gains; and they found the Greek language best suited to their empire-building purpose. Eventually Alexander judged that the Macedonian-Greek alliance was no longer adequate as a basis on which to sustain his empire. He sought a new fusion between Macedonians and Asians.

Despite their reluctance to fight for Alexander's empire, the Greek states were pushed into enormous change, like it or not. Sometimes the upheavals occurred because the Greeks were with the Macedonians, and sometimes because they were against them. There were huge troop movements, and movements of civilian populations to settle conquered areas. History tells us that "the Macedonian conquest of Greece and Persia involved such enormous social upheaval that the Greek cities found it impossible to revert to their old values. Alexander's career marks the end of the classical era in Greece and the beginning of the Hellenistic period."[50]

David Hogarth remarks that the Hellenes were thrust reluctantly into an international role, economically and politically, and this role was determined largely by Philip II.[51] Philip's reign was, therefore, the beginning of an era of international importance for the Greek language and culture. Hogarth writes:

> But Philip it was that forced the Hellene into the open sea, and therefore if it be found that "nothing moves in the world which is not Greek in origin," it is owed to no man more than the Macedonian.

4. The Great Ethnic Mix of Greece

Just as Macedonia and other Balkan states were invaded by Slavs and other peoples from the north and from within the Balkans themselves, so were the lands that eventually were to become modern Greece. We need to examine this issue, since the modern Greeks repeatedly argue that they are direct ethnic descendants of the ancient Greeks and Macedonians. The fact is that the ethnic, linguistic, and cultural developments that these invasions created simply built upon similar movements of peoples into and out of the Balkans in the ancient past.

The Myth of Greek Ethnic Purity

Greek writers give a great deal of emphasis to the idea of Greek racial purity. For instance, in speaking of the movements of Germanic tribes in the Balkans before the Slavs, the writer of *Macedonia History and Politics* says that the Goths were beaten off and the invasions in the fourth century did not lead to "ethnological adulteration." In speaking about more modern times the writer says (p. 43), "Greece became involved in the 'Macedonian disputes,' because of political pressure from the Bulgarians and Yugoslavs, and because of the sensitivity of the Greeks towards the historical continuity of their race." Clearly this view about racial purity amongst the Greeks, presented here in a magazine distributed by the Greek government in English-speaking countries, is important to the Greeks.

Macedonia has been represented as a buffer protecting Hellenism from the waves of the barbarians throughout the centuries. Thus it is argued by modern Greeks that the area of the present-day Republic of Macedonia was affected by these barbarian invasions, but the lands that are now Greece were largely unaffected.[1]

The Greek insistence on ethnological purity for its people is not unusual among expressions of nationalism. The American political scientist Buck explained that the notion of physical kinship implied in the word "nation" is the most conspicuous element in the popular conception of nationality. However, it is also the least realistic. Buck points out that we have only to think of the extent of invasion and colonization that has occurred in nearly every corner of Europe to realize that this notion could at best be only approximate. More importantly, from the viewpoint of historical analysis, it is not possible to demonstrate national family connections. Recorded descent is at best restricted to a few families that are notable for some reason or another. All that can be shown convincingly is linguistic descent, but this is often taken as evidence of national descent.[2]

Anthony D. Smith points out, specifically in reference to the modern Greek nation, "Greek demographic continuity was brutally interrupted in the late sixth to eighth centuries A.D. by massive influxes of Avar, Slav and later, Albanian immigrants." He adds that modern Greeks "could hardly count as being of ancient Greek descent, even if this could never be ruled out."[3]

It seems clear that Greek nationalists do not wish to examine evidence concerning the present state within Greece that may reflect on this question about the reality of ethnic purity. The editor of The Times, long the most prestigious of British newspapers, wrote in August 1993: "Since 1961, no Greek census has carried details of minorities. This is because successive Greek governments, 'à la mode japonaise,' subscribe to a myth of homogeneity. Today, the historical refusal to acknowledge ethnic or cultural plurality has transmogrified into a refusal to accept political dissent in relation to these ethnic or cultural questions."

Simon McIlwaine writes, "Modern Greek identity is based on an unshakable conviction that the Greek State is ethnically homogenous. This belief … has entailed repeated and official denial of the existence of minorities which are not of 'pure' Hellenic origin. The obsession with Greek racial identity involves the distortion of the history of the thousands of years when there was no such thing as a Greek nation state."[4]

Many of the views that follow explain that, whether the Greeks feel comfortable with the idea or not, their peoples are of diverse ethnic background, a great mix of the peoples of the Balkans, and have been for the past several thousand years. If all of the peoples of the Balkans were subjected to mixture of varying degrees with the invaders, as was certainly the case, then the argument might readily be made that modern-day Greeks are no more ethnically related to early Greeks than present-day Macedonians are to ancient Macedonians.

Ancient Greeks. A common assumption is that ancient peoples were ethnically homogenous. As has already been noted with regard to the peoples of Macedonia, the kingdom was undoubtedly a great mix of people, and the diversity increased with the expansion of the Macedonian Empire. There was probably a comparable mix of peoples in various Greek city-states. While the Greeks who came into the Balkan peninsula became the dominant people in that area, strong influences from the earlier inhabitants remained. "For certain areas of the Greek mainland and many of the islands, the names of some fifteen pre-Greek peoples are preserved in ancient traditions, together with a number of other references."[5]

A widely accepted view is that the Indo-European language moved into Greece from Anatolia with the spread of agriculture around 7000 B.C.[6] Thus a dialect of Indo-European would have been the language of the neolithic cultures of Greece and the Balkans in the fifth and fourth millennia. There were also infiltrations or invasions from the north by Indo-European speakers sometime during the fourth or third millennium B.C.[7]

Bernal suggests an explanation of ancient Greek development in terms of what he calls "the ancient model." Classical, Hellenistic, and later, pagan Greeks from the fifth century B.C. to the fifth century A.D. believed their ancestors had been civilized by Egyptian and Phoenician colonization and the later influence of Greek study in Egypt. Up to the eighteenth century A.D., Egypt was seen as the fount of all "Gentile" philosophy and learning, including that of the Greeks, and it was believed that the Greeks had managed to preserve only a part of this wisdom. Bernal suggests that the sense of loss that this created, and the quest to recover the lost wisdom, were major motives in the development of science in the seventeenth century.

Bernal argues that the ancient model was accepted by historians from antiquity till the nineteenth century, and was rejected then only for anti–Semitic and racist reasons. He sees the Egyptian and Phoenician influence on ancient Greeks as beginning in the first half of the second millennium B.C. He concludes that Greek civilization is the result of the cultural mixtures created by these colonizations and later borrowings from across the eastern Mediterranean. These borrowings from Egypt and the Levant occurred in the second millennium B.C. or in the thousand years from 2100 to 1100 B.C., which Bernal suggests is the period during which Greek culture was formed.[8] "The Ancient Greeks, though proud of themselves and their recent accomplishments, did not see their political institutions, science, philosophy or religion as original. Instead they derived them — through the early colonization and later study by Greeks abroad — from the east in general and Egypt in particular."[9]

"Pelasgians" is the name generally given by ancient writers to the peoples before the Hellenes. According to both Herodotus and Thucydides, Pelasgians formed the largest element of the early population of Greece and the Aegean, and most of them were gradually assimilated by the Hellenes. Herodotus saw this transformation as following the invasion by Danaos (the Egyptian), which he took to be around the middle of the second millennium B.C. Herodotus stated that the Egyptian Danaids taught the Pelasgians (not the Hellenes) the worship of the gods.[10] The idea that the Pelasgians were the native population, converted to something more "Greek" by the invading Egyptians, also occurs in the plays of Aischylos and Euripides, written around the same time as Herodotus' *Histories.*

The Ionians were one of the two great tribes of Greece, the other being the Dorians. In classical times the Ionians lived in a band across the Aegean from Attica to "Ionia on the Anatolian shore ... Herodotus linked the Pelasgians to the Ionians."[11]

Tiberius Claudius wrote about the movements of some Greek tribes into the Balkan peninsula:

> Among these Celts, if the word is to have any significance, (are included) even the Achaen Greeks, who had established themselves for some time in the Upper Danube Valley before pushing southward into Greece. Yes, the Greeks are comparative newcomers to Greece. They displaced the native Pelasgians ... This happened not long before the Trojan War; the Dorian Greeks came still later — eighty years after the Trojan War. Other Celts of the same race invaded France and Italy at about the same time.[12]

With regard to what is now called the Dorian Invasion, Bernal notes that in ancient times this was much more frequently called "the return of the Her-aklids." The Dorians came from the northwestern fringes of Greece, which had been less affected by the Middle Eastern culture of the Mycenaean palaces which they destroyed. Their use of the name Heraklids was a claim not only to divine descent from Herakles, but also to Egyptian and Phoenician royal ancestors. This is not simply a modern theory. Ancient sources show that the descendants of these conquerors, the Dorian kings of classical and Hellenistic times, believed themselves to be descended from Egyptians and Phoenicians.[13]

Bernal argues that the explanation of Greek development in terms of Egyptian and Phoenician influences was overthrown for external reasons, not because of major internal deficiencies or weaknesses in the original explana-tion, but because eighteenth- and nineteenth-century Romantics and racists could not tolerate the idea that the crown jewel of European civilization owed its beginnings to a racial mix of cultures. For such reasons the ancient model had to be discarded and replaced by something more acceptable to the politi-cal and academic views of the time.[14]

The Aryan model. The Aryan model, an alternative theory about the devel-opment of the ancient Greeks, first appeared in the first half of the nineteenth century. It denied any influence of Egyptian settlements and expressed doubt about a role for the Phoenicians. An extreme version of this model was pro-pounded during the height of anti–Semitism in Europe in the 1890s, and then in the 1920s and 1930s; this particular explanation denied even the Phoenician cultural influence.[15] According to the Aryan model, there had been an invasion from the north, an invasion not described by ancient writers, which had over-come the existing pre–Hellenic culture. Greek civilization was seen as the result of the mixture of the Indo-European speaking Hellenes and the older peoples over whom they ruled.

Bernal argues that four forces explain the overthrow of the ancient model as a description of the beginnings of Greek culture: Christian reaction to the threat of Egyptian ideas, the rise of the concept of "progress," the growth of racism, and Romantic Hellenism.[16] In particular, a tidal wave of ethnicity and racialism swept over northern Europe at the end of the eighteenth century. The view was established that humankind was made up of races that were intrinsically unequal in physical and mental endowment. Racial mixing could lead to degradation of the better human qualities. To be creative, a civilization needed to be "racially pure." It became accepted that only people who lived in temperate climates — that is, Europeans — could really think. Thus the idea that "Greece, which was seen not merely as the epitome of Europe but also as its pure childhood, [could be] the result of the mixture of native Europeans and colonizing Africans and Semites" could not be tolerated.[17] By the turn of the eighteenth century, the so-called "European" Greeks were considered to have been more sensitive and artistic than the Egyptians and were seen as the better philosophers, even the founders of philosophy. By the end of the nineteenth century, some popular German writers had come to see the Dorians as pure-blooded Aryans from the north, possibly even from Germany. The Dorians were certainly seen as very close to the Germans in their Aryan blood and character. Significant British historians of the time also were enthusiastic about the supposedly pure northern, and possibly Germanic, blood of the Dorians.[18]

These ideas were developing in Europe in the same period as the Greek War of Independence, which united all Europeans against the traditional Islamic enemies from Asia and Africa. This war and the philhellenic movement throughout Europe and North America, which supported the struggle for independence, helped refine the existing image of Greece as the epitome of Europe. Paradoxically, the more the nineteenth century admired the ancient Greeks, the less it respected their writing of their own history.[19]

Linguistic evidence and the ancient model. Bernal provides evidence in support of his view that Egyptian and Phoenician elements were powerful in the development of ancient Greek culture. He notes that it is generally agreed that the Greek language was formed during the seventeenth and sixteenth centuries B.C. Its Indo-European structure and basic lexicon are combined with a non–Indo-European vocabulary of sophistication. He argues that since the earlier population spoke a related Indo-European language, it left little trace in Greek; thus the presence of that population does not explain the many non–Indo-European elements in the later language. Bernal suggests that it has not been possible for scholars working in the Aryan model over the last 160 years to explain 50 percent of the Greek vocabulary and 80 per cent of proper names in terms of either Indo-European or the Anatolian languages supposedly related to "pre–Hellenic." Since they cannot explain them, they simply call them pre–Hellenic.[20]

Bernal suggests to the contrary: that much of the non–Indo-European element can be plausibly derived from Egyptian and West Semitic and that this would fit very well with a long period of domination by Egypto-Semitic conquerors.[21] He claims that up to a quarter of the Greek vocabulary can be traced to Semitic origins (which for the most part means the Phoenicians), 40 to 50 percent seems to have been Indo-European, and a further 20 to 25 percent comes from Egyptian, as well as the names for most Greek gods and many place names. Thus 80 to 90 percent of the vocabulary is accounted for, as high a proportion as one can hope for in any language.

Bernal argues that the Indo-European component of the Greek lexicon is relatively small. There is a low proportion of word roots with cognates in any other Indo-European language. Further, the semantic range in which the Indo-European roots appear in Greek is very much the same as that of Anglo-Saxon roots in English, another culture strongly influenced by invaders (in this case, the French-speaking Normans). These roots provide most pronouns and prepositions, most of the basic nouns and verbs of family, and many terms of subsistence agriculture. By contrast, the vocabulary of urban life, luxury, religion, administration, political life, commercial agriculture and abstraction is non–Indo-European. Bernal points out that such a pattern usually reflects a long-term situation in which speakers of the language which provides the words of higher culture control the users of the basic lexicon. For example, he claims that in Greek the words for chariot, sword, bow, march, armor, and battle are non–Indo-European.[22] Bernal explains that river and mountain names are the toponyms that tend to be the most persistent in any country. In England, for instance, most of these are Celtic, and some even seem to be pre–Indo-European. The presence of Egyptian or Semitic mountain names in ancient Greek would therefore indicate a very profound cultural penetration. Bernal presents many examples of these and notes that the insignificant number of Indo-European city names in Greece, and the fact that plausible Egyptian and Semitic derivations can be found for most city names, suggest an intensity of contact that cannot be explained in terms of trade.[23]

Bernal maintains that when all sources, such as legends, place names, religious cults, language and the distribution of linguistic and script dialects, are taken into account alongside archaeology, the ancient model, with some slight variations, is plausible today. He discusses equations between specific Greek and Egyptian divinities and rituals, and the general ancient belief that the Egyptian forms preceded the others, that the Egyptian religion was the original one. He says that this explains the revival of the purer Egyptian forms in the fifth century B.C.[24] The classical and Hellenistic Greeks themselves maintained that their religion came from Egypt, and Herodotus even specified that the names of the gods were almost all Egyptian.[25]

Using linguistic, cultural, and written references, Bernal presents interesting evidence connecting the first foundation of Thebes directly or indirectly to eleventh-dynasty Egypt. He argues that both the city name Athenai and the divine name Athene or Atena derive from Egyptian, and offers evidence to substantiate this claim. He traces the name of Sparta to Egyptian sources, as well as detailing relationships between Spartan and Egyptian mythology. He says that much of the uniquely Spartan political vocabulary can be plausibly derived from late Egyptian and that early Spartan art has a strikingly Egyptian appearance. For Bernal, all these ideas link up with the Spartan kings' belief in their Heraklid—hence Egyptian or Hyksos—ancestry, and would therefore account for observations such as the building of a pyramid at Menelaion, the Spartan shrine, and the letter one of the last Spartan kings wrote to the high priest in Jerusalem, claiming kingship with him.[26]

Bernal claims that there has been a movement, led mainly by Jewish scholars, to eliminate anti–Semitism in the writing of ancient history, and to give the Phoenicians due credit for their central role in the formation of Greek culture. A return to the ancient model is less clear with regard to Egyptian influence. However, Bernal proposes that the weight of the Aryan model's own tradition and the effect of academic inertia have been weakened by startling evidence showing that the Bronze Age civilizations were much more advanced and cosmopolitan than was once thought, and that in general the ancient records are more reliable than more recent reconstructions. He believes the ancient model will be restored at some point in the early twenty-first century. For our purposes it is sufficient to note that even the current acknowledgment of the significance of Phoenician influence in the formation of ancient Greek culture indicates some of the ethnic mix that made up ancient Greece.[27]

Influences in the Greek Ethnic Mix

Slavery in the ancient world. While it is difficult to gauge the intermixture that took place between the older established inhabitants and the infiltrating Greeks wherever they may have come from, the tradition of slavery in the ancient Mediterranean may have had an even greater impact on the physical nature of the people. It has been estimated that in classical times the number of slaves in Attica was roughly equal to the number of free inhabitants, or around 100,000.[28] In Sparta there was an even greater proportion of slaves, and most of them, the helots, were Messenians. While the slaves of Athens were a wide racial mix and therefore less likely to unite on the basis of a common language, these Messenian helots of Sparta all spoke Greek, and had a kind of group self-consciousness. Thus they presented "special problems of security for their Spartan masters, whose numbers were constantly on the decline."[29]

Changes in the ethnic composition of Greek city-states are illustrated by the comments about the case of Piso. Piso, who had been the recipient of an unhelpful decision by a vote of the Athenian city assembly, "made a violent speech in which he said that the latter-day Athenians had no right to identify themselves with the great Athenians of the days of Pericles, Demosthenes, Aeschylus, and Plato. The ancient Athenians had been extirpated by repeated wars and massacres and these were mere mongrels, degenerates, and the descendants of slaves. He said that any Roman who flattered them as if they were the legitimate heirs of those ancient heroes was lowering the dignity of the Roman name."[30]

Such historical ideas make it clear that even two thousand years ago the notion of ethnic purity amongst the Greeks was difficult to sustain. The ethnic mix continued over the next two thousand years. As Nicol has observed, "The ancient Greeks were, after all, of very mixed ancestry; and there can be no doubt that the Byzantine Greeks, both before and after the Slav occupation, were even more heterogenous."[31]

Celtic Influence. In 282–280 B.C., a Celtic army of about 170,000 led by Brennos and Achicorius entered Macedonia and, with Bolgios, overwhelmed the country. The Celtic army swept into Greece, defeating the Greeks at Thermopylae, and went on to sack the temple of Delphi, the most sacred site of the Hellenic world, before withdrawing. The Celtic army eventually withdrew in an orderly manner, taking their loot with them. No Greek army was strong enough to attack them. The Celtic invasions had a lasting effect on Greek consciousness, being commemorated in Greek literature.

Though some remained as mercenaries, the bulk of the Celtic armies moved north again, having found little room to settle in populated Greece and Macedonia. The Celts remained in Thrace, though they were Hellenized. The Scordisci had established a prosperous and strong kingdom around modern Belgrade, and one Celtic tribe settled on the slopes of Haemos. However, most went further north and east, some even settling in Asia Minor, in Galatia.

Greeks as Slavs. In recent historical time other Europeans have held the view that the people of modern Greece have little ethnic connection with the ancient Greeks. Robert Browning,[32] a writer who is sympathetic to the Greeks, discusses the writings of the Bavarian Johann Philipp Fallmerayer, who in 1830 proposed that the Slav invasions and settlements of the late sixth and seventh centuries resulted in the "expulsion or extirpation of the original population of peninsula Greece. Consequently the medieval and modern Greeks...are not the descendants of the Greeks of antiquity, and their Hellenism is artificial." Fallmerayer's view that not a drop of pure Greek blood is to be found in the modern Greek is often held to be extreme. A more moderate version of essentially the same idea was presented more recently by R.H. Jenkins.[33]

Browning concedes that the Slavic impact was considerable in the Balkan peninsula, and that there was great intermixture of races in Balkan Greek lands. He says Fallmerayer was right in drawing attention to the extensive Slav invasion and settlement in continental Greece. Despite the great attention given by the Greek government to renaming towns, villages, rivers and other geographic locations, there remain large numbers of place names of Slavonic origin. Even so, Browning suggests, the majority of the Greek-speaking people lived in Constantinople and Asia Minor, and in these more distant locations were not so strongly affected by the Slavs. He says also that the original population was not extirpated or expelled, since many remained in coastal regions, cities, and inaccessible areas.

Nicholas Cheetham is uncompromising in the language he uses to describe the Slav influence. He says that between the fifth and seventh centuries "a sharp and brutal revolution altered the whole character of Hellas... It also involved a steep decline of civilized life and an almost total rejection of former values... The most striking change affected the ethnic composition of the people and resulted from the mass migration of Slavs into the Balkans which began in the sixth Century."[34]

Cheetham explains that the eastern emperor held back the Slavs for decades. For instance, the emperor Constans II (642–68) successfully forced back the "Macedonian Slavs" (as Cheetham calls them) who were threatening Thessalonika. Later Constans' grandson, Justinian II, undertook a major campaign against the Slavs and settled many in Asia. But in the end there was a continuous infiltration followed by settlement. It seems that earthquakes and the bubonic plague had thinned the population on the eve of the Slav invasion. After the great plague of 744–747, Constantinople was repopulated with Greeks from the Balkan peninsula and the islands, and this may have made even more room for the newcomers. The land was repeopled, Cheetham says. The Slavs occupied the fertile plains and river valleys, while the original peoples were forced into the numerous mountain ranges. The Slavs remained rural dwellers, so the cities may have suffered less from their arrival. The Slav settlements extended the length and breadth of the Balkan peninsula. They overran the "whole of Greece," and more, Cheetham says. Their influence extended across the Balkans from the Danube to Cape Tainaron. In the process, Roman authority was submerged, and the remnants of classical culture and the Christian religion were extinguished. There were few areas remaining where the Greeks predominated, though at least in those early times Thessalonika was one of them. In the eighth century Strabonos Epithomatus wrote, "And now, in that way almost all of Epirus, Hellada, the Peloponnese and Macedonia have also been settled by the Skiti-Slavs."[35] In general, the lands that had been Greek in ancient times were commonly regarded by foreigners as a Slav preserve.

In 805 the Slavs came under imperial control. They learned the ways of Roman citizens and were probably being attracted to Christianity. Eventually, peasant farmers from Asia minor were brought in to recolonize coastal plains and river valleys of "Hellas." Those Slavs who did not assimilate were gradually pushed back into the more rugged and inhospitable regions of the interior.

The distinction between Romans and assimilated Slavs became blurred. As early as 766 Niketas, a (Macedonian) Slav, became patriarch of the Constantinople patriarchate.

Nicholas Cheetham claims that the Orthodox church made intense efforts to convert the Slavs in Greece, and that this took effect more or less in the period from A.D. 800 to 1000, only when the Greek language had ousted Slavonic. Again, this effect was stronger in the southern part of the peninsula than further to the north, since the Christianization of the Slavs as a whole was made possible only when some Slav monks from Thessalonika created a suitable script in their own language as the vehicle for this task. Yet the central point, that the ethnic mix was profound, is quite clear.

Another historian, Tom Winnifrith,[36] says that the Slav conquest of the Balkans was rapid, eliminating the Latin heritage. He says the Slavs "spread throughout Greece." However, it was not just the Slavs who created ethnic change at this time. Winnifrith says there were many Latin-speaking refugees from cities in the thickly populated areas of the Danube frontier and Illyricum who are likely to have gravitated to Salonika and Constantinople and exchanged their Latin for Greek. These refugees added another element to the constantly changing ethnic equation in the Balkans.

The extent of the Slavic inroad is evident on maps showing mediaeval population distribution. The map titled "Slavs in the Balkans" shows that by about the eighth century A.D., Slavs were settled along the whole length of the Balkan peninsula right to the tip of the Peloponnese and were especially strong along the western coast. Pockets of Greek inhabitants remained along the east coast.

The Byzantine emperor Constantine Porphyrgenitus openly says that the whole of Hellas had been Slavicized. The Slavonic tribes of the Ezerites and the Milingi were independent in the Peloponnese in the seventh and eighth centuries and did not pay tribute to Byzantium. Even today in the Peloponnese, one cannot go three miles in any direction without encountering a Slavonic place-name.[37]

Arnold Toynbee compares the Slavic invasion with the early Greek invasions, noting that "on the mainland itself, the Slav occupation was more nearly complete than the North-West-Greek occupation had been." He explains that Attica was not occupied in either historical invasion, but in the Peloponnese, "Arcadia, which had escaped occupation in the twelfth century B.C. was now overrun." For more than two hundred years, till the reconquest of the Peloponnese by the East Roman government around A.D. 850, the Slavs controlled almost all of it. "As late as the year A.D. 1204, the French invaders of the Peloponnese found that, after more than three centuries of East Roman rule, there were still two independent Slav peoples, the Ezeritai and the Melingoi, in the fastness of Mount Taygetos."[38]

There is much agreement among historians about the dramatic and

SLAVS IN THE BALKANS

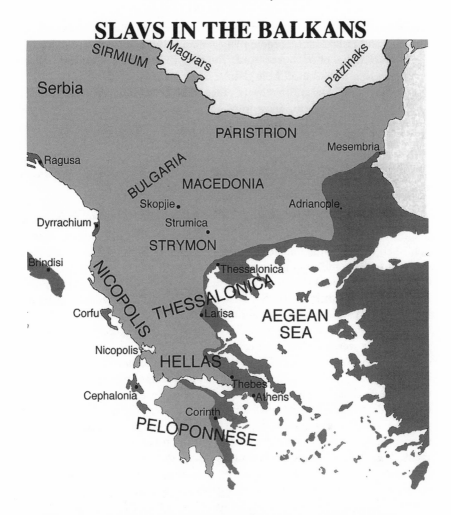

Territory occupied by the Slavs by the 8th Century
Territory that remained under Byzantine control

overpowering influx of Slavic peoples to Greece. These people often intermarried and were assimilated in the "Roman" culture. Some writers tend to
downplay the importance of the racial intermixture for Hellenization, suggesting that being a Hellene does not require particular racial antecedents. This
is a point that modern Greeks appear unwilling to believe. Their preference
seems to be simply to deny that "ethnological adulteration" ever took place. For
example, in *Macedonia, History and Politics* (a publication sponsored by the
Greek government and distributed throughout the English-speaking world) it

is acknowledged (p. 10) that after Basil II there was a "solid Slav element" in Yugoslav and Bulgarian Macedonia, but it claims there was no impact at all in Greek Macedonia, or in Greece itself. The analyses from other sources lead us inevitably to a rejection of these claims. The Slavic influence in what is now Greece is clear. However, there were other important influences also.

Greeks as Albanians. Slavs were not the only groups to move into the southern part of the Balkan peninsula. Many Albanians came in also. Albanians settled in Athens, Corinth, Mani, Thessaly and even in the Aegean islands. In the early nineteenth century, the population of Athens was 24 percent Albanian, 32 percent Turkish, and only 44 percent Greek.[39] The village of Marathon, scene of the great victory in 490 B.C., was, early in the nineteenth century, almost entirely Albanian.[40]

Nicholas Hammond,[41] a historian who is sympathetic to the Greek view that the ancient Macedonians were a Greek tribe and who has had several works published in Athens, is unable to support the Greek view on this matter. He says that by the middle of the fourteenth and early fifteenth century the majority of people in the Peloponnese were Albanian speakers. The fascinating point is that the people with whom they were competing for land were overwhelmingly not the original Greek-speaking Roman citizens, but the new breed of Greek-speaking Slavs. As Hammond says, many Greek-speaking people at that point in time were probably ethnic Slavs.

The continuing impact of this new ethnic and cultural force is indicated in Hammond's comments that the Albanian incursions into Greece continued under the Turkish system and went on right into the eighteenth century, and that the descendants of these Albanian people were still speaking Albanian when he was in Greece in the 1930s. This is not a reflection on the national consciousness of these Greek citizens, for as Hammond explains, they thought of themselves as Greek. Indeed Hammond points out that the Albanian role in the resistance to the Turks, and in the formation of the Greek nation, was significant. Like the Slavs, the Albanians became attached to their new lands, learned the new language, and began to think of themselves as one with the other peoples living there.

Greeks as Vlachs. Also quite numerous during the eighteenth century in Greek lands and in territories that were to become Greek were the Vlachs. Hammond says that the Vlachs came in with the Albanians and provided leadership. He suggests that the Vlach peoples probably originated in Dacia, an area that is now part of Romania. Hammond says that the Vlachs managed to acquire possession of the great Pindus area. In general, they stayed in northern Greece and were never assimilated in terms of language the way that other ethnic groups were, though some groups ended the nomadic life and settled in Macedonia and in Thessaly.

According to Tom Winnifrith, some Greek writers have claimed the Vlachs as ethnic Greeks.[42] He is skeptical about this idea, claiming that these Greek historians have "been at unfair pains to eliminate almost completely the Latin element in Vlach language and history." Winnifrith comments that one of these Greek writers, M. Chrysochoos, the first to suggest that the Vlachs living in the passes crossing the Pindus mountains were the linear descendants of Roman soldiers, is inspired by misplaced patriotism to insist that these Romans were really some kind of Greeks.

The Vlachs seem to have left Dacia as part of a wave of migration that spread throughout the Balkans from Greece, where they are known as Kutzo Vlachs, Tzintzars, or Aromani, through Bulgaria and Yugoslavia to the Trieste region.[43] Many of them are still in these areas today. They all speak varieties of Romanian, but represent the remnants of originally Dacian-, Illyrian-, Thracian- and even Scythian- speaking tribes. Vlachs settled in Thessaly, Roumeli, the Ionian islands and the Aegean islands.

The Romanian Balkan history professor Motiu has said that the Vlachs comprised 7 to 8 percent of the population of Greece, numbering seven to eight hundred thousand. There have been no population statistics regarding the Vlach minority since the Greek census of 1951. The census of 1935 and 1951 recorded 19,703 and 39,855 Vlachs respectively. Greece does not recognize the presence of a Vlach minority.[44]

Greeks as Turks. A recent issue that has engaged the vigorous attention of Greek politicians is the position and status of Cyprus. It is an area of conflict with Turkey, and one in which Greece has attempted to influence world opinion in its direction by fostering the theory of Greek ethnic purity. In 1964 German archaeologist Franz Maier argued that the Turkish Cypriots were a "people" and not a minority, and that Greek Cypriots and Greeks were not really racially Greek but a mixture.[45] Similarly the Cypriot sociologist Andreas Panayiotou has been quoted as saying that Cypriots were not Greek, but were a synthesis of Greek, Turkish and other elements. He advocated that the Cypriot dialect should become the island's official language.[46]

Some external observers (perhaps with their own case to make) have come to similar conclusions: "Greece, while denying the presence of ethnic and religious minorities within its borders, tries to convince the world that the Orthodox people living in its neighboring countries are ethnic Greeks. But this is not true. In Cyprus, the Southern Cypriot Orthodox whom Greece presents to the world as Greek Cypriots, are not ethnic Greeks."[47]

This material demonstrates that the Greek attitude towards ethnic purity in Greece, and all that follows from it, can be seen in various spheres of political interest, not only in the case of the ethnic Macedonians of Aegean Macedonia and in behaviors towards the new Republic of Macedonia. It is a mainstay of the Greek nationalist position.

The Cyprus position is something of a special case; nevertheless, it reminds us of the 400-year occupation of Greek lands by the Turks and the inevitable ethnic impact. It has already been noted that in the early part of the nineteenth

century the population of Athens was about one-third Turk. "Auberon Waugh
… wrote in The Daily Telegraph that the Greeks of today, with hairy popos,
flat noses and bushy eyebrows, are clearly a race of Turkish descent and have
nothing to do with the Greeks of antiquity sculpted on the Elgin marbles."[48]

The Greek independence movement. Just as interesting as the ethnic diversity of Greece is the idea that the new peoples in the southern Balkan peninsula learned Greek, became good Roman citizens, and identified a community
of interest with other peoples living in their land. Writing nearly one hundred
and fifty years ago, just a few years after the success of the Greek revolution,
George Finlay[49] noted that the local energies and local patriotism of all the
Christian municipalities in the Ottoman empire were able to readily unite in
opposition to "Othoman oppressions" whenever some kind of communication
or administrative structure to centralize their efforts could be created. In these
local institutions, Finlay suggested, a foundation was laid for a union of all the
Christian Orthodox races in European Turkey. This comment was made, of
course, a generation before Bulgaria achieved its autonomy from the Turks, and
long before a Macedonian state became possible. Greece was then still a very
small state at the bottom of the Balkan peninsula. Finlay recognized " the vigorous Albanians of Hydra, the warlike Albanians of Suli, the persevering Bulgarians of Macedonia, and the laborious Vallachians on the banks of the
Aspropotamos" who embarked together on a struggle for Greek independence,
"as heartily as the posterity of the ancient inhabitants of the soil of Hellas."
Nicholas Hammond tells us that in the Greek War of Independence the Albanians, above all, drove the Turks out.

The heroism and determination of the Greek revolutionaries alone probably would not have been enough to overcome the Turks and their allies. The
armed intervention of the European powers made a difference at crucial times.
With the beginning of the Greek War of Independence in 1821, the Turkish sultan gave Mohammed Ali (an Albanian general of the Turkish forces in Egypt
who had seized power in 1808) the provincial governorships of Crete and the
Peloponnese with a commission to exterminate the Greek rebels. The Greek
fleet kept them out till 1825, when the fleet mutinied over a lack of pay. A battle at Missolonghi, where Greek patriots were being besieged by the Turks, was
swayed in Turkish favor by the arrival of the Egyptians. The heroic defense and
the appearance of an Egyptian threat moved the governments of Europe to
support the Greek cause. In 1827 squadrons of British, French and Russian
navies destroyed the Turkish and Egyptian fleets at Navarin, and Greek independence was made certain.

According to anthropologist Roger Just, most of the nineteenth-century
"Greeks," who had so recently won their independence from the Turks, not only
did not call themselves Hellenes (they learned this label later from the intellectual nationalists); they did not even speak Greek by preference, but rather
Albanian, Slavonic, or Vlach dialects.[50] He held that their culture was similarly

remote from the culture of the ancient Greeks. Their "customs and habits might seem to bear as much if not more relation to those of the other peoples of the Balkans and indeed of Anatolian as they did to what were fondly imagined to be those of Pericline Athens."[51]

Maintaining the myth. Other Europeans have become irritated with the Greek myth of ethnic purity. For instance, in an editorial in *The Sunday Telegraph*, London, March 27, 1994, the Greek attitude is taken to task:

> What is the word for this obsessive Greek pseudo-relationship with their country's past (they even have a magazine, Ellenismos, devoted to the subject)? It is not quite pretentiousness. There is too much passion for that. No, the Greeks, the ancient ones, had a word for the modern Greek condition: paranoia. We must accept that Mr Andreas Papandreou (Greek prime minister) and the current EC presidency are the sole legitimate heirs of Pericles, Demosthenes and Aristide the Just. The world must nod dumbly at the proposition that in the veins of the modern Greek ...there courses the blood of Achilles. And their paranoid nationalism is heightened by the tenuousness of that claim.

The Editor of *The Sunday Telegraph* argues that Greece has been ruthless in erasing traces of ethnic diversity, and suggests that the desperation of its actions, including the Greek claim to a monopoly of the classical past (in which all peoples of European origins have a share) can be explained by the fact that the Greeks today are a mixture of Slavs, Turks, Greeks, Bulgars, Albanians, Vlachs, Jews and Gypsies.

One modern Greek intellectual who now lives outside of that country has reflected on the forces within Greece that foster and sustain the theory of Greek ethnic purity:

> In retrospect it is clear to me that my 12 years of Greek schooling, mainly in the 1970s, conspired to instill in me precisely one attitude: an almost unshakable belief in the purity and unity of the Greek people, language and culture...Belief in the continuity of Greece against all odds was enabled also by the method of withholding information and sealing off interpretive paths. We had, as children, neither the capacity nor the inclination to explore disunities and "impurities."[52]

Modern Greek citizens who try to assert their ethnic identity are not treated tolerantly in Greece even today. One of these recently said, "There are a million Macedonian speakers [in Greece]. We are entitled to rights, to associations, schools, churches, traditions ... I have a Macedonian ethnic consciousness ... I belong to an ethnic minority which isn't recognized by my State."[53] As a consequence of this statement and others like it, Christos Sideropoulos and another Greek Macedonian, Anastasios (or Tasos) Boulis, repeatedly faced the Greek courts. They were charged with spreading false rumors about the non–Greekness of Macedonia and the existence of a Macedonian minority on Greek territory which is not officially recognized, and with instigating conflict among Greek citizens by differentiating between the speakers of a Slavic language and Greeks. If convicted they faced possible terms of several years' imprisonment and heavy fines.[54] More will be said about charges of human rights abuses against Greece in a later chapter. At this point it is enough to recognize the continuing vigor with which Greece asserts an ethnic purity that cannot be substantiated by historical analysis.

Of particular interest are the population changes that have occurred in Aegean Macedonia during the twentieth century. The Greek position is that the Greek citizens of Aegean Macedonia have a genuine claim to historic connection with Macedonia and that the Slavs do not. It is implied that they have this connection since they are Greek and the ancient Macedonians are claimed to have been Greek. However, it is not commonly known, even among Greeks, that a majority of the "Greek" population of Aegean Macedonia can trace its immediate ancestors not to Macedonia, but to Anatolia, western Turkey, since they came from Turkey as refugees in the 1920s during one of the Greek-Turkish wars. The population of western Turkey at the time had been subject to many of the same forces that affected the populations of the southern Balkans, though for various reasons, including the tendency of the Byzantine Empire to move troublesome peoples to this area and the strong presence of peoples of Turkic origin, the mix was even more complex. If the connection of Balkan Greek speakers to the ancient Greeks and thence to the ancient Macedonians is tenuous, the links with the Turkish Greek speakers who came into Aegean Macedonia are even more dubious. This issue will be explained further in another chapter.

Nineteenth-century European attitudes toward Greece. In 1821, after the Greek War of Independence broke out, western Europe was swept by Philhellenism.[55] The Germans were the nationality most quickly and deeply involved. Over 300 Germans went to fight in Greece, but throughout Europe tens of thousands of students and academics were involved in support movements. Many Britons, French, and Italians went to Greece to fight, and there was a strong support movement in the U.S. Though only sixteen North Americans reached Greece, the widespread philhellenic feelings arising from the war provided a big boost for the "Hellenic"—Greek letter—fraternities in the U.S. Shelley wrote:

> We are all Greeks. Our laws, our literature, our religion, our arts all have their roots in Greece. But for Greece ... we might still have been savages and idolaters ... The human form and the human mind attained to a perfection in Greece which has impressed its images on those faultless productions whose very fragments are the despair of modern art, and has propagated impulses which can never cease,

through a thousand channels of manifest or imperceptible opera-
tion, to enable and delight mankind until the extinction of the
race.[56]

Throughout western Europe, the Greek War of Independence was seen as
a struggle between European youthful vigor and Asiatic and African decadence,
corruption and cruelty.

The Greek fight for independence had attracted European sympathy
because of European distrust of the Moslem Turks, sympathy with the Christian Greeks, a great respect for classical Greek scholarship, and views developing
in Europe that the ancient Greeks were "northern Europeans" and the origi-
nators of philosophy and science. Despite this favorable view of the ancients,
closer inspection of modern Greeks had left many western Europeans disappointed with their heroic, but superstitious, Christian and dirty, "descendants,"
whom some regarded as "Byzantinized Slavs."[57] These views were not isolated.
Mark Twain, for instance, "had thought modern Greeks a libel on the ancients."[58]
The English poet Byron was shocked when he came to Greece expecting to find
the tall, blond, blue-eyed heroes of antiquity.[59]

Cheetham[60] says that the new Greeks were regarded with vague suspicion
in academic circles, since their association with ancient Greece was not considered to be genuine. They were, in Robert Byron's words, "discounted as the
unmoral refuse of medieval Slav migrations, sullying the land of their birth with
the fury of their politics and the malformation of their small brown bodies."
Cheetham says that the classical master at his school commiserated with him
on the prospect of his having to consort on his holidays with what he called
"those nasty little Slavs."

It may be that European racist contempt for the Greek revolutionaries of
the nineteenth century goes some way toward explaining the persisting determination of the Greeks to create an alternative racial model for themselves. If
we juxtapose the nineteenth-century view of the ancient Greeks as Aryans with
attitudes towards the ethnic characteristics of the Greek revolutionaries, we can
see the enormous burden that the Greeks carried in their dealings with Europe.
While it has been a characteristic of new nation-states during the last century
and a half to manufacture a suitable cultural, linguistic and ethnic pedigree for
themselves, the Greeks have carried this process through to an extent that is
unparalleled in Europe. Even today, Greece clings to a European connection
via its rather tumultuous relationship with the European community. It is
ironic that a part of the continuing European mistrust of the Greeks, as is evident from influential editorial comments such as those cited above, has developed because of the very myths that the Greeks propagate in order to purify
their image. Greek myth-making today can be seen as inspired by the wider
European racism of the nineteenth and early twentieth century, and even a
continuation of that racism. The United States State Department and international human rights organizations have claimed that Greek suppression of eth-

nic minorities has come out of such policies. These claims will be elaborated in a later chapter.

The Continuation of Greek Culture?

Arnold Toynbee discusses the evolution of the meaning of the word "Hellene" in Greek literary usage, noting that it was originally given to a very specific group of northwest Greek-speaking people who lived in the interior of Epirus, but later came to be used to describe the association of twelve peoples in central and northeastern continental Greece that formed the Delphi-Anthela amphictyony. This was primarily a religious communality. Other Greek city-states joined this association and the name Hellene was applied to all who participated in this civilization. Toynbee points out that the principal distinctive feature of this new Hellenic civilization, a characteristic that distinguished it from the earlier Mycenaean civilization, was the city-state. This feature was more important even than language, as is evidenced by the admission of the Luvian-speaking city-states of Lycia and Caria.

Toynbee notes that Herodotus, writing in 479 B.C., put common race and language first in his definition of Hellenism, but acknowledged a role for a common culture. However, Isocrates, nearly 100 years later (380 B.C.), made the point that the Athenians "have given the name 'Hellenes' a spiritual connotation instead of its former racial one. People who share in our Athenian culture are now felt to have a stronger title to the name 'Hellenes' than people who share with us merely a common physical make-up."[61]

Robert Browning dismisses the significance of the Slavic influence in Greece by taking up this idea, arguing that being Hellene was not a matter of genetics or tribal membership, but of education. Thus Browning suggests that if you speak Greek and live like a Greek, you are Greek. Cheetham takes a similar tack, claiming that the "original" citizens of the Balkan peninsula were intensely proud of their Hellenic culture but adding that questions about racial origins would have appeared pointless to educated persons of the high Byzantine age, since they tended to indifference towards such matters. They had become quite accustomed to the enormous ethnic mixture that had characterized the empire since late Roman times. Both of these explanations, though intended to be sympathetic to the Greeks, are diametrically opposed to the present Greek government position.

Like Robert Browning, Cheetham makes the point that there was at least some continuity of culture in early medieval times, since the mixture of peoples was held together by the combined power of "Greek civilization, Roman law and the Christian religion." Cheetham argues that the Slav immigrants were progressively intermingled with the Greeks so that an eventual fusion took place.

Browning also notes that over time the Slavs were acculturated and were often converted to Christianity. A process of "re-hellenization" took place, led by the Greek Orthodox Church, using the vehicle of the Greek language. To use the words of Nicholas Cheetham, (in the south) "religion and Helleniza-tion marched hand in hand." The Slavs and Albanians, in particular, converted to Christianity and learned to speak Greek.

The nature of this re-hellenization must be questioned, since even its advocates recognize that Roman law and the Christian religion were in no sense contiguous with classical culture yet made up a large part of the character of this "new hellenic culture." If we strip away the religion of classical Greece and the unifying force of common shrines and rituals of the Delphi-Anthela amphic-tyony; eliminate the political structure of the city-state; and replace Greek law and administrative procedures with those of Rome, it seems unreasonable to assert that the remaining elements constitute a culture essentially the same as classical Greece. It is simply not plausible to suggest that the bulk of Greek-speaking Roman citizens in the Middle Ages, let alone the former Turkish sub-jects of nineteenth-century Greece, "lived like" ancient Greeks.

Making a case about the difficulty classical writers faced in distinguish-ing between dialects of Greek, Arnold Toynbee[62] offers an analogy. He suggests that a speaker of High German from Frankfurt am Main, or a speaker of Low German from Flanders or Holland, might find it difficult to believe that the lan-guage spoken by people in some rural district in Luxembourg, Alsace, or one of the forest cantons of Switzerland is a dialect of his own language. Perhaps the most interesting point about this example is how it demonstrates that although people may speak dialects of the same language, they can enjoy very different lifestyles and cultures. If we compare the Dutch seaman of the six-teenth century and a Swiss-German farmer of the same period, we might won-der whether the two would see any affinities between themselves except for a remote language similarity. We might also contemplate the absurdity of the idea of a Swiss-German of the present day saying to himself, "My (Dutch) ances-tors were among the greatest of sea navigators." It would be an anachronism.

Eric Hobsbawn reminds us:

> The most usual ideological abuse of history is based on anachronism rather than lies. Greek nationalism refused Macedonia even the right to its name on the grounds that all Macedonia is essentially Greek and part of a Greek nation–State, presumably ever since the father of Alexander the Great, king of Macedonia, became ruler of the Greek lands on the Balkan peninsula … it takes a lot of courage for a Greek intellectual to say that, historically speaking, it is non-sense. There was no Greek nation–State or any other single politi-cal entity for the Greeks in the fourth century B.C.; the Macedo-nian empire was nothing like the Greek or any other modern nation-state, and in any case it is highly probable that the ancient Greeks regarded the Macedonian rulers, as they did their later

Roman rulers, as barbarians and not as Greeks, though they were
doubtless too polite or cautious to say so.[63]

In the same way that it would be questionable for a modern Swiss-German to claim descendence from sixteenth century Dutch seafarers, it is questionable for modern Greeks to claim family affinity with the ancient Macedonians, even if the ethnological purity which such a claim requires could be established.

An appeal to continuity of Hellenism through the Greek language is similarly dubious. We have already seen Roger Just's comment that by the nineteenth-century most of the newly independent "Greeks" did not call themselves Hellenes, and did not even speak Greek by preference. Furthermore, the use of a form of the Slavic language was still widespread, perhaps dominant, in the territories that were not taken into the Greek nation until later in the nineteenth and twentieth centuries.

It has been claimed that the Greek language of the nineteenth century was a corrupted ecclesiastical version of classical Greek that the ancients might have had some trouble comprehending. George Finlay was extremely critical of this language and the role of the church hierarchy based in Constantinople in reducing it to the level apparent in the mid-nineteenth century.

If we consider the standard applied by Herodotus that ancestry, language and culture were the basis for Greek community, or even if we prefer the evolved definition of Isocrates that gives primary emphasis to culture, it is not an unreasonable conclusion that nineteenth-century Greeks failed to meet these criteria. After the establishment of independence, Greek intellectuals made a great effort to return their country to its Hellenic past. Classical place names were revived, and Turkish, Venetian and even Byzantine buildings were removed to reveal ancient ruins. The language was standardized in the nineteenth century as part of a concerted effort to create a new Greece. This brought some stability to the culture of the diverse "new Hellenic" peoples who could be recognized at that time. Since 1988 and the renaming of northern Greece as Macedonia, a whole new focus has been given to the Greek effort to identify with the classical and Hellenic past.

5. Aegean Macedonia

To better understand political development in "Macedonia" we need to specify the area of interest. The land in question, at least as far as the nineteenth century is concerned, was that area known by the Turkish rulers as the "three vilayets." These three areas were named Solun (now Thessaloniki), Bitola, and Kosovo, but were known to Macedonian nationalists and to much of the rest of the world as Macedonia. These days we might use the term "Greater Macedonia."

It is important to understand what happened politically to that land, and to the peoples who inhabited it. Macedonia was divided amongst other Balkan states after it was forcibly taken from the Turks in the Balkan wars early in the twentieth century. This division created the three major elements of Macedonia that are recognized today: the modern Republic of Macedonia (Vardar Macedonia), a portion of western Bulgaria (Pirin Macedonia), and the northern province of Greece (Aegean Macedonia). The Greek king at first recognized the latter as new territory conquered, rather than as Greek lands retaken, and it was not named Macedonia by its new political masters until more than seventy years later.

Ordinarily we might not make a distinction between a land and its peoples, since political change need not affect the make-up of the peoples living within particular boundaries. However, in the case of Macedonia there have been dramatic changes in the population as a consequence of changes in political control.

The world is now sadly familiar with the concept of "ethnic cleansing." The label has recently been employed to describe the practice in Bosnia of clearing out the population of an area by extermination or exile, and replacing them with peoples more suitable to the group in political control. This process was employed in many parts of Europe and the Balkans in the early part of the twentieth century, including Macedonia. The resettlement of Aegean Macedonia continues with the recent arrival of substantial numbers of "Pontiac" Greeks from the former U.S.S.R.

Ethnic and Language Groups
in Aegean Macedonia, 1870–1928

Before the Balkan wars of 1912-13, Macedonia was treated as a single administrative unit in many ways — for instance, for the purposes of census taking. There is a persuasive body of evidence and opinion suggesting that Slavs outnumbered all others in the "three vilayets" of Macedonia in the nineteenth century. Given the ideas presented earlier about the great influence of the Slavs throughout the Balkans, including Macedonia, this is no great surprise. Statistics collected by various authoritative groups at the time show an overwhelming majority of Slav-speaking peoples. In 1881 the Roumeliote government issued detailed statistics based on Turkish figures, commune by commune, which gave for Macedonia, from a total of 1,863,382 inhabitants, 1,251,385 Slavs; 463,839 "Mussulmans" of whom part were Pomaks (Slavs converted to Islam); and only 57,480 Greeks.

The statistics of the famous German geographer Ritter, towards the end of the century, identifying inhabitants largely in terms of their religious affiliation, are reasonably consistent with these figures. Ritter claimed 1,124,288 "Bulgarians"; 360,626 "Mussulmans, Turks and Pomaks"; 422,357 "Serbs, Albanians, and Wallacks"; and 59,833 Greeks. A census made by the authorities of the Orthodox Church that considered only the Christians showed 181,000 families or 905,000 souls who were Slavs of the eastern rite, and 20,300 families or 101,500 souls who were "Greeks and Valaques."

While there is some variability in these figures that may be explained in terms of changes over time and enrollment on parish registers, none of these estimates indicate that the "Greeks" were anything but a small minority, while Slavs were the major group. However, Mihailo Apostolski, who describes the changes in the ethnic and religious composition of Macedonia's population between 1900 and 1948,[1] states that the greatest changes were caused mainly by the Ilinden uprising of 1903, the Balkan wars of 1912 and 1913, and World War I. These changes need to be taken into account when one attempts to understand the modern history of the area.

Comparisons of population statistics that specify the ethnic composition for Macedonia in the late nineteenth and early twentieth centuries show that the area was inhabited by a very large number of disparate social and ethnic groups.[2] Italian writers Arbakke and Torre, who have examined the issue, have concluded that the problem of finding adequate ways to describe these populations is complicated by the contradictory criteria applied by competing national aspirations. These national claims were based on assumptions that were taken for granted and even considered more or less unchanging. Ethnic or national identity is often spoken of as if it were a stable personal feature, whereas history shows that ethnic adherence can vary. Thus different factors contribute to shaping national identity, including the options available for

LANGUAGE DISTRIBUTION IN THE BALKANS IN THE NINETEENTH CENTURY

—— Borders in the late 20th Century
--- The limits of territory in which a majority of
    Macedonian/Bulgarian speaking peoples lived.
AL Albanian speakers
GK Greek speakers
MB Macedonian/Bulgarian speakers
RO Roumanian speakers
SB Serbian speakers
T   Turkish speakers

identification. Given such options, ethnic or national identity may then be constructed by individual or external forces. Different forces have taken effect in different parts of Macedonia.

The Macedonian Bulgarian language was dominant in Aegean Macedonia, even south of Salonika, in the nineteenth century (see the map titled "Language Distribution in the Balkans in the Nineteenth Century"). By the middle of the century, there were clear signs that the Macedonian and Bulgarian languages were splitting. By the time the Bulgarian language was moving towards formal codification, the movement towards a separate Macedonian language had become significant. Nevertheless, the more important distinction here is that between Greek and Slavic speech.

The Greek historian Stavranios asserted that the population of Macedonia was distinctly Slavic "except for the border areas where members of the other Balkan nations can be found." Using religious affiliation to identify different groups (the choices for Christians were essentially the Greek or Bulgarian Orthodox religions), he said that "in Aegean Macedonia, just before the Balkan wars lived: 326,426 Bulgarians, 40,921 Macedonian Moslems, 289,973 Turks, 4,240 Christian Turks, 240,019 Greeks, 13,753 Greek Moslems, 5,584 Albanian Moslems, 3,291 Christian Albanians, 45,457 Christian Wallachians, 3,500 Wallachian Moslems, 59,560 Jews, 29,803 Gypsies, 8,100 other, or in total 1,073,549." Stavranios said that Salonika, claimed by the Greeks today as purely Greek, was made up of 45 percent Jews, 20 percent Bulgarians, 20 percent Turks, and 15 percent Greeks. A British writer, Simon McIlwaine, gives slightly smaller percentages for the Greek and Turkish populations of Salonika in the early twentieth century, eighteen and fifteen percent respectively.[3]

The great Macedonian leader of the uprising against the Turks at about the turn of the century, Gotse Delcev, was born right in the middle of what is now Aegean Macedonia, and so were many of those who fought beside him. Delcev was educated in Salonika. His first language was Slavic Macedonian. The Macedonia he knew was the Turkish administrative district later split apart by the Serbs, Bulgarians, Greeks and Albanians. Delcev and his compatriots throughout Macedonia were fighting not for a northern Greek state, but for a free (Greater) Macedonia. The Greek annexation of the southern part of Macedonia a few years later prevented the realization of this aspiration.

A point noted by Mihailo Apostoloski concerns the change in numbers of Macedonians after the Ilinden uprising. Newspaper reports of the time spoke of massacres involving 50,000 Macedonians. While there is uncertainty as to the numbers of people killed, there is no doubt about the murderous reprisals of the Turkish authorities against whole villages identified as sympathetic to the revolutionaries. To escape massacre, many thousands of Macedonians fled into Bulgaria, Serbia, and Greece. This shift in the population balance affected census data immediately after this period, though many of the refugees probably returned eventually. However, data taken around 1904 concerning the population balance in parts of Macedonia mu^st he considered of questionable value.

The Balkan Wars and the Partitioning of Macedonia

At the beginning of the twentieth century, Macedonia was a province of the Ottoman Empire, occupied primarily by Macedonians, though there were also Albanians, Turks, Romani (Gypsies), Vlachs, Jews, and Greeks. Until the Balkan wars, Macedonia had been a compact and coherent geographic, economic, and historic entity, but after the Balkan wars Macedonia was divided.

Greece, Serbia, and Bulgaria looked back to the past when their peoples, or those with whom they felt some historical association, had held great empires, and all hoped to resurrect a former glory. The great European powers had prevented Macedonian liberation before this time, sometimes even going so far as to send their own forces to assist the Turks against the Macedonians. Often the larger powers, like Russia, Austria, Britain and France, were pulling strings behind the scenes, protecting their own interests and usually, with one or two notable exceptions, holding little regard for the Macedonians. Thus Macedonia remained helpless, was frequently devastated under the Turks, and became an easy victim for these other Balkan states.

Before the outbreak of war, Macedonia was under pressure from Greeks, Bulgarians, and Serbs, who were preparing their case for their territorial expansion. All claimed that they were simply occupying lands inhabited by their own peoples — thus, in the view of Macedonian nationalists, creating Greeks, Bulgarians and Serbs where none had ever existed before. In the last two decades of the nineteenth century, armed gangs working on behalf of the Greek and Bulgarian churches struggled with each other, and intimidated Macedonians, in their efforts to achieve control. Through the construction of churches and schools and the assignment of priests and teachers, each state was conducting an intense propaganda campaign within Macedonia, aimed at shaping the sense of national identity of the Orthodox Christians of Macedonia towards their particular direction.[4] Harilaos Trikoupis, Greek prime minister from 1882 to 1895, said, "When the great war comes, Macedonia will become Greek or Bulgarian according to who wins. If it is taken by the Bulgarians they will make the population Slavs. If we take it, we will make them all Greeks."[5] In 1897, with the support of Russian diplomacy, Serbia obtained the right to have its own church in Macedonia, and then its own schools as well. From that time there was a three-way struggle for the hearts, minds, and bodies of the Macedonians, all against a background of continuing Turkish occupation. The Turks were able to turn this divided struggle to their own purposes, as always acting on the principle of divide and rule. They willingly cooperated in the "cultural and spiritual partition of this one people into three sections, finding in this the guarantees for its peace and power."[6] Meanwhile, agents of the Greeks, Serbs, and Bulgarians plotted against the Macedonian nationalists as much as against the Turks, often betraying them to the Turkish authorities. "The most characteristic feature of the history of cultural life in Macedonia proves to be the circumstance that the greatest enemy to its autonomy was not the barbaric Turks, but its brothers of the same stock and the same faith, who tried to dispossess and assimilate it with the help of the very culture the Macedonians themselves had created."[7]

The Macedonian struggle reached a climax in the Balkan wars of 1912-13. Serbia, Greece and Bulgaria formed a series of alliances to "liberate" Macedonia from the Turks. This objective was accomplished by their victorious armies in the first Balkan war, a brief struggle from October to December 1912. In the second Balkan war, sometimes called the Inter-Allied War, the other allies fought Bulgaria over the spoils between June and July of 1913.

Macedonians participated with enthusiasm in the Balkan wars, hoping that the battle against the Turks would give them the independence they had so desperately sought in the Ilinden uprising just a few years before. It is significant that their co-religionists in the neighboring Balkan states had offered no help to the Macedonian revolutionaries. An independent Macedonia was not on their agenda. In 1912-13 Macedonian emigre groups, and others organizing within the country, formed armed detachments which participated in the Balkan wars, sometimes as conventional troops, sometimes as guerrillas, or "terrorist bands," for example the mobile detachments of Sandanski. Macedonians of the time claimed that "more than 100,000 Macedonians participated in this war, not considering the help that the whole population offered to the allies for the liberation ... under the slogan 'Macedonia to the Macedonians.'"[8]

Before the end of 1912, Turkey had concluded an armistice with all Balkan allies except Greece, but a treaty was finally signed between all antagonists in May 1913. The Serbs had previously captured northern Macedonia (the Vardar basin, with Uskub/Skopje as the center) and Monastir. The Bulgars had taken Thrace as far as the Chataldja lines close to Constantinople. The Greeks took Salonika and Preveza in the west, and in February 1913 they had captured Jannina, completing their control over Epiros. However, an independent Albania was established by the great powers.[9]

A dispute arose between Bulgaria and its allies over Macedonia, and war erupted again. Bulgaria had tried to take over Serbia's portion of Macedonia including Uskub/Skopje and Monastir, and Greece's portion, the southwestern districts and Salonika, as well as Thrace. The Serbs and Greeks united against the Bulgarians, defeating them in their own theatre of war. The Romanians took advantage of the Bulgarian difficulties, declared war on them and took territory in the north while the Turks took back eastern Thrace. The Treaty of Bucharest on August 10, 1913, divided Macedonia between Greece, Serbia, and Bulgaria. In 1919 a small part of Macedonia was given to Albania by the Treaty

MACEDONIA IN THE EARLY PART OF THE TWENTIETH CENTURY

Boundary changes resulting from the Balkan wars are shown. Greece took the largest portion, Aegean Macedonia, from the south. Serbia took the next largest piece, Vardar Macedonia, calling it South Serbia. Bulgaria took Pirin Macedonia, and Albania took some small areas in the west.

of London. With minor adjustments, these borders have remained in force ever since.

That the Greek presence in Macedonia was considered by the Greeks of the time to be an occupation seems confirmed by the Decree of Occupation by the Greek king Georgios I, of October 31, 1912. The decree does not speak of territories which the Greek army had liberated or regained — which would have implied that Greece considered them Greek lands — but clearly speaks of "Macedonian territories occupied by the Greek army."[10]

It is instructive to see how more recent Greek publications speak of the partitioning of Macedonia. *Macedonia, History and Politics* explains that "Macedonia was divided up according to the following proportion: Greek Macedonia: 34,603 square kilometers or 51.57%; Yugoslavian Macedonia: 25,714 square kilometers or 38.32%; Bulgarian Macedonia: 6,789 square kilometers or 10.11%" (p. 17). Two small parts of Western Macedonia, the ones around Lake

Ohrid and Prespa and the other just south of Debar, were given to Albania a few years later.

The consequences of partition brought despair to Macedonian nationalists:

> A thousand Greek and Serbian publicists began to fill the world with their shouting about the essentially Greek or Serbian character of the populations of their different spheres. The Serbs gave the unhappy Macedonians twenty-four hours to renounce their nationality and proclaim themselves Serbs, and the Greeks did the same. Refusal meant murder or expulsion. Greek and Serbian colonists were poured into the occupied country... The Greek newspapers began to talk about a Macedonia peopled entirely with Greeks — and they explained the fact that no one spoke Greek by calling the people "Bulgarophone" Greeks ... the Greek army entered villages where no one spoke their language. "What do you mean by speaking Bulgarian?" cried the officers. "This is Greece and you must speak Greek."[11]

The Report of the Carnegie Endowment for International Peace on the Balkan Wars, initiated after "amazing charges of Bulgarian outrages attributed to the King of Greece," indicated that 161 Macedonian villages were burned down and more than 16,000 houses were destroyed in the Aegean part of Macedonia.[12]

Macedonia, History and Politics argues that most of the populace of the new province was Greek-speaking, a dubious suggestion given the material we have already considered, but this source acknowledges that there were significant numbers of Slavic-speakers in the territories taken over by Greece. It says that the new province of "Northern Greece" (as it was called for its first 74 years after partition) included "the majority of the Slav-speaking inhabitants who had retained a Greek national conscience." The implication here is that the Slavic-speakers in Aegean Macedonia had exercised some kind of choice about becoming part of Greece while others had left. In fact there was no occasion on which such choice could be exercised, and Slavic Macedonians' lack of enthusiasm for their new nationality is suggested by their large-scale participation in the Greek civil war a few decades later. In August 1988 Greece renamed "Northern Greece" as "Macedonia." Only since this renaming have Greek claims to Macedonian heritage gained widespread publicity.

The Greek writer of *Macedonia, History and Politics* also argues that the portion of Macedonia given over to Greece was approximately equal in extent with the "historical" Macedonia of the classical period, thus providing a justification for the expansion of Greek territory. There are good reasons to doubt this argument. Examination of the descriptions of Macedonia provided by ancient writers as well as modern historians shows that virtually all of what is now the Republic of Macedonia was included in ancient Macedonia at the time of Philip II.

It would appear that some Greek politicians would like to return to what they see as the good old days. "Prominent members of the Greek parliament expressed nostalgia for the simple old times when E. Venizelos of Greece (former prime minister) and N. Pasic of Serbia, after the Balkan wars in 1913, agreed on the Greek-Serbian frontier so that to the north there would be only Serbs and to the south only Greeks, and no 'Macedonians' on either side."[13]

Repopulating Aegean Macedonia

At the beginning of this book, we note Greek claims that Northern Greece, or Aegean Macedonia, is "more than 98.5% ethnically pure." The purity is held to be Greek. However, the statement is not accepted by reputable opinion outside of Greece. For instance, the 1987 edition of the *Encyclopaedia Britannica* indicated that there were still 180,000 Macedonian (Slav) speakers in this area, indicating a much greater percentage than 1.5. If Macedonian activists from these areas are correct, there may be as many as 1,000,000 people from Macedonian-speaking backgrounds in Aegean Macedonia. Perhaps even more interesting is the origin of many of the Greeks who inhabit Aegean Macedonia. There is no doubt that there is now a high proportion of Greeks, but many, perhaps a majority, have forebears who were relative newcomers to the area.

John Geipel explains that after the dismembering of the Ottoman Empire, of which Greece was a part for nearly four hundred years until 1832, "thousands of Greeks from Asia Minor were resettled in Hellas... Fresh genetic material must also have been introduced from Asia Minor when over a million Greeks from Turkey were resettled in their own country during the 1920's."[14] The events that brought these new settlers to Aegean Macedonia, and that forced out many of the existing inhabitants, were the Balkan wars between 1912 and 1913, and the continuing Greek struggles against the Turks into the 1920s. From 1920 to 1922 Greece fought a war against Turkey, attempting to add territories in Asia Minor, many of which had large Greek-speaking populations, to the Greek nation. Greece was defeated in this war and was forced into a population exchange that required the assimilation of 1.3 million Greeks from Asia Minor. Around half of these refugees were settled in Aegean Macedonia, where there was more habitable space than in other parts of Greek-controlled territory.

The largest numbers of new inhabitants came to Aegean Macedonia after the fall of Smyrna in August 1922. Hundreds of thousands of Greek inhabitants escaped from the city with the Greek army. A large majority of these people were women and children and old people, since the men of military age had either been killed or imprisoned by the Turks.[15] Between 1913 and 1923, Greece had particularly difficult minority problems to deal with among Bulgarians and Turks in Aegean Macedonia and Moslem Albanians in Epiros. However, they dealt with these problems to some extent by handing over northern Epiros to Albania, by slowly exchanging recognized Moslem Albanians for Christian "Greeks," and finally "by the disaster of Asia Minor which led to the final expulsion of the entire Greek population of Turkey, except that of Constantinople, and the compulsory exchange for them of the Moslem population of Macedonia..."

In 1923 an agreement was signed with Turkey (formalized as the Treaty of Lausanne) for an exchange of populations. Some 350,000 Moslems and "Bulgarians" left Greece,[16] and more than 550,000 of the Asia Minor refugees came to Aegean Macedonia between 1920 and the census of 1928. The overall population of the area increased by 330,000, or 33 percent, to 1,400,000. The numbers in Salonika increased by 70,000, or nearly 40 percent, to 244,000 in 1928, of whom nearly 100,000 were officially classed as refugees. No other part of Greece (except Athens) received anything like this proportion of refugees.

A.W. Gomme gives the population of Aegean Macedonia in 1920 as 1,070,000. If 350,000 people were removed, as he says, that leaves us with 720,000, of whom a small minority seem to have been of Greek-speaking background. Since the population was 1,400,000 by 1928, presumably most of this increase is due to the Greek speakers from Turkey who were settled there. It is quite clear that many more Greeks were brought in from Turkey (about 600,000 to 650,000) than were there already. Other refugee settlers came to Aegean Macedonia from Yugoslavia, Romania, and Russia.[17] Thus the population of Aegean Macedonia was changed by the introduction of Greek speakers from other lands, people who had no historical connection with the land of Macedonia. The case is similarly clear with regard to Salonika. We have already noted Stavranios' observation that Salonika, claimed by the Greeks today as purely Greek, was made up of 45 percent Jews, 20 percent "Bulgarians," 20 percent Turks, and 15 percent Greeks in the early part of the twentieth century. If 100,000 refugees were added to the population of around 175,000 people, as Gomme claims, the number of Greek speakers goes from around 26,000 to 126,000. While Greek speakers were in the minority before the Balkan wars, they were clearly the largest single group in Salonika after the population exchanges, even before allowing for the forced removal of many of the Salonikan Turks and "Bulgarians."

While the biggest influx of Greek speakers to Aegean Macedonia came as a result of the Greek-Turkish wars, a major exodus of Slavic-speaking Christians occurred as a result of fighting in the later period of the Balkan wars between Greece and Bulgaria. Bulgaria had attempted to take the lion's share of the spoils after the Turks had been forced out of Macedonia, and was successfully resisted by the Serbians and Greeks. Between 1913 and 1920, on the basis of voluntary and mandatory population exchanges between Bulgaria and Greece and Greece and Turkey, 130,000 Slavic-speaking Christians were driven from the Aegean part of Macedonia[18]; around 86,000 Macedonians were forcibly sent to Bulgaria, and among the Moslems sent to Turkey were more than 40,000 Macedonian Moslems who were Macedonian speakers.

Even Greek sources concede that during the years from 1913 to 1928 the enormous movements of population which took place in Greek Macedonia changed the ethnological composition of the area.[19] *Macedonia, History and Politics* acknowledges that perhaps 100,000 Slavic speakers "left" (i.e., were forced to leave), 77,000 of these in 1926 alone. These figures may well be an underestimate (by comparison with Gomme's estimates, for example), but this material does add weight to the idea that huge numbers of Slavs left and that even greater numbers of Greeks came in. The extent of the population movement out of Aegean Macedonia is emphasized in a report on March 30, 1927, in the Greek newspaper *Rizospastis*, which stated that 500,000 Slavic speakers were resettled to Bulgaria.

Thus the majority of the Greek-speaking population of Aegean Macedonia is descended from relatively recent Greek refugees from Turkey and other places. This being the case, Greece might be considered to have questionable claim on the name Macedonia. Remember, too, that the name Macedonia was not applied to the province by Greece until 1988. Thus much of the current population has lived at most some 70 years in a land that has been called "Macedonia" for less than a decade. Clearly they do not have the kind of historical claim to the land and to the name Macedonia as the Macedonian Slavs, Vlachs and Albanians whose ancestors have been there for 1,500 years or more.

Forced Assimilation

After the occupation of Aegean Macedonia by the Greeks in 1912 and the formal partition of 1913, the experiences of the Slavic-speaking inhabitants of Bulgarian (Pirin) Macedonia, Greek (Aegean) Macedonia and Yugoslav (Vardar) Macedonia varied considerably. In the beginning, however, "it was now the common lot of all Macedonians to have their language forbidden in public life (schools, the press, etc.) — In each part of the country the official language of the partitioning state, and it alone, was imposed as the cultural vehicle for the Macedonian population."[20] Each of the states — Bulgaria, Greece, Serbia and Albania — that occupied a part of Macedonia denied the existence of any national minority within its borders. The experience is described with considerable emotion by a modern-day Macedonian, the current president of the new Republic:

> The participants in this partitioning claimed right to parts of Macedonia, declaring Macedonians to be Southern Serbs, Bulgarians and Slavophonic Greeks. They changed their new subjects' names and surnames. They forbade the Macedonian language, forced Macedonians to learn in foreign languages and imposed their own interpretations of history. They forced them to go to their churches. In short, they turned them into second-rate citizens, subjected to systematic re-settling and permanent exile. The common denominator of

such politics was denationalization of the Macedonian people, erasing them from the Balkan's map of peoples, usurping its history, identity and desire for its own state. They forced upon us the fate of disappearing through assimilation.[21]

For most of the past eighty years, the Greek government has consistently denied the existence of both a Macedonian nation and a Macedonian minority in northern Greece and has adopted a policy of forced assimilation toward the Slavic-speaking inhabitants of Greek Macedonia. The degree to which this policy has affected the human rights of Macedonians who are Greek citizens has been a concern for various human rights agencies and the United States State Department for many years. As we shall see later, international concern was first expressed effectively through the League of Nations in the early 1920s, and is still being expressed just as vigorously today. In the 1920s, Greece was seen as having breached its human rights obligations under the international conventions to which it was a signatory. A similar situation holds today.

Part of the detail for the argument that follows comes, with little modification, from a Macedonian source, and for that reason might be expected to present a biased position. However, there are good reasons for considering it very seriously. Many of its conclusions are consistent with the observations of human rights organizations and the United States State Department in their recent criticisms of Greece's human rights record, and they were accepted without amendment by the international meeting of P.E.N. (the international society of writers) in 1986 and in subsequent years. Besides, some of the changes that came about are self-evident.

Population changes in Aegean Macedonia had an effect on the status of the languages in common use in those territories. Up until the period of the great population exchanges, the Macedonian (Slavic) tongue was the most commonly used language. "Out of a total population of 1,052,227 inhabitants ... 805,000 persons knew and used the Macedonian language in business and the marketplace in everyday life."[22] Greek was a minority language or family language, used daily by some 220,000 speakers. The situation reversed after the population exchanges.

Out of a total of 1,412,477 persons living in Aegean Macedonia after the great population exchanges, more than a million people used or tried to use the Greek language. Thus Greek became the common as well as the official language. The Macedonians suddenly found themselves a national minority within their own land. Some have estimated that about 370,000 Slav Macedonians were living in northern Greece after the partitioning,[23] many in the western part of Aegean Macedonia in the Kostur, Lerin, and Voden areas. These latter areas are still predominantly Macedonian-speaking today, though the people are often reluctant to admit this.

After the Greeks occupied Aegean Macedonia, they closed the Slavic-language schools and churches and expelled the priests. The Macedonian language and name were forbidden, and the Macedonians were referred to as Bulgarians, Serbians or natives. By a law promulgated on November 21, 1926,[24] all place-names (toponymia) were Hellenized; that is the names of cities, villages, rivers, and mountains were discarded and Greek names put in their place. At the same time the Macedonians were forced to change their first names and surnames; every Macedonian surname had to end in "os," "es," or "poulos." The news of these acts and the new, official Greek names were published in the Greek government daily *Efimeris tis Kiverniseos* no. 322 and 324 of November 21 and 23, 1926. The requirement to use these Greek names is officially binding to this day. All evidence of the Macedonian language was compulsorily removed from churches, monuments, archaeological finds and cemeteries. Slavonic church or secular literature was seized and burned.[25] The use of the Macedonian language was strictly forbidden also in personal communication between parents and children, among villagers, at weddings and work parties, and in burial rituals.

Despite this general policy, there were times when arms of the Greek government, in the face of international pressure, took quite a different position to the Macedonian language. However, it is now the position of the Greek government that the Macedonian language does not exist and never has existed.

The Macedonian primer of 1925 produced by Greece (ABCEDAR). After the Treaty of Versailles at the end of World War I, several treaties were supposed to be implemented (under the auspices of the League of Nations) requiring the Greek government to guard the rights of Macedonian Slavs in northern Greece (Aegean Macedonia).[26] For example, in Article 46 of the Treaty of Neuilly the Kingdom of Greece committed itself to defend the rights of national minorities within its borders. By the Treaty of Sevres, which was signed in Paris on August 10, 1920, the countries of Britain, France, Italy and Japan concluded an agreement with Greece on the protection of "non–Greek nations." Greece pledged full protection of the Macedonian national minority (and other minorities), its language and culture, and undertook to open Macedonian schools. In Section 2, Greece pledged to extend full care over the life and freedom of all citizens irrespective of their origin, nationality, language, and faith. Article 7 of this treaty states, "No restrictions may be sanctioned which restrict the free use by each citizen of Greece of any language." Article 8 says, "The citizens of Greece who belong to national, religious or linguistic minorities must be granted the right to equal treatment as citizens of Greece … for example, equal rights to open, manage and control institutions, schools and other educational institutions in which they are free to use their own language and confess their own religion." Article 9 refers to children who do not speak Greek and the requirement that they "receive primary schooling in their own language."

The Bulgarians claimed that the Macedonians in Greece were Bulgarian, and the Greeks for their part wanted to look after the interests of Greeks in

Bulgaria, so these two countries signed the Kalfov-Politis Protocol in 1924, agreeing to minority rights. One very good reason for Greece to give at least the appearance of meeting its international obligations was the financial aid that was tied to such cooperation. Greece needed loans approved by the League of Nations to resettle refugees from Asia Minor. On September 4, 1925, the office of High Commissioner for National Minorities was established at Salonika, for the observance of international agreements concerning national minorities. For a time, Greece seemed ready to go along with the treaties it had signed. It explicitly reassured the League of Nations of its willingness to fulfil the terms of articles 7 to 9 of the treaty in 1925 by submitting two copies of a primer published under the auspices of the Greek Ministry of Education for use in Slavonic-language schools. This primer, the *ABCEDAR*, was written in a central Macedonian dialect.[27]

Greece's ambassador at the League of Nations explained that the *ABCEDAR* was written in a form of Latin script "similar to that used by the Croats, Czechs, Slovenes." Given the common use of Cyrillic script in Aegean Macedonia, as in Vardar Macedonia, up until this time, the deliberate use of the Latin script suggests that this primer was intended to counteract Bulgarian influences among the Slavic Macedonian minority in Greece. Since the use of the local dialect in Vardar Macedonia had been banned by the Serbian authorities for official and educational use, the adoption of such forms suggests that the primer might also have been intended to encourage separatist feeling among the "South Serbs," as these Macedonians were called at the time.

Although it was presented to the League of Nations, the *ABCEDAR* never reached the Macedonian children. Most copies were immediately destroyed. Locally the *ABCEDAR* often arrived at the required towns but was destroyed by local police chiefs or met other (sometimes Bulgarian-inspired) misadventure. There have been recent reprints to show us what the Greek authorities achieved. The production of this little book, and the attitudes that surrounded it, indicate that at least some important Greek academics and politicians of the time recognized that Macedonian Slavs in Aegean Macedonia were a group of significant size, and a people distinct by culture and language from the Serbians and the Bulgarians.[28]

The *ABCEDAR*, the first and only Macedonian primer officially prepared in Greece despite Greece's international obligations to do much more, gained much favorable comment in the Greek press of the time. Nikolaos Zarifis, writing in *Elefteron Vima*,[29] said, "The Primer was printed in the Latin script, and compiled in the 'Macedonian dialect.'" Zarifis went on to say, "The compilers rejected the Bulgarian and Serbian Cyrillic alphabet, and followed the Macedonian speech of the Lerin-Bitola region." These comments make it clear that informed people of the time recognized both the language and the territory ("Macedonia") from which it originated.

The principles of the Treaties of Neuilly and Sevres were honestly supported by the Greek minister of foreign affairs, Rusos; an expert in international law, Nikolaos Politis; and the left-wing liberal leaders, Yoanis Sefianopulos and Papanastasiu, among others.[30] Nonetheless, the Greek government failed to distribute the book or to implement plans to open Macedonian schools. A Greek writer, Dimitrios Vogazlis,[31] said that the failure of the *ABCEDAR* project was caused by the Bulgarian and Yugoslav governments. He said the Greek government did not follow the lead given by the Bulgarian and Yugoslav governments, labeling the Macedonians Bulgarian or Serbs, since "it held to the opinion that they constituted a separate nation regardless of the names they were given." This attitude seems to have provoked the Yugoslav government into action. The *London Times* of March 12, 1925, also suggests that the Yugoslav government caused Greece to back away from fulfilling its treaty obligations towards the Macedonian minority. The Yugoslav government (the Kingdom of Serbs, Croats, and Slovenes), angered that the Slavs south of the Yugoslav-Greek border might be called "Macedonians," threatened to cancel the treaty of alliance with Greece and discussed with the Bulgarians a division of Greek Macedonia into spheres of influence.

Despite those few Greek voices of support for fair dealings with the Macedonian Slav minority in Aegean Macedonia, the *ABCEDAR* never reached any of the schools for which it was intended. The suppression was so complete, there must surely have been a highly coordinated campaign to make sure that the book was never used. Nevertheless, analysis of the circumstances surrounding the preparation of the book shows that in the 1920s the Greek government, perhaps reluctantly, recognized the Macedonian Slavs to be a separate ethnic group with their own "Macedonian" language. However, despite this acknowledgment, in the 1920s Macedonian schools were closed, not opened. Kindergartens were established in Macedonian localities so children could be inculcated in a Greek spirit. This was despite a November 11, 1930, press conference in Athens at which prime minister Eleaterios Venizelos said, "The problem of a Macedonian national minority will be solved and I will be the first one to commit myself to the opening of Macedonian schools if the nation so wishes."[32]

Metaxas. The dictatorship of Ioannis Metaxas (1936–1940) was especially brutal in its treatment of the Slavic speakers of Aegean Macedonia, who by this time had increasingly begun to identify themselves as Macedonians. On December 18, 1936, the Metaxas dictatorship issued a legal act concerning "Activity Against State Security." This law punished claims of minority rights. On the basis of this act, thousands of Macedonians were arrested, imprisoned, or expelled from Greece. On September 7, 1938, the legal act 2366 was issued. This banned the use of the Macedonian language even in the domestic sphere. All Macedonian localities were flooded with posters that read, "Speak Greek." Evening schools were opened in which adult Macedonians were taught Greek. No Macedonian schools of any kind were permitted. Any public manifestation of Macedonian national feeling and its outward expression through language, song, or dance was forbidden and severely punished by the Metaxas regime. People who spoke Macedonian were beaten, fined, and imprisoned.[33] Punishments in some areas included piercing of the tongue with a needle and cutting off a part of the ear for every Macedonian word spoken. Almost 5,000 Macedonians were sent to jails and prison camps for violating this prohibition against the use of the Macedonian language. Mass exile of sections of Macedonians and other "difficult" minorities took place. The trauma of persecution has left deep scars on the consciousness of the Macedonians in Greece, many of whom are even today convinced that their language "cannot" be committed to writing.[34]

Writing in 1938, Australian author Bert Birtles in his book *Exiles in the Aegean* said, "If Greece has no Jewish problem, she has the Macedonians. In the name of 'Hellenization' these people are being persecuted continually and arrested for the most fantastic reasons. Metaxas's way of inculcating the proper nationalist spirit among them has been to change all the native place-names into Greek and to forbid use of the native language. For displaying the slightest resistance to this edict — for this too is a danger to the security of the State — peasants and villagers have been exiled without trial."

Vardar and Pirin Macedonia

Like the other invaders of Macedonia, the Serbs had ambitions for a greater empire. One way of making that empire more cohesive was by "Serbianizing" the Macedonian population. In their part of Macedonia, which was officially referred to as "South Serbia," the Kingdom of Serbs, Croats and Slovenes (Yugoslavia) declared the Slavonic inhabitants to be Serbs. In these endeavors to carry out assimilation, the history of the Macedonian people was changed to have a Serbian emphasis, surnames were changed, newborn children could be given only Serbianized names specified by the authorities, names of places were altered, and the newly created colonies acquired names from Serbian history. The use of the Macedonian language in public was forbidden. In official use only the Serbian language was permitted.

Between the two world wars, Serbia also made considerable efforts to send Serbian settlers into Macedonia, thus giving them a stronger justification for being there and a larger base of support within that territory.[35] In 1992 we saw the consequences of such Serbian policies in Croatia and Bosnia-Herzegovina, where Serbians have carved out enclaves of "Serbian" territories. We can see the same kind of policy in action today as Serbia makes repeated representations to the government of the Republic of Macedonia on behalf of Serbians in that country, Serbian organizations within Macedonia repeatedly claim that their numbers have been officially underestimated, and the Serbian leadership consults with Greece about a possible division of Macedonia (see Chapter 10).

An important Serbian doctrine, expressed in 1784 as Serbs struggled to become free from the Turks, was that Serbian states should annex to Serbia all lands that had once been ruled by Tsar Dushan. Dushan ruled the great fourteenth-century Serbian empire, moving its capital to Skopje, before the Turks took over. The Serbian Vladimir Karich in the 1880s hoped to prepare the way for annexation of Balkan territories by having Serbian settlers colonize areas such as Macedonia — to "make this small yeast soon grow into great Serbian Bread."[36] Nikola Pasic, the president of the Serbian government, sent settlers to the cities with the task of creating there a favorable ground "to welcome us when we arrive there with the army." The outbreak of the First World War frustrated plans to settle 12,000 families in the Vardar region, but settlement occurred after the war, often under the guise of agrarian reform.

In the 1930s, while Metaxas was imprisoning Macedonians in Greece for speaking their native language, the Serbs were relatively liberal. Only Serbian was permitted in schools and in official government documents, but recognized literary *"belles lettres"* could be published, and it was permitted to perform dramas in the Macedonian "dialect." Peter Hill describes many examples of these.[37] He gives instances also of Macedonian poetry published in the 1930s that had enormous effects on school children, such as the work of "Kosta Racin (showing a clear striving towards a standardization of the Macedonian literary language), Kole Nedelkovski, Venko Markovski, and Aco Sopov, who all wrote in the central dialect, thus establishing a foundation for constructing the new literary language."

Except for a brief period following World War II, when Bulgarian behavior seemed guided by socialist ideology rather than narrow nationalistic interests, the Bulgarian government has officially denied the existence of a Macedonian nation, arguing implacably that all the Slavs of Macedonia are Bulgarians. The Bulgarian regime followed a policy similar to that of the Serbians, calling its Macedonians Bulgarians and refusing to acknowledge that the people and language had developed separately from Bulgaria. Thousands who wished to express a different view were jailed or exiled.[38] This attitude that Macedonians are Bulgarians is used to justify a continuing policy toward the Macedonians within Bulgaria of forced assimilation into mainstream Bulgarian society.[39] Bulgaria's possessiveness towards the Macedonians shows most clearly in the continued efforts to occupy the country, first in the actions that precipitated the second Balkan war, then during the First World War, and again in the Second World War. After the First World War, the Bulgarian government sponsored an organization that was ostensibly a Macedonian revolutionary group, VMRO, sending armed bands (*comitadjis*) from Bulgaria into Greek and Yugoslav Macedonia to terrorize communities and weaken potential resistance to Bulgarian forces.[40] Like the Serbians, the Bulgarians did not allow the use of the Macedonian language in official matters or in schools, but permitted poetry and drama in local dialects.[41]

World War II

Once war broke out in Europe in 1939, Bulgaria formed an alliance with the axis forces and was permitted to occupy Vardar Macedonia and eastern (Aegean) Macedonia. When the Italians pulled out of the war, the Bulgarians took the west of Macedonia as well. They enforced Bulgarianization and brought in Bulgarian-speaking settlers. Although the Bulgarians were greeted at first as saviors by the Yugoslav Macedonians, their harshness soon led to increased opposition.[42] The violent Bulgarian invasion and efforts to control the Macedonian population destroyed much of the remaining pro–Bulgarian sentiment.

Underground resistance movements appeared throughout the Balkans, with Communist groups having the greatest influence. Led by Josip Broz (Tito), the Communist partisans in Yugoslavia organized a war of national liberation. Macedonians fought on the side of the Communist-led resistance under General Svetozar Vukmanovic Tempo. They formed their own section of the resistance before the Yugoslav Communist party officially recognized them. The anti-fascist war of national liberation is considered to have begun in Vardar Macedonia on October 11, 1941, and this date has since been celebrated as Macedonian Revolution Day. In April 1942, Macedonian partisans organized an uprising against the Bulgarian occupation army in Vardar Macedonia, which was bloodily suppressed. The unarmed Macedonian population then poured into the streets to protest the Bulgarian actions and were likewise cut to pieces.[43]

In Aegean Macedonia, the Macedonians joined the left-led resistance to Nazi occupation. The resistance organizations in Florina and Edessa were largely Macedonian.[44] In 1944, the Slavic Macedonian People's Liberation Front (SNOF) was set up as the Macedonian arm of the Greek popular liberation army (EAM). One of the leaders of the underground government of the Greek resistance movement was a Macedonian, Keramitzev.

During the war, the Yugoslavian partisans won jurisdiction over Vardar Macedonia and followed Tito's policy of cultural autonomy by issuing leaflets and news bulletins in the local dialects. Various announcements, news bulletins, verse, and stories published by the partisans and their allies during the war were usually written in local dialects, but there was a continuing effort to use the central dialect. By the time the war ended, general agreement had been reached on the basic features of the literary language.[45] Church services were given in Macedonian, and Macedonian language schools were begun. The formal proclamation of Macedonian as a literary language on August 2, 1944, was merely official recognition of the status quo.[46]

Journalistic activity in Macedonian vernaculars, including efforts to standardize the form of the language used, occurred also in Aegean Macedonia. During World War II, the partisans in Aegean Macedonia set up Macedonian vernacular schools in liberated areas. From January through May 1944, the

Macedonian partisans in the village of Karcista in the district of Kastoria (Kostur) published the newspaper *Slavjanornakedonski glas* (*Voice of the Slav Macedonians*) in the local dialect. Later that year, in October, they published a primer, *Bukvar na Makedonskijazik* (*Primer of the Macedonian Language*) and distributed it to a number of schools in the Kastoria and Florina (Lerin) districts.[47] All of these activities were forbidden after the treaty of Vardkiza, February 12, 1945.

One of the great resistance leaders in Yugoslavia in the Second World War was General Tempo, who helped form and lead the Macedonian partisan brigades. In an interview with *Nova Makedonia*,[48] General Tempo notes that he had written in his memoirs how, during the war, the Macedonians in today's Macedonia and those living in northern Greece wanted to unite. He observed:

> If not people in Thessaloniki, then the people in Kostur (Kastoria), Voden (Edessa) and Lerin (Florina) are pure Macedonians and they do want to unite with Macedonians in Macedonia. I wrote that and I stand behind it now. But, let me make something clear here — we did not want to raise the question of uniting then, as peoples are mixed everywhere and no ethnically clean borders can possibly be drawn. This is not possible anywhere. We concluded that we could unite the peoples only by creating a Balkan confederation in which all nations could develop their own culture and language. It was wartime and we wanted to establish a Balkan unity between Greeks, Macedonians, Serbs, Montenegrins, Albanians, Croats and Romanians. The intention was to create conditions for a joint struggle throughout the region and to leave the borders issue for after the war. We wanted to form Macedonian partisan units in Greece in the same way that we wanted to form, for instance, Albanian units in Macedonia. The units were to have their own national marks and flags, but also the marks and flag of the state under whose command they were. The unity of the Macedonian people was understood in the context of this Balkan confederation. The idea was to establish this unity which would later on be a foundation stone of such a federation. But, the idea was never carried out since Greece was the first to cancel its participation in the joint Balkan headquarters, on a suggestion by Great Britain. Then, Bulgaria withdrew from the idea as ordered by Moscow and Tito also refused the idea, as he wanted (despite my advice not to) his headquarters to be recognized as the main Balkans ones by all other countries. That was how the idea for a Balkan headquarters and a confederation never worked.

On August 2, 1944, the Yugoslavian Communists formally decided to set up a Macedonian republic within the Yugoslav Federation and declared also that the vernacular speech of the Slav Macedonians would be the official language of the republic. After the liberation, the People's Republic of Macedonia was constituted as a state of the Yugoslavian Federation, with Skopje as its capital.

The Greek Civil War

With the ending of the Nazi occupation in Greece, the Stalinist leadership of the Greek popular liberation army acknowledged control of the new Greek government in 1945. The new government embarked on a "white terror" campaign against the recently organized Macedonians. There were widespread massacres of Macedonians, 7,000 of whom fled to Yugoslavia. A Macedonian resistance group, the successor of the SNOF, the National Liberation Front (NOF), was set up, strongly supported by Aegean Macedonian emigres returning from Vardar Macedonia. The aim of the NOF was to defend "the national rights of the Macedonian people within a democratic Greece."[49] From 1946 to 1949, it fought on the side of the Communist party against both the white terror regime of the Greek right, and Bulgarian nationalist groups in the region. By 1949, Macedonians made up 14,000 of the 40,000 troops led by the Communists against the Greek government. Greek sources concede that members of the NOF believed that they were fighting "a national liberation struggle for the Macedonians of the Aegean."[50] In passing, it might be noted that in order to field a force of 14,000 fighting men, from a community that was not universally convinced of the advantages of fighting a civil war, it would be necessary to have a population base of at least 100,000 to 150,000 people, but probably there would have been double this number.

During the civil war in Greece, in the period from 1947 to 1949, in the Aegean part of Macedonia, 87 schools were opened with 10,000 students, and Macedonian literature and culture flourished.[51] Macedonian territories controlled by Greek government forces did not fare so well. The headquarters of the Democratic Greek Army (the Alliance of Greek Communists and Macedonians) reported that from mid–1945 to May 20, 1947, in western Macedonia alone, 13,529 Macedonians were tortured, 3,215 were imprisoned, and 268 were executed without trial. In addition, 1,891 houses were burnt down and 1,553 were looted, and 13,808 Macedonians were resettled by force. During the war, Greek-run prison camps where Macedonians were imprisoned, tortured, and killed included the island of Ikaria near Turkey, the island of Makronis near Athens, the jail Averov near Athens, the jail at Larisa near the Volos Peninsula, and the jail at Thessaloniki. Aegean Macedonian expatriates claim that there were mass killings on Vicho, Gramos, Kaymakchalan, and at Mala Prespa in Albania.[52]

In 1947, during the Greek civil war, the legal act L-2 was issued. This meant that all who left Greece without the consent of the Greek government were stripped of Greek citizenship and banned from returning to the country. The law applied to Greeks and Macedonians, but in its modernized version the act is binding only on Macedonians. It prevents Macedonians, but not former Communist Greeks who fought against the winning side from returning to Greece and reclaiming property. On January 20, 1948, the legal act M was issued. This allowed the Greek government to confiscate the property of those who were stripped of their citizenship. The law was updated in 1985 to exclude Greeks, but it is still binding on Macedonians.

Among the refugees of the Greek civil war were 28,000 Macedonian children between the ages of 2 and 14. These were mostly the children of the Macedonian independence fighters whose parents were fearful for their safety after the war. The children were evacuated to the Eastern Bloc countries. Although the children of Greek fighters were officially pardoned in the 1960s and allowed back into Greece, this human right has not been extended to the Macedonians. On November 27, 1948, the United Nations issued Resolution 193C (III), which called for the repatriation of all child refugees back to Greece. However, Greek laws still prevent the free return of these and other Macedonian refugees.

While they received support from Yugoslavia and Bulgaria, the partisans and Communists were able to resist Greek government forces, at times staging some remarkable victories. However, after Tito's break with Stalin in 1948 and massive British and United States intervention, the Greek Communists deserted the Macedonian partisans, and Yugoslav support for the Macedonians was withdrawn. After the Greek Communists surrendered, Greek government forces quickly overcame Macedonian resistance.

After the defeat of the Communist and Macedonian revolutionaries, a reign of terror ruled over Aegean Macedonia. Many thousands more Macedonians fled Greece, seeking asylum in Yugoslavia and other countries in eastern Europe under extremely difficult circumstances.[53] Unlike Greek Communist refugees who have since returned, the Macedonians are barred from returning, even visiting relatives, and have not been permitted to reclaim family land and property.[54]

Official policies toward Macedonians in Greece and Bulgaria. Some villages in Aegean Macedonia were depopulated in the post–civil war period, but the bulk of the Slavic population stayed in their homes "looking after their fields, their gardens, their families, and their homes — and submitting to a barrage of official propaganda that being Slavonic meant being a communist, a traitor — and a barbarian. And who would admit to that in public?"[55]

In the decades following the Greek civil war, conservative Greek governments continued a vigorous policy of assimilation of the Macedonian Slavs and other minorities. The nature of this policy has in recent times led to international condemnations, some of which will be detailed later in this chapter. On August 23, 1953, the legal act 2536 was issued. This law allowed that all those who left Greece and who did not return within three years' time could be deprived of their property. This permitted the confiscation of Macedonian property. Around the same time, a decision was taken to resettle Macedonians out of Aegean Macedonia. A wide-ranging media campaign was launched to induce the Macedonians to leave their native areas voluntarily and to settle in the south of Greece and on the islands. The Greek intention was to separate

Macedonians living in Greece from their kin living in the Republic of Macedonia in Yugoslavia, and to create a 60-kilometer-wide belt along the border with then Yugoslavia where "the faithful sons of the Greek nation" could be settled. A firm reaction from Yugoslavia led to the eventual cancellation of the plan.

In 1959 the legal act 3958 was issued. This allowed for the confiscation of the land of those people not "Greek by birth" who left Greece and did not return within five years' time. The law was amended in 1985, but it is still binding on Macedonians.

In 1962 the legal act 4234 was issued. Persons who were stripped of their Greek citizenship were banned from returning to Greece. A ban on crossing the Greek border also extended to spouses and children. This law is still in force for Macedonians, including those who left Greece as children. In its June 1991 edition the *Atlantic Monthly* magazine ran an extensive story detailing many of the atrocities committed in Macedonia during the Balkan wars and following the partition of Macedonia. The author, Robert Kaplan, also said, "Greece, for its part, according to a Greek consular official whom I visited in Skopje, does not permit anyone with a 'Slavic' name who was born in northern Greece and now lives in Yugoslav Macedonia to visit Greece, even if he or she has relatives there. This means that many families have been separated for decades."

In 1969 a legal act was issued to allow the settlement by ethnic Greeks on Macedonian farms left behind. This has facilitated the recent relocation to Aegean Macedonia of over 100,000 immigrants of Greek origin, called Pontiac Greeks, from the former Soviet Union.

On December 29, 1982, the legal act 106841 was issued by the government of Andreas Papandreou. This allowed those who were recognized as ethnic Greeks who left Greece during the civil war to return to Greece and reclaim their Greek citizenship. Macedonians born in Greece and their families were excluded and remain in exile. Heads of various state administration departments received the right to use property left in Greece by Macedonian refugees.

On April 10, 1985, legal act 1540/85 was issued. This amended the previously issued acts regulating property relations, making it impossible for Macedonians to return. This act limits the definition of political refugees to ethnic Greeks and permits the recovery of illegally seized property to such ethnic Greeks. The Macedonian refugees from Greece are denied the same rights. In June 1989, the prime minister of Greece, Mr. Papandreou, said at a pre-election meeting in the Macedonian locality of Florina that if he won the election he would build a factory in which only the locals (i.e., Macedonians) would be employed. He also said that he would abolish law 1540 that he had been responsible for some years before. That promise has not been kept.

In 1987, Macedonian parents in Aegean Macedonia were forced to send their 2- and 3-year-old children to "integrated kindergartens" to prevent them from learning the Macedonian language and culture. The ruling was not implemented elsewhere in Greece.

On August 30, 1989, a legal act rehabilitating the participants in the Greek civil war of 1946–49 was issued. The act granted damages and disability pensions to fighters in the civil war who now have Greek citizenship. By this measure the Macedonian fighters living in exile — who earlier had been stripped of their citizenship — were rendered ineligible.

In 1990 the High Court of Florina under decision 19/33/3/1990 refused to register a Center for Macedonian Culture. An appeal on August 9 the same year against the decision was also refused. In May 1991, a second appeal was refused by the High Court of Appeals in Thessaloniki. In June 1991, the Supreme Administrative Council of Greece in Athens dismissed a further appeal. This refusal to permit a cultural center has drawn the criticism of several international human rights groups.

The Greek government has undertaken a range of measures to suppress the idea that there are minority ethnic groups in the country. Since 1961, no Greek census has carried details of minorities. The Greek position has come under harsh criticism from commentators outside the country, in part because as the *London Times* noted in August 1993, "the historical refusal to acknowledge ethnic or cultural plurality has transmogrified into a refusal to accept political dissent in relation to these ethnic or cultural questions."

The present public stance of the Greek government is that there is no minority group of Macedonians. There is acknowledgment that some people who live in areas bordering the Republic of Macedonia can speak another language apart from Greek, but the description of these people as "bilinguals" always implies that the use of the "Slavic idiom" is simply a matter of neighborly convenience rather than an ethnic identification. Greeks insist that these people are Greek by ethnicity.

The Greek argument about Greek nationality goes something like this: all the people in Greece, except the Moslem minority that was defined in a 1920s treaty with the Turks, are Greeks. Therefore, apart from these Moslems, there is no minority population within the country. There can be no issue about the human rights of non-existent groups. As we have seen, this was not the position held by the Greeks in the years following the Balkan wars when Aegean Macedonia was first taken over by Greek forces. Now, contrary to the earlier Greek position, it is Greek government policy to deny the existence of a language called Macedonian.

This denial of the Macedonian language is a problem from the international perspective since linguistics authorities generally recognize the language and the United Nations accepted the Macedonian language several decades ago, soon after the language was standardized. While Macedonia was a part of Yugoslavia, of course, Serbia accepted the existence of the Macedonian language. The only countries that do not accept the Macedonian language are

Bulgaria and Greece. (Bulgaria continues to insist simply that the Macedonian language is Bulgarian; thus Bulgarians regard Slavic peoples in Aegean Macedonia as a Bulgarian-speaking minority.) In 1994 the European Union recognized Macedonian as one of the languages spoken by minorities living within Union boundaries, that is in Aegean Macedonia (at that time Macedonia itself was not a part of the EU).[56] One might expect that this general acceptance of the Slavic language spoken by many Aegean Macedonian people would be a difficult stumbling block for the Greek government. However, Greece simply denies that the Macedonian language is internationally accepted. Thus the Greeks can argue that since there is no nation called Macedonia, and no language called Macedonian, there can be no national minority within Greece that is Macedonian or that speaks Macedonian or any other recognized language.

The United Nations, the United States State Department, Amnesty International, and various chapters of Helsinki Watch throughout the world disagree with the Greeks, in particular, about the presence of Macedonians (and other minorities) in Greece and have pressured them in recent times to change their behavior toward their Macedonian-speaking minority. There have also been significant condemnations of Bulgaria. Both the Greek and Bulgarian positions have remained unchanged in the face of increasing criticism. (Meanwhile, the Serbians may be reconsidering their previous recognition of their Macedonian-speaking population; in 1989, Serbian and Greek leaders discussed the issue of "assimilating" Macedonia.)

The Bulgarians argue that since Macedonians are simply Bulgarians under another name, they have no minority Macedonian group either. Yet a 1970 census in Bulgaria indicated there were 600,000 people who identified themselves as Macedonian. The Bulgarian human rights record has not attracted so much media interest, but it has been noted by various organizations. For example, the Finnish Helsinki Watch Committee, in its February 1991 report, denounced the Bulgarian government for a forced denationalization of the Macedonians similar to the activity in Greece.

Amnesty International described the official response to the 1993 commemorative assembly at Rozen Monastery in Blagoevgrad, an annual event, traditionally organized by OMO "Ilinden" (United Macedonian Organization "Ilinden") to commemorate the death of Jane Sandanski, a local hero of the struggle against Ottoman rule at the turn of the century:

> Special police units beat them with truncheons and rifle butts; they dragged people from their cars and knocked them to the ground.... We are concerned that the apparently unprovoked attack by officers of the special police units on the people who gathered in Lozenitsa and Spatovo represented a flagrant violation of international human rights standards, including the International Covenant on Civil and Political Rights (ICCPR), to which Bulgaria has acceded.

Such actions led to concern about police threats regarding future gatherings.

Amnesty International has written to Zhelyu Zhelev, the president of Bulgaria, urging him to initiate an independent and impartial inquiry into the alleged beatings in Blagoevgrad, to make public its findings, and to bring to justice anyone responsible for human rights violations. The human rights organization did not receive any reply to its letter of July 1993 to minister of the interior Viktor Mikhaylov, which expressed concern at the police violence at the 1993 assembly.

Despite Amnesty International's plea, the Bulgarian police again prevented Macedonians from gathering at the Rozen Monastery at the same anniversary in 1994. Macedonian Radio said the police used force and beat a large number of people. The leaders of OMO Ilinden were held in the village of Hitovo, on the claim that the buses they traveled on did not have valid documents. Bulgarian government officials (Interior Minister Victor Mikhaylov and Attorney General Ivan Tatarcev) undertook an intensive media campaign against OMO Ilinden, openly calling on the community to oppose the gathering of Macedonians. The Blagoevgrad group of skinheads threatened to take matters into their own hands if government bodies failed to prevent the gathering.[57]

The 1994 Helsinki Watch report said that neither Greece nor Bulgaria took a single step forward in improving the civil rights of its minorities in the preceding year. The report drew attention to the Bulgarian government's refusal of permission for several Macedonian organizations, including OMO Ilinden, to register, as they were regarded as separatist organizations; the refusal of Ilinden's request to celebrate the ninetieth anniversary of the Ilinden uprising; and actions of the police to prevent commemorative gathering of Macedonians. The report also claimed the Bulgarian government had put in place limitations on freedom of opinion and religion.

The *1994 Annual Report on Human Rights in Bulgaria* by the United States State Department was equally critical of the Bulgarian human rights record with regard to its Macedonian minority, noting confiscation of newspapers published by OMO Ilinden, denial of registration of OMO Ilinden, the arrest of activists George Solunski and Janus Sapundziev, and the withdrawal of the registration of another cultural group, TMO Ilinden. The results of a census conducted in December 1992 were also said to have caused controversy, since those who considered themselves ethnic Macedonians complained they were unable to identify themselves as such on the census form.

In March 1995, the coordinating committee of OMO Ilinden announced its intention to take Bulgaria to the European Court of Justice. Bulgaria is a signatory to the 1992 European Convention on Human Rights Protection. The organization said Bulgaria has done nothing to implement even the most basic rights of Macedonians in Bulgaria, and OMO Ilinden has already used all legal means available.[58]

The Persistence and Significance of the Greek Position

Several times during the 1980s the Greek government admonished over-seas officials for recognizing a Macedonian nationality. Greek authorities protested to the United States ambassador in what was then Yugoslavia for having uttered a few sentences in the "non-existent" Macedonian language while visiting the Republic of Macedonia. Minister for Macedonia and Trakia (previously for Northern Greece) Stelios Papatamelis sent a letter to Pope John Paul II admonishing him for having uttered his Christmas and New Year greetings in the same "non-existent" tongue. In 1986 former minister for Northern Greece N. Martis addressed a letter to the Australian prime minister, Bob Hawke, entitled "Falsification of the History of Macedonia," in which he denied the existence of a Macedonian nationality.

In June 1986 at its forty-ninth congress, the international writers' organization, P.E.N., condemned the denial of the Macedonian language by Greece and sent letters to the Greek P.E.N. Center and the Greek minister for culture. The Greek response was a denial of the existence of a Macedonian minority. In July 1989, the Athens Information Agency issued a leaflet in English entitled *The So Called Macedonian Problem*. This leaflet denies the existence of a Macedonian minority in Greece.

On May 20, 1989, Stelios Papatemelis appealed to the Greeks to wage a sacred war against the so-called Macedonians. At a rally in Salonika on July 29, 1989, President Sardzetakis said, "Macedonia was, is and will always be Greek." International travelers find this phrase emblazoned on walls in places usually visited by tourists. On March 25, 1990, in a television address, President Sardzetakis said, "Only native Greeks live in Greece."

On February 21, 1990, Constantinos Mitsotakis, then leader of the New Democracy party, said at a press conference in the town of Jannina that he is increasingly convinced that the Greek policy in relation to national minorities should be more aggressive. He said, "We have nothing to fear. We are clean because Greece is the only Balkan country without the problem of national minorities." He added, "The Macedonian minority does not exist, neither is it recognized by international agreements." On March 7, 1990, N. Martis, former minister for Northern Greece, declared that the Macedonian nation (meaning ethnic group) is an invention of the Communist party of Yugoslavia.

On March 19, 1994, a letter from the press counselor of the consulate general of Greece in New York titled "End the Intransigence" was published in the *New York Times*. The press counselor denied the existence of a Macedonian minority in Greece. He claimed that people in Greece who speak the Macedonian language, which he dismisses as "a Slavonic-oriented idiom," are all "fervently Greek." Similarly, in April 2, 1992, the ambassador of Greece to Australia, V.S. Zafiropoulos, wrote a letter to the *Canberra Times* (Australia) newspaper in which he said Macedonia, Greece's most northerly province, does not contain "a significant minority who are ethnically related to the Slavs across the border." He said, "In fact, Greece has the most homogenous country in Europe and if a small number of Greeks on the border speak, beside Greek, a Slavic idiom, this bilingualism does not constitute a minority."

The Greeks have taken their case overseas. Between June 26 and 30, 1989, at Columbia University in New York, Greeks held a symposium entitled "History, Culture and the Art of Macedonia." While the ostensible purpose of the symposium was a presentation of ancient culture, a major theme of the symposium and of the publicity that accompanied it was the Greek theory of the unbroken continuity of Greek ethnicity in Aegean Macedonia. The symposium occasioned strong protests from Macedonians in the United States and Canada. At about the same time, during the Bicentenary of Australia, Greece organized an exhibition in Sydney entitled "Ancient Macedonia: the Wealth of Greece." The Greek president Sardzetakis toured various Australian cities and frequently gave public statements denying the existence at any historical period of a Slavic-speaking Macedonian group in Aegean Macedonia. After a sharp reaction from Macedonians in Australia, the Greek government protested to the Australian government for letting the Macedonian protests occur.

The viewpoints of Greek government officials are reflected in some elements of the Greek press. In September 1989, the Athenian newspaper *Avriani* wrote that the demands of some members of Parliament for the abolition in Greek law of the term "Greek by origin" creates a serious threat to the national unity and territorial sovereignty of Greece. The newspaper also wrote that the "second group" of refugees, meaning Macedonian refugees as opposed to refugees of Greek ethnicity, could return to Greece under the condition that they unambiguously declare their Greek origin. This would require that they deny their Macedonian ethnicity. Taking an even more extreme position, the far-right Greek newspaper *Stohos* has written: "Everyone who will openly manifest his views concerning the Macedonian minority will curse the hour of his birth."[59]

Greek response to international criticism has often been vehement. A Greek magazine distributed in English-speaking countries through Greece's embassies and consulates published a bitter reaction to United States State Department comments:

> Both Ankara and Skopje are justly celebrating the State Department Report. Its American authors are attempting — and have managed in part — to undermine Greece by fabricating non-existing "ethnic minorities" in Greek Macedonia and Thrace... The Americans had similar imperial dreams based on Islam, when they reinforced the Shah of Iran and following his collapse, the Iraqi leader Sadam Hussein. The effect was in both cases, disastrous ... And when the State department invents a "Macedonian ethnic minority" in Greek Macedonia, it clears the way for a new Balkan tragedy ... There are, however, the Slav-speaking Macedonian Greeks who are not simply willing, but also ready to defend their national identity from all sorts of "protectors" and

conspirators ... Should the need arise the Macedonian Phalanx will still be here.[60]

Later editions take a similar line. The magazine noted that the reason for a meeting of the lawyers union of Thessaloniki "was the report of the Foreign Secretary of the U.S.A. with its historically groundless content... In the historical substantiation of the non-existence of the so-called "Macedonians"... There never have been "Macedonians" in our Macedonia... Never have a Slav people asked for a minority regime."[61]

On April 21, 1994, the U.S. Chapter of Human Rights Watch/Helsinki released its report entitled *Denying Ethnic Identity: The Macedonians of Greece* to coincide with the official visit of Greek prime minister Andreas Papandreou to the United States. The 84-page report describes in detail the existence and activities of the Macedonian national minority in Aegean Macedonia. The report concludes that ethnic Macedonians make up a large minority with its own language and culture. Responding to the report, Mr. Papandreou formally denied the existence of a Macedonian minority. The *Times* (London) judged this response "an example of intolerance which the more extreme members of his government and ... society have not been slow to exploit.[62]

The Greek government and press reacted bitterly to the United States State Department document issued October 18, 1994, claiming the existence of Slav and Albanian minorities in Greece and pointing to human rights violations against these groups, the Turkish minority, and certain religious minorities. Officials announced their intention to submit a protest to Washington. The Greek government spokesman Mr. Venizelos demanded an official explanation of the document by the United States.[63] According to the Greek newspaper *Ta Nea*, the document was an open provocation against Greece by bureaucrats in the American administration. Another newspaper, *Mesivremini*, pointed to the fact that this was the first time the United States had mentioned the existence of an Albanian minority in Greece. The paper reported that the State Department report of 1991 mentioned only a Slav-Macedonian minority, and added that the new position was a response to a request by Albanian organizations in the United States.[64]

During his stay in Salonika in November 1994, CSCE high commissioner for national minorities Max van der Stuhl stated that the position of the Macedonian national minority in Balkan countries deserves attention. This brought angry responses from the Greek press. The most bitter attacks came from *Elefteros tipos*, which spoke of the "rottenness" of the "anti–Greek" CSCE high official, who, instead of dealing with the position of the Greek national minority in Albania, talked to President Gligorov about the "presumed" Macedonian minority in Greece. When asked to comment on the statements by van der Stuhl, the Greek foreign minister, Mr. Papoulias, stated that "there is no other minority in Greece except for the Muslim minority."[65]

The official Greek government policy about the non-existence of Slavic-speaking Macedonians seems to have been widely believed within Greece. Certainly the government claims about the Republic of Macedonia have received widespread support. On October 9, 1994, a popular Macedonian newspaper, *Nova Makedonija*, reported that on the previous day the most popular Greek TV station "Mega" had broadcast live interviews between reporter Tanas Atanasiu and citizens of Florina, Greece.[66] For the first time, *Nova Makedonija* says, viewers in Athens heard Greek citizens claiming they are not "Greeks by birth," but Macedonians. The presentation was treated as sensational by the journalists running the interviews and by the TV station, who noted that the Greek authorities have so far denied the existence of a Macedonian national minority in Greece. Viewers from Athens and other parts of Greece heard that Florina (still called Lerin by the Macedonians) was populated by non–Greek people who speak a different language. When asked, "Are you a Greek?" Stavros Anastasiadis answered, "No, I am not. I don't feel like a Greek in the least bit." The reporter asked, "Then, what are you?" The answer was, "I am a Macedonian."

How Many Macedonians?

Macedonian writers claim that there are as many as one million Macedonians in Aegean Macedonia (See "Steve's Story" below). The 1987 edition of the *Encyclopaedia Britannica* put the number of Slavic-speakers in Aegean Macedonia at 180,000. The London newspaper the *Independent* suggests that there are anywhere from 50,000 to 300,000.[67] Recent observations by the United States State Department suggest smaller (though significant) numbers, perhaps between 20,000 and 50,000 Slavic-speakers in northern Greece, many of whom live in the area along the border between Greece and the former Yugoslavia.[68] The department says that although a majority of these people have a Greek national identity (they identify themselves as Greeks *and* as Macedonians, or as Greek-Macedonians), a significant number of them have a Macedonian national identity (they identify themselves as Macedonians but not as Greeks).[69]

The truth about the number of Macedonian speakers in Aegean Macedonia is difficult to determine. The Greek government says none; Macedonian activists claim more than a million. If Greece responds to international pressure to allow human rights and freedoms to its Macedonian speakers, we may gain a more accurate idea in the future about the number of people in Aegean Macedonia who consider themselves Greek-Macedonians or Macedonians. As we have seen, great pressure has been put on Aegean Macedonians to deny their language and culture. According to international commentators and others with obvious sympathy for the Aegean Macedonians, the resulting climate of fear makes any accurate analysis impossible.

It is also worthy of note that there may be close to a quarter of a million Aegean Macedonians living outside Greece. For instance, the Aegean Macedonian Human Rights Association of Australia claims it "represents the interests of an estimated 90,000 Macedonians in Australia who originate from the part of Macedonia which is now incorporated into Greece."[70] Similar numbers are claimed for Canada and the United States. Many of these people see themselves as refugees, and they maintain a strong interest in their native land. At the very least, they would like to visit their birthplace and their relatives again, and many would even resettle there if their human rights were recognized. "We emphasize, however, that our ethnic origin is Macedonian, not Greek: we speak Macedonian, identify as Macedonian, and have a separate, wholly Macedonian culture. The Aegean Macedonian community is ethnically related to the Macedonian immigrants from the Republic of Macedonia, which was formerly part of Yugoslavia. Many of the members of the Aegean Macedonian Association of Australia are political refugees from Greece, others are economic refugees due to the Greek policy of not developing Macedonian areas, and the majority still have family members in Greece."[71]

Anastasia Karakasidou is an academic of Greek extraction who was herself surprised to find a suppressed but surviving Macedonian culture in Aegean Macedonia. In the process she has learned about the lengths to which Greek government officials have gone to hide this group of people and to force them to assimilate with mainstream Greek culture. She has also been the target of threats from various Greek interest groups, including some in the United States, and of harassment from the Greek government security services. In an academic analysis of the situation in Aegean Macedonia, she discusses Greek efforts at nation building aimed at turning the peoples of its expanding territory into the citizens of a nation-state. She observes that "since the incorporation of Macedonia into the expanding Greek state in 1913, Greek authorities have attempted to wrest control of enculturation away from the private domain of the family and to place it under the control of state institutions. In the process, Slavic speakers of the area have found themselves forbidden to use their Slavic language or to engage in songs, dances and other public cultural activities. Some have resisted, protesting that such restrictions destroy their distinct local culture." Karakasidou investigates these charges, examining Macedonian claims to a distinct ethnic heritage and minority status, and reactions and counterclaims by Greek authorities.[72] She argues "that the politicization of culture in Greek Macedonia has directly contributed to the denial of ethnic identity among Slavic speaking inhabitants there."

When Karakasidou first began to explore such issues, she traveled to the western part of Aegean Macedonia with her husband to search for Slavic speakers. She visited Florina (Lerin) and traveled off the beaten path in the country around Edessa (Voden). For the first time she met people who identified themselves as Slavic speakers. They told her that the men of their village had first learned Greek in 1912. The women of their village were the last to learn Greek, and some of the older people, most of whom had died, never learned it at all. They told her that under the Metaxas regime, anyone caught speaking the local language was forced to drink retsinolado (castor oil) and some were tortured. Youths were beaten for speaking the language at school. In the evenings, spies listened for anyone speaking the language in the privacy of their homes. While talking to her, these Slavic speakers became nervous and suspicious and wondered why she was asking so many questions. Fortunately Karakasidou was able to calm their fears and begin the accumulation of a wealth of information about the Aegean Macedonians. She studied the present population, the history, and the nature of the territory that she was investigating.

Karakasidou concludes that Greece has confused ethnicity with nationality. In order to make sure that its citizens are loyal to the Greek state, she observes, the state has insisted that all its residents are ethnic Greeks. She says:

> In redefining ethnicity as nationality, the Greek state created the contradictions that form the basis of the minority problem in Northern Greece today... While assimilation and amalgamation in Central Greek Macedonia, where the process had its impetus a generation earlier, is now essentially complete, in the Florina region some local communities continue to display ethnic (i.e. Slavo-Macedonian) consciousness despite their national Greek identity... What most seek is simply recognition of their status as an ethnic minority within the greater nation-state, and thus the right to gain equitable access to jobs, to practice their own Orthodox religion, to speak their own language and to educate their children in the folklore and stories of their ancestors.

Karakasidou notes with concern that the Greek authorities have been implacable in antagonism to these "Slavo-Macedonians," having little regard for the loyalty of their own citizens in their concern for the principle of Pan-hellenism. She describes the takeover of Greek families by the Greek state, which uses them as an instrument for the building of Greek nationhood. She describes the arguments of Greek nationalist intellectuals, who attempt to build a Greek national consciousness based on a rewriting of history. She focuses on the "common blood" metaphor used by nationalists, identifying it as racism, a kind of social Darwinism and "pseudo-biology." She points out that such arguments have long been discredited in the social sciences, though they are still "the dominant ethnological, historical and political position of the overwhelming majority of Greek scholars who identify ethnicity with nationality." She argues that the so-called historical perspectives of Greek academics such as Kyriakidis and Vakalopoulos fall into the trap of anachronism, imposing the categories of the present on very different situations that existed in the past. This ideological meddling with the raw material of history, she suggests, cannot be given serious intellectual weight in modern times. She tells us that "the efforts of Greek intellectuals and politicians to construct a tradition of Greek heritage in Macedonia has led to a protracted campaign to denigrate or even

deny the existence of a Slavo-Macedonian ethnic minority in Northern Greece."
She suggests that the issue is more than just an "academic" debate, since it has
very real, and usually unpleasant, consequences for the lives of the people in
question as well as for the political stability of the Greek nation-state.

Karakasidou outlines the language struggle between the Slavic-speaking
peoples and the Greek authorities from the end of the nineteenth century. She
describes with near disbelief what she calls bizarre attempts of Greek scholars
to discredit the Macedonian language by saying it has no syntax or grammar.
She feels that such indefensible ideas only discredit Greek scholarship. She
writes: "The extremist and militant tone of most articles is alarming. It is striking that much of the rhetoric coming out of Greece on the issue has progressed
markedly little beyond the simplistic and reductionist notions that inflamed the
Balkan Crisis at the turn of the century." In particular, she says there has been
confusion between ideas about "nationality" and ideas about culture and ethnicity. She says that Greek scholars have frequently argued from historical
premises that are fundamentally misinformed. Some have claimed that since
there is no country called "Macedonia," there can be no "Macedonians." Such
simplistic notions are compounded when Greek scholars fail to recognize that
ethnicity and nationality are constructed, she says.

As is noted elsewhere in this book, to anthropologists, national identities
are constructed through complex historical processes. They are categories people use to classify themselves and others, categories subject to negotiation and
change over time.[73] Belonging to a particular ethnic group or national minority is a matter of individual choice which, signatories to United Nations conventions on human rights have agreed, must be freely exercised. Karakasidou's
argument suggests that neither the Greek government nor Greek academics are
willing to consider such distinctions.

Karakasidou's work has been received with great hostility by extremist
Greek nationalists. Leonard Doyle writes that in order to avoid unnecessary
controversy over the Macedonian debate in Greece, she decided not to publish
her dissertation, *Fields of Wheat, Hills of Shrubs, Agrarian Development and
Nation Building in Northern Greece.* However, Greek newspapers somehow
obtained copies of the manuscript, and since that time "Ms. Karakasidou, the
mother of two young children, has been mercilessly hounded by sections of the
Greek media and by the Greek-American community in the United States.[74] She
received a veiled death threat from a Greek-American newspaper in February
1994, in the form of an article it published describing a possible scenario for
her death. The article described an attack by a group of men, one of whom
drove a pointed stake, wrapped in the colors of the Greek flag, into her heart,
killing her as a traitor." Leonard Doyle says, "It is thought that the veiled death
threats were designed to frighten her away from academic research." The threats
against Ms. Karakasidou, 38, escalated early in May 1994 when *Stohos*, an
extreme right-wing Greek newspaper, published her address in Salonika. The

newspaper also provided details of the car she uses. Karakasidou does not believe that the government is behind the death threats but feels they are the work of nationalist extremists.

A Climate of Fear

Of considerable relevance to questions about the number of Macedonian speakers in Aegean Macedonia is Karakasidou's description of the terror of many Slavic speakers when asked if they know the language. After several generations of persecution, she says, they are hesitant to share their knowledge with outsiders, explaining that even today when inhabitants of some villages sing in their mother tongue, the "local" Greek policeman comes over and compels them to stop. Other commentators see the prosecution of Macedonian human rights activists as part of a process aimed at continuing the climate of fear. "By denying the existence of any minority group, except the Turkish community in Western Thrace, the government apparently hopes to extinguish any nationalist feeling among its ethnic Macedonian population."[75]

The *Spectator* magazine published an article on the same theme on August 15, 1992. The article, by Noel Malcolm, was titled, "The New Bully of the Balkans." The article discusses the plight of the main ethnic minorities in Greece, including the Macedonians, the Vlachs, and the Turks. On the Macedonians, Mr. Malcolm noted, "How many of these Slavs still live in Greece is not known. The 1940 census registered 85,000 'Slav-speakers.' The 1951 census (the last to record any figures for speakers of other languages) put it at 41,000; many who had fought on the losing side in the civil war had fled, but other evidence shows that all the censuses heavily underestimate the Slavs' numbers. The lack of a question on the census-form is not, however, the only reason for their obscurity." Mr. Malcolm says, "One group of these Slavs has started a small monthly newsletter, with an estimated readership of 10,000. But they have great difficulty finding a printer (even though it is in Greek), and they say that if copies are sent through the post, they tend to 'disappear.' 'Even if we find a sympathetic printer,' one told me, 'he's usually too scared to take the work: he's afraid of losing his other contracts, or perhaps of getting bricks through his window.'"

The following message was distributed to all subscribers to a Macedonian discussion group on the Internet. It followed a debate between a number of Aegean Macedonians and a person of "Greek" origin concerning the numbers of Macedonian speakers in Greece. A number of Macedonians with Aegean connections tried to explain the great disadvantages that could be suffered by Aegean Macedonians who publicly stated that they were not of Greek birth and who indicated that by preference they spoke a different language. They emphasized the deep distrust of Macedonians toward the Greek authorities, and their constant fear of punishment. It was in response to this discussion that the following story emerged. I have left it essentially intact. The anger and the profound unhappiness revealed in the story make their own point.

Sat, 23 Jul 94 13. Macedonian Discussion List From: SARAGIL STEVE
This is my story,

My family is from what is now a border village, Sveti German, Aegean Macedonia. It is a village on Lake Prespa directly south of the village of Bracino in the Republic of Macedonia. My family and all the other families of the village were and are of Macedonian descent. No Greek blood ever flowed in our village until the beginning of this century.

When Macedonia was one whole under the Ottoman empire, Sveti German enjoyed a glorious reign as the largest village in its region. It had just under 4000 people, which in those days (early 1900's) was considered a large town. Well to make a long story short, with the occupation by Greece of Macedonia's southern territory, everything and anything associated with being Macedonian was made illegal by persecution, abuse and ultimately (and the most common route) DEATH! The village name was changed from Sveti German to the disgusting name it holds today — Agios Germanos. All the villagers family names were changed to resemble Greek ones. My family name was changed from Saragilovski to Saragiopoulos. Some families names were completely changed to something totally different. (e.g. Mangov to Papoulias) Our street name was also changed to "Odos Pavlos Melas".

Everything was now Greek and one had to declare oneself a Greek person by citizenship (naturally), but also by blood. This made no sense to many people who continued to publicly call themselves Macedonian and publicly spoke the "forbidden" Macedonian language. Well ... these people also died publicly in open village executions to make examples of those who fought against the Greek regime.

The pearl of the Balkan peninsula was now in Greek hands and they would not let the fertile soil slip through their fingertips. Greece-proper is one huge rock that would be lucky to grow moss, let alone peppers, wheat, rice, etc. that Macedonia could. Without Macedonia, Greece would be a non-country; insignificant in the newly resource-based societies that would flourish in years to come.

Death was a common sight for Macedonians. It is impossible, literally impossible to find one family or person that did not suffer by losing at least one person at the hands of the Greek government. I lost my grandfather in WWII when the Greek army took him and all the other men from my village and made them fight the Italians in the Greek-Italian war. My grandfather lost his life defending a country he deplored — Greece. Greeks love to use the argument that they lost loved ones too. This is true ... however the difference is that we lost our loved ones at the hands of the Greek government and people. The Greeks lost theirs at the hands of the Italian government. We inflicted no offensive on the Greek government and people, but merely attempted to defend our land, homes, families and pride. The argument that Greeks lost a lot in those years falls on deaf ears here and on Macedonians around the world because they brought it on themselves. Macedonians NEVER gave a tenth of a percent of anguish that the Greeks gave to us.

In the years following WWII, the Greek government exiled all Macedonians that did not declare themselves Greek. Women and children were forced to Eastern Bloc countries and were forbidden to ever return to their homes. Today, my grandmother who lives in Skopje is forbidden to lay a flower at her husband's grave in Sveti German. She cannot return to her home, the land she was born and raised in — because she is a troublemaker — because she is Macedonian. The Greek government is SCARED that an 80-year-old woman who can barely walk will turn their government upside down if they let her in the country. They are COWARDS!!!!!! This is the same fate that many Macedonians living in Macedonia, Greece and other countries have had to deal with.

Today, it is estimated that there are over 1 million Macedonians in Greece and that is a VERY conservative estimate. Our stories will be heard and justice will be served to those in the Greek government and society that continue to spread lies and propaganda about the Macedonian people who are 100% NON-Greek. Only with the emergence of the Republic of Macedonia can this voice be heard. That little republic of 2 million will help its people from all borders make sure that their basic human rights, which are not guaranteed in Greece, will be met. Greece will never live in peace until Macedonians receive justice. Its funny ... why is it that of course some countries have enemies and some have none ... but Greece has deep wounds with ALL countries that it stole from. If you peel away all that Greece has taken from others, you will find an empty carcass of a people shocked to find that they have been living a lie — a lie that they invented and a lie that will ultimately destroy them.

In a communication following this story, Steve Saragil offered the following statement.

Just to let everyone know, I have all of this "unhappiness" of Macedonians in Greece documented on home video from our trip to the occupied land, namely Aegean Macedonia. A Greek would never be able to find this unhappiness because the Macedonians lie to the Greeks and say they are happy in fear of persecution if it is discovered that one is a Macedonian of non–Hellenic background. If you walk down the streets of Lerin (Florina), Kostur (Kastoria), Voden (Edessa), Solun (Salonika), and most of the towns/villages that were not burned or destroyed by the Greek authorities, with a video camera telling the people that you are a Macedonian from Canada, you will be amazed at the outpouring of emotions that you get from 80 percent of the people questioned on how they have been treated in the "democracy" of Greece.

The nashi (Macedonians) came out of the woodwork to tell us stories of their lives and how "they" (the Greeks) don't allow them to speak, sing or practice their beautiful Macedonian culture. And I have this all on video. Some of it is so sad that it breaks your heart... If they were talking to a Greek, almost all feel that they would be found out and persecuted until their final days. Macedonian is an underground culture and language in Greece and most Greeks to the south don't know and will probably never know how serious the problem really is.

The truth is that most of the people that we encountered, and mind you they were just normal people off the streets, dream of a day when there will be a united Macedonia. These are the people that keep the dream alive. But of course in this day and age, things are not that easy, especially with the bullies in Athens. The media are on the Macedonian side and they will show the rest of the world what the rest of Greece refuses to listen to.

Reasons for the Greek Position on Aegean Macedonians

As we have already noted, the Greek academic Anastasia Karakasidou argues that the suppression of the Aegean Macedonians has arisen out of Greek efforts at nation-building. After the takeover of Aegean Macedonia in 1913, a great effort was made to turn the inhabitants into the citizens of the Greek nation-state. In order to make sure that its citizens are loyal to the Greek state, politicians and intellectuals have rewritten history, creating a myth that all Greek residents are ethnic Greeks. Thus Greece confused ethnicity with nationality. This politicization of culture in Greek Macedonia led directly to the denial of Slavic Macedonian ethnic identity and the human rights abuses that followed. From the Greek nationalist perspective, a campaign of denigration and denial of the existence of a Slavo-Macedonian ethnic minority was necessary.

Editorials in prominent newspapers offer similar analyses. For instance, Toronto's *The Globe and Mail* said, "These repressive actions, shocking in a democracy, spring from complex roots. Since emerging from Ottoman domination in the early 19th century, Greece has been at pains to establish a Greek identity separate and distinct from that of its Balkan and Turkish neighbors. That has meant stressing the ethnic and linguistic purity of the nation (though most modern Greeks spring from mixed origins after centuries of immigration from Asia Minor, southern Russia and elsewhere), emphasizing links with the glorious Greek past, and underlining the centrality of the Christian Orthodox faith in determining Greekness." The writer notes that a recently leaked document of the Greek secret service suggested that only members of the Orthodox church could be considered true Greeks, and concludes, "The result is an often xenophobic strain of nationalism that is sadly typical of the Balkans."[76] The existence of a strong non–Greek Macedonian state on Greece's borders may be seen as a threat to this effort at nation-building. People living close to the borders who speak the same language may find it easy to identify with the new nation, and this nation might well be able to offer them some support (certainly this is the belief of Steve Saragil, quoted above). This would be a threat to the Greek view of how their nationality is constructed.

Other commentators offer additional reasons for the Greek desire to suppress the presence of Aegean Macedonians. The president of the Republic of Macedonia, Kiro Gligorov, says he believes that much of the Greek concern in the dispute with his country centers on the claim for land by Slav Macedonians who left Greece, or were expelled, after the Greek civil war. Thousands of exiles would like to reclaim their land and homes, which they were forced to abandon. Gligorov said, "This has weight in Greece because of the enormous number of people who left or were expelled, who are not able to receive their property or compensation."[77] In February 1993, Gligorov, speaking at the United Nations on the possible admission of Macedonia to the body, criticized Greece for its treatment of its Macedonian minority. Gligorov said, "It is surprising that the Republic of Greece disputes article 49 of our Constitution which refers to the concern of the Republic of Macedonia for our minority in the neighboring countries. It should be pointed out that there is a similar provision in the Greek constitution. It is a well known fact that the Republic of Greece does not admit the existence of a Macedonian minority there." Gligorov asked, "Why does Greece not fulfill at least the basic rights of this minority as provided in the UN Charter, the Helsinki Document, the Charter of Paris, etc., of which it is a signatory?" He also said, "Most important of all, is this the reason that the Republic of Greece opposes the recognition of the Republic of Macedonia under its constitutional name?"[78]

American journalist Chuck Sudetic, writing for the *New York Times*, is another who concludes that claims about land ownership are central to the present-day dispute.[79] He suggests that northern Greeks see Macedonia's actions with regard to the choice of name and flag, and support for Macedonians beyond the border, as a threat to their land. Sudetic interviewed one of the exiled and dispossessed Macedonians, Risto Yatchev, who is reported to have said, "It isn't just a question of the name or the flag, it's a question of the property... I had a house, 14 fields, a couple of vineyards and a chestnut grove. It was my family's property for 300 years, and I want it back."

Sudetic makes the case that many of the people who came to Aegean Macedonia after the wars with the Turks remember the losses of their homes in Turkey and do not want to see Greeks dispossessed again. Sudetic quotes a Greek journalist, Nikolaos Karamanavis, who said, "This land is ours. When they steal our name, it is a clear sign that they want to steal our land." Thus the very recognition of a neighboring republic with the name "Macedonia" can be seen as a kind of de facto recognition of the Slavic minority in Greece with a possible flow-on to the issue of property ownership.

American anthropologist Loring Danforth argues that denying Greek-Macedonians, who are not ethnic Greeks, the right to identify themselves as Macedonians could be called a kind of symbolic ethnic cleansing, since it not only denies the existence of a Macedonian nation and a Macedonian minority in Greece, but also tries to destroy the identity, language and culture of this minority. Danforth considers that this approach "is an expression of the same kind of ethnic nationalism that in times of economic chaos and political collapse can all too easily lead to a literal, not just a symbolic, form of ethnic cleansing, the kind of ethnic cleansing we are witnessing now, to our horror, in other parts of the former Yugoslavia."[80]

However, Danforth argues that the Greek strategy may not work. An anthropological perspective suggests that attempts by the Greek state to impose a homogeneous national culture on a group of people with different linguistic and cultural traditions may itself contribute to the creation of a national minority. By denying the existence of a Macedonian minority in northern Greece, the Greek state may be nurturing "the very nightmare it wishes to dispel."[81]

Human Rights for Macedonians: International Reports

The final document of the second CHD meeting held in Copenhagen in June 1990 affirmed that respect for the rights of persons belonging to national minorities, as part of universally recognized human rights, is an essential factor for peace, justice, and stability in the participating states. The signatories to this document affirmed that persons belonging to national minorities have the right to freely express, preserve and develop their ethnic, cultural, linguistic and religious identity and to maintain and develop their culture in all its aspects, free of attempts of assimilation against their will. Greece and Bulgaria were among the signatories. A Macedonian-speaking delegate from Bulgaria provided a list of human rights abuses within Bulgaria in relation to the Macedonian population of western Bulgaria (Pirin Macedonia). An Aegean Macedonian representative gave a similar list of human rights abuses in Greece. The Greek case is of particular interest since the representative, Christos Sideropoulos, has since been brought before Greek courts on more than ten occasions because of the statements made in this forum and repeated to the press (this case will be described in more detail later in this chapter).

In February 1991 the United States State Department, in its annual human rights report, sharply criticized Greece for its ill-treatment of the Macedonian and Turkish minorities. Since that time many international human rights organizations and the United States State Department have repeatedly drawn attention to the violation of the rights of Aegean Macedonians. Amnesty International (November 1992), Helsinki Watch (July 1993), and the United States State Department in its yearly reports are among the organizations that have criticized Greece for failing to grant minority rights to the Macedonians in northern Greece (see also *The Economist*, Aug. 14, 1993, page 44).

Naturally enough, there is much overlap between the human rights reports, so rather than going through these in turn I have chosen to summarize important issues that have been raised.

The United States State Department annual report (1994) notes that "organizations of self-identified Slavic Macedonians are not allowed to use the word "Macedonian" in their names, and that some Greeks of Slavic descent do not proclaim themselves Macedonian for fear of losing their jobs in the public sector or being penalized, e.g., through a punitive job transfer. The report also refers to an internal report of the Greek National Intelligence Service (NIS) about the dangers to Greece allegedly posed by non–Orthodox denominations. The NIS report argued that "any Greek who is not Greek Orthodox is not a genuine, incorruptible, pure Greek," and that the leaders and adherents of non–Orthodox organizations are characterized for the most part as having a "lessened national conscience."[82] Greek suspicion about non–Greek Orthodox religions will be seen later in the detailed description of the case of Father Tsarknias, political activist, member of the Macedonian Orthodox religion, who has been repeatedly sentenced to prison terms for wearing the robes of his church.

In May 1992, Australian journalist Richard Farmer visited Aegean Macedonia and published an article in the Sydney newspaper the *Sunday Telegraph*, entitled "Freedom Fragile in Macedonia." The article described numerous examples of human rights abuses witnessed by Farmer, including the jamming by Greek authorities of Easter religious services broadcast in the Macedonian language from the Republic of Macedonia and listened to by Macedonians in Greece.

The United States State Department and other observers note that Article 19 of the Greek Citizenship Code distinguishes between Greek citizens who are ethnic Greeks and those who are not. Greek citizens who are not ethnic Greeks may be deprived of citizenship if it is determined that they left Greece with the apparent intent not to return, though exile is unconstitutional. However, immigrants who are ethnic Greeks are normally recognized as Greek citizens and accorded full rights, despite years or even generations of absence from Greece. Those who lose Greek citizenship as a result of such hearings sometimes learn of this loss only when they seek to re-enter Greece. Despite repeated assurances of change since 1991, the law still stands. The existing legislation has been used against various minority groups. For instance, human rights groups see it being used to attack Macedonians who opposed the Greek government during the civil war, and against their children, as already noted. The 1994 report of the British section of the International Society for Human Rights (ISHR) notes the "official harassment and arrest of former (Slavonic) Greek nationals returning to Greece to visit their families." In *Denying Ethnic Identity: The Macedonians of Greece*, it is noted that ethnic Macedonian political refugees who fled northern Greece after the Greek civil war (1946–1949), as well as their descendants who identify themselves as Macedonians, are denied permission to regain their citizenship, to resettle in, or, for the most part, to visit northern Greece.[83] The Aegean Macedonian Human Rights Association of Australia has prepared a detailed submission concerning claims of human rights abuses in Aegean Macedonia.[84] This submission gives examples concerning the treatment of Macedonian-Greek citizens who have been affected by this particular Greek legislation.

Several of the human rights reports draw attention to the "use of laws dating from the Metaxas fascist period to outlaw Slavonic cultural associations, and the systematic imprisonment of members of such organizations for 'disseminating false information.'" Thus, Greece denies Slav Macedonians the right to identify themselves as such. Similarly there is the "use of official decrees to wipe out all expressions of non–Greek culture. The use of non–Greek surnames, place-names, and language is expressly forbidden and non–Greek cultural festivals may be broken up by the police."[85] Macedonians are not allowed to found schools where classes would be held in Macedonian language, and their children are not allowed to be educated in their mother tongue in the state schools.[86]

A common theme in the reports critical of Greece is that Macedonian activists are constantly watched and harassed by the Greek police and security forces, and subjected to economic and social pressures resulting from government harassment.[87] For instance, Macedonians who are Greek citizens are subjected to constant questioning on the northern Greek-Macedonian border.[88] "The variety of persons and groups subjected to government surveillance ... raised questions about safeguards. Targets included human rights monitors, non–Orthodox religious groups, and members of minority groups who meet with members of the diplomatic community. In one case, the security forces interrogated the family of a controversial academic who writes independently on such topics."[89] The academic referred to is Anastasia Karakasidou, mentioned above. Her suspected crime is her description of the existence of the Macedonians in Greece and her academic criticism of the Greek government position. The antagonism she has suffered from government authorities is reflected in the more extreme responses of Greek nationalists within Greece, and in the United States.

The United States State Department report for 1994 noted a system that suppressed academic freedom of speech and that kept foreign organizations, which are generally permitted to monitor the human rights situation in Greece, under constant surveillance. The missions of Helsinki Watch in western Trakia (Thrace) and the western Macedonian province were followed openly and on regular basis. The British newspaper *The Guardian* (May 12, 1994) noted the refusal of the Greek authorities to cooperate with international organizations concerned with minority rights. The paper also described a report by the Greek security services on one such human rights mission that concluded: "Learn the enemies of our nation and do not forgive them. God forgives. Greece never does."

Greek citizens who try to investigate violations of human rights are criticized and harassed in various ways. For example, those who bring up the question of the Macedonian minority are publicly vilified as "agents of Skopje," kept under surveillance, and often denied access to government functionaries. While the election for deputies to the European Parliament included an official list of Macedonian candidates, members of the Rainbow Party, the Supreme Court initially accepted the list only to refute it later on, and the party was deprived of the right to a national television campaign.

In fact, the human rights reports consistently note that Greece violates the freedom of speech of Macedonians in Greece. Cases of such violations are reported with varying degrees of detail. The Greek Monitor of Human and Minority Rights report of 1994 says there have been eight trials for "crimes of opinion" during the past 30 months, including those of opponents of government policy on Macedonia and a leader of the Turkish minority.[90] The report says that 18 individuals have been sentenced to prison by Greek courts since 1991, on grounds of denying the Greek thesis on minorities or criticizing Greek politics in the Balkans.

In Section 2 of the United States State Department report (1994), under the heading "Respect for Civil Liberties," it is noted that "significant exception to freedom of speech and press is provided for in the Constitution. Some legal restrictions on free speech remain in force and have been invoked the last 2 years in five cases concerning the politically sensitive topics of relations with the former Yugoslav republic of Macedonia and the question of ethnic minorities within Greece. On these so-called national issues, under the previous government, the authorities gave clear evidence of their intolerance of political dissent; the charges the prosecutors brought in court were based on what the defendants said or wrote, not on violent acts or other criminal behavior."[91]

The United States report points out that several Penal Code sections have been used to restrict free speech and press. It notes that "article 141 of the Penal Code forbids 'exposing the friendly relations of the Greek State with foreign states to danger of disturbance'"; Article 181, repealed in December, forbade "insulting authority." Article 191 of the code prohibits "spreading false information and rumors liable to create concern and fear among citizens and cause disturbances in the country's international relations and inciting citizens to rivalry and division, leading to disturbance of the peace." People were arrested for distributing leaflets or booklets denouncing government policy on Macedonia and asserting the existence and mistreatment in Greece of Macedonian and other minorities.

Some specific instances of human rights abuse. The United States State Department report says that in January 1992, a court sentenced six members of an organization to six and a half months' imprisonment. The group was charged with making slanders and insinuations against the government, and of causing anxiety among citizens by distributing leaflets and putting up posters which read: "No to Patriots. Recognize Slav-Macedonia." They appealed their conviction.

In April 1992, police in Athens arrested four students for distributing a leaflet entitled, "The Neighboring Peoples Are Not Our Enemies. No to Nationalism and War." The leaflet opposed the government's domestic policy regarding Greece's ethnic minorities. A court sentenced them in May to a fine and 19 months in jail. The charges were eventually dropped due to the lifting of some restrictions on freedom of speech and press.

In May 1992, police arrested five members of a socialist group, labeled "Trotskyites" by the prosecutors, for distributing a booklet about "working class" perspectives on Balkan issues, denouncing the rise of Greek nationalism, and asserting the existence of a Macedonian minority in Greece. The group was charged with "disturbing the peace through disharmony" and "spreading misinformation and rumors which could cause create unrest and fear among the population, and could damage the country's international relations." A court acquitted them on May 7, 1993, after a week-long trial. The public prosecutor's office appealed the unanimous verdict, but the charges may be dropped due to the new law that ends prosecution of offenses "committed by or through the press." This is the only known case of the prosecution appealing an acquittal on such charges.

The State Department report describes also the case of Michael Papadakis. In January 1993, Amnesty International published a report about the case titled, *Greece: Violations of the Right to Freedom of Expression: Further Cases of Concern*. Papadakis was a 17-year-old school boy who had been arrested on December 10, 1992, for handing out a leaflet that said, "Don't be consumed by nationalism. Alexander the Great: war criminal." In the leaflet, Alexander the Great was called a "miserable slayer of people." The leaflet also said: "Macedonia belongs to its people. There are no races. We are all of mixed descent." Papadakis was charged with attempting to incite citizens to divisions among themselves, disturbing the peace, and carrying a weapon. He was sentenced to a year in prison. *The Times* calls this the "most bizarre example" of Greece's denial of its mixed ethnicity.[92] The United States Human Rights Watch organization noted that Papadakis was accused of carrying an iron bar but stated that "it was not found, and no evidence was produced in court to corroborate the weapons charge." Papadakis remained free pending an appeal.

The case of Christos Sideropoulos. Amnesty International reported the case of Christos Sideropoulos and Anastasios Boulis in November 1992 in a report titled *Violations of the Right to Freedom of Expression*. The two Macedonian activists were due to attend court on December 10, 1992, after comments reported in an interview with a Greek magazine, *Ena* (March 1992). They had spoken of their ethnic identity as Macedonians, saying that they "feel Macedonian." Sideropoulos said, "There are a million Macedonian speakers (in Greece). We are entitled to rights, to associations, schools, churches, traditions... I have a Macedonian ethnic consciousness... I belong to an ethnic minority which is not recognized by my State." This case has been noted by many other reports including, most recently, the United States State Department report of 1994. Sideropoulos and Boulis were charged with spreading false rumors in the press about the non–Greekness of Macedonia and the existence of a Macedonian minority on Greek territory, and with instigating conflict among Greek citizens by differentiating between the speakers of a Slavic language and Greeks.

Christos Sideropoulos is a forester in his mid-forties, from the country's northern border area. He is president of the Movement for Human Rights of Macedonians. Mr. Sideropoulos, who calls himself "a Macedonian patriot," claims he and his family are constantly harassed by the Greek authorities for expressing their opinions. "My telephone is tapped and I am followed by the secret police whenever I meet fellow Macedonian activists or outsiders," he said. "I am accused of being an agent of Skopje." Sideropoulos says he comes from a long line of rebels against Greek rule. "My maternal grandfather was a schoolteacher and activist who was hanged by his tongue by the Greeks in 1913 to terrorize people not to go to Macedonian schools," he said. He claims that his father was also tortured for siding with the Communists in the Greek civil war. His descriptions of discrimination against Macedonians are consistent with the reports just mentioned. He adds that Macedonians are effectively denied freedom of religion as the Macedonian Orthodox Church is banned from operating within Greece's borders, and that there is also discrimination in employment.

In March 1993, a court convicted Sideropoulos and Boulis, sentencing them to five months in prison and a small fine. Both were freed on appeal. Later, the particular charges against Sideropoulos and Boulis were dropped due to the changes in law with regard to views published in the press. However, Sideropoulos and Stavros Anastasiadis still had to face charges arising out of similar statements made on June 10, 1990, in Copenhagen at the CSCE Conference on the Human Dimension (CHD). The Greek delegation at the Copenhagen conference had requested that the executive secretary of the conference remove the Macedonian Human Rights delegation's literature from the non-government organization's desk. The request was refused. Sideropoulos and Anastasiadis experienced official harassment upon their return to Greece. Sideropoulos was transferred through his work to Kefalonia, several hundred kilometers from his homeplace, and Anastasiadis was given discriminatory tax penalties and dismissed from his job.

The public prosecutor, Ilias Costaras, subpoenaed Sideropoulos, accusing him of "spreading misinformation and thus endangering Greece's international relations." The indictment describes the claims that Sideropoulos made at the CHD conference in defining his offense. Amnesty International and other human rights organizations condemned the continued prosecution against Sideropoulos. Amnesty International and Helsinki Watch requested the text of the indictment, which was due to be presented at the District Court in Lerin in May 1994, but was adjourned several times. Diplomatic representatives of several countries announced their presence at the Athens hearing due for November 1994. The president of the Greek Helsinki Monitor, Panajotis Dimitras, said that Greece's actions in this matter had been observed throughout the world and brought Greece into disrepute in the international community.

The legal action against Sideropoulos prompted a reaction from the International Helsinki Federation for Human Rights with its headquarters in Vienna, the Greek Helsinki Monitor, and the Norwegian Helsinki Committee, all of which expressed deep concern over the charges against Sideropoulos. The International Helsinki Federation on Human Rights issued a public announcement to express its deep concern with a prosecution. The committee claimed that the law applied violates the principles of freedom of speech.

In their view, Sideropoulos's statement was simply an expression of opinion, the right to which is protected by the Greek Constitution, by Article 10.1 of the European Convention on Human Rights, and by Article 19 of the Universal Declaration on Human Rights (both of the latter had been ratified by Greece). By prosecuting on such grounds, the committee said, Greece "has become the first CSCE member to prosecute one of its citizens for expressing a personal opinion during a CSCE conference." The Helsinki Federation appealed to all governments of CSCE member countries to demand from the authorities in Greece a withdrawal of the accusations as they present a direct attack on the CSCE's development and cause deep concern with regard to Greece's readiness to act in accordance with international minority and freedom-of-speech regulations.

Amnesty International (AI) claims that Sideropoulos is still to be tried on charges which seriously breach his right to freedom of expression. Moreover, AI says the prosecution against him should be legally inadmissible because Article 6 of the Greek Penal Code states that a Greek citizen can be prosecuted for a criminal act committed in a foreign country only if this "act is punishable under the laws of that country" or there is "an application from the government of the country wherein the misdemeanor was committed." Neither of these two conditions has been fulfilled.[93] Amnesty International believes that if Christos Sideropoulos is imprisoned, he will be a prisoner of conscience.

According to the United States Human Rights Watch group, the prosecutions against Christos Sideropoulos are part of an officially sanctioned policy of harassment of ethnic Macedonians living in Greece.[94] These actions help continue the climate of fear among ethnic Macedonians living in Greece. The report states that "prosecuting people for the peaceful expression of their views, popular or unpopular, is forbidden under international human rights laws and agreements." The treatment of Christos Sideropoulos has been said to "run counter to the most basic values of European society... Greece has tried to stifle his voice: Britain should offer him asylum."[95]

Violence and harassment against dissenters. Various human rights reports, including those of Amnesty International, note that individuals arrested for political reasons, including the Macedonians, are sometimes physically mistreated. There are other occasions on which Macedonians in Greece experience violence at the hands of the Greek authorities. Greek border authorities frequently take the law into their own hands in dealing with border crossings of which they disapprove. No Greek government functionary has ever been found guilty of impropriety in such cases.[96] For example, when representatives of the Cultural and Artistic Association, "Gotse Delcev," a folklore ensemble from Bitola in the Republic of Macedonia, attempted to enter Greece early in April 1994, they were denied entry.[97] The group of 30 dancers had been invited by the artistic association of the village of Meliti (Ovcarani) near Florina (Lerin), Greece, to participate in a cultural event, traditionally held every year in the village on the occasion of the religious holiday "St. Ilija." Entry was refused because the invitation from the Greek citizens of Meliti was addressed to a "non-existing state — the Republic of Macedonia." Even those members of the group with the old (Yugoslav) passports were refused entry. While petty, the behavior of customs officials up to this point seems within the law. However, when about 30 citizens of the village of Meliti — Greek citizens who had been at the border crossing to meet their guests — attempted to persuade customs officers to let the group pass, the police used clubs, violently dispersing the group of Meliti villagers. Vasilis Sieklis and Kosta Sozislis, members of the Meliti group, were taken into custody, and one of their cars was confiscated. Further examples of such harassment and violence can be seen in the case of the Archimandrite Nicodimos Tsarknias.

The case of Father Nicodimos Tsarknias. On May 10, 1994, Amnesty International wrote to the government of Greece expressing concern about human rights violations, noting in particular the cases of Christos Sideropoulos and two others whose human rights had reportedly been violated by the Greek authorities purely because of their non-violent activities on behalf of the Macedonian minority in Greece.[98] Archimandrite Nicodimos Tsarknias, a Macedonian human rights campaigner, and his sister, Maria Tsarknias, were reportedly beaten by Greek border guards on May 4 when crossing the border checkpoint of Niki between the towns of Bitola in the Former Yugoslav Republic of Macedonia (FYROM) and Florina in Greece. Father Tsarknias was leaving Greece to attend a religious event in Canada. Father Tsarknias was arrested and sent to the Regional Office of the Department of Defense in Florina for further interrogation. He collapsed there and was transferred to the General Hospital of Florina for medical treatment. It is not clear on what charges he was arrested; however, the charges were later dropped and he was released after Human Rights Watch/Helsinki, Amnesty International and other parties sent strongly worded protests to Athens. Father Tsarknias has been outspoken in defending the rights of the Macedonian minority in Greece, and Amnesty International believes that this may be the reason he and his sister suffered ill-treatment by the border guards. In its letter of May 10, Amnesty International urged the Greek government to ensure that the serious allegations of ill-treatment of Archimandrite Nicodimos Tsarknias and Maria Tsarknias were fully investigated by an impartial authority and that any persons found responsible were brought to justice.[99] The United States State Department report (1994) notes that no police official has been charged or punished for such behavior.

Father Tsarknias, a Macedonian citizen of Greece, lives in the town of Aridea (Subotsro). Father Tsarknias has publicly demanded freedom for Macedonians to proclaim their ethnic heritage, to be educated and to worship in their own language as well as Greek. For more than 10 years his movements have been monitored by Greek authorities. He has been criticized and ridiculed in the Greek news media. There has been, what the Greek chapter of Helsinki Watch calls, a campaign of character assassination, which included accusations that he engaged in pedophilic activities. He claims that in October 1989 he was offered a bishopric if he would side with the state on the Macedonian issue, and was told that he would pay dearly if he did not. Father Tsarknias continued to work for the rights of Macedonians.

In 1992, Bishop Apostolos dismissed Father Tsarknias from his parish. In July of that year, Father Tsarknias and a parishioner, Photios Tzelepis, were issued a writ of summons to appear in the Magistrate's Court of Thessaloniki. The priest was charged with insulting his archbishop. He was also accused of being a homosexual and a Skopjan (Republic of Macedonia) spy. However, a Greek Secret Service (KYP) report published in a Greek newspaper revealed that the minor charge in the summons was a pretext to harass the priest for his human rights activism. The report says the authorities "did not find the courage to say that they dismissed him from his parish for his anti–Hellenic stance and to ask for his committal to trial for high treason, but instead they removed him with the lukewarm 'justification' which we reveal today so that it will stain with shame all those who contributed to it." A new trial was set down for April 1994.

Father Tsarknias was ordered to appear in court, though his trial was repeatedly postponed, since (he maintains) there was no case against him. In 1993, after having served for twenty years in the Greek Orthodox Church, he was defrocked in absentia by the Holy Synod of the Greek Orthodox Church, officially for reasons of discipline, but (in the view of the Greek Helsinki Watch) in reality for his advocacy for the rights of the Macedonian minority in Greece.[100] At that time, Father Tsarknias joined the Macedonian Orthodox Church and became a member of the monastery of St. George the Great Martyr in the village of Kuckovo, Skopje. Since then, he has been persecuted for pretense of authority by the Greek government. This persecution has been noted by a variety of human rights observers, and by reports of the United States State Department over the past three years. Father Tsarknias was due to stand trial in June 1994 on charges that he resisted arrest in 1992.

On May 11, 1994, Father Tsarknias once again attempted to leave Greece to attend the Canadian religious event. He was informed by the border police in command at the time that if he attempted to leave Greece, he could "anticipate" the same treatment as before. The following day, Father Tsarknias wrote an open letter to the Macedonian organizations in America, Australia, Canada and Europe explaining what had happened. He added, "The primary reason why I am precluded from leaving Greece, according to a comment that Mr. Giorgios Lianis, Deputy Minister of State for Sport, made to Mr. M. Tsotskou and Mr. G. Gotsi, is that I 'defy Greece.' This comment seems to refer to my struggle for the national rights of Macedonians living in Northern Greece. I implore you to inform all the International Organizations of how I am forbidden to leave Greece, without any court order being issued."[101]

According to the *Macedonian Tribune*, Father Tsarknias reports that on June 18, 1994, he went to court in Edessa to answer charges of misrepresenting religious authority. The trial was postponed. On leaving the courthouse, he was again physically assaulted by Greek authorities, this time for wearing the robes of an Orthodox priest. When his sister, Stojanka, intervened, she too was physically attacked. They were both arrested for "obstructing justice" and interrogated at the Edessa police station. They both had to be treated in a hospital for the results of their detention. At Edessa General Hospital, the staff refused to treat them and shouted obscenities at them. A male nurse, named Haralambros, tried to choke Father Tsarknias while another attendant, Stylianos Selidis, threatened to "eliminate" him. Dr. Maria Varela, a staff pathologist, shouted to the police that the two Macedonians "should be thrown into the street."[102]

In November 1994, Father Tsarknias was summoned to a trial by the court in Edessa, Greece, on the grounds of wearing priest's garments after he had been defrocked by the Greek Orthodox Church. He was imprisoned two days before the hearing. There were unconfirmed reports that the Macedonian Orthodox Church undertook efforts to persuade the Greek Church to have the matter resolved in a way that would not violate basic human and religious rights.[103]

On December 2, 1994, Edessa's single-member circuit court (presided over by Vassilios Tsourdas) found Father Tsarknias guilty and sentenced him twice on the same charge repeated, to a total of six months imprisonment. Father Tsarknias was tried for pretense of authority, under article 176 of the Greek penal code; more specifically, for wearing a uniform of a clergyman of the Eastern Orthodox Church. This is the same uniform worn by clerics of the Macedonian Orthodox Church. Father Tsarknias was able to present documents confirming his affiliation with the Macedonian Orthodox Church. Nevertheless, the court ignored them and convicted him to three months in prison, which he appealed, but also had to "buy off" (a common procedure in Greek courts), since the alleged crime was committed in the court and the sentence was not suspendible. After the formal proceedings of the first trial, the court required Father Tsarknias to promise that he would never wear the priest's robes again. He declined to do so, stating that he would have to consult first with his lawyers and his spiritual counselor. The court decided to prosecute him again immediately. Father Tsarknias was tried summarily, as he did not participate in the proceedings. His lawyers resigned in protest at the behavior of the court. The court handed down a second three-month sentence which again Father Tsarknias appealed and bought off as before. The judge was then prepared to continue trying Father Tsarknias repeatedly until he promised not to wear priest's robes, but the public prosecutor intervened, stopping the process at this point.

The Greek Helsinki Monitor group condemned the double conviction of Father Nicodimos Tsarknias, describing it as a violation of religious freedom that sets a dangerous precedent of intolerance in the Balkans. The convictions against Father Tsarknias were based on the argument that, as a Greek citizen, he cannot invoke his affiliation to a non–Greek church. Until now, the clergymen of the various Orthodox churches, including those of the Macedonian Orthodox Church, which is considered schismatic by the other Orthodox churches, enjoyed freedom of movement around the region. Such a precedent may now be invoked by Albanian authorities to expel Greek clergymen who serve in the Albanian Orthodox Church; or by Macedonian authorities against either Serb clergymen who live in that country but adhere to the Serbian Church, or Greek clergymen who visit or travel through the Republic of Macedonia. The Greek human rights group called on the Greek government to see that such prosecutions stop immediately and to instruct judges to protect defendants, witnesses, and lawyers from verbal abuse like that observed in Edessa, which was not followed up with action against the offenders. During the trial, the Greek Helsinki Monitor spokesperson was called a traitor by a member of the audience while he was making a human rights experts' deposition. Greek lawyers in the court, but not involved in the case, called Father Tsarknias' lawyers — one from Athens and one from Salonika (local lawyers have been refusing to defend him) — "miasma" and "defenders of a foreign fatherland." The court took no action against them for these repeated outbursts.

The Greek Helsinki Monitor points out that clerics of the Church of Greece who have been demoted by the church or who are not recognized by the state because of illegal appointments and continue to wear their frocks and perform religious services are repeatedly violating article 175 (assuming without justification the service of a clergyman of the Greek Orthodox Church) and 176. They have never been arrested or prosecuted. Father Tsarknias has been singled out for attention.[104] They expressed the view that the true reason for the court's decision against Father Tsarknias was his support for the rights of the Macedonian minority in Greece. This is the twelfth court sentence against Tsarknias on grounds of disrespect for Greek Orthodox Church regulations. All convictions are being appealed, and therefore, the only time he has spent in custody was that following his arrests.[105]

In a joint statement, the national committees of the International Helsinki Federation in Albania, Bulgaria, Croatia, Greece, Montenegro, Kosovo, Romania, Serbia and Macedonia expressed deep concern over the decision of the Greek courts concerning Father Tsarknias. The committees said the court decision is based on the claim that a Greek citizen must not join a non–Greek church. The committees warned again that this as a dangerous precedent in the Balkans. The decision not only violates religious freedom, but may cause new conflicts in the region, the statement said. The national committees demanded that all charges against Tsarknias be dropped.[106]

On March 20, 1995, on a visit to the United States, Father Tsarknias traveled to Fort Wayne, Indiana, where he spoke with representatives of the *Macedonian Tribune* and other local Macedonians. He spoke on a variety of issues, but gave some insights into the pressures facing Macedonians in Greece. He said:

> It is difficult for people who are openly Macedonian to find a job, to work. Those who acknowledge that they are Macedonian are not allowed to advance professionally ... People can speak Macedonian amongst themselves... Strong, brave individuals speak Macedonian in public ... In pure Macedonian villages, there are no problems with speaking our language. In mixed villages, people are afraid to speak. In the cities, in Edessa and in Lerin, they speak freely in the cafes. If two to three million people live here, half of them are Macedonians, a million or more. People who feel they are Macedonian have to have the right to say so. If they were not afraid of losing their jobs, if they were not afraid of being attacked, arrested and beaten by police, they would call themselves Macedonian... There are many Macedonians in Greece. Ninety percent of the population in Lerin is pure Macedonian ... We say that we are Greeks to save ourselves and our children ... My father couldn't even speak Greek, but he became a Greek. That's a tragedy.[107]

How international commentators judge Greece. In January 1994 the British section of the International Society for Human Rights published a report on human rights abuses in Greece. The comments of Stephanie Snow, secretary general of ISHR (British section) at that time, were as follows:

> It was nothing short of a scandal that the state holding the Presidency of the European Community should be engaged in institutional violations of human rights on this scale. Within the context of the Council for Security and Cooperation in Europe (CSCE) Greece has committed itself to legal guarantees for minorities, and has also officially adopted the United Nations Declaration on Minority Rights. Yet in practice Greece is using its own laws and legislation to operate in direct contravention of the international Declarations it is supposed to have adopted. This cannot be allowed to continue. In the light of these revelations, I would urge the governments of the European Community to examine whether it was appropriate for a state with such a disregard for the human rights of its minorities to assume the presidency of the EC and indeed, whether Greece should remain a member of the EC at all.[108]

The outrage shown here is repeated in other human rights reports and in the comments of the international press.

The British Helsinki human rights group produced a report in August 1994 titled *Macedonian Minorities*. The report claimed that Greece is guilty of such serious human rights violations against the Slav minority in the north of the country that it probably does not deserve to be a sovereign state. A commentator in *The Times* suggested that "there is a matter in which Greece has, until now, escaped the censure it deserves: the treatment by Athens of its Slav Macedonian minority. Great resources, and greater energy, have been spent on 'proving' that there are no such things in Greece as a Macedonian people and language."[109]

The authors of *Macedonian Minorities* used the methods of the Badinter Commission as a standard for judging Greek actions with regard to the Aegean Macedonians. This commission was established in December 1991 to advise the European Community on the recognition of former Yugoslav republics as independent states. Its brief was to judge whether they satisfied the legal criteria for statehood, namely, a permanent population, defined territory, effective government, independence, and adequate constitutional protections for ethnic minorities. The commission found in favor of Macedonia, but Greece's opposition delayed Macedonia's admission to the United Nations. *Macedonian Minorities* concludes that with regard to the provision of adequate constitutional protections for minorities, Greece would fail to meet the criteria for recognition that were applied to Macedonia. "It is probably not an exaggeration to say that if Greece were to undergo the same process today, the Badinter Commission would be obliged, after considering the non-observance of minority rights by the Greek government, to recommend against recognizing Greece as a sovereign state."[110]

Macedonian Human Rights Groups

Since the mid–1980s, a small number of Macedonians (many of whose families experienced severe persecution during the Greek civil war) have become politically active and begun to demand human rights for the Macedonian minority in Greece. In 1984 the Central Organizing Committee for Macedonian Human Rights was established in northern Greece. In the next few years, similar organizations were formed by Aegean Macedonians in diaspora communities in Canada and Australia.

In the earlier mentioned live television interview of October 8, 1994, reporter Tanas Atanasiu addressed Greek fears that there are territorial pretensions from Macedonia by asking a citizen of Florina, "Do you want a unification of Greek Macedonia with Skopje?" Stravos Anastasijadis answered: "No, I do not think so, we are quite fine where we are." He pointed out that the Macedonians in Greece, particularly in Florina, are not asking for anything else except the right to open up schools, churches and culture centers in their mother tongue, along with rights to free expression of ideas, access to media, and participation in the government, all of which is guaranteed by Greece's international agreements. The show also interviewed Traianos Pasois, president of the party "Rainbow" and editor of the magazine *Dawn*, and Christos Sideropoulos, leader of the Macedonian Movement for Human Rights in Greece. They, too, spoke of problems faced by the unrecognized Macedonian minority in Greece. They expressed the hope that local election candidates in Lerin might be announced "bilingually."

Macedonian human rights groups seek recognition by the Greek government of the existence of a Macedonian minority. They are working to end discrimination against Macedonians in Greece in the fields of education and employment, as well as in other areas of social, cultural, and political life. They want Macedonians in Greece to have the right to attend church services in Macedonian, to receive their primary and secondary education in Macedonian, and to publish newspapers and broadcast radio and television programs in Macedonian. They also want the right to establish Macedonian cultural organizations, such as the Center for Macedonian Culture, which was formed in Florina in 1984. These groups have also protested against police interference with village festivals where Macedonian folk songs and dances are performed, as well as against the harassment and persecution of Macedonian human rights activists, some of whom have been dismissed from their jobs, denied entry into Greece, and deprived of their Greek citizenship.[111] Among the goals of these groups are the repeal of several specific laws, already noted, that discriminate against Macedonians on the issues of citizenship and property rights, and recognition of university degrees obtained in the Republic of Macedonia.

In 1984, the Movement for Human and National Rights for the Macedonians of Aegean Macedonia, operating in Greece illegally, issued a Manifesto for Macedonian Human Rights. This states, "In Greece, human rights are openly disregarded and our human existence is cursed. We, in the Aegean Macedonia, are determined to carry our struggle on various levels, employing all legal means until our rights are guaranteed." In the northern autumn of 1988, the newspaper *Alagi*, published in Florina, wrote that the Macedonians do exist and that they should have the full rights of a national minority. The newspaper pledged to fight for those rights until victory. After parliamentary elections in 1989, thousands of leaflets protesting against the disregard for human rights in Greece were placed in the ballot boxes in Aegean Macedonia. We have already seen something of the activities of Christos Sideropoulos, president of the Movement for Human Rights of Macedonians, in presenting a case to the CSCE conference in 1990 concerning human rights in Aegean Macedonia.

In January 1993, the Macedonian Movement for Prosperity in the Balkans held its first congress in Sobotsko, Greece. The MMPB issued a statement highlighting Greece's discriminatory policy towards its Macedonian minority and in particular, the denial of basic human rights. The MMPB said ethnic Macedonians in Greece and Macedonians in the diaspora should cooperate closely to further ethnic, religious, linguistic and social freedoms for all minorities in Greece. The organization urged the Greek government to allow Macedonian political and economic refugees to return to Greece if they desired.

A delegation of MMBP visited the European Parliament in Strasbourg during its regular session held from February 7 to 10, 1994. The visit came at the invitation of the European parliamentary group "Rainbow," which protects the interests of European minorities. During its visit, the delegation from Greece held numerous meetings with deputies in the European Parliament;

representatives of the Commission for Minority Languages; the president of the "Bureau for Less Often Used Languages," Mr. D. O'Reagan; the secretary of the European Council Section for Human Rights, Mr. Kruger; the commissioner for the provinces of the European Union, Mr. Albanese; and the leader of the Green party, Mr. A. Lager. During these meetings and the press conference that was held during the last day of the visit, the situation of the Macedonians in Greece was discussed. The Macedonian Greeks suggested a need for the Greek government to undertake appropriate measures to achieve human, cultural and language rights for the Macedonians in Greece, in accordance with Rainbow's aims. They also discussed the issue of returning the right of the Macedonians, both political and non-political emigrants, to visit their birth places in Greece.[112]

Later that same year, the MMBP submitted a request to register a political party of Macedonians in Greece under the name of Rainbow (Ouranio Tokso). Rainbow was founded on May 21. There were 23 ethnic Macedonians or sympathizers aiming to stand for election. Rainbow planned to run candidates in the June 12 European elections, in an effort to test their strength nationally and to explode the myth that there is no ethnic Macedonian minority within Greece. The Supreme Court in Athens at first (on May 29) decided not to let candidates of the Macedonian ethnic minority enter the coming elections for delegates to the European Parliament. The official reason given was that Rainbow had not stated its principles as being "opposed to any action aiming at the violent seizure of power, or the overthrow of the free democratic regime." (Law No. 59 from 1974 states that "parties will make a statement on use of non-violent means in realizing their political goals.") The United States State Department report of 1994 noted this particular failure to accord human rights to Macedonians. International commentators suggested that Rainbow was banned because the Greek authorities feared the possible success of Macedonians.[113] Even a moderate show of strength for the Rainbow party would have proved an embarrassment to the government since it represents a minority group that Athens says does not exist.[114]

In an interview for Radio Noma of Skopje, Traianos Pasios, coordinator of Rainbow and editor of the Macedonian paper *Dawn*, gave a statement on the Greek elections for the European Parliament, about the participation of Macedonians. Over 7,000 voters had chosen Rainbow candidates. Most of the votes came from the Lerin and Voden region.[115] Pasios thought the modest vote was a success. He pointed out that the media in Greece had published very little about the party, and many people were not even aware of its existence. He noted that the people are still threatened with loss of jobs, refusal of local government assistance to the villages, and so on for any opposition to the central government line. He suggested that what had been said on television and written in the papers had been mainly negative. For instance, party members had been described as "agents paid by foreign forces," "Gligorov's associates," "autonomists," "agents of Skopje," "well-known opposers to Greece." Party posters had been torn down. As well as these problems, the banning of the right to register Rainbow was widely published in the press, but the reversal of the decision just before the election received no exposure. Pasios stated it was quite clear the Macedonians would not succeed this first time, but stressed it was important the government recognize them as a party. He felt that Rainbow's time was yet to come.[116]

After the European elections, Rainbow announced that it planned the first congress of the Macedonian political movement in Greece during the European spring of 1995. The congress was aimed at defining the character of the movement, reorganizing it, preparing a statute and program, and electing a new leadership. The announcement of the congress stated that "every Macedonian and every Greek citizen who fights for essential democracy and social justice has the right to join 'Rainbow' and take part in the pre-congressional activities." This document indicated that Rainbow stood for a decentralized administration, and for respect of human rights and basic freedoms for all national, language, cultural, and religious minorities. It expressed the hope of appealing to all native Macedonians, and of conducting a struggle to end unjust Greek policy toward the Macedonians in Greece and Macedonian refugees.[117]

At the local elections in Greece in October 1994, the "Slav Macedonians" elected mayors in many villages in the vicinity of Florina. One of the leaders of the Macedonian group, Panos Voskopoulous, expressed satisfaction with these wins and pointed out also that Macedonians were in important positions in the mainline Socialist party in the region.[118] In October 1994, Rainbow president Traian Pasios said that since the European Union had recently recognized Macedonian as one of the languages spoken by minorities living within Union boundaries, the MMBP of Voden, Greece, will seek mediation by the High Commission on Minorities to help in introducing Macedonian as a second language in schools in Aegean Macedonia, as well as radio programs in Macedonian.[119]

Harassment of the Macedonian activists has come in many forms. Some of these have already been noted. The Greek Helsinki Watch organization reported that, without explanation, the Bank of Greece had blocked the account of the monthly magazine *Zora*, based in Arideja, published by the Slav Macedonian minority. This move had occurred one day after a very large street demonstration by Greeks through the streets of Thessaloniki in support of Athens' stance against Macedonia. The publishers of *Zora* received a letter from the director of their local bank, informing them that their account was blocked, but offering no explanation, according to Panayotos Dimitras, a spokesperson for Helsinki Watch.

The United States assistant foreign minister Nancy Ellie-Rafael, a human rights expert, met in Thessaloniki with representatives of the Macedonian national minority in January 1995. The leader of the MMBP at the time, Pav-

los Vaskopoulos, and Tashko Bulev met with the United States official and the
United States consul, exchanging opinions on ways in which they could change
the situation for the Macedonian minority in Greece.[120]

   A plea from Aegean Macedonians. At the end of July 1994, more than
5,000 citizens of Bitola and other Macedonian cities, including about 100 guests
from Pirin Macedonia (Bulgaria), Aegean Macedonia (Greece) and Mala Prespa
(Albania), participated in the fourteenth border meeting of Macedonians of the
Aegean part of Macedonia, traditionally held and organized by their association seated in Bitola, in the southwest of the Republic of Macedonia. This association had its first meeting in Skopje in 1980, when Aegean Macedonians from
around the world gathered to share their stories. A large proportion of these
peoples now live in Vardar Macedonia, where they have been warmly welcomed
and even provided with special housing and work opportunities. Many have
settled in Canada, the United States and Australia.[121] The following material
involves extracts from a message from the Association of Aegean Refugees to
the Secretary General of the United Nations and various international human
rights bodies, dated July 1994. The document should be read, keeping in mind
the fact that it is close to fifty years since these people have seen their birthplace. They have been forced to see the Macedonian nation as a worldwide phenomenon. They have often developed considerable loyalties towards their host
nations, Canada, the United States, Australia, and the Republic of Macedonia.

> After Macedonia was split among the Balkan countries, Serbia, Greece, and
> Bulgaria, on 10 August 1913, the national rights of the Macedonians from the
> Aegean part of Macedonia who live in Greece were constantly denied. Dur-
> ing the Greek Civil War, in the period from 1946 to 1949, reactionary Greek
> authorities committed mass genocide over the Macedonian people in that
> part of Macedonia, caring not about the manner or the means chosen for the
> extinction of the Macedonian people. In 1949 the Macedonian people faced a
> tragic exodus which included mass persecution, imprisonment on the unin-
> habited islands on the Aegean Sea, murders, rapes, and robberies. Four hun-
> dred seventy Macedonian villages were burnt down completely; innocent,
> helpless, old people, women and children were killed only because they were
> not Greeks by birth.
>   The Republic of Greece, which expresses pride in the ancient Greek demo-
> cratic ideal, by these acts, committed racial and national discrimination split-
> ting the citizens of Greece into those who were Greeks by birth and those who
> were not. The special regulation of the Ministry of public order and the Min-
> istry of internal affairs, No. 106841 of December 1982, and the law passed by
> the Greek government in 1985, No. 1540, both aimed at solving the question
> of the return of properties to Civil War refugees, allow only Greeks by birth
> to return to Greece. This is nothing else but a clear case of apartheid in Greece.
>   We, the expelled Macedonians from the Aegean part of Macedonia, are for-
> bidden to return to our birth-places in Greece. We are not allowed to enter
> even when we have to pay our respects to our relatives after a death in the fam-
> ily. We are forbidden to visit the homes of our ancestors because we are not
> Greeks by birth, because we are proud of our Macedonian name and because

we want to talk, write, rejoice, sing, and cry in our Macedonian mother tongue, in our birth places. All previous governments, including the present government of Mr. Papandreou, admitted the existence of Macedonian people in Greece. They had to recognize Macedonians, because they fought and died on the battlefield defending the Greek state; they had to admit Macedonians because they serve in the Greek army; and they had to admit Macedonians because they pay taxes and vote in the elections.

Amongst the requests from this organization were the following:

We ... ask from you the following:
That you impose pressure on the Greek government to respect international norms concerning the human and national rights and liberties of the Greek citizens who are Macedonians who live in Greece, in accordance with UN Declarations and Conventions on Human Rights, the Paris Charter, CSCE and Council of Europe Human Rights Documents, signed by Greece.
That you impose pressure on the Greek government to undo the land confiscation, returning the whole property of the Macedonians expelled from Greece between 1940 and 1949, because that property was taken away by force and by the illegal acts of the Greek government which are in contradiction with paragraph 17 of the Article 2 of the UN Declaration on Human Rights which says that: "Nobody has right frivolously to be deprived of his/her property."
...We want peace in the world and we are ready to struggle for this. We want equality for the Macedonians who live in the Aegean part of Macedonia, in Greece. We want complete recognition of their national rights (education, language, church, radio, TV, press) with regard to their mother tongue. We, the Association of the Macedonians from the Aegean part of Macedonia, struggle against any kind of discrimination and we are against any violence including the use of war as a means for solving problems. Our old and present determination is to support human rights and national equity for all people who are discriminated against in the Balkans, in Europe and, in the World. We fought and will fight for peace in the Balkans and peace in a United Europe.[122]

The Association of Children Refugees from Aegean Macedonia. For more than a decade, another grouping of refugees, the Association of Children Refugees from Aegean Macedonia, has met in the Republic of Macedonia to work on issues of common concern. The eleventh meeting was in May 1995. Representatives to the electoral assembly of the association came from many countries of Europe and other parts of the world. The association aims to give special attention to securing national, cultural, and other human rights of the Macedonians living in the neighboring countries and other countries around the world.

There is little doubt that elements of the population of Aegean Macedonia who have a Macedonian national consciousness, as well as surviving refugees from that territory in Europe and in other parts of the world, who may number in the hundreds of thousands, wish for a Greater Macedonia that will incorporate Aegean Macedonia. However unrealistic this wish, they continue to take actions that reflect this ambition. For instance, the Association of

Children Refugees from Aegean Macedonia publishes a "geography map of Macedonia in its natural boundaries, considerably bigger than its present boundaries." This map, authored by Todor Simovski, is made available on request. The map shows political, geographic and demographic changes caused by this century's historical processes. It shows names of places in Greece in both original Slavic and recent Greek form.

Greek Voices of Concern

In February 1988, the Athenian newspaper *Ergatiki Alilengii* criticized the discriminatory policy of Greek authorities towards Macedonians. It also criticized the anti–Macedonian hysteria in certain mass media. Later in that year, in November, the newspaper *Alagi,* published in Florina, printed a statement by one of the leaders of the Greek Communist party, Mr. Kostopoulos, who said that it was a fact that the Macedonian minority existed in Greece.

In its issue No. 1/89, the Athens monthly *Sholiastis* published an article by Mrs. Elewteria Panagiopoulou entitled "Nationalists and the Inhabitants of Skopje — the Gypsies," in which she demanded a halt to the discriminatory policy of authorities and abolition of the inhuman legal acts aimed against the Macedonians. In another article, the same author called Macedonians "the Palestinians of Europe." In the northern spring of 1989, 90 Greek intellectuals addressed a note of protest to the Greek government in connection with the common violation of human rights in Greece. In September of 1989, the newspaper *Ta Maglena* asked, "Why are the Macedonians discriminated against?" The newspaper also asked, "Why does Greece not observe international law?" At the same time, it warned Macedonians against the agents of the Greek security service, who were said to be numerous in Aegean Macedonia. In November 1989, *Sholiastis* published an interview with several members of the illegal Movement for Human and National Rights for Macedonians of Aegean Macedonia.

We have already noted the much more recent appearance of Macedonian speakers on mainstream television programs. While these appearances and the dissenting voices in the press are not commonly heard, their presence suggests the possibility for change.

Dr. Alexander Zaharopoulos left Greece after completing his secondary education, but returned frequently while studying at University College, London. He settled in Australia in 1992. He suggests that the controversy over Macedonia owes much to a mindset in Greece that is all-encompassing and all-consuming. In a letter to the *Sydney Morning Herald*, Australia's preeminent national newspaper, he presented the perspective of a Greek who had taken the opportunity to look at Greek society from the inside and from the outside. Zaharopoulos said that to those who have had a Greek education the dispute between the Greeks and the Macedonians was no trivial matter. "In retrospect, it is clear to me that my 12 years of Greek schooling, mainly in the '70s, conspired to instill in me, precisely one attitude; an almost unshakable belief in the purity and unity of the Greek people, language and culture." He explained that this attitude was taught at school using images from history of Greek success against the Turk and other "Eastern riff-raff." Alternative interpretations of events were prevented by withholding information or changing the description of historical events.

Dr. Zaharopoulos says he was once told by Government Minister, and one time film star Melina Mercouri, while working as assistant to her senior adviser, Vassilis Fotopoulos, that the importance of the Elgin marbles lay in the fact that they were the heart of a body of Greek culture inherited from the ancient past. Consistent with this, until her death, she believed that modern Greece had a duty to preserve the organic coherence of that body of culture. It was only when Zaharopoulos left Greece, he explains, that he understood the profound inadequacies of his education. He was surprised to learn of the strong Asian and Asiatic influences that operated upon early Aegean cultures and the influence of a Jewish culture in Salonika that rivalled Vienna's "before local Greeks collaborated in its extermination," and was shocked to learn of the existence of present day communities in the Greek provinces of Macedonia and Thrace who are still treated as outcasts because Greek is not their first language. He says he was horrified to realize that for decades these communities had resisted policies of forced "Hellenization." Zaharopoulos concluded his letter with the observation that the conventional method of perpetuating Greek identity "has no place in a modern, tolerant, culturally diffuse world."[123]

Around the time of the signing of the Interim Accord between Greece and Macedonia on September 13, 1995, there was an unsuccessful attempt to tear down the sign on the office of the Rainbow party, in Lerin. The next day, the offices of the party were set on fire. There had already been two burglaries in the offices, when the party documentation was stolen. At the same time, the public prosecutor of Lerin brought charges against Rainbow for causing "discord" among the people. The Helsinki Committee for Human Rights of Macedonia responded to the fire with a public announcement: "We are convinced that the nationalist way of thinking and acting does not lead to any resolution of problems, but to the inflaming of nationalistic passions and the use of violence as the cruelest way of violating human rights." The Helsinki Committee for the Protection of Rights of the Minorities in Greece also denounced the violations and burning of the office of Rainbow, saying, "This party includes Greek citizens who belong to the Macedonian national minority, which is internationally recognized everywhere, but unfortunately not in Greece. This event shows that Greece does not respect international principles of free expression and the rights of minorities." The International Helsinki Federation for Human Rights called on Greece to respect international human rights instruments in respect to its Macedonian minority. The federation welcomed the decision of a Greek court to withdraw charges against Macedonian human rights activist Christos Sideropoulos, but strongly criticized the Greek authorities for not investigating the case of the arson attack on the Rainbow premises.[124]

6. The Development of a Macedonian National Consciousness

The issue to be discussed in the next two chapters is the degree to which modern peoples are the legitimate inheritors, by race or ethnicity rather than by possession, of the ancient lands. It will be argued here that demonstrable connection with the ancient peoples who lived in their lands is tenuous for both the modern Macedonians and the modern Greeks. It will also be noted that if any case for continuity of race can be made it is for the Macedonians, though, naturally enough, this is a contentious issue. On the other side of the argument, the ethnic connection of the modern Aegean Greeks with the ancient inhabitants of Macedonia is particularly thin.

In dealing with these issues, it is necessary to understand that the development of nation-states attached to particular territories is a relatively new phenomenon in European history. It was not land that defined those feelings of unity expressed by the ancient Greeks, but a similarity of culture. In the Balkans, unity was imposed by a succession of empires that controlled more or less of the area at different points in time. The longest-lasting influence was that of the Roman Empire, but in the fourteenth century the Ottoman Turks held political sway and maintained their domination for five hundred years or more. People in the Balkans thought of themselves as subjects of a particular empire, as members of a particular religion, and as speakers of particular languages. They also recognized attachments to particular places, though hardly ever in the same broad way that citizens of modern nation-states might do. Villages or cities of origin were likely to have emotional meaning, rather than the kinds of nations that we are more familiar with today.

It is part of the task of these chapters to discuss the development of new ways of thinking about how similar peoples relate to one another and to the lands that they share in the Balkans. One way to do this is to start in the present, looking at current national sentiment, then uncovering the pathway that has brought us to this state of affairs.

After Tito's death in 1980, the Yugoslav government gradually relaxed the controls it had exercised over expressions of Macedonian nationalism. As moves for autonomy gained strength in various parts of the Yugoslav federation in the late 1980s, in parallel with increasing Serbian nationalism, the citizens of the People's Republic of Macedonia began to consider the possibility of independence. In a referendum held on September 8, 1991, Macedonians voted overwhelmingly (95 percent) in favor of establishing a completely sovereign and independent Macedonian state. Serbs and Albanians boycotted the referendum, which caused tension between Macedonia and the Serbian-controlled Yugoslav government, but armed conflict did not ensue. In April 1993 the United Nations recognized the republic under the name "the Former Yugoslav Republic of Macedonia." Members of the European Union and the United States followed suit soon after. Some countries, including China, Russia, Turkey, Bulgaria, Slovenia and Croatia, have recognized this country by its chosen name, the Republic of Macedonia.

The Greek nationalists say that the Macedonians have no right to this name. They say that Alexander the Great and other important ancient Macedonians were Greeks, and they claim a racial and cultural continuity between the ancient and modern Greeks. They argue that only modern Greeks have the right to identify themselves as Macedonians, not the South Slavs who settled in Macedonia in the sixth century A.D. and who, they say, were not recognized as Macedonians by anybody until 1944. Perhaps more significantly, in terms of modern historical analysis, Greeks argue that the Macedonian nation is a very recent artificial creation of that master politician Josip Broz (Tito). They claim that Tito applied the Greek name "Macedonians" to a diverse group of people who had never been given such recognition before, and more importantly, who had never seen themselves as a coherent group of people with a common purpose and a common attachment to their lands.

Although this argument was not vigorously promoted by the Greek government till about 1988, when the province of Northern Greece was renamed Macedonia, the Greek nationalist perspective now says that the use of the name Macedonia by the "Skopjans" is like an act of plagiarism against the Greek people. Some Greeks actually accuse the Macedonians of falsifying Greek history. A historian employed by the Greek foreign ministry told an American reporter, "It is as if a robber came into my house and stole my most precious jewels — my history, my culture, my identity."[1]

As we have seen, a strong historical case directly contradicts the Greek arguments about the Greekness of ancient Macedonians, the ethnic purity of Greeks at any time in history, and the continuity of the culture of ancient Greece. In this chapter we will confront questions about the "genuineness" of the modern Macedonian nation, the appropriateness of the use of the name Macedonian by the people who inhabit this portion of the lands of ancient Macedonia, and the development of a Macedonian national consciousness.

In particular, we might ask whether there were signs of development of a Macedonian national consciousness before the twentieth century. Can we find evidence of some earlier self-awareness of a grouping of Macedonian people, in the area of Greater Macedonia, people who acknowledged a common history, culture, and perhaps language? Was there at another time in history a group of Macedonians who shared a sense of community and who saw themselves as different from neighboring peoples?

This chapter will discuss opinions and evidence that show the development of a Macedonian national consciousness from the Middle Ages to the present time. It does not suggest that there was a linear growth process, but rather that the seeds were planted many centuries ago and in more recent times have blossomed. It will be useful to look at these developments alongside similar changes in nearby areas of the Balkans and even in other parts of Europe. These comparisons give us a context in which to understand the changes that were special to Macedonia. They lead to the conclusion that the emergence of Macedonians amongst Balkan ethnic groups, with a self-conscious recognition of their uniqueness, has been underway for at least the last two hundred years, and is very similar to the process that has occurred for the modern Greeks, Serbs, Bulgarians and Albanians.

Anthropologists say that national identities are constructed through complex historical processes. They are categories people use to classify themselves and others, which may change over time as a result of internal and external pressures. The important point is that identifying oneself with a particular ethnic group or national minority is a matter of individual choice.[2] Loring Danforth argues that from an anthropological perspective, the present dispute between Greece and the Republic of Macedonia can be seen as "a conflict between two opposing nationalist ideologies, both of which reify nations, national cultures and national identities; project them far back into the past; and treat them as eternal, natural and immutable essences." Clearly this process does not provide the observer with objective information about the way things really happened. We may well be presented with two rather different nationalist myths. But it may be possible to analyze with some objectivity the process of nation formation, the way that these particular national cultures and identities have been constantly reconstructed in recent history.

Ancient or even medieval history may be of little relevance to such an analysis. Nations in the process of constructing themselves seem always to claim connections with peoples and cultures of the distant past.[3] For instance, ethnic, linguistic and cultural continuity with the Romans has been part of the nation-building process in Romania. Bulgaria harks back to the great Bulgarian empires of the Middle Ages. Serbia sees its modern roots in a Serbian empire that existed some six or seven centuries ago. A current view among Albanians is that they are the twentieth-century survivors of the Illyrian people who lived on the eastern shores of the Adriatic sea 2,500 years ago. Indeed, by extension,

since the Illyrian tribes were the majority constituent people of the Great Macedonian homeland at the time of Alexander the Great, the Albanians see themselves as successors to the ancient Macedonians. Since we have reason to be
skeptical about ethnic purity anywhere in Europe, perhaps especially in the
Balkans, these appeals to the distant past, while fascinating, must be treated
with some caution. Because of the different allegiances that existed in the
ancient and medieval worlds, there was no concept of statehood. Thus references to romantic history may not be particularly helpful in examining problems of modern statehood. It may be better to consider instead the political and
social developments in those territories of concern during the past two or three
centuries.[4]

The formation of many states in Europe, particularly in the Balkan peninsula, occurred at the end of the eighteenth and the beginning of the nineteenth
century, with the breakup of the Austro-Hungarian and Turkish empires. This
process continued at the beginning of the twentieth century. Of course, we can
see a similar process at work today after the disintegration of the USSR. The
latter case demonstrates that national consciousness could survive even under
the overwhelming centralist authority of one of the most powerful totalitarian
states the world has ever seen, to reemerge with the demise of that state. This
shows that the late appearance of national sovereignty is no proof that the
potential for the development of a national consciousness has not been present
for generations or even centuries.

Thus we see that the time frame is not a significant basis on which to judge
the sincerity of national feeling. Does it matter if a state became independent
for the first time in 1991? Demonstration of a more or less unified national
intent must be taken seriously no matter how recent its appearance. In the
case of Macedonia, as with several other new European states, the early 1990s
was the time of first independence. The Macedonians in Vardar Macedonia
voted by an overwhelming majority to seek independence from Yugoslavia. The
strength of the vote was extraordinary and suggests a remarkable degree of
consensus. This political choice may represent merely the endpoint in a long
battle. It might be useful to look at the evidence concerning the length of that
struggle.

For the purposes of this chapter, in speaking about Macedonians, it will
be useful to consider those people who have inhabited the area that has been
called Greater Macedonia. This region is bounded by the Shar Mountains in
the north and the Aegean Sea in the south, by the lower Mesta (Nestos) River
and the Rhodope Mountains in the east, and by the Albanian highlands in the
west. Greater Macedonia thus includes the modern–day Republic of Macedonia, a portion of the northern part of Greece referred to here as Aegean Macedonia, a small area in the western part of Bulgaria (Pirin Macedonia), and a
few villages in the eastern areas of Albania. It is reasonable to choose this area
as the focus of attention because all of these territories over which the Serbs,

Greeks, Turks and Albanians fought in the later Balkan wars had a majority of Macedonian/Slavic speakers at the time of the forced partition in 1913. The history of the Republic of Macedonia is inextricably linked to developments in this larger region until the Balkan wars (1912-13), when it was divided amongst Bulgaria, Greece, Serbia and Albania.[5]

Naming and the Concept of Nations

During the period of Ottoman Turk rule in Macedonia, from the fourteenth century until 1913, the population of Macedonia included a broad number of different ethnic, linguistic, and religious groups. There were Slavic- and Greek-speaking Christians, Turkish- and Albanian-speaking Muslims, Vlachs, Jews, and Gypsies.[6] Toward the end of the nineteenth century, the population of Macedonia was increasingly being defined from various external nationalist perspectives as Greeks, Bulgarians, Serbs, Albanians, and Turks. The Turkish rulers had divided the population of their empire into administrative units, or *millets,* on the basis of religious identity rather than language, ethnicity, or nationality. Thus Macedonian Slavic speakers affiliated with the Bulgarian church were called Bulgarians, while their relatives affiliated with the Greek church were called Greeks.

Prior to the nineteenth century, however, such national identities did not exist because there were no Balkan nations. The peoples who inhabited different lands distinguished themselves territorially and culturally, but did not relate to each other on a national scale.[7] All were a part of the Turkish empire. Thus, to argue over what Macedonians "were" before the 1850s may not be particularly useful. Serbia was the first of the Balkan states to regain its independence in 1817 and Greece followed soon after in 1830. After popular uprisings in Macedonia and Bulgaria that led to shocking Turkish reprisals, the great European powers began once again to actively intervene in the Balkans. After the Russo-Turkish war in the 1870s, the Turks were forced to allow some autonomy to the Bulgarians. Though rejecting a proposal to set up a Bulgarian state more or less equivalent to the last medieval Bulgarian empire (this would have included Macedonia), international negotiators at the Treaty of Berlin (1878) allowed for northern Bulgaria to be an independent principality for which Sofia was later to become the capital. Southern Bulgaria became an autonomous province (Eastern Rumelia) within the Ottoman Empire with the administrative center in Plovdiv. Despite the wishes of the Russians, the other European powers did not want Macedonia to become a part of the Bulgarian (and therefore Russian) sphere of influence. Turkey remained in control of the three vilayets (administrative districts) of Skopje (Uskub), Bitola (Monastir), and Salonika (Selanik). Danforth reminds us that the expression "three vilayets" came to be used as a synonym for (Greater) Macedonia, and that the name Macedonia was banned by the Ottoman administration because of its nationalistic connotations. Clearly, nationalist aspirations were a reality in Macedonia in the late nineteenth century and were significant enough to inspire the Turks to take counter-measures. Yet those aspirations were not to bear fruit for another century, at least in part, because the other newly independent Balkan States divided Macedonia amongst themselves in the Balkan wars. It should be understood that the terms of the Treaty of Bucharest in 1913, which resolved the division of the three vilayets and consolidated other territorial gains from the Turks, added substantially to the territory of Greece, Serbia, and Bulgaria. If we think of territorial acquisitions as a part of the process of nation-building, we must recognize that this process was still underway in these Balkan states in the early part of the twentieth century. Indeed, with the events of the two world wars, we can consider territorial consolidation to have been incomplete throughout this region only shortly before the recognition of the People's Republic of Macedonia within the Yugoslav Federation.

An important issue is the appearance of the concept of a nation. During most of the last 1,500 years, the peoples of the central and southern Balkans were generally under the control of one great empire or another: Roman, Bulgarian, Serbian, Ottoman, Austro-Hungarian, or German. With that kind of experience as the norm, it is hard to imagine that the world view of the average Balkan peasant who never traveled far from the village of birth might extend beyond an awareness of a few neighboring villages, and the administrative structure of the prevailing empire. It is most unlikely that we are going to find the roots of nationalism in any Balkan nation springing from the illiterate peasant population. In the cities, and amongst those who were literate and therefore exposed to ideas from elsewhere in Europe, we are most likely to find the clearest indications of budding national consciousness. When we examine the personalities recognized as the most significant Macedonian revolutionaries, we find people who were broadly middle class, well educated, and keenly aware of the need to disseminate written ideas to people they wanted to recruit to their cause. In this respect the Macedonian case is not unique. The same was true for present-day Greece.

Modern Greece came into existence formally in 1830. It began in 1821 with a revolt on the Peloponnesus against Turkish rule. Especially in England, it caused a flood of romantic feelings, encouraged by poets such as Byron, who thought they owed some kind of cultural debt to the ancient Greeks. There was a great deal of popular support for the Christian Greeks in their revolution against the Moslem Turks. In 1827, the Christian European powers intervened on behalf of Greek rebels and forced the Turks to grant them independence. The newly recognized nation comprised an area almost equal to the territories that were unequivocally Greek in ancient times. It was an economically weak and politically divided country where the great powers of England, France and Russia competed for influence. In 1832, the same powers that established the first modern Greek state chose Prince Otto of Bavaria to be "King of the Hellenes" and sent him to Athens. Clearly Greek independence owed much to external support, even to the extent of having a head of state imposed from the outside. It might even be argued that in supporting a monarchy, the European powers structured the kind of Greek state that they thought they could deal with most effectively — a state that would further western European interests in the Balkans and further afield. One should consider these points when judging the role of external forces in the early development of the Macedonian nation.

We might ask, what was the national consciousness of the newly independent Greek kingdom? The most important identifying characteristics may well have been ideas of community coming from an earlier empire. It has been claimed that "modern day Greeks did not even call themselves 'Greeks' (Hellenes) before the nineteenth century. All through the middle ages the Greeks referred to themselves as 'Romans' (Romii) harking back to the Byzantine Empire — and even today *Romiosini* is the popular Greek for 'Greekness', not the artificial expression *Ellinikotita*."⁸ No doubt Greeks recognized their common Christian faith as a powerful unifying factor, but at this stage a Greek standard language was yet to be codified, so the uniting potential of modern Greek was some way off in the future. Antagonism to the domination by an outside group, the Moslem Turks, remains one of the most significant factors explaining the drive towards revolution.

Developments in Macedonia in the Middle Ages

Although some of the following viewpoints suggest the emergence of a Macedonian national consciousness predominantly in the nineteenth century, others suggest an awareness of Macedonians, especially the Slavic Macedonians, as a distinct group from as far back as the tenth century A.D. Even Greek sources acknowledge the common use of the name Macedonian to refer to people living there: "In medieval and modern times, the word 'Macedonian' lost its ethnic connotation, but continued to be used in a geographical sense to refer to any inhabitant of the geographical area of Macedonia in general."⁹

It is worth giving brief attention to the first part of this quote since it refers to a question that has been discussed earlier in this book, namely the ethnicity of the people who lived in ancient Macedonia. The quote suggests that, at some point in time, the word Macedonian did have a specific ethnic connotation. While that may be arguable, the time period for this was likely to have been around or before 500 B.C. Once Macedonian territory expanded, especially in the time of Philip II and Alexander the Great, the ethnic mix was considerable. The majority of people in Macedonia were not ethnic Macedonians. It seems unlikely that the name Macedonia would have been used during this period to denote a specific ethnic group. Certainly it was not used this way in the standing army of Philip II. Thus, for most of the past 2,500 years the name has been given to people who lived there rather than to people of a specific ethnic group.

In the era of Ottoman rule and after liberation, in all three parts of Macedonia, the inhabitants referred to themselves in their own languages, using the same geographical name. The Greeks of Macedonia called themselves *Makedones*, while the Slavs used the term *Makedonci,* and the Vlachs, *Macedoneni.*[10] The Greek source that notes this fact seems to hold that the practice somehow reduces the value of the label "Macedonian." The authors apparently feel that since the name does not necessarily indicate common ethnicity, it has no real power among its users, and therefore we need not take it very seriously. However, we should not underestimate the importance of attachment to particular territory in shaping human concepts about group belonging. Examination of psychological and sociological theory will show the belief that the use of labels, such as the place name Macedonia, by groups of people to describe and define themselves, implies a community spirit of some kind. At the very least, it means something like "those of us who live together in this land." It would not be unreasonable to argue that the use of a name is an expression of a common destiny insofar as that destiny is determined by territorial boundaries. It is a very short step from this idea to the notion of national identity.

If we apply our analysis to the great modern nation of the United States of America, we might question the reasoning of the Greek authors. The United States has been one of the great melting pots for people of diverse ethnicity. It has a strength shaped by the shared boundaries and common purpose of its peoples. It demonstrates clearly that seeing oneself as having roots in one land and sharing a common destiny with other inhabitants of that land can create the most powerful sense of national consciousness. Of course, a sense of national consciousness unconnected to ethnicity is not unique to the United States. There are many other examples among modern European nations. France, Spain, the United Kingdom, Italy, Belgium, and Germany are all cases in which ethnicity and language differences have been submerged, more or less effectively, beneath a common national consciousness. As we will see later, Greece is another case in point.

While Macedonia was under the control of the Turks, nationalist sentiment was perceived as revolutionary and was suppressed. When Macedonians were free from Turkish control, they sometimes gave public expression to feelings of national consciousness. These feelings were not always appreciated by rulers. Late in the sixteenth century and in years to follow, Macedonian emblems were being published in Europe. Diverse museums in Europe have displays of crests or insignias marked with the name Macedonia dating from 1595[11]—well before other Balkan nations achieved independence from the Turks.

Hristofor Zefarovik was a monk and writer born in Dojran (in the southeast of modern-day Vardar Macedonia) at the end of the seventeenth century.[12] Zefarovik was well educated, mostly in Ohrid and Thessaloniki, and traveled widely. In the early part of the twentieth century, the Serbian writer Stanoe Stanoevic recognized Zefarovik as Macedonian.[13] This was at a time when Serbian politicians preferred to define Macedonians as "South Serbians." Zefarovik was recognized as one of the most famous Macedonian and South Slavic authors. He was innovative as an artist but is best known for his *Stematography*, printed October 21, 1741, in Vienna. This work played a revolutionary role in awakening the national consciousness of South-Slavs in general since it distinguished between these groups and other Slavic peoples, and by claiming their uniqueness may well have inspired or encouraged nationalistic sentiment. The book was a heraldic handbook for the South Slavic world, written in Old Church Slavonic. It contains pictures of rulers and other famous figures and a total of 56 coats of arms applicable to various, mostly Balkan, peoples. The book was very popular and went through several reprintings. In the *Stematography* the Macedonian coat of arms appears three times. Zefarovik himself emphasized the fact that he initially took up the creation and printing of the book because of his own Slavic national feelings: "So that memory not be lost among the people, but be eternally with us, I have taken the liberty of writing this booklet."[14] The Austrian authorities banned the book and threatened its users with the death penalty.

In those areas of the Balkans controlled by the Turks, uprisings were not at all uncommon. Rebellion against Ottoman rule began in Macedonia as early as the 1560s.[15] Many Macedo-Vlachs were active in the Serbian independence movement in the first two decades of the nineteenth century. In 1807 and 1808, there were several uprisings in Macedonia and neighboring areas. The spread of revolutionary ideas at the beginning of that century was such that a distinct Macedonian drive for self-determination may have developed. Some claim this as a common theme that has run through all Macedonian political and national organizations since 1816.[16]

Macedonian National Consciousness in the Nineteenth and Early Twentieth Centuries

Just as Macedonian intellectuals were affected by the Serbian revolt to their immediate north, they were affected by, and had a positive sympathy for, the Greek War of Independence. After all, these were co-religionists with a common enemy, the Moslem Turks. Some authorities see clear signs of the growth of a "Slavic national consciousness" in Macedonia stimulated by the development of a Hellenic national consciousness among the Greeks during the Greek war of independence (1821–1829), by the spread of Russian influence, and by the ending of the Greek commercial monopoly.[17] There are two very important points here: first, that a national consciousness of some sort within Macedonia was clearly visible at the end of the eighteenth and the beginning of the nineteenth centuries; and second, that a Macedonian Slav national consciousness was developing concurrently with a Greek national consciousness.

Evidence of a distinct Macedonian national consciousness can be seen in the Constantinople Bulgarian newspaper *Pravo* of November 30, 1870, referring to the idea "that a Bulgarian and the Bulgarian language is one thing and a Macedonian and the Macedonian language is another."[18]

In 1876 the rebellion of the Christian peasantry of Bosnia-Herzegovina spread to parts of Macedonia and Bulgaria, where it was cruelly suppressed by the Turks. After the Turks butchered Macedonian and Bulgarian populations in reprisal for the uprisings, the Russians fought against the Turks and defeated them. At the Treaty of San Stefano, Russia proposed a greater Bulgaria, similar in extent to the Macedo-Slav empire of Tsar Samuil in the tenth century. It included practically the whole of Thrace, and Macedonia. France and Great Britain opposed this formulation, but argued that Greece should get Thessaly.[19] The great powers returned Macedonia to Turkey.

The involvement of Macedonians in the uprisings against the Turks, and the frequency of these uprisings at the end of the nineteenth century, is highlighted by Chupovski's account of Macedonian revolutionary activity.[20] He claims that at the time of the Russo-Turkish war of 1877-78, two-thirds of the volunteers from the Balkan Slavs, fighting in alliance with the Russians, were Macedonians. Chupovski says that the action of the Congress of Berlin in returning Macedonia to Turkish control "caused an explosion of despair and discontent in Macedonia. The whole people, like one man, rose up and started an unequal struggle against the Turks for their liberation. This uprising lasted for more than a year and ended, of course, with the triumph of the embittered Turks, who finally devastated that unfortunate country. Many villages, and even towns, were burnt down, many people were butchered, and some of the Macedonian intellectuals were killed while others found salvation in fleeing to the free states."

Prior to 1878, the peoples of Bulgaria and Macedonia shared a similar social, political and economic experience under the Ottoman Empire. The uprisings and the eventual partial independence of the Bulgarians stimulated similar ambitions in Macedonia. In 1878 and 1879, there was an uprising in Kresna by a group describing themselves as Macedonian. The Turks suppressed the rebellion, but the surviving rules of the Rebel Committee tell us about the distinctly Macedonian consciousness of those involved.[21] By the last two decades of the nineteenth century, the European powers were well aware of a spirit of national consciousness, based on ethnic and language differences from other Balkan areas, within Macedonia. The slogan "Macedonia for the Macedonians" was adopted by the English politician Gladstone in this period.[22]

With reference to the concept of a greater Bulgaria which included Macedonia, proposed by the Russians and Bulgarians at the Treaty of San Stefano in 1878, Michael Radis describes the recorded communiques of some of the Western powers at the Berlin conference that indicate their awareness of the ethnic, language, and sentiment differences between Macedonians and other peoples in the Balkans.[23]

Lord Salisbury, British foreign minister, dispatched the following telegram to his ambassador in Constantinople after the signing of the San Stefano treaty between the Russians and the Turks: "There is no question but that the Bulgarian principality as outlined in the treaty of San Stefano cannot remain with such extended borders, nor can it contain territory which does not belong to it ethnically" (18/4/1878). Similarly the Austrian minister of external affairs cabled his ambassador (17/4/1878) saying: "Let Nelidov (The Russian Ambassador) know that our government will under no circumstances tolerate an extended Bulgarian principality. The ethnic principle is not at all upheld in the preliminary text. We are aware, according to statistical data available, that Bulgarians and Serbs inhabit the region between the Black and Adriatic Sea. The territory of Macedonia is settled by a diverse population in which the Slav element predominates. However, it is known that a strong movement has emerged in the Slav population there which is endeavoring to make its own way. Our more recent interest dictates that we penetrate Macedonia to reach the Aegean Sea, taking advantage of the good will extended to us by the Slav population in Macedonia."

This is a definitive statement by a foreign observer acknowledging clear signs of an independence movement some time before Tito was born. The fact that the signs were so apparent even to foreigners despite tight Turkish control probably means that Macedonians had been discussing the issue for some considerable time before this. In the course of the nineteenth and twentieth centuries, at least up until independence in 1991, the name Macedonian came to be applied to the majority Slavic population.

Blazhe Koneski quotes Temko Popov's claim in 1888 that "the national spirit in Macedonia today has reached such a degree that if Jesus Christ himself came down from heaven he could not persuade a Macedonian that he is a Bulgarian or a Serb."[24] After 1885, Macedonian revolutionary groups were organized in Thessaloniki, Plovdiv, and Sofia.[25] Following a Macedonian uprising of 1895 (led by Trajko Kitanchev) and the (Armenian) slaughter in Asia Minor, the European states forced the sultan in 1896 to proclaim his famous "Irade" for reforms in the whole of European Turkey. According to Chupovski, these promised changes did not help the Christian population of Macedonia at all.

Chupovski says that despite the savage Turkish reprisals and the efforts of the great European powers in returning Macedonia to the Turks, the idea of liberation remained strong amongst the Macedonians. He describes the 35 years between the Congress of Berlin and the Balkan wars as "one bloody page of continuous struggle of the Macedonian people for their liberation." He says that in the five years from 1898 to 1903, there were more than 400 confrontations between the Macedonians and Turks. There were good reasons for Macedonians to feel anger and resentment at their Turkish overlords. Spiridon Blagoev describes European press reports — English, French, German, and Austro-Hungarian — concerning the acts of Turkish terror and violence perpetrated in Macedonia during the nineteenth century.[26]

The authority of the Greeks over the Orthodox Christian *millet* had been seriously challenged for the first time by the establishment of an independent Bulgarian Church in 1870. Orthodox communities in Macedonia now had the choice of affiliating with either the Greek or the Bulgarian national church. This led to a struggle between Greek, Bulgarian, and to a lesser extent Serbian interests, represented by their churches, over who would gain control over the people and the territory of Macedonia.[27] By the 1890s the three Balkan states each had supplied irregular bands of guerilla fighters who attacked the Turks, fought each other, and terrorized the local population. In addition, through the construction of churches and schools and the assignment of priests and teachers, each state was conducting an intense propaganda campaign whose goal was to instill the "proper" sense of national identity among the Orthodox Christians of Macedonia.

Meanwhile, within the population of Macedonia there were emerging signs of a Macedonian national identity as indicated by expressions of Macedonian ethnic nationalism on the part of intellectuals like Krste Misirkov, who by 1903 was calling for "the recognition of the Slavs in Macedonia as a separate nationality, Macedonians."[28] The Macedonian struggle reached its climax in the Balkan wars of 1912-13, involving a Serbian, Greek, and Bulgarian onslaught against the Turks and their European territory. Though Macedonians often fought with the anti–Turk forces with their own independence in mind, the wars ended with the partitioning of Macedonia among Bulgaria, Greece, Serbia (later Yugoslavia) and Albania.

Chupovski, who identified himself as a Macedonian patriot, wrote a lengthy plea for international help for the Macedonians in 1913 at the end of the Balkan wars.[29] His paper, titled "Macedonia and the Macedonians," was submitted by the Macedonian colony in St. Petersburg to the conference of the representatives of the Great Powers in London in 1913. Chupovski was calling for international intervention, especially for Russian help, for the Macedonian people who had simply swapped one ruler (the Turks) for another (the Serbians, Bulgarians, or Greeks). Chupovski's plea itself is evidence of significant Macedonian national feeling early in the twentieth century. There were many others who identified themselves as Macedonian and who organized politically or who wrote in support of Macedonian autonomy or independence. The journal *Macedonian Review* (vol. 14, no. 1 [1984] pp. 50–87) published a paper entitled "The Historical Truth" that presents 21 documents issued by various Macedonian figures and organizations between 1896 and 1930 on the struggle of the Macedonian people for liberation and self-determination.

The Internal Macedonian Revolutionary Organization (VMRO). Perhaps the clearest indication of a distinct Macedonian identity and of efforts to consolidate this was the formal creation of a widely supported revolutionary party in 1893. Two Macedonian schoolteachers, Gotse Delcev and Damian Gruev, were behind the founding of a secret society in Solun (Thessaloniki) that came to be known as the Internal Macedonian Revolutionary Organization. This group embarked on a program of educating Macedonians about the value of achieving autonomy, and they launched a systematic campaign of terror against the Turks. The terrorist action was not indiscriminate. The revolutionaries distinguished between the Ottoman authorities and sympathetic elements of the Turkish population, treating the latter in a progressive and pacifist manner even during the 1903 Ilinden uprising.[30]

There is some uncertainty about the date of their first formal meeting. Duncan Perry says that the Macedonian Revolutionary Organization (the MRO, as it was first called) began formally after a meeting in the Chelebi Bakal Street home of Ivan Hadzhi-Nikolov in Salonika on November 3, 1893.[31] The memoirs of the first chairman of the organization, Dr. H. Tatarchev, reported that "in the group, apart from myself, there were Gruev, Peter Arsov, Ivan Hadzhi-Nikolov, Andon Dimitrov (a teacher of Turkish in the High School, I think he was born in the village of Ayvatovo), Hristo Bastandzhiev (from Gyumendje, at the time teacher in the primary school and after that secretary to the Metropolitan bishop; he perished together with archbishop Evlogi in 1913, thrown into the sea by the Greeks). We exchanged ideas on the future political work and decided that each of us would try to influence other people and persuade them to work for the same cause, so that organized public activity could be prepared."[32] Later, perhaps early in 1894, the revolutionaries met at Andon Dimitrov's and made the decision to establish a revolutionary organization. As a guide, they used the memoirs of Zachary Stojanoff and took as a model the constitution of the Bulgarian Revolutionary Committee. During other meetings, a constitution was agreed upon and the first Central Committee was set up. Tatarchev was elected president and Damian Gruev was elected secretary and treasurer.

Damian Gruev wrote in his memoirs that the Constitution was based on the application of the Berlin treaty that had, in its Article 23, provided some autonomy for the people of Macedonia.[33] This suggests quite modest goals, falling short of complete independence from the Turks. Tatarchev wrote about the same issue in his memoirs. He said that the goals of the organization were for autonomy for Macedonia, though they did not favor the idea of the integration of Macedonia with Bulgaria, because they knew it would face the opposition of the Great Powers, neighboring Balkan countries, and Turkey. They considered that an autonomous Macedonia would be a rallying point for a future federation of the Balkan peoples. Under Gotse Delcev (1871–1903), the MRO (later Internal Macedonian Revolutionary Organization, IMRO, or, from the initials of its Bulgarian name, VMRO) put forward the slogan "Macedonia for the Macedonians." Although the MRO was predominantly a Slavonic organization with widespread sympathy, "Macedonians" was here intended to refer to all inhabitants of the region. Macedonia was to be a "Switzerland of the Balkans."[34]

Hristo Silijanov, who was very active in Lerin and Kostur, wrote *The Liberation Movement of Macedonia — The Ilinden Uprising*, describing the first steps of the organization. Silijanov claimed, "The organization was seen in the minds of its founders as Bulgarian. The first Constitution provided that members could include 'every Bulgarian.'" However, given the use of the label "Bulgarian" at the time it should probably not be understood with its modern meaning. It may be synonymous with "every Slav with Bulgarian Church affiliation," or it may simply reflect the fact that the conspirators used the Bulgarian constitution as their first model and gradually introduced changes. I suggest this because clearly some of the original conspirators were born in Macedonia of parents born in Macedonia; they used the Macedonian name for their organization; they planned for Macedonian autonomy; they spoke of "Macedonia for the Macedonians"; they said they wanted a Switzerland of the Balkans, implying acceptance of different ethnic/language groups. As well they had amongst their supporters even people of non–Christian background. Clearly they felt great sympathy and fellowship with the Bulgarians, often had their education in Bulgaria, and if they were members of the Bulgarian Orthodox Church, the Turkish government defined them as "Bulgarians." Silijanov says that according to the terms of the original constitution, only the "Bulgarian" element was deemed trustworthy by the founders. However, changes to the constitution show that after a while they willingly allowed membership to all Macedonian Christians who wanted to support the liberation movement. Presumably this was aimed particularly at Macedonian Slavs who were members of the Greek Orthodox Church (defined by the Turks as "Greeks"). The Greek Church was stronger in Aegean Macedonia. Given the presence of at least one Jewish revolutionary (Julius Rosenberg) amongst prominent Ilinden heroes, it would seem that membership was expanded even further at some point in time. This would not be particularly surprising, given the very large numbers of Jews in major cities of Macedonia at that time; probably more than 30 percent of the population of Solun was Jewish. It would also be consistent with revolutionary ideals that had been popular in Europe for a century and had been actively disseminated by leaders such as Gotse Delcev.

The small group of conspirators grew in time, and membership came from all over Macedonia. From its beginning it was affected by a division within its ranks, promoted by Bulgarian government interests aimed at bringing

Macedonia under Bulgarian control. A Bulgarian group, formally constituted as the Supreme Macedonian Adrianople Committee, took advantage of Bulgarian sympathies amongst Macedonians and infiltrated VMRO, sometimes creating effects that were destructive to the Macedonian cause.[35]

Meanwhile Greece, Serbia, and Romania sponsored guerilla bands to oppose Bulgarian influence. By 1902, VMRO was divided into two opposing factions: a right wing favoring union with independent Bulgaria and a left wing preferring Macedonian autonomy within a Balkan federation. We have already seen that the original conspirators and founders of VMRO wanted the latter outcome. Fearing the success of the left, the Supremists (Bulgarians) sought to provoke reprisals by the Turks against Macedonian villages in order to facilitate eventual Bulgarian intervention. It may have been such a motive that precipitated the great uprising at such an inopportune time. With more than 30,000 men under arms in Macedonia, VMRO initiated the Ilinden uprising in Macedonia and the Preobrazhenie uprising in the Adrianople region.

Ilinden: the great uprising. The uprising most celebrated by Macedonians occurred in August 1903. This uprising was internationally recognized as an event of significance.

Early in 1903 there was a secret nationalist congress at which Supremist agents in VMRO persuaded the delegates of the need to organize an uprising in the district of Monastir (Bitola) during the summer of that year. Gotse Delcev was not at that meeting but seems to have gone along with the decision. He was killed by the Turks before the uprising. On St. Elijah's day, August 2, the rebellion began. There were only 30,000 rebels, and by then it was well known that the Turks had sent additional troops into Macedonia to create an army of 300,000. For ten days the insurgents held out at Krushevo, where they set up a democratic commune, the "Krushevo Republic." The rebellion throughout Macedonia lasted only two months before the inevitable Turkish victory. Great Britain, Serbia, and Greece were not prepared to consider the possibility of autonomy for the region. They were convinced that an autonomous Macedonia would simply be a transitional stage before the inevitable unification with Bulgaria. Even the Russians — co-religionists, Slavic speakers, previously defenders of the Bulgarians — did not come to their aid, and the revolution collapsed. The Turks took terrible revenge, slaughtering whole villages.

After the failed uprising, the Supremist faction gained almost complete control of VMRO. Describing the popular and political reactions in Great Britain, France, and the United States to the Macedonian rebellion of 1903, Todor Dobrijanov notes that it received wide Western coverage, especially in ethnic newspapers with a large circulation. Clearly by the middle of 1903 other newspapers of the world knew that there was a revolutionary movement in Macedonia. Dobrijanov also gives a short narrative of diplomatic events, including a description of Austro-Russian compromises concerning the Macedonian rebellion.[36] With the failure of the rebellion and the Turkish reprisals, thousands of Macedonians from the district of Monastir emigrated to Bulgaria, Serbia, and the United States.

Activities by armed groups supported by the Bulgarian, Serbian and Greek governments continued after this time on a smaller scale. Greek sources report only portions of this history, speaking for instance of the VMRO uprising as "Bulgarian" and saying the armed "Macedonian struggle began in 1904 until 1908."[37] We can see from the sources cited above that this is a misleading comment. It refers to Greek-supporting Macedonians and others taking actions in support of Greek political ambitions. It gives some indication of the involvement of forces supported by the Greek government, active in Macedonia before the Greeks invaded during the Balkan wars. This Greek government source says that "volunteers from the Free Greek State, from Crete, and other areas poured in" to Macedonia to support other groups already active there, groups sympathetic to the Greek cause.

The great Macedonian revolutionary heroes. There are many figures revered by Macedonians today as revolutionaries who fought bravely for the Macedonian cause. One of the greatest was Gotse Delcev, who was born 120 years ago in eastern Macedonia (what is now Aegean Macedonia). He was a teacher, and is significant for helping build a network of shadow governments, schools and other institutions in the rugged mountain area, known before World War II as Nevrokop, just to the east of the present-day border between Macedonia and Bulgaria. This work was a preparation for the day when revolutionaries would be able to drive out the Turks. Delcev was captured and executed even before the Ilinden rebellion in 1903, but his work has won him enduring respect amongst Macedonians. The memoirs of Lazar Tomov[38] recall Gotse Delcev and the time when Gotse was a school principal in Bansko, Pirin Macedonia, and organized the revolutionary struggle of that whole region. As Tomov explains, during the school year Gotse traveled to many places to form revolutionary committees. He visited Mehomia (Razlog), Belitsa, Godlevo, Draglishta, Dobarsko, Banya, Dobrinishte, Yakoruda, Eleshnitsa, and Bachevo as well as Gorna Dzhumaya (Blagoevgrad) and Nevrokop (Gotse Delcev). Delcev believed that people should read literature. His couriers carried not only letters, but also newspapers, pamphlets and books. Among these were the biographies of Vasil Levski and Hristo Botev, the novels of Luben Karavelov, the memoirs of Zahari Stojanov, the history of the Sredna Gora Uprising, and books about the French Revolution, and so on. Delcev was described as being like a whirlwind. "He traveled all over Macedonia to fill its people with his passion for freedom. His great spirit shone in his high goals. He was a noble person whose words were always followed by his courageous actions."

Another revolutionary hero was Damian Gruev, who was born in the village of Smilevo, Bitola.[39] While working in the Solun print shop of K.G. Samardjieff in 1893, Gruev met with fellow students from Sofia University, where he had studied history. The group discussed the liberation of Macedonia, which they had talked about when they were still in Sofia. Gruev persuaded Dr. Hristo Tatarchev of Resen to join the group as well as other Macedonians living in Solun at the time. Gruev was elected the first secretary and treasurer of the new revolutionary organization.

Dr. Hristo Tatarchev, a founder of the Internal Macedonian Revolutionary Organization (VMRO), was born in Resen in the present Republic of Macedonia, in 1869 to Nicolo and Katerina Tatarchev. His father was a well-to-do businessman and banker. His mother came from a distinguished family of Yankovets, Resen. After graduating from primary school in Resen, young Hristo was sent to study in the high schools of Bratsigovo and Plovdiv, Bulgaria. After that he studied medicine in Zurich and Berlin. He was working as a doctor in the Bulgarian High School for Boys and the Bulgarian High School for Girls in Salonika when he met Damian Gruev and other intellectuals from Macedonia. In 1893 he was elected as the president of the Central Committee of VMRO. In 1901 he was arrested and sent into exile in Podrum Kale, Turkish Anatolia. Upon his return, he was elected, together with Hristo Matov, as a representative of the Foreign Committee of the VMRO in Sofia. In 1908 he was a delegate at the Kuystendil convention of the VMRO. He returned to Macedonia in 1915 when the Bulgarians had control, but was forced again to leave in 1918, after the Serbian occupation. He settled in Turin, Italy, never to return to occupied Macedonia. He died in 1952 in Torino, Italy.

Nikola Karev was born in 1877 in Krushevo. He went to elementary school in his home town. Since his extremely poor parents couldn't afford to pay for his further education, they apprenticed him to a cabinet-maker's workshop. While working there, young Nikola lost the use of his left arm and left leg, which became paralyzed. He was sent to Sofia for treatment, but his left arm remained paralyzed, as well as some of his toes. At high school in Bitola, he joined the students' revolutionary preparedness circle and learned about the liberation movement. After finishing the fourth year of high school, Nikola had to give up his studies due to lack of money. He was then named primary school-teacher in the village of Gorno-divyatsi, Krushevo region, and at the same time began his revolutionary activities. He was soon chosen as the revolutionary leader of the village and several surrounding villages, and quickly became popular among the local people. By 1902, he was teaching in Krushevo and a member of the regional revolutionary leadership. While working as a teacher, he spent many nights touring the region with his village fighting bands. He was the primary organizer of the Krushevo region, preparing it for the Ilinden insurrection. He is said to have been a master at encouraging and maintaining a revolutionary spirit. During the Ilinden insurrection, he took an active part in all the actions leading up to the capture of Krushevo and the Krushevo area. He was elected the first president of the "Krushevo Republic," the first and possibly the shortest-lived socialist state in the world. After Ilinden, he was forced to escape to Bulgaria and spent most of his time in Sofia. He worked there as a cabinet-maker. On April 23, 1904, he crossed the border into Macedonia with his band and was returning to his home territory. A few days later on April 27, his men and those of Petar Atzeff arrived at the village of Raycheni, Kratovsko, where they were planning to rest briefly. However, they had been betrayed to the Turks. As they arrived, the village was surrounded by Turkish troops, who were soon joined by irregulars from neighboring Turkish villages. The battle began at seven in the morning and lasted till two-thirty in the afternoon. During the bloody engagement, 18 members of the two bands were killed, including Nikola Karev.

Macedonian emigres between the wars. In his published memoirs, Ivan Mihailoff, a Macedonian who was forced to leave Macedonia for the relative safety of Sofia, explains that after the First World War he began working with Todor Alexandroff for VMRO's Representatives Abroad.[40] He says that there were many emigres dedicated to the Macedonian Liberation Movement, and that revolutionaries from the Greek- or Serbian-occupied territories, who kept up the struggle within Macedonia, visited the Sofia office from time to time. They brought written information about the conditions of "our enslaved people," which Mihailoff sent to Bulgarian and foreign institutions. Mihailoff says that there were many students from Macedonia living in Sofia at that time, though they were politically divided. Mihailoff and some friends decided to establish a new group that was called at first the "Vardar" society. This group started publishing the magazine *Ilinden*, distributing it to Macedonian emigres. The founders hoped that the society would become a training laboratory for future leaders of the Macedonia liberation movement. Their goal was "a free and independent Macedonia." They said that they were working for "the interests of all the people of Macedonia, for people from all social levels, groups and nationalities." Their political goal was the founding of "a Macedonian state, free and independent of all Balkan countries." Most of the leaders and many members of the Vardar organization (or "Shar" as it was later called) were executed by the Bulgarian communists in 1944.

The Macedonian Orthodox Church and the Development of a Macedonian National Consciousness

At the beginning of the Christian era in Macedonia, the cultural Christian center of Macedonia and of the Balkan peninsula in general was Salonika with its archbishopric. However, the Emperor Justinian (527–565) established the Illyrian archbishopric in western Macedonia, near present-day Skopje, as an autonomous unit. This church organization, called Prima Justiniana, had an authority equal to that of the Constantinople patriarchate. The whole of the Balkan peninsula was subordinate to it. Later Justinian decreed that the archbishop should be ordained by his own synod, with rights equal to those of the Roman Pope.[41]

Later, the most important center of the Christian national culture of Macedonia became the town of Ohrid, with its famous archbishopric of Ohrid, restored upon the ruins of the Justiniana by the Slavic Macedonian emperor, Samuil. This archbishopric was accorded the same rights as the Prima Justiniana. As a center of arts, letters and learning in general, the archbishopric took a significant role in defining and in defending a uniquely Macedonian Slav culture during the period from 995 to 1767. At the end of this period, the archbishopric was abolished by a decree of the sultan (the Ottoman Turkish ruler), at the urging of the Greek church leaders in Istanbul, and was placed under the jurisdiction of the patriarch of Constantinople. This development was seen by the Macedonian church as part of an effort by Hellenist church forces to extend their control over the Macedonian church. Only Greeks were appointed bishops and other senior officials; the schools were turned Greek; and the Slavic services were replaced by Greek ones.[42] Even today, based on this decree of the eighteenth century, the Macedonian area of northern Greece is, in theory, under the authority of the ecumenical patriarch, not under the Greek Orthodox Church.

The Greek church (patriarchate) in Constantinople was seen as an instrument of Turkish oppression in Bulgaria and Macedonia and in the southern Balkan peninsula. George Finlay explains that in Greece, "the two earliest institutions tending to national centralization after the Othoman conquest — the patriarchate of Constantinople and the official dragomans — were employed by the Sultan's government as instruments for enslaving the Greeks."[43]

The suppression of Christian Slavic interests gave rise to resistance by Slavs in the whole area of authority of the former Macedonian church, including Bulgaria. This struggle of Slavism against Hellenism led to the Bulgarians establishing their autonomous church (exarchate) in 1870. Many Macedonians joined this church since the Bulgarians were allowed to found churches and schools throughout Macedonia. The Macedonians really had little option. They chose the next best thing to their own church. At least they could use their own language in this church and educate their children in their own language in church schools. In doing so they were left open to the influence of the Bulgarian government, which used the exarchate to further its own political ambitions in Macedonia.

During the nineteenth century, the lower clergy in Macedonia, often of Slavic background, tended towards sympathy with local interests and suspicion of the Greek upper clergy. They played a primary role in the diffusion of Slavic consciousness among the Macedonian Slavs.[44] The Bulgarian church became the focus of opposition to the Turks and to their instrument, the Greek church. Some Bulgarians and Bulgarianized Macedonians used the exarchate and the schools to foster Bulgarian national consciousness among the Slavs of Macedonia and Old Serbia. After 1878, and especially after 1890, there was a war of churches — Bulgarian, Serbian, and Romanian — in Macedonia. In particular the Bulgarian church and the patriarchate competed to gain adherents. New Bulgarian schools and Bulgarian churches were set up everywhere. Armed bands were formed on both sides, supposedly to prevent the use of force by the other.[45]

For most of the early part of the twentieth century, the Macedonian Orthodox Church was placed under the authority of the Serbian church. During World War II, the Macedonian church supported aspirations towards a united Macedonia. The very first modern assembly of the Macedonian Orthodox clergy was held near Ohrid in 1943. This meeting was influenced by, and in turn fostered, a Macedonian national identity.[46] After the liberation from the Nazis, an independent Macedonian Orthodox Church was proclaimed under the leadership of the archbishop of Ohrid and Macedonia. After that the Serbian and Macedonian churches were at loggerheads.[47] In 1958, the Serbian church, no doubt under pressure from Tito, declared the Macedonian church to be independent. However, in recent times, since Macedonia's political independence, the Serbian church has been seeking to restore its control over the Macedonian church. The Macedonian church sees these efforts, supported by other orthodox churches, as closely connected to the Serbian government agenda.

Since the Republic of Macedonia became independent in 1991, the struggle between the Macedonian Orthodox Church and the Serbian Orthodox Church has continued, often with the support of the secular governments. In November 1993, the Yugoslav government Committee for Relations with Religious Associations accused Macedonian authorities of "roughly breaking civil rights and religious liberties by preventing Serbian church officials, the bishops Anatase and Pahomie, from crossing into Macedonia."[48] The Macedonians were very suspicious of Serbian efforts to interfere in Macedonian affairs in the lead-up to the national census and the national elections, both held in the latter part of 1994. They were prepared to permit the Serbian bishops to enter Macedonia as private citizens, but not as Serbian church officials wearing their formal robes.

Recently, Archbishop Mihail, the newly elected head of the Macedonian Orthodox Church (MOC), archbishop of Ohrid and Macedonia, stated that the Macedonian Orthodox Church wanted to cooperate with the neighboring Serbian, Bulgarian and Greek churches. The archbishop hoped, in particular, for understanding from the influential Russian Orthodox Church, though he saw it as "still under the influence of the misinformation of these, our neighboring churches."[49] He hoped "that we will find understanding after we give our true information about the restoration of the autocephaly of the Ohrid archbishopric and the activities of our dear Macedonian Orthodox Church... The Macedonians are an ancient nation, we are an ancient church, we did not create a church, we renewed our illegally abolished Ohrid Archbishopric."

After presenting historic assertions as to the relations with the Serbian Orthodox Church (SOC) and recent discussions with them, Archbishop Mihail pointed out that the SOC was acting in the interests of the Serbian government. They had asked for the Macedonian church "to regress to the former status as a part of the Serbian Orthodox Church," but there was no way that the MOC could go back to that situation. In fact, Archbishop Mihail argued, historically the Serbian church was under the authority of the Macedonian church for many centuries, so the MOC could be seen as the mother church. In any case, "the politics and church in Serbia are oriented toward non-recognition of our state, and of course, [non-recognition of] the autocephaly of our Macedonian Orthodox Church. In modern times the Serbian, Greek and Bulgarian churches in Macedonia have acted as advocates of the ideals of a great Serbia, a great Greece, and great Bulgaria." By contrast, Archbishop Mihail said, officials of the Vatican, including the Pope himself, had been most understanding of the Macedonian position. While the MOC was not under Vatican influence, it was true that the attitude of the Serb, Bulgarians and Greek churches was such that they were forcing the MOC to turn to the Vatican.

At its June 1994 session, the Holy Synod of the Macedonian Orthodox Church expressed concern about Serbian church attitudes[50] and rejected Serbian efforts to regain the authority they had relinquished in 1958 since the Serbian churches' regulations had ceased to be valid for the Macedonian church. The synod affirmed that "the autocephalous status of the Macedonian church and the interests of the Macedonian people and state are holy and inalienable values, which it has no intention of ever giving up."

Post–World War II Macedonia

Until the Second World War, the official view of the Yugoslav state was that the Slavs of Macedonia did not constitute a distinct ethnic or national group, but were all "South Serbs." This denial of Macedonian ethnicity occurred in all of the states, Serbia (Yugoslavia), Greece, Bulgaria and Albania, that had shared in the division of greater Macedonia in 1913. In all of these states dissent was crushed by harassment, imprisonment and often torture of "autonomists". All the occupying states attempted to eliminate signs of a distinct Macedonian culture or language. We have seen some of these efforts, especially with regard to Aegean Macedonia, in an earlier chapter.

We have already seen that the intention of the founders of VMRO was to create an autonomous Macedonian state, separate from Bulgaria, and with significantly reduced Turkish control. As will become clear when the issue of language is discussed in more detail, at the time of the founding of the revolutionary movement there were other voices speaking out in favor of a distinct Macedonian language. It is highly likely that the intellectual arguments pressed in favor of these ideas were familiar to the instigators of the VMRO. Nonetheless, there remained significant political sympathy with Bulgaria. That sympathy was probably affected negatively by the Bulgarian occupation of Macedonia in both world wars. The Bulgarian police who exercised control were inevitably seen as outsiders. The forced use of Bulgarian words in official documents and in schools and of the Bulgarian form of names was resented as much as the Serbian versions before. During the Second World War in particular, the enmity between Bulgarians and Macedonians grew. It was often Bulgarian police who, in their search for information, arrested and tortured the wives and families of Macedonian partisans fighting the Bulgarian and German forces. The degree of organization and strength of the partisans was itself a factor in effectively defining the Bulgarians as the enemy from outside. By the end of World War II, the Bulgarians' own efforts had effectively killed off their own prospects of unifying Macedonians with Bulgaria. In the immediate post-war period, flushed with socialist ideology, the Bulgarian socialist party recognized the nationalist aspirations of the Macedonians and their right to a distinct language and political independence. The Bulgarians soon reverted to their previous position, but their brief support at a crucial time probably helped the Macedonians, who were for the first time in a thousand years given some autonomy, this time within the Yugoslav federation.

The Slavic-speaking inhabitants of Macedonia had by now come to a stage in their national development when it was no longer possible to think of identification with either Serbs or Bulgarians.[51] During World War II Germany and its allies had invaded Yugoslavia and split it up between themselves. As we have already noted, Bulgarian forces took over much of Macedonia. The rest of the country was partitioned among the Germans, Hungarians and Italians.[52] The Croat fascist puppet state that was supported by Italy savagely suppressed Serbian resistance. The forces of Marshal Tito, himself a Croatian, fought against the fascist invaders throughout Yugoslavia. Within Macedonia an independent resistance movement was established against Bulgarian rule. The Antifascist Assembly of the People's Liberation of Macedonia (ASNOM, for Antifasisticko sobranie na narodnoto osloboduvanje na Makedonija) fought on the side of Tito. In August 1944, while the Allies worked with the various Yugoslav leaders who had emerged during the war, ASNOM formed an independent sovereign state called the Republic of Macedonia. By 1945, however, the government of Yugoslavia was formed with Tito as premier, and the various parts of Yugoslavia, including Macedonia, were reconciled into one country.[53] Tito's government was the first to recognize Macedonians as a distinct ethnic and political entity. When the Federal People's Republic of Yugoslavia was proclaimed in 1946, Macedonia officially became one of the country's six constituent republics. This new Yugoslavia was the first state in which Macedonians had been a distinct part. With central government support Macedonians were able to reestablish their own independent Orthodox church, and a Macedonian standard language was formally established. In 1945 Macedonian was internationally recognized as a literary and linguistic language.

The political motivation for the recognition of the People's Republic of Macedonia by Tito and the Communist party of Yugoslavia was no doubt pragmatic to a degree, since Macedonian national consciousness had been shown to be a powerful force that might be difficult to suppress. An increasingly progressive policy of the Yugoslav Communist party toward the "Macedonian Question" before the war — the result of the party's attempts to establish an anti-fascist people's front — had resulted in the strengthening of the Communist party in Macedonia.[54] However, the Macedonian anti-fascist alliance was not established as a Communist organization. The Macedonian uprising against the fascist occupation forces began on October 11, 1941, when the first partisan units in Prilep and Kumanovo made their first attacks. The Anti-fascist Council for the Liberation of Macedonia held its first session on August 2, 1942, but the formation of the Macedonian Communist party did not occur till 1943.[55] The Central Committee's first session in 1943 affirmed the Macedonian Communist party's adherence to the Yugoslav Communist party's revolutionary policy; its goals were the defeat of fascism in Macedonia, Macedonian national and social revolution, and the formation of a Macedonian federal state within a Yugoslav federation. Thus its expressed ideals at that time, necessary because of perceptions of popular demands, were for Macedonian liberation. Between 1943 and 1945, the Anti-Fascist Council for the National Liberation of Macedonia followed a program, with much popular support, that aimed for the expulsion of foreign occupiers of Macedonia and the creation of an autonomous Macedonian state, maintaining Macedonian culture.[56] Given this history and the very large number of fighting men put in the field by Macedonia, it would have been virtually impossible for Tito to do anything but seek to bring Macedonia into a federation. Recognition also served to de-legitimate both Serbian and Bulgarian claims to the area.[57]

In May 1995, a Macedonian delegation, led by president Kiro Gligorov, took part in celebrations in Paris, London and Moscow to mark the fiftieth anniversary of the end of the Second World War and victory over fascism in Europe. On that occasion, President Gligorov said, "During the Second World War, Macedonia had an army of 100,000 people, and 24,000 Macedonians gave their lives in that war. Not one allied soldier died on our territory, demonstrating that we liberated ourselves. On the other hand, I'd like to note that the Macedonian corps entered Zagreb and took part in the final operations, starting from the Srem front. Our units reached as far as the Austrian border." President Gligorov made the point that the inclusion of Macedonia, as an equal participant, in the fight against fascism contradicts claims that Macedonia was inaugurated by Tito. The character of this participation in the family of countries that fought against fascism indicates that Macedonia's fight was not an accident, that it occurred in continuity with other liberation battles fought in Macedonia before that time.[58]

Another Macedonian commentary about those times is more critical of the

Communist role in the Macedonian independence movement and tends to reinforce the idea that Tito allowed the Macedonians autonomy because he had to, but that he needed to somehow rein in Macedonian aspirations once the state was a part of Yugoslavia. The newspaper *Delo* wrote that "the Macedonian people joined the Communist partisan forces mainly because they were made to believe that the war was fought for the independence of Macedonia. While the Communist Party declared VMRO ideas and goals as its own ideals during the war, it suddenly dissociated itself from VMRO in the post-war period. The Communist Party of Macedonia joined the Yugoslav federation. Obeying directives from Belgrade, they declared all living (and deceased) independence-seekers to be pro–Bulgarian enemies of the federation. They imprisoned people expressing ideas of Macedonian independence. This attitude lasted as long as the former Yugoslavia."[59]

The current Macedonian position. A significant minority of people who live in Macedonia would like to see the restoration of a Greater Macedonia in the form that it took before 1913. They would like to actively participate in the liberation of the "occupied" portions of Macedonia. In the first free elections in 1991 about a third of Macedonian voters supported the political party advocating such action. The majority of Macedonians voted for political parties opposed to such views, some of whom came to form the governing alliance group. Kiro Gligorov, the first (and continuing) president of the Republic of Macedonia, has publicly acknowledged the inviolability of the Bulgarian, Greek and Albanian borders and has explicitly renounced any territorial claims against the three countries. He has attempted to explain Macedonia's concern about the welfare of people with a Macedonian ethnic consciousness in other parts of the world, including especially Bulgaria and Greece.

Some extreme Macedonian nationalists hold to the theory that the modern Macedonians are ethnically descended from the ancient Macedonians. Some of these deny that they are Slavs and claim to be the direct descendants of Alexander the Great and the ancient Macedonians.[60] They maintain that the connection with Slavic culture is explained by the fact that the Slavs adopted the language of the Macedonians. Others, taking a line that is historically more plausible, argue that the Slavs who came to Macedonia in the sixth century were simply Paeonians, former participants in the Macedonian kingdom of Alexander the Great, forced to leave Paeonia in the second century B.C. and now returning to their ancestral lands. President Gligorov presents a more moderate position, accepting that modern Macedonians have no relation to Alexander the Great, but are a Slavic people whose ancestors arrived in Macedonia in the sixth century A.D. Gligorov makes the point that the new peoples of Macedonia have their own proud history and have developed their own distinct language.

Though conscious of the strong Slav influence in their history, Macedonians within the Republic of Macedonia and in other countries of the world generally reject the label "Slav-Macedonian." They argue that such labels are not applied to Russians, Poles or the many other nations with a significant Slavic history; besides, the term is very close to the label "Slavophone" that the Greeks use to describe Greek citizens who speak what they prefer to call a Slavic dialect. Slavko Mangovski says he refuses to be labeled Slav by anyone.[61] He says he is not Slav but Macedonian. Although the language is undoubtedly Slavic, he says that this does not determine his ethnicity. He argues that ideas that Macedonians who claim to be Slavs are racist since they ignore the fact that through the ages different peoples lived and intermarried in the territory of Macedonia, and the product of this mixing is the modern Macedonians.

Macedonian president Gligorov, speaking in front of the French Institute for International Relations on the subject "Macedonia and the New Europe," said that a people's right to a name is a natural and an inalienable one.[62] He said that the Macedonian people came to the Balkans in the sixth and seventh century A.D. and are of Slavic origin. They have their own authentic culture, language and history. He explained that it was on Macedonian territory that the first Slavic letters and literature were born, and it was there also that the Slavs were first converted to Christianity. That, he said, is why the Macedonians "do not have to identify ourselves with the culture and civilization of other peoples, nor with their contemporary achievements."

Speaking in Sofia on November 7, 1993, Mr. Gligorov softened a claim made previously at the United Nations that the Macedonian nation gave the Slavs the Cyrillic script and Christianity, a statement which caused dissatisfaction in Bulgaria. He now said that the Slav script and Christianity originated from "these territories." He added that Cyril and Methodius as well as the first Slavs baptized somewhere around Stip were from "this region." He went on to say, "This does not mean that they are not yours as well. Even in the Constitution of Slovakia it is said that she is a Slav Republic of Cyril and Methodius... Christianity departed from here to Moravia and to Russia."[63]

Who Has a Macedonian National Identity?

Loring Danforth uses the term Macedonian to refer to Slavic-speaking people with a "Macedonian national identity" regardless of their country of origin. From this perspective (although Danforth does not put it quite this way), there can be several kinds of Macedonians: those who are citizens of the Republic of Macedonia, or those who are citizens of Greece, Bulgaria, Albania, the United States, Canada, Australia, and so on. Of course this categorization ignores the Macedonian citizens of a different ethnicity living within Macedonia (e.g. Albanians, Vlachs, Gypsies, Turks, Serbs) who may have some loyalty to the state in which they live. In terms of the current Greek-Macedonian dispute we might think of another dichotomy of Macedonians: on the one hand those citizens of Macedonia who live, or who could live, in the new Republic of Macedonia; and on the other hand Macedonians who are Greek citizens, many of whom live in Aegean Macedonia. I say "many" here since estimates of the numbers of these people in Aegean Macedonia range from around 20,000 (Greek sources) through 300,000 (international sources), to about one million (Macedonian sources). If we take the middle estimate to be most likely, then Aegean Macedonians with Greek or some other citizenship are at least as numerous in the United States, Canada and Australia particularly as they are in Greece. This leaves us, at a fairly conservative estimate, with around two and a quarter million Macedonians in the Balkans: a little less than one and a half million (Slavic) Macedonian people in the Republic of Macedonia; about a quarter of a million in Aegean (Greek) Macedonia; and perhaps 600,000 in Bulgaria, mostly in Pirin Macedonia. Overseas there are probably a little more than 500,000 Macedonians: about 250,000 from Vardar or Pirin Macedonia and 300,000 from Aegean Macedonia, in the United States, Canada and Australia. An obvious deficiency of this kind of classification is that it ignores around 30 percent of the population of the Republic of Macedonia — Albanians, Turks, Gypsies and Vlachs in particular.

In November 1994 a conference on "Macedonia — Next Balkan Tragedy or Model of Multi-culturalism," sponsored by the Forum against Ethnic Violence, was held in London. This was a gathering of experts from non-governmental organizations from a number of European countries and the United States, many of whom held opposing views. Professor John Olcock from the University of Bradford explained the historic process of the Macedonian national awareness and the creation of a Macedonian ethnic identity, under conditions of permanent usurpations and suppression. He argued that the common use of the Macedonian language was the strongest evidence of the existence of a Macedonian identity.[64] The role of language in the shaping of a national consciousness will be examined in a later chapter.

Loring Danforth argues that from an anthropological perspective the relatively recent date of the creation of a Macedonian state and the construction of a Macedonian nation does not mean, as Greek nationalists claim, that the Macedonian nation is "artificial," while the Greek nation is "genuine." Danforth takes the Greek government historian Kofos to task for what he sees as a misuse of earlier theory about the nature of national identity in his support of the Greek cause. Kofos claims that Macedonian national identity is only "imagined" (using Anderson's terminology), while Greek national identity is "real."[65] Danforth argues that both Macedonian national identity and Greek national identity are equally constructed.

A central problem Danforth sees in the dispute between Greeks and Macedonians is that two different national identities and cultures are being constructed from the same raw materials, from the same set of powerful national symbols. Danforth argues that while territory must be the mutually exclusive possession of one state or another — a particular village can be located only in Greece or in the Republic of Macedonia — not only can two cultures coexist in one place, but two different peoples with two different nationalities can share the same name. Thus he says there can be two kinds of Macedonians, Greek and non–Greek. Similarly, there can be a Macedonia which is an independent country and a Macedonia which is a region in another country. He concedes that such a solution may create some confusion, but believes it is preferable to denying Macedonians who are not Greeks the right to identify themselves as Macedonians. He sees the alternative position, the denial of the existence of a Macedonian nation and a Macedonian minority in Greece, as a kind of symbolic ethnic cleansing that could lead to the kind of active ethnic cleansing of which the Serbs have been accused in Bosnia.

Citizenship of the new Macedonian Republic. The Republic of Macedonia has established procedures for Macedonians living outside the Republic of Macedonia to formally gain recognition of citizenship. The law on citizenship treats as Macedonian citizens people of "Macedonian origin" who live in Bulgaria, Greece and Albania. To gain Macedonian citizenship such people have to demonstrate their recent family history and present a birth certificate, and possibly birth or death certificates of the parents. Other Macedonians living abroad need a little more evidence. They have to show a birth certificate, a citizenship certificate of one of the parents (or birth certificate of one of the parents and detailed information about their grandparents, or a death certificate of the latter). Macedonians now living in some part of the former Yugoslavia and originating from the Aegean part of Macedonia are automatically treated as Macedonian citizens, provided they have had a Yugoslavian citizenship. The children from marriages between Macedonian citizens and others also have a right to a Macedonian citizenship.

The Global Conflict Over Macedonia

Danforth makes the point that the present phase of the Macedonian question is taking place in many different parts of the world, not merely in the Balkans. This extends our understanding of national identity, since here we see national communities being constructed trans-nationally. We can observe the construction of trans-national communities in which homelands and diasporas are linked through a complex network of "global cultural flows" of people, information, money and images that have been made possible by the ease of international travel, new satellite telecommunications networks, fax machines, international electronic mail, and the video camera.[66] The trans-national dimensions of the conflict between Greeks and Macedonians can be seen in Greek references to "Greece of the Five Continents" and in descriptions by Greeks of the diaspora as "the most powerful weapon" in the arsenal of "World

Hellenism." Mike Featherstone speaks of a "global cultural war" between Greeks and Macedonians over which group has the right to identify itself as Macedonian.[67] This struggle includes the Greek and Macedonian diaspora communities in Europe, the United States, Canada and Australia. Danforth notes the concerted efforts of the different Balkan communities in various parts of the world. Political demonstrations in 1990–91 in Greece, the Republic of Macedonia, western Europe, Canada and Australia; international conferences sponsored by Greek organizations like the Australian Institute of Macedonian Studies in Melbourne in 1988 and the Pan-Macedonian Association in Thessaloniki and New York in 1989; and the lobbying efforts of Macedonian groups such as the Macedonian Information and Liaison Service in Brussels, the International Macedonian Lobby and the Macedonian World Congress are all a part of this international battle.

Macedonians and Greeks in North America. The Macedonian Patriotic Organization (MPO) has been established in North America since 1922. Its founders were "the freedom fighters of Ilinden, who were forced out of their motherland Macedonia by the exceedingly harsh new political, cultural, religious, economic and national enslavement initiated by the 1913 Treaty of Bucharest." The MPO's newspaper, *The Macedonian Tribune*, established in 1927, is published bi-weekly by the Central Committee of the MPO, in English and the old-script Bulgarian. It is circulated around the world.[68] It is said to be the oldest active Macedonian newspaper in the world. As well as being the voice of the MPO, it presents the views of the Macedono-Bulgarian Orthodox Churches of the United States and Canada. During most of its existence the *Macedonian Tribune* has been banned in Greece, Yugoslavia and Bulgaria.

In an article in *The Macedonian Tribune* early in 1994, Ivan A. Lebamov, president of the MPO, described something of the organization's history and purpose. He explained that the MPO was organized to work for a free and independent Macedonia — a Switzerland of the Balkans. In 1922, the first delegates met in Fort Wayne, Indiana. By the constitution of the MPO "the Macedonian Immigrants of the United States and Canada, as well as their descendants, regardless of nationality, religion, sex or convictions, realizing the necessity of joint organized activity for the liberation of Macedonia, formed the Macedonian Patriotic Organization with the slogan 'Macedonia for the Macedonians.'" The aim of the MPO is "to strive in a legal manner for the establishment of Macedonia as an independent state unit within her historic and geographic boundaries, which should constitutionally guarantee the ethic, religious, cultural and political rights and liberties for all citizens."

Lebamov claims that the MPO has been called the flagship of the Macedonian Liberation Movement. He says it was called the successor to VMRO by Dr. Tatarchev, a founder of VMRO, and that it has been recognized in the United States, Canada and Europe as the most dedicated and accurate historian of the Macedonian question for more than seventy years. During this period it has kept the Macedonian question alive through its petitions to governments, the League of Nations and the United Nations. When doors were closed by totalitarian Greek regimes, Tito's followers, even the Zveno, the MPO never wavered and never lost hope in its mission, Lebamov says.

This level of lobbying required donations and fund-raising from North American Macedonians. With respect to American recognition of Macedonia, Lebamov says "there were many trips to Washington, thousands of letters, hundreds of faxes and tons of paper used by *The Macedonian Tribune*" to further their cause. Recognition by the United States did not just happen, he says. The MPO helped make it happen. The MPO proved to the United States and many other countries that the recognition of Macedonia was in their own best interest. They worked with senators, congressmen and generals; they talked to politicians, statesmen and world leaders. They networked with Macedonian groups in the United States, Canada and the world. They talked with Albanians, Bosnians and democratic Croatians. The MPO has urged the leadership of the Republic of Macedonia to follow the example of Israel and to start a program of "Bonds for Macedonia." This would give Macedonians in the diaspora an opportunity to invest in the republic, giving it the hard currency necessary for growth and progress.

Delegates to the seventy-second Annual Convention of the MPO held in Toronto, Ontario, Canada, September 3–6, 1993, wrote an open letter that called for all Macedonians to work together so the Republic of Macedonia could flourish with ethnic, religious, cultural and political rights and liberties guaranteed for all. The MPO of the United States, Canada, Australia, Belgium and Brazil appealed to all Macedonians to respond to the needs of the new republic, whether these be medical, financial, political or cultural. All people from Macedonia were urged to support the Republic of Macedonia and democracy by writing letters urging recognition, and by providing financial and moral support to those still in Macedonia.

Delegates attended the convention from many parts of the United States and Canada, and from other countries of the world. There were delegates from 15 MPO chapters: MPO "Victory" from East York; MPO "Pelister" from Akron; MPO "Rodina" from northwest Indiana; MPO "Luben Dimtroff" from Toronto; MPO "Solun" from Springfield; MPO "Fatherland" from Detroit; MPO "Strumishkata Petorka" from Newark; MPO "Vardar" from Cleveland; MPO "Justice"— from Toronto; MPO "Damian Grueff" from Indianapolis; MPO "Balkanski Mir" from Lansing; and MPO "Kostur" from Fort Wayne. From other countries there was MPO "Todor Alexandroff" from Australia; MPO "Strumishkata Petorka" from Sao Paolo, Brazil; and MPO "Todor Alexandroff" from Belgium.

To commemorate the one-hundredth anniversary of the founding of the VMRO, the MPO invited several guests from Europe to the seventy-second convention. The names and history of these special guests shows us the links that the MPO has maintained with VMRO figures. They also show us the Bulgarian sympathies of the MPO. This is not to suggest that at the present time the MPO is in favor of a union of Macedonia with Bulgaria, but it is probably fair to say that the distancing from Bulgaria that has happened in Macedonia is not reflected in the attitudes of the MPO in North America and elsewhere. George Kenney, Robert Kaplan and Janusz Bugajski gave lectures about the Republic of Macedonia and the role of the diaspora in working for Macedonia's future. Each speaker encouraged the *Macedonian Tribune* to stop using the map of "Greater Macedonia" showing the three parts of divided Macedonia. Each discussed the need to work with the Macedonian government in its bid for recognition of the republic.

According to the MPO, the Ilinden flag carried by the Ilinden revolutionaries was made in 1903 by Masa Grancharova at Zagorichani, Kostur. After the Ilinden uprising failed, the flag was hidden from the Turkish and Greek authorities. After many years, it found its way to Ivan Mihailoff, who presented it for safekeeping to Metodi Chaneff of Canton, Ohio, a past president of the MPO Central Committee. The flag was repaired by Mrs. Jivko (Stephanka) Nickoloff of Canton, and passed into the care of Blaze Markoff of Toronto, a past vice-president of the MPO Central Committee, then to Dr. Asparuh Isakov of Clarks Summit, Pennsylvania, another past president of the MPO Central Committee, and finally to the Central Committee of the MPO for permanent safekeeping and display at conventions and in the MPO museum.

Basil Gounaris investigated Macedonian emigration to the United States in the 1910s, focusing on previous emigration trends, socioeconomic and political conditions that contributed to emigration, and the ramifications of continued emigration for the remaining population.[69] An entry titled "Macedonians in America" in the *Harvard Encyclopedia of American Ethnic Groups* (1980) describes Macedonian immigration to the United States between 1920 and 1980. Mihajlo Minoski's book *USA and Macedonia*, dealing with bilateral relations of the two countries between 1986 and 1991, was released in Skopje in May 1994 and provides an exhaustive listing of involvements at governmental and non-governmental levels. Further comment about United States attitudes to Macedonia and interactions with Macedonia over recent years is given in a later chapter.

Even at the state level, Macedonia has received attention in North America. According to journalist Virginia Nizamoff Surso, the state of Ohio, under the guidance of Governor George Voinovich, apparently at no expense to taxpayers, recently sent $10 million in medicine and medical equipment to the Republic of Macedonia.[70] Three rooms full of x-ray equipment were included in the shipment. According to Governor Voinovich's special assistant for multicultural affairs, August B. Pust, who coordinates activities with more than 50 ethnic groups, Macedonians throughout Ohio collected information about the whereabouts of unused medicines and medical equipment that medical facilities were happy to donate to a worthy cause. In all, 28 tons of supplies were shipped via Thessaloniki. Macedonian President Kiro Gligorov wrote a special thank-you to Governor Voinovich and invited him to visit Macedonia.

Macedonia is not the only former Yugoslav territory to receive help from Ohio. Shipments of similar supplies were planned for Slovenia and Slovakia, and other shipments had already gone to Croatia, Slovenia and Slovakia. Governor Voinovich believes that the friendships these shipments develop will lead to good international business and trade between Ohio and the recipients of the goods.

Various public protests have been made by Macedonian groups in the aftermath of Macedonia's efforts to gain international recognition, and the Greek economic blockade that followed recognition by the United States. An article in the *Toronto Star*[71] in March 1994 described a rally by about 2,000 Macedonians against the Greek economic blockade of the Republic of Macedonia. The Macedonians came from southern Ontario and from Buffalo, New York, to condemn the Greek government. They urged Premier Chretien to recognize the Republic of Macedonia as an independent state, following the lead of many other countries, including the United States. Speakers also asked for support for the basic human rights of Macedonians in Greek Macedonia, including their right to use their own language without fear of persecution. The United Macedonians Organization of Canada made the point that the blockade could cause the Balkans to explode into a greater regional war. Christine Repas, 50, said to Royson James that she joined the protest because she remembers her mother being slapped by a Greek police officer for speaking Macedonian. Chris Paliere, president of a Macedonian senior citizens group, told the reporter that Macedonians have nothing to celebrate on Greek independence day because there has been a "brutalization of human rights of Macedonians for every year since 1913."

Among well-known Canadian Macedonians is the Bitove family, who has been prominent in Canadian political and financial circles.

The Macedonian Canadian News is a 16-page English-language monthly newspaper distributed throughout North America.[72] Its editorial policy is to fight for the recognition of Macedonia and the Macedonian language. The paper has news from Macedonia, book reviews, people profiles, recipes, a calendar of events and a rather wry personal advice column.

In the United States a powerful Greek-American lobby has made its presence known. In the years between 1988 and 1992 public presentations of the Greek view about Aegean Macedonia increased in frequency in the United States, culminating in a very expensive publicity campaign during 1992. Various Hellenic organizations in the United States attempted to bring pressure to bear on their elected representatives in order to foster their view. For instance, there were two full-page advertisements placed in the *New York Times* by a group called Americans for the Just Resolution of the Macedonian Issue. In the advertisement on Sunday, April 26, 1992, the headline read, "Macedonia, What's in a Name?" The rest of the ad consisted of an "Open Letter to President Bush," which began by saying that Greece, "the mother of democracy," had always stood beside the United States whenever wars were fought in defense of freedom and democracy. The letter argued that there were now threats to Greece to which America should be sensitive. It was stated that recognizing the "Republic of Skopje" as "Macedonia" would be "the height of ingratitude," making a mockery of "the terrible suffering inflicted on the Greek people." The letter went on to urge the president not to allow the "remnants of Communist expansionism" to create a source of conflict for decades to come. "We urge you not to discount the concerns of the Greek people and three million Greek-Americans who stand united on this issue," the letter said.

The second ad appeared two weeks later (Sunday, May 10). The heading this time said, "The Name 'Macedonia' is a Time Bomb! Mr President, You Can Defuse It." Again, Americans for the Just Resolution of the Macedonian Issue asked the president to let the world know that the United States would not recognize "Skopje" as the "Republic of Macedonia."

Early in 1993, the United States recognized Macedonia under the name "The Former Yugoslav Republic of Macedonia," but Greek organizations in the United States continued efforts to turn things back. Late in 1993, Andrew E. Manatos, a member of the executive committee of the board of a national Hellenic group (UHAC National) in Washington, D.C., sent a letter to Congressman Frank McCloskey with an accompanying "fact sheet," to urge that President Clinton rescind American recognition of the Republic of Macedonia. A resolution to Congress sought to push the president to hold off on relations with Macedonia until Skopje complied with all Greek demands. More will be said about the Greek-American lobby in a later chapter. At this point it might be noted that the lobby was successful in pressuring the American president to retreat from his decision to establish diplomatic relations with Macedonia early in 1994. Coincidentally with the American back-down, Greece hardened its attitude to Macedonia and applied a trade embargo that gravely threatened Macedonian stability. Macedonians believe that the visible presence of a Greek-American close to President Clinton explained the United States reticence in the face of the Greek economic embargo.

Greeks in Canada have supported the Greek nation from time to time. For instance, *The Toronto Star*[73] reported a protest march by 1,000 demonstrators against *The Star*'s editorial support for Macedonian independence. Chanting, "No more lies," "Get your facts straight," and "Macedonia is Greek," the protesters tore up and burned copies of the paper outside the newspaper office. In the same article, reporter Royson James noted that more than 40,000 Greek Canadians have signed petitions and sent them to MPs demanding that the government not establish diplomatic ties with Macedonia.

Macedonians and Greeks in Australia. In 1930, the first Macedonian clubs were established in Australia, the oldest being the club "Edinstvo" (Unity) in Perth. In 1946, the Macedonian-Australian Association was formed. This group, widely accepted among the Macedonian community, acted on behalf of the interests of the Macedonians in Australia and their better integration into Australian society. Over 50 newspapers, magazines and radio-hours are currently published or broadcast in the Macedonian language in Australia. There is a Slavonic Studies department, teaching Macedonian language and history, at the University of Macquarie in Sydney. In the past 30 years, 16 Macedonian churches and 2 monasteries have been built in Australia. The oldest church is "Sveti Gjorgji" (St. George) in Melbourne, established on May 27, 1956, as part of the Macedonian Orthodox Church.

According to published estimates in the Macedonian press, some 200,000 Macedonians live in Australia. Estimates by the Australian authorities put the numbers somewhere in the vicinity of 75,000. However, this official estimate does not take into account Aegean Macedonians, many of whom have Greek citizenship and who would be recognized by anthropologists as "Macedonian" because of their "Macedonian consciousness." In any case the official estimate must be considered suspect since Australian census data generally did not allow for ethnic or regional identification of immigrants from Yugoslavia.

The most recent Australian census (1991) indicated that there were a little more than 300,000 Greeks in the country, though a large proportion of these are probably Aegean Macedonians. These Greeks are organized in over 500 societies, sports clubs and scientific and cultural associations. There are many prominent Greek-Australian politicians and other Greek-Australians with a high public profile in the broader Australian community. The Labor party in particular was successful in getting Greeks into its ranks, and some of these reached senior public office. The previous federal minister for immigration and ethnic affairs, Mr. Nick Bolkus, for example, is a Greek-Australian. The most populous state, New South Wales, also had until recently an ethnic affairs minister of Greek extraction, Mr. Photios. Macedonian-Australians believe that objective decisions about their situation have not been possible from government ministers who have such visible relationships with the group that is antagonistic to the Macedonian cause.

Although the numerical disparity between those who would identify themselves as ethnic Macedonians and ethnic Greeks in Australia is probably not so large, various government bodies seem to have accepted the Greek claim that there are around 700,000 Greeks in the country and only about 70,000 Macedonians. As indicated above, the numbers are probably more like 300,000 and 200,000, respectively.

After the United States and Australia recognized the Former Yugoslav Republic of Macedonia early in 1994, Greeks throughout the world protested. In Australia they had a special impact. Leading opposition politicians were able to use the occasion to rally Greek support by criticizing the position of the federal government, which was said to have broken promises to the Greek community in Australia. There were demonstrations in Australia's largest cities by tens of thousands of Greeks (some carrying Serbian flags) against the recognition of Macedonia and against the federal government. Concurrent with these demonstrations were several acts of extreme violence against Macedonian properties. Less than a week after Australia recognized Macedonia under the name Former Yugoslav Republic of Macedonia (FYROM), the Macedonian church Sveta Nedela, in a Melbourne suburb, was set on fire. The same day, a Molotov cocktail was thrown at Sveti Dimitrija Church in another Melbourne suburb; there was a bomb explosion in the club Macedonian House in Melbourne; and the premier of the state, Geoff Kennet, said that "the ones responsible are most probably Greeks." There were more bombings and public violence over following weeks. Before long politicians from the government side were trying to turn the issue to their own benefit by attempting to show solidarity with the Greek view. The government attempted to mollify Greek critics by formally adopting the label "Slav Macedonian" for Macedonians from Vardar Macedonia (FYROM).

Thus, partly through violent action, even though this was not publicly condoned by Greek spokespersons, the Australian Greek community as a whole was remarkably successful in causing the federal government to treat the Macedonians with more severity than has been possible in any other western democracy. An interesting side issue is that this seems to be but one possible arena in which Greek national interests might be supported. Other issues in which Greek-Australian pressures have been applied might affect United States national interests more directly.

A leading conservative political commentator in Australia, B.A. Santamaria, offered an analysis of a paper entitled *The Role of the Greek Communities in the Formulation of Australian Foreign Policy, with Particular Reference to the Cyprus Problem,* delivered to the Institute of International Relations Conference on the Greek Diaspora in Foreign Policy in Athens in May 1990. This paper, prepared by Dr. Andrew Theophanous, a member of the governing Federal Labor party, and Michalis Stavrou Michael, discussed both the methods and the significance of what they call the "mobilization" of the Greek community in influencing the development of Australian government policy in relation to Greek national interests. Two issues discussed in the paper were the defense installation at Pine Gap, in which the United States has a vital interest, and the Cyprus issue. In the latter case pressure was brought to bear for Australia to act in the interests of the Greek and Greek-Cypriot governments against Turkey — a NATO member, a United States ally, and a country that has friendly relations with Australia.[74]

According to Santamaria, the extraordinary aspect of the Theophanous paper is that it did not hide the fact that the purpose of the "mobilization" of the Greek community was to impose the policies of a foreign power (Greece) on the Australian government, without any regard to Australian interests. Theophanous and his colleague wrote, "The test comes when the ethnic imperatives clash with other goals of foreign policy, and require the government to adjust its foreign policy stance" (p.7). The Pine Gap Issue "illustrates the impact of the Greek community on the Australian Government, mainly through its Greek MPs and its general capacity to mobilize for political purposes, including in the area of foreign policy" (p.13). Santamaria took the view that in a democratic society demonstrations are to be tolerated, but violence (including bombing and arson) are not. He says that rewarding such violence gives an unfortunate message to other ethnic groups and encourages intelligence agencies of foreign governments to manipulate their own ethnic groups in Australia.

The Greek community in Australia is very aware of its power. Illias Rallis, a spokesman from the Greek community, stated,[75] "Greece is not a powerful country, but there are large Greek communities in countries like Australia. We have power. We can use it on behalf of Greece. This is what the diaspora should do." This very vividly supports Danforth's idea that the Greek and Macedonian diasporas represent a trans-national extension of the Balkan disagreements.

The Macedonian community in general has most often been on the defensive against Greek and Australian government actions. They have angrily rejected the label "Slav Macedonians" imposed on them by government agencies in the wake of the bombings, protesting that this is a Greek slogan of propaganda. They point out that no other country officially uses the term except Greece and that the offensive term does not adequately describe the ethnic mix or heritage of Macedonians. The Macedonian Council of Australia and the Aegean Macedonian Association of Australia emphasized in a press release that Australia was the only country, among 60 others that had recognized Macedonia at the time, that had imposed conditions on the recognition of the Republic of Macedonia, such as banning the displaying of Macedonian symbols and flags on the building of any Macedonian consulate. They claim that this represents a violation of Resolutions 817 and 845 of the United Nations, which provided for United Nations–sponsored mediation in the solving of the dispute between Macedonia and Greece.

Multiculturalism: an American idea. Multiculturalism is the concept of a Jewish-American philosopher named Horace Kallen, who in 1915 argued against the "melting pot" method of establishing a nation of immigrants.[76] He wrote, "Men may change their clothes, their politics, their wives, their religions, their philosophies: they cannot change their grandfathers, Jews or Poles or Anglo-Saxons. Jews or Poles or Anglo-Saxons, in order to cease being Jews or Poles or Anglo-Saxons would have to cease to be." Kallenism gained in strength in the United States in the 1970s, following the civil rights successes of African-Americans. Anglo-centrism became a target for attack. However, in the United States the vigorous demand for national loyalty seems to have modified the ways by which Greek-Americans seek to aid Greek national interests. With regard to the Greece-Macedonia dispute at least, a more or less normal democratic process seems in evidence in the American approach. Clearly that is not the case in Australia, given the level of violence, and the explicit description by Greek-Australians of strategies for furthering Greek national interests in the Australian context. If we come back to Danforth's ideas about the construction of trans-national national communities in which homelands and diasporas are linked, we might conclude that this process has flowered more completely in Australia than in North America.

The Flag of Macedonia

In 1991 Macedonia chose a flag based on the Star of Vergina, a symbol from the era of the ancient Macedonian kingdom. This symbol, a sun with sixteen rays, came to public awareness only after archaeological excavations in Aegean Macedonia in the twentieth century. It was adopted by Macedonians during the Second World War for use on battle flags. It was also used by Greeks who believed they had a special connection with ancient Macedonia. In recent times it became a particular focus of attention as the Greeks claimed exclusive use of the symbol. It actually appears on at least one other national flag (Uruguay), but the Greeks have been concerned about the flag of Macedonia. Mr. Gligorov, president of the Republic of Macedonia, says that the symbol has been used for centuries in Macedonian churches, but if true, this may simply be a coincidence.

It has been argued that since modern-day Greeks are not descended from ancient Greeks, "the Star of Vergina is not a Greek symbol, except in the sense that it happens to have been found on the territory of the present-day Greek state. The modern day Greeks appropriated ancient Greek cultural symbols because they happen to live in more or less the same part of the world as the ancient Greeks did."[77] It is widely recognized that "..national symbols are often modern creations which do not reflect the reality of the circumstances they purport to represent. Tradition can be invented. Modern Greece, for example, is a relatively new creation and bears little resemblance to the ancient Greece which is the source of much of its symbolism."[78] Thus we must consider the fact that national symbols are chosen by groups of people to make public statements about themselves. This is a normal phenomenon. It has no moral significance. In this case, the problem has arisen because two neighboring groups want to use the same symbol to tell the world something about themselves. They want to appeal to the same history.

As a consequence of the Greek embargo, Macedonia has been forced to back down on the issue of its flag, agreeing to change it by the terms of the

Interim Accord with Greece. Accordingly it abandoned the sun with sixteen rays and chose instead one with only eight. It is different enough so that the Greeks feel they have exclusive use of their chosen historical symbol.

However, some recent claims suggest all may not be what it seems in the matter of the Star of Vergina. Greek archeologist Liljana Suvaldzi claims to have discovered the tomb of Alexander the Great in Siva, Egypt. Archaeologists from Macedonia are visiting the site, paying particular attention to the tomb's symbol with an eight-ray sun on it. The notion that Greece and Macedonia are in a dispute over the "wrong" symbol has been raised.[79]

Perhaps coincidentally, an Italian-Macedonian research team of the International Federation of Research on Rock Art Organizations (IFRAO) recently discovered a stone carving of a Macedonian sun, about 3000 years old (at the end of the bronze and the beginning of the iron age), near Kratovo, in the Republic of Macedonia. The sun, carved with primitive tools, has eight rays and is in a square frame. The team, consisting of professor Dario Seglie, representative of IFRAO from Italy; Dr. Piero Ricchiardi, president of the Center of Study and Museum of Ancient Art of Pinerolo, Italy; Dr. Dushko Aleksovski, IFRAO representative for Macedonia; along with the representatives of the Italian Embassy in Skopje, Dr. Gianfranco Stillone and Gino Mucilli, claim this is an extremely important artistic work from ancient Macedonian culture. The discovery was described during IFRAO's congress in Torino, August 30–September 9, 1995. At the present, the carving is kept at the offices of the Italian Embassy in Skopje.

It is conceivable that the appearance of historical validation of a Macedonian eight-rayed sun has made it easier for Macedonia to abandon its original choice for a flag.

7. The Macedonian Language: The Mother of Written Slavic Languages?

The official Greek position is that there is no Macedonian language and never has been. The Greeks claim that the Macedonian language was invented in 1944 at the same time as the nationality "Macedonian" was created by Tito. They take the view that because the language spoken by the ancient Macedonians was Greek, the Slavic language spoken by the "Skopians" cannot be called "the Macedonian language." Official Greek writings refer to Macedonian as "the linguistic idiom of Skopje" and describe it as a corrupt and impoverished dialect of Bulgarian.[1] On the point about the relationship between Macedonian and Bulgarian, there is some agreement between the Greeks and the Bulgarians. The Bulgarians argue that the Macedonian language is really just a dialect of Bulgarian and it is the Bulgarian language that gave the world Slavic text.

Since Greece does not recognize Macedonian as a language it cannot be used officially in Greece. It is said that cases have been thrown out of Greek courts because some of the evidence was in the Macedonian language. One story in circulation amongst Macedonians holds that evidence in one case had to be translated from Macedonian to Croatian, then presented to the court; only then was the Greek court willing to permit translation into Greek.

As demonstrated in earlier chapters, Greek claims about a mid-twentieth century beginning for a Macedonian national consciousness are inconsistent with historical evidence. The same is true with regard to the language. Additionally, the Greek claim that there is no linguistic evidence that Macedonian is a distinct language and not just a dialect of Bulgarian, ignores the point, accepted without question by sociolinguists, that the decision as to whether a particular variety of speech constitutes a language or a dialect is always based on political rather than linguistic criteria[2] and that the only people who can make the choice are the ones who use the language. There are many instances in the world today of similar languages that are accepted as distinct by the international community. Organizations such as the United Nations have often been willing to accept that independent peoples of the world have the right to define their own language. At the present time we can see an acceleration of formal language development in nearby Croatia, Bosnia and Serbia, as all of these nations strive to distance themselves culturally from the others.

The Macedonian language is accepted by linguists everywhere in the world except in Serbia, Bulgaria and Greece.[3] It is recognized as a distinct language by various international authorities such as the *Encyclopaedia Britannica* and *The Cambridge Encyclopedia of Language*. It is one of the recognized 88 world languages, spoken by close to 1.5 million people in Macedonia, 250,000 people in Aegean Macedonia, 250,000 people in Pirin (Bulgarian) Macedonia, and around 500,000 people in other parts of the world, particularly North America and Australia.

Because the development of a standard language is marked by a political choice, it is conceivable that a new language could arrive on the world scene very rapidly. However, in a study of the development of Macedonian we see a lengthy growth process from its origins in common Slavic more than fifteen hundred years ago. Even the splitting of Bulgarian and Macedonian has been quite a long process. Evidence of this change has been available to the external observer for more than 120 years. Furthermore, since both nations and languages are perceived as "better" if they can trace back their pedigrees for many centuries, Macedonian nationalists seek to demonstrate that the Macedonian language has a history of over a thousand years, going back to the Old Church Slavonic language codified by Saints Cyril and Methodius in the ninth century.

Before describing some of the important stages in the development of a distinct Macedonian language, it may be useful to consider some more general issues about the role of language in a modern nation-state. The attitude towards a national language gives us additional information about the closely related issue of national consciousness.

Language, Nation-building, and Linguistic Nationalism

The terms *Abstand* and *Ausbau* have come to be used for languages that are, respectively, far enough apart that they are clearly different and mutual comprehension is not possible (like Serbian and Albanian or German and Hungarian) or mutually so similar that comprehension is usually easy across borders (like Danish and Norwegian, Macedonian and Bulgarian or Czech and Slovak).[4] The *Ausbau* languages are based on very similar speech patterns that have been codified as different standards for historical and political reasons. The process of codification helps separate one group from another, creating a sense of "them" and "us." In time, people become convinced that they are speaking the same language as other groups of people within their own nation and a different language from the people across the border.[5] Cross-border differences may in fact be much smaller than the people of neighboring nations believe.

One of the functions of language is to serve as a marker of nationality. With the rise of nationalism, a national language was considered evidence of the existence of a nation. Conversely, and except for the English-speaking nations, nations have generally felt impelled to have their own distinct "language." Furthermore the borders of such languages are imagined to coincide with national borders. This idea is more obviously realized in the case of *Abstand* languages. Where the differences between languages are small, other steps are necessary to affirm the separateness of national groups. These languages must be codified, a process that often takes deliberate advantage of existing differences between language usage in neighboring states. This is the process of developing a standard language. However, some preexisting support is required for popular acceptance of codified languages, just as it is necessary for the viability of nations.[6] There are a number of examples of imposed national federations that have failed: Yugoslavia and Czechoslovakia, for instance. Similarly, even the most severe suppression may fail to stamp out languages that have popular support, as is the case with the use of Macedonian dialects in Aegean (Greek) Macedonia.

Language has commonly been used as an instrument of nation-building by European states. "For Europe, the nineteenth century was the great time when languages were identified and codified in single forms, minority languages in part eliminated, consciously national literatures and musics invented …What becomes the English language starts as the dialect of a minority and is imposed upon the majority, usually by force, with legal punishments for those who refuse the schooling which will induct them in the national language. Thus, the definition of what is the national culture is the result of a pre-emptive strike by only one group of people."[7]

The concept of linguistic nationalism is relatively recent. In fact, use of the idea of nationalism to describe world affairs one thousand or two thousand years ago is anachronistic. Hobsbawn has pointed out that nationalism in the modern sense of the word "nation" is no older than the eighteenth century.[8]

Linguist Peter Hill explains that the "father" of linguistic nationalism is generally considered to have been Johann Gottfried von Herder, who lived in the latter part of the eighteenth century.[9] Von Herder identified language as the foundation of human society, the treasure trove of a nation. The idea of linguistic purism was strongly influenced by his ideas. Linguistic purists believe that languages should contain lexical material from only, or at least predominantly, a single source. There have been, and still are, strong linguistic purism movements in France and other countries in Europe. France is an example of a "nation-state that has been successful in homogenizing its population and eliminating regional identities and national minorities. The language policy of

France has been central to this process."[10] However, French did not become the universal means of communication until late in the nineteenth century (1881–1886) when free, compulsory, neutral and secular schooling allowed for the spread of a single standard language to every part of France.

This example shows us how recent the development of a national language has been for one major European power. It gives us a context in which to examine the Macedonian case. However, some twentieth-century examples may be even more helpful. In the eighteenth, nineteenth and twentieth centuries language was used as a way of consolidating central rule in the Russian empire and later in the Soviet Union.[11] After the Socialist revolution, Lenin and Stalin followed a policy that saw language as the most important distinguishing feature of a nation. Thus the establishment of union republics within the USSR was based largely on language. There were great political advantages to this move. Though the Turkic-speaking republics could have shared a common standard, and might even have accommodated to standard Turkish, these peoples were divided up into a large number of manageable individual republics with their own separate languages. At first the script was Latin-based as a strategy to limit Islamic and Persian influences. With a movement to greater centralization during Stalin's time, the Russian language was emphasized, and the required script became Cyrillic. These developments occurred only a decade before the appearance of Macedonian standard language (MSL). At the present time, as anti–Russian feeling is high in many of the central Asian republics of the former USSR, there are moves to undo some of these changes. We may see the codification of new standard languages in the years to come. The fact that they are codified now says nothing about how long the languages might have existed.

Language developments within the Balkans. The process of standardizing modern languages has typically occurred after national independence. Since southern Balkan nations achieved independence from the Turks, or the Austro-Hungarian empire during the nineteenth and twentieth centuries, this is the time period during which standard languages appeared in the Balkans. In the Macedonian case, the standard language appeared before independence, but at the beginning of a period of autonomy (in 1944) that had not been experienced in the previous one thousand years.

Sociolinguists accept that the Bulgarian standard language, which was not codified till the latter part of the nineteenth century, has the same history before that time as the Macedonian language. The oral version of the Serbian standard language was not established among the educated in Belgrade and Novi Sad until the end of the nineteenth century. This language was considerably influenced by French, which was dominant in Belgrade at that time.[12] The Albanians, while still under the rule of the Turks early in this century, had a language conference in 1908 that began a move towards the Latin orthography they were to adopt after independence. For a time the Turks quashed this development as the nationalist implications became clear. Thus Albanian was not codified until the early part of the twentieth century. Even the modern Turkish language with its new Latin-based alphabet was not established until Kemal Ataturk chose to use this development as part of the process of creating a new Turkish nation, separating it from any wider Islamic identification.

In Greece, what unified disparate ethnic groups in the course of the nineteenth and twentieth centuries was the Greek language and the cultural values emphasized along with it. Thus, in the case of the modern Greeks, language performed a double role: first, it served to support the initial claim to the ancient Greek heritage; second, it helped to pull various peoples into one — "Hellene" — nation.

The Greek language required much attention to enable it to fulfill this role. There were deliberate efforts to revive it in the years leading up to and immediately following independence from the Turks. British historian George Finlay, writing a few years after Greek independence,[13] noted that the people most influential in the establishment of the modern Greek language were Eugenios Bulgares and Adamantios Koraes. Both were opponents of "Orthodox bigotry." It seems that Koraes had great influence on the leaders of the Greek revolution. Greek nationalists seeking a national language employed to their advantage an idiom that, from the perspective of nineteenth-century theories of comparative linguistics, seemed to be descended from ancient Greek. Thus Finlay could say, "The fact that the Greeks have hitherto made greater progress in regenerating their language than in improving their moral condition, must be attributed to the superiority of the material in which they worked. The language retained its ancient structure and grammar; the people had lost their ancient virtues and institutions." Later Ioannis Psykharis sought Greek support for demotic Greek, saying,"Language and fatherland are identical. To fight for one's fatherland or one's language, the fight is one and the same." (Cited after Magner 1988, 109.)

The Development of Modern Macedonian

Modern Macedonian has a long history. Like other European languages, such as English, its form of fifteen hundred years ago is different from its modern form. Just as English speakers cannot comprehend old English, Macedonians cannot usually understand Old Church Slavonic, even though it was based on a Macedonian dialect. In considering the development of Slavic languages, it must be remembered that a dialect from western Macedonia was the basis of the first written Slavic language, and therefore exercised a powerful influence over all other Slavic languages. Because of this, Macedonians prefer to think of their language as the mother of Slavic languages.

When the Slavs moved west and south into the Balkans they replaced the administrative languages Latin and Greek and the earlier Illyrian, Thracian and Phrygian speech of the inhabitants with their own dialects. These were ancestral forms of Slovene, Croat, Serbian, Macedonian, and Bulgarian.[14] In the middle of the ninth century Macedonia was a part of the Bulgarian empire, though the Slavs in the west (in Macedonia) were often difficult to control and before long revolted against the rule of the Bulgarians and took over the empire themselves. The Bulgarians had adopted Slavic language and culture. It is paradoxical that the Bulgarians, a Turkic people who adopted Slavic language and customs, took a significant role in standardizing Slavic writing.

The advance of Christianity in the Balkans was slowed by the fact that there was no written Slavic language, and therefore no vehicle for the transmission of the Christian liturgy. In the ninth century the "Apostles to the Slavs," Constantine the philosopher (later St. Cyril, 826–869) and his brother Methodius (c.815–885), created a new alphabet for the use of Moravian Slavs. This alphabet was applied to the first unequivocally attested Slavonic script, known as Glagolitic. The lexicon for which it was used and the grammar which provided its structure were based on a dialect of southern Macedonia,[15] the Slavic dialect of Salonika, the birthplace of Cyril and Methodius. It then became possible to translate Christian scripture into the dialect of the Slavs of southern Macedonia.

Clement, a follower of Methodius, was sent to Macedonia about 886 and worked there as a missionary for thirty years. In 893 Naum joined him in Macedonia. Clement and Naum simplified the Glagolitic script devised by Cyril and Methodius, in the process inventing the Cyrillic script. The written language that they used is called Old Church Slavonic. The Macedonian archbishopric of Ohrid (Ohrida), recognized by the emperor as equal in rank to Constantinople, became the ecclesiastic center from which the Cyrillic script and the eastern Orthodox faith were spread throughout Serbia, Bulgaria, and Kievan Russia.[16] Old Church Slavonic eventually became the sacred idiom of a large section of the Slavs, the official state language of the Bulgarian empire, and the third international language of Europe. Simeon, Boris' son, continued his father's enthusiasm for Christianity. In particular he showed an enthusiasm for Slavonic letters alongside a devotion to Byzantine culture. The Slavonic liturgy was enthusiastically supported also by two Slav rulers in central Europe, Ratislav of Moravia and Kocel of Pannonia. Pope Hadrian II gave his unqualified approval to the work of Constantine and Methodius and publicly authorized the use of the Slavonic liturgy. Methodius was appointed archbishop to Pannonia, and his Slavonic liturgy and Slavo-Byzantine culture became a force for two centuries. Some writers claim that since the time of Cyril and Methodius[17] the Macedonian language has functioned without serious challenge as the principal literary, liturgical and colloquial language of Macedonia.

At the time of Cyril and Methodius and Clement and Naum, the Turko-Tatars Boris and Simeon, who spoke Slavic and had adopted Slavic customs, ruled over the Slavs of Macedonia. To some extent, therefore, Macedonia's experience was determined by Bulgarian political and cultural forces. However, Peter Hill argues that Old Church Slavonic was more than merely a written dialect.[18] It is naive, he says, to imagine that this construction of a written language was possible without established tradition. Therefore it can safely be assumed that there was at least some tradition on which Cyril and Methodius could build. Presumably their familiarity with this tradition derived from the fact that they were Slavic themselves. Cyril and Methodius were more than simply well-educated agents of the Greek church. They were themselves of Macedonian heritage.[19] The father of Cyril and Methodius, Lev, was a Macedonian Slav in the Byzantine service, occupying the post of assistant to the Salonika military commander.

Medieval development of the Bulgarian and Macedonian languages. Old Church Slavonic continued in use among the Orthodox Slavs for biblical and liturgical texts and for some other areas as well (sermons, moral tales, philosophical texts, chronicles, even secular romances) for a thousand years.[20] The language naturally developed somewhat separately in the different areas occupied by Slavic-speaking Christians.

Russian Church Slavonic became the model for use among the Serbs and the Bulgarians from the seventeenth century onwards. Apparently this language was not suitable as a colloquial or administrative language. Peter Hill says that from early times both Church Slavonic and written vernacular forms of the language existed side-by-side being used for such matters as legal documents. The vernacular that was used is likely to have varied from one dialect area to another.Written Greek was also used for such purposes.

Both the Bulgarian standard language and the Macedonian standard language can be seen as direct descendants of Old Church Slavonic. The Bulgarians see their language as directly descended from the first Slavonic written language. They consider that this gives their language a particular prestige and their nation therefore a cultural preeminence among the Slavonic peoples, and Bulgarian children are taught this at school as a significant part of their national education. Today there are continuing disputes between Bulgarian linguists on the one hand and some Macedonian and other linguists on the other over who can legitimately claim Old Church Slavonic as their own. The Bulgarian side refers to Old Church Slavonic as "Old Bulgarian," while the Macedonian side calls it "Old Macedonian." The Bulgarian side denies that Macedonian is a language and therefore that it could be a rival claimant to the Old Church Slavonic heritage. The Macedonians in turn consider that the use of a dialect from the Macedonian Slavs in the formation of "Old Macedonian" gives their language the preeminent claim.[21] For instance, Dimitrija Chupovski observed that the Macedonian dialect used as the basis for Old Church Slavonic "has not ceased for more than 1,000 years to resound in all Slav places of worship."[22] He also makes the point that "Slav literature came from there" and that all Slavic states owe a debt to the Macedonians not merely for the development of a written language and Christianity, but also for art, architecture and literature.

Other historians acknowledge that Macedonia became a renowned center of Slavo-Byzantine culture and its chief city, Ohrid, became the metropolis of Slavonic Christianity. The literary wealth that accumulated, including some original creations, "was to nourish throughout the middle ages the religious and intellectual life of the Russians, the Serbs and the Rumanians."[23] The existence of the Bulgarian state provided an alternative center of power from the Byzantine court at Constantinople and made Byzantine life less prestigious. After the conversion of Bulgaria and especially after the adoption by Tsar Simeon of the Slavonic liturgy for the Bulgarian church, it was possible to be a Christian, and therefore a part of the civilized world, without taking on Greek culture or a Byzantine allegiance.[24]

The first mention of the Church Slavonic used in Macedonia as simply "Macedonian" comes from 1603 in the work of the German humanist Hieronomus Megisser. A psalm is translated into 21 languages, one of which is marked as "Macedonian." Few texts approximating the spoken Macedonian language are known before 1790. However, one important historical record is a small dictionary of the dialect of Kostur with a folk song in it dating from the sixteenth century.[25]

Very soon after the first written Slavic language appeared, Macedonia fell under the control of empires using other official languages, or somewhat different Slavonic dialects. First there was the Eastern Roman (Byzantine) Empire, whose official language was Greek. In the fourteenth century the rulers were Serbians. Late in the fourteenth century the new power was Turkey, and the Turks stayed for more than five hundred years. During the fifteenth century, all of the Balkan states fell to the Ottoman Turks. The town of Salonika surrendered to Sultan Murad II in 1430. This date can be considered to mark the final incorporation of Macedonia into the Ottoman Empire. Thus the Turkish language became important in Macedonia. In the latter part of the eighteenth century, with the Turkish abolition of the Macedonian Orthodox Church, Greek was once again an officially sanctioned language in Macedonia, having its impact through churches and schools under the control of the Constantinople patriarchate.

The nineteenth century: Macedonian literature, folklore, and textbooks. Writings from Macedonia beginning in the first half of the nineteenth century contain signs of a vernacular language unique to this area. However, accomplished scholars may well have found it more straightforward to publish their ideas in other literary languages, such as Greek, that were widely in use at the time, and in which they were likely to have received advanced education. We see exactly this kind of thing in the writings of the Macedonian Grigor Parlicev

(1830–1893), who won acclaim as a second Homer and the national poetry prize for an epic poem in Greek. Despite this proficiency, Parlicev desired to encourage the use of a Macedonian vernacular (see comments later in this chapter).

Slavonic language specialist Peter Hill describes early developments of a school of vernacular writing.[26] The literary works of Joakim Karcovski (c. 1780–1820) and Kiril Pejcinovic (c. 1770–1845) together with those of Chadzi Teodosij Sinaitski (c. 1770–1840) are considered the first generation of modern Macedonian literature showing signs of prevailing vernacular traditions in Macedonia. Though these writings show a content, style and language that is heavily influenced by the prevailing religious vernacular writings, they contributed to a new vernacular written tradition. Their works were used in the "cell schools" and later in private schools opened in the houses of artisans and merchants. These schools appeared in Macedonia, particularly from the middle of the nineteenth century, as an alternative to church schools. In 1876 there were about 45 such private schools in the towns in Macedonia and about 118 in the villages. They used Serbian, Bulgarian and their own Macedonian teaching materials. It was partly through the influence of these schools that the works of both Karcovski and Pejcinovic reached a broad audience.

Hill says that analysis of Karcovski's works reveals distinct elements from western Macedonia, where he was born, and other elements from eastern Macedonia. The title pages of his books stated that the books were written in "Bolgarskijazik" ("Bulgarian"), but "Bulgarian" here probably means simply "vernacular." Pejcinovic's most famous work, published in 1816, was *Kniga sija zovornaja Ogledalo*, containing prayers and quotations from the Bible and sermons. This book became very popular all over Macedonia, where almost every priest owned a copy. Hill says that its popularity was due to the practical nature of the book and to the language in which it was written. While the prayers and quotations from the Bible were given in Church Slavonic, the sermons were written in a language based mainly on the vernacular of Tetovo. It seems also that Pejcinovic's language was livelier and closer to the vernacular than that of Karcovski. A peasant's son, Pejcinovic was a gifted teller of tales in the folk idiom. His *Sermon for the Holidays (Slovo za praznicite)* was written basically in vernacular with an especially high proportion of Turkisms, although there are many Church Slavonic terms and quotations. In 1835 Pejcinovic's last literary work was his epitaph, engraved on his tombstone. These verses have long been considered the first verses of modern Macedonian literature.

Another important influence was archimandrite Chadzi Teodosij Sinaitski, who began to translate different prayers and liturgical texts from Greek into a form of Macedonian in the 1830s. Sometime around 1838 he established the first press in Salonika. Although he is regarded as the first Macedonian publisher, Bulgarian writers also consider him their first publisher. Teodosij's press worked for four or five years, printing five books and other items such as public announcements. One of the books printed at Teodosij's press was Pejcinovic's *Utesenie gresnymb*. The title page of this work states that it was "translated into simple language," the folk language, in order to open the heart of the simple man.

Chadzi Teodosij's activities are seen as an important contribution to the establishment of a common Macedonian norm based on the simple language of Lower Moesia of Skopje and Tetovo that was accepted in the extreme south-eastern (Salonikan) wing of Bulgarian-Macedonian dialects. However, Hill notes that any linguistic outcome was probably incidental since Karcovski's, Pejcinovic's and Teodosij's purpose was to popularize works of a religious nature among the faithful. Their aims were religious, rather than linguistic. Nonetheless it is significant that they saw a local vernacular as the best medium to reach the common people. This implies an established tradition that they could use for this purpose.

Some other literary records from this early period are worthy of mention. There was a translation of the New Testament into Macedonian vernacular, the *Konikovo Evangeliurn*, printed in Salonika in 1852. There is also evidence of some Serbian influence in this work, both in the language and in cultural ideas. Zlatarski[27] reported on two other documents written in Slavonic script from 1814 and 1815. One was a letter written in the Veles dialect from the area of the village of Basino: the other was a business document written in Prilep. Thus even when Hellenism in Macedonia was at its strongest, some Macedonian merchants and artisans at least were using their own language in written communications rather than other, more formally sanctioned, literary languages.

From the evidence available to us today, we may conclude that a Macedonian vernacular was widely used for religous purposes in the first half of the nineteenth century, along with a few printed books based in various dialects, both eastern and western but still heavily influenced by Church Slavonic. There may well be other published materials yet to be discovered that will take our knowledge of language developments a step further. It might be noted also that the Constantinople Bulgarian newspapers, such as *Carigradski vestnik* and *Makedonija,* published contributions from their readers in Macedonian dialect or vernacular.

Grigor Parlicev, who at first wrote with such great success in Greek, later attempted to create a "common Slavonic" literary language based on Church Slavonic and Russian. He had little success in this effort but is significant for his speeches and sermons in the Ohrid dialect, which was refined syntactically and lexically as a part of this effort. Parlicev's writings probably indicate important elements of the urban educated speech of his time.

Folklore appeared in written form during the nineteenth century, when there were several significant efforts to collect and publish Macedonian folk songs. Widening knowledge of these songs played an important role in the

Macedonian national awakening.[28] The most famous collection was the Miladinovs' *Bulgarian Folk Songs (Balgarski narodni pesni)* published in Zagreb in 1861. Peter Hill tells us that Dimitar (1810–1862) and Konstantin (1830-1862) Miladinov, like many educated Macedonians of their time, studied in Greek schools and became Greek language teachers. Dimitar was teaching Greek in Struga in 1845 when the Russian scholar Viktor Grigorovic visited him at this school, asked him why he did not teach in his native tongue, and encouraged him to do so. From then on, Dimitar turned more and more toward his native Slavonic language and the Cyrillic alphabet, and became a firm opponent of Panhellenism. He had a number of famous pupils, his younger brother Konstantin, Rajko Zinzifov, Grigor Parlicev, and Partenij Zografski among them. He advised them to go to Russia for their education. Dimitar was influenced and inspired by the work of Vuk Karadzic, who encouraged him to collect Macedonian folklore. In his own original writings, he used a language form consisting of his native Struga dialect and elements of literary Bulgarian (the developing Bulgarian standard language). However, his brother Konstantin, twenty years his junior, had a rather different influence that might be taken as the beginning of modern Macedonian. Konstantin has been described as the "first real Macedonian poet."[29] When living in Moscow he wrote a poem, "Longing for the South" (Tdga za jug), which is among the most famous in Macedonian literature. Konstantin's version of vernacular literary language was based mainly on the western dialects, especially those of Struga and Ohrid. Dimitrovski (1981) sees indications of an effort consciously to broaden the dialect base of his written language, since Miladinov was in favor of a written language that would be based predominantly on the morphological and syntactic structure of the folk language.

The greatest achievement of the Miladinov brothers was their collection of Macedonian folk songs, which they referred to as "Bulgarian". In a letter to Viktor Grigorovic, Dimitar refers to "my efforts concerning our Bulgarian language and the Bulgarian folk songs."[30] The dialects used as a base for Konstantin's writings are of some interest given the elder Miladinov's view that they were writing in Bulgarian. The dialects do not come from an area to the center of what was then the broader Slavic community with Bulgarian sympathies, but from the far southwest of Macedonia. The use of the name Bulgarian may not be as significant as it first seems and perhaps should not be interpreted in its present-day sense.[31] Croats, Ukrainians, Byelo-Russians, in the early period of the development of their standard languages called the written dialects they used "Russian." Perhaps all this means, as in the Macedonian case, is that they had not yet formally recognized and named the differences that had developed between their own dialects and those of their Slavic neighbors.

Another Macedonian writer of significance, named by Peter Hill, is Marko Cepenkov, who was born in 1829 and began the collecting of folklore in 1856 or 1857. A tailor by trade, a man with little formal education, Cepenkov collected folk tales and retold them in his own style and language. In time he produced original creations, writing drama, poetry and prose.[32] Cepenkov's autobiography was written in Prilep dialect (again from the southwest of Macedonia) in Sofia in 1896, though it was not published until 62 years later and therefore had little effect on the development of the Macedonian language. Nevertheless it indicates the direction in which events were moving.

Significance has been given to the Veles (now Titov Veles) branch of the bookstore of the National Revival publisher Khristo Danov (1828–1911) and the work there of the Bosilkov brothers, Doncho, Georgi, and Konstantin. This was the first bookstore to be established in Macedonia and was important for the development of the book trade in general as well as for dissemination of National Revival literature. The bookstore was founded in 1867 by the Bosilkov brothers, who were sons of a Koprivshtitsa weaver. The brothers became important social and cultural activists during the latter stages of the National Revival.[33]

Textbooks, too, appeared in the nineteenth century. In 1838 Anatolij Zografski wrote the first Macedonian school primer, *Nacalnoe ucenie*. This book was published by Teodosij Sinaitski. However, Partenij Zografski (1818–1875), a pupil of Dimitar Miladinov, became the best known of the early textbook writers. In his textbooks Partenij used a literary language based on west Macedonian. He explicitly advocated the use of this language as a Macedo-Bulgarian compromise, describing it in detail in articles published in Bulgarian journals printed in Constantinople in 1857 and 1858.[34] Partenij's most active pupil, Kuzman Sapkarev (1834-1908), published eight textbooks between 1868 and 1874. His later works became more and more west Macedonian as he became a Macedonian nationalist.[35] Another textbook writer, Dimitar Makedonski (-1898), has been identified by Friedman as significant "among the list of those who contributed to Macedonian nationalism by publishing textbooks which attempted to synthesize Macedonian dialects into a literary language."[36]

Peter Hill reports that the commune of Kostur (Kastoria), which, like other communes in the Ottoman Empire, enjoyed cultural autonomy, planned to introduce the use of the vernacular in the local schools in 1892–93 and set up a committee to advise on teaching materials. They planned to use the vernacular texts where necessary. The "Macedonian dialect" was to be used also in municipal administration and for readings in church. This grass-roots movement was crushed when the Greek Orthodox metropolitan intervened, ostensibly because of the interference in church matters, and had the schools and the church closed.[37] This ended an experiment that must have had community support to have been contemplated in the first place.

The literary developments considered so far, though largely in the area of religious and literary communications, had an obvious political significance, and this point was increasingly attended to by Macedonian writers and political figures. In 1875 the *Dictionary of Three Languages (Recnik od trijezika)* was published in Belgrade by Georgi Pulev (1838-1894). This dictionary, covering "Slav-Macedonian, Albanian and Turkish," was the first published document of explicit Macedonian linguistic and political separatism.[38] Pulev argued that the Macedonians constituted a separate nationality, and he advocated a Macedonian literary language and a free Macedonia. The basis of Pulev's literary language was primarily his native dialect from Galicnik in the Debar District. Peter Hill suggests that this publication might be seen as an indication of a major division between Bulgarian and Macedonian. While it could be argued that before this time these two languages had a common history, this book presents an explicit recognition of differences between the two languages.

Evidence of a distinct Macedonian national consciousness firmly associated with language differences comes in the Constantinople Bulgarian newspaper *Pravo* of November 30, 1870, referring to the allegation "that a Bulgarian and the Bulgarian language is one thing and a Macedonian and the Macedonian language is another."[39]

The link between the increasing focus on a distinctly Macedonian literary language and political activism is shown in the establishment of the Young Macedonian Literary Society, which published a journal, *The Vine* (*Loza*), in the years from 1892 to 1894, using what was apparently intended to be a Macedonian variant of the Bulgarian standard language. This society, though on the surface a literary group, seems to have been primarily political in intent with separatist ambitions, since they had a public constitution published in Sofia and a secret one printed in Romania.[40] Although the society did not last long, other groups that it influenced were soon to follow. The student society Vardar, established in Belgrade in 1893, grew out of the society, including as members Krste Misirkov and Dimitrija Chupovski, who first began to develop their Macedonian nationalist ideas at that time.

The Inner Macedonian Revolutionary Organization (VMRO/IMRO) in Salonika was founded by members of *Loza* and similar groups. However, it is worth noting that Gotse Delcev and the Macedonian Revolutionary Organization used the Bulgarian standard language in all their correspondence, programmatic statements and so on.[41] They wanted an autonomous Macedonian state but do not appear to have been in any way interested in the creation of a separate Macedonian standard language.[42]

There was an active Macedonian scholarly and literary association in Belgrade, the Macedonian Club in the years 1901 and 1902, which influenced the appearance of the Macedonian Scholarly and Literary Society in St. Petersburg soon after. This society fought for the recognition of Macedonian autonomy from 1902 until the death of its most important figure, Dimitrija Chupovski, in 1940.[43]

After the failure of the Ilinden rebellion, Misirkov returned to St. Petersburg, and in 1905 he launched the journal *Vardar* in Macedonian. Although the journal failed, Peter Hill says that the language shows a further development of Misirkov's (and his circle's) codification, including increasing evidence of the idea of separation from Bulgarian. In a work published in 1903 in Sofia but confiscated by the Bulgarian police (*Za makedonskite raboti*), Misirkov argued that modern Macedonian should be based primarily "on the Prilep-Bitola dialect which is equidistant from Serbian and Bulgarian, and central to Macedonia," with enrichment of the lexicon by collecting material from all Macedonian dialects.[44] His work was lost, and had no influence. Thus the standardization had to begin all over again. However, Peter Hill suggests that the forces for this particular kind of standardization of the Macedonian language must have been broadly established by the end of the nineteenth century since Friedman notes that these were "the same principles which were ultimately arrived at in 1944 in ignorance of his (Misirkov's) work." Misirkvo's 1903 book was actually written in Macedonian standard language that was finally codified in 1944–45, thus we might place the beginning of MSL at this point in time. However, it should be stressed that Misirkov was working within an established tradition. For more than fifty years the dialects of the Ohrid-Bitola-Prilep area had predominated in published Macedonian vernacular writing.

The twentieth century. The use of a contemporary Macedonian literary language was clearly evident in the area of drama. In a review of the performances by Vojdan Cernodrinski's troupe in Belgrade, in an article in *Brankovo Kolo* in 1904, Andra Gavrilovic said that the language of the plays marked the debut of a fourth south Slavonic literary language, not just a *patois*.[45] *Macedonian Blood Wedding (Makedonska krvava svadba)* was described as "a tragedy in five acts in Macedonian dialect." The play created the basis for an indigenous vernacular tradition in drama and has remained one of the most popular Macedonian pieces to this day.[46]

After the Balkan wars and the partitioning of Macedonia there were four official languages — Greek, Bulgarian, Serbian, and Albanian — in the area of Greater Macedonia. The four controlling powers attempted to suppress the Macedonian form of the Slavic tongue. "It was now the common lot of all Macedonians to have their language forbidden in public life (schools, the press, etc.). In each part of the country the official language of the partitioning state, and it alone, was imposed as the cultural vehicle for the Macedonian population."[47]

In their part of Macedonia, which was officially referred to as South Serbia, the Kingdom of Serbs, Croats and Slovenes (Yugoslavia) declared the Slavonic inhabitants to be Serbs. In official use only the Serbian language was permitted. While only Serbian was permitted in the educational and public spheres, *belles lettres* could be published and dramas performed in dialect. Hill describes many examples of these. He gives instances also of Macedonian poetry published in the 1930s that had enormous effects on schoolchildren in Vardar Macedonia. Hill indicates that the work of Kosta Racin showed a clear striving towards a standardization of the Macedonian literary language. Other writers of significance were Kole Nedelkovski, Venko Markovski and Aco Sopov, who also wrote in the central dialect, thus broadening the base for the consolidation of the new literary language.

Except during a brief period following World War II, the Bulgarian government has officially denied the existence of a Macedonian nation, arguing instead that all the Slavs of Macedonia are Bulgarians. Its policy toward the Macedonians in Bulgaria has been one of forced assimilation into mainstream Bulgarian society.

While poetry and even drama in the vernacular were permitted in Bulgaria and Yugoslavia as "dialect literature," things were different in Greece. After 1913 all Slavic personal and place names were Hellenized, and all evidence of Slavic literacy was destroyed. Under pressure from the League of Nations to fulfil its treaty obligations to minority ethnic groups after the Balkan wars, Greece had initially adopted a tolerant policy and even published a Macedonian primer for use in schools in the new northern territories. However, the primer never reached the schools (see Chapter 5). Meanwhile, the authoritarian regime of Ioannis Metaxas explicitly banned the use of the "Slavonic *patois*" even in the home, imposing fines or torture on offenders. Peter Hill says that the trauma of persecution has left deep scars on the consciousness of the Macedonians in Greece, many of whom are even today convinced that their language "cannot" be committed to writing. The Greek government has consistently denied the existence of both a Macedonian nation and a Macedonian minority in northern Greece and has adopted a policy of forced assimilation toward the Slavic-speaking inhabitants of Greek Macedonia. One example of how this policy is carried out comes from Stoyan Pribichevich:

> I subsequently secured back issues of Athens and Salonika newspapers which confirmed imposition of the Greek language oaths on the three villages. The oaths were taken in the summer of 1959, collectively and in public, before representatives of the Church, the government, the police and the army. The "Slavophones" swore en masse that from then on they would never again speak Slav among themselves, only Greek. For instance, the *Athens Vima* of July 8, 1959, said in part, "The Macedonian Slav language should have been abolished earlier. But it is still not too late, and this should be emphasized and used as an example for other Greeks inhabiting Macedonia and still using that language." According to the Salonika *Hellenikos Vorras* of July 8, 1959, the collective public oath ran as follows: "Before God and man, as faithful successors of the ancient Greeks, we swear that in the future, voluntarily, at no place and at no time shall we use the Slav language dialect."[48]

The literature of the liberation movement advanced the development of the written standard language. During the Second World War, Bulgaria formed an alliance with the fascist forces and occupied Vardar Macedonia. The Yugoslavian partisans, including the Anti-fascist Assembly of the People's Liberation of Macedonia (ASNOM) took control over Macedonia and, following a policy of cultural autonomy, issued leaflets and news bulletins in the local dialects, [49] though there was a continued effort to use the central dialect. By the time the war ended, general agreement had been reached on the basic features of the literary language.

Writings in the Macedonian vernacular, including deliberate efforts at codification, occurred in Aegean Macedonia as well as in Vardar Macedonia. From January through May 1944, the Macedonian partisans in the village of Karcista in the district of Kostur (Kastoria) published the newspaper *Voice of the Slav Macedonians (Slavjanornakedonski glas)* in the local dialect. During both World War II and the Greek civil war that followed, the partisans set up Macedonian vernacular schools in the liberated areas. In October 1944, the partisans in the Kostur district published a *Primer of the Macedonian Language (Bukvar na makedonskijazik)* and distributed it to a number of schools in the Kostur and Lerin districts.[50] At about the same time a partisan by the name of S. Spirovski from the village of Nikiforovo/Gostivar, while in prison in Tirana, compiled a Macedonian-Albanian-Italian dictionary based on the Miladinovs' collection and the poetry of the nineteenth century writer Rajko Zinzifov.[51]

Macedonian Standard Language

On August 2, 1944, in the monastery of Prochor Pcinjski, ASNOM made the decision to set up a Macedonian republic within a planned People's Federal Republic of Yugoslavia. The official language of the People's Republic of Macedonia was to be a new standard language based on Macedonian vernacular speech. It was resolved that the central Macedonian dialects were to be the basis of the standard language. This new standardized language was to replace other standard languages previously used in Macedonia, such as standard Bulgarian, Serbian and Greek. The Macedonian standard language is the youngest of the south Slavic standard languages, though its appearance was delayed primarily by the political power of Macedonia's neighbors rather than by any lack of community acceptance of the literary language on which it was based.[52]

That literary language was in turn based on a group of dialects which until 1944 could be formally classified only as Bulgarian.[53] This was simply because they had not been formally codified and Bulgarian standard language was the codified language closest to them. The creation of the Macedonian standard language turned "these dialects into 'Macedonian' dialects and their speakers together with the new generation educated in the MSL — into 'Macedonians.'"[54] The formal proclamation of Macedonian as a literary language on August 2, 1944, may have been merely official recognition of the status quo.[55]

The choice of script for the new Macedonian standard language was a source of bitter dispute. The issue at stake was the choice between certain letters used either in the Bulgarian or in the Serbian script. Some, including Venko Markovski, argued for a distinctive Macedonian alphabet, while others, notably Blazhe Koneski, were for the adoption of the Serbian script and orthography. Three commissions examined possibilities, with the final one recommending that MSL be based on the central Macedonian dialects that were most widespread and most likely to be adopted by the speakers of other dialects. The alphabet was to be basically Serbian Cyrillic. The language recommendations were finalized on May 3, 1945, published two days later and promulgated on June 7. The final codification of 1952–54 established MSL as we know it today, a synthesis of many different elements.

MSL quickly developed into a standardized literary language. It was used immediately in the daily press, in schools, in the theater and on the radio. By the time the *Macedonian Orthography* appeared in March 1951, the language had achieved a great uniformity and almost universal acceptance. In a very short time a standard language, comparable to that of other Balkan languages, was defined and put into formal use.[56]

The accelerated acceptance and use of MSL allowed it to compress into less than 50 years a level of development that had taken the other south Slavic languages about 100 years. The mass media (radio, television, newspapers) undoubtedly played a significant role in this rapid change. Peter Hill notes that literary works have played an important role in the affirmation of MSL, since an impressive amount of innovative literature in MSL has been produced over the past half-century. The relatively free intellectual climate in Tito's Yugoslavia, compared with the more rigidly controlled Bulgarian system, favored this development and gave Macedonian literature a clear advantage.

The affirmation of MSL remains a favorite topic of public speakers on solemn occasions. While some Macedonians were displeased by the appearance of MSL, since they saw themselves as Bulgarian or Serbian, today the place of MSL seems assured. The break with the Bulgarian tradition seems complete, and even in today's democratic Macedonia there have been no demands for turning back. Macedonians still keenly appreciate the distinction. At a ceremony in May 1995, the Macedonian Academy of Arts and Sciences (MANU) awarded honorary membership to Dr. Victor Friedman, an American expert known worldwide for scholarship in Macedonian and other Slav languages. Dr. Friedman gave a lecture on "Differentiation Between the Macedonian and Bulgarian Language in a Balkan Context." Friedman is known for his work in the field of codification of the Macedonian language and his bitter debates against its detractors.[57]

Though it might have been possible to construct a Macedonian standard language that was virtually incomprehensible to speakers of the neighboring tongues, this did not occur. Friedman says that if anything, over the past 45 years MSL has moved closer to Bulgarian and Serbian. Serbian influence in particular has been considerable, especially in the administrative styles of the language and in the press. These effects have been weakest in the best works of artistic literature.[58] The dialect of Skopje, which is closest to Serbia, has been strongly influenced by neighboring Serbian dialects, but less by standard Serbian. Some Macedonians have publicly expressed concern about the Serbian inroads, and have sought to bolster up support for MSL.[59]

Finally it must be noted that MSL is increasingly accepted by Macedonians outside the Republic of Macedonia — in Aegean Macedonia, North America and Australia — as their language, irrespective of their political stance or their attitude towards Yugoslavia. It is significant that even such an anti–Yugoslavian group as the Movement for the Liberation and Unification of Macedonia produced all its publications in MSL.[60] Moreover, those Macedonian nationalists from Aegean Macedonia who have drawn the attention of the outside world look on MSL as their standard language.[61]

Some publications using other forms of Macedonian language have appeared over the years. The oldest Macedonian newspaper in the world is the *Macedonian Tribune (Makedonska Tribuna)*, published by the Macedonian Political (later Patriotic) Organization of Indianapolis (later Fort Wayne), Indiana, since 1927. For most of its existence the *Macedonian Tribune* has been banned in Greece, Yugoslavia and Bulgaria. Since the members of the MPO, even today, consider themselves to be Bulgarians from Macedonia or "Macedo-Bulgarians," the *Macedonian Tribune* has always been published in the Bulgarian standard language (or English), even retaining the pre-war (non–Communist) Bulgarian orthography.[62]

From 1946 through 1956, the Australian-Macedonian People's League, a group of Macedonian nationalists, published a newspaper, *Makedonska iskra (Macedonian Spark)*, in Perth and then Melbourne. They aimed to write in Macedonian, but the texts were not truly standardized. Articles were in the dialects of the individual writers.[63] However, the presence of this newspaper helps to show us that written forms of a language can be alive and well and widely understood even if they do not adhere to a codified standard.

As codified in Yugoslavia after 1944, MSL has proved a vital and successful language form. Linguists argue that language standardization, even if it does contain artificial or arbitrary elements, succeeds only if there is widespread acceptance of the language. It has to be acceptable to people, and factors that increase its acceptance include both popular and political elements. Popular elements are such things as a history of exposure and acceptance of a language within communities. Political factors include such elements as the degree to which the newly codified language can be distinguished from neighboring but politically unacceptable forms. For instance, when the Macedonian alphabet was being defined there was a strong political desire to distinguish Macedonian script from Bulgarian, the language of the most recent invaders of Macedonia. The use of one particular letter, which is considered typically Bulgarian, has since become synonymous with treason.[64] This gives some indication of the strength of feeling in Macedonia about separateness from Bulgaria, and the importance of having a language that defines that separation.

8. Macedonia Today

Macedonia today is a tiny country. Its total area is a little less than 28,000 square kilometers, or 9,928 square miles. This is less than half the size of the nation of Ireland, slightly larger than the state of Vermont in the United States and about 40 percent of the size of Tasmania, the smallest state of Australia. It is a landlocked country, bordered to the north by Serbia and Montenegro (221 km), to the west by Albania (151 km), to the south by Greece (228 km) and to the east by Bulgaria (148 km). The Republic of Macedonia is sometimes called Vardar Macedonia, after the Vardar River. The capital of Macedonia, Skopje (pronounced Skop-yeh), is the largest city with a population of close to 600,000 people.

Macedonia is a country of rugged mountains and wide, fertile valleys. In the mountainous areas the summers are very hot and dry and the winters are cold with heavy snows. Of course, spring comes sooner to the valleys and basins, where the climate is milder. Skopje has a considerable annual rainfall. Along Macedonia's western borders are great forests including beech, pine and oak trees. In other areas the trees have been largely removed for cultivation of the land. The Vardar River, the longest in the country, originates in the northwest and flows southeast through the length of the country. In Greece it becomes the Axios and drains into the Aegean Sea. The Vardar has become the focus of many patriotic Macedonian folk songs. In the south there are three significant lakes, Ohrid and Prespa in the west, and Dojran in the east.

Other important cities are Ohrid, Bitola and Prilep, in the southwest; Tetovo, Kumanovo, and Titov Veles in the north; and Strumica in the southeast. Although some of these cities are small by modern standards, they were often of historical significance and are seen by their peoples as centers of importance.

The economy is predominantly agricultural, but Macedonia has a variety of natural resources including zinc, lead, manganese, nickel, chromium, and tungsten. Mining operations scar the landscape and, together with metallurgical plants, pollute the air and the waterways. Until recently there has been little awareness of the dangers of poisoning the environment. There are now

211

THE REPUBLIC OF MACEDONIA

active groups working to reduce the damage to the biology of Lakes Ohrid and Prespa. Mineral and thermal springs, some of which have been developed for public use for the past two thousand years, are common in Macedonia. Earthquakes are relatively common, and Skopje experienced a devastating earthquake in 1963.

In the recent past Macedonia was the major transportation corridor from western and central Europe to the Aegean Sea. A freeway and a railway line run through the country from north to south. East-west transport is much less developed. While there are good road links with Bulgaria, there is no developed railway connection. There are plans to develop both road and rail to improve access to Bulgaria's Black Sea ports. Roads through Albania to the

Adriatic port of Durres are much less developed than Bulgarian roads, and though it is only a third of the road distance to the Adriatic, travel from Macedonia takes as long as the journey through Bulgaria to the Black Sea. Macedonia has at least 125,000 telephones.

According to the census of June and July 1994, the Republic of Macedonia had a total population of 1,936,877. Of these, 1,288,330 or 66.5 percent were Macedonians, 442,914 or 22.9 percent were Albanians, 77,252 or 4 percent were Turks, 43,732, or 2.3 percent were Rhomas (Gypsies), 39,260 or 2 percent were Serbs, and 8,467 or 0.4 percent were Vlachs. A total of 34,960 people or 1.8 percent said they belong to some other nationality, while 1,962 or 0.1 percent did not want to express their ethnic affiliation. There were 503,456 households, 582,981 dwellings and 177,447 agricultural holdings in the Republic of Macedonia at that time. Living abroad were 138,319 people (figures from Yugoslavia could not be gathered), in about the same proportions with regard to ethnic groupings. There were 13,395 persons with a residence permit in the Republic of Macedonia less than a year, including refugees, persons under humanitarian care and others. Of this group, 3,145 said they were Macedonians, 5,966 said they were Albanians, 36 said they were Bulgarians, 1,160 said they were Muslims, 581 said they were Serbs, 130 said they were Croats, 37 said they were Montenegrins, and 127 did not state their ethnic affiliation.[1]

The United States State Department reports no governmental interference with the practice of religion in Macedonia.[2] The dominant faiths are Eastern Orthodox and Muslim, but many others are active. The Macedonian Slavs are mostly members of the Christian Macedonian Orthodox Church. The Turks and most of the Albanians are Muslims. A small proportion of Macedonian speakers are Muslims. Around 70 percent of the people speak Macedonian as their primary language, 21 percent speak Albanian, 3 percent speak Turkish, 3 percent speak Serbo-Croatian, and the remaining 3 percent speak a variety of other tongues. Approximately 59 percent of the people are members of the Christian Orthodox Church, 26 percent are Muslim, 4 percent are Catholic, 1 percent are Protestant, and 10 percent are of unknown religious affiliation.

The Macedonian Orthodox Church does not enjoy any special legal status. That church and all other religious communities and groups are separate from the state and equal under the law. The Muslim community complains about the placement of crosses on the facades of public buildings in some towns, and criticizes the reproduction on the national currency of cultural monuments, such as churches with crosses. However, some denominations of the currency also portray monuments from the period of Ottoman rule.[3]

Figures from 1992 indicated that the literacy rate in Macedonia was somewhat different for males and females, with 94.2 percent of males and 83.8 percent of females aged 10 and over able to read and write. This gives an overall figure of 89.1 percent.

Education is compulsory through grade eight. In 1994 there were 1,067 elementary schools in Macedonia, with a total of 7,175 classes. Of those, 718 were Macedonian schools, attended by 188,051 Macedonian pupils. The 279 Albanian schools taught 72,121 Albanian pupils, while the remaining 55 elementary schools were attended by 5,342 Turkish children. Of the teachers, 8,990 were Macedonians, 3,571 were Albanians, and 288 were Turkish. Approximately 70 percent of the population also completes secondary or tertiary education. There were 97 high schools in Macedonia in 1994, with a total of 2,296 classes. Of these, 90 were Macedonian, with 2,218 classes; 5 were Albanian, with 72 classes; and 2 were Turkish, with 6 classes. There were 67,975 Macedonian, 2,535 Albanian, and 186 Turkish high school students. Of the high school teachers, 4,060 were Macedonians, 148 were Albanians, and 19 were Turks. The University of Skopje, which was founded in 1949, and various other institutes of higher learning provide schooling for those seeking degrees of bachelor of arts and higher.

According to the United States State Department, the Macedonian Parliament was first elected in free and fair elections in 1990.[4] Following its declaration of independence from Yugoslavia on November 20, 1991, the Macedonian government began adopting many elements of democratic government. The Parliament adopted a constitution on November 17, 1991, effective November 20, 1991, which guarantees civil rights to Macedonian citizens. The issue of citizenship has been a difficult one to define. In general citizens are those who have lived in the republic for at least 15 years. However, people born in Macedonia or having parents born in Macedonia have the right to citizenship even if they live out of the country. They can demonstrate such eligibility through family biographies. Macedonians now living in some part of the former Yugoslavia and originating from the Aegean part of Macedonia are automatically treated as Macedonian citizens, provided they have had Yugoslavian citizenship.[5]

The first and current president of Macedonia is Kiro Gligorov. He was born on May 3, 1917, in Stip, the Republic of Macedonia, about an hour's drive south of the capital Skopje. He is married to a doctor and has three children. He originates from an urban family, with a history of active involvement in the national liberation movement in Macedonia. He completed his secondary education at the Skopje Gymnasium and graduated from the Faculty of Law in Belgrade in 1938. During the period of his studies, he actively participated in the students' movement in Belgrade. After graduation, he returned to Skopje, where he worked as an attorney in a private bank. At the outbreak of the Second World War, he actively took part in the anti-fascist and people's liberation movement in Macedonia. He published an underground wartime manifesto demanding independence for Macedonia during this period. He was a member of the People's Liberation Struggle from 1941 and a member of the Antifascist Assembly of the National Liberation Movement of Macedonia. In the years 1944–1945, he was placed in charge of finances of the Presidium of ASNOM, at the time of the proclamation of the Macedonian state. After

Macedonia joined the Yugoslav federation, Gligorov became a member of the Anti-fascist Assembly of the National Liberation Movement of Yugoslavia. At the end of the war, he was sent to Belgrade. As Tito created the state of Yugoslavia, he offered the young Gligorov various party positions in Belgrade, "well away from the hub of Macedonian politics."[6] Clearly Tito was aware of demands by talented young Macedonians for independence. He took Gligorov away from Macedonia to harness his skills for the broader federation and to prevent him from stirring up problems in Macedonia itself. From 1945 to the beginning of the 1960s, he held specialized executive functions in the spheres of economy and finance. He was assistant general secretary in the government of the People's Federal Republic of Yugoslavia from 1945 to 1947, assistant minister of finance from 1952 to 1953, deputy director of the Federal Institute for Economic Planning from 1953 to 1955, secretary of the Federal Executive Council for Economic Issues and federal secretary of finance from 1962 to 1967, and vice-president of the Federal Executive Council from 1967 to 1969.

Gligorov was one of the leading economists supporting the advancement of a market economy in Yugoslavia. He became the head of the federal government team that conceptualized and carried out the first market-based economic reform in Yugoslavia in the 1960s. It was the first such attempt at economic reform in the "socialist world." Though the reforms were suspended, he became active in conducting theoretical research and socioeconomic studies pertaining to the necessity of the development of a market economy. Throughout this period he was involved as a member of the Council of the Institute for International Politics and Economy, president of the Institute for Social Sciences, and a participant in numerous specialized conferences in Yugoslavia and internationally. He published numerous articles in specialized publications.

At the beginning of the 1970s, Gligorov was elected a member of the presidency of the Socialist Federal Republic of Yugoslavia (1974–1978) and President of the Parliament of the Socialist Federal Republic of Yugoslavia. Immediately following his time as president of the Parliament, he was virtually removed from political life in Yugoslavia, but pursued theoretical research as a professor of economics at Belgrade University. Almost 15 years later, in the late 1980s, he was once again included in the government team of Ante Markovic for the implementation of a new market economy in Yugoslavia. At the onset of the crises of Yugoslavia (1989–1990), he made a comeback to political life in Macedonia, promoting multi-party elections and the introduction of a market economy. These activities resulted in his election as president of the Republic of Macedonia. Some consider Gligorov a part of the discredited Communist past. Nevertheless, he gained a majority of the popular vote in the first free, multi-party elections (the constitution guarantees universal suffrage to those 18 and over) on January 27, 1991. In 1994 he faced no serious opposition in his bid for reelection. His victory was overwhelming, suggesting that his moderate policies have broad appeal for Macedonian voters.

The Republic of Macedonia has a multi-party system. In the general elections in October 1994, a large number of parties and individuals sought election to the Parliament. The Macedonian Parliament has a 120-member unicameral National Assembly, which is elected by popular vote to create laws and develop policy. As has been noted, the first and continuing president of the republic, appointed by the old Parliament on January 27, 1991, is Kiro Gligorov. The president and members of the National Assembly are elected for four-year terms. In the 1994 elections Gligorov was reelected president by popular vote. The president makes policy for the republic and appoints a prime minister, who must be approved by the National Assembly, to manage the day-to-day business of government. In addition to being the head of state, the president is also the chairman of the Security Council and the commander-in-chief of the armed forces. The prime minister is the candidate of the party or parties that are in the majority in the Assembly. The prime minister and the other ministers do not have to be members of the Assembly, but most of them are. The constitution provides for legislation by initiative and referendum. The first prime minister, Nikola Kljusev, was appointed by the president in March 1991. The National Assembly appoints judges to the nation's Judicial and Constitutional Courts. There are also lower-level trial and appeal courts. The legal system is based on civil law and includes judicial review of legislation. The court system is three-tiered: municipal, district, and the Supreme Court. The constitutional court deals exclusively with matters of constitutional interpretation.

Following the dissolution of the Macedonian government in the middle of 1992, President Kiro Gligorov appointed Branko Crvenkovski, leader of the Social Democratic Alliance (SDA) party, the "new Communist" group, as prime minister and gave him the authority to create a new government. Crvenkovski participated in the formation of a coalition government, consisting of the Social Democratic Alliance, the Albanian Party for Democratic Prosperity (PDP), and the Alliance of Reform Forces of Macedonia-Liberal Party (MARF). This coalition was elected to government on September 7, 1992. The coalition controlled 73 out of the 120 seats in the National Assembly. The single largest party, the Internal Macedonian Revolutionary Organization (VRMO-DPMNE), which won 37 seats in the Parliament, remained outside the governing coalition. The position of VRMO-DPMNE is of some significance because this group is considered the most extremely nationalistic of the Macedonian political parties. Stojan Andov became president of the Assembly.

The economy of Macedonia is based on agriculture, mining, and light industry. In former years, this economy was closely tied to those of the other Yugoslav republics, especially Serbia, and Macedonia was the poorest of these republics. In recent years, regional conflicts and the imposition of international sanctions against Serbia/Montenegro, coupled with dislocations caused by the transition to a market economy, have severely disrupted the economy.[7]

In the first year of independence, the country's gross domestic product (GDP) per capita was US$1,140, one-third the rate of Slovenia, the richest of the former Yugoslav republics. The total GDP shrank 14 percent in 1992. Twenty percent of workers were unemployed in 1991, and the rate of unemployment increased to around 36 percent through 1994. Agriculture and the coal industry allow Macedonia to provide for its basic food and fuel needs, but other fuels, machinery and transport equipment, and manufactured goods have to be imported. Macedonia has two international airports, at the capital city of Skopje and at Ohrid, a tourist destination. Agriculture provides 12 percent of Macedonia's GDP. Its principal crops are rice, tobacco, wheat, corn, and millet. Other crops are grapes, sunflower, cotton, sesame, mulberry leaves, citrus fruit, and vegetables. Macedonia is one of the seven legal cultivators of the opium poppy for the world's pharmaceutical industry. Agricultural production depends on a work force using simple hand tools rather than machinery. As you travel south from Slovenia down though Serbia and then into Macedonia, you see more and more people using hand-tools, rather than tractors, in the fields. The minimum wage, set in March 1993, was approximately $50 (denars 1,500) per month. The 1995 United States State Department report on Macedonia said that the average monthly salary as of October 1994 was about 6000 denar, or US $200, and the minimum salary was 4,000 denar (US$133). Despite these rises in income, the cost of living generally far exceeds the minimum wage.[8]

The Council of Trade Unions of Macedonia (SSSM) is the successor organization to the old Communist labor confederation. It continues to maintain the assets of the Communist group and remains the government's main negotiating partner. An active observer of labor issues has termed it "independent of the Government and not associated with any party." The constitution guarantees the right to strike. Strikes were common in 1993 because of difficult economic conditions. The constitution implicitly recognizes employees' right to bargain collectively. Anti-union discrimination has not been observed.[9]

The government has enthusiastically adopted many free-market measures in its constitution, reformed its currency and begun a massive drive for privatization under the direction of privatization minister Jane Miljovksi. To some extent this drive has been accelerated by the preference of Macedonian consumers to deal with private enterprises offering service, rather than state-owned businesses that retain their indifference to customer needs. At the end of 1992, more than 85 percent of Macedonia's industries, but only 15 percent of the country's capital, was privately owned. In April 1992 the national bank was established and a new floating currency, the denar, was introduced.

A great threat to Macedonian economic viability arose from the lack of recognition by the international community. Foreign loans and capital could not be obtained without recognition.[10] The barrier was imposed after Greeks opposed the use of the name and flag and certain statements in the constitution expressing concern about the welfare of Macedonians in other countries.

Greece blocked recognition till the temporary compromise name "Former Yugoslav Republic of Macedonia" was accepted by the United Nations. After this Macedonia was able to join the International Monetary Fund and to gain observer status in the Conference on Security and Cooperation in Europe (CSCE).

Greece continued to block Macedonia's membership in various European organizations, including the CSCE, that might have been helpful in stabilizing Macedonia's economy through into the middle of 1995. After the United States expressed the intention to open diplomatic relations with Macedonia early in 1994, Greece imposed a trade blockade. Since Thessaloniki, a few kilometers to the south, had been the main port for Macedonian imports and exports, this embargo had a profound effect. The effect was enhanced because of the United Nations economic embargo on Macedonia's major trading party, Serbia. Macedonia's trade north and south was blocked. Though simple survival prevented complete Macedonian adherence with this ban on trade with Serbia, trade was severely curtailed.

Compliance with the United Nations embargo on Serbia probably hurt Macedonia more than Serbia. As a part of Yugoslavia, Macedonia conducted around 60 percent of its trade with Serbia. The international community has not come close to compensating Macedonia for its losses. The effects of the sanctions were described as "crushing economic damage."[11] The sanctions cut off Macedonia not only from its major trading partner, but also from its direct trucking routes and its only rail link to most of the rest of Europe. The Greek embargo was an additional burden at a time of heightened vulnerability. More than 80 percent of other industrial exports, materials not going into Serbia, were shipped through the Greek port of Thessaloniki. The effect of the two embargoes was the devastation of an already frail Macedonian economy. This left Macedonia vulnerable to pressure from powerful neighbors, particularly Serbia.

The problem for Macedonia was and still is the lack of alternative transport infrastructure through Bulgaria to the Black Sea, or through Albania to the Adriatic port of Durres. There is no east-west rail link, and east-west road transport is more complicated than through Thessaloniki and more costly. The transport of goods, raw materials and semi-manufactured goods via the roundabout east-west corridor has resulted in a drastic rise in business costs, according to Macedonian businessmen. As a result, an increasing number of companies faced bankruptcy, while others were forced to halt production.[12] Government funds were provided for a widening of two bottlenecks at the border crossings of Deve Bair (to Bulgaria) and Chafa San (to Albania). Shipping agents in Macedonia are aware that the corridor through Bulgaria and in particular the one through Albania cannot be compared to the routes towards Europe via Serbia. Although the distance between the border crossing at Chafa San and the Albanian port of Durres is only 148 km, trailer trucks need over nine hours to cover that section because it is in a very bad condition. Moreover, they are in constant fear from road bandits or police "controls." It is easier to transport goods from Birmingham to Moscow than from Skopje to Durres, according to one observer.[13] In any case the port of Durres is unable to meet all of Macedonia's requirements. Durres cannot handle more than a million tons a year, while output from Skopje ironworks in 1993 was 2.5 million tons. While transport charges in the world amount for 5–12 percent in produce costs, the transport of Macedonian goods to Europe via Albania and Bulgaria pushes up these costs to as much as 50 percent. Crude oil, which used to come 240 kilometers from Thessaloniki, now comes by truck from Bulgarian ports over 700 kilometers away. This has threatened employment within Macedonia. Fuel for Macedonian power stations used to come from Serbia or Tuzla in Bosnia. Now it is imported from countries outside Europe, with increased risks concerning quality and a variety of increased costs. Construction has started on an American-backed rail link with Bulgaria, but further international finance that has been planned from European sources for transport infrastructure has been blocked by Greece.

Six weeks after the Greek blockade began, the *Financial Times* reported that Macedonian authorities estimated the monthly cost of the blockade at some $80 million. This figure, roughly equivalent to 85 percent of the country's total export earnings, is the result both of lost trade opportunities and of more expensive transportation.[14]

Macedonian and Greek businessmen were still doing some trade despite the economic embargo, Macedonia's foreign trade representative, Dimitar Delcev, was reported as saying.[15] They transported goods through Bulgaria using companies in Sofia as fronts to get around the blockade. "Some Greek goods still make it to our market, and I know some Macedonian raw materials are still accepted in Greece by our traditional customers," Mr. Delcev said. Macedonian shops sold Greek milk, olives, olive oil, eggs and consumer goods. Macedonian firms were able to export shoes, yarn, fabrics, plywood, furniture, transformers, welding machines and raw materials to Greece through Bulgaria, Delcev said. "They are exporting to phantom companies in Bulgaria." Nevertheless, the costs to Macedonia were high.

By early 1994, exports had dropped to only 15 percent of the bulk that was being shipped before the United Nations imposed the trade embargo on Serbia and Montenegro. As a result, many factories were unable to find a market. Farmers too were unable to find foreign buyers for their produce. The anti–Yugoslav blockade alone had cost Macedonia three billion United States dollars by mid–1994. The Greek blockade was costing Macedonia some $60 million monthly, according to government estimates, further weakening an economy already damaged by United Nations sanctions against Serbia. Because of the combined effects of the sanctions against Serbia and the Greek trade embargo, millions of liters of wine were poured out in 1994, and hundreds of tons of lamb rotted. Macedonia faced economic disaster. Officially there was 30 percent unemployment, and the number of families on welfare doubled in 1993 to 50,000. Unemployment compensation was being paid many months in arrears in mid–1994 because of the rising deficit of the state unemployment fund.

The special rapporteur of the United Nations Committee on Human Rights, Tadeusz Mazowiecki, expressed concern at the negative influence of the economic situation on the social stability of the country and its impact on broader social issues. He said that the persistent economic deterioration might destabilize the current coexistence of different ethnic groups. He reiterated his belief that Macedonia should receive adequate compensation for losses connected with the implementation of the sanctions against the Federal Republic of Yugoslavia (Serbia and Montenegro), that the Greek embargo should be lifted immediately, and that equal and fair treatment should be given to Macedonia (which he described as FYROM, of course) in regard to its applications to join international organizations. He said it was particularly important that Macedonia be promptly allowed to join all relevant security mechanisms, particularly the Conference on Security and Cooperation in Europe.[16]

In order to survive, Macedonia did not comply completely with sanctions in 1993 and 1994. The country conducted some trade with Serbia. The United Nations seemed willing to turn a blind eye to these violations. "They say they have no choice, that it is a matter of survival for them," said the head of the sanctions-monitoring mission, Pierre Gravel.[17] Reuters (July 7, 1994) reported that United Nations mediator Thorvald Stoltenberg cautioned the Security Council on tightening a trade embargo against Serbia because of its impact on neighboring Macedonia. The United Nations itself was forced into tolerating Macedonian trade with Serbia because of its inability to compensate Macedonia for complying with its regulations. In August, the European Union mediator for Bosnia, Lord Owen, asked for a complete blockade of Serbian territory, but pointed out that Macedonia must be given considerable financial aid if the border was to be closed.[18] Soon after, the Macedonian government completely halted all cargo traffic on all border crossings with the Federal Republic of Yugoslavia.[19] The unofficial easing of United Nations sanctions against Serbia-Montenegro early in 1995 boosted trade, especially in food, construction materials and spare parts.[20]

United Nations secretary general Boutros Boutros-Ghali submitted a report to the Security Council on the economic and political situation in Macedonia and the problems it was currently facing. In his report, Mr. Boutros-Ghali said the military situation in Macedonia had "remained relatively peaceful and able." For the first time, he referred to the Greek embargo as an "imposed economic blockade," noting that the unresolved differences with Greece, its blocking of Macedonia's entry into various international organizations, and Federal Yugoslavia's refusal to recognize Macedonia's borders were the main threats to the stability in the country.[21] (He also noted increased tension between Macedonians and ethnic Albanians.)

Macedonia was positively evaluated at the regular session of the United Nations Sanctions Committee held in Vienna early in June 1995. The cooperation between the Macedonian Customs and the team from the United Nations mission for the implementation of the sanctions in Macedonia also received a "thumbs up."[22]

Economic change is underway in Macedonia. Under pressure from the IMF and World Bank, which have been insisting on swift changes, the new government has given priority to economic stabilization and speeding up the pace of structural reform. The trade blockades have added to the difficulties of making the transition to a market economy. Reform of Macedonia's banking system continued slowly in 1994. The system was technically insolvent as banks were burdened with more than $1 billion in (frozen) foreign-currency liabilities, without foreign-currency assets to back them. This was in addition to the Macedonian government's foreign debt of more than $500 million. There were no available detailed figures on foreign trade by mid–1995. The current-account deficit in 1994 was estimated at less than $100 million. After a 15 percent fall in industrial production in 1993, there was a further decline of 14.6 percent in the first half of 1994. However, the government did not expect the level of production to decline further and predicted that gross social product (GSP) would decrease by around 8–10 percent in 1994. The budget deficit was held at 4 percent of SP, in 1994, against a target of 5.8 percent. The government aimed to reduce the deficit to below 2 percent in 1995. The government had some success in meeting inflation targets agreed with the IMF. The year-end inflation rate for 1994 dropped below 60 percent from 230 percent the previous year, and was projected to fall to 30 percent in 1995. The Macedonian denar remained stable, at around 30 denar to one deutsche mark (DM) in the six months to April 1995.[23]

Potential foreign investors continued to show interest in Macedonia, mainly in the tobacco and textile sectors, in 1994, but the uncertain political and economic climate was an inhibiting factor. The prospect of receiving sizeable amounts of aid in 1995 persuaded the government to speed up the pace of privatization. Skopje planned to privatize about 900 state-controlled enterprises through auction sales, starting with Macedonia's tobacco processors. The government hoped that successful sales would open the way for sales to foreign buyers of companies in other sectors, including tourism and hotel companies, textiles and marble producers, and food processors.

The respected international magazine *Emerging Market* wrote in superlatives of the Republic of Macedonia, describing it as a leading star in reform processes in eastern and central Europe, and its national bank's activities as identical with those of western institutions.[24] The paper underscored a conclusion by the World Bank's deputy executive concluding that Macedonia needed aid in cash or oil, instead of blankets and bread. The article ended in a statement by Macedonian finance minister Trpevski, stressing the point that Macedonia was managing to keep its currency stable despite its various difficulties.

In matters of defense, Macedonia employs an army, air force, and air defense force. The republic has approximately 15,000 lightly armed troops and 7000 special police members. In the first half of 1993, the United Nations sent 1000 peacekeeping troops to Macedonia. Seven hundred of these troops, from Scandinavia, arrived in February, and a further 300 United States troops arrived in June. Although the generally expressed intention regarding the presence of these troops has been to prevent the war in Bosnia from spreading to Macedonia, they are mostly positioned on the border with Serbia, where the greatest threat is expected.[25]

The Ministry of Interior oversees the internal security organizations, including uniformed police, border police, and the domestic and foreign intelligence services. By law, the ministry is under the control of a civilian minister and the civilian government. A standing parliamentary commission oversees operations. Charges of excessive use of force in connection with the handling of an early 1993 demonstration and public disturbances in late 1992 led to a formal parliamentary review and debate.[26]

The Media in Macedonia

The constitution forbids censorship and guarantees freedom of speech, public access, public information, and freedom to establish institutions for public information. These freedoms are generally respected. There are several daily newspapers in Skopje and numerous weekly political and other publications. An Albanian-language and a Turkish-language newspaper are also published nationally and are directly subsidized by the government. Other cities publish their own dailies or have them printed in Skopje. Some critics complain that the government, through the powerful national daily *Nova Makedonija* and affiliates, monopolizes local press coverage. The government's ability to present its views through this influential medium has led to the criticism that it manages the news. *Nova Makedonija* receives income from its near monopoly on printing, rental space, and kiosks.[27]

By early 1995, Macedonia had at least 211 radio and television stations. The number of stations has fluctuated, increasing with increased private involvement and interest particularly at the regional level, and decreasing in the face of greater governmental efforts at regulation. Much of the television programming involves material relayed from Skopje or nearby countries, or obtained from satellite broadcasts by other European operators. There are at least 370,000 radios, and 325,000 television sets. Macedonian Radio-Television (MRT) in Skopje, which is state-owned, transmits programs in the Macedonian, Rom, Turkish, Albanian, Serbian, and Vlach languages. In 1993 there were three television and four radio stations under MRT's control. In addition, there are many private radio and television broadcasters throughout the country. Towards the end of 1993, a private radio station with an all–Albanian format reportedly began broadcasting in Skopje. The Albanian minority had complained of insufficient Albanian-language broadcasting on state television, only some five hours per week. VMRO, the Macedonian nationalist party, complained of unequal access to the media. However, several journalists claimed VMRO does not understand that a free press has editorial freedom. There are no legal barriers to setting up independent media outlets.

Foreign books and publications are freely available, principally in larger cities. Academic freedom appeared to be respected despite the fact that the university in Skopje relies on government funds. No government interference with professorial latitude in research or publishing was observed by the United States State Department in 1993 or 1994.

There have been some efforts to censor the printed media in Macedonia. On July 4, 1994, the Macedonian Interior Ministry banned the import, distribution and sale of the Belgrade daily *Vecernje Novosti*, after previously banning a number of publications produced in Serbia, such as *Politika Ekspres*, *Tempo*, *Politika Zabavnik*, *Sportski Zurnal*, *Bazar*, *Ilustrovana Politika*, *Svet Kompjutera*, and *Mikijev Almanah*. *Vecernje Novosti* was banned because "their global approach does not present objectively the situation in the Republic of Macedonia. That is their articles have a tendentious approach."[28] The Serbian press expressed annoyance at this censorship.

A 1995 report by the United Nations special rapporteur, Tadeusz Mazowiecki, on the freedom of press in Macedonia said that the national television and radio, A1 Television, and Radio NOMA were the most influential media in the country. The report pointed to *Nova Makedonija* and *Vecer* as the most influential daily newspapers in Macedonia, along with the Albanian-language *Flaka e Vlazerimit* and the Turkish *Birlik*. Mazowiecki stressed the absence of regulations to support article 16 of the constitution, which regulates freedom of press. He remarked that a large number of laws issued before Macedonia gained independence were still in effect. He said that the media in the country were not setting out to increase ethnic and nationalist tension on purpose, but ethnic origin was a factor in reporting. The report mentioned the banning of some magazines published in Belgrade. The conclusion of the report reads, "The situation in the former Yugoslav Republic of Macedonia is characterized by attempts of political forces to impose influence over the media, so as to secure their political power. Thus, journalists in the country are facing the challenge of establishing professional and independent media through which democracy and human rights can actively be promoted."[29] The United

States State Department made similar observations in its 1995 annual report. It was noted that freedom of speech and the press are guaranteed by the constitution, and in general the government respects it. However, newspapers can be imported from Bulgaria, Serbia and Albania only with formal approval from the Interior Ministry.

A current-affairs program on "Macedonian Television" in May 1995 took a very different view from Mazowiecki in commenting on the chaotic situation in radio and TV broadcasts. The commentator, Nikola Cunihin, noted that the existence of 211 registered radio-television stations in Macedonia could be taken as an indicator of the rate of democratization and liberalization of electronic communications. However, Cunihin noted with concern that some television stations presented full broadcast programs of foreign national television stations. "Super SKY" from Tetovo transmits the programs of Albanian radio-television, including the program for Albanians living outside their native country. On some occasions official Albanian government stances in relation to the dispute in the PDP were presented, giving open support to the radical wing of Taci and Dzaferi. Another recent broadcast was the program of the private TV station MI-FI "TG-RT," a program in the Turkish language, which due to extreme fundamentalism had been banned in the Republic of Turkey. Some private TV stations in Tetovo, Kumanovo and Kavadarci transmit the central information news from Serbia during the scheduled broadcast of the Macedonian information program, as well as every current affairs program from Serbia. The Greek media in particular "bombards" the southern part of Macedonia with various news and information programs, using very strong signals. The situation is similar in the written media, which Cunihin called "propaganda." Extensive distribution of Bulgarian newspapers in Macedonia has developed. The most frequently seen newspaper is *Makedonija*, an organ of the Bulgarian VMRO alliance of the Macedonian associations, which Cunihin describes as "a well-known product of the Bulgarian Security Service." The "psychological-propaganda campaign" is also carried out with the distribution of religious literature, particularly that designed for Muslims. The book *The Path of the Saved Nation*, which vigorously promotes the idea that "the handling of weapons is the holy duty of every Muslim," has been widely distributed in Macedonia. A brochure with the same title as this book states that "every Muslim has been ordered to fight against unbelievers until they admit that Allah is the only God." All these books and brochures are printed in Middle East countries and translated in Macedonia. Funds to pay Albanian radio-television have been raised by the PDP and the Democratic Alliance of Kosovo, according to Cunihin. Apparently the government has no plans to ban or control such activities. It has no personnel to supervise the output of the private radio-television stations, or print media, and it has no guidelines by which they should operate. Cunihin saw this as a threat to the independence and sovereignty of the Republic.[30]

In May 1995, the Ministry of Traffic and Communications closed the TV station in the Albanian-language "ERA" in Skopje, without any previous warning. According to the director of the TV station, Abdula Mehmeti, the only TV station in the Albanian language working in the Skopje area was "closed for no reason." Sources from the Ministry of Traffic and Communications claim that "ERA" did not possess a work permit. This TV station had been working in Skopje for more than six months and broadcasting programs of TV Tirana, intended for viewers abroad. The director of TV "ERA" said that "none of the TV stations in Macedonia have special work permits, as there is no law for radio diffusion." Mehmeti feels that "the same criteria should exist for all."[31]

Human Rights

During a three-day visit to Macedonia in July 1994, Tadeusz Mazowiecki, United Nations representative for human rights in the former Yugoslavia, gave a press conference in Skopje during which he stated that progress has been made towards greater implementation of human rights in Macedonia. However, he said progress had been slow in the area of greatest concern to minority groups, the field of education. Yet progress was evident in the participation of minorities in the government as well as in the formation of the Inter-ethnic Council within the Parliament. He said changes were required in regard to criminal laws and the law regulating the courts. He noted too that the country had no regulations to enforce the freedom of press.[32] Similar comments were made in a 1995 report to the Council of Europe. He made a distinction between the constitution, which goes beyond the minimum set in European human rights conventions, and the practice, which as yet falls short of the standards set in the constitution.[33]

Fundamental human rights are provided for in the constitution and are generally respected, but there continue to be occasional reports of police abuse of detainees and prisoners. Government authorities seem responsive to criticism. Disciplinary action against police officers for exceeding their authority has often led to dismissals or other punishment. Prison treatment of some ethnic Albanian prisoners at the Idrizovo prison near Skopje improved after investigation by the monitoring mission of the Conference on Security and Cooperation in Europe. The United States State Department said that "informed independent sources describe prison mistreatment as rare."

There were no reports of political killings during 1993, though an Albanian national implicated in the smuggling of arms for an Albanian paramilitary group (the All-Albanian Army) died while undergoing interrogation, possibly from the effects of a beating, and an Albanian died in a violent confrontation with police in February 1995. A parliamentary commission that investigated the November 1992 riot in Skopje exonerated the police involved.

There were no reported disappearances or confirmed reports of arbitrary arrest in 1993 or 1994, according to the United States State Department. Despite opposition claims of political murders, arrests and harassment, there has been no proof of such police actions. No cases of inhuman treatment or punishment of citizens have been observed.[34]

There is little or no systematic use of detention as a form of nonjudicial punishment. Incommunicado detention is not practiced in Macedonia. Speedy arraignment in court is required, and the accused is entitled to contact a lawyer at the time of arrest and to have a lawyer present during police and court proceedings. A person illegally detained has the right to compensation. There were no known trials on purely political charges in 1993, and no political prisoners were known to be held. According to the constitution, the courts are autonomous and independent. The 1995 United States State Department report on Macedonia emphasized that no political influence on the work of the courts had been observed.

The State Department report says that generally speaking, the government does not interfere in the field of freedom of religion. All churches and religious communities can establish schools, social and philanthropic organizations.

Despite these relatively favorable observations by the United States, some problems remain. In the "Conclusions and Recommendations" section of his report to the United Nations Commission on Human Rights, Tadeusz Mazowiecki stated that

> the human rights situation in the former Yugoslav Republic of Macedonia continues to be impaired by delay in the enactment and implementation, according to the Constitution and the Constitutional Act, of some of the basic laws upon which the juridical and institutional structure of the State is based. These laws are essential for an effective enforcement of the rule of law and thus for the adequate protection of human rights. The Special Rapporteur therefore calls upon all political forces in the former Yugoslav Republic of Macedonia to concentrate on the implementation of the Constitution and the Constitutional Act and thus successfully complete the structural transition to a democratic system based on the supremacy of the rule of law and the protection of human rights... The Special Rapporteur continues to be concerned by the reports received regarding a limited enjoyment of the right to a fair trial and the persistence of cases of excessive use of force by police. While recognizing that the use of force cannot be avoided in certain circumstances, the Special Rapporteur believes that the police should spare no efforts to restrain its use to the level strictly necessary for the performance of their duties.[35]

The constitution gives the rights to privacy of person, home, and correspondence. Although no instances of abuse were substantiated in 1993 or 1994, officials of the VMRO opposition party claimed that their telephones were tapped and other communications interfered with.

The constitution provides for freedom of peaceful assembly and association.

Groups and political parties may not advocate the forcible overthrow of the constitutional order, encourage the commission of military aggression, or promote national, racial, or religious hatred or intolerance. The United States State Department reports over the past few years have stated that advance notification for an assembly is required to ensure adequate security, but add that this requirement does not seem to have been used to restrict public demonstrations. However, following the 1995 report, Dime Gjurev, undersecretary in the Ministry of Interior, gave an interview for Macedonian A1 television. He said that while respecting the United States State Department's work, he needed to refute certain statements in the report, particularly the claim that the police must be notified beforehand of any intended public gathering. This is just not true, he said. The police do not require any organizations to do this although some have voluntarily done so. Gjurev said the police act strictly by the regulations when summoning people for informative talks and hold them no longer than 24 hours. A small number of cases of detention longer than 24 hours by police officers were investigated, and appropriate disciplinary measures had been undertaken. According to the Ministry of the Interior, such incorrect reports are due mainly to inaccurate reporting to the State Department by monitors in the field. Regarding the report by Tadeusz Mazowiecki concerning the rights of the Serbian minority in Macedonia to exercise religious ceremonies, Gjurev said the problem was a result of the failure of the Serbian Orthodox Church to register in Macedonia, which disallows Serbian clergy from giving services within the territory of Macedonia.[36]

Political parties and nongovernmental organizations are required to register with the Interior Ministry. Over 50 political parties and associations have registered. The Ministry of the Interior has sought the deregistration of two parties for advocating the "forcible change of the constitutional order and/or promoting ethnic or religious intolerance"; one opposed independence and supported reintegration with Yugoslavia, while the other was allegedly advocating the establishment of a fundamentalist Islamic state. There was no change in the United States State Department's conclusions about this issue in its 1995 report.

Human rights groups and ethnic community representatives meet frequently with foreign representatives without government interference. The Forum for Human Rights was established in 1990 by a group predominantly made up of academics to propagate a culture of respect for human rights. While their effort is primarily educational, they work with the government and institutions to improve protection of human rights. The government has cooperated fully with visits or investigations by international human rights groups. Tadeusz Mazowiecki asserted that nongovernmental organizations constitute an indispensable source of feedback in the efforts of the government for the effective promotion and protection of human rights. He welcomed the recent creation of a Human Rights Helsinki Committee in Macedonia.[37]

Women have the same legal rights as men. However, Macedonian society, both in the Christian and Muslim communities, is traditionally patriarchal, and the advancement of women into nontraditional roles is still limited. Little is known of the extent to which violence against women, including domestic violence, occurs. In 1993 a few fledgling women's advocacy or support groups began to organize.

There are no reports of child abuse in Macedonia. Macedonia's commitment to children's rights and welfare is limited by its resources. The state does have social welfare programs to support children, but the economic crisis brought on by the sanctions against Serbia and the Greek embargo so restricted funding that they could not operate. Despite these problems there was a children's vaccination program in the spring of 1993 that reportedly covered at least 95 percent of the country's children.

Minorities in Macedonia

A 1995 report to the Council of Europe said Macedonia is a country facing numerous difficulties due to the dispute with Greece, the Greek embargo, United Nations sanctions on Yugoslavia and interior ethnic problems. The ethnic problems were considered the most dangerous of all. The report pointed out the fact that Macedonia was undergoing a transition without bloodshed, but underlined the potential danger of a spillover of the war in this region. The reporters were impressed by the scope and dynamics of the reforms, as well as with the willingness of authorities to carry them out with technical aid from the Council. A great deal remained to be done at that point, they said, but Macedonia was in a position analogous to many other east and central European countries currently in transition.[38]

Some things about Macedonia may be unique. The Macedonian weekly magazine *Puls* reported statements by Slovenian sociologist Rastko Mocnik about the sociopolitical situation in Macedonia. He said, "These new Balkan states are nothing but an instrument for establishing new forms of exploitation and domination. They all have terrorist attitudes towards themselves, military intentions towards their neighbors and servile behavior towards international imperialism. Macedonia is an interesting exclusion. The Macedonian case should be carefully studied, not in regard to recognizing this state, but in connection with its attempt to establish a multicultural and multiethnic system."[39]

All citizens are equal under Macedonian law. The constitution provides for the protection of the ethnic, cultural, linguistic, and religious identities of minorities. Thus in principle, minorities in the Republic of Macedonia enjoy all the basic freedoms of self-identification, expression, congregation and political expression. There are programs on the radio and TV in the languages of the minorities — Albanian, Turkish, Vlach — which are financed by the state, while classes at schools are carried out in Albanian, Turkish, and the Roma language.[40] However, ethnic tension and prejudices between groups are still apparent. The government seems to want to address the concerns of national groups without provoking a backlash from extreme nationalists. Various minority groups, including Albanians, Turks, and Serbs, have raised various credible allegations of human rights infringements and discrimination at the hands of the ethnic Macedonian population. When it comes to government jobs, in civil administration, education, the court system, the armed forces, and the police, ethnic Macedonians are overrepresented in terms of their numbers in the overall population.[41]

Albanians. The Albanian community, because of its size, has been the most visible in complaints of discrimination. Before the 1994 census, their claims were particularly strident as they claimed to account for as much as 40 percent of the population. The census data showed that the Albanians were really about 22 percent of the population, as the government had suggested for several years. However, they held far fewer than 10 percent of positions in government employment and were particularly underrepresented at senior levels. They also claim economic discrimination and unequal political rights, particularly with regard to representation in local administration. They demand increased Albanian-language instruction, greater representation in public sector jobs, and enhanced media access. The government has acknowledged underrepresentation in the military and police, and the Ministries of Defense and Interior have begun moderate measures to respond to the imbalance. The minister of the interior says that the army, around 16,000 troops, is now 26.5 percent Albanian, and the police, 7,000 strong, are expected to reach 15 percent within 2 years.[42] On the question of Albanian education, the minister noted that primary and secondary education are provided, as well as Albanian-language courses at the college level to prepare primary and secondary schoolteachers.

From time to time there have been widely publicized incidents of conflict between ethnic Macedonians and ethnic Albanians. For instance, on June 19, 1994, a street fight broke out about 9:00 p.m. near the Colourful Mosque in Tetovo, involving a group of about 12 teenage Macedonians and about 15 Albanian adults, which ended in the death of 18-year-old Vase Trpcevski, who was stabbed near his heart. The group of young Macedonians was coming back from a party and was attacked by the bigger group of Albanians. Two of the attackers, Suleiman Skenderi and Adnan Sediu, were arrested at the border crossing of Deve Bair during an attempt to leave for Turkey. The police also imprisoned Rusit Rusiti and Menduh Zendeli, suspected of murderer. Eight Macedonians were treated at the Tetovo medical center. Two of them were kept for hospital treatment, and the others were released. Tetovo Macedonians condemned the crime and criticized the city police who had prevented doctors from providing first aid for the injured Macedonians on the spot. Trpevski's family received telegrams of condolence from President Gligorov, Parliament president Andov and prime minister Crvenkovski. Earlier the same day, interior minister Frckovski had spoken of the security situation in the country, at a press-conference in the Tetovo Culture Center. He said Macedonia could be an example to the world and that ethnic groups do not have to love each other, but should live in mutual tolerance, side by side.[43]

In a public announcement about the murder, VMRO-DPMNE expressed deep concern and revulsion at the "mad Schiptar chauvinists and separatists." This terrorist act, the party said, is only a logical and direct consequence of the anti–Macedonian politics carried out by the coalition government and President Gligorov, who were just too lenient towards Albanian aspirations, including their attempts for partitioning Macedonia. The Macedonian World Congress, seated in Gevgelia, also expressed deep concern over the tragic event in Tetovo. This organization's statement describes the murder as a continuous pressure on Macedonians in their own state. The Congress demanded that the government reexamine its policies towards the influx of Albanians from Kosovo and its granting of citizenship to these Albanians, as all this changes the ethnic structure of the country's population and endangers the survival of the Macedonian people.[44]

Another contentious issue is the so-called "All-Albanian Army." Three years ago, before the departure of the Yugoslav army from Macedonia, President Gligorov had encouraged Macedonian and Albanian groups to form paramilitary forces. Once the peaceful departure of Yugoslav forces had been negotiated, support for the paramilitary groups was withdrawn. However, nine ethnic Albanians were charged with arms smuggling for the All-Albanian Army. Macedonian nationalist politicians questioned the loyalty of ethnic Albanians to Macedonia. In an effort to placate angry Albanian politicians Gligorov at first said there was no connection between the alleged conspirators and the leadership of the main ethnic Albanian Party. Leaders of the Albanians responded with calls for unity and allegiance to the Republic of Macedonia, but matters became strained when one of the alleged conspirators died (of heart attack) while being interrogated. In the course of interrogations the other charged Albanians implicated Mithat Emini, who had recently been the secretary of the PDP. Emini was arrested. Albanian officials in Tirana claim that the former chairman of the PDP, Nevzat Halili, who had irritated Albania from time to time, was implicated in the conspiracy. The Albanian government claims that any gun-running was done during the time of the former Communist government.[45]

On June 27, 1994, the second municipal court in Skopje passed sentences between five and eight years in jail on the Albanian conspirators. Mithat Emini, the former secretary-general of the PDP, and Hasan Agusi were sentenced to eight years in jail; Ejupi Rezni, Selam Elmazi and Sinasi Redzepi, to seven years in jail; Husein Haskaj, the Macedonian deputy defense minister, Akif Demiri and Abdiselam Arslani, to six years in jail; and Burim Murtezani and Eugen Cami, to five years in jail. Agusi will be expelled from Macedonia after his term in jail. Under the indictment, all of the accused associated in order to engage in hostile activity, and their aim was to topple the Macedonian state. Emini, Agusi and Haskaj were identified as the ringleaders. The indictment says that the accused had established a state-of-the-art computer center, a courier service and a program of setting up paramilitary units in Kumanovo and towns in western Macedonia.[46]

There are many other instances of conflict between Albanians and ethnic Macedonians. Some of these are tit-for-tat actions in response to perceived grievances. For instance, the agricultural cooperative in Tetovo held a press conference in mid–December 1994 informing reporters that deliberate damage to crops and pastures in the region had increased. State-owned land in the most fertile parts of the Polog region, used by the cooperative, has been savagely destroyed in the past few days by organized citizens of Albanian nationality, "in accord with the ethnic cleansing policies of the Albanian leadership of local authorities and the head of the Tetovo Property Department," the cooperative said.[47] It is just as likely that the destructive actions were a response to perceptions of oppression held by Albanians at that time.

At a local level we can see that divisive withdrawal from participation in legislative procedures may occur on the part of any group that feels unfairly treated. In December 1994 the Tetovo local assembly had voted to protest at the activities of the state organs directed against those struggling actively for a university in Albanian language. By itself this is not unexpected. However, as an expression of protest the session was held exclusively in the Albanian language, though this is apparently contrary to the constitution. Macedonian members, unable or unwilling to understand the Albanian language, left the session and did not participate in debate concerning the local council's forthcoming activities, or the budget.[48]

Soon after the events in Tetovo in mid–February 1995, 35 Muslim graves were destroyed in the city of Kumanovo, presumably by ethnic Macedonians. The Kumanovo Islamic religious community leaders issued a statement to say the barbarous and uncivilized act deeply offended and embittered ethnic Albanians of Kumanovo and other towns. Therefore, they expected that the police would find and punish those responsible. They said the case had caused anxiety among all citizens of Kumanovo, as this was the first such instance of desecration.[49]

The most dramatic and wide-reaching series of recent events dealing with the status of Albanian-Macedonians and their conflict with the Macedonian community has been the affair of the Albanian language University at Tetovo, which is described later in this chapter.

Serbs. Serbs, who comprise about 2 percent of the population, have long complained of discrimination. Despite the fact that Serbian minority rights have generally been observed, Serbs have demanded explicit constitutional recognition as a guarantee that they will have equal minority rights. On August 27, 1993, an agreement between the government and the ethnic Serbian community provided equal rights with other, larger minorities and specified an 18-month time frame for amending the constitution. The "agreed minutes" negotiated between the government and representatives of the ethnic Serbian community provided for treatment for the Serbian Orthodox Church equal to that accorded to other faiths. According to the United States State Department 1994 report, after criticism from Serbia/Montenegro, a new Serbian leadership emerged and abrogated the agreement.

On New Year's Day, 1994, ethnic Serbs clashed with Macedonian police in a village with a Serbian majority, and Serbs charged that police used excessive force. Macedonian authorities alleged that a Serbian guard had provoked the police by hurling stones.[50]

Even after the 1994 census, the Democratic Party of Serbs in Macedonia claimed that "the census of population in Macedonia was unrealistic and the figure of 39,000 Serbs living in the country is not in accord with the true figures, as there are 250,000 Serbs in Macedonia." The party leader, Dragisha Miletich, said: "There are 2 deputies in the new parliament of Serbian nationality, but they are representatives of the Alliance of Macedonia and the ruling apparatus, serving merely as camouflage in the eyes of the world."[51]

Turks. Around 4 percent of the Macedonian population (around 77,000 people) are ethnic Turks. They too have complained of governmental, societal, and cultural discrimination. Major concerns are a lack of Turkish-language education, exclusion from Macedonian political life, inadequate media access, and insufficient representation in government jobs. They campaigned for primary and secondary education in Turkish for their children. However, since in many cases the children did not speak Turkish, the government refused to teach in this language. Citizens have begun to teach their children Turkish in the hope of changing this decision.

As with other national minorities, the Turks have occasional direct contact with government officials from their national affiliation. For instance, in February 1995, Turkish president Suleiman Demirel received a delegation from the Democratic Party of Turks in Macedonia, headed by its leader, Erdogan Sarac. The delegation spoke of the position of the Turkish minority in Macedonia.[52]

At a meeting with officials of the European Court and Commission on Human Rights early in 1995, representatives of the Democratic Party of Turks pointed out several examples of disrespect for the basic rights of Turks in Macedonia. They said classes in the Turkish language at elementary schools in Radovis, and indeed throughout the entire country, have been banned. In the Debar region, four teachers who demanded to teach classes in Turkish lost their jobs as a result. The party claimed Macedonia was assimilating the Turkish minority by adding suffixes as "ov," "i," and "ski" to people's last names. They said no state institution, such as the constitutional or Supreme Court, had employed an ethnic Turk, despite the fact that proposed candidates met all requirements.[53]

Roma. The Roma, or Gypsy people, comprise about 2.3 percent (43,732) of the population of the Republic of Macedonia, though their own estimates before the 1994 census suggested a percentage as high as 10. President Gligorov has repeatedly and explicitly recognized Roma as full and equal citizens. There is a commendable lack of tension between the Romany population and the Macedonian Slav majority. There has been progress on important issues, such as education. There is good communication between the Romany community and the Ministry of Education. A Romany primer has been prepared for use in schools, along with a Romany educational program, with considerable input from the Roma community, that included two hours a week of instruction in the Romany language in grades one to eight. A 40,000-word Macedonian-Romany dictionary, based on the most widely spoken of the three main Romany dialects in the country, has been completed. The government television station MRT provides some daily programming in the Romany language, including instruction, news, and music.

Many of these activities have been spearheaded by the main political party of the Roma, the Party for the Complete Emancipation of Romanies in Macedonia (PSERM), which has local branches throughout the country and a membership as high as 36,000. Its president is a member of the Macedonian Parliament, representing the predominantly Romany town of Suto Orizari, located on the outskirts of Skopje.[54]

April 8, the Day of Romas in the World, is celebrated annually under the motto "All Under the Same Sun," at the St. Clement of Ohrid Public and University Library in Skopje. In his 1994 address, the president of the World Union of Romas, Iliaz Zendel, said that Macedonia sets an example to the world, being the only country in the world to allow Romas to fully implement their human rights. On that occasion, Macedonian president Kiro Gligorov sent a telegram of congratulations to all Romas in Macedonia for their special day.[55]

Vlachs. In the 1994 census, 8,467 or 0.4 percent of the population described themselves as Vlachs. Despite their small numbers, Vlachs have been able to achieve a considerable degree of parity with ethnic Macedonians, with primary schools in their own language, and even radio and TV broadcasts from government stations in the Vlach language. Radio Krushevo started broadcasting a radio program in the Vlach language called "Panorama" in April 1994. The program includes Vlach culture and art.[56] The important religious holiday for the Epiphany of St. John the Baptist was commemorated in Krushevo in the Vlach church St. John in October 1994. For the first time since the war, the holy liturgy was held in two languages, Macedonian and Vlach.[57] Because of their small numbers and their integration with the ethnic Macedonian community, and perhaps because they have been less dissatisfied with their treatment, there has been little political pressure exerted by the Vlach community.

Bosnians. Macedonia accepted a number of refugees from the war in Bosnia, more in the early stages of the war. Since the middle of 1992 the government has restricted the entry of refugees. The government believes that if troubles break out in Kosovo (southwestern Serbia, on the Macedonian border), greatly increased numbers of refugees from that region could destroy Macedonia's ethnic identity and its fragile economy. While the number of Bosnian refugees is small, they have been the center of ethnic tensions in some areas. In February 1993 there was a clash between ethnic Macedonians and Bosnian Muslim refugees at a camp in Skopje in which a number of people were injured. There was an angry demonstration in the Gjorce Petrov suburb of Skopje against the construction of a refugee camp for Bosnian Muslims in the neighborhood. Fourteen people, including eight policemen, were injured during the protest. Given the number of policemen hurt, it would seem that the demonstrators produced a large amount of violence. Parliament investigated police actions in the incident and exonerated the police of wrongdoing.[58]

In the middle of 1995, villagers from the Skopje village of Batinci and other neighboring villages, including a large number of refugees from Bosnia and Sandzak on one hand and the authorities on the other, struggled over an illegally built mosque in Batinci. The villagers at first staved off an attempt by the police to tear down the mosque.[59] The police were blocked by a barricade of heavy agricultural machinery and some 2000 villagers. They explained that they were simply protecting the mosque in which religious services were held in a Bosnian language. Other disputes involving the Bosnians seemed to be brewing.

Macedonian Muslims. Within Macedonia, groupings of ethnic Macedonians who are Muslim by religion play a visible role in political affairs. These people often feel themselves torn between other ethnic Macedonians, towards whom they feel national loyalty, and co-religionist Turks and Albanians, whose political positions they often find unacceptable. Some observers have suggested that the marginalization of the Macedonian Muslims by Albanian and Turkish groups has greatly encouraged their nationalistic feeling.[60] The State Association of Cultural and Scientific Manifestations of Macedonian Muslims has acted as the sole representative of these people for over 20 years. Fostering cultural tradition and customs, it played a large role in the process of a national awakening of the Macedonian Muslims. Its president, Ismail Boyda, says, "The association is not a political party, but an independent organization with its own cultural and national features, aimed at preserving the national identity of the Macedonian Muslims." The association formed separate groups to work on different problems in areas populated by Macedonian Muslims. It plans to undertake special efforts to overcome problems in education, science and culture; to improve the economic and social position of the people; and to ensure their inclusion in government agencies and in the work and influence of the Islamic religious community.

According to officials of the association, during the latest census, most Macedonian Muslims declared themselves clearly as Macedonians, without the Muslim suffix. Their religious affiliation was registered only where requested in the census forms. According to Boyda, the suffix Muslim is considered to be somewhat superfluous, but it is left in the official name of the association for those for whom this process of national awakening goes more slowly. According to data gathered by the association from village birth registers, there are between 100,000 and 120,000 Macedonians of Islamic religion in the country. This would make them about 5 to 6 percent of the population. If this is true, it means there are significantly more Macedonian Muslims than Turks. The association has suggested a forum of Macedonian Muslim intellectuals might contribute to the national awakening of these Macedonians. The association seeks aid from the state to achieve this. They say the state has to find ways to revitalize income production within this group and to assist efforts of these small communities to achieve a greater degree of self-government. An important problem is the work of the Islamic religious community in Macedonia. Ismail Boyda points out two possible ways to reduce the influence of the Albanian and Turkish factions. One is to formally recognize a distinct Macedonian Islamic community, which would allow the Macedonian Muslims to seek secession from the broader Islamic community.

The association pointed to Albania's attempts to cover up the existence of as many as 200,000 Muslim Macedonians they claimed were living in compact regions in Golo Brdo, Kuks, as well as several thousand Muslim Macedonians living in 20 larger towns in Albania, particularly in Tirana, Elbasan and Duress.[61]

Boyda bitterly condemned the act of the State Census Committee and the State Statistics Institute for having allowed the Macedonian mother tongue to be replaced by the Turkish language in the villages of Plasnica, Preglovo and all other villages surrounding Kicevo, as well as some villages on the outskirts of Skopje, populated by Macedonians of Muslim religion with Macedonian as their mother tongue. Retreats made under pressure from the Democratic Party of Turks, who, they claimed were attempting to assimilate this part of the population, were extremely humiliating, and were leading towards denationalization of part of the Macedonian population in their own home country.

The president of the Association of Islamized Macedonians strongly condemned the misuse of Islam and of Muslim believers in Macedonia in support of the Greater-Albania idea. The association said that the head of the Islamic religious community in Macedonia, Suleiman Redzepi, had for several years congratulated the so-called president of "the Republic of Kosovo," Ibrahim Rugova, on September 7 — "Independence Day" of the nonexistent republic.

Such congratulations to Rugova could have only negative consequences on relations between Macedonia and the Federal Republic of Yugoslavia, the statement warned, and it was noted in particular that Greater-Albanian forces claim a large part of Macedonia for "the Republic of Kosovo." The association demanded an urgent convocation of the assembly of the Islamic religious community so that it could distance itself from Redzepi's actions, which openly made use of Islam to work for Greater-Albanian aims.[62]

Early in 1995 Boyda condemned what he called the latest political radicalization of the Islamic religion in Macedonia, involving the use of mosques throughout the country to raise funds for Muslim political causes, calling for Islamic solidarity and unity of all believers in the resistance against the Macedonian state.[63] Similarly, in the middle of 1995, the leadership of the National Association of Macedonian Muslims issued a statement of protest against the decision of the Islamic religious community in the country to suspend the Macedonian language from its administrative documents. All official letters of the community are written solely in the Albanian language, and members speak only in Albanian during sessions. Macedonian Muslims said this was an attack on the Macedonian language.[64]

At the same time the president of the association stated that the letter sent by PDP to the Council of Europe was just another anti–Macedonian gesture inspired by Greater-Albania ideas. Blinded by large ambitions, the Macedonian Muslims claimed, parties of Albanians in Macedonia failed to see the enormous step the Macedonian state has made toward securing equality for ethnic groups, and especially for ethnic Albanians in the country.[65]

Steps toward conflict resolution. In June 1993, a 13-member Council for Interethnic Relations, provided for in the constitution, was established in Macedonia. The council has a mandate to study interethnic issues and suggest solutions for problems observed. Parliament is required to consider the implementation of the council's recommendations. The council is comprised of the president of the Assembly and two representatives each from six national and ethnic groups (Macedonians, Albanians, Turks, Serbs, Roma, and Vlach). The council has had only limited influence to date.[66]

A conflict resolution program called Search for Common Ground was planned for the Republic of Macedonia once the Agency for International Development (AID) made funds available. Former United States ambassador to the Conference on Security and Cooperation in Europe Robert Frowick will act as executive director of the project, and John Marks as president. The general aim of the program is to create within divided societies a climate of peaceful resolution of conflict and equitable resolution of grievances, through a multi-faceted approach including (1) Macedonian TV, which will produce a series of ten programs seeking common ground in the most contentious issues facing Macedonia; (2) a training program to teach journalists to cover conflict in post–Communist Macedonia in non-inflammatory ways; (3) a pro-active mediation program, planned after discussions with opposition leaders including Ljupcho Georgievski, leader of VMRO-DPMNE; Albanian leader Nevzat Halili, leader of the Democratic Prosperity Party; and Turkish Democratic Party leader Erdogan Sarac; (4) a Parliamentary Council for Ethnic Relations, begun by Stoyan Andov, president of the Parliament and leader of the Liberal party, who agreed that his organization would receive training and other assistance in dealing with ethnic conflict; and (5) a Center for Ethnic Relations at Saints Cyril and Methodius University in Skopje, which deals primarily with ethnic, religious and social problems and is interested in including more hands-on practical activities.[67]

The census in 1994. The census that began on June 21, 1994, was designed to answer the difficult question of just who the Macedonians really are.[68] If we were to add together the numbers claimed for just the largest minority groups, Albanians (40 percent claimed), Serbs (12–13 percent claimed), Turks (10 percent claimed) and Roma (10 percent claimed), there would be very few ethnic Macedonians at all. As the day for the census approached, Albanians raised objections about "technical difficulties." Some said they feared the census would enable authorities to claim that many Albanians were not Macedonian citizens because they had come from the Serbian province of Kosovo, but it was suggested that their real fear was the loss of political influence when their true numbers became known. President Gligorov is reported to have said, "I understand their problem. The leaders claimed the numbers to be far greater than they are, and now they are facing difficulties explaining this to their party members."[69]

According to Macedonian government statements, the census was "organized and conducted in line with the European standards and methodology, with the active participation of European and international experts."[70] The European Council formed an expert group, which cooperated with the Macedonian government on all aspects of the census. This expert group made many recommendations that were accepted by the Macedonian Parliament. Expert observers were provided for all phases of the conduct of the census. Forty foreign observers from a number of European countries were organized in seven different towns, ten in Skopje, four in Bitola, five in Kumanovo, six in Ohrid, five in Stip, six in Tetovo, and four in Titov Veles. Financial support for the census came from the European Union, and representatives of the CSCE took an active part in preparations for the census. There were disagreements between the government and Albanians about the criteria that should apply to determine the citizenship status of people living in the country, and about the use of bi-lingual teams of census takers for some areas. Compromises were achieved with the help of the European expert group.[71]

The census was carried out in six languages, and the state employed 11,000 people to conduct the survey. Western diplomats acknowledged that some Albanians, who lack legal citizenship, might refuse to cooperate with the census because they feared authorities could deport them due to their illegal status. President Kiro Gligorov said he hoped the census would defuse political tensions and pave the way for discussions based on accurate statistics. "The census should put a stop to all the controversies and provide real facts for talks," Gligorov said.[72]

Abdurahman Aliti, the president of the PDP, the largest political grouping of Albanians, said in regard to speculations about the accuracy of the census: "We firmly decided the census had to take place and I believe we fulfilled all our obligations." He criticized aspects of the "technical organization" of the census, but said that the international team of experts had successfully resolved some of the issues.[73] Nevertheless in some quarters they challenge the accuracy of the 1994 census of population, according to which Albanians constitute 22.9 percent of the total population. The challengers continue to claim that ethnic Albanians make up over 40 percent of the population in Macedonia.[74]

Before the 1994 census, the Association of Serbs and Montenegrins in Macedonia said they could not accept the results as accurate. The association president, Nebojsa Tomovic, said the census would be just another step towards federalization of Macedonia and meeting the demands of Albanians at the cost of the Serbian population in Macedonia, whose real number would be minimized. The association announced an inner census only for the Serbian minority, in order to come up with the "real figures" for Serbs living in Macedonia.[75]

With regard to the census form, the Association of Egyptians in Macedonia expressed bitter protest against the fact that they had not been included in the list of nationalities living in Macedonia, despite their efforts over two decades. The association claimed that earlier statistics showed 3,169 citizens declared themselves as Egyptians, but there were really 30,000 Egyptians in the country.[76]

In Sofia, the independent daily the *Standard* (9th June) quoted the leader of Macedonia's pro–Bulgarian Party for Human Rights, Iliya Ilievski, as warning his party would not recognize the census since the Bulgarian language is not going to be mentioned among the questions.[77]

A press conference in Skopje featured Avdija Pepic, leader of the Macedonian Party of Democratic Action (Stranka Demokratske Akcije, or SDA), a Muslim party initially founded by Alija Izetbegovic, leader of the ruling party in the Bosnian government that had established branches in all former Yugoslav republics before the break-up of Yugoslavia. Pepic distributed copies of a letter sent by the Ministry of Foreign Affairs of the government of Bosnia-Herzegovina in Sarajevo to the Macedonian Parliament. The letter insisted that a Bosniak category be introduced in the Macedonian census questionnaires, and demanded that a representative of the Bosnian government should take part in the census. This letter followed demands from the SDA itself.[78] The Bosniak category was supposed to refer to all Muslims, but given the variety of Muslims in the country, many of whom are staunchly Macedonian, it stood little chance of being adopted.

The international team of experts and its president, Werner Haug, held a press conference after the collection of census data. He said, "We believe that, despite certain problems which occurred during the census, the overall results are acceptable and accurate. I would like to especially underline the idea that our research indicates that the figures regarding the different ethnic groups are realistic, and the international group sees no point in continued dispute about how large certain ethnic groups are. The determination of these primary results and the control of the scope were carried out in accordance with international standards and methodology. The data on the population are also in accord with latest demography trends."[79]

Political Parties and Developments in Macedonia, 1994–1995

Some indication of the attitudes of Macedonians to their government and specific political issues is given in the fourth *Eurobarometer* analysis, dated March 1994.[80] The central and eastern *Eurobarometer*, surveys of political attitudes in individual countries, involved interviews with around 1,000 people in the 15+ age group, face-to-face in their homes. A majority of people believed that their personal financial situation had gotten worse, and as many people expected things to stay the same as expected them to improve.

Half of those interviewed were suspicious of a free-market economy, and less than 30 percent thought it was the right way to go. There was a strong feeling that economic reforms were going too fast. People were evenly divided (satisfied/not satisfied) about the way that democracy was developing in Macedonia, and about the human rights situation in the country. Respondents saw Macedonia's future more closely tied to the United States than to the European Union, to the west rather than to former eastern bloc countries. Respondents thought both Russia and Turkey would be significant in the future.

The major party in the previous coalition government, the Social Democratic Alliance of Macedonia (SDSM), headed by Branko Crvenkovski, were mostly former Communists. Influenced by nationalist values, but experienced in the ways of Communist bureaucracy, this group remains a relatively conservative element in Macedonia. Nevertheless, the pragmatic politics of leaders such as Kiro Gligorov and Branko Crvenkovski have led this group to embrace democratic processes and a free-enterprise economy.

Possible sources of instability in the political functioning of the country are the Albanian parties, the largest of which have been the Party for Democratic Prosperity (PDP) and its splinter; the Macedonian nationalist group, the Internal Macedonian Revolutionary Organization-Democratic Party of

Macedonian National Unity (VMRO-DPMNE); and the Democratic Party of Serbs in Macedonia (DPSM). The Albanian political groups represent a very large minority that feels it has not yet received its political due. Albanian members of the ruling coalition made government impossible by withdrawing support from the parliamentary process. VMRO-DPMNE has received great popular support in the recent past, being the largest single party represented in the first Parliament of the Republic of Macedonia. Because of the strength of public support for nationalist values and the threat that this poses for Balkan politics in general, this group is of considerable interest. The Serbian party, though small in size, has significance because of the possibility that it takes direction from outside of Macedonia, and because it represents a group that may be used by Serbia to justify direct involvement in Macedonia.

The Albanian parties. Internal political and ethnic tensions flared in the period before recognition of Macedonia by the United Nations as the Former Yugoslav Republic of Macedonia. The country's Albanian minority began lobbying for more recognition, with one part of the community demanding more political representation, and the other part boycotting all participation. Many Albanians refused to participate in a national census in 1991, arguing that it would not give a fair estimate of their numbers. Because of increased tension between the Albanian and Macedonian community, there were public demonstrations in the capital, Skopje, during the latter part of 1992. The PDP experienced internal conflict at this time, with the emergence of a more radical faction led by Menduh Taci. The PDP split into two factions at the second party congress on February 1, mainly over the issue of cooperation with the government. Since then, both groups have claimed to be the legitimate successor to the PDP.[81] The appearance of the distinct radical group probably increased the militancy of Albanian groups generally.

There have been many occasions when tension was high in meetings of the national Parliament. Albanian representatives have often chosen the tactic of walking out, or not showing up at all.

A major ambition of Albanian parties has been for Albanians to be declared a constituent nation of the republic. They argue that they had more rights as citizens in the Yugoslav state than they have in the new Republic of Macedonia. The preamble to the Macedonian constitution recognizes the constituent nation status of the Macedonians alone. Macedonian officials argue that the preamble has no legal force but is simply a statement that Macedonia is the only state that the Macedonians have.[82] PDP president Abdurahman Aliti addressed Albanian concerns about the constitution: "The constitution preamble speaks of the historical, cultural, etc. heritage of the Macedonian people and its desire to have its own state, and only afterwards does it mention the category of citizens. Claims that the preamble is not a part of the constitution are theoretically wrong. On the contrary, it determines the character of the constitution. If this is so, and I assure it is, then Macedonia has a national constitution, instead of a civil one. The Republic of Macedonia is not constituted and conceptualized as a state of equal citizens, but as a one-nation state. This is where all the problems begin." In a statement directed at both the Albanian and Macedonian voters, he said that the country's future lay only in coexistence.[83]

Recognition as a constituent nation has implications beyond the treatment of Albanians themselves. For instance, it will affect the issue of the languages used in the country. Albanians may stand beside Macedonian as an official language. However, many Macedonians see much more troubling implications of a move towards recognition as a constituent nation. They see this as the first step towards autonomy for the Albanians, to be followed by federalization of Macedonia, and perhaps eventual independence of the Macedonian Albanians.

In November 1994 the Data Press survey agency published the results of a survey conducted just before the elections asking Macedonians and Albanians several questions regarding inter-ethnic relations in Macedonia. The survey showed that three-quarters of the Macedonians, but less than half of the Albanians, believed that the constitution was satisfactory and that Albanian demands for national recognition were the main source of conflict between Macedonians and Albanians. Only minorities, from all groups, thought that the roots of conflict lay in religious and cultural differences.

Gert Arens, who was authorized to monitor ethnic relations in the former Yugoslavia on behalf of the European Union, said "Albanians in Macedonia are well aware of the fact that they have good prospects in Macedonia. Nowhere in the entire Balkans have the Albanians lived as they do in Macedonia."[84]

The question about the real ambitions of Albanians in Macedonia is constantly raised because of conflicting views among Albanians themselves. Albanians had conducted a referendum on views about "political and territorial autonomy" among Albanians in Macedonia between January 15 and 16, 1992. This dealt with the idea of federalization of Macedonia. Prior to the referendum, Nevzat Halili, then president of the PDP (a party which at that time stated it had nothing to do with conducting polls among Albanians), stated: "No one even thinks of secession at the moment, but I could not guarantee this will continue to be the case in the future."[85]

The PDP and NDP regarded the demand for political and territorial autonomy as a legitimate claim based primarily on the "European document on human dimensions in Copenhagen (point 30), guaranteeing national minorities their right to autonomy" and in protocols issued by the European Convention on Human Rights. However, the mediator for the conference on the former Yugoslavia on ethnic issues in Macedonia, Gert Arens, had said in regard to the affair of "attempts to forcefully overthrow the constitutional order in Macedonia" that he would never support demands for federalization of Macedonia or forming "some autonomy there."[86]

Mohammed Halili of the PDP had first said, early in 1994, "I think it is more acceptable to insist on the demand for a constitutive status for Albanians here. All around the world, constitutive peoples are those who play the main roles in society. Whereas, an autonomy would mean a right of a national minority to self-organize itself within a state... What is most important for us is that Albanians are made equal with Macedonians, regardless of the form in which it is realized." However, during 1994, according to *Nova Makedonija*, the parties were demanding autonomy. Mohammed Halili seemed to have changed his position and was quoted in the Albanian political weekly magazine *Zeri*, saying, "The option for federalization of Macedonia is becoming increasingly current in this former Yugoslav republic." At about the same time the leader of the Kosovo Albanians, Ibrahim Rugova, stated to the Serbian paper *Borba* that the Albanian political parties in the former Yugoslavia were all interested in an Albanian confederation which would include the Republic of Albania, Kosovo and western Macedonia.

PDP branch leader Nevzat Halili said Macedonia ought to be transformed into a two-nation country and a state of peoples instead of national minorities. Speaking at the founding assembly of the party branch in Tetovo early in February 1995, Halili said, "What we need are radical changes in the Macedonian Constitution. Albanians in Macedonia should be recognized as a constitutive people. There are three categories of citizens in Macedonia," he said. "Macedonians are first-class citizens, Albanians are second class, and Serbs, and others are third class. Our goal is an autonomy and a special status for Albanians in Macedonia."[87]

An exception to this repeated reference to "autonomy" comes from an Albanian outside Macedonia, Shkelzen Malichi from Kosovo, who suggested that an independent Kosovo would facilitate stability in Macedonia. He said that the "strengthening of the Albanian factor (through gaining independence for Kosovo) can by no means change the basic geostrategic relations which resulted in creating Macedonia. Albanians have never shown aspirations for destroying Macedonia, but have constantly proved to be vividly interested in improving their status in their common state."[88]

During December 1993 and January 1994, several leaders of the PDP, including Nevzat Halili and general secretary Mithat Emini, resigned in the face of accusations that their policies had proven ineffective in obtaining the desired special constitutional status for Albanians. In an interview given to *Rilindja* on January 10, 1994, Dr. Zydi Bilalli, who also resigned, said he looked to the upcoming party congress to elect "a leadership with clear aims, professionally prepared and with a clear national orientation."

Menduh Taci, leader of the Tetovo PDP group, together with other radicals attempted to take over control of the PDP at the second party congress in Tetovo on February 1, 1994. Members of the moderate Albanian group, including the five ministers in Gligorov's coalition government and all 23 deputies in Parliament, were not allowed to enter the hall where the congress meeting was held. Taci sought greater control for his group. The moderates survived, but from that time there have been in effect (if not always in name) two PDP parties. After this split at the party congress both groups claimed to be the legitimate successor to the PDP.

Taci is 29 years old, the son of a construction worker, and a student of dental medicine. He is reported to have said, "I'm sad to say, but if the Macedonians continue to reject the Albanian demands, there will be bloodshed here. Only Albania and the Albanians hold the key to the stability of this country. We are in a strong position and have many, many unplayed cards." He has remarked that "only one spark is necessary for the southern Balkans to light up." Taci is said to be supported by the Albanian government. "Most of our political leaders were corrupt collaborators. They were not there for the Albanians, but simply because of the power," Taci said. "We are in a very important strategic position. Stability in Tetovo, means stability in Macedonia, and stability in Macedonia means stability in the region."[89]

The head of Skopje University's Center for Ethnic Relations, Professor Emilia Simovska, suggested that the tensions appearing at the time were the result of interference by neighboring countries. She saw external manipulation of ethnic and religious feelings as the source of the current conflict between Albanians and Macedonians. Macedonian government officials agree, noting contacts between politicians from the state of Albanian and leaders of the radical Albanian faction in Macedonia. Albanian president Sali Berisha, interviewed by VOA, said that although he thought the demands would be for the good of Macedonia he was actually trying to tone down the stridency of the Albanian's demands.

Menduh Taci gave an interview to the newspaper *Vecer* in February 1994. He said his group was not so radical really, but that they did criticize the Albanian participation in the government, because the Albanians had entered the coalition without a platform and their participation had not led to any improvement of the situation of the Albanians. He said that Albanians in Macedonia thought of Tirana as a "close and friendly neighbor," especially with its recent move towards democracy and closer cooperation with the West. Concerning the media attention he had received he said, "It is true that I am new, young, and uncorrupted, and that I do not suffer from recidivism, atavism, and complexes. With me, new people and new ideas will appear on the Macedonian political scene."[90]

Menduh Taci's group accused the Albanian parliamentarians of dogmatism, poor judgment and nepotism. The differences between the two Albanian factions may be more a matter of age and emphasis than policy, but nationalist Macedonian groups (e.g., VMRO) see radicalization of the Albanian community as a threat to Macedonia's territorial integrity. The chairman of PDP's radical wing, Arben Dzaferi, says solutions could be found through dialogue and by treating people as equal partners. He said Macedonia must be a multinational, multicultural state with a genuine political pluralism. Albanians would defend such a state, he said. If this approach failed, real radicalism would emerge and Macedonian Albanians might resort to civil disobedience. Abdurahman Murati, leader of the traditionalist wing of the PDP, played down differences between his group and that of Mr. Dzaferi. He emphasized the need for unity amongst Albanians and said Macedonians must accept that the Albanians are an indigenous population.

Early in April 1994 riots were being predicted for Macedonia by the London *Times*. Macedonia was said to be on the same path that pushed Bosnia into war. It was predicted that any violence would be much bigger than that in Bosnia, because of the risk of the conflict spreading to other countries. The greatest threat to peace was said to be the Albanian minority, particularly the radical splinter group led by Menduh Taci. The only way to avoid the war, according to the *Times*, was to make concessions to the Albanian minority, to introduce United Nations mediation and to appoint a United States diplomat who would make it clear to all sides that war in this part of the Balkans would not be tolerated.[91]

By the middle of 1994, Menduh Taci was presenting himself as a constructive factor in Macedonian-Albanian relations. "I am for a step-by-step advancement of Albanian rights," Taci said, "We want to be part of this country — to build it up together with the Macedonians." The new softness in the ranks of the extremist Albanian political wings in Macedonia may have been related to pressure put on Sali Berisha, President of Albania, by the United States and the western allies with the goal of reducing the tension in the neighborhood of the Balkan war.

At the end of September 1994, even as the national elections approached, the two hostile factions of the PDP were fighting over the right to keep the party name.[92] Abdurahman Haliti's faction, which continued to participate in the coalition government, launched legal proceedings against the group headed by Arben Dzaferi. Meanwhile, Menduh Taci, brought a lawsuit against Haliti's group. Both factions had the same program and said they would participate in the elections.[93]

The Serbian party. Boro Ristic was the first president of the Democratic Party of Serbs (DPS), founded in March 1992. They have been outspoken in their criticisms of special treatment given to Albanians in Macedonia. They have been seen as having a Serbian orientation with an open dislike for the authorities in Macedonia, and as refusing to accept Macedonian independence from the former Yugoslavia. There were several battles between the police and the militant part of the party membership, especially in the Skopje village of Kuceviste. At one of these disturbances, at which Boro Ristic was prominent, slogans such as "Long live Arkan!" "Long live Seselj!" and "Serbia, Serbia!" were shouted by the Serbian protesters. The DPS announced at a press conference on January 15, 1993, that "unless the discriminating situation of Serbs in Macedonia is resolved through democratic means, we will be forced to undertake measures of self-defence, counting on aid from the homeland."[94] The party demanded Serbian equality with all other nationalities in Macedonia, and the status of a constitutive people in Macedonia. At this press conference the party expressed dissatisfaction with government statistics on the number of Serbs in Macedonia. Official figures of the time suggested around 40,000 Serbs, but the party insisted on a "realistic" figure of between 200,000 and 300,000 Serbs in Macedonia. Ristic could hardly be seen as a moderate force, having invited the Russian ultra-nationalist Vladimir Zirinovski to Macedonia.[95] However, even more extreme Serbian forces took over the Serbian party. The party is accused of conspiring together with the Serbian Orthodox Church, especially with the bishop of Grange, Pahomie, against Macedonian interests.

With the assistance of mediation by EU representative Gert Arens, an agreement was signed in 1993 between the Macedonian government representative Ljubomir Frckovski, who is believed to have some sympathies with Serbia, and Boro Ristic on behalf of the DPSM. This agreement dealt with processes for resolving disputable issues concerning the position of Serbs in the country. Serbia and Montenegro immediately criticized this agreement, and a "radical stream" (as Ristic called it) of Serbs in Macedonia described the agreement as a "betrayal of Serbia." In the period following the signing of these minutes, visits of Serbian priests in Macedonia became more frequent, particularly in the Kumanovo region. At the same time, the presence of people belonging to the top party leadership of the Seselj Serbian Radical Party was noticed in this region. *Nova Makedonija*, the national daily newspaper, concluded that there were continuing efforts to create an "extended hand" of a Serbian political organization in Macedonia, which would lead to policies being determined by instructions from the North. Boro Ristic seemed to agree. The "radical stream" became stronger by the day and resulted in his resignation at the end of 1993 "on grounds of too strong influences from outside and interference in creation of the party's politics, especially by the Socialist and the Radical Party from Serbia, as well as by the Serbian Church, whose 5 senile old leaders cannot comprehend the fact that there is a Macedonian nation, Macedonian state and Macedonian Orthodox Church."[96] Dragisha Miletich was appointed the new president.

In the middle of 1994, Miletich announced a Serb boycott of the census unless the government met their demands. In particular the party was concerned that 85 percent of the Serbs had not received citizenship certificates. Miletich said the government's desire to prove there are only 15,000 Serbs in Macedonia would not be successful. Miletich announced further struggle for Serbs' rights, claiming his party had the support of the Macedonian people.[97]

Some elements of the Macedonian press have been highly critical of the role that Serbian church leaders have played in Macedonia.[98] The Synod of the

Serbian Orthodox Church has, in turn, expressed concern about the treatment of Serbian Orthodox priests in their efforts to cross into Macedonia, and efforts of the Macedonian church to express its independence from the Serbian church. Actions of the Serbian church, including threats against the Macedonian church and unwillingness to use the constitutional name of the country in communications with President Gligorov, have been seen as impudent and arrogant in Macedonia.

Macedonian nationalists. The largest ethnic Macedonian nationalist party is VMRO-DPMNE, the Democratic Party for Macedonian National Unity. The party declares itself a "national party with exclusively liberating, national-patriotic and democratic goals." The party does not define itself as right-wing, but acknowledges opposition to left-wing forces. When first formed it aimed to achieve "state sovereignty and complete independence" for Macedonia, gaining wide support, as shown by its winning 38 seats in the first Parliament. On the occasion of the one-hundredth anniversary of VMRO, the party president, Ljupcho Georgievski, said the most significant tasks for the party were defining the Republic of Macedonia's international position, liberating it from the blockade imposed by the country's southern and northern neighbors, removing the dangerous pro–Yugoslav influences and Communism in Macedonia, defining the status of and relations with the Albanian minority, and, finally, consolidating the country's economy. The main stated goal of VMRO-DPMNE is the struggle to reestablish the pride and dignity of the Macedonian people and state. The party aims for "complete spiritual, political, economic and ethnic uniting of the partitioned Macedonian people" in an independent national state. This has led to the conclusion that the party does not accept the present Macedonian borders. Attacks on the party in regard to this analysis have been so fierce that the party leaders have softened their position. VMRO has been particularly critical of former Communist president Gligorov.

VMRO has argued for the Macedonian state to be defined as a national state of the Macedonian people, down-playing the constitutional recognition of minorities. One change to the constitution proposed by VMRO and accepted by the Constitutional Committee stated that the Macedonian language would remain the official language and Cyrillic the official script. Consistent with this, statements foreshadowing future discussion on the language issue were removed. At the time there were violent demonstrations (not organized by VMRO) supporting the VMRO position. At first VMRO was a part of the government, but the party went into opposition during the third extension of the twenty-seventh Parliament session, when Parliament accepted the resignations of Georgievski (the vice-president) and Dragi Arsov, previous vice-president in the Parliament. By this move VMRO missed out on a sequence of opportunities to take a part of the government cake and to participate formally in government. This seemed to raise a general doubt amongst Macedonians about whether VMRO was simply too inflexible to be able to achieve the party's stated objectives.[99]

Elections 1994

The 1994 elections for the 120 members of the Macedonian Parliament were held in accordance with laws passed by the former Communist government. These laws were used for the first multiparty elections in 1992 and again in 1994.[100] The first elected government failed to pass a new electoral law in time because the ethnic Albanian parties boycotted Parliament earlier in the year. This boycott paralyzed the activities of the ruling coalition of President Gligorov.

On September 17, 1994, Kiro Gligorov was put forward as the presidential candidate of the Social-Democratic Alliance (SDSM), the Liberal Party (LP) and the Socialist Party(SP)— the three parties that then formed the coalition government— for the first presidential elections, to be held on October 16. The leaders of the three parties— Branko Crvenkovski (SDS), Stojan Andov (LP) and Kiro Popovski (SP)— announced that their parties would present a single list of candidates at the second multiparty parliamentary elections, also to be held on October 16. They announced the formation of an "Alliance for Macedonia."[101]

The "Alliance for Macedonia" campaigned under the motto "Definitely!" Addressing the participants in the assembly in the overcrowded hall of the Macedonian National Theater, Gligorov suggested that the formation of the Alliance for Macedonia was a major event. Gligorov emphasized that these three parties were the "bearers of the peaceful and legitimate way of independence and that they won Macedonia's place in the UN and the internal stability of the state." Mr. Gligorov underlined the three basic goals of his program as market reforms, democratic development and international affirmation of the Republic of Macedonia. He appealed for an election campaign without false promises and inflated passions and without inter-ethnic hatred.[102]

International analysts believed it was never likely that a single party would win an overall majority in Parliament, but the coalition partners considered they would have a reasonable chance of doing so as a united front. The government had lost popularity during its two years in power, mainly because of worsening economic conditions. However, the main opposition, VMRO-DPMNE, lost even more support and broke up into rival factions. Talks between Petar Gocev, an ex–Communist, leader of the small Democratic Party, and VMRO leaders might have led to a rival nationalist election alliance that would have presented a much stronger challenge to the Social Democrats and their partners at the election, but VMRO-DPMNE intransigence seemed to prevent this.[103]

Pre-election polling by Brima, an associate of the Gallup organization, showed that Macedonians had more confidence in Gligorov than any other politician. Seventy-seven percent of Macedonians expressed confidence in Gligorov, while only 44 percent felt confidence in another national figure, Vasil Tupurkovski. Further behind were Stojan Andov (41 percent), Branko Crvenkovski (40 percent) and Ljubomir Frckovski (40 percent).

Most of those who supported the Alliance for Macedonia favored Gligorov, but so did 80 percent of those who planned to vote for VMRO-DPMNE. Analysis by social groups showed that the clerks and intelligentsia (88 and 86 percent) held the greatest degree of trust in him, while the private businessmen trusted him the least (62 percent and 68 percent). People over 65 years of age had the most trust in Gligorov (84 percent) compared with those between 25 and 39 years of age (71 percent). Ninety percent of those with Macedonian ethnicity had a positive opinion regarding the president, compared with 35 percent of Albanians respondents, and 96 percent from the other nationalities.

By mid–September 1994, three candidates had announced their intention of running for the presidency at the upcoming elections. These were Kiro Gligorov from the "Alliance for Macedonia"; Ljupcho Georgievski, the leader of VMRO-DPMNE; and an independent candidate from the United States, George Atanasovski.

Kiro Gligorov was the first president of the Republic of Macedonia. His survival and success in the broader Yugoslavian Communist political context offers testimony to his personal competence, but was seen by critics as a reason to be suspicious about his willingness to tolerate real democracy. He was not expected to encourage future elections within Macedonia. However, his enthusiasm for the democratic process and for a free-market economy seemed to remove some of the doubts people held about him, and weakened the political platform of the hard-line nationalist groups. He was seen by other governments as a force for moderation and stability in the Balkans. He was reported to "know and understand intimately" the mind of the Serbian leader Slobodan Milosevic, which may partly account for his political success.[104] He is reported to have said, "If we are strong inside, no pressure from the outside will influence the internal situation."

Ljupcho Georgievski is a member of the Forum for Freedom of the Press, a supporter of Macedonian independence for many years, and one of the promoters of a platform for economic prosperity in Macedonia. Georgievski repeatedly claimed that the government tended towards secrecy and Macedonians faced "media totalitarianism." His party, VMRO-DPMNE, was fully aware of the popularity of Gligorov but aimed to use the media to improve Georgievski's position. By his candidacy they hoped to promote VMRO principles and thus help in the total election marketing of his party.[105]

George Atanasoski was one of the founders of the Macedonian World Congress and financier of the magazine *Macedonian Sun*. This American with

Macedonian citizenship is a successful businessman from Florida who contributed to certain NASA programs. Atanasovski met with Vlado Ralev, the vice-president of the so-called Ohrid Macedonian World Congress, aiming to overcome the differences between the two congresses in order to integrate them into one united nonparty and nongovernment organization. Apparently the other organization was less willing to interfere in Macedonian politics, and negotiations were not finalized. For a time it seemed that VMRO-DPMNE might consider Atanasovski as their presidential nominee.[106] In his statement for the public, Atanasovski claimed that the country needed fundamental changes to complete its democratization process, maximal development of the economy and the establishment of a functional legal system. According to him, Macedonia's future lay in a wide political coalition, able to give legitimacy to potential economic development programs and to contribute to the preservation of internal peace and stability.

Signatures from 30 deputies or 10,000 citizens were required in order to make presidential candidatures official. Both Gligorov and Georgievski fulfilled the legal requirements for candidature, but Atanasoski was rejected by the State Electoral Commission because he did not raise enough signatures and was said to have uncertain residence qualifications. Candidates were required to have lived in Macedonia for at least 10 of the last 15 years. Critics within Macedonia stated that Atanasovski was unknown in Macedonia, thus regardless of his abilities and good intentions he had little support. Atanasovski claimed that he had fulfilled all the necessary conditions for nomination as a candidate for president of the Republic of Macedonia. He said he had faced "certain difficulties and obstacles, created by the bureaucracy" and that in a complaint to the State Election Committee he had pointed out "certain irregularities and oversights." However, despite his legal efforts he was unable to become a recognized presidential candidate.[107]

The law on the presidential election states that the victory goes to the candidate who wins 51 percent of the total number of votes, providing that at least half of all voters take part in the elections. Should no candidate win the required number of votes, there must be a second round of voting.

According to figures from the Ministry of the Interior (where political parties must register), there were nearly sixty political parties in Macedonia by August 1994.[108] Fifty parties nominated 1,766 candidates for Parliament, and a total of 284 independent candidates also ran. As far as the election of Parliament members is concerned, candidates who win the majority of votes are elected, as long as they have received at least one-third of the total number of votes. If this does not happen, a second round is required. The second round, scheduled for October 30, included only candidates who had won at least 7 percent of the votes in the first round.[109]

The presidential and parliamentary elections in Macedonia were observed by 540 monitors. One hundred and fifty of these were from the CSCE and the

European Council, and the others were domestic monitors and representatives of various nongovernmental organizations. Monitors were distributed throughout Macedonia and present at most of the 2,000 polling places.[110] As well as the official observers there were about 150 foreign reporters following the election process in Macedonia.

The representatives of the European Council, Lambert Kestermans and Doris Hevik, said: "We can say that the elections were fair and free, and that this Parliament will be freely elected. This is a great step towards the membership of Macedonia in the Council of Europe." They noted that the organization was not as good as it might have been, but ascribed this to the fact that Macedonia is a young democracy and that these things take time. The Macedonian Helsinki Committee for Human Rights demanded that the State Electoral Commission and the government examine in detail all criticisms regarding the inaccuracy of electoral lists and evaluate the degree to which this problem had a negative influence on citizens' right to vote. The committee issued a public statement appealing to competent government agencies to act in accordance with the CSCE Parliamentary Assembly monitors' suggestion to correct all irregularities before the second round, so that the procedure would be completed as free and fair.[111]

Response to the first round. Prime Minister Branko Crvenkovski, from the Alliance for Macedonia, assessed the elections as exceptionally successful. The response of the voters was much higher that the response at the first elections. He added that stability of the electoral body was confirmed at these elections, and that the results from the public opinion polls were almost identical with the results from the elections. Crvenkovski said that the irregularities in the elections were of a technical nature and did not influence the results. They included electoral rolls which were not brought up to date, lateness in delivering the electoral invitations, and mistakes that occurred when parts of some streets were transferred from one electoral unit to another. Irregularities reported to the Electoral Committee included breaking of the ballot boxes and the taking of the electoral rolls by the voters, which led to results from the polling station in Kisela Voda being declared invalid; and, in Valandovo, finding one ballot paper more in the ballot box than the number of voters, which also led to the voting being declared invalid.[112] In such cases, the prime minister said, most probably the voting would be repeated, under the guidance of the State Election Committee.[113]

The spokesman of the Alliance for Macedonia, Tito Petkovski, warned citizens not to be provoked by the opposition's moves resulting from their poor electoral results. He claimed that the party most affected by the irregularity of the elections was the Alliance for Macedonia, since many of its candidates could already have become MPs were it not for those irregularities. "We don't go about solving the problems on the street with populism, but through the institutions of the system."[114]

The VMRO-DPMNE and the Democratic Party attempted to arrange a public demonstration against the election process, leading the Macedonian Interior Ministry to appeal to the public to behave in an orderly and peaceful manner. The Democratic Party, headed by Petar Gosev, claimed this appeal was further proof of the involvement of government organs in the "filthy" election campaign of the Alliance for Macedonia, since it was, he said, typical of Stalinistic methods of inciting fear among the population. The Democratic Party guaranteed the peaceful character of this meeting, and said that expressed fears of violence were libels against the opposition groups.[115]

Ljupcho Georgievski stated that the government had committed fraud on a national level, a "unique election putsch" and a degree of manipulation unseen before in Europe. He furthermore emphasized that VMRO-DPMNE would continue to insist on an annulment of the first round and the establishment of an administrative government that would prepare the elections in a thorough manner. Georgievski said that unless this was done, his party would abstain from the elections completely.[116]

The VMRO-DPMNE and the Democratic Party organized a public protest at Macedonia Square in the center of Skopje. Reporters estimated that there were 8,000 to 10,000 people in attendance. VMRO-DPMNE leader Georgievski stated that the meeting was for democracy. He promised to gain power, not through a clash between Macedonians themselves, but through democratic, free and fair elections. The "March for Democracy" ended without incident.[117] Other parties expressed dissatisfaction with aspects of the first round of the elections, but stopped short of claiming manipulation by the government.

On the international scene, observers were generally satisfied. On the ninth of November, British observers concluded that the first-round elections were generally free and fair. Although there were many regrettable technical irregularities, they said, they saw no evidence of a concerted campaign of manipulation. According to the embassy, the British government believed that threats of a boycott of the second round of elections were unjustified and urged all parties to participate in the second round on October 30. The government of Great Britain looked forward to continuing to work closely with President Gligorov, to improve the political and economic stability of his country, the Foreign Office statement said.[118]

After the first round of the elections, the president of the Macedonian Parliament, Stojan Andov, met with Hugo Anson, representative of special United Nations envoy Yasushi Akashi, who expressed satisfaction with the way elections were being conducted, adding the hope that all inadequacies would be corrected by the second round. At a following press conference, all citizens and political parties were urged to continue participating in the elections. It was noted that while public demonstrations were part of the political process, democracy must be expressed through voting and not on streets. These views were echoed by the head of the United States Liaison Office in Skopje, Victor

Comras, who added, "We note that a number of people have been critical of various irregularities... This is part of the growing pains of any republic and we believe that Macedonia is committed to the democratic process... We do not believe that anyone is seeking to thwart that process ... it is in everybody's interest to proceed with these elections ... we believe it is very important for Macedonia to move through and complete this very important election; that no party should boycott the election."[119]

The European Council issued a report concerning the elections in the Republic of Macedonia prepared by Mr. Lambert Kestermans (Belgium EPP), rapporteur of the parliamentary monitoring mission of the European Council. The report states that "within the existing legislative system these elections can be considered to be an important step towards democracy ... the delegation feels that the government has gone to great lengths to secure fair elections." The members of the mission visited more than 60 polling stations in Skopje and throughout the country. They were present at the opening of the electoral units and during the counting of the votes. The delegation observed that the clerks in the election units performed their duties correctly. Certain complaints concerning the irregularities of the electoral rolls and confusion as to what documents were required to prove citizenship were lodged with the observers by political parties and voters.[120]

At a press conference on October 20, the State Electoral Commission announced the official results of the presidential elections. Out of the total 1,360,729 registered voters, 1,058,130 citizens actually voted. 713,729 voters (52.44 percent) gave their votes to the candidate of the Alliance for Macedonia, Kiro Gligorov, while Ljubisha Georgievski obtained 196,936 votes (14.47 percent). Ljubisha Georgievski immediately submitted a formal complaint.[121]

Following the official announcement of the presidential election results, Kiro Gligorov held a conference for the press. He expressed great satisfaction with the large turn-out of voters. He said that the trust his people has shown in him was a great responsibility and honor. He promised to treat all citizens equally, regardless of their political, national or religious affiliation. "I think Macedonia must rush. We have a great deal to do. The situation in the region is still very complex, and solutions for issues decisive for our peace and stability have not yet been found... We have to take large strides towards reforms in the political system, move quickly towards a free market economy with accelerated privatization, reconstruction, modernization and establishing of a government administration that can cope with the complex problems. It must not be forgotten that we will have the option of becoming a part of Europe in the future. This means all reforms must be in accord with standards of the EU member countries." As for relations with neighboring countries, President Gligorov said Macedonia will continue its peaceful politics, oriented towards friendly relations with all, but giving no privileges to any in particular. He called on all citizens to vote during the second round, so that the elections could be completed in the best possible democratic and civilized manner.[122]

The British Embassy in Macedonia immediately stated, "The British Government welcomes the re-election of President Gligorov as Macedonian President. His long political experience will be invaluable as his country confronts the problems that threaten its stability and also that of the region."

In Assembly results, the necessary majority for continuing the race in the second round was secured by a total of 389 candidates out of 1,765, representing 16 political parties and 67 independent candidates. The coalition Alliance for Macedonia went into the second round with 86 candidates, VMRO-DPMNE with 84, the Democratic Party with 68, and the PDP with 31. As well, there were 13 candidates from the NDP, 7 from the LP (Liberal Party), and four each from the Democratic Party of the Turks and the MAAC (Movement for All-Macedonian Action). Minor parties accounted for the remaining candidates.[123]

The second round: boycott. State Electoral Commission president Mr. Najdanov gave assurances that electoral lists would be made accurate for the next round of voting by adding citizens who were unjustifiably excluded in the first round. 1,058,130 citizens voted, which represents 77.76 percent of the total number of voters in the country. This figure includes an additional 125,473 citizens who were not on the lists, but proved their right to vote by various identification documents.[124]

The two major opposition parties, VMRO-DPMNE and DP, at a joint press conference, stated they would boycott the second round of elections as a protest against the "organized plotting" of the government. The parties withdrew their candidates from the election, and in case they were elected, said they would not participate in the work of Parliament. MAAK and the independent deputy Todor Petrov joined their initiative. Thus a total of 157 candidates planned to boycott the second round of elections: 84 VMRO-DPMNE nominees, 68 of DP, 4 of MAAK, and Todor Petrov. The opposition planned to organize protest meetings throughout Macedonia, demanding new elections. VMRO-DPMNE leader Georgievski described the presidential elections as one of the biggest forgeries in the country, implying that Norman Anderson, head of the CSCE Mission in Macedonia, was also involved in it. Georgievski said, "We will help them win 100 parliament seats, in order to prove the absurdity of the situation to the world."[125] With the explanation that they did not want to take part in the "electoral farce," these opposition parties planned to organize a protest vote at all town squares in the larger towns in Macedonia. According to the leader of DP, Petar Gosev, 116 objections with general and specific remarks were addressed to the electoral commissions by the opposition candidates. After being rejected, the objections were submitted to the Supreme Court, where they were again rejected. They claimed that 120,000 non-citizens voted and that going into the second round of voting would mean "support and legitimacy of an anti-democratic situation."[126]

In the voting on October 30, 109 electoral units voted for candidates in the second round only. In 11 other electoral units both first- and second-round voting occurred during the same day to overcome the irregularities that had occurred in the first round two weeks before. After the final results were considered for the presidential elections in 120 electoral units, Kiro Gligorov had won 715,774 votes or 52.60 percent, while Ljubisha Georgievski had won 197,210 or 14.49 percent.

Radio Skopje said that the Alliance for Macedonia had won over 89 seats in Parliament. SDSM won 57 at least; the LP won 27, and the SP won 5. The PDP gained 12 seats in the new Parliament, and joined the new government.[127] Another nine seats were shared among candidates of the other Albanian parties, the NDP and the Taci-Dzaferi group. Minor parties and independents won the remaining seats.[128]

The CSCE Parliamentary Assembly, CSCE Office for Democratic Institutions and CSCE Mission in Macedonia all stated at a press conference that the second round of elections was conducted regularly and in a peaceful manner. The nine-member American delegation of the International Republican Institute (IRI) regarded the elections in Macedonia as a significant step towards the country's transition to democracy, in the view of the head of the delegation, Donald Roomsfeld, former United States secretary of defense. The institute monitoring teams paid unannounced visits to 80 polling stations throughout Macedonia, and although they did not discover any problems big enough to undermine the electoral process, they did find certain problems they said should be resolved before the next elections. The IRI mission stated that despite the boycott by "certain parties," the response of voters was high enough to yield legitimate election results.[129]

The Bureau of the Council of Europe's Parliamentary Assembly discussed the report by the monitors and concluded that the elections were a significant step towards democracy in Macedonia. It was judged that the elections were free and fair. It was recommended that the newly elected Parliament should revise the electoral legislation before the next elections.[130]

Norman Anderson, head of the CSCE Mission in Macedonia, sent a telegram to President Gligorov to say: "Your election for a president was a direct result of the will of your people. Your strong support for peace and stability is highly respected by the CSCE and we expect an even closer co-operation on these issues in the future..." Telegrams of congratulations were also sent by Hugo Anson, special envoy of the United Nations secretary general, and Tryggve Tellefsen, commander of UNPROFOR troops in Macedonia: "Your constantly impressive and wise leadership will be of great importance in the years to come, for both the international community and the people in FYROM... You can be assured that the UN and UNPROFOR will continue to do all in their power to help this country in its efforts to achieve prosperity and peaceful co-operation with its neighbors."[131]

Mr. Gligorov and the Government's Platform

After the elections, on the occasion of taking a formal oath of office, Gligorov addressed the newly elected members of the Macedonian Parliament. He explained the presidential program, the tasks which stood ahead of him, for the new five-year mandate. He stated that Macedonia was "dealing with problems in international relations in the only possible way — in the spirit of our tradition of co-existence and tolerance, and on basis of international standards and practice." As matters of utmost concern he listed "deep economic changes and the stabilization of our economy." He went on to note:

> It is similarly important to create equality and the rule of law, to enable the judicial system to come fully to life, our executive power to become more efficient and the legislature to be strengthened. Further development of ethnic relations in the spirit of mutual understanding and tolerance and implementation of the rights of minorities is a goal. All these are the main buttresses of internal stability and development in the Republic of Macedonia.[132]

With regard to interethnic rivalries, Gligorov insisted that minority rights could be protected only by participation in the democratic process, and not by non-parliamentary actions. Pledging to "remain consistent to the concept of development of ethnic relations," he emphasized his "firm determination to carry out the presidential function in concordance with the constitutional authorities, as a president of all citizens, regardless of their party, political, ethnic or religious affiliation."[133]

While these are the kinds of statements to be expected of a politician, it is encouraging to observe the emphasis given to the issues recognized as critical to Macedonia's future, such as the place of minority groups, the future of democracy, and the move towards a free-market economy. However, only a few months after the government was elected, the Macedonian press was complaining bitterly. *Nova Makedonija*, a daily national newspaper supposedly very much under government control, strongly attacked the government's performance.[134]

Nova Makedonija argued that the Macedonian people had wanted a competent and energetic government and a vigorous opposition, but had been disappointed by the apparent lack of harmony and competence of the new ministries, and the lack of an opposition. The newspaper complained that democratic process in the country was developing very slowly, that the lawmaking process was far behind schedule, especially in the civil rights area. *Nova Makedonija* suggested that the Alliance for Macedonia had apparently ceased to exist after a struggle for power, creating a political crisis. The ruling parties had diametrically opposing views on future investment in the country, on the way in which the economy was to be privatized, on the way that privatization should occur, on liberalization of the economy, on taxation, on the functioning of banks, and even on the role of the army and police. A bitter struggle was underway to determine what banks would gain influence. The parties differed widely on the ways of resolving problems with ethnic relations. *Nova Makedonija* argued that there had been a ruthless battle for power and influence within the new government, and an atmosphere of deep distrust had developed. The paper suggested that the elected members of Parliament put their responsibility to their country ahead of their personal ambitions.

One element in the new political atmosphere, according to the newspaper *Delo*, was an echo of the unhappy history of the independence movement in Macedonia.[135] The newspaper lamented the violent divisions within Macedonian politics over the last one hundred years. *Delo* pointed out that it was the desire for independence that led Macedonians to join the Communist party resistance to the invaders in the Second World War. It noted also that once in power, for fifty years the Communist rulers of Macedonia attacked Macedonians who expressed the very same ambition for Macedonian independence, "declaring all living (and deceased) independence-seekers to be pro–Bulgarian enemies of the federation. Splits in foreign interests again brought about splits among the Macedonians themselves, giving birth to antagonism and hatred whose influence can still be felt today... Daily political interests have again divided the Macedonian nation into pro–Bulgarian and pro–Serbian oriented groups. Faced with the possibility of losing power, the current ruling party played the old card of ... declaring an entire party (VMRO) to be pro–Bulgarian." Arguing that it was high time to stop labeling people in this way, *Delo* asked for a national reconciliation platform to unite all significant groups in the country. The issue that prompted government attacks on VMRO was a move to rehabilitate Macedonians who had been charged with pro–Bulgarian (i.e. independence) sympathies during Communist times. *Delo* claimed that the newly elected government bore primary responsibility for the fact that the national reconciliation had not yet been achieved. The opposition was marginalized during the election process, and leading political figures seemed to be ignoring the "aching" need for national reconciliation. *Delo* suggested that the Macedonian Orthodox Church might be the only organization under which such national reconciliation would be possible.

The Dispute Over an Albanian-Language University

The struggle to establish an Albanian-language university in Tetovo is an instructive demonstration of the currents of conflict between Albanians and Macedonians at both the political and popular levels. The pressure to establish the university, though to some extent in the hands of an Albanian from Kosovo (the would-be rector of this university) who might be expected to have less sensitivity to Macedonian developments, no doubt indicated the importance of the educational issue for the Albanians. The events that unfolded show how easily a course of action that seems reasonable to one side in a dispute can be interpreted as provocative and outrageous by the other. They show how easily violence can break out in Macedonia. The fact that a greater conflict did not ensue is probably attributable to the caution of moderate Albanian political groups, and a genuine desire by Macedonian politicians to bring about the changes that are demanded.

The session of the Tetovo township assembly scheduled for November 2, 1994, was to discuss the initiative for opening an Albanian language university, with departments for natural sciences, Islamic studies, arts, philology, philosophy, economy and law. The assembly president, Shakir Aliti, was among the co-signers of the initiative for an Albanian university.[136] However, the session was delayed due to the lack of a quorum, largely because the ethnic Macedonian members refused to attend. This attitude was reflected throughout Macedonia. Nearly a hundred scientists, intellectuals and public figures in Macedonia submitted a memorandum to the government, expressing their disagreement with attempts to establish a parallel educational system in the Albanian language in the higher education sphere. They stated that they refused to be merely silent observers of "anti-constitutional, illegal and politically forced solutions" for change in the educational system in Macedonia. They saw this as the beginning of a process of federalization of the country. They demanded that the government prevent all activities aimed at establishing a parallel educational system in the Albanian language in higher education institutions.[137]

On December 14, 1994, three days before the planned public opening of an Albanian university in Tetovo, the president of the initiative committee for establishing the university, Fadil Suleimani, and the president of the Forum for Human Rights in Gostivar, Miljaim Fejziu, were arrested and police broke into the administrative offices of the proposed university.

Signs of police activities aimed at preventing the establishment of an Albanian-language university could also be seen in the nearby village of Mala Recica. According to the PDP radical group, a building authorized by the previous municipal committee, but probably illegal, had been torn down in the presence of some 250 policemen early on the same day. It was in this structure that the university lectures were to be given. A larger group of infuriated villagers told reporters that a curfew had been introduced in the village the previous night. They claimed that a big meeting would take place in Tetovo if arrested villagers were not released. In the afternoon the Taci-led party held a conference for the press. The "Tacists" stated that their premises had also been searched with no warrant or explanation. Agni Dika, one of the organizers of the university, stated: "They can tear down all the buildings they want, but we will still open the university on December 17. What this state knows how to do best is to harass and oppress non–Macedonian nationalities in the country."[138]

Arben Dzaferi told reporters that the police had also been active in cities other than Tetovo. He said that similar interventions took place in Kumanovo, where the police hunted for the organizers of the fund-raising for the university and even confiscated part of the money. He also said that Sami and Enver Bekhiri were arrested at the print shop "Aza," where materials for the work of the university had allegedly been printed. Dzaferi claims all this was a planned and controlled destabilization of Macedonia. He said his party was undergoing strong pressure by their supporters who, infuriated by the previous day's events, demanded that the party withdraw from Parliament. These people were ready to protest publicly. "But, we will not allow a chaos," he said. "We will respond with responsible behavior to this irresponsibility shown by the government. It does not really matter who has the matches in a room full of gunpowder; what matters is that the matches are taken away." The Tacists advised that they were acting in coordination with the NDP and the initiative committee of the PDP (the moderate groups). They said there was a consensus among the political parties of Albanians in Macedonia on the question of the university.[139]

A joint statement by several Albanian associations from Gostivar criticized government efforts to prevent the opening of the Albanian university and the unnecessary politicizing of the issue. They similarly criticized efforts to organize protests by Macedonian youth groups and students who publicly opposed the initiative, as well as public statements by the majority of Macedonian political parties and associations. The Albanians said that the Macedonian constitution and laws do not ban higher education institutions of other national groups. They said that the university in Tetovo was supported by many international conventions, including the constitution of the Republic of Macedonia itself. In practice, Albanian students were hardly ever able to gain entry to Skopje and Bitola universities, and in any case lectures at them were given only in Macedonian.

On December 17, at the headquarters of the Party for Democratic Prosperity in Tetovo, despite a ban by the Interior Ministry, a formal opening of the Albanian-language university took place. Representatives of all the political parties of the Albanians in Macedonia, the municipal assemblies from western Macedonia, MPs and ministers in the old and candidates for ministers in the new government attended the event. "The University in Tetovo has been founded. This university will contribute to the well-being of all the nations in Macedonia. Everyone should rejoice, not only the Albanians," stated the president of the University Council, Fadilj Suleimani, at a press conference. The Minister of the Interior, Ljubomir Frckovski, characterized the event in Tetovo as a "private party" and a "blown up balloon." At the headquarters of the political grouping led by Dzaferi and Taci, it was announced that on that Friday night, several people were taken in to the Tetovo police station for "informative discussions." Among them were two members of the council of the university, Agni Dika and Murtezan Ismaili, as well as the owner of the private

TV station ART from Tetovo. University spokespersons said that classes were due to begin around January 20, 1995.[140]

The Interior Ministry, which controls the police, persisted with its ruling that establishing an Albanian-language university in such a manner was illegal, but at this stage, before any actual classes were in session, restricted its involvement to questioning of those involved and examining their documents. The CSCE Mission in Skopje said it was seriously concerned about possible disturbances in connection with the announced opening of a university in Tetovo. The mission said that as long as both Macedonians and Albanians were committed to development in the republic, there were no problems involving higher education which could not be solved through negotiations. The CSCE Mission appealed to political leaders and all groups involved in the dispute to exercise restraint and offered to help establish a dialogue to work toward bridging the differences.[141]

The Macedonian Helsinki Human Rights Committee issued a statement arguing the need for public debate on the origins of the problems surrounding the issue, as well as on finding optimal constitutional and legal solutions for higher education of teachers needed in the elementary and high school education in Albanian language. The committee was gathering objective information on the initiative itself and the activities undertaken by the state thus far. The committee claimed that Article 45 of the Macedonian Constitution allows establishing of private educational institutions at all levels except elementary schools. However, the committee believed that direct action by Albanians had contributed to an escalation of misunderstandings.[142]

In January 1995 the Tetovo university committee submitted an official application for a court registration of the institution with the Skopje district court.[143] According to Dr. Fadil Suleimani as quoted by Radio Tirana, "The university is functioning, the entry exams have started, premises have been provided, professors have been engaged and everything is going smoothly." But, he stressed, "we are being obstructed by the Macedonian police, who intend to prevent the university from working by use of force and pressure just as the Communists used to. We firmly believe that all they will do is compromise themselves. The university will never cease its work, and the political forces of Albanians ... have never been more united than at present." A1 television cited the Pristina (Kosovo) paper *Bujku* that described entry exams were being held in Tetovo, despite efforts by the police to prevent it. The paper stated that 400 regular and 100 part-time students would enroll at the university.[144]

The government did not want the Albanians to set up their own university. They wanted the Albanians to stay within state educational structures, and were prepared to accelerate educational change to allow this to happen. Early in February 1995, students of Albanian nationality, who had boycotted all classes in the previous three months, returned to the Teachers' College "St. Clement of Ohrid" in Skopje with the promise of being taught in the Albanian

language. It seemed that the Ministry of Education was taking a more conciliatory approach towards the Albanians than the Ministry for the Interior.
Albanian language classes were soon to be available after the completion of the
formalities concerning the part-time employment of Albanian teachers. On
this understanding, students of Albanian nationality attended classes in the
Macedonian language.[145] The council of the Teachers' College followed the
Ministry of Education directive to permit students of Albanian nationality to
do their classes in their mother tongue for the summer semester. Dr. Dzeladin
Murati was appointed as a professor of pedagogy in the Albanian language,
Redzep Balaci as a professor of psychology, and Dr. Seifedin Suleimani as a pro-
fessor of educational sociology.[146]

The people behind the Albanian-language university continued with their
own plans. Fadil Suleimani informed Radio Tirana that the university would
begin its work on February 15. Saying they would never give up the initiative
to establish the university, Suleimani stressed that a delegation of United States
politicians would attend the opening ceremony and would try to persuade
Macedonian authorities of the need for such a university. The delegation was
to be led by former United States congressman Joseph Dioguardi, vice-president of the United States–Albanian Friendship Association and leader of the
Albanian lobby in the United States. Meantime, the Tetovo university had
signed an agreement on bilateral cooperation with George Washington University in Washington, D.C. During his visit to the United States, Suleimani
met with deputy secretary of state Richard Holbrooke to inform him of the
problem with and pressures against the university.[147] The day before the opening, Suleimani was quoted as saying that they would not wait for the Tetovo
university to be incorporated into the Macedonian educational system. "The
police should not be involved in this affair otherwise they would bear the
responsibility of some possible incidents that might occur."[148]

Nearly 2,000 people, including about 100 enrolled students, attended the
official opening of the Albanian-language university on February 15, 1995.
Official guests included former United States congressman Dioguardi, Yugoslav
dissident and representative of George Washington University Mihajlo Miha-
jlov, and Jerry Klein, member of the United States delegation. Leaders and representatives of ethnic Albanian political parties with branches in Tetovo, Gostivar and Debar, along with Albanian deputies in Parliament and a large group
of OSCE officials, also attended the ceremony. Albanian ministers in the government did not attend. The event went peacefully, without police presence. The
promotion was opened by Dr. Suleimani, who emphasized that the university represented a victory for educational principles over daily politics. The university,
he said, had been supported by universities in Heidelberg, Bonn, and Zurich as
well as George Washington University. He warned that should the police obstruct
the university's activities, 200,000 Albanians stood ready to defend it.[149]

The initial response of the Macedonian government was measured. Government spokesman Gjuner Ismail said, "The government will move only within the legally established educational system and recommends the same to all those people and organizations desiring to establish any institution... What they are doing is nothing but an impudent violation of the constitutional framework and flagrant disrespect of the political reality. Their activities are political and they must be fully aware of the possible consequences of their interfering in the sphere of politics." Asked about Joseph Dioguardi, Mr. Ismail said he was simply an ex-congressmen and a president of a citizens' association who has been received in Macedonia as a guest. "His attempts to be involved in politics in this region probably result from his inability to perform well as a politician back home now that he is no longer in the U.S. Congress."[150] Macedonian Radio said that Dioguardi had not been a polite guest, and his actions involved "direct interference in the internal affairs of a sovereign state." Macedonian Radio said Dioguardi "had long ago proved his personal lack of principles when dealing with issues concerning Macedonia and the Macedonian people, openly taking the side of separatist forces among the ethnic Albanians in the country."[151]

There was some foreign support for the position of the Macedonian government. According to Risto Nikovski, Macedonian ambassador to London, who discussed the issue with several British Foreign Office officials, the British government viewed the opening and functioning of the university in Tetovo as going beyond the legal framework of the country and therefore considered it unacceptable. The British officials said that Great Britain was deeply concerned by the establishment of the university. The official British standpoint regarding the initiative of ethnic Albanians in Macedonia was that solutions must be sought within the legal framework and educational system. London did agree that some demands by ethnic Albanians in Macedonia might be justified and should therefore be taken into consideration.[152]

The Albanian university started classes on the day after the official opening. The undersecretary in the Macedonian Interior Ministry, Dime Gjurev, confirmed that an attempt was made in the village of Poroy to start the classes at the "illegal" university in Albanian language. Gjurev stated that around 80 citizens congregated in a "religious structure" located in the village of Poroy, and that this meeting was also attended by the self-proclaimed rector Suleimani and the Albanian lobbyist and former Republican congressman Joseph Dioguardi. Police sources claimed that Suleimani called on the villagers from the surrounding villages to protect the students. The undersecretary said that the legal significance of Suleimani's activities was still being examined. The police interrupted classes in philosophy and the theory of literature, which were held by professors Rahmed Duda and Ismet Hodza, according to the private TV station ART from Tetovo. The same source claimed that the police did not use force, but that Suleimani told a Ministry of Interior representative that the university would continue working at any cost.[153]

The faculty of Economics within the Albanian-language university was opened in the Tetovo village of Poroy on the morning of the following day, without any incidents or police intervention. Around 1,000 villagers congregated in front of the building, observed by about 100 police officers. Representatives of UNPROFOR and the United Nations also attended the event. After the end of the lesson, rector Suleimani asked the congregated people to peacefully disperse. He announced that the classes on philology and philosophy would continue the following week.[154]

On the afternoon of February 17, near the rector's office of the Albanian university in the village Mala Recica, a large group of Albanians came into conflict with the police. The incident began when police tried to enter the building while lectures were in progress. A1 television reported that 30 police officers and about 100 villagers were already at the spot by 2:00 p.m. Two buses soon arrived carrying police reinforcements, accompanied by OSCE and UNPROFOR representatives. The OSCE official made efforts to mediate between the two sides, but to no avail. Several inhabitants of Mala Recica tried to do the same, but failed as well. The police then began vigorously pushing the crowd away from the building, and the villagers started throwing stones at them. The police tried using nightsticks, tear gas, and warning shots in the air to move the crowd. The Tetovo police headquarters claims it was the crowd which started shooting automatic weapons. The crowd was soon dispersed, but not before damaging the two police buses and a vehicle belonging to Macedonia Television. At about 4:00 p.m., a PDP delegation, led by Abdurahman Haliti, arrived at the scene. NDP parliament deputy Bekhir Kadriu persuaded the crowds to go to their homes. The situation calmed down during the evening hours. Armed police troops were deployed along roads going into Tetovo and into Mala Recica.[155] The on-duty surgeon, Ljubomir Jankovski, told Macedonian Radio that five persons were severely injured in the incident, including a reporter of the Skopje paper *Vecer*, and one ethnic Albanian, 33-year-old Emini Abdulselam, who had died.[156]

PDP president Abdurahman Aliti condemned the police intervention, calling it an "act for destabilization of Macedonia and a direct attack on inter-ethnic relations." He blamed the police actions on the political institutions in Macedonia and President Gligorov, who had opposed the request to open a university in the Albanian language. Aliti called on the Macedonian Albanians to "maintain peace and quiet, so that irresponsible persons do not take the situation in their own hands." The radical leader Menduh Taci stated that evening that people were still gathered in Mala Recica. "We are trying to convince them to disperse, and I think we will succeed." The number of injured persons being reported by that time had grown to 19, of whom 9 were police officers. One police officer had been seriously injured.[157]

Kiro Gligorov sent a telegram to the family of Emini Abdulselam, in which he expressed his deepest condolences and emphasized his respect for "the peace and security of all our citizens."[158]

After the death in Mala Recica on Friday the situation in Tetovo remained tense. The police spent the night in the suburb, surrounding the university building, but withdrew in the early morning hours after the Interior Ministry responded to a request from the Tetovo assembly, addressed to President Gligorov, the prime minister and the foreign minister. The Macedonian government reportedly agreed to withdraw police troops guarding the university sites, after a promise made by the political parties of Albanians that no lectures would be given for the time being.[159] The funeral for Emini Abdulselam was attended by over 10,000 people. The police were not present. Representatives from the OSCE, as well as a large number of reporters from Macedonia and abroad, were in attendance at the cemetery, while the entire happening was monitored by members of UNPROFOR from the surrounding hills. After the funeral, a large number of citizens headed for the police station in the town to demand the release of Fadil Suleimani, who had been arrested by the police during the night. The situation in front of the police station was tense. However, after some initial chanting of the name "Fadil," the crowd dispersed peacefully after they were addressed by Sali Ramadani, an Albanian member of the Macedonian Parliament. Mr. Ramadani told them that the release of the people taken in by the police would be negotiated, and that, if necessary, they would come to the same place again, but with "one hundred thousand people."[160]

The following day villagers set up barricades around the village of Poroy and around the local mosque where the university was planning to hold lectures for its economic and law departments. Redzep Seljami, president of the local community, stated that "the protection of this place is the will of the people, who decided to take this course of action on their own initiative." He said, "This building will not fall as long as we are alive."[161]

During this very sensitive time, Serbian symbols were sprayed on the walls of the university buildings in Mala Recica. The local villagers say these symbols were written by the police, a charge the Ministry of Interior denied.

At first the Interior Ministry laid charges against five people: Fadil Suleimani, the rector of the university in Tetovo; Miljaim Fejziu, president of the Human Rights Forum of Gostivar and member of the university council; Arben Ruse, a member of the executive of the Taci group and president of the humanitarian organization "El Hilal"—Tetovo; and Shaban Kemal and Arben Murtezani, participants in the demonstration. Criminal charges were brought against these men, according to articles 205, 206 and 218 of the criminal law of the Republic of Macedonia, namely, inciting people to resist the police, belonging to a crowd that was preventing police officers from exercising their duties, and the illegal possession of weapons. Undersecretary Gjurev emphasized that Shaban Kemal possessed two firearms, an automatic rifle and a gun with ammunition. The charges were submitted to an investigative judge.

The undersecretary in the Interior Ministry, Dime Gjurev, announced that according to the forensic report, Emini Abdulselam had died from a single gunshot wound to the chest. He had been shot from a distance of only 60 cm, with a 7.62 mm calibre gun called an M-57. Gjurev explained that a very small number of police officers owned such a weapon, but also that they can easily be bought cheaply. He said it was possible that it could have been used by the police, but also by some person in Mala Recica. "The competent department … is continuing its efforts to determine the participants in the Mala Recica incidents."

The Democratic Party of Turks in Macedonia expressed deep concern with the events in Mala Recica, appealing to the Macedonian authorities to introduce a serious approach for resolving problems by democratic methods and dialogue, and avoiding the use of force. The party insisted that President Gligorov use his authority to contribute to a peaceful solution for the problems. The party also appealed to all political structures of ethnic Albanians in Macedonia to avoid the use of vocabulary which could add to the current tension. The party demanded that if it were proven that the police abused their authority, the guilty parties should be held responsible. Conversely, the Democratic Party of Macedonians of Tetovo said that government measures to deal with the university in Tetovo were just and rightful, but too late. This party believed that the university issue was only a part of the Greater-Albania strategy to create "Ilirida," which involved annexing the western part of Macedonia to Albania. The party said Fadil Suleimani's claim that 200,000 Albanians would defend the university was in fact a call to all Albanians to come out into the streets.[162]

The leadership and executive committee of the Tetovo municipality issued a public statement appealing to all citizens of Tetovo to refrain from violence and avoid quarrels and provocation of any kind, in order to preserve peaceful coexistence in the area. The statement was signed by Shakir Aliti, Tetovo township committee president.[163]

Asked whether he would start negotiations with government officials and temporarily cease all activities of the university, Suleimani answered that the school year must not be lost and people who want to learn would not harm anyone. He said the law must be changed right away, and that new laws on education must be created urgently. The Pedagogical Academy in Skopje, Suleimani said, had never met the basic educational needs of Albanian students. "It is a ridiculous political school of no use to us."[164]

All sorts of rumors were being reported by various media after the violence in Tetovo. Radio Tirana reported the possibility of organized gatherings of Macedonians in Tetovo. These claims were never shown to be true.[165] *Nova Makedonija* asked about Fadil Suleimani's political connections. The newspaper said, though he had come from Kosovo, the Albanian enclave in Serbia, he had never been on the "black list" of the Serbian police, and members of his family still live and are employed in Pristina. This implied that he might be an ally of Serbian interests. *Nova Makedonija* went on to say, "Our available information indicates that Suleimani is in the service of the Serbian regime and its secret intelligence agency, KOS. His mission in Macedonia is not that of an educator. He has been assigned to transfer the focus of the international attention from Kosovo into Macedonia, as this would be in the interest of Serbia now that it is attempting to present itself as a peacemaker in order to achieve lifting of the UN sanctions."[166]

International reactions to the incidents at Tetovo. After the violence in Tetovo, Mr. Hugo Anson, representative of United Nations special envoy Yasushi Akashi, issued a statement to the press expressing regret at the violence and urging dialogue.[167] Ambassador Tore Bogh, head of the OSCE Mission in Skopje, made a similar statement at about the same time. Following a meeting with President Gligorov, the OSCE high commissioner for inter-ethnic issues, Max van der Stoel, who visited Skopje a few days after the shooting of Emini Abdulselam, urged restraint on all sides and expressed the hope that the government would attend to the educational needs of minority groups as it had promised.[168]

Max van der Stoel was interviewed by *The Macedonian Times* at the end of January 1995.[169] He was asked about his impression of the "globalization of the Albanian issue in the Balkans," and how events in Macedonia might be a replication of those in Kosovo, with extremist actions on both sides. He responded by saying, "I think that nationalist extremism is the worst enemy here in Macedonia. Any extremism, regardless of where it comes from, is harmful for the future of Macedonia." He made a plea for "fruitful cooperation between the various ethnic groups here." He stated that while members of minority and national groups within a state have the right in principle to establish private educational institutions, including universities, the criteria of OSCE and the Council of Europe make it clear that this can only happen within the legal framework of the country. His view was that Suleimani and the others who launched the initiative failed to take this into account.

In the regular session of the Permanent Council of the OSCE in Vienna on February 23, particular emphasis was placed on developments in Macedonia connected with the recent events surrounding the "so-called University in Tetovo." The Permanent Council expressed regret over the tragic incident in Tetovo on February 17 and also expressed support for the territorial integrity, sovereignty and stability of Macedonia. It acclaimed the attitude of the Macedonian government and those representatives of the Albanian minority who contributed to the reduction of possible tensions. The Permanent Council called for restraint and dialogue, for overcoming the problems in accordance with the constitutional system of Macedonia, and for adherence to the principles and decrees of the OSCE.[170]

At the time of the death in Tetovo, a spokesman for the Albanian government said, "Albanian public opinion is deeply embittered about this chauvinistic act of violence against the Albanians and their legitimate rights. The

Albanian Government regards this incident as a criminal act of violence, filled with destabilizing effects, and demands that the Macedonian Government undertakes measures for the rights of the Albanians to be respected, on the basis of international conventions and obligations."[171]

Commentators in Serbia were equally outraged by the Tetovo incident but had rather different interpretations of what was behind it all. *Vecernje Novosti*, a Belgrade daily newspaper, wrote that the events in Tetovo were part of a well-prepared plan already used in Kosovo. Intentions of the Albanian groups to make in Macedonia what it had failed to create in Kosovo were being thwarted by government action. According to the paper, ethnic relations in Macedonia had been radicalized because Macedonia opened its borders with Albania too soon, and also because Tirana had offered official support of the university in Tetovo.[172]

Yuri Petrovich Trushin, the Russian chargé d'affaires in Macedonia, visited the Macedonian Ministry of Education for discussions on the educational problems of ethnic Albanians. Stating that Russia considers the university in Tetovo illegal, Trushin repeated his country's interest in the preservation of stability in Macedonia, which required an unconditional respect by all citizens for the constitutional order.[173]

The Italian paper *La Vocce* wrote, "Thus far the tolerant policy of President Gligorov has succeeded in maintaining peace, thanks to allowing representatives of ethnic Albanians to hold office in the Macedonian government. Yet fears are held that Tirana is trying to increase ethnic tensions and even cause conflicts in the region... More than anywhere else, the dream of a Greater Albania is alive in Tirana. Albanian extremists in Macedonia are apparently provided with guns by Tirana. Knowing Albania is supported by Turkey, and Greece by Serbia — historic enemies — it is easily predictable what kinds of scenarios are possible in this region of the southern Balkans."[174]

Slowly, but surely, Macedonia is being turned into a second Kosovo, the Greek paper *Elefterothipia* wrote (February 22, 1995) in an article entitled "Tension Eased, Crisis Still There." The Athens paper said there were no signs the crisis in Macedonian-Albanian relations had been overcome. Ethnic Albanians in Tetovo had taken a bold step and had caused incidents and riots. Comparing Skopje to Pristina (in Kosovo), the paper concluded that the last thing President Gligorov wished was to see was his state turning into another Kosovo.[175]

Comments and developments within Macedonia. The Tetovo township assembly president, Shakir Aliti, blamed the government for the direct clash between police and citizens. Prime Minister Crvenkovski and Minister of Interior Frckovski were bitterly criticized. "Mr. Frckovski's police are pro–Serbian Chetnicks, with or without his being aware of it," said Muzafer Kamberi, committee member and president of the municipality of Mala Recica. Other ethnic Albanian members spoke in a similar way. Following the open and direct support of the university in Tetovo by all ethnic Albanian members, the

Macedonian committee members walked out of the city hall. On behalf of all of the Macedonians, member Zoran Stojanovski said, "The Macedonian committee members are of a common view that the disturbed political and safety situation in Tetovo results from the illegal activities of the so-called rector's office of the university in Tetovo and its wide support by all parties of Albanians in Macedonia. Statements about the Macedonian police by ethnic Albanians in this committee are tendentious and lead to the further destabilization of ethnic relations."[176] *Nova Makedonija* observed that the relative calming of the passions in Tetovo was partly owing to the announcements issued by the political parties of the Albanians and the appeal from the Tetovo assembly to citizens to keep their dignity "and not to succumb to any kind of provocations, by any side, so as to keep the peace and co-existence in these regions." The Albanian political parties, the PDP, NDP and Albanian Democratic Alliance — Liberal party (ADA-LP), as well as Albanian ministers and parliamentary members, along with representatives of the assemblies of the municipalities of Tetovo, Gostivar, Debar and Struga, held a joint meeting in the early morning hours, behind closed doors. The only ones not to attend this meeting were representatives of the radical PDP wing. This meeting discussed the university issue as well as a proposal to walk out of the institutions of the government system and to proclaim political autonomy.[177]

A joint statement made at this meeting said the Albanian political movement in the country would consistently support the future work of the university in Tetovo, and university directors would decide how lectures would continue in light of the new situation. The Albanian political groups in Macedonia insisted that Fadil Suleimani and the four others had been arrested without any legal grounds. A committee of representatives of political parties and the Association of Albanian Women in Macedonia was formed to contact representatives of the Macedonian authorities and demand their immediate release. PDP president Abdurahman Haliti said the representatives of all political parties of Albanians in Macedonia had reached a consensus. He also said he had the impression, after talks with President Gligorov, Parliament President Andov and Prime Minister Crvenkovski, that "there are realistic chances to work out an agreement and come up with a just solution." He said the university ought to continue its work, but through appropriate models and methods, leaving time for the problem to be resolved within the framework of the forthcoming higher education law. "What we all now need is space, a peaceful atmosphere to enable us all to help resolve problems in a suitable way, without any ultimatums from either side."[178] Muhamed Halili, a member of the PDP leadership, said, "We believe the police intervention was a brutal act against the right of a people to an education in its native language. The main parties to be blamed for the incident are those who were too slow in dealing with the issue of higher education in the Albanian language, including President Gligorov and the entire cabinet as well."[179]

Mr. Haliti from the Albanian party, the NDP, said demands for an immediate release of Suleimani were justified. Charges brought against some of the imprisoned Albanians could also be laid against some VMRO-DPMNE leaders for their activities of two years ago, when they called the Macedonian people to a rebellion. Suleimani's statements were mild compared with such statements, he said.[180]

Menduh Taci, on behalf of the radical PDP group, said his party continued with its firm support for the university and Fadil Suleimani. Taci said all parties of Albanians ought to reconsider their participation in all spheres of life in Macedonia. Asked whether this would not mean creating a Kosovo-like situation, Taci agreed, listing all elements, such as boycotts and civil disobedience, that might occur in common. He also said he would suspend the participation of his party's deputies in the Parliament for an indefinite time. Still, he appealed for a "cool-headed approach to the new situation, appealing to the people to avoid being provoked." Taci said to *Nova Makedonija* (February 18, 1995) that "the blame for the tragic outcome must be carried by the Government and Gligorov as they did not find it necessary to conduct talks about the proposed university."

On February 20 the block of Macedonian political parties and associations in Tetovo held a meeting to discuss the political and security situation in the region. They passed resolutions supporting the law-and-order protection measures undertaken by the Macedonian government and the Ministry of Interior. They requested that all activities connected with the university in Tetovo be forbidden and efforts be aimed at reaching a consensus between all Macedonian political parties in Tetovo and western Macedonia. While this looks very hard-line, they also decided to start a direct dialogue with all leaders of parties of Albanians, and appealed to citizens in and around Tetovo to contribute to peace and stability.[181]

The Democratic Party of Serbs reacted bitterly to the news of the alleged involvement of Serbs in events in and around Tetovo, as well as rumors that Fadil Suleimani was a KOS agent. According to the party leader, Dragisha Miletic, the media in Macedonia were full of lies and fabrications, and they should stop blaming Serbs for every unrest in the country. "I would like to remind people that our party was the first in Macedonia to warn the Macedonian government against its very suspicious coalition with the Shiptares (Albanians), some two and a half years ago. We also told them there would come a time when this coalition would bring nothing but trouble to the Macedonian people... This is only the beginning, as this is a scenario already seen in Kosovo. However, Serbia has already dealt with this problem. According to this scenario, the university is the first step to be followed by demands for cultural autonomy, then a secession and finally creation of their desired 'Ilirida' state. Why have they chosen Tetovo? Because they are counting on a large number of students from Kosovo; according to our calculations, this university would have up to 50,000 regular students. Why is the Macedonian government tolerating this and why is Minister Frckovski giving such casual statements?"[182]

Miletic denied claims of Serbian police involvement in Mala Recica, saying the Serbian signs on the walls could not have been written by Serbs, as the entire place was under the control of the Macedonian police. Miletic said Serbs in Macedonia were not demanding a university in their native language as they already have a university in Belgrade. He added that Serbs in Macedonia stood for coexistence, while the university in Tetovo was only a facade to cover up what is already happening in Kosovo: autonomy to be followed by secession. He promised protection to all Serbs in Macedonia should the conflict spread.[183] The day after this statement, the Macedonian Ministry of the Interior reported that it had discovered who wrote offensive graffiti on the walls of houses in the village of Mala Recica. It was police officer Goran Stanojkovich (the name is close to a Serbian form), who had been dismissed and would be the subject of disciplinary proceedings.[184]

Dosta Dimovska, vice-president of VMRO-DPMNE, was not convinced that Serbs played no role in the Tetovo affair. Dimovska said, "The recent events surrounding the so-called university in Tetovo show that all this was a premeditated scenario between the parties in the Alliance for Macedonia and parties of Albanians. The reason was to cause incidents and intimidate the Macedonian population in western Macedonia into accepting the policy of retreat and concessions toward the Albanian minority in Macedonia. This will increase the number of immigrants from Kosovo to Macedonia. In my opinion, this is part of the plan by Mr. Gligorov, who intends to help alleviate Albanian-Serbian tension in Kosovo and then give the Albanians in Macedonia a territorial and political autonomy. Finally, the remaining part of Macedonia would be annexed to Serbia and so complete the Belgrade-Skopje-Athens axis... The official policy, allegedly led in the name of peace and coexistence, will lead exactly to the opposite — disturbance of peace and stability in the country, turning it into another Bosnia."[185]

Petar Gosev, leader of the Democratic Party, took the view that the tragic outcome of the university dispute arose because the Albanians acted outside the legal framework. In any case, he thought it inappropriate to form a third university in the country, when the other two were "far from meeting European educational criteria."[186]

Macedonian prime minister Branko Crvenkovski expressed deep regret for the "tragic events" in Tetovo concerning the university in Mala Recica and Poroy. He said that such events showed what could result from going outside the legal framework noting that "the government had made its position on the issue clear" and had warned all concerned of the likely consequences. He referred to the leaders of the university as "self-declared messiahs" with no regard for human life. He pledged that "all activities violating the Constitution and law" would be punished. At the same time, Crvenkovski acknowledged a constitutional responsibility to provide trained Albanian teachers for elementary and high schools.[187] He was critical of the University of Saints Cyril and Methodius, which, he suggested "should have pushed forward educational reform within the framework of the Constitution."[188]

As for suggestions that a process of "Kosovization" was taking place in Macedonia, or that there was knowledge that Fadil Suleimani was an agent from KOS, Crvenkoski called them "speculations" and implied the government had no information on the latter issue. He said there was no danger in Macedonia from "Kosovization" for a number of reasons. Macedonia had a different history of coexistence between ethnic groups than Kosovo; the degree of tolerance between citizens is higher than in Kosovo; and government policy and the way it is enforced varies considerably from what happens in Kosovo.

Student opinion about the right way to respond to the Tetovo events was split, with some wanting to support the government position and others (the Liberal Youth group) seeking to make a stand against interethnic conflict in any form.[189] Nearly 2,000 students of the Saints Cyril and Methodius University in Skopje held a peaceful protest in front of the Parliament building. They issued a declaration against the establishing of an Albanian-language university in Tetovo. Among the many slogans was, "Let the damn Shiptares know the Macedonian name will never die." Only one professor, Dimitar Dimitrov, participated in this protest. The Students' Council at the "St. Clement of Ohrid" university in Bitola sent a telegram of support to their colleagues from Skopje. The day after the demonstration the Students' Council of Skopje dissociated itself from the chauvinist slogans used during the protest, since they were held to be contrary to the principles proclaimed by the council.[190] The government also criticized the student protest, with spokesman Gjuner Ismail saying, "This protest only encourages activities by Albanian extremists, feeding on nationalism which inevitably leads to a bottomless pit of nationalist hysteria... Claims that an entire nation is 'damned' are the best proof of one's own damnation."

For a few days after the killing at Tetovo, courses at the Albanian university were halted until results of negotiations with Macedonian authorities were known.[191] However, by the end of February, the senate of the university in Tetovo told the Albanian-language media that a way had been found to continue the work of the university and to inform enrolled students. The senate appealed to citizens not to gather in front of buildings in which the lectures were taking place. *Nova Makedonija* claimed that lectures were again being held, probably within the mosque in the village of Poroy.[192]

Early in May, the Rector's Office of the University of Saints Cyril and Methodius in Skopje held a round table discussion on the topic of "Possible Alternatives for Meeting Educational Needs of Ethnic Albanians in Macedonia." The debate was organized by the Ethnic Relations Center of the Sociology and Political Research Institute in cooperation with the Open Society Institute (also known as the Soros Institute). George Soros, an American businessman involved in a number of efforts at international dispute resolution and cooperation, spoke at this meeting. Soros had previously had several personal meetings with President Gligorov, and had loaned Macedonia 25 million dollars at a difficult time. At this meeting he argued for the resolution of educational problems within the legal framework of the society and suggested opening classes in Albanian language at the Pedagogical Academy in Skopje. He expressed readiness to provide financial backup for multilingual studies.[193] Tirana Radio took up the idea that an Albanian-Macedonian-English university financially supported by George Soros would be established in the near future, with government approval.[194] Soros was accused by the Skopje daily *Nova Makedonija* of interference in Macedonian affairs and supporting Albanian claims to constituent nation status. He also upset Mr. Gligorov by using the term "Macedonian Slav" to distinguish between Albanian Macedonians and ethnic Macedonians. Soros denied *Nova Makedonija's* claims and argued that an insistence that all citizens of Macedonia are Macedonians was the same kind of crime against the Albanians that the Greeks committed against Slavic Macedonians in Greece. He nevertheless pledged to continue his support of the Open Society Institute.

Macedonian Television commented that an influx of personnel from the Kosovo political environment, in the last year or two, had brought a disruptive radicalization of Albanian political activity in Macedonia. The "new political actors ... want everything and they want it immediately, regardless of existing laws, in contradiction to the existing constitution and most important of all, in contradiction to the existing Macedonian political reality." The commentator said that Fadil Suleimani was "a typical representative of the Kosovo political school," who, after a decade and a half of working and living with his family in Kosovo, without making any political impact, returned to Macedonia and "immediately thinks that he knows better than all of us," how to achieve what the Albanians need. In Kosovo, the commentator said, he was "a political zero for year," while in Macedonia he had become "a prominent political actor in only a couple of months." Suleimani was said to be telling everyone that the "so-called university" would be a factor for bringing Macedonians and Albanians closer together, though "Suleimani himself cannot make even half a sentence in the official Macedonian language." The commentator was angry at the outcome of Suleimani's actions, saying, "The tragically lost young life cannot be replaced or justified by even three universities open throughout the Tetovo villages!" The commentator concluded by saying that there were lessons for the Macedonian side in this matter: Educational improvements for the Albanians must be more rapid. If the public does not support the reforms to the educational system, they must expect angry Albanian agitation.[195]

The trial of Fadil Suleimani and Miljaim Fejziu began in late April. In addition to the earlier charges, they were also accused of having continually incited people to resistance and disobedience of a formal decision of the Macedonian government and appropriate measures of the Ministry of the Interior concerning the university in Tetovo. For instance, the indictment cited Fadil Suleimani as saying, "Should the Macedonian government try to stop us, everything will go to hell," in an interview with the paper *Nova Makedonija* on December 2, 1994, and Miljaim Fejziu was charged with calling for disobedience to the government decision during a television show at the end of January 1995, warning that the university would be defended with all means possible.[196]

Nevzat Halili, leader of a new party of Albanians in Macedonia, PDP — Party of National Unity, and professor at the "Kiril Pejcinovic" school in Tetovo, had also been taken into custody. Halili, a close associate of Suleimani, was directly involved in the events surrounding the university, especially in the village of Poroy.[197]

On April 27, 1995, the day the Tetovo municipal court opened the hearing against Fadil Suleimani, and Miljaim Fejziu, there was a large, orderly protest march outside the courtroom starting at noon, involving nearly 10,000 citizens.[198] Demonstrators demanded that all accused be unconditionally released. The crowds were addressed by leaders and representatives of various Albanian political groups, and monitored by OSCE and UNPREDEP officials. On May 3, Suleimani was sentenced to two and a half years' imprisonment, and Miljaim Fejziu was sentenced to six months in jail. Fejziu was released on bail until the verdict came into effect, but Suleimani was kept in prison, although his defense offered a bail of 50,000 German marks. The court held that Suleimani's bail should be decided by the criminal council of the court.[199]

Three weeks later, the Tetovo district court sentenced Musli Alimi, former professor at the Pristina university (in Kosovo, Serbia), to eight months in prison, on grounds of participation in crowds and preventing police officers from exercising their duty during the February events in Mala Recica. In the meantime bail of 200,000 German marks (about 700 times the annual wage in Macedonia) had been set for Suleimani. His defense lawyer argued that the bail was too high and would suit murderers and drug-traffickers, but not a man who was struggling for science. He said the amount was set so high in order to keep Suleimani in jail. Nevertheless, efforts would be made to raise the money.[200] Nevzat Halili and Arben Ruse were sentenced at the same time. Both had been accused of participating in crowds and preventing police officers from exercising their duty. Halili was sentenced to one and a half years in prison, and held in custody until the decision came into effect.[201] Ruse was sentenced to eight months in prison.[202]

The university in Tetovo started its second academic year on October 19, 1995. At the formal opening ceremony, which was attended by the various professors as well as representatives from UNPREDEP, the president of the university, Fadil Suleimani (who had been released from prison on bail of

100,000 DM) said that 1,254 students had been enrolled, of whom half were female. He added that 150 professors had been engaged to hold classes in 17 lecture halls. The official government position on the university seemed to have softened, after international pleadings, with the authorities saying little more than that the so-called university was not under the jurisdiction of the Ministry of Education and Physical Culture, and therefore not the Ministry's concern. They noted that certificates from this organization would not be recognized.[203]

Albanian Agitation Continues

The PDP parliamentary group sent a letter to the Council of Europe dated May 17, 1995, in which it said that Republic of Macedonia does not meet the criteria to be accepted by this organization or any other international organizations, and that acceptance should follow only "after the true democratization of Macedonia begins, with the equal treatment of all its citizens... After Macedonia's gaining of independence, the members of the Albanian minority were deprived of the rights they enjoyed with the 1974 Constitution, such as the right to a constitutive nation and the status of the Albanian language as official, in parallel with the Macedonian language." The PDP considered also that the way in which education in the mother tongue was being dealt with ruled out the possibility of higher education, in contradiction to the constitution. "The Electoral Law, as it presently stands, prevents Albanians from being represented in parliament in the percentage that corresponds with their numbers... Judges are not independent at all. The police, especially in dealing with the Albanians, overstep their competence and easily turn to the use of force... The Law on citizenship ... has denied citizenship to 100,000 members of the Albanian minority," according to this letter.[204]

At about the same time, Abdurahman Haliti, vice-president of the Macedonian Parliament and current president of the PDP, resigned from his position in Parliament. The reasons he gave were his dissatisfaction with government-proposed laws to regulate the status and rights of ethnic Albanians and other minorities in Macedonia, and the fact that members of Parliament express their views only through voting, instead of through "open dialogues and sincere discussions."[205]

Albanian members of Parliament refused to take part in the Parliamentary vote, early in May 1995, as the Macedonian Parliament passed laws on personal identification, birth registration and personal names, traffic regulations and public gatherings. These were sensitive issues, but the reason for the walk-out lay elsewhere. Albanians had been upset a few days before, during the debate, when the session was stopped by the president of the Parliament after deputy Sali Ramadani began speaking in Albanian with Macedonian translation.

This had been an acceptable procedure previously, but the president said that on this occasion reasonable notice had not been given to allow for simultaneous translation, so the session could not go on. As a result the NDP announced that their members would no longer participate in the work of Parliament. Ismet Ramadani of PDP said the PDP sympathized with this position; therefore, the PDP also refused to take part in voting, and the radical PDP members joined the other Albanians as they left the hall.[206]

Sali Ramadani, whose speech had precipitated the move by Albanian politicians, said that the leading Macedonian politicians of the time were pro–Serbian and openly expressed anti–Albanian views. Therefore, Ramadani said, Albanians in Macedonia ought to join forces with VMRO, as it was the only Macedonian national party.[207]

In the latter part of 1995, Abdurahman Aliti, Arben Dzaferi and Iliaz Halimi wrote to United States president Bill Clinton, complaining about the position of Albanians within Macedonia. Some Albanians were upset by this action. The independent MP Hisen Ramadani and the president of the Albanian Democratic Union — Liberal Party (ADS-LP) Dzemail Idrizi claimed that it was against Albanian interests.[208] Ramadani said, "As an Albanian, I don't want to create the impression that I don't recognize the Macedonian nation and that I don't accept the Macedonian state as my own. Anti-Albanian forces will use the letter to present the Albanians as a destabilizing factor in the region." Idrizi emphasized that the majority of Albanians were committed to peace and stability in Macedonia and would never become the source of a crisis in the region. The ADS-LP and the Union of Albanian Intelligentsia had been opposed to the boycott of the referendum for independence, against the referendum for territorial autonomy for Albanians ("Ilirida") and against the boycott of the recruitment of Albanians into the Macedonian Army. They suggested that the letter to Clinton advocated a division of the state which the writers had no mandate to do.

VMRO-DPMNE's Position Changes

VMRO-DMPNE became known as a party that was uncompromising. It seemed radical in its political philosophies and in its political actions. International observers had been concerned at its decision not to participate in the new Parliament, fearing the divisive effects from its nonparticipation in the parliamentary decision-making process. An already extremist party with considerable public support was seen as having become even more marginalized, and therefore more of a destabilizing force. During the first part of 1995 VMRO gradually changed its public position, moving towards a new pragmatism.

On February 8, 1995, VMRO attempted to justify its boycott of the elections to a skeptical interviewer from *Nova Makedonija*. The newspaper stated that VMRO-DPMNE had pompously announced its withdrawal from the second round of the previous October's election race, explaining that it would not be a part of the "dishonest game" imposed by the parties of the Alliance for Macedonia. The media had seen this as a betrayal of their supporters, who ended up without their own representatives in Parliament. Three and a half months after the elections, VMRO-DPMNE still maintained that the party had done the right thing and that the state must suffer the consequences of the party's absence in all spheres of life. To feel the effects of the VMRO's absence would take time, they argued, but this was necessary to achieve their higher purposes. Dosta Dimovska, vice-president of VMRO-DPMNE, insisted that the boycott had not been a mistake. By boycotting the elections, VMRO-DPMNE and the other opposition parties destroyed the plans to manipulate the second part of the voting process, she said. She claimed that the government intended to keep the number of opposition representatives in Parliament small so it could include Macedonia in Yugoslavia and conclude agreements with Greece on changing the name and flag.

Dimovska insisted that VMRO-DPMNE would not be a decoration in an illegal parliament or be an alibi for the Alliance for Macedonia in its negotiations and deals with the PDP. She argued that since "half of the electorate" was not represented in Parliament, the government could not be considered legal. She reiterated the VMRO claim that the election results were a sheer fabrication and could not be a basis for constituting a legal government supposedly representing the interests of the nation. Dimovska said it was fitting that the government should move into the building of the old Central Committee of the Communist Party of Macedonia, since this symbolically revealed its true nature. She interpreted moves to use the Albanian language at university level in Skopje as a step towards the federalization of Macedonia. She predicted economic disaster characterized by a drastic decline of production, an absence of investments and a domination of the economy by a black market and higher taxes. Privatization was continuing through a massive theft of state capital, and the new unemployed were thrown out in the streets without any social protection, she claimed.

Dimovska said there was only one truly independent weekly magazine in Macedonia and all other media were government-controlled. No daily newspaper was independent and there was no freedom of the press. Almost all media either had been attacking VMRO-DPMNE or launching misinformation about it, continuing its marginalization. Two months later, Ljupcho Georgievski, leader of VMRO-DPMNE, expressed similar views to a *Puls* reporter (April 21, 1995). Georgievski acknowledged that many Macedonians had been somewhat frightened by the uncompromising ways in which VMRO described the situation in the republic and by the ideals they expressed. He said that Albanian support of his party was clearly possible since all VMRO expected was a commitment to primary loyalty to the state of Macedonia. He said that few

Albanians had been prepared to make such a commitment so far. He said, "If we only once heard them declaring themselves to be loyal citizens of Macedonia, it would be much easier to sit down and discuss any problem. However, if we keep hearing demands for recognizing Albanians here as a nation or if they continue to present conditions of all kinds and speak of federalization ... this leads nowhere."

Early in May 1995, 223 party delegates of VMRO-DPMNE and several hundred guests from Macedonia and abroad held "the tenth congress of continuity of the Interior Macedonian Revolutionary Organization" in Kicevo.[209] This was the occasion of a major change in the public position of VMRO. In his speech reporting on the activities of VMRO since the last congress, Ljupcho Georgievski pointed out this was the first congress of a VMRO held in a free, independent and autonomous Macedonia. He claimed that there was no political party in Macedonia whose fundamental principles and goals had been achieved as fully as those of VMRO-DPMNE, but he recognized failures and mistakes, in particular the fact that VMRO-DPMNE had missed two chances to participate significantly in forming a government in the country. He said, "We were building an image of a party which refused to have anything to do with ex-communists or extreme parties of Albanians, but we lost the sense of pragmatism and missed a chance to form a government." The most recent and biggest mistake, he said, was that sufficient efforts were not undertaken before the second elections in the country to create a strong coalition and win the elections. For the future he proposed active cooperation with three or four parties to defeat the current government by democratic means. "We are aware that, despite the huge support for our party, we cannot come out as absolute winners of any elections all by ourselves." He said that this is possible "only with a strong coalition of opposition parties. The basic goal of VMRO-DPMNE in this period will be to schedule new elections in the country," by organizing a general referendum on new elections to be held next year.

Georgievski announced a new strategy of the party, consisting of correcting past mistakes and introducing a philosophy of political pragmatism to win political power in the Republic of Macedonia. On the second day of the congress, Georgievski was reelected party leader by an overwhelming majority (195 to 11). A vote was taken, though he was the only candidate for the position. The congress concluded with the adoption of several declarations, including one on the unity of the Macedonian nation, one on the place of Islamic Macedonians as an integral part of the nation, and one on the need for the national reconciliation of Macedonians scattered throughout the world. From this time, VMRO-DPMNE acknowledged that it would be acting as a party of the right center, very close to the philosophical position of other European Christian-democratic parties.

The new pragmatism of VMRO-DPMNE was demonstrated in June 1995 when party president Georgievski started negotiations in Tetovo with the

Albanian PDP on a possible coalition at a local level.[210] It was in this western area of Macedonia, where the Albanian influence was strongest, that VMRO had received its most enthusiastic support in the past from Macedonians seeking some counter to the Albanian influence. During the first free election campaign in this region, Georgievski had coined a famous slogan: "We will cut off the claws of the Albanian eagle." *Puls* remained skeptical about the possibility of cooperation between the PDP and VMRO, pointing out that Shakir Aliti, president of the Tetovo township committee, has neither the authority nor the reputation of Abdurahman Aliti, leader of the PDP at a national level. Nevertheless, the dialogue went ahead. The discussions came after talks between the Democratic Party and the splinter group PDP-A, led by Dzaferi and Taci. *Puls* saw this willingness to engage in discussions with Albanian groups as an admission that Macedonia is a multiethnic state and a recognition that Albanian parties must be involved in government if federalism is to be avoided.

While having many differences with regard to the constituent peoples of the nation (and such issues as the employment of minorities and the languages of education), confederation versus possible federation, social versus private ownership of production, and the rights of Macedonians abroad (i.e., in Greece, Bulgaria and Albania), both parties agreed that the potential "Serbianization" of Macedonia was the greatest danger. Their mutual enemy seemed to be the Macedonian police and their "inclination toward the use of excessive force." *Puls* judged the likelihood of successful negotiation to be slight. Nevertheless, this development suggests that VMRO may return to center stage in the democratic political process in Macedonia. It allows for more optimism about Macedonia's future political stability.

VMRO saw the threat of Serbian influence as the most dangerous problem for Macedonia. It claimed that results in the 1994 elections had been fabricated by a clique with Serbian sympathies. James Pettifer, writing in the *Wall Street Journal*, suggested that the electoral result pointed to a much closer relationship between Macedonia and Serbia. The bureaucracy in Skopje was said to be "one of the most unreconstructed in the ex-communist states, and many top officials who were alleged to be involved in the election manipulation have close links to Belgrade."[211] It is arguable, too, that the sanctions against Serbia and the Greek embargo brought Macedonia and Serbia closer together. The two governments cooperated during the embargo in order to survive. One consequence of this was increased Serb influence in Macedonia's Interior Ministry, and in the police and paramilitary forces. The Minister of the Interior was Ljubomir Frckovski, often accused by VMRO of Serbian sympathies. Frckovski, a man in his early forties, was considered a possible successor to President Gligorov. As noted earlier, Frckovski scored quite highly in the public opinion polls in Macedonia, and in the absence of a national unity candidate was thought likely to become the Alliance candidate in following elections.

9. The Course and Meaning of the Greek Embargo Against Macedonia

In November 1993, the Greek foreign minister, Mr. Papoulias, wrote to the United Nations secretary general, Mr. Boutros Boutros-Ghali, informing him about his new government's attitude toward talks between the Republic of Macedonia and the Republic of Greece. The following is an extract from the letter:

> I would like to point out that the premature recognition of Bosnia and Herzegovina, not preceded by previous overcoming of ethnic problems, led to civil war and brought foreign countries into the crisis. I fear that this example given in Bosnia could be repeated in the case of Skopje. You know very well that two ethnic groups in this region are antagonistic one towards the other, and that there is always a possibility of a worsening of their relations. Skopje emerged as a result of certain geopolitical speculations in the past, ideas that could still destabilize the region... Peace in the region is threatened not only by the name of this new state, but also by a series of actions, resulting from the usurpation of the name Macedonia, and with an aim of creating a new, historically non-existent country, with territorial pretensions as its fundamental policy, especially towards Macedonia, a northern region in Greece... We emphasize that the new government in Skopje adopted and continues with enemy propaganda against Greece ... we call your attention to the fact that the primary goal of the strongest political party in the Skopje Parliament is "uniting Macedonia," i.e. inclusion of neighboring territories in its own ... Mr. Gligorov's Government, with the agreement of his Parliament, accepted a national flag with symbols from the history of Greece. The Greek Government will no longer tolerate the disinformation that the Macedonian Government releases in international circles, because Macedonia has clearly shown that it has no genuine desire for a peaceful solution of the differences, defined by the Security Council. I believe that it is my duty to emphasize again and clearly state that the Greek Government and the Greek people will never recognize a state whose name has Macedonia in it, nor any other words generated from that name.[1]

Teodoros Pangalos, Greek deputy foreign minister, said, "We live in a dangerous neighborhood... Their flag is a provocation. Claiming you are descendants of ancient Greeks is very flattering for us, but please find something from your own territory."[2] Pangalos said that if the flag issue were settled the rest would fall into place. "What we ask is not much: they have to abandon the dream of uniting Macedonia under their leadership."

Nearly eighteen months later, in the first interview that the new Greek president, Kostas Stefanopoulos, gave for the TV station Euronews, he said very similar things: "Greece is not the reason for any kind of problems in the region, but others are creating problems for her."[3] Asked about the Republic of Macedonia, he said that there had been several wars in the twentieth century centered in this area and that Greece is sensitive about the region because so much blood was shed there. He noted that there had also been, in Greek Macedonia, "an autonomist movement, which claimed that Macedonia was a wider region, that it encompassed not only Greek Macedonia, but also today's territory of Skopje, a part of Bulgaria and therefore, a new autonomous state had to be formed, which would engulf that entire region." This is the explanation for the appearance of "some kind of nation" called Macedonia, "which no historian found until a couple of years ago." He said this began with Tito from 1945, when he formed one of the republics of federal Yugoslavia under the name Macedonia. Stefanopoulos said that today Skopje is continuing with this tactic by insisting on the name, which has an expansionist character, and by using symbols which are purely Greek. By using such symbols they confirm their intentions for expansion to "all of Macedonia." In addition, the constitution expresses the obligation of the Skopje state to take care of that so-called Macedonian population. He said that what really concerned him was the claim that "a part of that Macedonian population exists in Greece." Skopje continued with propaganda against Greece, and therefore Greece was forced to defend itself. When many other nations recognized the Skopje state under the name Macedonia, "Greece was forced to impose an embargo in order to turn the world's attention to the question that is destabilizing the Balkans." Stefanopoulos said that Greece was the only Balkan country that made no claims on the territory of Skopje, that wanted it to exist as an independent country, but not with such aggressive dispositions towards Greece.

In the winter of 1993, Greece blocked Macedonia's petrol supply through the port of Thessaloniki, holding a tanker with enough Macedonian petrol to last three full months. This created political destabilization in Macedonia, which was forced to obtain its petrol supplies from Bulgaria and Turkey. This was but one of many occasions on which Greece had blocked trade with Macedonia. During 1992 and 1993, Greece frequently closed its border to goods being transported from Macedonia to Greece and vice versa, and threatened a full blockade.[4]

Just after Christmas in 1993, at a meeting held in Kozani at the Macedonian-Greek border, the city mayors from northern Greece requested the direct closing of the border with Macedonia, the revoking of the consular representation from Skopje, the cancelling of all sorts of trade and economic concessions given to the Republic of Macedonia, and the full blocking of the Aegean part of Macedonia and Thrace.[5] Soon after this, trade unionists at the Esko refinery in Salonika decided to suspend the delivery of oil to the refinery in Skopje, as a protest against the establishing of diplomatic relations between Macedonia and several European Union countries.[6] These developments suggest that the Greek community had become well informed about the nature of the Greek argument with Macedonia, and agreed with the government position.

Some public statements by Greek leaders suggested they would follow a moderate path. Deputy foreign minister Pangalos told *Reuters*, "Greece can survive without the direct settling of the question of the name of the neighboring Republic... We asked them to change the symbol on their flag, the Constitution and to proclaim that the borders are definitive." Pangalos said that these are elementary matters that do not require any great sacrifice. He suggested there was no sense in Greece continuing to insist that the name "Macedonia" be excluded from the name of the "neighboring Republic." Greece could live without the direct resolution of the name issue.[7]

The London newspaper the *Economist* speculated that Greece was inching towards a compromise in the dispute with Macedonia because they could not win and had become thoroughly unpopular with their allies. A "certain bending" had already taken place, the paper noted, since Greece now accepted the title "Former Yugoslav Republic of Macedonia," under which it had sponsored Macedonia's admission to the United Nations in 1993.[8]

However, on January 24 a majority of the Greek Parliament supported the view that Athens should continue to exert pressure on the Republic of Macedonia in order to safeguard vital national interests. Prime minister Andreas Papandreou demanded that before negotiations on a normalization of bilateral relations could begin, Macedonia must remove what Greece regards as a traditional Hellenic symbol from its flag, amend its constitution to make it unequivocally clear to Athens that no territorial designs were intended, and end "hostile propaganda" directed against Greece. Both Papandreou and Adonis Samaras, leader of the Political Spring party, reiterated the position that Greece would never recognize a state called Macedonia. Miltiadis Evert, chairman of the conservative New Democracy party, while echoing that demand, warned that if the new state were to collapse Greece could be facing a Greater Albania and a Greater Bulgaria on its northern border. Evert said Macedonia was not only crucial to stability in the southern Balkans but, due to its geostrategic position, may one day hold the key to Greece's relations with western Europe.[9]

Explanations for the Greek Attitude

After the establishment of full diplomatic relations between Washington and Skopje in September 1995, special envoy of the United States President Matthew Nimitz gave a press conference at the International Press Center in New York. His response to a journalist from the *Christian Science Monitor* makes an interesting point about the way that other nations have been able to maintain comfortable working relationships despite having disagreements of a similar nature to that between Greece and Macedonia.[10] He noted that the Irish do not accept the name "United Kingdom of Great Britain and Northern Ireland," and that the British do not accept the Irish-language name "Eire," which refers to all of Ireland including the North. Each country has stood by its own usage since the 1920s, yet the countries are able to cooperate without formal agreement on names.

Analysts Janusz Bugajski and David Augustyn argued that the Greek government could reap domestic political advantage from nationalistic fervor. The real reason, they said, for the Greek attitude toward Macedonia was the strategic advantage that this antagonism gave Greece and its major ally, rump Yugoslavia.[11] They said that Greece, on the threshold of a more crucial role in the Balkans as a strong local power, could become either a pillar of stability or an agent of escalating strife in the area. They concluded, early in 1994, that Greece was taking the latter course. Instead of drawing the "fragile and non threatening" Macedonians into a close alliance, the conservative Mitsotakis government had provoked nationalist feeling by aggravating fears over alleged Macedonian expansionism. In turn this stimulated nationalist feelings and ethnic divisions in Macedonia itself. The Mitsotakis government had been pushed in this direction after Adonis Samaras was dismissed as foreign minister in April 1992. Samaras had taken a very hard line with virtually no possibility of compromise. After he was sacked, he left the ruling New Democracy (ND) party and established an extremist rival faction, Political Spring. Political Spring gained support by taking advantage of nationalist feeling, so the government needed to appear tougher with Macedonia. When the government lost its majority in Parliament after two ND deputies defected to the Samaras party in September 1993, it was forced to resign. With Greek nationalism determining foreign policy, Athens was in no position to moderate its stance. Nationalism gained ground as a result of these events, "manipulated by ambitious politicians from across the political spectrum who may seek to distract attention from more immediate economic problems."

Bugajski and Augustyn noted that Macedonia explicitly renounced any territorial pretensions to northern Greece and in any case was not in any position to threaten Greece. Despite this move, Athens continued to insist that the new country change its name, claiming, "contrary to the historical record" that the name Macedonia had an exclusively Hellenic heritage. Bugajski and

Augustyn concluded that "such spurious justifications have led to suspicions that the name issue is merely a smoke screen for strengthening the Belgrade–Athens axis and repressing demands for the recognition of the sizable Slav minority in Greece itself." The Greek dispute with Macedonia suited Belgrade since it kept Skopje off balance and encouraged suspicions that Athens wanted to take a part of the country for itself. While cooperation between Greece and Yugoslavia had been limited in the early Cold War years because of Yugoslav assistance for Communist forces during the Greek civil war in the 1940s and Belgrade's support of a distinct Macedonian nationality, things improved after Tito's death in 1980 and the success of the Panhellenic Social Movement (PASOK) government. Relations improved so much that during the war in Croatia and Bosnia, Greece, while nominally adhering to the United Nations–imposed sanctions, maintained cordial and often supportive relations with Belgrade.

William Dunn, another American analyst, also took the view that Greek policies toward Macedonia were understandable in light of the politics of cultural purity which dominated the country.[12] He said the three major Greek parties were driven by policies based on a myth of continuity with classical antiquity and a notion of exclusive entitlement to symbols, conquerors, kingdoms, and territories of the ancient world. Dunn pointed out that while it was true that ancient Greece was the cradle of Western democratic civilization, it was equally true that Philip of Macedon and his son, Alexander the Great, did not consider themselves Greeks, that Alexander conquered Athens, and that today's Macedonia was never a part of Greece. Dunn also noted that Greece did not refer to any part of its current territory as Macedonia until 1988, when Papandreou's government officially adopted the name Macedonia to replace that of Northern Greece. This point added weight to the notion that the dispute with Macedonia was a manufactured one.

The grip of nationalist fervor seemed to reach out widely in Greece. A research study financed by the European Union, and published late in 1994 in the daily Greek newspaper *Avgi*, concluded that most Greeks were xenophobes, racists and anti–Semites. According to the study, Greeks expressed the most aversion to Turks, then Albanians, Jews and Gypsies. Sixty-two percent of Greeks did not like the Greek Muslims of Turkish origin who lived in Thrace, and 52 percent wanted them to go back to Turkey. Sixty-six percent of Greeks in this study said that they would never marry a Muslim, while 64 percent said the same for the Gypsies. Eighty-four percent of Greeks disapproved of having foreign workers (mostly Albanian) in Greece, and 90 percent of them believed that these workers took jobs from Greeks.[13]

Some American analysts believed that the Greeks were concerned about the influence Skopje might have on Macedonians living in northern Greece, encouraging their political aspirations and human rights demands.[14] According to Macedonian president Kiro Gligorov, much of the Greek concern in the dispute centered on the possibility of land claims by Slav Macedonians who left Greece, or were expelled, in the Greek civil war. Thousands of exiles would like to reclaim their land and homes, which they had to abandon. Some houses were torn down, others confiscated. Gligorov said, "This has weight in Greece because of the enormous number of people who left or were expelled, who are not able to receive their property or compensation."[15]

In an earlier speech before the French Institute for International Relations on the subject "Macedonia and the New Europe" at the end of October 1993, President Gligorov said that a people's right to a name is a natural and an inalienable one. He said the Macedonian people had a Slavic origin and had come into the Balkans in the sixth and seventh century A.D. They had their own authentic culture, language and history. It was on this territory that the first Slavic letters and literature were born, and it was also here that the Slavs were converted to Christianity for the first time in history, he said. That is why "we do not have to identify ourselves with the culture and civilization of other peoples, nor with their contemporary achievements." He said it was of great interest for Macedonia to overcome the dispute with Greece, and that is why Macedonia agreed to direct talks with Greece in the United Nations. Gligorov observed that Macedonia is the road to Europe for the Greeks, and Greece is Macedonia's exit to the sea. Greece is also a member of the European Community. Gligorov expressed the hope that realism would shape the talks with the new Greek government.[16]

Gligorov said he thought a realization that an independent Macedonia had advantages for Greece would spread more widely, adding, "We have much more reason to cooperate fully, as good neighbors, than to create a new region of anxiety in the Balkans. With the independence of our country, Greece's security perimeter is extended to over 200 km to the north." He said that "no force" could now deprive Macedonia of its hard-won independence and that the Republic of Macedonia is a constitutional reality.[17]

The willingness of Macedonia to participate in discussion on the dispute is indicated in comments by foreign minister Stevo Crvenkovski. For instance, in an interview given to the Belgian newspaper *Free Belgium*, Crvenkovski noted that the future of talks was uncertain only because there had been no response from the Greek side. He stated that the new Greek position was unclear, and that continuation of the dialogue was the only possible way to solve the conflict. "We are neighbors and have to go on living together. The dispute over the name is irrational, because up to 1988 the north of Greece was called Northern Greece, and not Macedonia, as it is now. The Macedonian Constitution clearly states that we have no territorial pretensions. We have insisted on talks since the very beginning, because it is the only way out of the situation."[18]

The previous round of talks involving Macedonia and Greece had ended in June 1993 with no agreement on the central issues. It is possible that the

Macedonians felt constrained in their negotiations by the fact that a two-thirds majority in Parliament is needed to change either flag or constitution, and following the 1992 elections, VMRO, Macedonia's most strongly nationalist party, which even today remains adamantly opposed to any compromise, had enough deputies and parliamentary allies to prevent any change.

The Embargo Begins

On February 16, 1994, after a specially convened session of the Greek government, the Greek prime minister Andreas Papandreou announced that Greece was cancelling all trade links with Macedonia and was closing its consulate in Skopje. Mr. Papandreou stated that "Greece is forced to take this step due to the consistent adamant stance of Skopje." Analysts in Macedonia believed that this Greek step was synchronized with a visit of the Greek Foreign Minister to Belgrade.[19]

The trade blockade of Macedonia seems to have been applied in response to the American offer of diplomatic recognition of Macedonia. One week after the United States recognized the country under the name "the Former Yugoslav Republic of Macedonia," and one day before the announcement of the embargo, tens of thousands of protesters filled the streets of Thessaloniki, waving banners proclaiming, "Macedonia is Greek," along with Greek flags and stars of Vergina (the same symbol that was on the Macedonian flag).[20]

The prominent Greek newspaper *Katimerini* described "great anti–American demonstrations" in the streets of Thessaloniki on the afternoon of February 15, "exactly three years since the great rally at the Aristotle Square in Athens, now called Agea Sofia." The protest was organized by the church, but explicitly supported by the nationalist right-wing party Political Spring, as well as by PASOK and New Democracy. Thessaloniki metropolitan Panteleimon led the 20,000 demonstrators, mostly students (there was no school that afternoon), who rallied in front of the United States General Consulate. Alongside the familiar signs reading, "Macedonia is Greek," there were others showing the words "Axes and fire for the Skopje dogs." The door of the consulate was not opened, though "the angry metropolitan constantly banged at the door ... with his scepter."[21]

President Clinton of the United States was denounced as a traitor, and protesters attacked the United States consulate with eggs, coins and other objects. The metropolitan Panteleimon II read a letter of protest addressed to President Clinton. The Greek government later stated that any expression of feelings by citizens is their personal matter, provided it is within constitutional limits. Government ministers were also present at the protest, in a private capacity. The Greek Communist party criticized the protest for spreading nationalism.[22]

In an interview published in *Balkan News* on February 20, Greek deputy foreign minister Teodoros Pangalos, while not backing down from Greek demands, made apologies for the government's behavior. Among other things, he said that the government should stop letting the issue dominate its concerns, instead placing it "within the context of the country's wider Balkan policies, which in turn should be put in the context of our global policies... We have an underdeveloped approach to international relations, proved by the fact that we have let the FYROM issue dominate public opinion, replacing all other issues of concern... Greece has suffered a fall in international esteem over the issue... We could not convince people abroad, as our position was not strong enough, and we ended up giving the impression that we were ultra-nationalists and fanatics... We have to look at the whole issue again, see what is actually the truth of the matter, not have false hopes, not be demagogic, and not fool around."

In Strasbourg, however, about two weeks later, Greek foreign minister Karolos Papoulias stated that "the Greek embargo against the neighboring country has been implemented due to its aggressiveness and uncompromising stance. It is a political measure of self-defense. Our vital interests were endangered by the uncompromising attitude of Skopje and its refusal to give up its imperialistic demands!"[23] Papoulias stressed that his government would resist international pressure aimed at having Greece lift the embargo and emphasized that Macedonia had to make concessions, which include changing its name, before Athens would be willing to negotiate.

A month after this, Prime Minister Papandreou, in a statement for the *New York Times*, stressed that his country had been forced into such action because Greece's national security was endangered. He said "this is a real threat to our national security, because Skopje's aim is to gain an exit to the Aegean Sea. We closed the border after 6 EU countries recognized Skopje... We had to remind the world there is a problem concerning stability and security in the region."[24]

Macedonian responses. A week after the Greek embargo was announced, Mr. Gligorov wrote to the Greek prime minister offering explicit assurances concerning Macedonia's borders, and inviting dialogue over all issues in the dispute between the two states. He stated that Macedonia was ready to "sign an agreement ... which would guarantee the permanency of the borders between the two countries." Though he warned that continuation of the embargo would "create unwanted consequences regarding peace and stability in this part of the Balkans, which unavoidably leads to the need for us to address the Security Council," he added that he was "deeply convinced that, taking into account the seriousness of these questions and the responsibility we carry, a quick resolution will be found, on a principled and lasting basis, and in the interest of the two countries and peoples."[25]

After the imposition of the embargo, Macedonian premier Branko Crvenkovski said, "Greece is responsible for every deterioration in relations between the two countries. The Greek government wants to exert economic and political pressure. The one-sided and unacceptable measures from Greece are very worrying."[26] Foreign minister Stevo Crvenkovski said his government was not prepared to enter direct talks while being threatened in this manner.[27]

On February 28, Kiro Gligorov said the Greek blockade was having "very serious effects" on Macedonia's economy, in particular its energy supply. He asked the European Union to pressure Greece to stop "an act unknown except in war." Gligorov said, "I believe that the ancient Macedonians were a special ethnic entity, which does not necessarily mean they were Greek. As to the Greek historical heritage, we do not wish to steal it. We settled this region in the 6th and 7th centuries A.D. Unlike other tribes, we took the name of the territory we settled, Macedonia, and that does not mean we have any pretensions to the history of ancient Macedonia. We have our own history and our own heritage."[28]

Speaking to the New York–based (nongovernment) Council for International Relations, a group comprised mainly of leading journalists in the field of foreign politics, Gligorov said it was good that Prime Minister Papandreou would be meeting with United States president Clinton soon. He said the United States had kept a balanced position regarding this question and was showing interest in maintaining peace and security in the Balkans. He expressed the hope that the same position would be presented in these talks. He said American efforts to help find a just solution for both sides were important in encouraging an emphasis on good will by both sides, rather than the use of embargoes and threats, "because reasonable people sit down and talk." Concerning the Greek reservations over part of the Macedonian constitution, Gligorov said that "before the Badinter Commission came out in favor of the recognition of Macedonia, we changed the Constitution and put it in writing that we have no territorial pretensions and that we will not interfere in the internal affairs of other countries." He noted that in Article 108 of its constitution, Greece also had maintained that the Greek state would take care of all Hellenes, regardless of where they lived in the world, though they had criticized such an item in the Macedonian constitution. President Gligorov added, "Besides this, we proposed an agreement to Greece for a permanent settlement in regard to the border, that would be guaranteed by the EU and the UN."[29]

Shortly after this very diplomatic statement, Gligorov was quoted as saying rather tougher things about the dispute with the Greeks. In an interview for the Dutch newspaper *Algemein Dagblad,* he said Macedonia would not accept any of the conditions set by the Greek side, and accused the Greek leaders of nationalism. He also said that Macedonia would now agree to negotiate only on an agreement securing integrity of its borders, and that Greek demands to change the name would never be accepted. He explained the Greece antagonism as related to the fact that Greece denies the existence of the Macedonian minority that lives in its territory. As for the Vergina Star flag symbol, Mr. Gligorov pointed out it that can be seen in many Macedonian churches.[30]

Macedonian prime minister Crvenkovski said, "We cannot establish a dialogue on an equal basis with Greece as long as a rope is tied around our neck."[31] In an address to the Economic Forum in Switzerland, Mr. Crvenkovski urged "more energetic steps by the international community," adding that the most serious blow to the Macedonian economy "is given by a country member of the EU, at a time when it presides over the Union. The losses to the Macedonian economy due to the Greek embargo in just the first month reached 60 million dollars, with an additional 40 million every month after that. The result is a suddenly worsened economic situation and 25,000 people out of work." Stressing that Macedonia is inferior to Greece in its territory, population and economy, Crvenkovski said it seemed amusing "to repeat that Macedonia does not intend to conquer Greece." He went on to warn that a "coordinated Serbian-Greek political strategy towards Macedonia" could lead to a Balkan war and to urge the European Union to "take timely action."[32]

A number of Macedonian politicians were interviewed by Macedonian Radio after announcement of the European Union decision to take Greece to Court for its embargo.[33] Dosta Dimovska, vice-president of VMRO-DPMNE, said, "The European Commission's decision is first of all a moral and political condemnation, but it is also controversial, because, besides condemning Greece, it requests that Macedonia make retreats on exactly those issues that led to the introduction of the embargo. This party considers the demands for changes in the constitution and flag unacceptable."

Blagoja Handziski, a leading figure in SDSM, said, "We are ready to negotiate. The controversial issues can be resolved under UN mediation, but it is absolutely unacceptable to go into negotiations while the embargo is in effect. Our readiness to negotiate does not mean all Greek proposals are acceptable for us, especially not the one suggesting Macedonia should change its name."

Petar Gosev, leader of the Democratic Party, said, "The decision appears to be positive, but we should pause before we get too excited about the solution. This is a hesitant decision, and the part justifying the Greek demands is very concerning, as it implies we should give up the name, flag and parts of the constitution. I personally expect Macedonian diplomacy will face a hard battle."

President Gligorov held talks in Geneva in November 1994 with UN secretary general Boutros Boutros-Ghali and mediator Cyrus Vance. Public announcements explained that no progress was made at the talks. However, for the first time in an official statement, Gligorov mentioned "the right of our people to promote its constitutional name at an international level and thus resolve the matter." He said, "Everything else is negotiable." This is of some interest because the United Nations Security Council Resolution 817 specifies negotiations on the name.[34] At about the same time, American analysts were saying that "Skopje is unlikely to drop the word Macedonia from its country's name."

It was suggested that after the 1994 elections, President Gligorov might agree to a name change like the "Republic of Macedonia, Skopje" or "Vardar Macedonia," but not the removal of the name "Macedonia." It was suggested he might also agree to modify the flag, since that seemed to be a lesser issue.[35] Three months later, in an interview for the newspaper *Figaro*, Gligorov said that it was "the right moment for France, as chairman of the EU, to put forward an initiative to settle the Macedonian-Greek dispute." He reiterated that his government was ready to compromise over all other questions, if Athens accepted the name Republic of Macedonia.[36]

European responses. The European nations were already irritated with Greece before the embargo against Macedonia. Criticizing the statement by deputy foreign minister Pangalos that Germany, one of the European Union's most powerful member states, was "a bestial giant with a child's brain," the *Financial Times* had suggested that a Greek presidency of the European Union was "widely seen as a loose cannon on the deck of a European ship." Greece was seen as obstinate in its opposition to Macedonia, and suspicious because of its close ties with Serbia. However, these factors only partly explained European irritation with Greece. Having also blocked aid to Turkey, Greece had hampered the European Union effort to put into effect a more coherent Mediterranean policy, important now because of Turkey's new role on the borders of former states of the USSR in central Asia. In a widely reported statement revealing Greek animosity towards the Turks, Pangalos had described the Turkish government as "muggers" who were "dragging bloody boots across the carpets of Europe."[37]

A common assessment of prime minister Constantine Mitsotakis' repeated demand that the European Union oppose recognition of Macedonia was that it lost Greece much European sympathy. Six European Union states showed their attitudes by opening diplomatic relations with Macedonia by the end of 1993. The name issue was by then seen as a lost cause. It had caused bad feeling among Greece's European partners and prevented Greece from being a force for stability in the Balkans. Some Greeks shared this analysis. Robert Marquand, writing in the *Christian Science Monitor*, cited examples.[38] One Greek diplomatic source said, "We were once the English of the Balkans, but we have wasted our positive role on Macedonia, whose actual threat to us isn't just a shadow, but a shadow of a shadow." Marquand concluded that the explanation for the Greek intransigence was the state of domestic politics. A young Athens lawyer acknowledged that the name issue was absurd, but pointed out that no one could say this publicly because it had become a test of patriotism. An Athens correspondent made the point that for Greeks, "some issues are more important than truth."

Just days after Greece announced its economic blockade of Macedonia, six of Greece's partners in the European Union — Great Britain, France, Italy, Holland, Germany and Denmark — requested that Athens bring the blockade to an immediate end. The new European Union president, Jacques Delor, sent an official note to the Greek prime minister stressing the Union's concern and the seriousness with which the European Commission was examining the latest Greek measures. The Union wished to determine whether grounds existed for bringing legal charges against Greece at the European Court in Luxembourg. The prime minister was asked for a justification of his position. In response to this request, the Greek minister of law and order, Stelios Papatemelis, stated that the blockade would remain in power until Macedonia gave in to the Greek demands.[39]

The commissioner for foreign policy of the European Union, Hans Van den Broek, had a series of meetings in Skopje and Athens concerning the embargo. Calling the situation "very difficult and very urgent," he said that Greece should lift the embargo so that the negotiations between the two states could go on.[40] He concluded that the border is closed not only for Macedonian oil, but also for humanitarian aid.

On February 28, European Union parliamentarians told Greece that its action could lead to more fighting in the Balkans. The assembly's presidential committee backed Union attempts to mediate in the crisis and welcomed Italian, Albanian and Bulgarian efforts to help Macedonia economically.[41]

The Council of Europe's Parliamentary Assembly on March 1 criticized Greece for imposing the economic blockade on the Republic of Macedonia. In a strongly worded statement, the assembly said that the embargo could have "a destabilizing effect in a region particularly vulnerable at this time."[42] British foreign secretary Douglas Hurd traveled to Athens a few days later with a stern message from Greece's eleven European Union partners. "We understand the anxieties and concerns of Greece ... They do not, in our opinion, justify the Greek measures which harm the Former Yugoslav Republic of Macedonia and in our view are illegal and certainly harm the reputation and the authority of Greece," Mr. Hurd said.[43]

On April 6, Hans Van den Broek announced that the European Commission had decided to take Greece to the European Court of Justice in Luxembourg over the embargo against Macedonia. The commission appealed to Macedonia to review its position over the controversial issues, but the arguments of Greece, based on Article 224 of the Maastricht Agreement, were dismissed by the commission. The commission determined that Greece was threatened neither by war nor by destabilization, hence the measures it was undertaking against Macedonia could not be justified.[44]

Greece threatened that it might walk out of the European Union if the European Court endangered the Greek national interests. Deputy Foreign Minister Pangalos, speaking at the Congress of the ruling socialist party, PASOK, said that "if the European Court brings a decision which could bring the Greek nation to the brink of disintegration, we would prefer to walk alone."[45]

The European Union opposition continued throughout the time of the embargo. In the summer of 1995, French president Jacques Chirac, using his position as host of the half-year European Union summit, said Greece was alone in its refusal to lift the embargo on Macedonia, and opposed the opinions of 14 other members. "Fourteen countries have approved my stance," he said, but "we did not manage to convince the Greeks to lift the embargo."[46] Greek prime minister Andreas Papandreou characterized the proposal of the French president to lift the embargo as a provocation directed against him personally, as well as Greece.[47]

The European Commission initiated proceedings on April 22, 1994. An interim judgment ordering the lifting of the embargo was not granted, since the court decided that the injury suffered by the FYROM could not be taken into consideration because the commission's responsibility is the protection of the community's interests, not those of a third country. However, the court considered that the unilateral measures taken by Greece were in contradiction with community rules on the free movement of goods and the common competition policy. The court continued to consider the issue of the legality of Greece's actions.[48] Accusing Commissioner Van den Broek of using "immoral methods" in bringing the European Union court action, Teodoros Pangalos demanded that he resign, although Van den Broek was immediately supported by the rest of the 17-member commission.[49]

At the end of June 1994, in an emergency debate, the parliamentary assembly of the European Council in Strasbourg (a pan–European organization responsible for promoting human rights) discussed the Greek embargo on Macedonia. Except for the Greek speakers, almost all of the 28 deputies who took the stand, both liberal and conservative, denounced the blockade. The discussion itself began with the introduction by Briton David Atkinson, who presented a short summary of the embargo, reminding the Parliament that in spite of the amendments that Macedonia had made to its constitution, Greece was still not backing down from its position, which placed it in violation of European Union rules. He said, "The young Macedonian republic is seized in a vice between Serbia and Greece. This can only spark internal tensions. In addition, various incidents make us fear that Macedonia could in future become the target of Serbian territorial ambitions." At the conclusion of his comments he proposed that the next meeting of the Commission of the European Council be held not in Thessaloniki, as planned, but in Macedonia, providing Greece had not lifted the embargo by that time. British liberal-democrat Russel Johnston said Macedonia's military capacity was nil (a sentiment echoed by many of the speakers) and added: "People mustn't give an exaggerated importance to symbols." Jean Seitlinger of France's center-right Union for French Democracy (UDF) called on the European Union to punish Greece for misconduct. He asserted that the Greek embargo was in violation of Article 113 of the agreement from Rome, and that therefore Greece violated the sovereignty of the European Union in an economic plan. In his address, the deputy in the

Macedonian Parliament, Lambe Arnaudov, explained Macedonia's difficult economic position caused by the Greek embargo. The representative from Finland reminded the Parliament that Macedonia, as a special guest at the Council of Europe, fulfilled all conditions for admission to this organization. Danish liberal Hanne Severisen accused Greek politicians of "throwing oil on the fire for domestic political reasons."[50] Mr. Demirel from Turkey emphasized that Macedonia deserved to become a full member of the international community, while Mr. Panov from Bulgaria noted that regardless of some misunderstandings, Bulgaria was still able to have good neighborly relations with Macedonia, and asked Greece to follow that example. At the end, the Swiss representative, Mr. Rufi, remarked that there could be no monopoly regarding names, and urged Greece to return to the negotiating table.[51]

European ministers discussed the embargo in Brussels at the end of June. The issue was raised by the current European Union chairman, German minister Klaus Kinkel. He stressed it was high time to do something about it, as the economic situation in Macedonia was increasingly worsening and could destabilize the region. Kinkel's initiative was supported by the head of the British Foreign Office, Douglas Hurd, and the French minister for European affairs, Allain Lamassour.[52]

On June 30, the European Liberal, Democrat and Reform parties issued a press release stressing that whatever the strictly legal position, the action by the Greek government on a frontier of the European Union endangered both the political and economic stability of a small democracy which threatens nobody, and risked extending conflict to parts of the Balkans which have so far been spared the horrors of the war in Bosnia-Herzegovina and Croatia.

Western European nations individually often made very strident criticisms of Greece while offering support for Macedonia. The British deputy foreign secretary, Douglas Hogg, summoned Greek ambassador Alijas Gounaris to the Foreign Office to convey to him the government protest in relation to the recent Greek actions toward the Republic of Macedonia. Hogg told the Greek ambassador that the embargo presented a threat to the stability of Macedonia, which Britain regarded as very important, as well as a great risk of an outburst of conflict in the already tense region. Hogg also called upon Greece to resume negotiations, without setting prerequisites.[53] A few months later, Britain reaffirmed its interest in finding a quick solution to the conflict.[54]

France had officially established diplomatic relations with Macedonia on December 27, 1993, by sending an envoy to Skopje. By that time, Slovenia, Turkey, Bulgaria and Britain had also set up diplomatic missions in Skopje.[55] France formally summoned the Greek ambassador, Dimitris Makris, and delivered a note of protest after introduction of the Greek economic sanctions against Macedonia.[56] French foreign minister Alain Juppe appealed for a reasonable behavior by Greece, stressing that a solution must be reached through · dialogue, and not through confrontation.

The German foreign minister, Klaus Kinkel, said that the Greek embargo was "contrary to acceptable behavior among civilized European countries."[57] Later he said, "I expect Greece to immediately withdraw its decision," and added that Bonn would not allow a destabilization of Macedonia.[58] Following an August meeting and talks with the Macedonian president, Mr. Kinkel said, "Macedonian-German relations are developing exceptionally well ... In our opinion, the Republic of Macedonia is extremely important for the Union and what is essential at the moment is to help it overcome its economic difficulties... Although the (European) Court has rejected the European Commission's accusations, it still does not mean the embargo is legal and politically justified. We believe in the urgent need to resolve this dispute and to have the blockade lifted... Macedonia is successfully proving it can function as a multiethnic and democratic state, even in these extremely hard conditions, and that is why we believe it deserves our full support."[59]

The prime minister of Italy, Silvio Berlusconi, said that the Greek embargo against Macedonia was irrational and that, as a man who puts the economy to the forefront, he simply could not accept this as a form of communication with another country. Italy offered financial aid and participated in the East-West project, which includes sub-projects, such as the gas line and a highway.[60]

A Danish parliamentary delegation, led by the president of the Committee for Foreign Affairs, Peter Doetoft, visited Macedonia soon after the embargo was applied. In talks with President Gligorov, the Danish deputies voiced their concern and condemnation regarding the embargo. On a separate occasion, in New York, Danish foreign minister Helveg Petersen called the embargo "seriously alarming." He promised to raise the issue at a European Union meeting, saying, "I must suggest the Greek government regain its composure and withdraw its decisions regarding Macedonia — especially the one about economic measures."[61]

Other nations' responses. Support for Macedonia, and criticism of Greece, has also come from the United Nations. In his 1994 report on Macedonia, the special envoy on human rights in the former Yugoslavia, Tadeusz Mazowiecki, demanded from the Security Council that the Greek embargo against Macedonia should immediately be lifted, and that Macedonia be given compensation for its losses due to the United Nations sanctions against Serbia and the current Greek embargo.[62] "The authorities in Macedonia want peace and complete stability in the Balkan region," secretary general Boutros Boutros-Ghali stated during a visit to Australia. Speaking of the positive and preventive role of the United Nations forces there, he referred to Macedonia by its constitutional name, the Republic of Macedonia.[63]

In an interview for the Greek TV station "Mega," American secretary of state Warren Christopher said Greece's economic blockade was an exaggerated and unjustified action.[64] He added that Macedonia was in a critical economic position and its having been recognized by the United States and the European

Union did not justify the Greek behavior.[65] While the United States continued to verbally deplore the Greek embargo, its actions to support Macedonia were often more subtle. Nevertheless, efforts at persuasion continued through to the time the first agreement was reached in September 1995. For instance, during a congress concerning economic cooperation on the Balkans, held in Salonika in February 1995, new American-British pressure was exerted on Greece. The United States ambassador, Thomas Niles, and the ambassador of Great Britain, Oliver Miles, warned that the Greek embargo against Macedonia, as well as the crisis in the relations with Albania and Turkey, presented obstacles to investment activities of their countries through Greece and therefore should be resolved as soon as possible.[66]

In talks with the leader of the opposition, Miltiadis Evert, at the end of February 1994, the Russian ambassador to Greece repeated an offer for Russia to act as a mediator in the Greek-Macedonian dispute.[67] A spokesman from the Russian Foreign Ministry stated in Moscow that the economic blockade was not acceptable in international relations, adding that Russia wanted to maintain friendly relations with both Macedonia and Greece, but that it had no intention of interfering in the settling of the "historic problems."[68] Russia's interest in Macedonia and the Russian attitude toward the use of the name were indicated in the enthusiastic congratulatory telegram from the president of the Russian Federation, Boris Yeltzin, sent on the occasion of Gligorov's reelection as president of Macedonia. "Receive my sincere congratulations on the occasion of your election as President of the Republic of Macedonia. By supporting you again, the Macedonian people voted for strengthening peace and stability not only in the Republic, but also in the Balkans. I take this opportunity to express the conviction that friendly relations and cooperation between the Russian Federation and the Republic of Macedonia will develop successfully in the interest of the people of both our countries."[69]

In the Balkans, Bulgarian president Zelju Zelev, in an interview for the TV show "Panorama," pointed out that the latest Greek blockade against Macedonia was "not contributing to relieving of the tensions in the region." At the same time, Bulgaria offered Macedonia the use of its port of Burgas on the Black Sea, as it had done during the previous blockade.[70] Albanian president Berisha placed all services of the port of Durres at Macedonia's disposal. Turkish president Suleiman Demirel offered Macedonia the use of Turkish ports and promised Turkish assistance. During the previous year's Greek blockade of Macedonia, Ankara had supplied Macedonia with fuel, including an entire tanker of petrol. Meanwhile, Turkey urged Athens to rethink its extreme position, calling Greece's actions unfair to the 2 million people of Macedonia.[71]

The twentieth meeting of the seven most developed countries in the world ended in Naples early in July 1994 with the adoption of an economic and political declaration. The official Japanese delegation presented the New Countries'

Government program, which included a section on relations with Macedonia. The program stated Japan's readiness to aid Macedonia economically and included preparation of a project for economic cooperation between the two states.[72] China established diplomatic relations with Macedonia soon after the Greek embargo, recognizing Macedonia under the name of the Republic of Macedonia. By September 1994, a new Chinese embassy had been established in Skopje.[73]

One international commentator who fully supported the Greek side of the dispute was Mikhail Gorbachev, former president of the USSR. Gorbachev said that no Macedonian question exists and that the Greek stand is firmly founded in history. Some Macedonians were skeptical about the value of this contribution, pointing out that Mr. Gorbachev could have a similar stand on the Lithuanian question, the Estonian question and the Latvian question, but might have been more willing to voice his opinion in the case of Greece because the Greeks paid for his cruise among the Greek islands and appointed him honorary professor at the Athens and Salonika universities.[74]

The Council of Europe. The Greek dispute with Macedonia led also to Greece blocking Macedonia's efforts to join the Council of Europe. Through 1994 and 1995, Macedonia made repeated efforts to meet the criteria for admission to the council, but did not advance past observer status.

In May 1995, a delegation of the Council of Europe visited Macedonia and met with President Gligorov and other government ministers. It was agreed that Macedonia's admission to the Council of Europe was of key importance for the further development and international affirmation of the Republic of Macedonia, as well as for stability in the region at large.[75] Discussions were held regarding concrete issues connected to the legislative system of Macedonia and its compliance with European standards. The delegation expressed great satisfaction with advances made, and at a news conference emphasized that "Macedonia is a democratic country. Perfect democracies are rare even in the Council of Europe." They gave a positive evaluation on the internal situation in Macedonia, noting ethnic disputes, including the case of the Albanian-language university, but said after discussions with minority groups that they did not see a substantial obstacle to Macedonia's admission to the Council of Europe. Recognizing Greece's opposition in this matter, they also said that the council as a whole wanted to overcome this problem. This view was confirmed during a visit to Macedonia by Miguel Martinez, president of the Council of Europe's Parliamentary Assembly.[76] The admission of Macedonia to the council should be a unifying factor for all political subjects in the country, Martinez said. All that remained was for the Macedonian government and Parliament to ratify the Declaration for Local Self-government and the Conventions for Human and National Minority Rights. Asked why he had insisted on Macedonia signing the Convention when a number of council members — including Macedonia's neighbors — have not signed it, Martinez said the Convention is a good initiative, adding that all other member countries are pressed to sign it and that the Parliamentary Assembly would be completely satisfied to see a greater participation of ethnic Albanians, as well as women, at all levels of governing within the country.

Press reactions to the trade blockade. Reactions of the non–Greek press to the dispute between Greece and Macedonia have been less cautious than those of the international diplomats. Many commentators have been extremely critical of the Greek embargo and the case that the Greeks have tried to make against the Macedonians.

The London *Times* wrote a lengthy and detailed editorial argument (February 21, 1994), claiming that the Greek action "was in violation of the Treaty of Rome, the Maastricht treaty, the United Nations Charter, resolutions of the UN General Assembly, the 1982 Law of the Sea Convention, and the basic norms of morality which govern civilized international relations." The *Times* pointed out that at the Edinburgh Summit of the European Council in December 1992, Greece had made a commitment to ensure that Macedonia received a "regular and properly monitored supply of oil." The embargo was in obvious violation of this commitment. The *Times* pointed out that Macedonia had not acted unlawfully in any way and concluded that no "legitimate interest" of Greece was at issue in the dispute. Greece's "obsession" with the name issue and the question of the flag could not be regarded as "legitimate" by any legal, moral or political measure. The *Times* insisted that the Greeks should end their blockade of Macedonia.

In another editorial (April 8, 1994), the *Times* called on Greece to give up its presidency of the European Union in order to prevent even greater damage to Europe than it had already caused. It said Greece had placed its own interests above those of the Union by introducing the embargo against Macedonia, thus abusing its position and damaging the Union's reputation. The *Times* said that bringing Greece to the European Court was not a suitable response since Macedonia needed help immediately. Concluding that Mr. Papandreou aimed to cause damage to a Balkan country that already faced great economic difficulties, and to increase tensions around it, the *Times* took the embargo as evidence that the Greek prime minister was more concerned with domestic political interests than with the need to prevent a wider regional conflict.

Other British newspapers took a similar stand against Greece. The *Spectator* said that the Greek government's actions to "further its vendetta" against tiny Macedonia represented "a curious mixture of farce, tragedy, the theater of cruelty and the theater of the absurd."[77] Greece had become more extreme in the face of European complaints, as though the European presidency had made it invulnerable to criticism, the *Spectator* said. Its behavior towards Macedonia was a first step towards destroying the country's stability, which could lead to internal violence and war. The *Spectator* concluded that this destabilization was the long-term aim of Greek policy, and that the greatest causes of instability in the Balkans were Serbia and Greece, acting more or less as allies. The paper argued that Greece was a "geopolitical liability" to Europe and should have its membership in the European Union withdrawn.

The *Daily Telegraph* (Feb. 19, 1994) said Greece's presidency of the European Community was degenerating into "an unseemly and dangerous farce." The trade embargo against Macedonia typified Greek truculence and insecurity. The Greek government seemed intent on pursuing "a narrowly nationalistic agenda," which compromised European Community institutions and treaties and threatened stability in the Balkans. In a later editorial (September 12, 1994) focused on Greek antagonism to Albania, the *Daily Telegraph* said that with both Macedonia and Albania "Athens has revealed itself as a vindictive, short-sighted bully of poorer and weaker neighbors," and argued that the European Community should intervene because of the instability in the Balkans that Greece had created.

The *Economist* wrote that the blockade violated Greece's treaty obligations and was imposed simply to protect Prime Minister Papandreou from domestic criticism after the United States recognized Macedonia.[78] The *Guardian* said the Greek action against Macedonia "would be suitable material for a diplomatic farce if it were not so disturbing," and was critical of Greek claims to exclusive use of the name, of the issue concerning the constitution that Macedonia had already addressed, and of Greece's avoidance of the issue of minority rights of Slav-Macedonians in Aegean Macedonia. The *Guardian* concluded that because of the disparity in the size of populations and armies in Greece and Macedonia, and Macedonia's landlocked vulnerability to blockade, the idea of expansionist actions from Macedonia is absurd.[79]

William D. Montalbano, writing in the *Los Angeles Times* (March 4, 1994), said, "Even Greece's best friends say the embargo is improvident, incendiary for the powder keg Balkans and embarrassing for the Athens government." An editorial in the *New York Times* a few days later said, "Greece is fueling tensions in another former Yugoslav republic, Macedonia, by imposing a strangling economic blockade. Greece's Western allies understand that Athens has had serious problems with Macedonia in the past. But they are losing patience with Greece's bullying tactics against a much weaker neighbor already suffering ethnic tensions."[80] A few weeks later, on the issue of recognition of Macedonia, the *New York Times* wrote, "Greece, the country that introduced Europe to comedy and tragedy, now leads its European Community partners into a shameful diplomatic farce."[81] The editorial went on to say Alexander the Great had no qualms about the spreading of the Macedonian name, since he left behind at least 10 Alexandrias in various parts of the ancient world. The article rejected the notion that Greece faced any military threat from "this ministate with no army" and concluded that "Washington has given its ally's temper tantrum more deference than it deserves. It ought to recognize independent Macedonia without further delay."

The *Christian Science Monitor* (April 15, 1994) said that Greece had made something of a laughingstock of itself in the international community for two years by demanding that its "enfeebled" northern neighbor not use the name of Macedonia. The *Monitor* added that the manner in which the blockade had stoked nationalist feelings in Greece was no laughing matter, being a significant factor aggravating the overall Balkan crisis. The *Monitor* noted that many in both of Greece's leading parties recognized that the "name issue" was blown out of proportion by the Mitsotakis government, and suggested that a way must be found for Athens to escape the corner it had painted itself into, but added that the United States administration ought not be a mere agent of the Greek lobby in Congress.[82]

The *Chicago Tribune* was particularly scathing in its attack on the Greek claims. It asked, "Would Mexico threaten a trade embargo against the United States to force New Mexico to change its name? Would the British huff and puff in the high courts of world opinion because a section of our Atlantic seaboard chose to call itself New England?" It concluded that there was little logic to Greece's argument and that furthermore, Greece's claim that full recognition of Macedonia would lead to Balkan instability could not be taken seriously while Greece continued to ignore United Nations sanctions against Serbia. The paper expressed distrust of Greek and Serbian urgings that the world not recognize the independence of Macedonia, and asked, "Why in the world is the world listening?"[83]

Like other United States analysts, William Dunn rejected the Greek claim that Macedonia is a military threat.[84] He pointed out also that the Macedonian constitution had been amended in 1992 to conform to recommendations of the Badinter Commission, which had then concluded that Macedonia fulfilled all conditions for recognition. He cited Article 3 of the constitution as explicitly excluding territorial ambitions, and explained that while the constitution expresses a concern for the status and rights of Macedonians in neighboring countries, in Article 49 it affirms explicitly the principle of noninterference in the internal affairs of other states. He adds that portions of Article 49 are virtually identical to Article 108 of the Greek constitution, which likewise seeks to support Greeks living outside Greece. Dunn noted that the relatively favorable United States State Department report on human rights in Macedonia contrasted with the unfavorable reports on Greece.

The Globe and Mail of Toronto had expressed concern about Greece's attitude to Macedonia before the embargo. In an editorial on October 25, 1993, the paper said that while it recognized Greek anxiety about the possibility of a war in its area of the Balkans, Greece in its fear was "succumbing to the same virus that caused that turmoil in the first place: unreasoning ethnic nationalism." Three months later *The Globe and Mail* (January 10, 1994) was again critical of the Greek position, noting that Greece's European allies had lost patience with its behavior and its claims. The paper said the European Community rightly believed that recognition of Macedonia and its stability were tied together. It also noted the paradox of the situation for Canada, since troops were sent as part of a United Nations contingent to defend the territorial integrity of a state whose existence Canada did not recognize.

An editorial in *The Toronto Star* (March 12, 1994) said, "Greece is giving its 3,000-year-old democracy a bad name with its continued bullying of Macedonia, its tiny neighbor to the north." The paper said that since losing its diplomatic war against international recognition of Macedonia, Greece had broadened its attack with the trade blockade, which the paper described as a crude attempt to starve the impoverished republic into submission. The *Star* said it was irrational of Athens to continue to lay sole claim to the Macedonian name, history and culture which have existed on both sides of the Greek-Yugoslav border for much of this century. The paper saw Greece as the malicious party in the crisis.

The Australian national newspaper, *The Australian*, approved of its government's decision to recognize Macedonia and noted that Greece's "punishing trade embargo" had been condemned by every other European Union government.[85] In an editorial titled, "On Recognizing Macedonia," *The Sydney Morning Herald* (March 7, 1994) said, "Greece's demand that Macedonia should delete a [constitutional] clause regarding the rights of Macedonians outside the country is ridiculous, since Article 108 of the Greek Constitution says much the same."

On its front page, the Torino newspaper *La Stampa* published an editorial entitled "The Vampires from 1914 Are Returning to the Balkans." According to this newspaper, Greece was the one to break off all relations and then light up another fuse, similar to that in Bosnia. The newspaper asked, but could not answer, the question, "Why are the Greeks so much against Macedonia?"[86]

The German press also criticized the Greek move. *Suddeutsche Zeitung* said: "This young country, which achieved its independence with great hardship, is weak economically and politically, and cannot present any danger to Athens." *Brausweirgere Zeitung*, in an article entitled "Athens Provocation," wrote that Greece has a tendency to blame others for its own economic and political crises.[87] The German press was unanimous in the assessment that Greece had taken the aggressive lead. German newspapers wrote that the Greek policy toward Macedonia had "nothing in common with the policy of responsibility"; that it violated the "unity of the EU" and spread paranoia in the Balkans; that "Papandreou's demagoguery [did] not comply with the international policy of peace," and that Greece was "playing with fire."[88]

After the European Commission's decision to bring Greece to the Court of Justice, the Paris newspaper *Liberation* concluded that the European Union seemed unable to cope with problems in the former Yugoslavia. The paper stressed that the Greek embargo endangered the Union trade policy, but even more seriously endangered the foreign politics of the EU, especially its concern for common security for its members. Another French newspaper, *Quotidien*, underlined the fact Greece was the first member country brought before the court since the Rome Treaty to establish the European Community was signed. Even the conservative Paris daily *Figaro* agreed that the Greek embargo was illegal.[89]

Changes in Greek public attitudes. From time to time Greek voices have expressed disagreement with the policies of their government, and more and more of these have been heard as time passed. In January 1994, the president of Cyprus, Mr. Kleridis, disassociated himself from the politics of Athens towards Macedonia, emphasizing that the essential issue was inviolability of borders, not the name dispute. He said the name issue was primarily an emotional matter, and recognized that a Macedonian state had existed for a number of years as a part of Yugoslavia.[90] In March, about two weeks after the imposition of the embargo, a group of 21 prominent Greek intellectuals, including university professors, former ambassadors, economists, journalists and students, sent an open letter to the media in Greece, harshly condemning the Greek measures, calling them a "revengeful act" aimed at covering up the weakness of the government by turning against countries that recognized Macedonia. The writers pointed out that never in its history had Greece been so isolated or disliked, and reminded readers of Greece's international obligations.[91]

Sissy Volu, a member of the Forum of Left-Oriented Feminists in Greece, visited Skopje in May 1994 as a guest of the Civilian Forum for Dialogue Between Greece and Macedonia. Volu, who comes from Athens, was making efforts to bring representatives of the Greek Organization of Women to an international conference of women in Skopje. She described herself as an active member of the anti-war and anti-nationalist movement in Greece, which had made attempts to organize demonstrations in Salonika, with the goal of "putting an embargo against nationalism, and not against Macedonia." She said, "Ever since the very beginning of the Greek campaign against Macedonia, we firmly took the view that the Republic of Macedonia must be recognized under its constitutional name." She said many of her group had been arrested without any legal grounds, but they had tried to keep in contact with several like-minded intellectuals from Macedonia.[92] The same group that organized Volu's visit to Macedonia organized a visit from a group of 80 Greeks in June 1994, financed by the Soros foundation's "Open Society" group.[93]

By April, Prime Minister Papandreou had moderated his public demands, saying that Greece would lift the trade embargo against Macedonia if it would stop using the disputed symbol on the flag and if it would change its Constitution. Papandreou's proposition does not include the dispute regarding the name of the country. He stated that he would retain "the question with the name, which is hard to solve," as a topic for further negotiations. United States president Bill Clinton stated, "It is very important for Greece and Europe, as well as for the world community, that the dispute between the two states is solved and I think that can be achieved." He added, "I think that the easiest way to achieve this is to soften the rhetoric, to consider minority rights and not to allow the war that is raging in Bosnia to spread to neighboring regions in which the situation is equally tense."[94]

Three and a half months after the introduction of the embargo, doubts about its effectiveness were growing throughout Greece. The assistant foreign minister, Yorgos Papandreou, stated that "the blockade has no effects." Some of the Athens press blamed the United States, especially after the decision of that nation's Congress to hold back 25 percent of the military help intended for Greece because of the embargo, and after the announcement of the forming of an American-inspired "customs corridor" to connect Macedonia with western Europe through Hungary, Romania and Bulgaria.[95]

A leading member of London's Greek community, Costas Carras, said Athens' existing rigid policy towards Macedonia must be modified, not to suit FYROM, but to preserve other priorities of Greek foreign policy. He believed Athens had lost influence in Europe by remaining inflexible on the issue.[96]

In August the Greek newspaper *To Vima* (July 29, 1994) published a lengthy argument titled "Eight Truths We Refuse to Accept," in favor of a more pragmatic approach to Macedonia.[97] Eight points were listed in the article: (1) Macedonia was partitioned amongst Greece, Serbia and Bulgaria — which received the smallest portion — after the First World War. (2) Following that partitioning, at least as early as 1919, the names "Vardar Macedonia" and "Pirin Macedonia" were in virtually universal use by diplomats, historians, and other writers including those living in Greece. (3) Since the population exchanges of the 1920s, Slavic Macedonian minorities in Greek Macedonia had been "insignificantly small." (4) Territory annexed to Serbia in 1919 kept the name Macedonia as a republic of Socialist Yugoslavia, and people in that area had "been living with the idea of being Macedonians" ever since. (5) Refusal to allow Skopje the use of any form of the name "Republic of Macedonia," began with former foreign minister Adonis Samaras and spread to the two main parties through his influence. (6) Greece's request that Skopje not be recognized under any form of the name Macedonia flew in the face of "basic democratic rules" of self-determination. (7) Even if Greece or an ally managed to persuade the Macedonian president to accept a ban on the use of the name Macedonia, Gligorov's own parliament would never vote in favor of such a proposal. (8) The Greek claim that "Macedonia is Greek" or that "there is only one Macedonia" only fueled suspicions that Greece planned to annex the two parts of Macedonia lying outside Greek borders.

The paper went on to say that whatever the behavior of Skopje, Greece should not stoop to irrational behavior in response, nor should it "support views unbecoming of a country with such a cultural tradition." And, the paper added, "above all, there can be no reason whatsoever to hide basic information … from the Greek people. Such systematic misinforming does not only underestimate the Greek people's reasoning power, but is also based on undemocratic and regressive ideas. What is more, it prevents us from an objective evaluation of our present situation."

In conclusion, said *To Vima*, only two strategies were possible for Greece: Continued insistence on Greece's sole ownership of the name Macedonia, or acceptance of some derivative form of the name, combined with an offer of economic aid dependent on changes in the constitution and flag as well as a halt to "irredentist propaganda." The results of the first would be continued isolation and loss of diplomatic opportunities for Greece, and increased international sympathy for and recognition of Skopje as the "Republic of Macedonia," particularly by Turkey, whose influence in the area would increase. With the second strategy, "Greece would be able to demand and would easily be granted guarantees for its present borders." The paper called for an end to "self-destructive politics" and to politicians placing "their own interests and status above national interests."

There were some opportunities for the Greek and Macedonian governments to cooperate on humanitarian issues during the blockade. For instance, in August 1994, the Macedonian government appealed to Athens for help in fighting an enormous forest fire in the area of Jasen. The Greek government placed special planes at Macedonia's disposal, and the planes arrived at the scene as soon as the following day, though by then the fires had already come under control. The Macedonian Foreign Ministry sent a note of gratitude expressing its desire for and confidence in the further improvement of such neighborly relations. The largest Greek opposition party, "New Democracy," reacted bitterly to this news.[98]

In November 1994, Greek government spokesman Mr. Venizelos said that Greece expected to resume talks on the dispute with FYROM now that the elections in that country were completed. He believed greater flexibility might now be possible for the FYROM side. The media were speculating about possible terms of an agreement that would include the removal of the embargo by Greece, support for FYROM to join the CSCE, and the dropping of the flag and changing of the constitution by FYROM. The name issue would be left for some future negotiations.[99] Soon after this, in an interview for the paper *Mesimevrini*, the leader of the largest opposition party in Greece, Miltiadis Evert, stated that he had never agreed with the embargo on Macedonia. He noted that the blockade against Macedonia had proved unsuccessful. He explained that the New Democracy party was left no choice in public discussion of the issue, and could have changed nothing by saying it would be a wrong move.[100]

Some of the Greek press, and even well-known personalities, began to express opinions completely opposite to those of the government on the embargo, following a statement by Teodoros Pangalos that it had been a total fiasco. In December 1994, even the opposition paper *Elefteros tipos*, known for presenting a hard line toward Macedonia, said that dock workers in Salonika were feeling the consequences of the Greek embargo on their pockets and backs even more than the Macedonian population.[101] The first Greek politician to visit Macedonia since the embargo was imposed, the head of the left-wing coalition, Nikos Konstandopoulos, said, "All the questions between the two countries have to be placed on the table, without any prerequisites. This initiative of Greek left wing forces is aimed at showing how ... a different approach is necessary. The ice has been broken in relations between the two countries."[102]

In January 1995, Constandinos Pilarinos, a deputy of the New Democracy party, claimed that Macedonian citizens could now freely enter Greece with passports bearing only a seal that reads "Macedonia," instead of "FYROM." He also said that foreign embassies in Athens confirmed that Greek customs officials no longer insisted on changing of the "MKD" seal in the passports of international travelers. He pointed to examples of violations of the Greek embargo as proof of the absurdity of the blockade for Greece itself.[103]

Former Greek prime minister Konstantinos Mitsotakis said in Athens that the dispute with Macedonia was at a dead end, and he recommended that Greece accept the proposals of mediator Cyrus Vance for a "complex name for Macedonia." He said that he had not had the opportunity of imposing a solution to the problem with Macedonia in April 1992 because the rest of the leadership, including President Konstantinos Karamanlis, though privately believing that the problem with the name was not the main issue, nevertheless refused to support the policy for a direct resolution of the problem with the "Pinneiro package." Mitsotakis also said that he had found himself alone in facing attacks by Andonis Samaras and his group, who threatened to create divisions within the party leading to early elections — which is exactly what happened. Mitsotakis added that his biggest mistake was failing to remove Samaras from the party at that time.[104] According to the Greek Foreign Ministry's *White Book on 1995*, Greece had no fears of military incursions from the north, although it might get militarily involved if wider alliances were formed in the region that could threaten the country's integrity. At the promotion of this book on Greece's Foreign Policy, former foreign minister Mikhalis Papaconstantinou condemned the view that "all sides have some plans against Greece." Briefly mentioning the Macedonian issue, Papaconstantinou said, "The name is a sovereign right of every country." He disagreed with the Greek official policy on minorities, saying the government is so afraid of the issue that it prohibits any research on it to the point of never mentioning national groups such as Vlachs. He spoke of a misunderstanding regarding the "Slavophone Greeks," explaining that "only the misinformed deny their Greek nationality. Language is not a necessary element for defining national affiliation." Papaconstantinou insisted on a solution for problems with Macedonia, which, he said, is populated by Slavonic people different from both Serbs and Bulgarians.[105]

There was discussion in the Greek press late in January 1995 about the possibility that Greece might lift the embargo if the European Commission withdrew its charges. This would enable Macedonia to give up its unyielding stance. The president of the left-wing Coalition of Progress, Nikos Konstandopoulos, wanted the embargo against Macedonia to be lifted immediately, as a sign of "good will." "Anyway," he said, "it's just the same as if it doesn't exist at all, because Macedonia has neither changed its stance, nor does it have any particular difficulties in securing supplies."[106] At the same time Thessaloniki businessmen were saying that the blockade greatly damaged them, especially the general northern Greek market and the port of Thessaloniki.

Further public discussion of such issues occurred throughout the next few months, with periods when an agreement seemed imminent, and other periods of apparent withdrawal by both sides. In March there were reports of a draft agreement being signed, though without direct dialogue.[107] In April there were reports that agreement had been reached on terms that had been floating about in the media since November, though a Macedonian government spokesman said this was all speculation.[108]

A softening of Greek behavior at the borders. When the dispute was at its peak, the treatment of people of various nationalities who attempted to cross from Macedonia into Greece was complicated by the fact that they had markings in their documents that the Greek government did not accept. Ethnic Macedonians from either Greece or Macedonia were often beaten by border guards, and Macedonians generally were denied entry to Greece. For example, in the summer of 1994, a number of Australian citizens, many of whom were ethnic Macedonians, were barred from crossing the Greek-Macedonian border, and in some cases passengers were physically abused, according to reports from the Australian Broadcasting Corporation (ABC). The ABC reported criticisms of Greece for not respecting international conventions at border crossing. One radio correspondent, not an ethnic Macedonian, described having had an unpleasant experience himself, and called on the Australian government to examine such cases since Australia and Greece have an agreement for non-visa entry.[109] The Australian minister for foreign affairs, Gareth Evans, made representations to his Greek counterpart over the issue. Soon after this event, CSCE officials from Great Britain and Canada were barred from entry to Greece at the Dojrani crossing, on the grounds that they had car insurance papers mentioning the name "Republic of Macedonia."[110]

By January 1995, however, Greek customs police were showing more tolerance to the Macedonian seal in international documents. Passengers who were not citizens of Macedonia were allowed through despite the fact that their traveling documents contain the Republic of Macedonia seal. Exceptions to this rule were certain members of Macedonian official or sports delegations, and on such occasions, the Greek visa was generally issued on a piece of paper.[111]

The End of the Embargo

In the first week of September 1995, the United States assistant secretary of state, Richard Holbrooke, stated that an agreement to put an end to the dispute between Macedonia and Greece had been formulated in which both countries had agreed to reach a compromise in the name of peace in the Balkans. He added that both sides wanted the United States to safeguard the agreement. At the same time, Cyrus Vance said that all elements of an agreement to end the dispute between Greece and Macedonia had been settled except for the name. He said it was a comprehensive agreement with every detail arranged. As a consequence of this development, the special envoy for the United States president, Matthew Nimitz, said in a statement for Macedonian radio, "I hope to be soon establishing diplomatic relations between our countries. The standing of your country is firm and good." He expected a formal arrangement the following week. He noted that United Nations secretary general, Boutros Boutros-Ghali and other members of the United Nations wanted the problem to be solved as soon as possible.[112]

An opinion poll published in the newspaper *Etnos*, in Athens, a few days later indicated that more than 60 percent of Greeks were against the signing of an agreement which would lift the economic embargo against Macedonia. Thirty-two percent out of 600 people sampled said the agreement would unavoidably lead to the recognition of Macedonia under that name, while 28 percent accused the Greek government of "selling itself" to the United States if it negotiated any kind of deal. Only 18.5 percent of those polled said the name issue had no significance and should be forgotten.

At about the same time, Greek prime minister Andreas Papandreou stated that during the talks to be held the following week in New York, Greece would not discuss the name issue. "This time we will talk about the small package," he stressed, adding that the name issue demanded more effort and time. He indicated that his government would not recognize "the neighboring country" under the name Republic of Macedonia or any other name that would include the word Macedonia. The leader of the New Democracy Party, Miltiadis Evert, strongly attacked the government for its actions. "After endless irresponsibility and recklessness, the Government begins a direct dialogue with Skopje for solving the issue, without confronting the issue of the name which is the major aspect of this great problem," he said. The Greek Committee for Dialogue Between Citizens in the Balkans and the Macedonian Civil Committee for Greek-Macedonian Dialogue and Understanding had already adopted a joint statement in which they expressed their satisfaction about the determination of the two governments to reach an agreement.[113]

The Interim Accord

On September 13, 1995, an Interim Accord was signed between the representatives of Greece and Macedonia. Minister Karolos Papoulias, representing Greece, described in the agreement as "the Party of the First Part," and Minister Stevo Crvenkovski, representing Macedonia, described as "the Party of the Second Part," agreed that Greece would recognize Macedonia as an independent and sovereign state, to establish diplomatic relations at an agreed level with the ultimate goal of relations at an ambassadorial level at the earliest possible date. The two sides confirmed their common existing frontiers as an enduring and inviolable international border, and each undertook to respect the sovereignty, the territorial integrity and the political independence of the other party. They agreed that they would not support the action of a third party directed against the sovereignty, the territorial integrity or the political independence of the other party. They agreed to refrain from the threat or use of force, including the threat or use of force designed to violate their existing frontiers, and they agreed that neither party would assert or support claims to any part of the territory of the other, or claims for a change of their existing frontier.

As well the two sides agreed to continue negotiations under the auspices of the secretary general of the United Nations with a view to reaching agreement on the issue of the name of Macedonia. Despite their differences on the issue each agreed to cooperate with a view to facilitating their mutual relations in various practical ways, including normal trade and commerce.

Macedonia affirmed that nothing in its constitution, and in particular in the preamble, would ever constitute the basis for any claim to any part of Greek territory, or for interference in the internal affairs of Greece. Macedonia agreed to stop using the Star of Vergina on its national flag.

Both sides agreed to prohibit hostile activities or propaganda by state-controlled agencies and to discourage acts by private entities likely to incite violence, hatred or hostility against each other, and to remove restrictions on the movement of people or goods between their territories.

On the questions of cultural and human rights, both sides agreed to be guided by various existing international charters, and to encourage contacts between their peoples at all appropriate levels in accordance with international law and custom.

Greece agreed not to object to any application by Macedonia to join international organizations so long as Macedonia used the name "Former Yugoslav Republic of Macedonia," and agreed that Macedonia's economic development should be assisted by developing a close relationship with the European Economic Area and the European Union.

With respect to treaty relations, the two sides agreed to follow provisions of earlier bilateral agreements between the former Socialist Federal Republic of Yugoslavia and Greece in the areas of legal relations, judicial decision, and hydro-economic questions, and to establish new agreements similar to these and in other areas of mutual interest.

Greece agreed to abide by the United Nations Convention on the Law of the Sea with respect to Macedonia's status as a landlocked state.

Both sides agreed to encourage the development of friendly and good-neighborly relations between them, particularly with regard to road, rail, maritime and air transport and communication links, and to strengthen their economic relations in all fields including scientific and technical cooperation, as well as cooperation in the field of education. There was even agreement to take steps to cooperate in eliminating all forms of pollution in border areas and more generally to protect the environment.

Both sides agreed to improve and promote business and tourist travel, to accelerate customs and border formalities, to modernize existing border crossings or construct new border crossings and to cooperate in the fight against crime, terrorism, economic crimes, narcotics crimes, illegal trade in cultural property, offenses against civil air transport and counterfeiting.

Finally, both sides agreed to abide by United Nations procedures in settling disputes.

The Interim Accord was to remain in force for seven years, until superseded by a definitive agreement, after which either party could withdraw by giving 12 months' notice in writing.

On the occasion of the signing of the Greek-Macedonian accord, Cyrus Vance said: "I can confirm that the accord, according to the new conditions, cancels the measures imposed by Greece on February 16, 1994, and replaces these measures with open and cooperative economic relations." Vance also explained that the document would come into force 30 days after its signing. Kiro Gligorov said, "I particularly greet the realistic attitude that neighboring Greece has shown in the signing of the agreement... It is especially important now, in the implementation of the agreement, to show good will, readiness and fairness in realizing of the agreement which is in the interest of both sides. I'm deeply convinced that this act can become a turning point for the future of the Balkans." Greek and Macedonian leaders offered one another their congratulations.[114]

The occasion of the signing of the agreement was also the occasion for the establishment of diplomatic relations at embassy level between the United States and the Republic of Macedonia.[115] In an interview for the private TV station "A1," Prime Minister Branko Crvenkovski said, "The establishment of full diplomatic relations with the U.S.A., at ambassadorial level, is an event of exceptional, I'd say historic, significance for the Republic of Macedonia. It's something we have been anticipating for a long time, aware that this would contribute, to a great extent, to the strengthening of Macedonia's position not only on a bilateral basis in relations with the U.S., but overall in the international community, as well."

World reactions. In the United States, President Clinton welcomed the agreement between Greece and Macedonia, stressing that it was of great importance for both countries and would significantly enhance international stability. U.S. negotiator Matthew Nimitz said, "I'm always an optimist but regarding the name issue, it will not be easy. We should do all that we can. The beginning of the negotiations for the name issue is expected to start in the second half of October, but the negotiations will not be easy. The Greek Prime Minister got everything he asked for. That is not only concerning the embargo but the very agreement which gives possibilities for full economic and cultural relations and cooperation in the region. FYROM will now be included in the NATO program. It is good for Greece to have such a friendly neighbor."

A little more than a week after the signing of the accord, a delegation from the United States Defense Department came for a one-day visit to the Republic of Macedonia. The military delegation, including the commandant of the United States Army for Europe, was received by President Gligorov, who welcomed the current development of the cooperation between the two countries in the defense field. The United States secretary of the army repeated the readiness of the United States to promote cooperation between the two armies and said the United States would stand by Macedonia in this field at an international level.[116] The chief of staff of the United States Army, John Shalikashvili, visited Skopje early in October, saying, "I'm glad to be again in the country in which our soldiers are so warmly welcomed." Both countries expressed their mutual satisfaction with the developments in the military cooperation, through the program "Bridge to America" and other educational programs of Macedonian officers in the United States. The mutual conclusion was that the mission of UNPREDEP should remain as it is in Macedonia.[117]

Embassies and foreign ministries of Great Britain, Germany, and Russia issued statements expressing their enthusiasm for the Interim Accord. Reactions in Athens, however, were divided. The pro-government newspapers spoke of "a new chapter" in relations between Greece and the "Former Yugoslav Republic of Macedonia," while the right-wing newspapers, including *Adesmaftos*, described the accord as "treason," a "humiliating compromise" in which "Greece is giving up its only weapon — the economic embargo." Evangelos Venizelos said, "The Greek government is absolutely satisfied. Positions which it formulated from the outset, positions which it firmly stuck to, were accepted." Stressing that Greece would not back down from its position on the name, Venizelos noted that the interim agreement would not be annulled if the two sides failed to reach agreement on the name. "Commitments have been taken," Mr. Venizelos said, adding that liaison offices would be opened in both Athens and Skopje. Karolos Papoulias said, "This is a very important agreement and a step forward after long and hard negotiations and the Greek government welcomes it... There is only the name issue left. I predict extremely difficult negotiations for the name issue, which are to begin right after the termination of the thirty day term set forth in the agreement. The embargo will be lifted on the same day that FYROM changes the flag and gives a reassurance concerning the Constitution." He said there would be no change of the Greek attitude regarding the name issue.

Miltiades Evert, leader of the largest opposition party in Greece, predicted an "endless discussion" would begin on the question of the name "which will in the end lead nowhere." He disapproved of the terminology of the agreement which avoided naming the two countries. In the last week of October, the Greek extremist leader Adonis Samaras called for division and cantonization of Macedonia, using Bosnia as an example. A former official of the Greek government, Evangelos Kofos, stated that the agreement should have covered the name issue, and should have acknowledged the Macedonian minority in Greece and the matter of allowing the return of Aegean Macedonian refugees. He observed that in the last 40 or 50 years a nation had been formed and it was evident that the people in it did not feel like Bulgarians, Serbians or Albanians. He said the problem was that this nation had taken the name of the native land, which has often happened elsewhere, and the geographical name is a name that can be used by any inhabitant in that region. But Greece did not allow these differences to be understood by the Greek people.[118]

Mayors of cities of northern Greece asked Prime Minister Andreas Papandreou not to make any compromises concerning the name Macedonia. Should their demand be rejected or should they leave the meeting with Papandreou dissatisfied, they threatened to organize mass demonstrations, this time against Athens instead of against Skopje.[119] The All-Greek Association of Northern Macedonia ("Makedonomasi") appealed to the citizens of Thessaloniki and Greek Macedonia, and the associations of Macedonians living in Greece, to join the "third greatest meeting in preserving Greek holy rights." The proclamation, published in the magazine *Elefteros Tipos*, called for united opposition to the "planned sale of Macedonia to Skopje's Slavs who came in this region 1000 years after Alexander the Great and Aristotle." The association accused Skopje of already announcing its intention to expel the Greeks from Macedonia.[120]

Opinions of Macedonians were similarly divided. A survey conducted by the NIP Agency "Nova Makedonija-Data Press" with 1,200 citizens indicated that a change of the name of the republic was unacceptable for 79.33 percent of the citizens of Macedonia. In contrast, some 56.33 percent stated that a change of the flag was acceptable.[121]

At a press conference of the Democratic Party, its leader, Petar Gosev, warned that signing of the agreement would produce catastrophic consequences for the future of the state, would be a total fiasco for Macedonian diplomacy and was an agreement of a national shame. He stressed that the agreement denies the existence of Aegean Macedonians. At the Universal Hall in Skopje, there was a meeting of representatives of VMRO-DPMNE, the World Macedonian Congress, the MAAK-Conservative party, the Association "Dignity," the Labor Party, and the Union of Independent Syndicates to express protest and disagreement about the accord. In the presence of some 100 people, the leaders of these parties expressed their discontent with, as they put it, "the signing of the disgraceful document against Macedonian national dignity, on which the opposition was not even consulted." A declaration was read in which the government was accused of excluding the Macedonian public from the negotiations. The meeting announced a major protest in front of the Macedonian Parliament for the day when the Parliament was to ratify the document.[122] Ljupcho Georgievski, leader of VMRO-DPMNE, said, "I assure you the Greeks will start with blockades against Macedonia again, and our delegation doesn't even know what it's signing. What's happening is a shameful defeat of Macedonian foreign policy." The leader of the Macedonian Orthodox Church in Macedonia, Father Mihail, also expressed disapproval of the accord.

City Hall of Prilep, at a special session, said that it did not agree with the Macedonian leadership and Kiro Gligorov as its leader about "accepting of the Greek ultimatum" for the change of the flag, constitution and name of Republic of Macedonia. It demanded that the government, Parliament and president of the republic urgently and energetically seek to terminate the negotiations in New York.[123]

Outside Macedonia, the Rainbow party of the Macedonian ethnic community in Greece welcomed the accord and asked for a similar dialogue between the Greek government and ethnic Macedonians in Greece. However, a delegation of the Organization of United Macedonians and the Macedonian Community of North America came to Skopje to voice their concern about the accord. On behalf of the organization, President Vlado Grozdanovski explained, that they viewed any kind of concession as a defeat for Macedonian foreign policy. It requested that the flag not be changed and stated that the demand for a change of the constitution was an insult and interference in the internal affairs of the Republic of Macedonia. Also, losing the right of the home state to care for the rights of Macedonians from the occupied parts of Macedonia would be a national insult and an act of treachery to the nation's own people. At the same time, in New York, in front of the United Nations building, a small group of Macedonians held a peaceful protest, waving the Macedonian flag. Disagreement about the signing was expressed also by Macedonian church communities and the Organization of United Macedonians of Toronto, Canada, the Australian-Macedonian Committee for Human Rights, and the Council of Macedonia of West Australia.

At the twenty-seventh session of the Macedonian Parliament, on October 5, 110 parliamentarians voted in favor of a proposal for a new flag for Macedonia, featuring a red base and a gold sun with eight sunrays. Only one delegate voted against this proposal, while four abstained. The flag became official immediately after publication of the decision in the *Government Gazette*. Greek Prime Minister Andreas Papandreou voiced his satisfaction at the decision as an integral part of the efforts for normalization of relations between the two countries.[124] VMRO-DPMNE released a statement criticizing the move and declared it unacceptable.[125] With 102 votes "for," 1 "against" and 2 abstentions, the Parliament of the Republic of Macedonia adopted the law on the ratification of the accord between the Republic of Macedonia and the Republic of Greece on October 9.[126] In his address, Prime Minister Branko Crvenkovski emphasized that with the accord, the Republic of Greece recognized the independence and territorial integrity of the Republic of Macedonia. Crvenkovski assessed the adoption of the law on the flag as the expression of an honest desire on behalf of Macedonia to implement the accord, and to restore normal neighborly relations. According to Crvenkovski, the document paved the way for a full normalization of relations with Serbia.

Macedonia was admitted as a member in the OSCE by a decision of the Standing Committee of the Organization held in Vienna on October 12.[127] Towards the end of October, talks began with Greece and United Nations negotiators about the name of Macedonia, and after Greece offered the European Union verbal assurances about lifting the embargo, the Union decided to withdraw legal charges against Greece. The embassy of the Republic of Turkey in Skopje informed the Macedonian Foreign Ministry that the Republic of Macedonia had been accepted as a full member of the Black Sea Convention for cooperation in the field of culture, education, science and information, alongside the governments of Albania, Armenia, Azerbaijan, Belarus, Georgia, Moldova, Romania, Turkey, Ukraine and Russia.[128]

A month after the signing of the accord, some movement began at the Macedonian-Greek border points, though there were some problems. At one stage the Greek border authorities started charging border insurance of 160 Deutsche marks for cars (25,000 drachmas), and 500 DEM (80,000 drachmas) for cargo vehicles, though this was soon abandoned.[129] People from the Republic of Macedonia originating from the Aegean part of Macedonia (northern Greece) were at first not being issued visas on the Macedonian-Greek border. It later emerged that the major issue was the writing of the Greek birthplace in the Macedonian script and following the Macedonian nomenclature.

Within days of the formal parliamentary approval of the new Macedonian flag, it was hanging in front of the United Nations building in New York. The Macedonian delegation, led by the Macedonian Parliament president, Stojan Andov, was present at the ceremony of the first raising. The ceremony was opened by the secretary general, who stressed: "There are not so many images that express such a collective strength as the flags near the U.N. building... The act of hanging up the Macedonian flag symbolizes the truth and understanding, the friendship in the region and in the international community because its colors are among those of other flags." In conclusion, Mr. Boutros-Ghali wished for Macedonia "to live in peace as a full member of the family of nations."

10. Macedonia in the South Balkans: Theories About War

In order to become independent in 1991, Macedonia had to negotiate with the remnants of Yugoslavia, Serbia and Montenegro. This process was not without its difficult periods. At one stage Macedonians were encouraged by Kiro Gligorov, the first elected president of an independent Macedonia, to arm themselves in case of the need to fight for independence. However, the withdrawal of the Yugoslav army occurred essentially without problems. At this point Macedonia needed to establish friendly relationships with other nations in order to support its economy by maintaining or developing trading relationships, and in order to protect itself from possibly hostile forces. As we have seen, Greece blocked this process. Since stability in Macedonia is widely considered to be of crucial importance to peace in the Balkans, this conflict with Greece is an extraordinary affair. However, relationships with some other neighbors at around the same time also were less than smooth.

In this chapter we will briefly examine the nature of relationships between the Republic of Macedonia and its Balkan neighbors in the first half of the 1990s, and in particular theories about the focal position of Macedonia in a possible future southern Balkan war. For this purpose attention must be given to Serbia (or FRY), Bulgaria, Greece, and Albania, as well as Turkey. Since the United States is now a significant element in Balkan events, we will also look at the development of relationships between the United States and Macedonia before, during and after the Greek embargo, and the significance that those relations have generally been accorded. While the particular events that are discussed may be forgotten quickly, the underlying issue, Macedonia's importance in Balkan affairs, is likely to be of significance for many years to come.

In an interview for the Information Center for the Balkans in Sofia, Kiro Gligorov talked about Macedonia's wish to avoid war, the stability of the state, a possible new Balkan conference, and relations between Bulgaria and Macedonia. Macedonia wants no war with any country and is determined to build

THE BALKANS IN THE EARLY 1990s

friendly relations with all neighboring countries, Gligorov said. Macedonia had no territorial disputes with any country. Gligorov pointed out that Bulgaria was among the first countries to have recognized Macedonia, and therefore it was strange that after such a long period, Bulgaria had no embassy in Skopje. He also pointed out Macedonia's readiness to raise the level of relations with Bulgaria. Maintaining peace in the Balkans was a priority, and closing the page of Balkan history, burdened with wars and conflicts, should be a primary goal now, Gligorov concluded.

"In order to secure stability in the region, it is best for Macedonia to remain an independent state and not join any federation," Gligorov told a fifteen-member group from the New York nongovernment Council for International Relations in the spring of 1994. Gligorov said this would avoid dispute about possible alliances. "However, that does not mean that we want to remain isolated. It is our firm determination to join the European associations."[1]

The Zagreb newspaper *Vjesnik* published an in-depth interview with

Gligorov on December 28, 1994. The interview was published under the title "No Confederation — See You in Europe." When asked to comment on Belgrade's latest offer to form a confederation on the Belgrade-Skopje-Athens axis, Gligorov replied, "Macedonia is interested in cooperation and good neighborly relations with all our neighbors, but not in plans which are aimed at creating some new confederations or axis, because every such attempt would end with a new tragic division of the Balkans." He reminded his audience of the "policy of equidistance" which demonstrated Macedonia's desire for good relations with all neighboring countries.

Nevertheless, Macedonia is seen as a flash-point for a war that could embrace much of the Balkans and perhaps many other countries because of the historic connections between Macedonia and its neighboring countries, all of whom have in previous decades participated in the dismembering of Macedonia, and all of whom are still interested in Macedonian territory. Other issues have arisen out of the settlements from the five wars that have embroiled the Balkans in the last hundred years. The Treaty of Versailles created a multi-ethnic Yugoslavia. Today, with the outbreak of war in Bosnia and Croatia, we have become aware of the complexity of the ethnic and religious mixture in these areas. The mix is even more complex in Macedonia. The Versailles treaty also created an Albanian state that contained only one-half of the ethnic Albanian nation; the other half was scattered among neighboring Yugoslavia (in Kosovo and Macedonia) and Greece. In the period following the First World War, in the Second World War and after the Greek civil war, the region experienced tragic and destabilizing ethnic migrations, and various forms of ethnic purification. As a result the flash-points for a south Balkan war are Macedonia and the immediately joining territory of Kosovo.[2] The risk of conflict existed from the late 1940s, but the break-up of Yugoslavia, and Serbian efforts to create a greater, "ethnically pure" Serbian state, intensified the risk at the latter stage of the twentieth century.

The prime minister of Macedonia, Branko Crvenkovski, said, "Any war in Macedonia at the very least would be a Balkan war drawing in our neighbors Serbia, Greece, Bulgaria, Albania and Turkey... We are determined that our state should be oriented toward Europe. Any other orientation be it an Eastern Orthodox, Muslim, or Pan-Slavic alliance, would only foment conflict and confrontation among Macedonia's inhabitants."[3] It seems that other important world powers agree with Crvenkovski's analysis. At the conclusion of the twentieth meeting of the seven most developed countries in the world in Naples, early in July 1994, Italian Prime Minister Silvio Berlusconi stated that all seven countries were making efforts to prevent the Bosnian conflict from spreading, because "if it does, it will include Albania, Macedonia, Greece and Turkey."[4]

Some Russian politicians also suggested a role for the United States in initiating a future Balkan, and perhaps wider, war. The extreme nationalist, Mr. Zirinovski, claimed that the presence of United States soldiers in Macedonia is a problem since Macedonia will be used as a beachhead for the United States Army, and future conflict between East and West will start in Macedonia. He said, "Unfortunately, Macedonians will be on the opposite side, but that's their problem." Alexandar Lebed, a deputy in the Russian Duma, also expressed a negative attitude toward the American soldiers in Macedonia. Lebed was one of the potential candidates for president and one of the most charismatic figures in Russian politics.[5]

In December 1995, the United Nations Security Council unanimously approved a six-month continuation of the mandate for 1,100 United Nations soldiers, including almost 500 Americans, in the Former Yugoslav Republic of Macedonia.[6] However, Russia spoke against the resolution, noting that this established a precedent, and that it was a very expensive exercise. The Russians argued also that the mission had been successful and that there was no threat to Macedonia. The Russian initiative was not supported, and accordingly there was no debate on the issue. Western analysts see a threat in the forces that organized the attempt on President Gligorov's life, and in the present situation in Kosovo. Serbia's intentions remain unclear. The Russian position is seen as reflecting Russian fears that Serbia may come more under United States and European Union influence.[7]

A theory of the early 1990s about the spark for a new Balkan war was that instability in Macedonia, meaning conflict between the Albanian minority and the ethnic Macedonians, could lead to war in which all four principal neighbors, Serbia, Greece, Albania and Bulgaria, were likely to become involved. Given that there was considerable agitation among Albanians in the west of Macedonia for an autonomous state, this was not a far-fetched proposal. At the end of 1993, former United States diplomat George Canny, an expert on the former Yugoslavia, said that in a few months the Balkan war would spread to Macedonia, Albania, Bulgaria, Greece and Turkey. This would all start in Macedonia, because the country was exhausted by the sanctions and the nationalist party VMRO was ready to take over power in the coming elections. The turmoil that would follow from this, in particular the dissension among the Albanians, would be used by Serbia as a pretext to intervene, which would involve the other Balkan countries.[8] Canny's predictions did not come to pass in the time frame he predicted, but the underlying internal difficulties remained.

In the latter part of 1994, United Nations secretary general Boutros Boutros-Ghali submitted a report to the Security Council on the position of UNPROFOR units in the former Yugoslavia, including a thorough analysis of the economic and political situation in Macedonia. According to this report the most serious difficulties facing the former Yugoslavia Republic of Macedonia in the middle of 1994 were economic and social. Social stability was endangered by high unemployment figures and economic decline, resulting from the economic blockade imposed by Greece, and the United Nations sanctions against Federal Yugoslavia — the main trading partners of this country in the past.

Internal political tensions between Macedonians and ethnic Albanians also had increased. Boutros-Ghali said that continuing differences between Greece and the former Yugoslav Republic of Macedonia concerning the name, flag and constitution blocked the latter's full membership in international organizations and continued the threats to its economic stability and border security, all worsened by the continuing Greek economic blockade and Federal Yugoslavia's refusal to recognize the borders of the Former Yugoslav Republic of Macedonia.[9]

The London *Times* said Macedonia was "creeping inexorably towards an internal collapse similar to that which prefaced the war in Bosnia."[10] The London *Daily Telegraph* suggested that economic collapse would eventually offer opportunities for Macedonia's Serbian and Albanian neighbors to fan intercommunal tensions. This could lead to its disintegration, in which case it might be shared between its neighbors, or in Serbian control over a rump state. Such disturbances could increase the flow of economic migrants from southern Albania into Greece, who already numbered several hundred thousand. Worse, the *Daily Telegraph* proposed, the danger existed that such a prospect would prompt Turkish intervention, so igniting a general Balkan conflict.[11]

However, the way that other Balkan states might become embroiled in the case of a civil war is not at all clear. It depends on what happens next. The course of action most likely to cause other nations to enter the fray is the involvement of Serbia. In the case of fighting between Albanian Macedonians and ethnic Macedonians, Serbia could come into Macedonia to discourage a similar uprising in its own state of Kosovo. Or, in conjunction with Greece, it might decide to take the opportunity to reestablish control over its former province of "South Serbia" at a time when it would be most vulnerable. Greece has previously been interested in discussions of such issues, so its involvement cannot be ruled out. Bulgaria would not wish to become directly involved in a Macedonian civil war, but Bulgaria might not be able to keep its people out if the Serbs were to come in, whether or not the Greeks were involved. However, if the Bulgarians tried to defend the Macedonians from the Serbs, that almost certainly would bring the Greeks into the situation.

It is not at all clear how Turkey might respond to an Albanian insurrection. While there may be some interest in supporting the Muslim Albanians, there are somewhere between 100,000 and 200,000 Muslim ethnic Macedonians who show no special affinity with the Albanians. Turkey would not wish to fight against these people. While Turkey may wish to support the small group of Turkish Macedonians, it is not clear that this group would support the Albanians. Greek intervention would probably bring the Turks in; not so much to support the Albanians, but to gain an advantage over the Greeks. Maintaining a Macedonian state would be one way to do this.

The demographic growth rate of Albanians in Macedonia has been one of the highest in the world at almost 3.5 per cent per year. Albanian numbers have been swollen also by the number of unofficial citizens from Kosovo living in Macedonia. As we have already noted, Albanian Macedonians feel excluded from participation in public affairs in Macedonia because of their persisting belief that they are more numerous than census figures show, because they are not adequately represented in government jobs of one kind or another, and because their aspirations with regard to education in their native language have not been adequately addressed. Their present attitude about their numbers is that at least 100,000 Albanians were denied citizenship and were therefore denied the opportunity to vote in the 1994 elections. Though the government has taken some steps to correct the imbalance in employment ratios between Albanians and ethnic Macedonians, change has been slower in the educational sphere, and serious confrontations have occurred. There are loud voices clamoring for autonomy or even independence for an Albanian region in the West. There is a perceived split within the state of Macedonia, since Albanians do not unreservedly see themselves as having a future in a united Macedonia, and ethnic Macedonians do not see them as willing participants in the new republic. This perception is the basis for speculation that the split could become more profound. It is widely feared that unrest due to economic difficulties could increase agitation from Albanians in Macedonia, leading to serious conflict. Some American analysts argue that the weakness of the country at that point would be an invitation for others to become involved. Unless an international force prevents them, Serbs, Greeks and others could seize the opportunity to fill the power vacuum in Macedonia, and once the process begins, an expanded Balkan war could be difficult to prevent.[12]

Albanian commentators considered the census in Macedonia a fiasco. Instead of producing accurate statistical data about the ethnic structure of Macedonia, they said, the results of the census deepened distrust and division. It was predicted that because there would be no internal stability after the census, the elections would cause an eruption of feeling and would break the "already fine thread" of Macedonian-Albanian consensus. It was also predicted that the coalition government would fall.[13] Neither of these pessimistic expectations was fulfilled. While there were some serious confrontations between Albanians and the police, and great unrest in the Albanian community about educational issues, the Albanians chose to deal with the conflict by negotiation rather than by escalation. As for the coalition government, it did more than just survive. It was in a stronger position than before the elections because of the temporary withdrawal of VMRO from the parliamentary electoral process. If the negotiations between VMRO and the Macedonian Albanians, inspired by a common fear of Serbia, go ahead, perceptions of unity may increase in Macedonia.

A variation on the theme of a civil war in Macedonia leading to a more general South Balkans war proposes an Islamic Albanian motive that can be realized in Macedonia. This theory holds that a Macedonian civil war will be prompted not by inequalities within Macedonia, but by more sinister and more widely spread forces.

Robert Kaplan, author of *Balkan Ghosts: A Journey Through History*, says that the Balkans entered the twentieth century as the powder keg of Europe. At the end of the century, it could again possibly serve as the powder keg, igniting warfare between Slavic and Greek Orthodoxy and the "world-wide house of Islam." "Macedonia is at the center of this cataclysm. It is the crossing point between two historic alliances."[14]

The controversial Serbian politician, leader of paramilitary groups, and head of the Serbian Radical party, Voislav Seselj, said early in 1994, "Serbia does not present any threat at all to Macedonia, regardless of the fact that we are not recognizing the Macedonian nation. The real threat to them comes from the West, from Albania." He added, "The people who think that the Albanian uprising will start in Kosovo and Metohija are wrong. The Albanians know that we have strong army and militia forces concentrated there, and assume that we can hardly wait for them to try something, so that we can clear up all misunderstandings with them. Therefore, their rebellion will begin in the western part of Macedonia, which is mainly inhabited by Albanians. From there they will try to spread it to Kosovo, as then they will be able to strike from more sides. If one is asking what they are waiting for, why they don't strike already, it should be known that they are waiting for a sign from the West, which wants them to keep calm, for the time being."[15]

A Serbian radio broadcast in mid–1994 clearly indicates the Serbian position regarding Albanians in the Balkans. The commentator started by saying, "The slogan, 'a republic by hook or by crook,' with which the Shiptars [Albanians] set out to break up Yugoslavia as early as 1981, remains the essence of their behavior." He claimed that the general aim of Albanian action in Serbia was an independent Kosovo that would subsequently join Albania. It was said that the more numerous Albanian faction in Kosovo, led by Ibrahim Rugova, was advocating secession through pressure from abroad and, if possible, through foreign military intervention. The hardline faction, in which the leadership of Rexhep Qosja was increasingly being threatened by the former leader of the provincial branch of the League of Communists, Mahmut Bakali, took the view that the Shiptars should resort to an armed rebellion. After a visit to the United States, Bakali was said to have secured five million American dollars for the Shiptars' paramilitary. He was said to be in close contact with the Shiptars in western Macedonia who said they would set up their own republic, called Ilirida, after the census and then start a war against the Macedonians. The commentator said that if the Albanian Macedonians were to get support from foreign forces, they would spread the war to Kosovo-Metohija. However, Rugova was more cautious because of the power of Serbs and Montenegrins and was moderating his hatred by constantly harboring the illusion among the Shiptars that a state would be handed to them as part of the general settlement

of the war in the former Yugoslavia. The Serbian Shiptars were said to be losing trust in Rugova as the parallel system that he had tried to set up was failing. Dissenting Albanians faced assassination. Imer Leka, a member of the
Socialist Party of Serbia who publicly criticized the policy of Albanian separatism, was ambushed near Glogovac and killed. This was allegedly done to
demonstrate the fate of those who do not obey the rules of the movement. The
Shiptars do not seem to care about more serious talks, it was said.[16]

Vecernje Novosti wrote about "the fierce Islamization of the neighboring
former Yugoslav Republic of Macedonia (FYROM) in the last ten years, especially since the break-up of former Yugoslavia," and claimed that in recent
years Turkey had been approaching the FYROM in an increasingly aggressive
manner.[17] It was claimed that Turkey's objective was to recover areas in the
southern part of the Balkans that the Ottoman empire lost about 70 years ago.
Businessmen from Ankara and Istanbul were said to be offering the Macedonian government around 200 million dollars as a non-recurrent investment to
build a railway line to Albania within six months. This would finalize a "green"
Muslim front around Serbia, opening up the possibility of military-transit
communications towards Serbia's southeast and the Yugoslav republic of Montenegro. According to *Vecernje Novosti*, some leaders of nationalist parties in
Macedonia had confirmed that Turkey had bought the silent approval of the
Macedonian government for its projects by giving substantial loans when Macedonia was striving for independence.

Within the framework of strengthening Macedonian-Turkish military
cooperation, a delegation of Turkey's general staff visited Skopje in March
1994. Observers in Serbia drew the conclusion that Turkey "has already set one
foot on the soil of Macedonia."[18] FYROM citizens were said to fear that United
States troops and Turkey's influence would not only deprive them of their cen-
turies-old identity but also lead to a confrontation between Macedonia and
other nations in the Balkans. It was said that precisely because of this well-
developed Macedonian-Turkish cooperation the Macedonian authorities did
not oppose the arrival of Turkish troops to join the UNPROFOR contingent
in the ex–Yugoslav republic of Bosnia-Herzegovina.[19]

Former United States diplomat George Canny suggested that an explosion
of events in Kosovo could be the other way of initiating war in the South Balkans.
To prevent this from happening, he argued, the United States should support
Macedonia economically and diplomatically. They must stop underestimating
Milosevic, who is a typical Stalinist, and help Macedonia to preserve peace in
this part of the Balkans.[20] Views of other American analysts in the mid–1990s
seemed to be consistent with this position. The United States expert from the
Institute for National Strategic Research from the University of National Defense
in the United States, Jeffery Simon, speaking at an international conference for
deterring conflicts in southeastern Europe, said that the main danger for the
Balkans came from the situations in Macedonia and Kosovo.[21]

In Kosovo, the Albanians constitute about 90 percent, and the Serbs less than 8 percent, of the population of a little more than two million. Under the 1974 constitution, Kosovo was an autonomous region of Yugoslavia. During the early 1980s the Serbs began to restrict the rights of the Kosovar (Albanian) minority in Kosovo. In 1989 there were very large, often violent, public demonstrations against Serbian actions. In breach of the Yugoslav constitution, Serbian president Milosevic revoked Kosovo's autonomous status. After 1992, the Serbs maintained control through the presence of 40,000 regular military troops and 30,000 paramilitary and police in Kosovo. Serbs and Kosovars shared the same territory in a state of high tension and in virtual isolation from each other. Kosovars were driven from key jobs in industry and government, and Kosovo's Albanian-language school system was shut down. Within Kosovo an "underground movement" has formed, led by Ibrahim Rugova of the Democratic Alliance of Kosovars (LDK) Party.[22]

The denial of human rights and harshness of Serbian control led many Kosovars to escape from Serbia. The Council for the Defense of Human Rights in Kosovo reported 13,431 cases of human rights violations in the Serbian province in 1993, many of these against children.[23] According to the human rights group, during that year 15 ethnic Albanians were killed by Serbian police and 14 wounded. At the same time some 2,305 people were arrested, but just 62 were charged with crimes under the penal code. Raids allegedly took place on 1,994 family homes, and 1,777 people said they had been physically tortured. The main targets of raids were members of ethnic Albanian political parties or other Albanian cultural, educational and scientific institutions.

The level of confrontation between the Kosovo Albanians and the Serb authorities reached such a height that wide-scale armed conflict seemed quite possible. United States State Department advice to American travelers in the spring of 1994 tells us something about conditions in Kosovo: "Ethnic tensions are especially acute in this southern Serbian province (called Kosovo Metohija by Serbian authorities). Demonstrations, sometimes violent, can occur without warning. In recent months, there have been several armed attacks on Serbian police, resulting in death and injury. Security forces are at a high state of alert and police check points are widespread. Travelers are routinely subject to police search and interrogation."[24]

Serbia claimed that Kosovo had historical and cultural importance for the Serbian people, who for this reason could not think of giving up this territory. However, the Albanians claimed that the Serbs were really interested in the province's mineral wealth. The repression in Kosovo seemed aimed at increasing conflict, perhaps with a view to justifying an even greater crack-down, with the possible effect of "ethnically cleansing" Kosovo. This would be a truly extraordinary undertaking given the size of the Albanian population in Kosovo, though enthusiastic Serbian ethnic cleansing further north in the Balkans, supported by Belgrade, gives no confidence about a capacity for moderate behavior.

The international community gave approval to autonomy, but not necessarily independence, for Kosovo. Belgrade insisted on only a limited autonomy, while the Albanians said that autonomy was no longer enough.[25] Some European analysts were hoping for a division with a border that would cut Pristina into three parts, giving Pec to Montenegro; the territory in the north of Pristina, which contains the mining center of Trepca, to Serbia; and the southern part to the Albanians.[26] This idea was supposedly supported by former rump Yugoslav president Dobric Cosic, who, in 1991, openly raised the question of partition. In theory, partition would have given Serbia important cultural sites and mining areas, while saving the population centers for the Albanians. The moderate leader of the Kosovo Albanians, Ibrahim Rugova, took the view that "a division of Kosovo and Metohija is unacceptable to Albanians." Rugova persisted in seeking to have Kosovo placed under an international protectorate.

For some time Belgrade attempted to construct the image of itself as a peacemaker. It no longer placed stress on its determination to defend Kosovo at all costs, but emphasized the theory that Kosovo must remain within Serbia, because independence for Kosovo would lead to war for the annexation of Albanian Macedonia.[27] Some European analysts seemed to accept the idea that an independent Kosovo would jeopardize the existence of Macedonia, because of the example it would set for the Macedonian Albanians, because of the support the Kosovars could then provide for them, or because the Kosovars and Albanians might wish to include western Macedonia in some kind of Greater Albania.[28]

Albanian commentators argued the opposite, suggesting that an independent Kosovo would increase stability in Macedonia.[29] It was argued that if Kosovo were to become independent while Macedonia remained under international protection, there would be an end to serious tensions in the region. The Albanians would not be interested in the fragmentation of Macedonia and the outbreak of a major war. It was said that not only Tirana, but Pristina and Tetovo too, were interested in the existence of Macedonia as a multiethnic state open to its neighbors, with direct access to Albania and Kosovo. A central idea in this argument was the proposition that the Macedonian Albanians had shown no ambitions to destroy Macedonia, but had merely demonstrated their vital interest in advancing their own status in a common state. This statement had some weight. Nevertheless, there were many separatist voices in western Macedonia.

United States presidents Bush and Clinton warned Milosevic that civil war in Kosovo could lead to United States–Serbian confrontation. Milosevic restrained the activities of Serbian ultra-nationalist paramilitary leaders, such as Voislav Seselj, but hindered humanitarian assistance to Kosovo. Kosovar radicals challenged Rugova's moderate policies. Albanians in western Europe and the United States provided economic assistance to Kosovars, and arms were stockpiled.[30]

It was feared that if armed conflict occurred, as many as 400,000 refugees would pour out of Kosovo, mostly into western Macedonia. This issue, more than any other, was expected to lead to unfriendly foreign troops entering Macedonia. The risk of internal unrest caused by such a number of refugees would be extreme, but this was seen as just one among many factors that could lead to invasion. It was considered likely that some of these refugees would arm themselves and return to fight Serbs in Kosovo. In turn the Serbs would probably move into northern Macedonia to deal with them.

In such a scenario, Macedonia, because of its own difficulties, could not offer much aid to any of the refugees. In an effort to find safe access to the West, many of these people would probably continue moving south, towards Greece, or might even be moved south by Macedonia to reduce the provocation to Serbia. The Greeks would probably come into southern Macedonia to keep Kosovar refugees out of Greece. For a long time Macedonians have been hearing stories about plans for a Greek-controlled zone 30 km wide inside the southern Macedonian border, which would be used to stop Kosovar refugees. Since Macedonia had no ability to resist, Bulgaria was considered likely to intervene to protect the Macedonians for reasons we have already seen. Albania would not confront either Serbia or Greece directly in such an affair, but might encourage volunteers and send weapons to assist Albanians in Kosovo or Macedonia.

A second wave of interventions, involving states that do not share a border with Macedonia, was expected to follow this sequence of events. If Greece entered Macedonia, Turkey would probably take direct armed action against Greece either in Macedonia or in the Aegean Islands.[31]

An anonymous Albanian politician, a self-proclaimed close associate of Ibrahim Rugova, purportedly told the *Telegraf* (the Belgrade weekly) that Milosevic would use the resettlement in Kosovo of Serbian Kraijna refugees, accustomed to war and antagonistic to non–Serbian Muslims, to send a message to Kosovars that they had no future in Serbia, as the spearhead of a Serbian move to ethnically cleanse Kosovo, and as a major irritant in his strategy to provoke Kosovars to armed reaction.[32] The informant said that the radical forces in the Albanian movement had become convinced that nothing could be achieved by peaceful means, so they were now urging an armed option, or the scenario he had described, which is something in between revolution and peaceful waiting. The informant gave weight to the role of American assistance for the Albanian army and said Albanians were counting on the help of United States troops now deployed in Macedonia. He saw this as likely to be influenced by a Bob Dole victory in the 1996 United States presidential elections, and the efforts of the Albanian lobby in America.

American analysts have suggested that positive international influence in the South Balkans might be exerted by providing direct aid to Macedonia, and by encouraging and advising Macedonia in making internal changes that will take away the causes of conflict.[33] Reducing the likelihood of internal disorder in Macedonia leading to a Balkan war may require sustained economic support for Macedonia. The lifting of the Greek embargo would undoubtedly have a positive effect in this regard. Long-term economic assistance to help Macedonia develop an east-west transportation infrastructure, relieving its dependence on its north-south axis, and increasing trade interdependence with Albania and Bulgaria may also be very helpful. To relieve internal ethnic tensions and improve external relations with Albania, Macedonia might also be urged to reform its constitutional description of citizenship.

If the international community is to deal with the risk of a Balkan war starting from Kosovo, a strategy for avoiding or controlling massive refugee flows into Macedonia might be prepared. If Serbia were to be persuaded that driving Kosovars south as refugees would carry a high price, the Serbs might reconsider this option. However, if refugees did eventually arrive in Macedonia, it would be helpful to have a contingency plan in place, developed in cooperation with Macedonia, Albania, Greece, Turkey and Bulgaria, and known to all NATO allies. Part of this plan would be keeping the refugees in the northwest of Macedonia, and developing a way of assuring that the refugee camps did not become base camps for guerrilla activity back in Kosovo.[34]

In the Balkans, the view is widely held that Milosevic may wish to strive for the kind of success in Kosovo that eluded him in Bosnia. At the same time, if the Kosovars were to feel abandoned, they might be more inclined to seek an armed solution to their problems. Getting OSCE monitors into Kosovo could ease tensions and give better information about what is going on.[35]

Potential Territorial Conflicts

Soon after Macedonia had gained admission to the United Nations as an independent country, a Macedonian official was said to have suggested jokingly that the country should redesign the flag with a map of Macedonia in the middle surrounded by four wolves — Serbia, Greece, Bulgaria and Albania, since they all claimed a piece of it.[36] Theories about the territorial ambitions of Macedonia's neighbors abound. Some of these theories have been taken so seriously, they have led to the United States sending troops to Macedonia to prevent "adventurers" from invasion. Others seem so bizarre that they stretch credulity. However, since actual events in the Balkans have often gone far beyond what outside observers thought possible, some of these theories will be examined in the context of facts about present and past relationships between Macedonia and the neighboring states.

In broad terms we might first consider the possibility of invasion by any of the states that share a border with Macedonia. In every case there is a distant historical imperative that might be invoked to justify such actions. All of these states could argue that at some time in the past the Republic of Macedonia was a part of some entity in which their own nation was prominent. Since Greece has been given a hearing in many international arenas by arguing just such a position, is it not likely that the arguments of these other states would be given the same kind of attention?

Serbia would like to take over Macedonia because in the fourteenth century the capital of the Serbian empire was located in Skopje. Serbian nationalists expressed their interest in bringing Macedonia into the Serbian embrace in the late eighteenth century, and introduced a strategy — the sending of colonists into the area — that was applied even in the twentieth. From 1913 till 1944, Macedonia was under Serbian control and was called "South Serbia." Serbian families were encouraged to settle in Macedonia at this time, though with only marginal success. In speaking of the kind of relationship that rump Yugoslavia might have with Macedonia, Serbian leader Slobodan Milosevic has sometimes rather enigmatically made reference to agreements that would follow the terms of the 1913 treaty — the treaty at the end of the Balkan wars by which Macedonia was handed over to Serbia. In 1989 Milosevic held talks with Greek prime minister Mitsotakis about sharing Macedonia between Greece and Serbia. One of the grounds for so doing is the Serbian claim that there is a population of around 300,000 Serbs in Macedonia, though Macedonian census figures indicate about 10 percent of this number.

Bulgaria might wish to take control of Macedonia because Macedonia was a part of the first Bulgarian empire in the ninth century A.D., and even if the "Bulgarian" empire that followed was really a Slavo-Macedonian empire, since it was controlled from Ohrid by Samuil, a Macedonian Slav, the close association between Macedonians and Bulgarians is undeniable. Bulgarians have expressed their interest in incorporating Macedonia into the Bulgarian fold several times this century, in the Balkan wars, and in the First and Second World War. Bulgarians consider that Macedonians are really Bulgarians; thus the whole of the Slavic-speaking population is seen as part of the greater Bulgarian family. Bulgarian paternalism seems to make it difficult for Bulgaria to comprehend the idea that Macedonians see themselves as independent. Bulgaria's last great effort to control significant portions of Macedonia in the Second World War undoubtedly created a huge store of animosity that is not understood in Bulgaria and apparently not reciprocated.

Albania might wish to take over Macedonia because Albanians consider themselves the true descendants of the Illyrian tribes who controlled upper Macedonia — essentially the same lands that make up the modern Republic of Macedonia — during the time of Alexander the Great. In modern times large numbers of ethnic Albanians live in the western part of Macedonia, in the areas adjoining the Albanian border. Though census data suggest that these people make up around 23 percent of the population, Albanians inside and outside of Macedonia claim 40 percent. Albania has often expressed interest in the well-being of these people, amongst whom the idea of separating from Macedonia and forming some kind of close relationship with Albania has sometimes emerged.

Although relationships with Greece have proved the most difficult of all its Balkan relationships, currently Macedonia probably has less to fear in terms of unilateral invasion from Greece than from other Balkan nations. Greece might be interested in acquiring a part of Macedonia since in ancient times it formed a part of the Macedonian homeland. During the Balkan wars, Greece occupied the southern parts of the Republic of Macedonia, notably the cities of Ohrid and Bitola in the southwest, and Strumica in the southeast. When treaty arrangements forced Greece to retreat from Strumica, Greek troops burned the city to the ground, which suggests an emotional rather than a pragmatic attachment. In modern times some Greek nationalists, choosing to ignore census data, claim that much of the population in the Bitola district is actually Greek-speaking and of the Greek Orthodox faith. Nevertheless, Mitsotakis seems to have turned down Milosevic's suggestion to split Macedonia between Greece and Serbia.

It is probably significant that Macedonia is where the United Nations, for the first time since its creation, introduced UNPROFOR as a preventive presence, before any kind of armed conflict appeared. It may be that Macedonia's strength lies in a weakness that demands external help, and in its position as a critical point that must be under international control. At the present time Macedonia might be seen as being under a kind of international protectorate.[37]

These viewpoints suggest the immediate relevance of concepts of a Greater Serbia, a Greater Bulgaria, a Greater Albania and even a Greater Greece. However, there are all sorts of other reasons why any one of these countries might invade Macedonia. For instance, Greece might see invasion of the southern part of Macedonia to be in its interests if another nation invaded first, or if events occurred within Macedonia that created a threat to Greece. In turn, other nations, such as Turkey and Russia, might also become involved in Macedonia if other nations get involved first. Some of these matters will be explored in the following pages.

The following population figures for South Balkan nations in 1994 show us how small Macedonia really is in relation to its neighbors:

Country	Population ('000s)
Albania	3,374
Bosnia-Herzegovina	4,651
Bulgaria	8,800
Croatia	4,698
Greece	10,565
Macedonia	2,214
Montenegro	667

Country	Population ('000s)
Serbia	10,093
Slovenia	1,972
Turkey	62,154

Besides being one of the smallest Balkan nations on a population basis, Macedonia is also extremely poor. These are important considerations in weighing up military potential, since population largely determines the potential size of a fighting force, and wealth may determine equipment levels. It should be remembered here that in the Second World War, Macedonia put 100,000 fighting men into the field (including Albanian-Macedonian troops), an extraordinary ratio given the population base. Some of these men were used as shock troops against elite German divisions. This tells us something about the motivation of the Macedonians when fighting for their independence. It would not be unreasonable to expect a similar level of enthusiasm in the future. In 1993 the Macedonian army had about 10,000 soldiers, but was being reorganized to comprise a standing strength of 15,000 to 20,000, with a reserve force of 80,000. The army had no heavy weapons such as tanks, artillery or combat aircraft, and was unlikely to obtain substantial quantities of such armaments so long as the United Nations embargo on arming the Balkans continued. All the tanks, fighter aircraft and heavy artillery stationed in Macedonia before the break-up of Yugoslavia were taken to Serbia by the Yugoslav Army.[38] Although Macedonia had 60 pilots for fighter planes, it had no aircraft for them to fly.[39]

Greater Serbia

Serbia has about five times the population of Macedonia, and though it was severely weakened by the United Nations embargo in the early 1990s, it was probably less affected than Macedonia, and in any case was much more powerful to begin with. The Serbian army is extremely well equipped and can field approximately 75,000 troops. It has at its disposal most of the equipment from the former Yugoslav army, including 900 tanks, 800 armored personnel carriers and 1,300 artillery pieces. The Serbian air force has about 300 combat aircraft and 150 helicopters. All Serbian aircraft have an operating range enabling them to cover all the territory of the former Yugoslavia, including Macedonia.[40]

Serbia designs and produces light, middle and heavy weapons. It has shown an interest in becoming the main missile power in the Balkans, building on Indian-developed earth-to-earth missiles, and using Iraqi experience in the field of medium-range missiles. Serbia has also tried to purchase advanced Russian helicopters and planes, and continues its domestic production of attack planes.[41]

If the Serbians chose to invade Macedonia they could probably do so with little real local opposition. Serbia could have held on to Macedonia and kept it within the fold of Yugoslavia with little effort had it wished. The risk at that time would have been the development of an armed Macedonian resistance, involving an alliance between Slavic and Albanian Macedonians, as occurred in the Second World War against the Bulgarians and Germans. Such a resistance might well cooperate with armed Albanian resistance in Kosovo, which would create considerable pressures on Serbia. Presumably Serbia decided in 1991 that other forms of integration with Macedonia could suit Serbia's needs. The risk of widespread and prolonged armed conflict as a result of direct Serbian invasion now is much greater since Bulgaria would certainly become involved one way or another, and the United States, which has troops in place to prevent this very development, seems committed to provide support. Thus seeking direct military control in the middle of the 1990s must be even less attractive to Serbia than it was at the time the Macedonians sought independence. A strategy for war that involved Macedonia seeking a military alliance with Serbia would be more likely to achieve Serbia's aims. It may not otherwise receive support from its most powerful sponsor, Russia.

Commenting on border incidents between Macedonia and Serbia, the Moscow newspaper *Izvestia* (June, 18 1994) noted that Serbian radicals had territorial aspirations towards their southern neighbor, but *Izvestia* concluded that the possibility of the conflict between Skopje and Belgrade turning into a war was small. Even if it was true that authorities in Serbia were engaged in some plotting with regard to Macedonia, President Milosevic was not likely to undertake any military action. If Serbia did provoke a war with this Slav and Orthodox Christian country, it would not receive support from Moscow, *Izvestia* concluded.[42]

Janusz Bugajski, associate director of East European Studies at the Center for Strategic and International Studies, suggests that Serbia is the main threat to Macedonia. He says both Milosevic and the radical party opposition led by Draskovic wish to lay claim to Macedonia, seeing it as southern Serbia. He concluded they would try to destabilize Macedonia, to provoke conflicts within the republic between the Slavic majority and the Albanian minority.[43]

There seems no question that the Macedonia policy of the Former Republic of Yugoslavia is based on the proprietorial attitude of Serbia towards Macedonia. Serbia is the most powerful of the states of the former Yugoslavia and was involved, in at least a supporting role, in the wars in Croatia and Bosnia, with the intention of maintaining a strong and centralized Serbian state. Serbia sees Montenegro as Serbian, and will not permit Montenegro to leave the Yugoslav federation. It may have similar feelings about where Macedonia should be positioned.

Many Macedonians believe that Milosevic seeks to implement "historical Serbian rights" over Macedonia in any part of the region where there are living or dead Serbs, and that the quest for a Greater Serbia, seen in the fighting in Bosnia, will include Macedonia. Consistent with this are the comments of Milosevic's political allies. Zeljko Simic, the president of the Yugoslav government and Milosevic's protege, who may become foreign minister, said: "Macedonia is nothing but a demarcation line, and is former, not only as a state, but as a nation and culture, as well."[44]

In the latter part of 1994 it seemed to some commentators that Serbia was going to lose some of its occupied territories in Bosnia and in Croatia. This seemed even more certain a year later. However, in 1994 Serbia began to speak again of an alleged Belgrade-Skopje-Athens axis. The Belgrade Institute for Strategic Research had been promoting Serbia's interests in Macedonia, in accord with the Serbian belief that Macedonia is a Serbian province. It published the statement that "Serbia is nothing without Macedonia and no expansion on the Bosnian and Croatian territories will be worthwhile, unless it gets Macedonia."[45]

Macedonian suspicion about Serbia's intentions even led to criticisms of efforts to lift the United Nations sanctions on Yugoslavia, despite the obvious economic benefit to Macedonia.[46] For example, Macedonian minister Jovan Andonov was "frequently attacked by the media in Macedonia due to his pro-Yugoslav view for resolving Macedonian problems, as he believes the way out for Macedonia from its current alarming situation is not achievable without a closer co-operation with the Serbian economy." Some Macedonians saw a need to be ready for Serbian takeover attempts that they expected in the near future, particularly after the lifting of the international trade embargo on Yugoslavia. Serbian promotion of an upturn in Macedonian-Serbian relations before the 1994 elections in Macedonia has been seen by some Macedonians as a part of Serbia's plotting against their nation.[47]

It has been argued that it is in Serbia's interests to see a Macedonian-Albanian conflict, which could end in an ethnic slaughter. The main historical protector of Serbianism is Russia, but a military alliance with Greece gives Serbia a counterweight to Turkey, Bulgaria and Albania, and at the same time isolates Macedonia.[48] Therefore, Milosevic was expected to attempt to get closer to Salonika, at Macedonia's expense.[49]

According to Vladislav Jovanovic, Yugoslavia's foreign minister, speaking in the middle of 1994, "There are certain open issues in the relations between the FRY and Macedonia that require a minimal civilized effort by the Macedonian authorities to be solved." Among them are the equal treatment of the Serbs in Macedonia, who according to the Yugoslav minister "are discriminated against in comparison to the Turks, Albanians, Vlachs and other nationalities."[50] Other issues include recognition by Macedonia of FRY's right to succeed the previous Yugoslavia. With regard to relations with Macedonia, Jovanovic said, "Normalization will follow the moment Macedonia resolves its problem with Greece and acknowledges our right to succession and continuity."[51] He also said that in its succession with the rest of the Yugoslav republics, "Serbia will divide everything created after 1974, and with Macedonia everything after 1913." Macedonians wonder if this reference to the Treaty of Bucharest, which at the end of the Balkan wars assigned Macedonia to Serbia, reveals Milosevic's true ambitions towards Macedonia.[52]

"We will easily recognize Macedonia, once it settles its dispute with Athens. There is no other problem between us," Milosevic stated for CNN at the end of 1994. Milosevic added that all Yugoslav peoples should have stayed within Yugoslavia, since they will never find a better future for themselves elsewhere. He said Slovenia is a second-rate province of Austria, Croatia is a satellite of Germany, Bosnia-Herzegovina practically does not exist, and Macedonia has lost its sovereignty before it even acquired it. This rather sour comment refers to the influence of outside nations, specifically of the United States on Macedonia.[53]

In an English-language broadcast from Belgrade, the Tanjug News Agency described concerns about increasing "Americanization" in Macedonia — the increasingly expanding American political and diplomatic engagement and military presence. The presence of United States troops in the UNPROFOR contingent was seen as proof of American plans to become established in the south Balkans. This "Americanization" had been supported by the ruling Macedonian, ethnic Albanian and major nationalist opposition parties, but Tanjug suggested there was a growing number of people resisting the process.[54]

In November 1993, after a meeting with Greek foreign minister Papoulias, Milosevic said: "Currently over there [meaning Macedonia], there are processes which are antagonistic to the interests of the citizens. Thanks to the current government in Skopje, there is a very well developed separatist movement." Milosevic claimed that the government in Skopje would soon receive a request by the Albanians to define the republic as a state of two nations. This in turn would lead directly to the secession of western Macedonia. "I'm afraid that if Greece does not hurry up, it will not have anyone to recognize."[55]

Puls suggested that Serbia was constantly intimidating the Macedonian people with alleged Islamic and Albanian dangers, and seeking ways for bilateral and multilateral associations with Macedonia's neighbors — even openly proposing a new partition of Macedonia (to Konstantin Mitsotakis).[56] Early in 1995, Milosevic, apparently with Russian support, was proposing a "weak confederation" between Belgrade, Skopje and Athens that would entail military, communications and trade cooperation and an explicit warning that Greece would be directly involved in a war against Albania, should a conflict arise in Kosovo.[57]

On June 1 a United States diplomat heading a CSCE monitoring team to Macedonia said, "There has been no overt Serb aggression ... but there is a feeling of menace."[58] Interviews with Macedonians in the streets of Skopje, and observations by Americans working in the city, suggest that many Macedonians are afraid of the Serbs. "Today the Serbs are selling to us so they can survive; tomorrow they might be killing us."[59] Some expected a Serbian invasion; others thought Serbia would appeal to the International Court of Justice in the Hague, referring to international agreements dating from the Balkan wars, to try and get Macedonia back.

An editor with the Skopje newspaper *Vecer*, Goran Mihajlovski, commented to an American journalist that Macedonians were afraid of Slobodan Milosevic because "he is crazy" and because he is powerful. The allies of the Serbs are the Greeks, who were already showing great antagonism towards Macedonia. These views were conformed by Susan Krause, director of the American Center in Skopje, who concluded that Macedonia is a joke to the Serbs and the Greeks who believe it has no real right to exist.[60]

The Macedonian newspaper *Puls*[61] compared Slobodan Milosevic with Hitler, arguing that his talk of liberation and peace was not to be trusted. *Puls* pointed out that Serbia did not have the justification of protecting a substantial Serbian population in order to begin interference in Macedonia, but was using the Serbian Orthodox Church and the border points for the same purpose. *Puls* said that when Milosevic says he wants peace, simultaneously an article appears in his newspapers claiming that Macedonia is illegally using several thousands of hectares of pasture land, and Serbian priests suddenly appear on Macedonian territory "to arrange our spiritual life." *Puls* feared that Macedonia would meet the same fate as Bosnia unless the international community did a better job of holding back Milosevic.

Thus there are several fronts, identified by Macedonians, on which Serbia has been working to extend its grasp over Macedonia. It has repeatedly presented Macedonians with the specter of Albanian plots to divide the country; it has provoked tension and fear on the border with Macedonia; it has supported efforts by the Serbian Orthodox Church to reassert control over the Macedonian Orthodox Church; and it has attempted to establish a powerful fifth column of senior Serbian military officers as Macedonian citizens.

With such ideas as the background, incidents on the border between Macedonia and Yugoslavia might be expected to provoke particular anxiety. In the middle of November 1993, five armed men, three dressed as civilians and two in military fatigues, abducted a patrol consisting of two police officers and a soldier from just inside the Macedonian border with Serbia near the village of Lojane.[62] According to Macedonian descriptions of events, the patrol was watching for fuel smugglers when it stopped two vehicles with Serbian markings. The drivers were evidently attempting to cross into Serbia with some 400 liters of gasoline. At this point, the five men from the Serbian side entered Macedonia in two cars and abducted the patrol. The three Macedonian men claimed that they had been beaten and that the Serbs attempted to force them to sign documents claiming responsibility for the incident. The Macedonians were later released, though one of the policemen had sustained head injuries.

The Macedonian government lodged a protest with the Belgrade government. The Yugoslav version of events was that the three Macedonians actually made an incursion into Serbian territory and were detained.[63]

In the following months there were further claims by Macedonians of border abductions,[64] and UNPROFOR personnel were arrested by Yugoslav troops.[65] General Tryggve Teleffsen, commanding officer of UNPROFOR for Macedonia, stated that an increased number of Serbian border patrols had been noticed in April, May, and the beginning of June. Recently, they had even started crossing the border, he said.[66] Writing in May 1994 about the border tensions, *Nova Makedonija* noted a doubling of incidents in the previous six months, coinciding with a heightened bitterness in the reactions of senior military officers in the Yugoslav army after every incident. Out of a total of a 231 km of the border with Serbia, 140 km were being disputed.[67] The London *Times* described an incident in which a Yugoslav MIG plane intercepted an UNPROFOR helicopter deep inside Macedonian air space.[68] Vlado Popovski, the Macedonian defense minister, said there had been nine border incidents by the spring of 1994.[69] Despite denials by Yugoslav authorities, Macedonian, UNPROFOR and other observers concluded that there was a dramatic upsurge in Serbian-provoked border incidents. In June, Popovski said that 19 Serbian-provoked border incidents had occurred since April, a much higher rate than before. Some of these incidents involved intrusions onto Macedonian territory by Serbian troops, and others involved confrontations between UNPROFOR and Serbian patrol units. The Republic of Macedonia had sent protest notes to the Yugoslav authorities on all these incidents, but all had been rejected.[70] Speaking in Vienna, the head of the CSCE Mission in Macedonia, Norman Anderson, criticized the increased military pressure on the Republic of Macedonia, pointing out that Serbia "has introduced a strong military pressure on its borders with Macedonia," while at the same time Macedonia was facing a possible danger of "threats of explosion in Kosovo."[71]

At the June 1994 meeting of the town government in Kriva Palanka, citizens expressed grave concern at the fact that Serbian troops had been stationed near Cupino Brdo, in the border area, but 250 meters deep into Macedonian territory. There were reports that 10–15 Serbian soldiers had put up tents near the border villages Luke and Podrzikonj, occupying strategic points for the observation of Macedonian territory. Serbian soldiers were also digging trenches, and transport vehicles were coming and going. For security reasons, the Kriva Palanka township committee members demanded that the Interior Ministry report on the situation in this border area and call an urgent session to discuss the problem.[72] Macedonian sources said that the Serbian soldiers, who had taken positions on the peak of Straza, were between 550 and 600 meters inside the territory of the Republic of Macedonia. This was concluded from maps from the Kriva Palanka Geodesic Center. The maps were made in 1967, and show the peak at Straza as 550 meters from the boundary of the neighboring county Surdulica, which is on FRY territory.[73] "As far as we can tell it is Macedonian territory," United Nations spokeswoman Elisabeth Baldwin said in Skopje.[74] UNPROFOR observers noted that there appeared to be a steady increase in the number of troops on the Serbian side. Macedonian troop strength in the area was reinforced also.[75] NATO observation patrols, made up of United States soldiers, stationed themselves near the Macedonian army camp in the area soon after the Serbian presence was noted, and their intention was to stay in this volatile region for a while.[76] Elisabeth Baldwin said, "We do not see any military threat building up, but if you add up all the incidents you can see a trend. It causes concern, not alarm, but concern."

The Macedonian army had been able to force most of the Serbian patrols out of Macedonian territory without violence, although both sides had pointed guns at each other at times. As for the peak of Straza, the decision was to try to resolve the situation through diplomatic means. The incidents could be interpreted as an attempt to destabilize Macedonia before the upcoming census and elections, Popovski stated. This pressure was complemented by the threats of the Serbian church to introduce cannon measures against the Macedonian church. These moves can be seen as an organized mechanism of political and psychological pressure on Macedonia.[77]

Popovski said that the Serbian-Macedonian border had been determined by the First Constitution of the People's Republic of Macedonia, and affirmed by a joint Macedonian-Serbian committee, in the period from 1945 to 1948. All peak elevations had been marked, and the Serbian side had never disputed the borders with Macedonia.[78] *Nova Makedonija* claimed the border between Macedonia and Serbia had previously been determined on several occasions, and there had never before been any serious controversy. In the period 1952 to 1954, a thorough delimitation of the boundaries between the two republics had been determined. The remeasuring that took place afterwards had simply confirmed these initial decisions without changes. After gaining its independence, the Republic of Macedonia accepted this territorial division as a factual situation, and suggested to the government of the newly formed FRY that a joint commission be set up to define borders and solve any controversies. The FRY had not responded to these proposals. A new FRY commission was acting without consultation with Macedonia, and its spokesman, Colonel Tihomir Stojanovich, had made provocative statements about border disputes with Macedonia. He also claimed that border problems with Macedonia had not started till June 1993, with the arrival of American troops.[79]

Vecernje Novosti concluded that the border incident near Kriva Palanka was simply an attempt to hide the true Macedonian domestic reality before the census and the fact that Macedonia refused to grant citizenship to 90 percent of the Serbs living there. The diplomatic attack on Serbia and Yugoslavia could also be interpreted as an intention to justify the American presence before its public, the paper said.[80] Popovski said that the border violations were causing increased tension in the area that could lead to more serious incidents. He described the incidents as "a form of military pressure." *Nova Makedonija* concluded similarly that the regime in Belgrade was intentionally provoking high tension on the border, perhaps to affect the balance of political relationships in the Balkans.[81] Western diplomats in Skopje also concluded that the situation on the border amounted more to some sort of psychological game than to serious military maneuvers.[82] Pointing out that Serbian troops had been stationed on Macedonian territory at Chupino Brdo during the Census, and that similar tactics might be used to pressure the international community to achieve concessions for Serbia, *Nova Makedonija* suggested there would be even greater border troubles when the "Kosovo question" came to the fore.[83]

According to Macedonian president Kiro Gligorov, the purpose of the Yugoslav troops at the border was "to create a feeling of uncertainty and fear among the people... There are figures in Serbia who cannot come to terms with Macedonia as an independent state and who think they should have a common border with Greece." Serbia's president, Slobodan Milosevic, had not "officially made such claims," said Gligorov, "but one can presume such actions [by Serbian troops] are not taken independently."[84] Asked by the Croatian newspaper *Vjesnik* whether tensions could ignite war in light of his defense minister's warning to the Serbs to withdraw or be "pushed," Gligorov said, "No. I do not believe so and I see no reason for it." He acknowledged that Macedonia's tiny army was no match for the Serbian military but said the presence of 1,000 United Nations peacekeeping troops, including Americans, would be an important deterrent to further Serbian action.[85]

At the end of June, the Macedonian mission to the United Nations delivered a letter by Foreign Minister Crvenkovski to Secretary General Boutros-Ghali concerning the border incidents. The letter gave information about "numerous incidents" on the northern border caused by Yugoslav army troops, and stressed Macedonian concern with the escalation of incidents in the previous three months. Crvenkovski wrote, "Should negative intentions continue, we will be obliged to ask of you and especially of the Security Council to introduce firm steps and measures to help avoid unwanted consequences."[86]

Early in July, Brigadier General Tryggve Tellefsen, commander of Nordic and United States peacekeepers, proposed that the Serbian army move back 100 meters from that peak at Struza and that the Macedonian army also move 100 meters back. Yugoslav authorities in Belgrade agreed, and tensions in the border area were reduced. The UNPROFOR troops were placed between Macedonian and Serbian soldiers. Macedonia's defense minister said that the Serbian withdrawal had eased tensions and paved the way for an agreement on the border line.[87] The Yugoslav army deputy chief of staff, Lieutenant General Blagoje Kovacevic, and Tryggve Tellefsen said that the small incidents on the border that had occurred there in the past had been successfully resolved, and cooperation between the two forces was now good.[88]

However, a few weeks later two Yugoslav citizens, apparently smugglers, were killed by Macedonian soldiers inside the Macedonian border. This time it was Yugoslavia's turn to complain to the United Nations. In a letter to Secretary General Boutros-Ghali, the Yugoslav government said that the killing of unarmed civilians could not be justified and that such actions escalate tensions. The letter said the government of the Yugoslav Federation firmly believed that the frequent border incidents were a result of provocation by the Macedonian authorities, aimed at drawing the attention of the international public to the fabricated danger from the north, in order to justify the presence of the foreign troops on Macedonian territory and to procure the lifting of the arms embargo.[89] Only days later a Macedonian farmer was shot by a Yugoslav military patrol inside the Macedonian border.[90] The FRY Foreign Ministry claimed that the incident did not take place at all.[91]

In September 1994 Boutros Boutros-Ghali submitted a report to the Security Council on the position of the UNPROFOR units in the former Yugoslavia, including a thorough analysis of the economic and political situation in Macedonia, as well as problems it was currently facing. Mr. Boutros-Ghali wrote,

> The military situation in the former Yugoslav Republic of Macedonia remains relatively peaceful and stable. There have been several border violations on the border-line with Federal Yugoslavia by military or police patrols. Since April, however, patrols from federal Yugoslavia and the former Yugoslav Republic of Macedonia have met frequently along the border. Most of the meetings went without any mutual confrontation, which indicates no side seems inclined to cause an incident. Yet, the number of the incidents may increase, due to Federal Yugoslavia's continued refusal to recognize the border. Although both sides have already formed commissions to work out this issue, the date of a bilateral meeting has not yet been set. As there is a threat to the stability due to unsettled border issues, it is more than obvious that an international border commission would be welcome here.[92]

The United States weekly newsmagazine *Time,* in two editions during November 1995, said United States troops might be deployed in Macedonia after finishing their peacekeeping task in Bosnia. Macedonia was seen as a more immediate problem than Cuba, Taiwan, Kurdistan, and various other world hot spots. *Time* said that the reaching of peace in Bosnia did not guarantee the peace in Macedonia and Kosovo. Serbs might again start ethnic cleansing and initiate a new crisis.

In its political analysis of the Republic of Macedonia, the independent weekly *Monitor* of Podgorica, Montenegro, suggested that Macedonia's neighbors were adopting the policy of waiting for internal ethnic chaos in order to start to realize their goals.[93] In an article headlined "Priests First; Guns to Follow" (an allusion to problems between the Macedonian and Serbian Orthodox churches), the paper wrote that Serbian military officials kept referring to the Macedonian-Serbian border as merely an "administrative one" and claiming that every incident, regardless of how deep into Macedonian territory, had taken place on Serbian land. The paper also suggested that an independent Macedonia would bother "certain neighbors," because the Macedonian referendum on independence "seriously threatens, and even annuls the 1913 Bucharest Treaty." Serbian efforts at controlling Macedonia could be seen also in Serbian church activities in Macedonia. Serbian priests had crossed the border into Macedonia in full clerical garb, gone into Macedonian churches and conducted services without any permission from the local bishop or priests. In reaction, Macedonia had closed its border to all Serbian clerics unless they were dressed in lay clothing.

In 1993 the Serbian Orthodox bishop Pahomije Gacic, metropolitan of Vranje, and his companion were denied entry to Macedonia on grounds of Article 18 of the Law on the Legal Status of Religious Communities, which allowed entry to foreign priests to give services only with previously issued permission.[94] Father Gacic had recently been appointed an administrator of the Serbian Orthodox Church in Macedonia. He was to deliver a message to the head of the Macedonian Orthodox Church, Father Mihail, from the Serbian Holy Synod, calling on the Macedonian church to reestablish unity with the Serbian church in three months. The police refused to let the bishop and his companion cross the border even after they took off their mantles, explaining they had no written permission to visit Macedonian colleagues. The Vranje eparchy reported the incident to the Holy Synod and the governments of both Serbia and Yugoslavia, describing it as a direct attack on and disrespect for the Serbian church and a human rights violation. The incident was given great publicity in Belgrade. Yugoslavia's Committee for Relations with Religious Associations accused Macedonian authorities of "roughly breaching civil rights and religious liberties."[95]

It was the Macedonian view that the appointment of Serbian bishops to Macedonia was a political act, according to Slav Nikolovski Katin, the deputy president of the Macedonian Commission for Religious Questions.[96] Though the FRY government had complained about the banning, Katin doubted that the FRY would permit entry to Macedonian Orthodox Church bishops, or change its position about refusing the registration of the MOC in Yugoslavia. The Macedonian Commission for religious questions strongly condemned the political activities of the Serbian priests and said it would gladly help settle the problems through negotiation with an adequate commission from the FRY. However, this seemed unlikely since an important task of the Serbian bishops had been to deliver an ultimatum to the leaders of the Macedonian Orthodox Church. The Holy Synod of the Serbian Orthodox Church sent a "brotherly appeal" to the "self-declared autocephalous Church" in the Republic of Macedonia, to "re-enter the church canon establishment" in three months, or "canon measures will be enforced against it."[97] This might have led to the defrocking of Macedonian bishops, even excommunication, and a ban on communications with other Orthodox communities. Reentering the church canon establishment meant the unwelcome prospect of acknowledging the control of the Serbian Church over the Orthodox community in Macedonia. The Greek Orthodox Church had supported various Serbian efforts in Macedonia, and had also given special honors to the Bosnian Serb Radovan Karadzic, who had been defined by the United Nations as a war criminal.[98]

Fears that a Serbian fifth column might be developing in Macedonia were raised in the lead-up to the 1994 census, when Macedonian residents were seeking official citizenship papers. Some of those seeking citizenship looked suspicious to the Macedonian government. "Beside the common citizens, lines before the citizenship windows have recently also been created by ... somewhere between 320 and 540 well-trained military personnel from the Yugoslav Army... How come they are suddenly so interested in Macedonia?"[99] It seems that very few of these applications were likely to achieve success since there was no innocent explanation as to why such a large number of senior officers (very few were under the rank of lieutenant colonel) suddenly became so interested in becoming Macedonian citizens. *Puls* points out that this is equivalent to about half of the officer corps of the Macedonian army. All had left Macedonia with the Yugoslav army, many had fought for Serbia in both Croatia and Bosnia, but they had left their families in Macedonia so that they would not lose apartments, jobs and other benefits. They all retired from the Yugoslav army at the same time in order to meet certain requirements for Macedonian citizenship. The list of applicants for Macedonian citizenship included General Nikola Uzelac, a signatory of the agreement for the peaceful withdrawal of the Yugoslav National Army (YNA) from Macedonia; Rajko Balach, a colonel in Radovan Karadzic's army, who at the time of YNA's withdrawal from Macedonia was known as a Serbian chauvinist, openly denying the existence of the Macedonian people and state; and Djuro Djurica, an active officer in Radovan Karadzic's army. Others were Vlado Milovanovich, a member of Ratko Mladich's immediate staff; Dusko Mladich, Radenko Akimovich (lieutenant colonel), Veselin Vidovich (lieutenant colonel), Branislav Petkovich, and several others, who in one way or another became well known both in Macedonia and the Bosnian battle grounds. The list also included officers who made up the nucleus of the top leadership of the former-Yugoslav intelligence service (KOS). The constitution might give such people the right to Macedonian citizenship on the basis of marriage or of permanent residence in Macedonia for more than 15 years. However, Macedonians were fearful that the bringing in of such a contingent of high-ranking, war-experienced officers would represent a real time-bomb for a small state such as Macedonia, and dubious applicants were being rejected.

Where do the Bosnian Serbs stand on Macedonia? An examination of the attitude of senior Bosnian Serbs to Macedonia may give some indication of wider Serbian ideas about Serb-Macedonian relationships. "After the war in the regions of the former Yugoslavia, some kind of a confederation is possible, which will be comprised of the Serbian Kraina, the Serbian Republic, Montenegro, and probably Macedonia." This statement by the leader of the Bosnian Serbs, Radovan Karadzic, was published in the Bulgarian newspapers *Twenty Four Hours*, *Trud* and *Duma*.[100] Karadzic went on to say, "Macedonia cannot be protected or survive without Yugoslavia. It would be best for Macedonia to become part of Yugoslavia as a sovereign state in some sort of confederation." Responding to the question regarding the consequences from the sanctions, Radovan Karadzic said that the sanctions were not only an evil for former Yugoslavia, but also for all neighboring countries, except for Macedonia, which is making a profit on them. "The Macedonians did not treat us decently," he said. "What they did to the Serbians was very bad. I officially state that the activities in Macedonia are not honest, and if at any time anything depended on us, we would never, never forget about this. We will always remember this, and we will pay them back some day."

Karadzic was still thinking in terms of Macedonian participation in a Yugoslav federation in the summer of 1995. In an interview with the Athens TV station STAR, Karadzic answered several questions regarding the Greek-Macedonian dispute. Expressing gratitude for the support and aid from "the brotherly Greek nation," Karadzic underlined his full understanding for the sensitivity of Greece concerning the name Macedonia. He said the only possible way out for Macedonia is to become annexed to Yugoslavia.[101]

Greater Greece

Some Macedonian commentators say the Greek-Serbian plans for Macedonia are well known, namely that Greece does not want a Macedonian state, and that it intends to intercept Turkish influence and interest in the Balkans and to regain its former influence in the area. Greece has long played the card of ethnic conflicts in Macedonia, trying to provoke conflicts amongst Macedonian parties.[102] One of the consequences of such conflicts might be a Greek presence in Macedonia. Despite its denials, Macedonians believed Greece was harboring territorial aspirations towards Macedonia that would embrace territories south of a line from Lake Dojran to Lake Ohrid, including the cities of Bitola, Krushevo and Strumica, and towards Albania, specifically Northern Epirus.[103] Greece has been seen as supporting such an approach primarily through economic measures of destabilization against Macedonia, while planning direct military destabilization steps later on. It continues to oppose Turkey at every opportunity, despite the policies of its European partners, and the fact that Turkey is a partner in NATO, in order to prevent rebirth of the "anti–Serbian and anti-Greek" Balkan military alliance (Ankara, Sofia, Tirana, Bucharest). In this scenario, Romania is seen as Greece's weakest enemy, and Belgrade as its strongest and most reliable ally. In accord with this view, Greece is expected to keep troops deployed near its borders with Macedonia and Albania, ready for immediate response.

At the very least, official Greek policy seems to include an invasion of Macedonia in the event of the outbreak of war in Kosovo. Officials of the Greek Ministries of Defense and Public Order held a meeting in Greece early in December 1994 at which they agreed on coordination of the actions of the military and police in the event of fighting breaking out in Kosovo. The meeting, presided over by the ministers Gerasimos Arsenis and Stelios Papatemelis, agreed that in case it did come to conflict in Kosovo, they would do everything to prevent Kosovar refugees from crossing the Greek border. This included having Greek troops cross into Macedonia to create a barrier within that country.[104]

Greece is a significant military power in the Balkans. The United States provided enormous military assistance to both Turkey and Greece in the early 1990s, amounting to an average of $1 billion each per year. This arms build-up came through the NATO-approved policy of "cascading." In October 1993, the United Nations Register of Conventional Arms listed the two countries as the world's largest importers of conventional weaponry. Both nations obtained armaments ranging from artillery pieces to warships.[105] In the course of 1992 and 1993, Greece received 1,163 tanks and 23 military planes, and Turkey was given 1,509 tanks, 54 planes and 28 helicopters, from discarded arsenals in Europe, as well as direct military funding.[106] Cascading led to an arms race between Greece and Turkey with the potential to affect other Balkan nations if these weapons had been supplied to any of the possible belligerents. This might then have brought Greece and Turkey into an open confrontation.[107]

So spurious did the justifications Greece used in setting up its trade embargo against Macedonia seem to American observers Janusz Bugajski and David Augustyn, that they suspected the name issue was merely a smokescreen for strengthening the Belgrade-Athens axis and suppressing the Slav-Macedonians in Greece.[108] The Macedonian question had become a component of the increasing nationalism within the Greek domestic political debate that showed signs of persisting through the 1990s.[109]

Certain extreme nationalistic forces in Greece proclaimed territorial ambitions in Macedonia.[110] For example, the Skopje paper *Vecer* described several "messages," sent to nongovernment organizations in Macedonia by a Greek group calling itself the Organization of Greek National Unity, claiming "Liberty for Slavonized Greek territories!" and "Cantons — the only just solution for the Balkan crisis." Among other things, this propaganda material stated that out of the entire 68,000 square kilometers of the Macedonian territory, 26,713 square kilometers (Vardar Macedonia) were under occupation by Skopje and 8,000 square kilometers (Pirin Macedonia) were under Bulgarian occupation, leaving only 34,203 square meters (Greek Macedonia) "free." The cantonization scheme of this organization proposed a division of the "Republic of Skopje" into four cantons — "Southern Serbia," "Monastir," "Ilirida," and "Strumica." Describing the dominant languages in the first three cantons, the "messages" named Serbian, Greek, Albanian, and Macedonian. They claimed also that the majority of the population in the proposed "Monastir" canton was of Greek Orthodox religion, while both the Eastern Orthodox religion and Islam occurred in all other cantons.[111]

However, although the Macedonian question was large in the minds of Greek politicians in the early 1990s, disputes with Albania seemed even more explosive, leading to the expulsion of tens of thousands of Albanian seasonal workers, and limited armed engagements on behalf of Greece that some have called "acts of state terror." The status of the sizeable Greek minority in southern Albania fueled nationalist sentiments in both countries.

Bugajski and Augustyn noted that some Greeks, including Panhellenic extremists within the Greek Orthodox Church, had called for the annexation of southern Albania, which the Greeks had been calling "Northern Epirus," and encouraged provocations. Tirana may have played into their hands by overreacting to such provocations. The Mitsotakis government "pandered to nationalist and xenophobic passions by expelling thousands of Albanian refugees." There were also suspicions that the Mitsotakis government coordinated its policy with Serbia to keep Albania destabilized in order to reduce pressures against Serbia for its repressive policies in the Albanian-majority province of Kosovo.

While the machinations of Greek extremists with regard to provocations directed towards Albania seem almost too far-fetched to be believed, there are other, even more bizarre, stories about what was going on in Greece. According to the Agency on International Affairs in Northern Cyprus, Greece had sent several hundred secret military agents disguised as priests to Macedonia, Albania and Bulgaria. The agency claimed that members of the secret organization ESEK (Union of Greek Religious Workers), established by the Greek Orthodox Church, were being trained for spying in a military base near Salonika. The secret agents were said to operate in orthodox churches in Macedonia, Albania and Bulgaria, recruiting members to further their intelligence network.[112]

Greece and Albania. Interactions between Greece and Albania in the early 1990s were affected by powerful forces of nationalism in Greece, the same forces that brought economic devastation to Macedonia. There was also the emergence of an issue of the rights of a minority group in Albania, but in this instance the group receiving the greatest attention identified itself as ethnically Greek. Greek determination to affect the well-being of this group of Greek-Albanians was remarkable given Greece's rejection of its neighbors' concerns about non-Greek populations in Greece. The significance of the dispute between Greece and Albania, as far as the South Balkans are concerned, rests in the expressed intentions of mainstream Greek political parties to directly affect the well-being of ethnic Greeks in Albania, and anywhere else that they may be identified, and in the desire of extreme nationalists to assert Greek political control over parts of Albania and Macedonia. In this latter ambition, the land mass that is the target of territorial expansion is an undivided territory that includes southern areas of Macedonia. Thus territorial ambitions in Albania imply such ambitions in Macedonia.

In the three to four years after Communism collapsed in Albania, 400,000 Albanians poured into Greece. At first the emigres were welcomed, but growing crime and unemployment were blamed on Albanians and soon created a backlash against them.[113] Even so, Albanian immigrants helped keep down labor costs on Greek farms and building sites and sent home hundreds of millions of dollars a year (in 1993, $330m, more than twice Albania's official export earnings). For Greek businessmen, southern Albania is an attractive place to invest, with great incipient development in infrastructure (funded by the World Bank), and cheap labor for manufacturing.[114]

Greece calls southern Albania "Northern Epirus," implying links with its Southern Epirus province. While Albania accepts the presence of an ethnic Greek minority in the Orthodox minority population in southern Albania, Greece does not accept the presence of the Albanian minority within its borders. Albania brought the situation of the ethnic Albanian minority in Greece to the agenda of the CSCE Human Dimension Meeting in Moscow in September 1991. Among other complaints it was said that Greece exerted pressure on the Albanians coming to Greece seeking work to become Orthodox Christian and change their names to Greek ones in order to be employed.[115] In the northern Greek town of Konitsa, a radio station backed by the local Orthodox bishop was broadcasting Greek propaganda to southern Albania.[116]

The Macedonian newspaper *Puls* noted what it called "a new Greek political line" in the writings of the right-wing magazine *Stohos*, which called on Greece to conquer the port of Saranda (directly opposite Crete), then to take over all of what it calls Northern Epirus. *Puls* saw these developments as ominous for Macedonia and for the Balkans as a whole, and suggested Macedonia start asking for UNPROFOR soldiers to be deployed along the southern border with Greece. *Puls* says that these actions should be analyzed alongside Greek plans to form a zone of some 30 km inside Macedonian territory with the aim of "preventing the flood of refugees toward Greece" in a future war in Kosovo. *Puls* claimed, "It is quite certain that our two neighbors (Greece and Serbia) have the same aim in mind: to force the country to return to the embrace of Serbia." Each is "interested in the restoration of a bipolar world, which explains the flurry of talk about an invasion by Islam."[117]

Athens accused Tirana of persecuting its Greek minority, estimated at 300,000 by Greece and at 60,000 by Albania. A central issue for the ethnic Greeks was education. The Albanian authorities shut down some village primary schools that taught in Greek, claiming there were not enough pupils. The

Greek-Albanians said they were not permitted to establish Greek-language high schools. They claimed several hundred ethnic Greek officers had been removed from the Albanian army and many Greek-Albanian civil servants also lost their jobs. Ethnic Greeks had also been prevented from bidding for privatized businesses.[118] Tirana accused its neighbor of fomenting unrest among its ethnic Greeks. Tensions increased in the summer of 1993 when Greece expelled thousands of illegal Albanian workers. On April 10, 1994, a new crisis erupted when gunmen (who Tirana said were ethnic Greek separatists) attacked an Albanian barracks near the border, killing two soldiers and stealing weapons.

Greece and Albania were due to discuss the shooting incident in mid–April 1994, but Albanian authorities imprisoned 11 Albanian citizens of Greek ethnicity for "anti-constitutional activities" and promoting "Greek expansionist designs and plans to annex parts of Albania." There were also charges involving arms and drugs. One of the men was an official of the Greek minority's Omonia party based in Gjirokaster.[119] These arrests prompted bitter complaints from Greek prime minister Andreas Papandreou and foreign minister Karolos Papoulias.[120] Papoulias said in part that Athens "condemns and denounces ... the unprecedented and continuing persecution of the Greek minority by Albanian authorities." Papoulias repeatedly warned Albania not to mistreat the ethnic Greeks. "I want to again warn Tirana that Greece has the capability to stop any barbaric attacks ... against the Greek minority," he said.[121]

At the end of May 1994, Athens cancelled planned talks between the two foreign ministers, alleging further persecution of the Greek minority. After Greece had blocked a European Union aid package, Albanian foreign minister Alfred Serreqi appealed to ambassadors of European Union countries and current members of the United Nations Security Council to prevent Greece from blocking his country's integration into Europe, and pledged to cooperate in defusing the crisis with Albania's Balkan neighbor.[122] At about the same time, Greek defense minister Gerasimos Arsenis announced plans to create a special force to seal Greece's northern border to stop thousands of illegal Albanian immigrants from entering the country. The new 5,000-strong force was to join an unspecified number of commandos and police squads, some of whom were to scout the region posing as shepherds. In response, Tirana said Athens was inciting its 59,000 Greeks to separatism.

By mid–August 1994, Greece announced it had closed its borders with Albania and would expatriate all Albanians working illegally in the country. Greek foreign minister Karolos Papoulias stated that the Greek answer to Albanian president Berisa's provocation would be harsh, but within the framework of international law. Nikos Kouris, deputy minister of defense, explained both political and economic countermeasures would be undertaken against Albania. In turn the Albanian Foreign Ministry denied Papoulias's claim that Albania was oppressing the Greek minority in the country. The Albanian ministry stated that Greece was leading a tendentious and provocative campaign towards Albania and its other neighbors.[123] On September 7, five prominent Omonia members were sentenced to between six and eight years in jail on charges of spying for Greece and illegally possessing weapons.

The *Economist* took Greece to task for its responses to Albania. The paper said that even after 13 years in the European Union and aid worth $6 billion a year the Greeks were still out of step with the rest of Europe, so much so that when Jacques Delors was president of the European Community he said he would be happy to see Greece leave. Greece's European partners had been annoyed because Greece permitted trade with Serbia despite United Nations sanctions, tried to block European Union recognition of Macedonia, broke Union rules by its trade embargo on Macedonia, then ignored Union requests to smooth over the difficulties with Albania. The Greek threat to block Union aid to Albania until ethnic Greeks in Albania were freed and minority rights for Albania's ethnic Greeks were guaranteed seemed an extraordinary effort to interfere in the internal affairs of a foreign country, the kind of interference that Greece has claimed it fears from Macedonia.[124]

On September 19, the Albanian president, Sali Berisa, participated in a commemorative celebration of the fiftieth anniversary of the liberation of Gjirokaster City from occupying Greek forces. In a speech to mark the occasion, he said that the men of Gjirokaster rose to arms when Greek nationalists annexed Gjirokaster and Korce, arresting and deporting Albanians who opposed the annexation. The actions of the Greek police against Albanian refugees over the preceding few weeks had stirred the human and national consciousness of the Albanian people, Europe and the civilized world. Serbian and Greek nationalism had increased, he said. "The collapse of the communist dictatorships in the Balkans has been accompanied by the immediate powerful wakening of the nationalist demons." This was a chauvinistic nationalism based on the violation of the freedom of others, on hatred of other nations. This nationalism was the enemy of democracy, of the genuine values of civilization. It represented a totalitarian ideology. Berisa said that Serbian and Greek nationalism constituted a real threat to the Balkans. Both these nationalisms aimed at the destruction of the Albanian nation. Serbia and Greece had established a secret cooperation between them, which was aimed first of all against Albania. Serbian nationalism had led to aggression in Bosnia for the creation of a Greater Serbia, and the tightening of apartheid in Kosovo. The Albanians of Kosovo had been deprived of all their rights. Serbian nationalism rejected any sort of dialogue while brandishing weapons and tanks and organizing police terror.

However, Berisa said, the greatest threat to Albania today was Greek nationalism. Through a series of maneuvers, Greece had sought to paralyze the reforms in Albania and to destabilize the country. To create conditions that would give an advantage to Serbia, it expressed territorial claims towards Albania. Greek nationalism had become more and more a part of official policy, and Greece had become the main supporter of Serbian nationalism. Berisa saw evidence of this in the blocking of recognition of Macedonia and the trade embargo against that country. He said it was Greek-Serbian nationalism that had frozen European Union aid to Albania, further aggravating Albania's economic situation. Berisa noted that the Mitsotakis government had officially demanded the autonomy of "Northern Epirus." The Papandreou government had declared that the southern half of Albania would be occupied if necessary for defense purposes. Berisa said that Albania would try to normalize relations with Greece. However, he said, it is the Greek nationalists in power, who expelled 60,000 innocents and killed, maltreated or tortured thousands of others just because five ethnic Greek Albanian citizens had been imprisoned for very serious offenses after a proper trial. Albania would defend itself, he said, but at the same time would continue on its path to democracy and integration to Europe. He said he would continue to invite dialogue with Greece.[125]

Greater Albania

Albania has a population about 50 percent larger than Macedonia but is equally poverty-stricken. In the mid–1990s it had an army of 30,000 regulars and 150,000 reservists. In addition there were 5,000 security police. Military equipment was largely obsolete, but the army had a few hundred tanks, APCs, mortars and artillery.[126] Like Macedonia it could not rearm substantially without the cooperation of nations willing to break the United Nations arms embargo on the Balkans at the time. While it might have been able to occupy a part of western Macedonia successfully at the time, without significant local cooperation this would have been difficult. American analysis suggested that Albania's poorly trained and poorly equipped forces were deployed only defensively. It was suggested that the United States resist providing lethal equipment to Albania at the time, since such equipment could easily end up in Kosovo, but that transfer of basic non-lethal equipment (from Germany, for instance) would gain support for United States policies.[127] If Macedonia could become stronger militarily, and United States involvement increase, the possibility of direct invasion from Albania becomes less likely. The counter to such an invasion in any case would be Serbia, which occupies neighboring Kosovo with large numbers of troops. Serbian troops could easily retake Tetovo from an external Albanian force if there was a need. Early in 1995, the Macedonian press was claiming the existence of an Albanian plan for causing unrest in Macedonia. A top secret CIA report was cited as the source of this idea.[128]

For a time Albania was making direct public contact with the most extreme group of Albanian Macedonians, the Dzaferi/Taci group, and was claiming that "one million" Albanians lived in Macedonia. Under pressure from the United States, Albania withdrew support for the Dzaferi/Taci faction of the PDP and was helpful with Macedonia's problem of finding a trading outlet to the sea.[129]

Albania had been seeking NATO membership and technical enhancement for its armed forces. It permitted NATO and the West European Union (WEU) access to its territorial waters in operations designed to strengthen the embargo against Montenegro and Serbia. Albania wanted close military cooperation with Turkey, sought modern weapons including aircraft and heavy artillery, and was sending officers to training courses in Turkey. Albania had cooperated with the land and air military presence of NATO and permitted the presence of United States troops on its territory. American analysts suggested Albania's major fear was of an all-out war with Greece. Although Albania sympathized with Albanians in Macedonia, it did not believe that partition of Macedonia was in its immediate interest.[130]

In an address to deputies in the Bulgarian Parliament as part of an official visit to Bulgaria in April 1994, Albanian president Sali Berisa said, "Albania and Bulgaria have recognized Macedonia and are of the opinion that its stability is necessary for preventing conflict in the southern part of the Balkans." He described Serbian chauvinism and Greek nationalism as the two basic threats to peace in the region. He added that the Greek economic blockade against Macedonia contravened modern European principles. He said the "Albanian problem is the most important in the Balkans," but he emphasized that Albania was against changing borders by force, preferring the creation of a "democratic space in which the human rights of the Albanians would be protected, regardless of where they lived."[131]

When handing over his credentials to President Gligorov in May 1994, the Albanian ambassador to the Republic of Macedonia, Saban Murati, said it was in both countries' interest to develop cooperation as much as possible since both Albania and Macedonia were facing danger from the north and could work together to prevent the risk of war.[132] According to the *Guardian*, Albanian president Berisa had given up the dream of a Greater Albania, at least temporarily.[133] The paper cited Berisa as saying that existing borders with Serbia and Macedonia should remain unchanged. He is said to have appealed to Albanians in Kosovo and Macedonia to somehow come to an arrangement with Belgrade and Skopje. The *Guardian* claimed that Washington had pressed Albania to cease its support of the radical Albanian fraction in Macedonia, led by Menduh Taci.[134] The Macedonian press saw Albania's change of tack as forced by "the ruthless Greek enemy." Berisa said, "Macedonia is a key factor to the stability and peace in the region, and stability in Macedonia depends on its attitude towards the Albanian population there."[135]

A month later a leaflet printed in Tirana, urging ethnic Albanians in Macedonia and Greece to fight for a Greater Albania, was being distributed widely, according to the Belgrade daily *Politika Ekspres*. The map of the proposed Greater Albania included the eastern part of the Yugoslav republic of Montenegro, including its capital of Podgorica, a good part of Serbia's Raska region, all of Serbia's province of Kosovo-Metohija, a part of southern Serbia, over a half of Macedonia, including the capital of Skopje, and a part of western Greece all the way to the port of Salonika. *Politika Ekspres* said the leaflet demonstrated Tirana's readiness to assist the secessionist attempts of ethnic Albanians in neighboring countries.[136] Clearly this Serbian view was a misrepresentation of stated Albanian government intentions at that point in time, though it indicates something about the force of Serbian antagonism to any hint of Albanian territorial ambitions.

Kiro Gligorov was seen by the independent weekly *Monitor* of Podgorica, Montenegro, as reducing the likelihood of a war between Macedonians and Albanians, through a meeting with Berisa in the summer of 1994. In turn, *Monitor* said, Albania had offered Macedonia more than any other neighbor — the shortest way to the sea, oil storage space, and support in the conduct of the census, all without any preconditions whatsoever.[137]

Some Macedonians were less impressed with Albanian policies. The president of the Association of Macedonian Ethnologists, a pressure group of Macedonian Muslims, bitterly protested against the Albanian government's "one-sided decision" to expand rights in education only for the Greek minority in the country, and not for the "enormous number" of Macedonians who had also demanded a right to have their elementary education in the mother tongue.[138] The Macedonian Association of Cultural and Scientific Manifestations of Macedonian Muslims also expressed surprise at this Albanian government decision. They said Macedonians living outside the area of Mala Prespa, an area with a large proportion of Macedonian speakers, had been deprived of their rights and their Macedonian origin was denied. The association believed the Macedonian government should raise the issue with the Albanian government and ask for reciprocity in ensuring rights for Macedonians in Albania and for the Albanian population in Macedonia. VMRO-DPMNE also suggested that the coalition government should undertake diplomatic steps for the protection of the national and human rights of Macedonians in all neighboring states.

Speaking at the Union Nations General Assembly in October 1994, Albanian foreign minster Alfred Serechi said his country was building relations of sincere friendship with Macedonia.[139] However, the affair of the Albanian university in Macedonia led to increased irritation towards Macedonia from Albanian politicians. The Albanian ambassador to the United Nations, Zef Mazi, spoke mainly of Macedonia in a January 1995 Declaration to the United Nations Security Council. He said an independent Macedonian state, truly stable and democratic, would contribute to Balkan stability, but that "it cannot be achieved without full respect for, and implementation of, the rights of Albanians in Macedonia."[140] This more critical attitude persisted after the shootings in Tetovo.[141]

In reaction to such attitudes, Macedonian Radio said Tirana wanted the status of constitutive people for Albanians in Macedonia to be followed by autonomy and new borders within Macedonia, all in pursuit of the dream for a Greater Albania in twenty-first-century Europe. Whenever this goal was threatened Tirana became more critical in its relations with Macedonia. Macedonian Radio was critical of Tirana's open support for the initiators of the university in Tetovo and its urging for disrespect towards the laws of Macedonia. Students at the university in Tirana were frequently organized to demonstrate against Macedonia, it was claimed, with slogans like "Tirana-Pristina-Tetovo." At about the same time, Albanian prime minister Mexi had said that all Albanians living in Montenegro, Kosovo, Macedonia, and Greece should gather together under one roof, in an Albanian state. Accordingly, Macedonian Radio was skeptical about Berisa's more conciliatory public statements.[142]

Berisa himself upset Macedonians soon after this when he said, "There is a Slav group living in Albania, but it is disputable whether its origin is Bulgarian or Macedonian." The Macedonian daily, *Nova Makedonija*, saw this as marking Berisa's evolution from a "well-intended friend" of Macedonia and "peacemaker" in the Balkans into a militant advocate of a Greater Albania. Even Enver Hodza had not denied the existence of a Macedonian minority in Albania. *Nova Makedonija* pointed out that such dilemmas are quite easily resolved in truly democratic countries by allowing the "disputable" population to declare its origin through an honest and properly scrutinized census, which Albania had never conducted. The denial of the origin of Macedonians was seen as "quite poisonous," indicating that Tirana accepted at the very least the Bulgarian argument that Macedonians are really Bulgarians who simply aren't aware of the fact. The reason for Berisa's 180-degree turn in his policy on Macedonia was seen to be the Tetovo University affair. Berisa hoped to gain something from a weak Macedonia.[143]

The statement by Berisa caused bitter reactions among Macedonians living in Albania. Alim Saitovski, secretary of the Macedonian Association "Brotherhood" of Tirana, said there were large numbers of Macedonians in Albania, especially in Golo Brdo, Prespa and Gora. There could not be Bulgarians in Albania, Saitovski said. Macedonians in Albania were gathering signatures to determine the exact number of Macedonians in Albania, which he said was much larger than official figures. Kimet Fetaku, president of the association "Peace," said Macedonians of Golo Brdo and Gora were recognized as a Macedonian minority even before 1947. He said Macedonians in Albania are loyal citizens and should be allowed to act as a factor for friendly relations between Macedonia and Albania. "President Gligorov is keeping silent about Albania's interfering in Macedonia's internal affairs. The association calls on Mr. Gligorov to dissociate himself from such statements by Berisa."

Greater Bulgaria

Bulgaria has a small but strong military force.[144] However, it seems the least likely of all Macedonia's neighbors to consider an invasion. In the early

1990s it acquired a reputation in Europe as a force for stability and peace, quite a contrast from the time not so long before when it was the Soviet Union's most slavish follower in Europe, and from earlier in the century when it invaded Macedonia on several occasions.

Bulgaria was helpful to Macedonia from the time of its independence, which brought important economic advantages to Bulgaria. Macedonia was Bulgaria's second largest trading partner in the Balkans, and the fourth largest in Europe. Trade between Macedonia and Bulgaria multiplied several times after 1991. *Nova Makedonija* said American analyses in 1993-94 indicated that Bulgaria was seeking to step back from Serbia and Greece, through a threat to sign a military pact with Turkey, because of its special interest in Macedonia. Bulgaria had concluded that partition of Macedonia was not in Bulgaria's interest, as it believed that an independent Macedonia would be a pro–Bulgarian ally. This meant that direct invasion of Macedonia was not an immediate option, since any such invasion would probably prompt a response from all of Macedonia's neighbors, so that Bulgaria would end up controlling only a portion of Macedonia at best. If there was a major internal conflict between Albanians and Macedonians, Bulgaria would support the Macedonian side by delivering sufficient arms for effective defense, and would keep its elite land and air forces in a state of readiness for military intervention should that be seen as necessary.[145]

Bulgaria offered support to Macedonia in a number of ways in the aftermath of the Greek blockade of Macedonia's southern border. During 1994 the European Union assembly's presidential committee welcomed Italian, Albanian and Bulgarian efforts to help Macedonia economically during the crisis.[146] The Bulgarian president, Zelju Zelev, in an interview for the TV show "Panorama," spoke out against Greek actions, pointing out that the Greek blockade against Macedonia was "not contributing to relieving of the tensions in the region." At the same time, Bulgaria offered Macedonia use of its port of Burgas, as it had done during the previous blockade in 1993.[147] Bulgaria also participated in plans for a "customs corridor" to connect Macedonia with western Europe through Hungary, Romania and Bulgaria.[148]

Bulgarian concern for Macedonia was indicated in the comments of foreign minister Stanislav Daskalov, who became chairman of the Committee of Ministers of the Council of Europe in May 1994. At his investiture Daskalov stated that his priority task would be admitting new members in this organization. Among the eight states to be urgently admitted to the council, he included Macedonia.[149] Less than two weeks later, in Athens, Daskalov said that the independence and stability of the former Yugoslav Republic of Macedonia were in the interests of Bulgaria and broader Balkan stability.[150] Later, even after he had resigned his ministry, Daskalov gave an interview for the paper *Kontinent* in which he said, "The Republic of Macedonia is a key factor for stability and peace in the Balkans. Bulgaria does not wish to see Macedonia turn into an apple of discord between Balkan states again." That is why "our efforts are aimed at strengthening Macedonia as a sovereign and independent state."[151]

Bulgaria was concerned that its efforts to assist in the maintenance of Balkan stability should be acknowledged. In April 1994, the Bulgarian embassy in Washington distributed a letter written by the Bulgarian ambassador, Stanimir Alexandrov, that had been published in the *Washington Post* on April 28, 1994. Citing a *Post* editorial of April 18, which had stated that Serbia, Albania and Bulgaria are conducting policies that call into question the integrity of Macedonia and that invite a broader war extending even to Greece and Turkey, Alexandrov complained that his government's policy had been sadly misrepresented. He staunchly denied that Bulgaria had any "territorial claims either on the Republic of Macedonia or on any of its neighbors," and pointed to his country's "policies of peace and cooperation" as evidence. The *Post*, he said, had failed to report on Macedonian president Gligorov's recent visit to Sofia, or on the fact that Bulgaria allowed UN convoys to cross the country with supplies for peacekeeping forces in Macedonia. "It is time," he concluded, "to explain why the international community, the United States included, considers Bulgaria a major stabilizing force in the Balkans. That might help *Post* readers understand why my country's policies cannot be seen as a cause for other countries' foreign policy failures."

Despite protestations made in the international arena, the idea of a "Greater Bulgaria" still remains close to the heart of Bulgarians at all levels of government, and it is never forgotten by Bulgaria's neighbors. Senior members of the Bulgarian government have publicly expressed the view that Macedonians are Bulgarians, separated from their own people a century ago by the machinations of the great European powers of the time, England, France, Austria-Hungary and Russia. As Nikolai Slatinski, president of the Bulgarian Parliament's Committee for National Security, puts it, "As far as every normal Bulgarian is concerned, the Slav-Macedonians are Bulgarians, with our culture and our blood. A century ago, the great powers, severely and mercilessly, cut off a peace of our fatherland's flesh." Slatinski also said that "Bulgaria's primary concern at present is to have Macedonia become subject to international laws and to confirm its separation from Yugoslavia as it falls apart."[152]

Georgi Prvanov, deputy president of the High Council of the Bulgarian Socialist Party, has lobbied strongly for development of Bulgarian-Macedonian relations. Discussing ways that Macedonian-Bulgarian relations could become smoother, Prvanov said, "Macedonians have to admit that they are Bulgarians in order to be recognized as Macedonians by Bulgaria." Prvanov also pointed out that Macedonia ought to recognize the "historic facts," that is, that all events in Macedonia have Bulgarian roots, and Bulgarians should deal with the reality of this shared nationhood. One of the consequences of this principle was that Macedonia is "the most natural ally and partner." Prvanov said that Bulgaria "must support the affirmation of the Republic of Macedonia at an international level and categorically put an end to all pretensions of a Macedonian national minority in the Pirin area."[153]

At a time when the Macedonian and Bulgarian governments were having a mild dispute about signing official agreements, the most popular Bulgarian newspaper, *24 Hours*, accused Macedonia of disrespecting and distorting Bulgarian history. The basic thesis of the article was that there is no Macedonian nation and language, and that Macedonia is a "twin state," a second Bulgarian state in the Balkans. The situation that existed previously in Germany was held to be an example of such a "twin state" arrangement. Theories of two German nations and languages vanished only one day after the Berlin Wall was brought down, the article noted. "This is an example of a situation in which a politically imposed border separates one and the same people and language." The "Macedonianism" was said to be just a transition phase in the movement away from the Serb assimilation of the Bulgarian people in Macedonia. The new written form was created by Belgrade and Moscow, the article claimed, but was still Bulgarian in its spirit and essence. It was pointed out that the Macedonian census forms did not include a reference to a Bulgarian minority, which some see as an indication of Macedonia's anti–Bulgarian attitude. The article points out that others say no such category is necessary, as the Macedonian language is simply a dialect of the Bulgarian.[154]

Goran Gotev, editor of the newspaper of the Bulgarian Socialist Party, Bulgaria's most powerful political party, was also the editor of the Bulgarian newspaper *Duma*. He took up the "twin state" idea in an article in *Duma* on September 17, 1994, arguing that now that there are two Romanian, two Croatian and three Serbian states, the time had come to inform the world that there were several Bulgarian states. Gotev suggests that post-war and Helsinki treaties were not to be highly respected and followed, as it was because of the disrespect the world showed towards them that Germany and Vietnam were united today and Korea would be tomorrow. "We would be glad to read or hear the Bulgarian president say to Mr. Kiro Gligorov, or our foreign minister to his Macedonian counterpart, that we look upon Macedonia as a second Bulgarian state." The article goes on to say that this does not mean that Bulgaria has any territorial aspirations, but simply what no one in Bulgaria denies, that the so-called Macedonians are in fact Bulgarians. Accordingly, Bulgaria was obliged to state clearly (even without waiting for a formal agreement with Macedonia) that it would regard any attacks on Macedonia as direct attacks on Bulgaria. The first to hear this, Gotev says, should be Macedonia's neighbors — Albania, Serbia and Greece.[155]

Asen Agov was a member of the Bulgarian government that decided Bulgaria would be the first to recognize the independence and territorial integrity of the Republic of Macedonia. At the end of 1994, Agov was deputy president of the National Coordinating Council of the Alliance of Democratic Forces (SDS) in Bulgaria. He publicly stated that Bulgaria's national ideals remained unfulfilled after the Berlin Congress in 1789, when the great powers refused to recognize the "Greater Bulgaria" proposed by Russia. Agov said, "Mizia, Thrace and Macedonia are the 3 words of the Bulgarian dream." He emphasized the intention of SDS to reaffirm this national ideal within the framework of the European alliance. Agov attacked the Socialists for having recognized the Macedonian national minority in Bulgaria after the war (in 1947), under pressure from the Communist International.[156]

The idea of a Greater Bulgaria has not been forgotten by Greece, perhaps because Bulgaria offers reminders from time to time. Greece developed a close relationship with Bulgaria after the two states signed a treaty of friendship and cooperation in 1964. Both were wary about Turkish intentions with regard to Thrace and the Aegean and Black Seas, and their concern was strengthened after Turkey invaded Cyprus in 1974 to protect ethnic Turks. An "Athens-Sofia axis" developed after 1986 following a security agreement that prohibited the territory of either country from being used for military attacks on the other. Anti-Turkish policies displayed by the Bulgarians in the 1980s were welcome in Athens.[157]

Even after the political changes in Bulgaria in 1989, the relaxation of repressive policies against the Turkish minority and an improvement in relationships with Turkey, Greek-Bulgaria relations remained stable until Bulgaria gave support to Macedonia's independence. At that point doubts began to arise about Bulgaria's long-term ambitions since, although Sofia recognized Macedonia as a state partly in order to balance the Serbian influence, it did not recognize the existence of a distinct Macedonian nation. Bulgaria continued to view the Macedonians as a sub-group of Bulgarians, and the language as a dialect of the Bulgarian language. Had this paternalism been expressed too vigorously, by some kind of attempt at integration, Greece would have felt under great threat, since historically Bulgarian interest extended to Aegean Macedonia and Thrace. Greek awareness of this possibility was shown in concerns expressed by Miltiades Evert, chairman of the major Greek opposition conservative New Democracy Party. While supporting Greece's stand against Macedonia, Evert warned that if the new state were to collapse Greece could be facing a Greater Albania and a Greater Bulgaria on its northern border.[158]

Macedonians in Bulgaria. In the summer of 1995, the Macedonian newspaper *Nova Makedonija* carried out an analysis of the experiences of the Macedonian organization in Bulgaria, OMO "Ilinden," on the prosecution and discrediting of its activists, on the characteristics of what it called an anti–Macedonian campaign in Bulgaria, and on the official Bulgarian position of not recognizing the Macedonian nation and language. This article brought a bitter response from the Sofia daily newspaper, the *Standard* which claimed that "Serbian mentors are poisoning the souls of the people in Macedonia," and that "the authorities in Skopje are financing an anti–Bulgarian campaign in the country." The *Standard*, also claimed that "one per cent of the population [in Macedonia] violently determines the feelings of the remaining 99 per cent."

Provoked by this criticism, *Nova Makedonija* weighed in against the "Greater Bulgarian" philosophy that was displayed here, and suggested that "even Bulgarian analysts are arriving at the clear conclusion, now that the borders are more open and historic deceptions can be seen through, that not only do the Macedonians exist as an autonomous nation, but they also have a minority in Bulgaria." The Bulgarian attack was likened to earlier efforts to block information published by *Nova Makedonija* about Macedonians in Pirin Macedonia. On one of these occasions the process of assimilation of Macedonians in the Pirin part of Bulgaria was "unpretentiously explained and supported with exact data taken from Bulgarian archives. The text told of how the 200,000 Macedonians registered in the 1946 census of population simply and inexplicably disappeared in the two following census surveys."

Nova Makedonija said that the Bulgarian authorities would like Macedonian reporters to avoid writing about the existence of a Macedonian minority in Bulgaria, to ignore the human rights organization OMO "Ilinden," to keep quiet about the promoting of the Greater Bulgaria cause, to consider the Bulgarian fascist occupiers in the Second World War as liberators of Macedonia, to overlook the frequent provocation of the Bulgarian national-chauvinist propaganda and to go along with the newly refloated thesis that all Macedonians feel as Bulgarians but are suppressed by the "pro-Serbian" Gligorov regime.[159] "The Greek and Bulgarian governments do not recognize the existence of the Macedonian people, since if they did, they would have to recognize the existence of the Macedonian minority in their territories."[160]

Bulgaria and Serbia. According to Albanian president Sali Berisa, "Bulgaria refused to take part in a secret meeting between Greece and Serbia in 1991, thereby sparing Macedonia from what could have become another conflict in the Balkans." Berisa discussed this question with Bulgarian president Zhelju Zhelev during his stay in Sofia in the spring of 1994, when he thanked Zhelev for turning down the invitation to take part in the meeting. Berisa explained that former Greek prime minister Mitsotakis had invited Mr. Zhelev and the Serbian president Slobodan Milosevic to attend a secret meeting in Athens, to discuss Macedonia. The meeting was supposed to begin around the time of the dissolution of the Yugoslav Federation and the first signs of a war between Croatia and the rebel Serbs. Berisa stated that discussion of the creation of a Greek-Serbian-Bulgarian axis was planned for the meeting, which was also to review Macedonia's fate and could have brought about the division of the Republic among its three Balkan neighbors. According to Berisa, "Milosevic agreed to take part in the meeting, but Zhelev... said, 'No, I will not come without Macedonia being present.'"[161]

Apparently there were further approaches from Serbia making similar offers to Bulgaria. During talks with President Zhelev, Parliament president

Alexander Jordanov and other Bulgarian leaders in April 1994, representatives of the Macedonian VMRO-DPMNE party, who were visiting Bulgaria, were told that the Serbian Academy of Science and Art and Serbian president Milosevic's advisers had offered Bulgaria a division of Macedonia between them. Bulgaria had refused the offer, preferring to support the independence of Macedonia.[162]

Government officials in Sofia made no official comment about the entry of Serbian troops onto Macedonian territory in the summer of 1994. However, General Stefan Dimitrov, chief of the president's army cabinet, told a Bulgarian paper the incident did not endanger Macedonia's sovereignty. The general stressed the fact that United Nations troops were deployed in the region, with the aim of preventing a spillover of the Yugoslav crisis. Nevertheless, the media in Bulgaria were closely following the development of events and finding anti–Bulgarian motives. The paper *Duma* wrote of a "Serbian-Greek scenario to destabilize Macedonia." The paper argued that Bulgaria was obliged to react to this and to warn the two countries it could not tolerate such threats near its state borders. *Duma* suggested there was a Serbian-Greek conspiracy against Bulgaria, and that the coming census would be an occasion to further destabilize Macedonia. As a part of this process, Belgrade was claiming there were up to 600,000 Serbs in Macedonia, and the Greek media were claiming several hundreds of thousands of Macedonian Greeks. If Albanian claims concerning an alleged million to million and a half Albanians in Macedonia were taken to be true, it would turn out that there were no Macedonians (i.e. Bulgarians) in Macedonia. Therefore, *Duma* concluded, the border incidents and the coming census of the population offered an opportunity for Athens and Belgrade to move closer to their strategic goals to secure Macedonia's return to Serbia/Yugoslavia and establish a common border between Greece and Serbia.[163]

The Bulgarian interest in establishing a feeling of community with Macedonia is indicated in the great attention it gives to sympathetic groups within Macedonia. In April 1994, a delegation from VMRO-DPMNE made a three-day visit to Bulgaria. The visit took place after an invitation by the "Fatherland Alliance," which is a nongovernment organization interested in collaboration between Bulgarians and others, such as Macedonians, that it sees as coming from a common heritage. VMRO-DPMNE president Ljupcho Georgievski and vice-president Dosta Dimovska met with a number of parliamentary and non-parliamentary individuals and groups, including President Zhelev, Parliament president Alexander Jordanov, and representatives of the Holy Synod of the Bulgarian church. This is quite an extraordinary level of access for a party that has never even participated in government in Macedonia. The VMRO-DPMNE representatives stressed that Bulgaria had shown even greater interest in closer political and economic ties with Macedonia than in 1992.[164]

The language dispute. In a speech before the United Nations, Kiro Gligorov had said that the Macedonian nation gave the Slavs the Cyrillic script and Christianity. This statement caused objections in Bulgaria, where the matter is expressed differently. Bulgarians say that Bulgaria gave the world the Cyrillic script and brought Christianity to the Slavs. In a statement anticipating an official visit to Macedonia by Bulgarian president Zhelev late in 1993, Gligorov changed his previous formulation of these ideas. He said, "The Slav script and Christianity originated from Macedonian lands," which is historically accurate and undisputed. He went on to say, "Cyril and Methodius as well as the first Slavs baptized somewhere around Stip are from this region. This doesn't mean that they are not yours as well. Even in the Constitution of Slovakia it is said that she is a Slav Republic of Cyril and Methodius." Gligorov suggested that the common script and civilization should bring Macedonia and Bulgaria together, rather than divide them. He said, "Let's look into the future and not return back into the history burdened by so many prejudices. For the modern person it does not have the great meaning that it used to have in times gone by."[165]

Gligorov also said, "I have no reasons to support any other position except the one for as good as possible relationships with Bulgaria and the Bulgarian people," and added that he had many relatives in Sofia and Gorna Oryahovitsa, a town in northern Bulgaria. Asked about his attitude towards Bulgaria, which some Bulgarians did not see as positive, Mr. Gligorov said, "Bad relations with Bulgaria would be against the interests of Macedonia. In your country there are some people or certain circles who think about Greater Bulgaria, just as there are Macedonians who talk about Greater Macedonia. In Bulgaria there are societies, who claim that we are not a separate nation and we are not Macedonians." Yet, he said, these are not arguments that should cause any change in Macedonia's friendly attitude towards Bulgaria. "I continuously repeat that Bulgaria was the first to recognize us, and that this is a historic act forever appreciated by every citizen of our country... However, I cannot explain to myself completely why Bulgaria has not established full diplomatic relationships with the Republic of Macedonia and why after she recognized us as a country, she does not have yet an embassy in Skopje."[166]

The diplomacy of the language used by Gligorov on this occasion, and the pragmatism of his approach were often not reciprocated by his Bulgarian counterpart and other Bulgarian spokespersons in the months that followed. In an interview for the French paper *Liberation*, President Zhelev, reminded that Bulgaria recognized Macedonia as a state but did not recognize a separate Macedonian nationality, commented, "We have one history, one culture, one religion, and one and the same language."[167]

An official visit by the Bulgarian minister of education and science, Marko Todorov, to Macedonia was alleged by the Macedonian media to have ended in a fiasco. In response to such claims, the Macedonian Foreign Ministry issued an announcement about the affair: "In accordance with the practice of successful cooperation with the Republic of Bulgaria in all spheres, a number of agreements and protocols have been signed. The texts of these documents were drawn up in the Macedonian and Bulgarian languages, without any problems arising in relation to the acceptance of these texts by one or the other side, as valid for cooperation in the concrete field. Unfortunately, in recent times, the efforts of the Bulgarian side to change this practice and to avoid the direct mentioning of the Macedonian language have become more evident. In that sense, it is insisted on using the formulation which states that such documents are signed in the official languages of both countries." The Macedonians wanted the names of both languages to be mentioned. The visit by Todorov was actually cut short after these unsuccessful talks about signing a protocol for cooperation between the Education Ministries, and in turn, a scheduled meeting between Minister Todorov and Macedonian prime minister Crvenkovski was cancelled.[168]

A little more than a week following this incident, Gligorov made his first official visit to Sofia. This two-day visit to Sofia was attended with great ceremony. The Macedonian national anthem was played, and its controversial flag was raised. A joint statement by the two leaders at the end of the visit said, "There is no field in which Macedonia and Bulgaria cannot co-operate. Mr. Gligorov's visit is of a historic character, not only because it is a first formal visit by a Macedonian president to Bulgaria, but also because this opens a new period in Macedonian-Bulgarian relations." Despite the appearance of agreement between the two leaders, the visit ended in disarray because of the failure to sign the many documents of agreement between the two countries. The problem was the same one that had affected previous efforts at reaching written agreements: The Macedonians insisted on a statement that the agreements were written in both the Macedonian and Bulgarian languages, while the Bulgarians would concede only that the documents were signed in the "official languages of the two countries." Gligorov stated that Macedonia could not sign an agreement that brought into question the language of the Macedonian people, though Zhelev said that despite the problems he was sure the agreements would be signed very soon. In an uncompromising interview with the Bulgarian *Standard*, Macedonian ambassador Gjorgi Spasov stated, "The Macedonian language is the official language of all of us living in Macedonia. If someone refuses to acknowledge or see this fact, that is their problem."[169]

Explaining why no documents were signed during the visit, President Zhelev noted that "the documents were to be signed in the official languages of the Republic of Macedonia and the Republic of Bulgaria which implied that they were two different languages. However, the Macedonian party insisted on the clear formula 'Macedonian language' and because of present public opposition, which I believe is quite artificial, we refrained from signing anything at this stage. I believe that the problem will be settled; I am sure it will be."[170]

This seems to clarify Zhelev's personal opinion. Zhelev had just had a book titled *Fascism* published in Skopje in the Macedonian language. Thus at a personal level he did not appear to have difficulties with pragmatic acceptance of the language. As head of state he was representing other interests. The newspaper *Otechestven Vestnik* wrote that "it is one thing to have your book translated in Skopje, and another thing to legitimize a phantom language with your signature." The Sofia newspaper *24 Hours* claimed that Prime Minister Berov, who in accord with protocol was to meet with Gligorov, refused to see him. Gligorov met instead with the deputy prime minister, Evgenii Matinchev.[171] The excuse given to Gligorov was that Professor Berov was still recovering from surgery, but Bulgarian sources said he was meeting with a breakaway group from his ruling party. It has not been revealed whether knowledge of this snub preceded or followed the difficulties in signing the protocol of agreement.

Neither Bulgaria nor Macedonia gave up on efforts to communicate after this setback. Representatives of parliamentary groups of the parties in the Alliance for Macedonia (SDSM, Liberal Party and Socialist Party), led by Parliament vice-president Tito Petkovski, arrived on a two-day visit to Sofia in June, after an invitation from parliamentary members of the left-wing Bulgarian Democratic Party. MPs from both countries agreed that the visit should initiate an intensified development of Macedonian-Bulgarian relations, especially in the fields of economy and culture, where there had been misunderstanding over the language to be used in signing agreements between the two governments. The Macedonian delegation was received by President Zhelev, who stressed the good relations between the two countries as a basis for stability in the Balkans, expressing a strong personal belief that Macedonia's independence is a guarantee of the peace and stability in the region. All neighbors, he said, must realize this and recognize Macedonia.

In a long article, the Bulgarian paper *24 Hours* accused President Zhelev and Education Minister Todorov of "pouring additional gasoline into the already burning dispute over the Macedonian language" by refusing to sign the prepared documents on cooperation with Macedonia. According to the paper, Bulgaria entangled itself into its own mess when it recognized the Macedonian state without recognizing the nation and the language. The article appealed to Bulgarian politicians not to seek "elastic formulas" (President Zhelev's expression), but to find a permanent solution, based on the principle of "respect for political realities" (a principle insisted on by President Gligorov). Otherwise, the paper warned, neighboring Balkan states would be encouraged in their malicious intentions towards Macedonia, and Skopje would start an anti–Bulgaria campaign.[172]

Nevertheless, the Bulgarian government held to its position on signing in the "official languages of the two countries," rejecting the proposal of one of its ministers to have the agreements with Macedonia signed in English. The Bulgarian ambassador continued to speak in terms of "the people in Macedonia" rather than "the Macedonian people."[173] Bulgarian prime minister Lyuben

Berov and deputy foreign minister Todor Churov met with Macedonian prime minister Branko Crvenkovski in Trieste on July 15, 1994. The prime ministers discussed Macedonia's economic problems, the prospects for expanding cooperation, and some controversial issues in the two countries' relations. Crvenkovski thanked the Bulgarian prime minister for Bulgaria's understanding and its help in mitigating the effects of Greece's embargo on Macedonia. In the course of discussions Professor Berov said, "We are more than neighbors, but a cold wind has been felt from Skopje of late, caused by persistence in regard to the formulation of the language used in the bilateral documents." Crvenkovski said this was not something that should affect Macedonian-Bulgarian relations.[174]

Bulgarian national TV broadcast an interview with President Kiro Gligorov made immediately after his reelection in the first round of the 1994 elections. President Gligorov emphasized that the existence of the "independent Republic of Macedonia has helped prevent the spreading of the war from north to south." He said Macedonia could be a factor of stability in this part of the Balkans. He said he had reason to expect support from Bulgaria for Macedonia's acceptance to the Council of Europe and the CSCE since Bulgaria held the chair of the Council of Ministers. President Gligorov said that the two close neighbors aimed for mutual cooperation. In relation to the language dispute with Bulgaria, the Macedonian leader insisted that every nation has the right to name its own language as it pleases, and the fact that there are some languages "with mutual similarities" does not mean that one country can claim ownership of all these varieties of language. He said, since the Republic of Macedonia and the Macedonian nation are reality today, it would be appropriate for language to be a non-issue in relations between Macedonia and Bulgaria. He saw the dispute as irrational, as a matter that could be settled through mutual respect and tolerance for the other's position. President Gligorov expressed gratitude to the Republic of Bulgaria for its support in helping Macedonia overcome the embargo imposed by Greece as painlessly as possible, and assessed the building of the railroad and the entire east-west corridor as a project of great significance.[175]

A year after the Bulgarian public outrage at the Macedonian attitude regarding the signing of intergovernmental documents, public opinion seemed to have softened. *Duma*, the paper of the ruling Socialists in Bulgaria, which had previously taken a harder line on the question, published an article demanding changes in the country's official policy on the "language dispute" with Macedonia. Reiterating the Bulgarian stance on "common national roots," the paper suggested that the authorities in Sofia accept documents signed in the Macedonian language.[176]

At a special press conference in Sofia in September 1995, Bulgarian foreign minister Georgi Pirinski declared that Bulgaria hoped for maximum, fast and wide development of bilateral relations with Macedonia, and offered concrete proof of such readiness in a willingness to sign 23 agreements with Macedonia that had previously been suspended because of the problem of acknowledging the Macedonian language.[177] However, some Bulgarian MPs pointed out that the signing of the agreements did not necessarily mean recognition of the Macedonian language, because it was still possible to adopt the attitude that the documents in Macedonian were really in a "Bulgarian dialect." Indicating the intransigence of Bulgarians on the issue of the language, the deputy president of the Foreign Political Commission of the Bulgarian Parliament made a public statement in which he emphasized that if Bulgaria were to recognize the Macedonian language it would "automatically erase its own history."

The Bulgarian military position. Early in 1995 the Greek newspaper *Apogevmatini* was claiming the existence of secret documents from the Bulgarian chief of staff, General Cvetan Totomirov, detailing plans for entering Macedonia should the war in the Balkans spread south. General Totomirov denied that such documents or plans existed.[178]

Although the different perceptions about the Macedonian nation and language have caused problems between Macedonia and Bulgaria, there are reasons to believe that Bulgarians would rally enthusiastically to Macedonia's aid if it came under attack. Some of the strongest support would come from Pirin Macedonia, from people acknowledged by the Macedonians as their kin. But the rest of Bulgaria may not be far behind, since, regardless of what the Macedonians say, the Bulgarians think that they are all one people. Writing in the *Los Angelos Times*, journalist Carol Williams argues that "the call of blood" may well decide the involvement of Bulgarians in a defense of Macedonia.[179] She quotes Hari Mavrodiev, a paramilitary commander from the Pirin area of Bulgaria, saying, "We must go and defend our relatives if this war touches them. If war spills to Macedonia, every man in this region will go there to fight." Mihail Ivanov, adviser to Bulgarian president Zhelev on ethnic and religious issues, is quoted by Williams as saying that "the Bulgarian government would oppose any involvement (in war), but things would be out of control." Williams suggests that the need to stand by ethnic brothers, no matter how hopeless the fight, is "the defining measure of nationalist dignity," an idea that explains why the violent history of the Balkans is compelled to repeat itself.

Williams says that the Internal Macedonian Revolutionary Organization is arming and training volunteers for an anticipated battle. Another VMRO member, Anatoly Velichkov, told Williams it was not simply a matter of protecting a country, but of looking after "our own brothers." Williams found evidence of the stockpiling of arms for battle, and food and clothing to cater for refugees. It was expected that Serbian repressions in Kosovo would provoke the war to come. If Serbian forces were to enter Macedonia, these Bulgarians said, hundreds of thousands of Bulgarians would rush to the defense. This particular group of activists opposed the Macedonian view about a separate identity, seeing the Macedonian nation as an artificial creation of Marshal Tito.

Turkey

Although Turkey does not share a border with Macedonia, it remains an active element in the South Balkans. In particular it is seen as a threat to the Serbian-Greek axis. It is a focus for Greek concern, since Turkey has shown a willingness to engage its NATO ally in battle if its perceived interests are sufficiently threatened. There are many territories that could become new sources of dispute between Turkey and Greece. Greece has been active in politically obstructing Turkey in various international affairs. Turkey is also seen as a possible threat to Serbia since it is identified as an ally of Muslim interests in the Balkans, and a potential barrier to the spread of Serbian power.

Macedonian news sources report that Turkey's policy was to oppose the Serbs in Bosnia, as well as in Kosovo, Sandzak and Macedonia, preferably in alliance with Bulgaria, Romania, Albania, Macedonia and Bosnia-Herzegovina, thus neutralizing Greece's influence. Turkey is perceived as a potential strategic ally to Macedonia, though this is complicated by the fact that there are no direct border contacts. Turkey is seen as wishing to avoid involvement in any spillover of conflicts in the former Soviet Union, in the Kavkaz and Black Sea regions, since Russia is perceived as potentially its strongest and most dangerous enemy.[180]

Consistent with this analysis of Turkey's possible role as an ally of Macedonia are Turkish efforts at increasing contacts with Macedonia at various levels, and the adoption of international postures about Macedonia that Greece has seen as threatening. In November 1993, on the occasion of a visit by the Macedonian defense minister Vlado Popovski to Turkey, Turkey's new defense minister, Mehmed Golhan, stated for Macedonian Radio that Turkey would get involved in a war in the Balkans if military clashes spread to Macedonia. Mr. Golhan warned, "If Serbia does not give up the idea of creating some sort of greater Serbia, the war will spread to Macedonia. Whether we want to or not, Turkey will be forced to intervene in this unwanted war." Golhan also asserted that Turkey would give its support to Macedonia's application for admission to NATO.[181] Turkey also provided aid to Macedonia during the Greek embargo in the form of thousands of tons of maize, and offered a special trade relationship with Turkey.[182]

The *Turkish Daily News* suggested, in June 1994, that an increased Serbian military presence on the border with Macedonia was instituted by agreement with Greece and aimed to isolate Macedonia, forcing the changing of the national Macedonian flag and then the name of the country. It was expected that these concessions would be followed by demands for larger and more complex retreats. The paper claimed that this was the reason for deploying American troops in Macedonia, and that preservation of Macedonian independence and sovereignty was of key importance in preventing a wider conflict in the Balkans.[183]

A delegation of the People's Assembly of Turkey, led by the president of the Turkish Parliament, Husametin Djindorluk, visited Macedonia on a three-day official visit early in August 1994.[184] Djindorluk said, "Turkey sincerely wishes all the best for Macedonia and supports its territorial integrity... We will listen to all the Macedonian government's wishes, particularly in the military field." Djindorluk said Macedonia had a historic right to the name, and that the name could not be a debatable issue on an international level. Djindorluk also said that Turkey would strongly support Macedonia's being granted membership into the CSCE, the European Union and other international organizations; that it wished to see Macedonia included in cooperative organizations of the Black Sea countries; and that it sought to deepen its own relationships with Macedonia.[185]

At the end of his visit to Macedonia, Djindorluk said, "I wish to underline two principles that the state and national politics of Turkey towards Macedonia is based on: Firstly, our respect for Macedonia's territorial integrity and the inviolability of its borders, along with its natural right to its own name and the right to choose a flag based on its history." He stressed that the Turkish and Macedonian people were "close and united." The Turkish press emphasized the identical points of view of the two countries as regards regional and world events. Ankara expressed regret at the fact that the Greek government was continuing with its "unjustified" embargo against Macedonia. Turkey was ready to aid the Macedonian economy, Djindorluk said.[186] Djindorluk's statement on Macedonia's right to its own name was described in the Greek media as a "provocation" and a "direct attack on Greece."[187]

The Turkish foreign minister, Muftaz Soisal, expressed very strong support of the Republic of Macedonia in his speech at the United Nations General Assembly. He said Macedonia was suffering because of the illegal economic blockade imposed by Greece. Furthermore, he said it was time that Macedonia was represented at the United Nations under the name and flag that it had chosen — making Turkey the first United Nations member to explicitly request such representation for Macedonia.[188]

In November 1994, the Macedonian-Turkish Friendship Association held its constitutive session in Bitola. To mark this occasion, the Bitola museum opened a commemorative room devoted to Mustafa Kemal Ataturk, the father of modern Turkey.[189] Mr. Ataturk's favorite mosque when he was a young officer of the Ottoman Turk Empire in Macedonia had been in Bitola.

Turkish president Suleiman Demirel visited Macedonia in July 1995. He met President Gligorov and gave a speech at the Macedonian Parliament. Several agreements were signed to regulate issues concerning friendship, cooperation and neighborly relations, and investment protection, and to form a joint commission for economic cooperation and a business council for cooperation between chambers of commerce. The delegation included foreign minister Erdal Ineni, a group of Turkish businessmen and representatives of the Chamber of Commerce and humanitarian organizations.[190]

Clearly Turkey has shown great interest in Macedonia, and has provided aid to match its diplomatic words. While Macedonia has willingly sought a relationship with Turkey, it is unlikely that this relationship will assume a significance above other international relationships. Macedonia has repeatedly indicated that it seeks friends in every part of Europe, and indeed in every part of the world. This even-handedness may be necessary to prevent being drawn into one or other of the antagonistic camps in the Balkans.

The Development of United States Relationships with Macedonia

The United States supported Macedonia's admission to the United Nations in 1993 under the temporary label, "the Former Yugoslav Republic of Macedonia" and had encouraged Macedonia and Greece to engage in negotiation through the United Nations to resolve their differences. However, during 1993 the United States had not yet formally recognized Macedonia. Late in 1993, after a socialist government replaced the Mitsotakis regime in Greece, George Stefanopoulos, a senior adviser to President Clinton, met with Greek-American representatives in New York to explain the president's policies. The Greek press had been speculating that the "special mission" in the Balkans of the new United States ambassador to Greece, Thomas Niles, was to weaken the Athens-Belgrade axis and to influence Greek foreign policy to a closer match with American ideas. The Greek newspaper *Elefteros tipos* claimed that the United States had planned the fall of the Mitsotakis government in order to destabilize the relationship between Greece and Serbia and in order to settle the Macedonian question. In support of this idea the newspaper cited a message, held by the Greek Foreign Ministry, from the former United States ambassador in Sofia to the United States State Department, which stated that the Macedonian issue could be settled to the advantage of the United States only if the Mitsotakis government was replaced by the socialists (PASOK). If PASOK was to abandon the United Nations–mediated negotiations with Macedonia, this would make way for the United States to recognize the Republic of Macedonia without obstruction from Greece. Stefanopoulos stressed that the White House would continue to cooperate with the new government in Athens in the settling of the "Macedonian question," while still making sure that Greek national interests would be protected. Stefanopoulos confirmed that the United States stance was unchanged, but refused to answer what Washington would do if Greece broke off the United Nations-mediated negotiations with Macedonia.[191]

The United States first offered to establish diplomatic relations with the Former Yugoslav Republic of Macedonia on February 9, 1994, in a letter from President Clinton to President Gligorov. This is the way that diplomatic relationships are established in international circles. Gligorov responded immediately to Clinton's letter, meeting all Clinton's conditions and assuring the United States of his country's readiness to continue negotiations with Greece.[192]

The United States State Department expressed its satisfaction with Macedonia's cooperative and peaceful stance, as well as its efforts toward the implementation of democratic principles and open-market reforms. Finally, the State Department stressed its belief that establishing diplomatic relations between the two countries would "help strengthen the stability in the region."[193]

There was international acclaim for the American move. Victor Comras was tipped as the first American ambassador to Skopje. Then a meeting with the Greek-American political lobby was followed by a reversal by the American government.[194] It was decided not to establish full diplomatic relations after all, and not to send an ambassador yet. Jim Hoagland said in the *Washington Post* that the sudden turnabout added weight to criticism of the United States administration "for letting domestic political interests take precedence over foreign policy priorities." United States interests were at stake in Macedonia, Hoagland wrote. Greece's actions threatened to destabilize President Kiro Gligorov's centrist regime and put at risk President Clinton's decision to send American troops to participate in the United Nations peacekeeping program. Hoagland suggested that Clinton's presidential adviser, George Stefanopoulos, who was present at the meeting with the Greek-American lobby, was of particular influence in the turnaround.

Other American analysts also have seen this "flip-flop" as a response to pressure from the Greek lobby and a sell-out to domestic interests.[195] Influential participants in the Greek lobby on this occasion were Senator Paul Sarbanes of Maryland, Representative Michael Bilirakis of Florida and lobbyist Andrew Manatos. Manatos had worked for the Carter administration and had once been paid $100,000 by Greece for "advice on tourism." In the few days after American recognition of Macedonia, the American Hellenic Educational Progressive Association (AHEPA) had produced a protest petition with 30,000 signatures. The Greek-Americans persuaded fourteen members of the House Foreign Affairs Committee to sign a letter urging President Clinton to delay implementation of the policy for two weeks. Then, apparently with the help of other influential Greek-Americans, including California businessman Angelo Tsakopoulos, the president of Greek-Americans for Mr. Clinton, and Chicago businessman Andy Athens, they were able to arrange a meeting with the president, with vice-president Al Gore and with national security adviser Anthony Lake. Also at the meeting were Orthodox archbishop Iakovos and thirteen other leading Greek-Americans. It is significant that no representative from the State Department attended, despite Warren Christopher's earlier urgings to the Greek government that it should lift the embargo against Macedonia. It seems that Clinton had already decided to change his position, since he read to the meeting his new policy position. He announced he would not establish an embassy in Skopje until the problems with Greece had been sorted out.

Manatos said, "The policy he outlined there is very consistent with what Greece would like it to be."[196] Nevertheless, Bilirakis later sponsored a bill that would prevent the United States from ever establishing diplomatic relations with Macedonia. In commenting on the case put by the Greek-Americans, Hanna Rosin used the expression "propaganda" to dismiss the accuracy of the information, concluding that claims of a military threat were illusory, given Greece's enormous military superiority, and that the Greek government had grossly overreacted to Macedonia.

The following month the Greek leader Andreas Papandreou was due to visit President Clinton in Washington. Few diplomatic visits had ever threatened to damage United States interests as much as this one, according to the *New York Times* in April 1994.[197] President Clinton was urged by the *Times* to publicly criticize Greece for its economic embargo against Macedonia and to get firm assurances that the Greek leader would be less supportive of Serbia. Papandreou was said to have replaced his former anti–Americanism with national chauvinism, achieving internal support by destabilizing Macedonia.

Other opinion was also harshly critical of President Clinton's Macedonian policies, but proposed a relatively novel solution. Michael Radu, a resident scholar at the Foreign Policy Research Institute in Philadelphia, writing in *Insight*, stated that the American troops should not be in Macedonia. He acknowledged that the Balkans was an explosive mixture, but took the view that the most dangerous element in the mix came from America's "supposed ally," Greece. Greece, he said, consistently pretended that Macedonia did not exist, claiming that this "pathetically weak country" was a threat to its security, and was trying to suffocate it economically and politically. With "anti-American demagogue" Andreas Papandreou back in control in Greece, Radu saw even greater potential for "Greek mischief."

Like other critics of American policy, Radu noted the powerful influence of the Greek lobby. He argued that the American decision to send troops defied logic, since the virtually unarmed troops had no clear mission, there was no immediate Serbian threat, and, in any case, any Serbian invasion would require cooperation from Greece and would not be stopped by 300 lightly armed troops. If a Serbian invasion came about, Bulgaria, Albania and Turkey would become involved, and this would draw in more United States troops.

Radu's conclusion was that the American policy in Macedonia was "an absurdity." A more sensible approach would have been to recognize the country under its chosen name, provide economic assistance, and bring the troops home. Though this might not have stopped Macedonia's "greedy neighbors" or persuaded Greece, "the greediest and nastiest of them all," to change its behavior, American interests were not sufficient to put the lives of any American soldiers at risk.[198]

At the end of April 1994, former United States foreign secretary James Baker told *USA Today* that "if Macedonia is endangered, the USA should be making preparations for war." According to Baker, if the conflict in former Yugoslavia were to spread to Macedonia, there would be a war likely to involve Bulgaria, Albania, Greece, Turkey and probably Hungary. It was unlikely that the United States would have been able to avoid an involvement in such a war. Baker also felt that the United States should have made it clear to any "adventurers," meaning invaders of Macedonia, that they would be dealing with the full force of NATO power.

In an article published in the Opinion/Essays Section of *The Christian Science Monitor* in May 1994, William N. Dunn, a professor at the University of Pittsburgh's Graduate School of Public and International Affairs, severely criticized America's policies towards Macedonia.[199] In particular, Dunn suggested that President Clinton's meeting with Greek prime minister Papandreou should have been used as an opportunity to press Greece to lift the embargo because of its effects on Macedonia's fragile economy and government. Dunn discussed one possible war scenario that included internal agitation in Macedonia promoted by economic difficulties, and Serbian moves in Kosovo. Either factor could lead to war in Macedonia, if Albanians in Macedonia attempted to secede. Albania was likely to become involved if Albanian peoples were under threat of war. This in turn might well bring in Greece, Bulgaria, and Turkey. Like James Baker, Dunn believed that a more immediate and forthright support for Macedonia might have served to reduce the threat to United States interests in Balkan peace. The United States government chose a different path.[200] Like Baker, Dunn said that the Greek-American lobby continued to shape United States foreign policy at a time when Macedonia's stability and independence were critical for averting disaster in the southern Balkans.

Dunn suggested that while Greece could have no reasonable military fears about Macedonia, Macedonia had legitimate concerns about the economic, political, and military threat posed by Greece. For instance, Greece had developed plans for a 20-kilometer "security zone" within Macedonia should Greece's ally, Serbia, crack down on Kosovo's Albanians, leading to a flood of southward-moving Albanian refugees. Greece had also conducted military maneuvers on the border with Macedonia. Dunn said that although Greece was supposed to have declined a 1992 proposal by President Milosevic to split up Macedonia between them, Greek actions suggested support for a "Greater Serbia" and attacked the stability and viability of Macedonia, increasing the risk of a war that would involve the United States.

In a June 1994 newspaper interview, James Baker said, "What we have to recognize now ... is the very real danger of a wider Balkan war. The key to this is Macedonia... Because if we do get a wider Balkan war, we'll be back. Forget that reduction of US troops in Europe. We'd be back."[201] Baker continued with this theme at the opening forum of a series of summer debates in El Escorial, near Madrid. He warned that Macedonia was on the brink of war and said Greece's policies threatened to destabilize its smaller neighbor. To prevent such a war, NATO needed to make explicit warnings to potential invaders while the United States had to take a leader's role instead of squandering United States credibility by not backing words with force.[202]

A bipartisan, independent delegation of prominent Americans and Europeans sponsored by the Action Council for Peace in the Balkans visited Macedonia and Greece in May 1994. Members of the Action Council came from every ideological persuasion on the American political spectrum. The steering committee included Morton Abramowitz, William Brock, Zbigniew Brzezinski, Frank Carlucci, Hodding Carter, David Dinkins, Geraldine Ferraro, Barbara Jordan, Max Kampelman, Lane Kirkland, Jeanne Kirkpatrick, Edmund Muskie, George Shultz, Susan Sontag, George Soros, Paul Volcker, Elie Wiesel, and several members of the Senate and the House of Representatives. The executive director and program director of the Action Council were, respectively, Marshall Freeman Harris and Stephen Walker, two of the three officials who resigned from the state department in August 1993 to protest United States inaction in Bosnia. After surveying Macedonia's internal situation and external threats, including Greece's economic and diplomatic embargo, the delegation reported they had found that the situation in Macedonia was urgent, serious, yet solvable.[203] The report said that the very existence of an independent Macedonian state was "seriously called into question by the combination of increasing interior and exterior political threats."

Internal dissent was likely to be encouraged by the deteriorating economic situation, while externally, "the country faces an ultranationalist and expansionist regime to the north, unrest and the realistic possibility of violence in Kosovo, economic sanctions imposed on Serbia by the United Nations, the Greek embargo, and poor communication and transport links over east-west routes now that traditional north-west roads are closed by embargoes." The report went on to say:

> Conflict or disintegration in Macedonia, whether sparked internally or externally, could ignite a full-scale war involving several neighboring countries. Unrest in Kosovo, in particular, would have unavoidably adverse consequences in Macedonia. Also, as history has shown through wars in the Balkans, the great powers could be easily drawn into such a conflict.
>
> Disputes over the name, constitution, and national symbols do not, in and of themselves, threaten peace in the region. The way in which Greece has chosen to deal with them up until now, however, does threaten regional security and stability. Greece has linked the disputes to issues that affect not just Macedonia's nomenclature and insignia, but also its very viability... [Athens has] resorted to coercion — its economic embargo — and thereby hardened resistance to compromise and, more ominously, created sparks in a tinder box... Greece's actions are weakening Macedonia's economy and social fabric ... and working against peace.

The Action Council pointed out that the Greek embargo amounted to an international blockade because of the closure of the northern border and the lack of east-west transportation routes. The council strongly condemned Greece's actions as being in violation of widely acknowledged principles of international relations as well as undermining United States policy of maintaining regional stability by supporting the internal cohesion and territorial integrity of the Republic of Macedonia. The council urged "the United States and its partners to respond firmly to Greece's deliberately destabilizing acts." It called for immediate steps from the United States administration, including calling for an urgent meeting of the United Nations Security Council to condemn the Greek government actions and demand their immediate and unconditional reversal; pressing for Greece to drop its veto on the admission of Macedonia to the CSCE; sending an ambassador to Skopje; recalling the United States ambassador from Athens for consultations; and issuing a strong public statement of protest on embargoes. The council suggested sanctions against Greece if it did not respond appropriately to these demands, including the barring of Greek ships from entry to United States ports, cutting United States security assistance to Greece and delivering direct United States aid to Macedonia.[204]

Speaking before the United States Congress' Subcommittee for International Security, International Organizations and Human Rights, American businessman and founder of the Open Society Fund George Soros pointed out that in Greece

> a frenzied national feeling over the name Macedonia has been created. The small and weak northern neighbor has been turned into a threat for Greece's territorial integrity. I accept that there is a small number of people in Macedonia who do have certain irredentist dreams as a result of ethnic sufferings in the past, but it is only a minority, whereas the Macedonian government is entirely devoted to creating a multinational democratic state. It is ready to make retreats, but it is not ready to give up its own identity. Greece is using this issue for domestic purposes, and in the meantime, the Macedonian economy, already greatly damaged by the sanctions against Serbia, finds itself facing a collapse under the burden of the Greek embargo... Macedonia could easily disintegrate, and if this happens, we will have a Third Balkan War... Macedonia is a clear example where only an ounce of prevention could save us tons of problems. Our priority must be to help this small country with a democratic multinational government which is on the edge of an economic collapse, through reasons beyond its control.[205]

In October 1994, Senator Dennis de Consini and Congressman Stanley Hoer, in the role of chairman and co-chairman of the CSCE in Europe, wrote to President Clinton insisting that the United States establish full diplomatic relations with Macedonia as soon as possible. The United States was requested to put pressure on Greece to lift the blockade on the border and to stop blocking Macedonia's acceptance to the CSCE. The letter said that from the beginning, Macedonia had fulfilled all the criteria that Europe set for the recognition of the other Yugoslav republics. In the development of bilateral relations, the forming of a United States embassy in Skopje was necessary, as was support for the full integration of Macedonia in Europe.[206]

At a hearing of the Congressional committee for international relations early in January 1995, James Baker said Macedonia was a "particularly dangerous zone," and he felt that NATO should send a clear message, supported by a convincing threat of force, that the alliance would not allow Macedonia to become the focus of a broader Balkan conflict. He said that this should include a clear signal to Greece that its NATO partners would not tolerate the "unfounded and illegal" embargo against Macedonia any longer, and that the administration should immediately send a fully accredited ambassador to Skopje. He said that if the Bosnian war were to spill over into Macedonia there would be a broader Balkan war that would inevitably entangle the United States. If there was war in Macedonia, Bulgaria, Serbia, Albania and Greece were likely to become involved. The only way to prevent that was by encouraging NATO to redefine its mission to encompass the maintenance of peace and stability in Europe, and "to tell those who are tempted by adventures in Macedonia, that, if they do that, they will face all the force and fierceness of the Alliance."[207]

Baker repeated his argument in the *Washington Times* a few months later, calling the Clinton administration policy confused and inconsistent and accusing the president of failure to stand up to pressure from the Greek-American community in the United States. As before, he urged a central role for NATO in ensuring peace in the region, and he pointed out that NATO advisers were warning that Greece must be forced to lift the embargo.[208]

The Washington Times of May 12, 1995, agreed with much of what Baker had proposed, saying Macedonia was a "time bomb." The paper agreed that Macedonia's geographic position and the presence of a large Albanian minority placed it in a critical position to determine whether peace could be maintained in this part of the Balkans. Noting that at that time the most serious threat to stability came not from the Serbs but from Greece's aggressive policies towards Macedonia, the paper urged the government to stand up against the Greek-American community; to condemn the Greek blockade, which was destabilizing a "friendly and democratic country"; and to open formal diplomatic relations with Macedonia.

American concern for the stability of Macedonia was shown in the presence of American troops as part of the international peacekeeping force. A letter from President Clinton to the speaker of the House of Representatives, dated January 10, 1994, explained something of the history of American forces in Macedonia, as a part of the larger United Nations contingent. He said that "our U.S. armed forces personnel have served with distinction in Macedonia continuously since their arrival in early July 1993... Upon receiving orientation and training on the mission at UNPROFOR headquarters in Skopje, the U.S. unit began conducting observation and monitoring operations along the northeastern section of the Macedonian border with Serbia. The U.S. contribution has thus enhanced UNPROFOR's coverage and effectiveness in preventing a spillover of the conflict, and has underscored the U.S. commitment to the achievement of important multilateral goals in the region." He was able to report that United States forces assigned to UNPROFOR Macedonia had encountered no hostilities, and there had been no United States casualties since the deployment began. The original U.S. troops were redeployed and replaced in December 1993. The president continued:

> The approximately 300-person replacement unit — Task Force 1-6, from 1st Battalion, 6th Infantry Regiment, 3d Infantry Division (Mechanized), Vilseck, Germany — assumed the mission on January 6, 1994. The U.S. contribution to the UNPROFOR Macedonia peacekeeping mission is but one part of a much larger, continuing commitment towards resolution of the extremely difficult situation in the former Yugoslavia. I am not able to indicate at this time how long our deployment to Macedonia will be necessary. I have continued the deployment of U.S. Armed Forces for these purposes in accordance with section 7 of the United Nations Participation Act and pursuant to my constitutional authority as Commander in Chief and Chief Executive.

A few days later, a delegation of United States congressmen, led by Republican congressman John Murtha, met with President Gligorov's cabinet. Murtha said, "I was the person that made the recommendation to President Clinton to deploy U.S. forces to Macedonia, and it is working very well. The reaction that I have from the President Kiro Gligorov and from the UNPROFOR Commander is that there has been good reception of the U.S. forces and that they are doing a good job in Macedonia. The tension at the border between Serbia and Macedonia has been lessened because of the presence of the U.S. forces." Murtha added that he was impressed with President Gligorov and the dialogue in Macedonia between people of different ethnicity. "This should be an example of how people get along and do well."[209]

Similarly, United States secretary of state Warren Christopher said to the Congress that the United States considered Macedonia with respect. "As you know, it was recognized by the U.S.A. recently. We have still not established diplomatic relations, however, that process is underway. Again, we emphasized that we favor the maintenance of the territorial integrity of this country. We have 300 soldiers over there and at the moment we want all countries in the region to be concerned about Macedonia. I believe that its future is important for the U.S.A. We are telling the Serbs that if they influence Macedonia's independence in any way, that will create a strong response from the U.S.A."[210]

When the Greek embargo was applied to Macedonia, the United States immediately tried to convince the Greek government to lift it, as it aggravated the already serious situation in the region, as the official spokesman of the State Department, Christine Shelly, stated at a regular briefing in Washington early in March 1994.[211] Jim Bright, former member of the CSCE Mission in Macedonia, was appointed military representative of the United States Liaison Office in Skopje in April 1994.[212] Soon after this, President Clinton said, "The entire (Balkan) region is a powder keg, which is why we are paying so much attention to it, and are attempting within the UN and NATO to confine the conflict."[213]

Some sign that Americans were willing to match rhetoric with action was indicated in decisions of the congressional Subcommittee for Military and Financial Issues, which preconditioned the year's military aid for Greece with lifting of its embargo against Macedonia. The Athens news agency reported that this decision was brought about under pressure from the Turkish lobby in the Congress.[214]

As part of his European tour, United States defense secretary William Perry made a one-day visit to Macedonia in July 1994. Addressing the troops deployed in Macedonia as part of UNPROFOR, he said that their presence in Macedonia was of both American and international interest, and that their task was to preserve peace in Macedonia. Perry and his Macedonian counterpart, Popovski, also announced a defense cooperation agreement which would allow Macedonia to receive excess United States military equipment and send some of its officers for training in the states. Perry said, "We believe Macedonia is the key to stability in the region, and peace and stability in the Balkans are the key factor for stability in the entire world."[215]

According to the Greek media, Washington was insisting on the quick settlement of misunderstandings between Skopje and Athens in the summer of 1994. The United States was seen to be distancing itself from Athens' problems with its neighbors, according to *Elefteros tipos.* Washington was said to have warned Athens that the "well is drying up" in relation to help for solving these problems. As Greece was not threatened by Macedonia militarily or economically, "being stronger," Greece could settle the question through dialogue, thus avoiding the demise of the moderate president Kiro Gligorov and an increase in Turkish influence in Macedonia.[216]

Upon returning from his visits to the United States and Germany, soon after this, President Gligorov stated at the Skopje airport: "The meeting with the U.S. vice-president Al Gore assured me that their interest for preserving the stability, sovereignty and peace in Macedonia continues. Macedonian-U.S. relations, practically functioning at all levels, will continue to develop in the future. This will be manifested by a larger U.S. support for Macedonia at international financial institutions, along with specific economic aid."[217] A few weeks later, American president Bill Clinton sent greetings to Gligorov on the occasion of the celebration of Macedonia's Independence day, in a letter of congratulations and recognition for Gligorov's "historic role in leading your country toward full integration into the international community of nations."[218]

President Clinton's special adviser, Alexander Verrsbou, who was also director for European issues at the American National Security Council, said Greece's disputes with its neighbors prevented it from being a factor for stability in the Balkans. He said the United States insisted on Greece being open and tactful towards its neighbors. In Verrsbou's view, a significant and urgent measure by Greece would have been to lift its embargo against Macedonia. "We hope Greece will realize the wisdom in having the Former Yugoslav Republic of Macedonia admitted into the Partnership for Peace program as soon as possible, as a guarantee it will adopt a responsible security policy," he added.[219]

American officials formally asked Greek government representatives to partially lift the embargo on Macedonia as a gesture of good will before the elections in Macedonia, scheduled for October 16. The Greek press believed that Washington's intention was to strengthen the position of Gligorov before the elections.[220] The United States Ambassador to the United Nations, Madeleine Albright, stated in New York following her meeting with Macedonian foreign minister Stevo Crvenkovski that "the contribution of the Macedonian Government and President Gligorov in keeping the peace and stability in this part of the continent is enormous." According to the United States assessment, Macedonia was very important for stabilizing the situation on the Balkans.[221]

American sources gave an evaluation of the role of United States troops in Macedonia in October 1994.[222] At that time, as part of a United Nations mission, the United States had 525 troops deployed along the eastern half of the border between Serbia and Macedonia. The Nordic Battalion patrolled the western half. Relations between United States and United Nations commanders were generally smooth except for American reluctance to place troops between Serb and Macedonian forces in some areas. Procedures for evacuating United States troops in the event of a large attack were constantly exercised. The United States commanders were said to consider that there were sufficient numbers of troops and adequate armaments to carry out their task. It had been concluded that the greatest risk to American forces came from possible border conflict with poorly trained Serb forces.

The United States gave Macedonia humanitarian as well as military aid. For instance in October 1994, the Head of the United States Liaison Office in Macedonia, Victor Comras, formally handed over a humanitarian medical package, provided by the United States Development Agency, at the Skopje army barracks. Comras emphasized the importance of this help, estimated at around U.S. $500 million, in the contest of the Greek embargo, which was preventing the continued supply of medical materials.[223]

The White House issued a statement from President Clinton on October 25, 1994, regarding the results of the presidential elections in Macedonia. He congratulated Gligorov on his victory and stated that he had "instructed ... special envoy Matthew Nimetz to double his efforts during the coming few weeks, in order to help Athens and Skopje, assisted by UN mediator Vance, to overcome their differences.[224]

Relations between the United States and Macedonia in the sphere of military defense moved faster and further than diplomacy, as shown by the high level of the meetings and the importance of the arrangements concluded between the two ministries of defense. In November 1994, the United States' intentions were formalized by the Memorandum for Military Cooperation. The memorandum symbolically laid foundations for a long-term, continuous, diverse cooperation that was to be further strengthened by new defense treaties. The memorandum was said to include training of Macedonian officers in the United States and at NATO educational centers in order to facilitate the transformation of the Macedonian army and adapt it to NATO, sending mobile American training teams to Macedonia and providing communications equipment. It has been suggested that Macedonia is a unique example of a country that is being helped to build a complete NATO-compatible military structure, having previously had no equipment at all. Thus the embargo against providing arms to Balkan states did not seem to be such a serious obstacle to the initial efforts of the United States to equip the Macedonian army and enable it to defend the country. According to Macedonian commentators, the most important features of the memorandum for military cooperation were that it imposed no limits and that its assistance in transforming the Macedonian army to match Western European standards led Macedonia through the back door right into NATO's security system, despite the veto and blockade imposed by Greece.[225]

The previous head of the CSCE Mission in Macedonia, American Norman Anderson, speaking about the security of Macedonia early in December 1994, said that it would take a lot of time, effort and money for Macedonia to build up a truly defensive army. He said he was not convinced that this was a realistic goal, and that it would be wiser for Macedonia instead to depend on the support of the United Nations and of the international community, which would guarantee its security.[226] A few days later, in a speech to the Macedonian-American friendship society explaining United States policy in the Balkan regions and toward Macedonia, Victor Comras, chief of mission of the United States Liaison Office in Skopje, stressed the importance of good relations between Serbia and Macedonia, saying that the United States could not foresee its own normalization with Serbia until such relations were achieved. He also urged both Greece and Macedonia to work diligently with mediator Cyrus Vance until their relationship was "mutually beneficial." Comras reminded his audience that Macedonia's economy had suffered "tremendous shocks," including the move from a controlled economy to a free market; the United Nations sanctions against Serbia; the reduction of business activity in neighboring countries emerging from Communist rule; and the Greek embargo. While urging Macedonia to continue its own progress toward economic reform, Comras listed United States efforts to help in the process:

We have devoted over 30 million dollars in favorable loans and grants to support the Macedonian economy since 1992. This has included direct financial
assistance and a full range of USAID programs amounting to more than 20
million dollars in the last two years. The USAID program for 1995 is expected
to provide an additional 13 million dollars. Our assistance has focused on
helping to establish the basic financial and economic systems critical to a market economy. This has included advice and assistance on macro economic
policy, the national budget, banking and taxation. We have also assisted the
agencies responsible for the privatization of social enterprises, and training
of Macedonian entrepreneurs in business management. Particular attention
has been paid to the Macedonian agricultural sector. Several of our programs
help Macedonian farmers increase their yields, gain access to new markets, and
improve the efficiency of their packaging and processing systems. This fall we
provided Macedonia with a special 7.5 million loan on very advantageous
terms to permit the acquisition of needed agricultural commodities. We envis-
age a similar loan earlier next year.[227]

On December 23, President Clinton addressed the Senate, stating that the
United Nations force in the Former Yugoslav Republic of Macedonia was successfully deterring the expansion of the conflict on the Balkans without any loss
of life among American forces.[228] In the middle of February 1995, a congress
was held in Salonika dealing with economic cooperation in the Balkans. At this
conference, new American-British pressure was exerted on Greece to lift the
embargo against the Republic of Macedonia. United States ambassador Thomas
Niles and British ambassador Oliver Miles warned that the Greek embargo
against Macedonia, as well as the crisis in the relations with Albania and Turkey,
presented obstacles to the investment activities of their countries in Greece
and therefore should be resolved as soon as possible.[229]

By early 1995, the newly elected Republicans in the United States were
saying they would support the idea to open an American embassy in Macedonia to help stabilize the situation in the Balkans.[230] Washington was indicating
that the establishment of full diplomatic ties between Macedonia and the United
States no longer depended on the outcome of Greek-Macedonian negotiations,
but on dealing with internal problems in Macedonia, such as improving the
democratic process and providing conditions for the Pedagogical Academy to
start courses in the Albanian language.[231] Construction began on a United States
embassy building in Macedonia. This was formally announced in June by Victor Comras.[232] Meanwhile, Macedonian A1 Television said Macedonia and the
United States were to establish diplomatic ties in September 1995, with the ele-
vation of the U.S. Liaison Office in Skopje to a consulate.

In May 1995, after a meeting between the new Macedonian defense minister, Blagoj Handziski, and William Perry, Perry continued to emphasize the
importance of Macedonia as a security interest in the Balkans and repeated the
United States desire for "close working and military relations with the
region."[233] A few weeks later, State Department spokesman Nicholas Barns
spoke to the press regarding the United States presence in Macedonia: "As you

know, at this moment, there are approximately 540-550 U.S. soldiers in the former Yugoslav Republic of Macedonia... The mission of our troops is to observe and inform about incidents along the northern border of the former Yugoslav Republic of Macedonia with Serbia... The presence of U.S. troops is intended to be a stabilizing factor and a warning against Serbian adventuring in this region. There is no reason to change or alter the UN mission. We will certainly keep our troops in Macedonia. We are doing so with the support of the Congress."[234]

At the end of May, Joseph Creusel, assistant secretary of defense of the United States, told the Macedonian independent weekly *Puls* that the recent United States visit of defense minister Handziski had been successful. "This was the first ever official visit of a representative of the Macedonian Government to the United States ... a way to underline the importance of our relations with the Government of Macedonia and to point out just how essential security in Macedonia is, not only for your country but for the entire Balkan region as well."[235] In June, United States assistant secretary of state Richard Holbrooke, visiting Macedonia as part of his Balkan tour, again stressed his country's readiness to "support Macedonia economically and technically" and reiterated America's desire to prevent the spread of conflict in the Balkans, "which is why we have troops in the former Yugoslav Republic of Macedonia."[236]

The presence of United Nations troops in Macedonia may have had some value in reducing the likelihood of a Serbian invasion. However, given Serbia's record in recent times, it seems unlikely that the troops would be a deterrent if the Serbs firmly decided that taking Macedonia was in their best interests. While Macedonians and Bulgarians seem to believe that the United States will come to their aid if the Serbians move against them, the United States has shown such a reluctance to get its troops directly involved elsewhere in the Balkans, and has been so heavily influenced by the domestic Greek-American lobby, that this does not seem very likely. America would prefer to try and strengthen Macedonia now, before any conflict, so that she can offer enough resistance to deter an invader, or even an Albanian secession movement.

Assassination Attempt

On October 3, 1995, an attempt was made to assassinate the president of Macedonia. An explosive device was placed in a car and activated by remote control as his vehicle passed by. Gligorov had disobeyed instructions from his security advisers to sit in the back seat and was sitting alongside his chauffeur. His driver took the full force of the blast, apparently shielding Gligorov, who suffered serious injury but survived. Immediately after the assassination attempt, Gligorov was taken to the city hospital in Skopje. He had suffered injury to one eye and had some pieces of metal lodged close to his brain stem.

Surgical teams were flown in to Macedonia from Greece, the United Kingdom, France, the Former Yugoslav Republics and Slovenia, though a Macedonian team seems to have done the required work, with the help of some imported high-tech equipment.

The explosive, a commonly available industrial material, had been placed in a Citroen Ami, with sandbags placed in such a way as to direct the blast in the appropriate direction. The car seems to have been chosen deliberately as the kind of vehicle most likely to fly apart in an explosion, thus creating shrapnel that could create the maximum damage.

There was much speculation about the perpetrators of the attack, and police experienced in terrorism investigations came to Macedonia from Britain, the United States, Greece and Germany. All sorts of groups were suspected of the outrage, including Bulgarian extremists, Macedonian nationalists opposed to the accord with Greece, and criminals hurt by Gligorov's crack-down on crime. The Bulgarian interior minister, Ljubomir Nacev, apparently picked up some gossip from Macedonians traveling through his country and claimed knowledge of the identity of the attackers. This appearance of inside knowledge did not make Bulgaria look good, but the comments were so clumsy that they were seen almost as clearing Bulgaria of involvement. The Bulgarians saw the possibility of a Serbian plot.[237]

On the day of the attack, the speaker of Parliament, Stojan Andov, said, "Today, a most devious attempt on the life of the President of the Republic of Macedonia Kiro Gligorov was made. As you have already been informed, the necessary surgical steps have already been taken and at this time, the President is not in a critical condition. The assassination attempt on the President of the Republic of Macedonia is a terrorist act with calculated political aims to destabilize the Republic of Macedonia." He said all efforts would be made to track down those responsible and appealed for calm.[238]

All Macedonian political parties reacted with horror to the attack, seeing it as a deliberate attempt to destabilize the country. VMRO-DPMNE called off a planned demonstration against the accord with Greece because of this event. International commentators seemed to expect that Macedonia would fall into ferment. Some feared that without Gligorov's gifted leadership, Macedonia would be diverted from its path to democratization and a free enterprise economy, or perhaps would sink into civil war. However, the Macedonian Parliament followed constitutional requirements and elected Andov as the interim president the day after the attack. The senior American diplomat in Macedonia, Victor Comras, said that Andov was "pro–American and pro–Western" and that he was committed to a market economy. Macedonian commentators were irritated by the pessimism of outside observers, and noted the determination of Macedonians to follow their chosen path to a Western-style democracy. They were not surprised at all at the continuing stability of the country.

Concern about the attack on Gligorov was expressed by a variety of foreign leaders, including those from the United States and Greece. In Athens, where news of the assassination attempt briefly interrupted the first official contacts between the two countries, the government expressed its relief that the attempt had failed and wished Gligorov a speedy recovery.[239] The attempted assassination was immediately condemned by Prime Minister Andreas Papandreou and opposition leaders. A C-130 military transport plane left Thessaloniki for Skopje early the same evening carrying a team of specialists and surgical equipment to assist doctors treating Gligorov. In his message to Gligorov, Papandreou expressed his view "that acts of terrorism should not obstruct the continuation of efforts for the strengthening of stability in our region."

At the end of October, the interior minister of the Republic of Macedonia, Ljubomir Frckovski, announced at a news conference that he had offered his written resignation to Prime Minister Branko Crvenkovski as a result of the assassination attempt on President Gligorov. He also suggested knowledge of those responsible. He said the attack was organized by a well-known multinational corporation based in a neighboring country, and that a representative of the suspected corporation had arrived in Skopje on September 28 and prepared the explosive in a building in the outskirts of the city. He was helped by perpetrators from Macedonia, described as "fanatics, criminals and the political underground of the country." According to the minister, the motivation of the assassins was to eliminate the president and to create a so-called controlled instability. Weakening political and economic sovereignty would then leave room for the conspirators to make their own impact. The next step of the "inspirers" would be to remove the existing government and replace it with another. Frckovski said the conspirators would fail in their plans.[240]

Analysts at the Macedonian newspaper *Puls* noted that the assassins planned to ruin the president's policy of "equidistance" in Macedonia's relations with other countries, which narrows down the field of conspirators to those who might desire such an outcome.[241] It was noted that the intention of the assassins was to change the political orientation of the state from political and economic independence (not oriented to local alliances, pro–Western), and turn it to pro–Eastern sympathies. Thus the commentator asked whether Gligorov was going too fast toward the West, toward new Europe and the United States, rather than toward the traditional ally, Russia. Macedonia did not offend Russia's pride directly, but it refused Russia's offer to send soldiers under United Nations auspices to mediate in the Macedonian-Greek negotiations, and made a defense agreement with the United States. The newspaper claimed it was obvious that the conspirators were "among those who are turned toward the east, those who are politically defeated in Russia itself and the other former East-European Communist countries." The Macedonian police, were cooperating with twelve intelligence services but excluded Serbian, Bulgarian and Russian police from the list of those giving (or being asked for) such aid. Since two of those intelligence services were from neighboring countries, maybe that was the reason the Ministry had not received any information about the responsible multinational group with its base in a neighboring country. The Macedonian commentator noted that these kinds of corporations are formed by former intelligence services and have the capacity to take such actions. There are tens of thousands of former intelligence operatives from former Communist countries looking for "business" throughout Europe. *Puls* noted that the chief of Securitate in Romania, though sentenced to twelve years in prison, has been released, and that Securitate had more than 15,000 spies. Similarly, the Bulgarian chief of the former intelligence service spent only ten months in prison for destroying certain documents and was now acting in a senior position in the private economic conglomerate "Multigroup." There had been many affairs in the Czech Republic in connection with the former members of the STB. Many officials of the Hungarian Intelligence Service were forced to withdraw after the elections in 1990. Polish former spies are now businessmen. The former Albanian minister of internal affairs had been sentenced to five years' imprisonment but had already been released. Thus it is easy to find an organizer who might use citizens of Macedonia to assist him in an assassination attempt. *Puls* suggested that if Macedonia is moving to defend its independence through Western systems of defense and security, then this attack was aimed to prevent it. If Macedonia joins NATO, it clearly means that the former focus of Yugoslavia towards both Eastern and Western spheres of influence has been readjusted. Macedonia obviously has made such a decision. The Russian daily *Nezavisimaya Gazeta'* says that the Russian army is ready to direct nuclear projectiles toward the Czech Republic and Poland if they join NATO. *Puls* asked why the West remains silent on this issue since it is unlikely that the Western intelligence services had no idea about the attempt if it was organized by such interests. In Sofia the Socialist daily *Duma* cited BBC claims that the attack was carried out by the KGB and Russian Mafia.

In any case, Macedonia remained stable and peaceful after the assassination attempt. Gligorov recovered sufficiently to be able to return to his normal duties. There were signs that with modest support from the international community, Macedonia might well survive and prosper.

Notes

Introduction

1. *Canberra Times,* Thursday, March 12, 1992, p. 9.

Chapter 1

1. Traian Stoijanovich, "Macedonia," *Colliers Encyclopaedia,* p. 154.
2. E. Badian, "Greeks and Macedonians," in *Macedonia and Greek in Late Classical and Early Hellenic Times,* Studies in the History of Art, vol. 10 (Washington, DC: National Gallery of Art).
3. "Macedonia."
4. *The Canberra Times,* Thursday, March 12, 1992, p. 9.
5. R.A. Crossland, "Linguistic Problems of the Balkan Area in Late Prehistoric and Early Classical Periods," in *The Cambridge Ancient History,* 2d ed., vol. 3, pt. 1, ed. by John Boardman, I.E.S. Edwards, N.G.L. Hammond, and E. Sollberger (Cambridge: Cambridge University Press, 1982).
6. Badian, "Greeks and Macedonians," p. 847.
7. Martin Bernal, *Black Athena: The Afroasiatic Roots of Classical Civilization* (London: Free Association, 1987).
8. Arnold Toynbee, *Some Problems of Greek History* (London: Oxford University Press, 1969).
9. Bernal, *Black Athena.*
10. Personal communication.
11. Toynbee, *Some Problems of Greek History,* p. 57.
12. Slavko Mangovski, electronic communication, MakNews List.
13. Crossland, "Linguistic Problems."
14. Pierre Jouguet, *Alexander the Great and the Hellenistic World* (Ares, 1985).
15. Demosthenes Crationes, from *A History of Diplomacy,* vol. 5 (Diodor Sikelioi, Biblioteka Historica), p. 49.
16. Peter Green, *Alexander of Macedon* (Weidenfeld and Nicholson, 1972), p. 84.
17. E. Badian, "Greeks and Macedonians."
18. In the Third Olynthiac, 3.24.
19. Badian, "Greeks and Macedonians."
20. Fear, personal communication.
21. Peter Berresford Ellis, *The Celtic Empire* (London: Constable, 1992).
22. Jouguet, *Alexander the Great,* p. 5.

23. Demosthenes Crationes, from *A History of Diplomacy*, vol. 5, p. 53.

24. Green, *Alexander of Macedon*, p. 7.

25. David G. Hogarth, *Philip and Alexander of Macedon* (London: John Murray, 1897).

26. *The New Illustrated History of the World, the Triumph of the Greeks 800 B.C.–321 B.C.,* ed. by Esmond Wright (New York: Hamlyn, 1970), p. 98.

27. In "Successors of Alexander the Great" (Ares, 1985), p. 47.

28. *New Illustrated History*, p. 399.

29. Michael Dimitri, *Macedonian Canadian News*, June 1993.

Chapter 2

1. John Geipel, *The Europeans: An Ethnohistorical Survey* (London and Harlow: Longmans, Green, 1969), pp. 62–70.

2. Traian Stoijanovich, "Macedonia," *Collier's Encyclopaedia*, p. 157.

3. Jacques Bacic, electronic communication, MakList.

4. N.G.L. Hammond, "Migration and Assimilation in Greece," chap. 4 in *Greece Old and New*, ed. by Tom Winnifrith and Penelope Murray (London: Macmillan, 1983), p. 44.

5. Bacic, electronic communication, MakList.

6. N.G.L. Hammond, "Illyris, Epirus and Macedonia in the Early Iron Age," in *The Cambridge Ancient History* (Second Edition) Vol. III Part 1. Edited by John Boardman, I.E.S. Edwards, N.G.L. Hammond, and E. Sollberger. Cambridge University Press, Cambridge, 1982), pp. 649–655.

7. Bacic, electronic communication.

8. N.G.L. Hammond, "Illyris, Epirus and Macedonia."

9. Tom Winnifrith. "Greeks and Romans" in *Greece Old and New*, edited by Tom Winnifrith and Penelope Murray (The Macmillan Press, London, 1983).

10. Geipel, *The Europeans*, pp. 62–70.

11. Stoijanovich, "Macedonia," p. 157.

12. David G. Hogarth, *Philip and Alexander of Macedon* (London: John Murray, 1897), p. 12.

13. F.W. Wallbank, *Philip V of Macedon* (Archon, 1940; reprinted, Cambridge University Press, 1967), pp. 2–7.

14. Winnifrith, "Greeks and Romans," pp. 65–75.

15. Winnifrith, "Greeks and Romans," pp. 71–73.

16. Peter Green, *Alexander of Macedon* (Weidenfeld & Nicholson, 1972).

17. Hogarth, *Philip and Alexander*, pp. 4–10.

18. Arnold Toynbee, *Some Problems of Greek History*, pt. 2 (London: Oxford University Press, 1969), pp 94–103.

19. Polybius 23.10.

20. Bacic, electronic communication.

21. R.A. Crossland, "Linguistic Problems of the Balkan Area in Late Prehistoric and Early Classical Periods," in *The Cambridge Ancient History*, 2d ed., vol. 3, pt. 1, ed. by John Boardman, I.E.S. Edwards, N.G.L. Hammond, and E. Sollberger (Cambridge: Cambridge University Press, 1982), p. 840.

22. Peter Berresford Ellis, *The Celtic Empire* (London: Constable, 1992), p. 73.

23. Ellis, *The Celtic Empire*.

24. Winnifrith, "Greeks and Romans," pp. 78–84.

25. Winnifrith, "Greeks and Romans," pp. 85–87.

26. Stoijanovich, "Macedonia."

27. Stepjan Antoljak, *Samoil's State* (Skopje: 1969), pp. 78–80.

28. C. Porphygenitus, *De thematibus* (Citta del Vaticano: 1952).

29. Geipel, *The Europeans,* p. 43.

30. Anastasius Bibliothecarius, *Chronographia Tripertita*, p. 282, 20–21. This matter is described similarly in the *Chronographia of Theophanes the Confessor*, I, p. 430, 21–22.

31. Dimitrija Chupovski, "Macedonia and the Macedonians," *Makedonskij Golos*, 1913.

32. Chupovski, "Macedonia and the Macedonians."

33. H. Gregoire, "The Amorians and Macedonians, 842–1025," in *The Cambridge Medieval History*, vol. 4, pt. 1, ed. by J. M. Hussey (Cambridge: Cambridge University Press, 1966), p. 116.

34. A. A. Vasiliev, *History of the Byzantine Empire 324–1454* (Madison: University of Wisconsin Press, 1952), p. 301.

35. Bacic, electronic communication.

36. Stoijanovich, "Macedonia."

37. Stoijanovich, "Macedonia," p. 158.

38. Clement, *Vita* (XX, 62), *Kirilo-Metodievska enciklopedija*, vol. 1, p. 656.

39. Stoijanovich, "Macedonia."

40. Stoijanovich, "Macedonia."

41. D. Anastasijevic, "A Hypothesis of Western Bulgaria," *Bulletin de la Societe Scientifique de Skoplje* 3, (1927), pp. 1–12; in French, Melanges Uspensky. Also J. Ivanov, "The Origin of the Family of the Tsar Samuel," volume in honor of V.N. Zlatarsky, 55.

42. D. Obolensky, *The Byzantine Empire and Its Northern Neighbors,* p. 517.

43. *Macedonian*, Feb. 15, 1992, pp. 20–21.

44. John Cametinae, *On the Capture of Salonika* (Sofia 1976: J. K. Begunov, Kozma Prezviter v slavjanskih literaturah), p. 297.

45. G. H. Pertz, Annales Barenses, Monumenta Germaniae historica, Scriptores V, p. 53.

46. Vizantiiski Vremenik, Moscow VI 1953, p. 367.

47. Ephraimi, Chronologici caesares; Ed. J.P. Migne — PG 143, Paris 1891, p. 198.

48. J. Pitra. Analacta sacra et classica specilegio Solesmensi parta, t. VI Juris ecclesiastici graecorum selecta paralipomena. Parissis et Romae 1891, col. 315.

49. Georgii Acropolitae Opera, Recensuit A. Haisenberg vol. I, Lipsiae 1903, pp. 74–75, 77.

50. Bertrand de la Brocuiere, Putovanje preko mora, Beograd 1950, pp. 134–135, 140–141. III.

51. Jovan Radonic, Gjurac Kastriot Skenderbeg and Arbanija u XV veku — Spomenik XCV (1942), pp. 128–129.

52. Gio Mario degli Angiolelo, A. Matkovski and P. Angelkova, Nekolku kratki patopisi za Makedonija, Glasnik na INI, VXI/1 (1972), pp. 246–247.

53. Issued in Vienna, April 26th, 1690. Representatives: defenders of the Macedonian people…. J. Radonic, Prilozi za istoriju Srba u Ungarskoj u XVI, XVII and XVIII veku. Knj. I, Matice srpske, 25 and 26, Novi Sad 1908, pp. 52–53.

54. Felix de Beaujour, *Voyage militaire dans l'Empire Othoman*, vol. 1 (Paris: 1829), pp. 127–128, n. 1; p. 130, 132.

55. Geipel, "The Europeans."

Chapter 3

1. Tom Winnifrith, "Greeks and Romans," in *Greece Old and New*, ed. by Tom Winnifrith and Penelope Murray (London: Macmillan, 1983), p. 71.

2. Robert Collins, *The Medes and Persians* (New York: McGraw-Hill, 1972), pp. 155–156.

3. Henri Berr, Foreword, in *Alexander the Great and the Hellenistic World* by Pierre Jouguet (Ares, 1985), p. xi.

4. London: Rex Collings, 1975, p. 52.

5. Pierre Jouguet, *Alexander the Great and the Hellenistic World* (Ares, 1985), p. 68.

6. R. A. Crossland, "Linguistic Problems of the Balkan Area in Late Prehistoric and Early Classical Periods," in *The Cambridge Ancient History*, 2d ed., vol. 3, pt. 1, ed. by John Boardman, I.E.S. Edwards, N.G.L. Hammond, and E. Sollberger (Cambridge: Cambridge University Press, 1982).

7. Traian Stoijanovich, "Macedonia," *Collier's Encyclopaedia*.

8. Peter Green, *Alexander of Macedon* (Weidenfeld & Nicholson, 1972), pp. 8–9.

9. E. Badian, "Greeks and Macedonians," in *Macedonia and Greece in Late Classical and Early Hellenic Times*, Studies in the History of Art, vol. 10 (Washington DC: National Gallery of Art).

10. Andy Fear, personal communication.

11. Badian, "Greeks and Macedonians."

12. Fear, personal communication.

13. Badian, "Greeks and Macedonians."

14. Green, *Alexander of Macedon*, p. 7.

15. Jouguet, *Alexander the Great*, p. 68.

16. Jouguet, *Alexander the Great*, p. 70.

17. Badian, "Greeks and Macedonians."

18. Herodotus, 5.72.

19. Badian, "Greeks and Macedonians."

20. Badian, "Greeks and Macedonians."

21. Badian, "Greeks and Macedonians."

22. Badian, "Greeks and Macedonians."

23. Green, *Alexander of Macedon*.

24. Green, *Alexander of Macedon*, pp. 49–50.

25. Badian, "Greeks and Macedonians."

26. David G. Hogarth, *Philip and Alexander of Macedon* (London, John Murray, 1897), p. 9.

27. Green, *Alexander of Macedon*, p. 83.

28. Jouguet, *Alexander the Great*, p. 87.

29. Jouguet, *Alexander the Great*, pp. 85, 86.

30. Badian, "Greeks and Macedonians."

31. Jouguet, *Alexander the Great*, pp. 20, 70.

32. Hogarth, *Philp and Alexander*, p. 177.

33. Jouguet, *Alexander the Great*, p. 7.

34. *Alexander of Macedon* (London: Robert Hale, 1946), p. 18.

35. Thomas W. Africa, "Alexander the Great," *The World Book Encyclopaedia* (Chicago: World Book, 1984), p. 326.

36. Jouguet, *Alexander the Great*, p. 15.

37. Jouguet, *Alexander the Great*, p. 20.

38. Jouguet, *Alexander the Great*, p. 70.

39. "Alexander the Great," p. 327.
40. Badian, "Greeks and Macedonians."
41. Badian, "Greeks and Macedonians."
42. *The New Illustrated History of the World, the Triumph of the Greeks 800 B.C.–321 B.C.*, ed. by Esmond Wright (New York: Hamlyn, 1970), p. 98.
43. *Voice of the Macedonians*, issue 63, p. 14.
44. Badian, "Greeks and Macedonians."
45. Badian, "Greeks and Macedonians."
46. Hogarth, *Philip and Alexander*, p. 50.
47. Henri Berr, Foreword, in *Alexander the Great* by Jouguet, p. xiv.
48. Badian, "Greeks and Macedonians."
49. Africa, "Alexander the Great," p. 327.
50. *The New Illustrated History of the World.*
51. Hogarth, *Philip and Alexander*, p. 157.

Chapter 4

1. *Macedonia and Its Relations with Greece* (Council for Research into South-Eastern Europe of the Macedonian Academy of Sciences and Arts, 1993), p. 14.
2. Carl Darling Buck, "Language and the Sentiment of Nationality," *The American Political Science Review* 10 (1916), pp. 44–69.
3. Anthony D. Smith, *National Identity* (London: Penguin, 1991), p. 29.
4. Simon McIlwaine, "The Strange Case of the Invisible Minorities — Institutional Racism in the Greek State" (International Society for Human Rights, British Section, Dec. 1993).
5. M.B. Sakellariou, *Macedonia, 4000 years of Greek History*, p. 23.
6. Georgieve, V. I., "The Arrival of the Greeks in Greece: The Linguistic Evidence," in R. A. Crossland and C. Birchall, *Bronze Age Migrations in the Aegean: Archaelogical and Linguistic Problems of Greek Prehistory* (London: Duckworth), pp. 243–254.
7. Martin Bernal, *Black Athena: The Afroasiatic Roots of Classical Civilization*, vol. 1 (London: Free Association, 1987), p. 14.
8. Bernal, *Black Athena*, pp. 10–11.
9. Bernal, *Black Athena*, p. 120.
10. Cited in Bernal, *Black Athena*, p. 79.
11. Bernal, *Black Athena*, p. 83.
12. Tiberius Claudius, in *Claudius the God*, by Robert Graves.
13. Bernal, *Black Athena*, p. 21.
14. Bernal, *Black Athena*, p. 2.
15. Bernal, *Black Athena*, p. 2.
16. Bernal, *Black Athena*, p. 189.
17. Bernal, *Black Athena*, p. 29.
18. Bernal, *Black Athena*, p. 2.
19. Bernal, *Black Athena*, p. 441.
20. Bernal, *Black Athena*, p. 47.
21. Bernal, *Black Athena*, p. 21.
22. Bernal, *Black Athena*, p. 59.
23. Bernal, *Black Athena*, p. 49–50.
24. Bernal, *Black Athena*, p. 23.
25. Bernal, *Black Athena*, p. 72.

26. Bernal, *Black Athena*, pp. 19, 50–54.

27. Bernal, *Black Athena*, p. 400.

28. *The Oxford History of the Classical World* (London: Oxford University Press, 1986).

29. *Oxford History of the Classical World*.

30. Tiberius Claudius, in *I Claudius*.

31. *Studies in Late Byzantine History and Prosopography* (1986).

32. Robert Browning, "The Continuity of Hellenism in the Byzantine World: Appearance or Reality," in *Greece Old and New*, ed. by Tom Winnifrith and Penelope Murray (London: Macmillan, 1983), p. 11.

33. *Byzantium and Byzantinism* (Cincinnati, 1963).

34. Nicholas Cheetham, *Mediaeval Greece*, (New Haven CT: Yale University Press, 1981), p. 13.

35. C. Muller, *Geographi Graeci Minores* (Paris: 1882), p. 574.

36. "Greeks and Romans," in *Greece Old and New,* ed. by Tom Winnifrith and Penelope Murray (London: Macmillan, 1983).

37. Cited in *Macedonia and Its Relations with Greece*, p. 14.

38. Arnold Toynbee, *Some Problems of Greek History* (London: Oxford University Press, 1969), pp 54–55.

39. McIlwaine, "The Strange Case."

40. Editorial, *The Sunday Telegraph*, London, March 27, 1994.

41. "Migration and Assimilation in Greece," Chap. 4 in *Greece Old and New*, ed. by Tom Winnifrith and Penelope Murray (London: Macmillan, 1983).

42. Winnifrith, "Greeks and Romans."

43. John Geipel, *The Europeans: An Ethno-Historical Survey* (London and Harlow: Longmans, Green, 1969).

44. *Greece in the NATO and the EC, and the Relations of Greece with Its Neighbors* (Istanbul: International Affairs Agency, 1993).

45. *The Cyprus Weekly*, March 5, 1992.

46. *The Cyprus Weekly*, April 10, 1992.

47. *Greece in the NATO and the EC.*

48. George Lanitis, *The Cyprus Weekly*, May 1, 1992.

49. *The History of Greece Under Othoman and Venetian Domination* (Edinburgh and London: William Blackwood, 1856).

50. Roger Just, "Triumph of the Ethnos," in *History and Ethnicity*, ed. by Elizabeth Tonkin, Manyon McDonald, and Malcolm Chapman (London and New York: Routledge, 1989), pp. 71–88.

51. Just, "Triumph of the Ethnos," p. 85.

52. Alexander Zaharopoulos, "Greece a Land of Heroes — and Distortions," *Sydney Morning Herald*, March 23, 1994, p. 15.

53. Christos Sideropoulos, *Ena*, March 1992.

54. Amnesty International, Greece: *Violations of the Right to Freedom of Expression* (November 1992).

55. Bernal, *Black Athena*, p. 282.

56. P. B. Shelley, Preface to *Hellas* (London, 1821).

57. Bernal, *Black Athena*, p. 292.

58. Bert Birtles, *Exiles in the Aegean* (1938).

59. Peter Hill, "Levelling the Levendis," *The Age*, Melbourne, April 20, 1994.

60. *Mediaeval Greece*.

61. Isocrates, *Panegyrilos*, 50 (translated by Norlin, p. 149).

62. *Some Problems of Greek History*, p. 61.

63. Eric Hobsbawn, "Fact, Fiction and Historical Revisionism," *New York Review of Books*, reprinted in *The Australian*, December 8, 1993.

Chapter 5

1. Mihailo Apostolski, "Etnickite Promeni Vo Makedonija Vo XX Vek" [Ethnic Changes in Macedonia in the 20th Century], *Istorija* (Yugoslavia) 20, no. 2 (1984), pp. 55–72.

2. Vemund Aarbakke and Angelo Torre, "Ethnic Identity and Irredentist Claims in a Changing Political and Social Setting: Macedonia in the Late 19th and Early 20th Centuries, *Quaderni Storici* (Italy) 28, no. 3 (1993), pp. 719–744.

3. Simon McIlwaine, "The Strange Case of the Invisible Minorities — Institutional Racism in the Greek State" (International Society for Human Rights, British Section, Dec. 1993).

4. Loring M. Danforth, "Competing Claims to Macedonian Identity: The Macedonian Question and the Breakup of Yugoslavia, *Anthropology Today* 9, no. 4 (August 1993), pp. 3–10.

5. Harilaos Trikoupis, *History of the Greek People*, vol. 14 (Athens Publishing), p. 18.

6. Dimitrija Chupovski, "Macedonia and the Macedonians," *Makedonskij Golos*, 1913.

7. Chupovski, "Macedonia and the Macedonians."

8. Chupovski, "Macedonia and the Macedonians."

9. A.W. Gomme, *Greece* (London: Oxford University Press, 1945), p. 43.

10. Interview with Kole Mangov, *Fokus* (Skopje), September 22, 1995.

11. John Reed, *The War in Eastern Europe; 1916.*

12. *The Other Balkan Wars* (The Carnegie Endowment for International Peace; reprinted by the Brookings Institute, Washington, 1994).

13. Stoyan Pribichevich, *Macedonia, Its People and History* (University Park: Pennsylvania State University Press, 1982).

14. John Geipel, *The Europeans: An Ethno-Historical Survey* (London and Harlow: Longmans, Green, 1969), p. 218.

15. Gomme, *Greece*, p. 30.

16. Gomme, *Greece*, pp. 82–86.

17. *Macedonia, History and Politics*, (Athens: George Christopoulos, John Bastias, printed by Ekdotike Athenon S.A. for the Center for Macedonians Abroad and the Society for Macedonian Studies, 1991), p. 42.

18. Macedonian P.E.N. Centre, *The Status of the Macedonian Language in the Aegean Part of Macedonia in Greece* (1986); cited in Slave Nikolovski, "A Document on the Macedonian Language," *Macedonia* no. 402 (1986).

19. *Macedonia, History and Politics*, p. 19.

20. Blazhe Koneski, "Macedonian," *The Slavic Literary Languages*, ed. by A. M. Schenker and E. Stankiewicz (New Haven: 1980), p. 62.

21. *Macedonian Information and Liaison Service (MILS) News*, Skopje, August 3, 1994.

22. Macedonian P.E.N. Centre, *The Status of the Macedonian Language.*

23. Stojan Ristevski, *Sozdavanjeto na sovremeniot makedonski literaturen Jazik* (Skopje; Studentski zbor, 1988), p. 90.

24. Ristevski, *Sozdavanjeto*, p. 96.

25. Peter Hill, "Language Standardization in the South Slavonic Area," *Sociolinguistica* 6 (June 1992), p. 108.

26. Hristo Andonovski, "The First Macedonian Primer Between the Two World Wars—The ABCEDAR," in *The 1986 Almanac for Overseas Macedonians* (Skopje: 1986).

27. Ristevski, *Sozdavanjeto*, pp. 91–95; Peter Hill, "Different Codifications of a Language," in *Slavistische Linguistik*, ed. by Wg. Girke (Munich: 1981), pp. 48–63.

28. Andonovski, "The First Macedonian Primer."

29. Nikolaos Zarifis, "The Minorities in Greece," *Elefteron Vima*, October 19, 1925.

30. Andonovski, "The First Macedonian Primer."

31. Dimitrios Vogazlis, *National and Religious Minorities in Greece and Bulgaria* (1954).

32. The Aegean Macedonian Human Rights Association of Australia, *Submission to the Australian Parliamentary Inquiry into Human Rights* (1994).

33. Hill, "Language Standardization," p. 108; and Mike Karadjis, *Green Left*, Australia, April 1, 1992.

34. Hill, "Language Standardization," p. 108.

35. Aleksandar Apostolov, "Colonization of Vardar Macedonia Between the Two World Wars," in *The 1991 Almanac of Overseas Macedonians* (Skopje).

36. Apostolov, "Colonization of Vardar Macedonia."

37. Hill, "Language Standardization," p. 108.

38. Karadjis, *Green Left*, April 1, 1992.

39. Danforth, "Competing Claims."

40. Traian Stoijanovich, "Macedonia," *Collier's Encyclopaedia*, p. 160.

41. Hill, "Language Standardization," p. 108.

42. *Macedonia, History and Politics*, pp. 23, 24, 26.

43. Karadjis, *Green Left*, April 1, 1992.

44. Karadjis, *Green Left*, April 1, 1992.

45. Horace G. Lunt, "The Creation of Standard Macedonian: Some Facts and Attitudes," *Anthropological Linguistics* 1, no. 5 (June 1959), p. 23.

46. Lunt, "Creation of Standard Macedonian," p. 23.

47. *Makedonija* (Skopje), Dec. 1984, pp. 28–29; Risto Kirjazovski, *Povod* (Sydney), Jan. 1984, pp. 26–27.

48. Interview with General Tempo, *Nova Makedonija*, July 2, 1995; reported in *MILS Special Supplement: Macedonia Is a Reality*, July 3, 1995.

49. Karadjis, *Green Left*, April 1, 1992.

50. *Macedonia, History and Politics*, p. 28.

51. Macedonian P.E.N. Centre, *The Status of the Macedonian Language.*

52. Aegean Macedonian Human Rights Association of Australia, *Submission to the Australian Parliamentary Inquiry into Human Rights* (1993).

53. Evangelos Kofos, *Nationalism and Communism in Macedonia* (Thessaloniki: Institute for Balkan Studies, 1964), p. 186.

54. Karadjis, *Green Left*, April 1, 1992.

55. Hill, "Language Standardization," p. 108.

56. *MILS News*, Skopje, October 25, 1994.

57. *MILS News*, Skopje, April 15, 1994.

58. *MILS News*, Skopje, March 20, 1995.

59. Aegean Macedonian Human Rights Association of Australia, *Submission* (1993).

60. *Macedonian Life* (Thessalonika), no. 231 (March 1991), English supplement, pp. 1,2.

61. *Macedonian Life* (Thessalonika), no. 232 (April 1991), English supplement, p. 1.

62 *The Times*, London, Aug. 22, 1994.

63. *MILS News*, Skopje, Oct. 30, 1994.

64. *MILS News*, Nov. 18, 1994.

65. Macedonian Information Ccenter (MIC), Skopje, November 14, 1994.

66. "We Are Fine Where We Are," *MILS News*, Skopje, October 10, 1994.

67. "Macedonian-Greek Relations in British Media," *MILS News*, Skopje, May 13, 1994.

68. United States Department of State, *Country Reports on Human Rights Practices for 1990*, p. 1172.

69. Danforth, "Competing Claims," and the breakup of Yugoslavia. *Anthropology Today*, Vol 9 No. 4, August, 1993, 3–10.

70. Aegean Macedonian Human Rights Association of Australia, *Submission* (1994).

71. Aegean Macedonian Human Rights Association of Australia, *Submission* (1994).

72. Anastasia Karakasidou, "Politicizing Culture: Negating Ethnic Identity in Greek Macedonia," *Journal of Modern Greek Studies* 11, no. 1 (May 1993).

73. Loring Danforth, *The Age*, Melbourne, March 5, 1994.

74. Leonard Doyle, *The Independent*, May 10, 1994.

75. Leonard Doyle, *The Independent*, May 11, 1994.

76. *The Globe and Mail*, Toronto, Oct. 25, 1993.

77. Robert Fox, "Macedonia: International — Macedonia Fears 'Another Cyprus' in Athens Dispute," *The Daily Telegraph*, London, June 7, 1994.

78. *MILS News*, Skopje, March 1, 1993.

79. Chuck Sudetic, "'Real' Macedonia Issue is Real Estate," Nov. 3, 1994.

80. Danforth, *The Age*, March 5, 1994.

81. Danforth, *The Age*, March 5, 1994.

82. United States Department of State, *Annual Report: Greece* (1994).

83. Lois Whitman, *Denying Ethnic Identity: The Macedonians of Greece*, Report of the United States Chapter of Human Rights Watch/Helsinki (New York: April 21, 1994).

84. Aegean Macedonian Human Rights Association of Australia, *Submission* (1994).

85. *British Helsinki Human Rights Group Report*, Aug. 1994.

86. *British Helsinki Human Rights Group Report*.

87. Whitman, *Denying Ethnic Identity*.

88. United States Department of State, *Annual Report: Greece* (1994).

89. United States Department of State, *Annual Report: Greece* (1994).

90. "Greece Under Attack for Violating Human Rights," *The Guardian*, London, May 12, 1994.

91. United States Department of State *Annual Report: Greece*, Section 2 (1994).

92. *The Times*, London, Aug. 22, 1994.

93. Amnesty International Index: Eur 25/Wu 02/94 10 May 1994.

94. Whitman, *Denying Ethnic Identity: The Macedonians of Greece*.

95. *The Times*, Aug. 22, 1994.

96. United States Department of State, *Annual Report: Greece* (1994).

97. MIC, Skopje, April 4, 1994.

98. Amnesty International Index: Eur 25/Wu 02/94 10 May 1994.

99. Amnesty International Index: Eur 25/Wu 02/94 10 May 1994.

100. "Tsarknias Speaks Out," *The Macedonian Tribune*, May 18, 1995.

101. Nikodimos Tsarknias, handwritten personal letter, Saint Sophias 14, Aridea — Vellis Postcode 58400, May 12, 1994.

102. "Tsarknias Speaks Out."

103. *MILS News*, Skopje, Nov. 25, 1994.

104. *MILS News*, Skopje, Dec. 8, 1994.

105. *MILS News*, Skopje, Dec. 6, 1994.

106. *Nova Makedonija*, quoted by *MILS News*, Skopje, Jan. 27, 1995.

107. "Tsarknias Speaks Out."

108. *MILS News*, Skopje, Feb. 21, 1994.

109. Eve-Ann Prentice, Greece Accused of Slav Rights Abuse," *The Times*, London, Aug. 22, 1994.

110. Prentice, "Greece Accused."

111. Danforth, *The Age*, March 5, 1994.

112. MIC, Skopje, Feb. 16, 1994.

113. Leonard Doyle, "Greece Blocks Ethnic Party," *The Independent*, May 31, 1994.

114. *MILS News*, Skopje, June 1, 1994.

115. MIC, Skopje, June 14, 1994.

116. *MILS News*, Skopje, June 14, 1994.

117. MIC, Skopje, February 7, 1995.

118. MIC, Skopje, Oct. 24, 1994.

119. *MILS News*, Skopje, Oct. 25, 1994.

120. MIC, Skopje, Jan. 16, 1995.

121. *MILS News*, Skopje, Aug. 3, 1994.

122. *MILS News*, Skopje, July 29, 1994.

123. Alexander Zaharopoulos, "Greece a Land of Heroes — and Distortions," *Sydney Morning Herald*, March 23, 1994, p. 15.

124. *MILS News*, Skopje, Oct. 12, 1995.

Chapter 6

1. Evangelos Kofos in *The Boston Globe*, Jan. 5, 1993, p. 9; cited by Loring M. Danforth, "Competing Claims to Macedonian Identity: The Macedonian Question and the Breakup of Yugoslavia," *Anthropology Today* 9, no. 4 (August 1993), pp. 3–10.

2. Danforth, "Competing Claims."

3. Eric Hobshawm and Terence Ranger, eds., *The Invention of Tradition* (Cambridge: Cambridge University Press, 1983); also, Richard Handler and Jocelyn Limekin, "Tradition, Genuine or Spurious," *Journal of American Folklore* 97 (1984), pp. 273–290.

4. Dr. Andrew Rossos, reported in *The Macedonian Tribune*, Feb. 19, 1994.

5. *Macedonia: History*, Microsoft Encarta, 1991.

6. Loring Danforth, "Competing Claims."

7. Michael Radis, *IMRO and the Macedonian Question 1893-1934*.

8. Peter Hill, *The Canberra Times*, April 12, 1992, p. 9.

9. *Macedonia, History and Politics*, (Athens: George Christopoulos, John Bastias, printed by Ekdotike Athenon S.A. for the Center for Macedonians Abroad and the Society for Macedonian Studies, 1991), p. 33.

10. *Macedonia, History and Politics*, p. 33.

11. *Almanac for Macedonians Overseas* (Skopje: 1987).

12. Tome Sazdov, *Macedonia,* vol. 468 (April 1992).

13. *National Encyclopaedia* (Belgrade: 1929).

14. Cited in Sazdov, *Macedonia.*

15. Traian Stoijanovich, "Macedonia," *Collier's Encyclopaedia,* p. 159.

16. Rossos, in *The Macedonian Tribune,* Feb. 19, 1994.

17. Stoianovich, op. cit. p. 159.

18. Blazhe Koneski, "Macedonian," in *The Slavic Literary Languages,* ed. by A. M. Schenker and E. Stankiewicz (New Haven: 1980), pp. 53–63; cited by Peter Hill in "Language Standardization in the South Slavonic Area," *Sociolinguistica* 6 (1992), pp. 108–150.

19. A. W. Gomme, *Greece* (London: Oxford University Press, 1945), p. 43.

20. Dimitrija Chupovski, "Macedonia and the Macedonians," *Makedonskij Golos,* 1913.

21. "Rules of the Macedonian Rebel Committee," *Macedonian Review* [Yugoslavia] 13, no. 2 (1983), pp. 159–176.

22. *The Times,* London, June 2, 1897.

23. Radis, *IMRO and the Macedonian Question.*

24. Koneski, "Macedonian," p. 59.

25. Stoijanovich, "Macedonia," p. 160.

26. Spiridon Blagoev, "The Foreign Press on the Terror and Violence in Macedonia Before the Ilinden Uprising" (1903), *Macedonian Review* [Yugoslavia] 14, no. 2 (1984), pp. 140–152.

27. Danforth, "Competing Claims."

28. Krste Misirkov, *On Macedonian Matters* (Skopje: Macedonian Review Editions, 1974), p. 73.

29. Chupovski, "Macedonia and the Macedonians."

30. Jusuf Hamza, "Relations of the Internal Macedonian Revolutionary Organization (IMRO) with the Turkish Population in Macedonia, 1893-1903," *Istorija* [Yugoslavia] 21, no. 2 (1985), pp. 119–130.

31. Duncan M. Perry, *The Politics of Terror: The Macedonian Liberation Movements 1893–1903* (Durham NC: Duke University Press, 1988), p. 38.

32. Cited in *The Macedonian Tribune,* Jan.-April 1994.

33. Cited in *The Macedonian Tribune,* Jan.-April 1994.

34. Peter Hill, "Language Standardization in the South Slavonic Area," *Sociolinguistica* 6 (June 1992), pp. 108–150.

35. Stoijanovich, "Macedonia," p. 160.

36. Todor Dobrijanov, "The Echo of Ilinden-Preobrazenie Uprising of 1903 in Great Britain, the United States and France, *Bulgarian Historical Review* [Bulgaria] 8, no. 3 (1980), pp. 78–88.

37. *Macedonia, History and Politics.*

38. Cited in *The Macedonian Tribune,* Jan.-April 1994.

39. Borislav Ivanoff, *The Macedonian Tribune,* January 1994.

40. Ivan Mihailoff, *Memoirs,* vols. 1 and 2.

41. Chupovski, "Macedonia and the Macedonians."

42. Chupovski, "Macedonia and the Macedonians."

43. George Finlay, *The History of Greece under Othoman and Venetian Domination* (Edinburgh and London: William Blackwood, 1854), p. 350–351.

44. Stoijanovich, "Macedonia," p. 160.

45. A. W. Gomme, *Greece,* pp. 30–31.

46. Done Ilievski, "The First Assembly of Macedonian Orthodox Clergy, 1943." *Macedonian Review* [Yugoslavia] 13, no. 3 (1983), pp. 304–310.

47. *"Relazioni Religiose,* An Interview with Dr. Dragoljub Zivojinovic," trans. by Slave Nikolovski-Katin, in *Makedonski,* no. 398, VI —1986.

48. *Macedonian Information and Liaison Service (MILS) News,* Skopje, November 8, 1993.

49. From an exclusive interview for the Macedonian Information Center (MIC), Skopje, Nov. 17, 1994.

50. *MILS News,* Skopje, June 24, 1994.

51. Henry R. Wilkinson, *Maps and Politics: A Review of the Ethnographic Cartography of Macedonia* (Liverpool: Liverpool University Press, 1951), pp. 299–300.

52. *Macedonia: History,* Microsoft Encarta, 1993.

53. *Delo,* Skopje, June 23, 1995.

54. Vladimir Kartov, "Treatment of the Macedonian Question in the Platform of the Yugoslav Communist Party, 1935-36," *Istorija* [Yugoslavia] 21, no. 2 (1985), pp. 189–200.

55. Strahil Gigov, "The Formation of the Macedonian Communist Party," *Istorija* [Yugoslavia] 19, no. 1 (1983), pp. 33–41.

56. Aleksandar Hristov, "The Anti-Fascist Council for the National Liberation of Macedonia and the Building of the Foundations on Which the Macedonian People Have Made a Common Life with the Yugoslav Peoples and Minorities in the Yugoslav Federation," *Istorija* [Yugoslavia] 20, no. 1 (1984), pp. 159–169.

57. Danforth, "Competing Claims."

58. MIC. Skopje, May 5, 1995.

59. *Delo,* Skopje, June 23, 1995.

60. Danforth, "Competing Claims."

61. Internet communication from 71334.3243@CompuServe.COM.

62. *MILS News,* Skopje, Oct. 26, 1993.

63. *RFE/RL Report* no. 215, Nov. 9, 1993.

64. MIC, Skopje, Nov, 14, 1994.

65. Evangelos Kofos, *Nationalism and Communism in Macedonia* (Thessaloniki: Institute for Balkan Studies, 1989), p. 262.

66. Danforth, "Competing Claims."

67. Mike Featherstone, ed., *Global Culture: Nationalism, Globalization, and Modernity* (London: Sage).

68. *The Macedonian Tribune,* 124 West Wayne, Fort Wayne, Indiana 46802, U.S.A. Telephone: (219) 422-5900; telefax: (219) 422-4379.

69. Basil C. Gounaris, "Emigration from Macedonia in the Early Twentieth Century," *Journal of Modern Greek Studies* 7, no. 1 (1989), pp. 133–153.

70. Virginia Nizamoff Surso, quoted in *The Macedonian Tribune,* February 1994.

71. by Royson James, March 28, 1994, p. A3.

72 *The Macedonian Canadian News,* P.O. Box 536, Mississauga, Ontario, L5M 2C1.

73. James, March 28, 1994.

74. B. A. Santamaria, "New Home Not Old Battleground," *The Australian,* March 19, 1994.

75. Quoted in *Weekend Australian,* March 12, 1994.

76. Cited by Frank Devine, "Take It from the Irish, Assimilate or Perish," *The Australian,* March 31, 1994.

77. Peter Hill, "Levelling the Levendis," *The Age,* Melbourne, April 20, 1994.

78. Jeremy Moon, *Making Macedonia* (Department of Political Science, University of Western Australia, March 1994).

79. *MILS News,* Skopje, Feb. 16, 1995.

Chapter 7

1. Loring M. Danforth, "Competing Claims to Macedonian Identity: The Macedonian Question and the Breakup of Yugoslavia," *Anthropology Today* 9, no. 4 (August 1993), pp. 3–10.

2. Peter Trudgill, *Sociolinguistics: An Introduction* (Harmondsworth, England: Penguin, 1974), p. 15.

3. Danforth, "Competing Claims."

4. Heinz Kloss, "Abstand-Languages and Ausbau-Languages," *Anthropological Linguistics* 9, no. 7 (1967), pp. 29–41.

5. Peter Hill, "The Role of Language in Nation Building in Europe."

6. Hill, "The Role of Language."

7. Nigel Harris, *National Liberation* (London and New York: Tauris), p. 5.

8. Eric J. Hobsbawn, *Nations and Nationalism since 1780: Programme, Myth, Reality* (Cambridge and New York, 1990).

9. Hill, "The Role of Language."

10. Douglas Johnson, "The Making of the French Nation," in *The National Question in Europe in the Historical Context*, ed. by M. Teich and R. Porter (Cambridge: Cambridge University Press, 1993), pp. 51–53.

11. Hill, "The Role of Language."

12. Hill, "The Role of Language."

13. George Finlay, *The History of Greece Under Othoman and Venetian Domination* (Edinburgh and London: William Blackwood, 1856), p. 350.

14. John Geipel, *The Europeans: An Ethnohistorical Survey* (London and Harlow: Longmans, Green, 1969), pp. 62–70.

15. D. Obolensky, *The Byzantine Empire and Its Northern Neighbors, 565–1018*, p. 497.

16. Traian Stoijanovich, "Macedonia," *Colliers Encyclopaedia.*

17. Jacques Bacic, electronic communication, Maklist.

18. Hill, "The Role of Language."

19. Dimitrija Chupovski, "Macedonia and the Macedonians," *Makedonskij Golos,* 1913.

20. Hill, "The Role of Language."

21. Hill, "The Role of Language."

22. Chupovski, "Macedonia and the Macedonians."

23. Obolensky, *The Byzantine Empire*, p. 501.

24. Robert Browning, "The Continuity of Hellenism in the Byzantine World: Appearance or Reality," in *Greece Old and New*, ed. by Tom Winnifrith and Penelope Murray (London: Macmillan, 1983).

25. Stojan Ristevski, *Sozdavanjeto na sovremeniot makedonski literaturen Jazik* (Skopje: Studentski zbor, 1988), p. 96.

26. Hill, "The Role of Language."

27. V. Zlatarski, "Kak sa pisali makadoncite predi 115 godini," *Makedonski pregled* 5, no. 1 (1929), pp. 117–120.

28. Hill, "The Role of Language."

29. Horace G. Lunt, "A Survey of Macedonian Literature," *Harvard Slavic Studies* 1 (1953), pp. 363–396.

30. *Macedonia* (1978), p. 137.

31. Blazhe Koneski, "Macedonian" in *The Slavic Literary Languages*, ed. by A. M. Schenker and E. Stankiewicz (New Haven: 1980), p. 62; Victor Friedman, "Macedon-

ian Language and Nationalism during the Nineteenth and Early Twentieth Centuries," *Balkanistica: Occasional Papers in Southeast European Studies* vol. 2, pp. 83–98.

32. Gane Todorovski, *Pretchodnicite na Misirkov* (Skopje: Misla, 1968), p. 143.

33. Kremena Bosilkova-Zotova, "Khristo Danov's Bookstore in Veles and the Work of the Bosilkov Brothers," *Istoricheski Pregled* [Bulgaria] vol. 48 (1992), pp. 116–130; abstract by L. L. Nelson.

34. Hill, "The Role of Language."

35. Friedman, "Macedonian Language"; Ristevski, *Sozdavanjeto*.

36. Friedman, "Macedonian Language," p. 87.

37. Ristevski, *Sozdavanjeto*.

38. Hill, "The Role of Language."

39. Koneski, "Macedonian," p. 58.

40. Friedman, "Macedonian Language," p. 90.

41. Blagoja Korubin, "K. P. Misirkov i prasanjeto za makedonskiot literaturen jazik vo negovo vreme," *Makedonski Jazik* 25 (1974), p. 23.

42. Ristevski, *Sozdavanjeto*, p. 74.

43. Blaze Ristovski, *Dimitrija Cupovski (1878–1940)* (Skopje: Kultura, 1978).

44. Krste P. Misirkov, *Za Makedonskite raboti* (Sofija: Pecatnitsa na "Liberalnija Klub," 1903); *Jubilejno izdanie po povod na stogodisninata od rag'anjeto na avtorot* (Skopje: 1974), p. 145.

45. Friedman, op. cit., p. 92.

46. Ristevski, op. cit, p. 66.

47. Koneski, "Macedonian," p. 62.

48. Stoyan Pribichevich, *Macedonia, Its People and History* (University Park: Pennsylvania State University Press, 1982), p. 246.

49. Horace G. Lunt, "The Creation of Standard Macedonian: Some Facts and Attitudes," *Anthropological Linguistics* 1, no. 5 (June 1959), p. 23.

50. *Makedonija* (Skopje), Dec. 1984, pp. 28–29; Risto Kirjazovski, *Povod* (Sydney) Jan. 1984, pp. 26–27.

51. Ristevski, *Sozdavanjeto*, p. 126.

52. Hill, "The Role of Language."

53. Henrik Birnbaum, "Language, Ethnicity and Nationalism: On the Linguistic Foundations of a United Yugoslavia," In *The Creation of Yugoslavia 1914–1918*, ed. by D. Dordevic (Oxford: S. Barbara, 1980). p. 173.

54. Hill, "The Role of Language."

55. Lunt, "Creation of Standard Macedonian," p. 23.

56. Lunt, "A Survey," pp. 372–373.

57. *Macedonian Information and Liaison Service (MILS) News*, Skopje, May 24, 1995.

58. Victor Friedman, "The Sociolinguistics of Literary Macedonian," *International Journal of the Sociology of Language* 52, *Yugoslavia in Sociolinguistic Perspective* (1985), p. 46.

59. V. Mechandzijski, *Nova Makedonija*, Aug. 3, 1990; and Jonce Josifovski, *Nova Makedonija*, Aug. 10, 1980.

60. Hill, "The Political Significance of the Macedonian Standard Language," *Australian Slavonic and East European Studies* 1, no. 1 (1987), p. 58.

61. Hill, "The Political Significance."

62. Peter Hill, "Language Standardization in the South Slavonic Area." *Sociolinguistica* 6 (June 1992).

63. Hill, "Language Standardization."

64. Hill, "Language Standardization."

Chapter 8

1. Macedonian Information Center (MIC), Skopje, November 15, 1994.

2. United States Department of State, *Annual Report on Human Rights: Macedonia* (1992-1995).

3. United States Department of State, *Annual Report on Human Rights: Macedonia* (1994).

4. United States Department of State, *Annual Report on Human Rights: Macedonia* (1994).

5. *Macedonian Information and Liaison Service (MILS) News*, Skopje, Oct. 26, 1993.

6. *The European*, March 4–10, 1994.

7. United States Department of State, *Annual Report on Human Rights: Macedonia* (1994).

8. United States Department of States, *Annual Report on Human Rights: Macedonia* (1994); *Annual Report on Human Rights: Macedonia* (1995).

9. United States Department of State, *Annual Report on Human Rights: Macedonia* (1994).

10. Mark H. Solsman, *World Fact Book* (Documentation Training and Publications, Center for Academic Computing, October 19, 1993).

11. Vince Beiser, "The Next Bosnia? Another Balkan Country Teeters on the Brink," *Maclean's*, Feb. 7, 1994.

12. Tanjug News Agency, Belgrade (in English), 1041 gmt, June 9, 1994.

13. *The Daily Telegraph*, London, June 17, 1994.

14. *The Financial Times*, London, April 6, 1994.

15. Dan De Luce, "Macedonia: Greek Embargo on Macedonia Fails to Halt Trade," *BBC Monitoring Service: Central Europe & Balkans*, June 28, 1994.

16. United Nations Commission on Human Rights, *Ninth Periodical Report on the Situation of Human Rights in the Former Yugoslav Republic of Macedonia*, submitted by Tadeusz Mazowiecki (Oct. 1994).

17. Yigal Chazan, "Impoverished Macedonia Flouts Sanctions on Serbs," *Guardian*, London, July 2, 1994.

18. *MILS News*, Skopje, Aug. 3, 1994.

19. Tanjug News Agency, Belgrade, Sep. 7, 1994.

20. "Economist Intelligence Unit News Analysis — Macedonia," April 17, 1995.

21. *Nova Makedonija*, Skopje, Sept. 27, 1994.

22. MIC, Skopje, June 15, 1995.

23. "Economist Intelligence Unit News Analysis — Macedonia," April 17, 1995.

24. Cited by MIC, Skopje, Oct. 3, 1994.

25. *Macedonia: Republic*, Microsoft Encarta, 1993.

26. United States Department of State, *Annual Report on Human Rights: Macedonia* (1994).

27. United States Department of State, *Annual Report on Human Rights: Macedonia* (1994).

28. Tanjug News Agency, Belgrade (in Serbo-Croat), 1416 gmt, July 5, 1994.

29. *MILS News*, Skopje, Feb. 15, 1995.

30. "Propaganda, as Part of the Special War Against Macedonia," *Review of the Macedonian Press: Macedonian Television* (Skopje: MIC, May 8, 1995).

31. MIC, Skopje, May 5, 1995.

32. *MILS News*, Skopje, Aug. 3, 1994.

33. *MILS News*, Skopje, May 5, 1995.

34. United States Department of State, *Annual Report on Human Rights: Macedonia* (1995).

35. United Nations Commission on Human Rights, *Ninth Periodical Report.*

36. *MILS News*, Skopje, Feb. 7, 1995.

37. United Nations Commission on Human Rights, *Ninth Periodical Report.*

38. *MILS News*, Skopje, May 5, 1995.

39. *MILS News*, Skopje, May 4, 1994.

40. *British Helsinki Human Rights Group Report: Macedonia* (1994).

41. United States Department of State, *Annual Report on Human Rights: Macedonia* (1994).

42. United States Department of State, *Annual Report on Human Rights: Macedonia* (1994).

43. *MILS News*, Skopje, June 20, 1994.

44. *MILS News*, Skopje, June 20, 1994.

45. Jolyon Naegle, "Macedonia-Albania Guns," Radio VOA Report no. 5-17050, May 11, 1994.

46. "Macedonia: Ethnic Albanians Sentenced to Jail for 'Hostile Activity,'" Tanjug News Agency, Belgrade, June 29, 1994.

47. "Land in Tetovo Area Continually Destroyed," *MILS News*, Skopje, Dec. 14, 1994.

48. MIC, Skopje, Dec. 29, 1994.

49. *MILS News*, Skopje, Feb. 21, 1995.

50. United States Department of State, *Annual Report on Human Rights: Macedonia* (1994).

51. *MILS News*, Skopje, Nov. 21, 1994.

52. *MILS News*, Skopje, Feb. 9, 1995.

53. *MILS News*, Skopje, Feb. 9, 1995.

54. United States Department of State, *Annual Report on Human Rights: Macedonia* (1994).

55. *MILS News*, Skopje, April 11, 1994.

56. *MILS News*, Skopje, April 11, 1994.

57. MIC, Skopje, Oct. 13, 1994.

58. United States Department of State, *Annual Report on Human Rights: Macedonia* (1994).

59. MIC, Skopje, June 29, 1995.

60. *Vecer*, Skopje, May 31, 1995.

61. MIC, Skopje, Sept. 5, 1994.

62. Tanjug News Agency, Belgrade, 1955 gmt, Sept. 11, 1994.

63. *MILS News*, Skopje, Feb. 28, 1995.

64. *MILS News*, Skopje, May 29, 1995.

65. *MILS News*, Skopje, June 13, 1995.

66. United States Department of State, *Annual Report on Human Rights: Macedonia* (1994).

67. Virginia Nizamoff Surso, "Search for Common Ground," *The Macedonian Tribune*, Dec. 1993.

68. *The Economist*, June 25, 1994.

69. *The Economist*, June 25, 1994.

70. MIC, Skopje, June 17, 1994.

71. MIC, Skopje, June 24, 1994.

72. Reuters, transmitted 14:56, June 21, 1994.

73. *MILS News*, Skopje, Aug. 15, 1994.

74. United States Department of State, *Annual Report on Human Rights: Macedonia* (1995).

75. MILS News. Skopje, 16th June, 1994.

76. *MILS News*, Skopje, June 16, 1994.

77. Ismije Beshiri, "Albanians in Macedonia Criticize Census," RFE/RL report no. 111, June 14, 1994.

78. Tanjug News Agency, Belgrade, 0918 gmt, June 29, 1994.

79. MIC, Skopje, Nov. 15, 1994.

80. "Public Opinion and the European Union 16 Countries' Survey," no. 4, March 1994; cited in *MILS News*, April 21, 1994.

81. Fabian Schmidt, RFE/RL report no. 186, Sept. 29, 1994.

82. Jolyon Naegle, "Macedonina/Albanians," Radio VOA report no. 5-17095, May 16, 1994.

83. *MILS News*, Skopje, Aug. 15, 1994.

84. *MILS News*, Skopje, Feb. 14, 1995.

85. *Nova Makedonija*, Aug. 11, 1994.

86. *MILS News*, Skopje, Feb. 13, 1995.

87. *MILS News*, Skopje, Feb. 13, 1995.

88. *MILS News*, Skopje, Feb. 13, 1995.

89. *MILS News*, Skopje, March 4, 1994.

90. *Vecer*, Feb. 5-6, 1994.

91. Misa Gleni, "Time Passes for Balkan Powder Keg," *The Times*, London, April 7, 1994; cited by MIC, Skopje, April 8, 1994.

92. *Rilindja*, Sept. 23, 1994.

93. Fabian Schmidt, RFE/RL report no. 186, Sept. 29, 1994.

94. "MILS Special Supplement: Political Parties in Macedonia. The Democratic Party of Serbs in Macedonia," *MILS News*, June 24, 1994.

95. "What Boro Wants to Hear from Vlado?" *Review of the Macedonian Press: PULS* (Skopje, MIC, May 13, 1994).

96. "MILS Special Supplement: Political Parties in Macedonia. The Democratic Party of Serbs in Macedonia," *MILS News*, June 24, 1994.

97. *MILS News*, Skopje, June 21, 1994.

98. "MILS Special Feature: Lesson on Behavior," *MILS News*, Skopje, Oct. 27, 1993.

99. "MILS Special Supplement: Political Parties in Macedonia. VMRO-DPMNE — Part I," *MILS News*, Skopje, June 20, 1994.

100. Fabian Schmidt, RFE/RL report no. 180, Sept. 21, 1994.

101. "Macedonia: Ruling Coalition to Present United Front at Parliamentary Elections," *BBC Monitoring Service: Central Europe & Balkans,* From Tanjug News Agency, Belgrade, 1821 gmt, Sept. 17, 1994.

102. MIC, Skopje, Sept. 19, 1994.

103. "Economist Intelligence Unit News Analysis: Macedonia," September 20, 1994.

104. *The European*, March 4–10, 1994.

105. *Puls*, Skopje, Sept. 9, 1994.

106. *Puls*, Skoopje, Sept. 9, 1994.

107. *MILS News*, Skopje, Sept. 30, 1994.

108. *MILS News*, Sept. 16, 1994.

109. *MILS News*, Skopje, Oct. 17, 1994.

110. MIC, Skopje, Oct. 17, 1994.

111. MIC, Skopje, Oct. 19, 1994.

112. MIC, Skopje, Oct. 19, 1994.
113. MIC, Skopje, Oct. 18, 1994.
114. MIC, Skopje, Oct. 19, 1994.
115. *MILS News*, Skopje, Oct. 19, 1994.
116. MIC, Skopje, Oct. 19, 1994.
117. *MILS News*, Skopje, Oct. 20, 1994.
118. *MILS News*, Oct. 20, 1994.
119. MIC, Skopje, Oct. 20, 1994.
120. MIC, Skopje, Oct. 20, 1994.
121. MILS News. Skopje, 21 October, 1994.
122. *MILS News*, Skopje, Oct. 21, 1994.
123. *MILS News*, Skopje, Oct. 24, 1994.
124. *MILS News*, Skopje, Oct. 25, 1994.
125. *MILS News*, Skopje, Oct. 25, 1994.
126. MIC, Skopje, Oct. 25, 1994.
127. MIC, Skopje, Dec. 28, 1994.
128. "Electoral Commission News Conference," *MILS News*, Skopje, Nov. 1, 1994.
129. *MILS News*, Skopje, Nov. 1, 1994.
130. *MILS News*, Skopje, Nov. 11, 1994.
131. *MILS News*, Skopje, Nov. 1, 1994.
132. "Special Supplement: Gligorov's Platform for the Future (Part 1)," *MILS News*, Skopje, Nov. 21, 1994.
133. Special Supplement: Gligorov's Platform for the Future (Part 2)," *MILS News*, Skopje, Nov. 22, 1994.
134. *Nova Makedonija*, Jan. 6, 1995.
135. *Delo*, June 23, 1995.
136. *MILS News*, Skopje, Nov. 3, 1994.
137. *MILS News*, Skopje, Dec. 14, 1994.
138. *MILS News*, Skopje, Dec. 15, 1994.
139. *MILS News*, Skopje, Dec. 15, 1994.
140. MIC, Skopje, Dec. 19, 1994.
141. MIC, Skopje, Feb. 28, 1995.
142. *MILS News*, Skopje, Dec. 29, 1994.
143. *MILS News*, Skopje, Jan. 16, 1995.
144. *MILS News*, Skopje, Jan. 5, 1995.
145. MIC, Skopje, Feb. 17, 1995.
146. *MILS News*, Skopje, Feb. 22, 1995.
147. *MILS News*, Skopje, Feb. 14, 1995.
148. *Flaka*, Feb. 14, 1995.
149. *MILS News*, Skopje, Feb. 16, 1995.
150. *MILS News*, Skopje, Feb. 16, 1995.
151. *MILS News*, Feb. 16, 1995.
152. *MILS News*, Skopje, Feb. 16, 1995.
153. MIC, Skopje, Feb. 16, 1995.
154. MIC, Skopje, Feb. 17, 1995.
155. *MILS News*, Skopje, Feb. 20, 1995.
156. *MIC Update*, Skopje, Feb. 17, 1995.
157. *MIC Update*, Skopje, Feb. 17, 1995.
158. MIC, Skopje, Feb. 19, 1995.
159. *Nova Makedonija*, Skopje, Feb. 16, 1995.
160. MIC, Skopje, Feb. 19, 1995.

161. MIC, Skopje, Feb. 19, 1995.

162. *Nova Makedonija*, Skopje, Feb. 20, 1995.

163. *MILS News Special Edition*, Skopje, Feb. 18, 1995.

164. *MILS News Special Edition*, Skopje, Feb. 18, 1995.

165. MILS *News Special Edition*, Skopje, Feb. 18, 1995.

166. MILS *News Special Edition*, Skopje, Feb. 18, 1995.

167. *MILS News Special Edition*, Skopje, Feb. 18, 1995.

168. MIC, Skopje, Feb. 20, 1995.

169. *The Macedonian Times*, Jan. 28, 1995.

170. MIC, Skopje, Feb. 24, 1995.

171. MIC, Skopje, Feb. 20, 1995.

172. *MILS News*, Skopje, Feb. 23, 1995.

173. *MILS News*, Skopje, Feb. 24, 1995.

174. *MILS News*, Skopje, Feb. 21, 1995.

175. *MILS News*, Skopje, Feb. 23, 1995.

176. *MILS News*, Skopje, Feb. 23, 1995.

177. MIC, Skopje, Feb. 19, 1995.

178. *Nova Makedonija*, Skopje, Feb. 20, 1995.

179. *Nova Makedonija*, Skopje, Feb. 20, 1995.

180. *MILS News*, Skopje, Feb. 21, 1995.

181. *MILS News*, Skopje, Feb. 21, 1995.

182. "MILS Special Supplement: Opposition Views on University in Tetovo," *MILS News*, Skopje, Feb. 24, 1995.

183. *MILS News*, Skopje, Feb. 27, 1995.

184. *MILS News*, Skopje, Feb. 28, 1995.

185. "MILS Special Supplement: Opposition Views on University in Tetovo," *MILS News*, Skopje, Feb. 24, 1995.

186. "MILS Special Supplement: Opposition Views on University in Tetovo," *MILS News*, Skopje, Feb. 24, 1995.

187. *MILS News*, Skopje, Feb. 22, 1995.

188. MIC, Skopje, Feb. 22, 1995.

189. *MILS News*, Skopje, Feb. 23, 1995.

190. *MILS News*, Skopje, Feb. 24, 1995.

191. *MILS News*, Skopje, Feb. 21, 1995.

192. *Nova Makedonija*, Skopje, Feb. 28, 1995.

193. *MILS News*, Skopje, May 11, 1995.

194. *MILS News*, Skopje, May 22, 1995.

195. *Review of the Macedonian Press* (Skopje: MIC, Feb. 20, 1995).

196. *MILS News*, Feb. 21, 1995.

197. *MILS News*, Skopje, Feb. 22, 1995.

198. *MILS News*, Skopje, April 27, 1995.

199. *MILS News*, Skopje, May 4, 1995.

200. *MILS News*, Skopje, May 25, 1995.

201. *MILS News*, Skopje, May 25, 1995.

202. *MILS News*, Skopje, May 25, 1995.

203. MIC, Skopje, Oct. 18, 1995.

204. MIC, Skopje, June 12, 1995.

205. MIC, Skopje, June 12, 1995.

206. MIC, Skopje, June 12, 1995.

207. MIC, Skopje, June 12, 1995.

208. *Vecer*, Skopje, Sept. 11, 1995.

209. *Nova Makedonija*, Skopje, May 7-8, 1995.
210. *Puls*, June 23, 1995.
211. James Pettifer, *The Wall Street Journal*, Feb. 4, 1995.

Chapter 9

1. *Macedonian Information and Liaison Service (MILS) News*, Skopje, Nov. 8, 1993.
2. *The Financial Times*, London, Dec. 22, 1993.
3. Macedonian Information Center (MIC), Skopje, May 8, 1995.
4. MIC, Skopje, Feb. 16, 1994.
5. MIC, Skopje, Dec. 30, 1993.
6. Fabian Schmidt, RFE/RL report no. 8, Jan. 13, 1994.
7. MIC, Skopje, Jan. 20, 1994.
8. *The Economist*. London, Jan. 29, 1994.
9. Kjell Engelbrekt, RFE/RL report. no. 16, Jan. 25, 1994.
10. *Puls*, Skopje, Sept. 22, 1995.
11. Janusz Bugajski and David Augustyn, "Greek Nationalism Gains Ground," *Greece: New Power in the Balkans*, in *The World & I* (Washington, DC: Washington Times, Jan. 1994).
12. William N. Dunn, "Macedonia: Europe's Finger in the Dike," *The Christian Science Monitor*, May 9, 1994, p. 19.
13. MIC, Skopje, Dec. 12, 1994.
14. *Strategic Forum*, no. 9 (Oct. 1994).
15. *MAK-NEWS*, Skopje, June 26, 1994.
16. *MILS News*, Skopje, Oct. 26, 1993.
17. MIC, Skopje, Dec. 30, 1993.
18. *MILS News*, Skopje, Nov. 8, 1993.
19. MIC, Skopje, Feb. 16, 1994.
20. Lou Panov, "Greece Shuts Door on Trade, Travel to Punish Macedonia," *Macedonian Tribune*, March 1994.
21. MIC, Skopje, Feb. 16, 1994.
22. *MILS News*, Skopje, Feb. 16, 1994.
23. MIC, Skopje, March 10, 1994.
24. *MILS News*, Skopje, April 8, 1994.
25. MIC, Skopje, Feb. 24, 1994.
26. Panov, "Greece Shuts Door," *Macedonian Tribune*, March 1994.
27. Kjell Engelbrekt, RFE/RL report no. 37, Feb. 23, 1994.
28. *Macedonian Tribune*, April 1994.
29. MIC, Skopje, April 15, 1994.
30. *MILS News*, Skopje, April 21, 1994.
31. Jolyon Naegele, Voice of America, no. 5 16799, April 27, 1994.
32. *MILS News*, Skopje, June 20, 1994.
33. *MILS News*, Skopje, April 8, 1994.
34. *MILS News*, Skopje, Nov. 9, 1994.
35. *Strategic Forum*, no. 9 (October 1994).
36. MIC, Skopje, Jan. 31, 1995.
37. *The Financial Times*, London, Dec. 22, 1993.
38. Robert Marquand, "Greece Wants to Be European," *The Christian Science Monitor*, Feb. 9, 1994.

39. MIC, Skopje, Feb. 21, 1994.

40. MIC, Skopje, Feb. 28, 1994.

41. *Macedonian Tribune*, April 1994.

42. RFL/RE report no. 42, March 2, 1994.

43. William D. Montalbano, *Los Angeles Times*, March 4, 1994.

44. MIC, Skopje, April 7, 1994.

45. MIC, Skopje, April 18, 1994.

46. MIC, Skopje, June 29, 1995.

47. MIC, Skopje, June 29, 1995.

48. Agence Europe, Luxembourg, June 29, 1994.

49. Christopher Lockwood, "EC Backs Off as Macedonia Feels Squeeze." *The Sunday Telegraph*, London, July 3, 1994.

50. *Reuters*, June 30, 1994.

51. MIC, Skopje, June 30, 1994.

52. MIC, Skopje, June 30, 1994.

53. MIC, Skopje, Feb. 23, 1994.

54. MIC, Skopje, May 13, 1994.

55. RFE/RL report no. 247, Dec. 28, 1993.

56. *MILS News*, Skopje, Feb. 23, 1994.

57. Boris Johnson and Paul Anast, *The Daily Telegraph*, London, Feb. 19, 1994.

58. *The Macedonian Tribune*. April 1994.

59. *MILS News*, Skopje, Aug. 15, 1994.

60. MIC, Skopje, May 27, 1994.

61. MIC, Skopje, March 11, 1994.

62. *MILS News*, Skopje, Aug. 5, 1994.

63. *MILS News*, Skopje, May 22, 1995.

64. MIC, Skopje, Feb. 15, 1995.

65. *MILS News*, Feb. 23, 1994.

66. MIC, Skopje, Feb. 15, 1995.

67. *MILS News*, Skopje, Feb. 23, 1994.

68. MIC, Skopje, Feb. 24, 1994.

69. MIC, Skopje, Nov. 10, 1994.

70. MIC, Skopje, Feb. 21, 1994.

71. *The Macedonian Tribune*, April 1994.

72. *MILS News*, Skopje, July 11, 1994.

73. *MILS News*, Sept. 20, 1994.

74. Ivan A. Lebamoff, editorial, *The Macedonian Tribune*, Sept.-Oct. 1993.

75. MIC, Skopje, May 22, 1995.

76. *MILS News*, Skopje, June 9, 1995.

77. *The Spectator*, London, April 9, 1994.

78. The *Economist*, London, Feb. 26, 1994.

79. The *Guardian*, London, April 10, 1994.

80. The *New York Times*, March 8, 1994.

81. The *New York Times*, April 5, 1992.

82. *The Christian Science Monitor*, April 15, 1994.

83. *The Chicago Tribune*, April 14, 1995.

84. Dunn, "Macedonia: Europe's Finger in the Dike."

85. *The Australian*, March 28, 1994.

86. Cited by *The Macedonian Tribune*, April 1994.

87. Cited by *The Macedonian Tribune*, April 1994.

88. MIC, Skopje, Feb. 23, 1994.

89. Cited by MIC, Skopje, April 8, 1994.

90. *MILS News*, Skopje, Jan. 21, 1994.

91. *MILS News*, Skopje, March 4, 1994.

92. *MILS News*, Skopje, May 13, 1994.

93. MIC, Skopje, June 15, 1994.

94. MIC, Skopje, April 25, 1994.

95. MIC, Skopje, May 27, 1994.

96. Peter Ellingsen, "Greece: Greece Weighing the Cost of a Tough Line on the Republic," *BBC Monitoring Service: Central Europe and Balkans*, June 28, 1994.

97. Translated by *MILS News*, Skopje, Aug. 5, 1994.

98. *MILS News*, Skopje, Aug. 20, 1994.

99. *MILS News*, Skopje, Nov. 3, 1994.

100. *MILS News*, Skopje, Nov. 16, 1994.

101. MIC, Skopje, Dec. 14, 1994.

102. MIC, Skopje, Dec. 20, 1994.

103. MIC, Skopje, Jan. 9, 1995.

104. MIC, Skopje, Jan. 19, 1995.

105. *MILS News*, Skopje, Jan. 23, 1995.

106. MIC, Skopje, Jan. 24, 1995.

107. *MILS News*, Skopje, March 20, 1995.

108. MIC, Skopje, April 21, 1995.

109. *MILS News*, Skopje, July 11, 1994.

110. *MILS News*, Skopje, Aug. 3, 1994.

111. MIC, Skopje, Jan. 10, 1995.

112. *MILS News*, Skopje, Sept. 7, 1995.

113. *MILS News*, Skopje, Sept. 11, 1995.

114. MIC, Skopje, Sept. 4, 1995.

115. MIC, Skopje, Sept. 15, 1995.

116. *MILS News*, Skopje, Sept. 21, 1995.

117. MIC, Skopje, Oct. 13, 1995.

118. *MILS News*, Skopje, Sept. 18, 1995.

119. *MILS News*, Skopje, Sept. 20, 1995.

120. *MILS News*, Skopje, Sept. 26, 1995.

121. *MILS News*, Skopje, Oct. 5, 1995.

122. *MILS News*, Skopje, Sept. 14, 1995.

123. *MILS News*, Skopje, Sept. 13, 1995.

124. *MILS News*, Skopje, Oct. 6, 1995.

125. *MILS News*, Skopje, Oct. 6, 1995.

126. MIC, Skopje, Oct. 10, 1995.

127. *MILS News*, Skopje, Oct. 13, 1995.

128. MIC, Skopje, Oct. 26, 1995.

129. *MILS News*, Skopje, Oct. 30, 1995.

Chapter 10

1. *Macedonian Information Center* (MIC), Skopje, April 15, 1994.

2. *Strategic Forum*, no. 9 (Oct. 1994).

3. Jolyon Naegele, report no. 5-16811, Radio Voice of America, April 28, 1994.

4. *Macedonian Information Liaison Service (MILS) News*, Skopje, July 11, 1994.

5. MILS News, Skopje, 30th October, 1995.

6. MIC, Skopje, Dec. 4, 1995.

7. *Nova Makedonija*, Skopje, Dec. 8, 1995.

8. *MILS News*, Skopje, Nov. 8, 1993.

9. *Nova Makedonija*, Skopje, Sept. 27, 1994.

10. *The Times*, London, April 6, 1994.

11. *The Daily Telegraph*, Feb. 19, 1994.

12. *Strategic Forum*, no. 9 (Oct. 9, 1994).

13. Shkelzen Maliqi, "An Independent Kosovo—A Stable Macedonia," *Rilindja*, Tirana, Aug, 18, 1994.

14. *The Macedonian Tribune*, Jan. 1994.

15. *MILS News*, Skopje, Feb. 1, 1994.

16. Milorad Roganovic, Radio Serbia, Belgrade, July 2, 1994.

17. *Vecernje Novosti*, Belgrade, June 28, 1994.

18. *Tanjug* News Agency, Belgrade, March 29, 1994.

19. *Tanjug* News Agency, Belgrade, March 27, 1994.

20. *MILS News*, Skopje, Nov. 8, 1993.

21. MIC, Skopje, May 31, 1995.

22. *Strategic Forum*, no. 9 (Oct. 1994).

23. *Rilindja*, Tirana, Jan. 7, 1994.

24. United States Department of State "Consular Information Sheet: Serbia & Montenegro," April 29, 1994.

25. *MILS News*, Skopje, May 23, 1995.

26. *Politika*, Belgrade, Jan. 21, 1994.

27. Maliqi, "An Independent Kosovo."

28. Maliqi, "An Independent Kosovo."

29. Maliqi, "An Independent Kosovo."

30. *Strategic Forum*, no. 9 (Oct. 1994).

31. *Strategic Forum*, no. 9 (Oct. 1994).

32. *Telegraf*, Belgrade, Aug. 30, 1995.

33. *Strategic Forum*, no. 9 (Oct. 1994).

34. *Strategic Forum*, no. 9 (Oct. 1994).

35. *Strategic Forum*, no. 9 (Oct. 1994).

36. Sherry Ricchiardi, *The St. Louis Post-Dispatch*, Nov. 8, 1993.

37. Maliqi, "An Independent Kosovo."

38. *Strategic Forum*, no. 9 (Oct. 1994).

39. Agence Europe, Luxembourge, July 1, 1994.

40. *Strategic Forum*, no. 9 (Oct. 1994).

41. *Nova Makedonija*, Skopje, Sept. 6, 1994.

42. *MILS News*, Skopje, June 20, 1994.

43. *The Macedonian Tribune*, Jan. 1994.

44. *Puls*, Skopje, Oct. 29, 1993.

45. *Puls*, Skopje, Sept. 1, 1994.

46. *Puls*, Skopje, Sept. 1, 1994.

47. *Puls*, Skopje, Sept. 16, 1994.

48. *Nova Makedonija*, Skopje, Sept. 6, 1994.

49. *Puls*, Skopje, Sept. 1, 1994.

50. MIC, Skopje, June 27, 1994.

51. *BBC Monitoring Service: Central Europe & Balkans*, May 23, 1994.

52. "Citizens in a Grey-Olive Uniform," *Puls*, Skopje, May 27, 1994.

53. *MILS News*, Skopje, Dec. 22, 1994.

54. *Tanjug News* Agency, Belgrade, March 29, 1994.

55. MIC, Skopje, Nov. 9, 1993.

56. *Puls*, "Citizens in a Grey-Olive Uniform," *Puls*.

57. MILS *News*. Skopje, 6th February, 1995.

58. Kjell Engelbrecht, RFE/RL report no. 105, June 6, 1994.

59. Sherry Ricchiardi, *The St. Louis Post-Dispatch*, Nov. 8, 1993.

60. Sherry Ricchiardi, *The St. Louis Post-Dispatch*, Nov. 8, 1993.

61. Mirka Velinovska, "Balkan Spindle," *Puls*, Jan. 21, 1994.

62. Duncan Perry, RFE/RL report no. 222, Nov. 19, 1993.

63. Duncan Perry, RFE/RL report no. 223, Nov. 22, 1993.

64. MIC, Skopje, April 4, 1994.

65. MIC, Skopje, April 7, 1994.

66. *MILS News*, Skopje, June 16, 1994.

67. *Vecernje Novosti* , Belgrade, cited by *MILS News*, Skopje, 30th May, 1994.

68. *The Times*, London, May 30, 1994.

69. Mircela Casule, "Macedonia Accuses Belgrade of Border Violations," *Reuters*, Skopje, May 30, 1994.

70. *MILS News*, Skopje, June 20, 1994.

71. *MILS News*, Skopje, June 1, 1994.

72. *MILS News*, Skopje, June 14, 1994.

73. MIC, Skopje, June 17, 1994.

74. *Reuters*, Zagreb, June 29, 1994.

75. Duncan Perry, RFE/RL report no. 112, June 15, 1994.

76. MIC, Skopje, June 17, 1994.

77. *MILS News*, Skopje, June 20, 1994.

78. *MILS News*, Skopje, June 20, 1994.

79. *Vecernje Novosti*, Belgrade; cited by *MILS News*, Skopje, May 30, 1994.

80. *MILS News*, Skopje, June 27, 1994.

81. *Vecernje Novosti*, Belgrade; cited by *MILS News*, Skopje, May 30, 1994.

82. Dan De Luce, "Macedonia: U.N. Says Serbs Violate Macedonian Border," *The Age*, Melbourne, June 26, 1994.

83. *Nova Makedonija*, Skopje, May 30, 1994.

84. *The Economist*, London, June 25, 1994.

85. *Reuters*, Zagreb, June 29, 1994.

86. *MILS News*, Skopje, June 27, 1994.

87. *Reuters*, Skopje, July 4, 1994.

88. *Tanjug* News Agency, Belgrade, July 1, 1994.

89. MIC, Skopje, Sept. 5, 1994.

90. MIC, Skopje, Sept. 5, 1994.

91. *MILS News*, Skopje, Sept. 14, 1994.

92. *Nova Makedonija*, Skopje, Sept. 27, 1994.

93. "Priests First; Guns to Follow," *Monitor*, Podgorica, Sept. 5, 1994.

94. MIC, Skopje, June 15, 1994.

95. *MILS News*, Skopje, Nov. 8, 1993.

96. MIC, Skopje, June 15, 1994.

97. *MILS News*, Skopje, June 6, 1994.

98. Lou Panov, *The Macedonian Tribune*, April 1994.

99. "Citizens in a Grey-Olive Uniform," *Puls*.

100. MIC, Skopje, Nov. 9, 1993.

101. *MILS News*, Skopje, May 22, 1995.

102. *Puls*, Skopje, Sept. 1, 1994.

103. *MILS News*, Skopje, Sept. 6, 1994.

104. *MILS News*, Skopje, Dec. 8, 1994.

105. Janusz Bugajski and David Augustyn, "Greek Nationalism Gains Ground," *Greece: New Power in the Balkans*, in *The World & I* (Washington DC: Washington Times, Jan. 1994).

106. *The Macedonian Times*, Nov. 30, 1994.

107. Bugajski and Augustyn, "Greek Nationalism Gains Ground."

108. Janusz Bugajski is associate director of East European studies and David Augustyn is a policy analyst in East European affairs at the Center for Strategic and International Studies in Washington, D.C.

109. Bugajski and Augustyn, "Greek Nationalism Gains Ground."

110. Janusz Bugajski, speech to the Macedonian World Congress, Seventy-second Annual Convention, reported in the *Macedonian Tribune*, Jan. 1994.

111. MIC, Skopje, April 7, 1994.

112. *MILS News*, Skopje, Feb. 27, 1995.

113. Helena Smith, "Life on Greece's Border Is Not a Bowl of Cherries," *The Guardian*, London, June 6, 1994.

114. "Greece v. Albania," *The Economist*, London, Sept. 17, 1994.

115. *Greece in the NATO and the EC, and the Relations of Greece with Its Neighbours*, (Istanbul: International Affairs Agency, 1993).

116. "Greece v. Albania," *The Economist*.

117. "Fatal Political Overture," *Puls*, Skopje, April 15, 1994.

118. "Greece v. Albania," *The Economist*.

119. *MILS News*, Skopje, April 21, 1994.

120. Duncan Perry, RFE/RL report, April 21, 1994.

121. *Reuters* Limited, Tirana, June 1, 1994.

122. *Reuters* Limited, Tirana, June 1, 1994.

123. *MILS News*, Skopje, Aug. 18, 1994.

124. "Greece v. Albania," *Economist*.

125. *BBC Monitoring Service: Central Europe & Balkans*, Radio Tirana, foreign service, 1800 GMT, Sept. 19, 1994.

126. *MILS News*, Skopje, March 6, 1995.

127. *Strategic Forum*, no. 9 (Oct. 1994).

128. *MILS News*, Skopje, March 6, 1995.

129. *Strategic Forum*, no. 9 (Oct. 1994).

130. *MILS News*, Skopje, Sept. 6, 1994.

131. MIC, Skopje, April 29, 1994.

132. *MILS News*, Skopje, May 20, 1994.

133. *The Guardian*, London, May 30, 1994.

134. Cited in *MILS News*, Skopje, May 31, 1994.

135. *Puls*, Skopje, Sept. 1, 1994.

136. *Tanjug* News Agency, Belgrade, June 28, 1994.

137. *MILS News*, Skopje, June 6, 1994.

138. *MILS News*, Skopje, Aug. 20, 1994.

139. *MILS News*, Skopje, 6th October, 1994.

140. *MILS News*, Skopje, Jan. 23, 1995.

141. *MILS News*, Skopje, Feb. 22, 1995.

142. *MILS News*, Skopje, Feb. 23, 1995.

143. *Nova Makedonija*, Skopje, March 5, 1995.

144. *MILS News*, Skopje, March 6, 1995.

145. *Nova Makedonija*, Skopje, Sept. 6, 1994.

146. *The Macedonian Tribune*, April 1994.

147. MIC, Skopje, Feb. 21, 1994.

148. MIC, Skopje, May 27, 1994.

149. *MILS News*, Skopje, May 13, 1994.

150. Radio Bulgaria, Sofia, May 24, 1994.

151. *MILS News*, Skopje, Sept. 19, 1994.

152. *MILS News*, Skopje, May 31, 1994.

153. *MILS News*, Skopje, Dec. 8, 1994.

154. *MILS News*, Skopje, June 6, 1994.

155. *MILS News*, Skopje, Sept. 19, 1994.

156. *MILS News*, Skopje, Dec. 15, 1994.

157. Janusz Bugajski and David Augustyn, "Greek Nationalism Gains Ground."

158. Kjell Engelbrecht, "Greek Parliament Supports Relentless Attitude Toward Macedonia," RFE/RL report no. 16, Jan. 25, 1994.

159. *Nova Makedonija*, Skopje, May 18, 1995.

160. *Relazioni Religiose*, trans. by Slave Nikolovski-Katin, in *Makedonski*, No. 398, VI —1986.

161. MIC, Skopje, May 13, 1994.

162. *MILS News*, Skopje, April 8, 1994.

163. *MILS News*, Skopje, June 20, 1994.

164. *MILS News*, Skopje, April 8, 1994.

165. Stefan Velev, RFE/RL report no. 215, Nov. 9, 1993.

166. Stefan Velev, RFE/RL report no. 215, Nov. 9, 1993.

167. *MILS News*, Skopje, Jan. 21, 1994.

168. MIC, Skopje, April 15, 1994.

169. *MILS News*, Skopje, April 26, 1994.

170. *BTA News* Agency, Sofia, April 26, 1994.

171. *BTA News* Agency, Sofia, April 27, 1994.

172. *MILS News*, Skopje, May 9, 1994.

173. *MILS News*, Skopje, May 9, 1994.

174. Lili Todorova, *BTA News* Agency, Sofia, July 15, 1994.

175. MIC, Skopje, Oct. 25, 1994.

176. *MILS News*, Skopje, June 19, 1995.

177. *MILS News*, Skopje, Sept. 25, 1995.

178. *MILS News*, Skopje, Jan. 26, 1995.

179. Carol Williams, "Bound by 'the Call of Blood,'" *The Los Angeles Times*, Feb. 2, 1994, p. 1.

180. *MILS News*, Skopje, Sept. 6, 1994.

181. MIC, Skopje, Nov. 9, 1993.

182. *Tanjug* News Agency, Belgrade, June 20, 1994.

183. *MILS News*, Skopje, June 6, 1994.

184. MIC, Skopje, Aug. 3, 1994.

185. *MILS News*, Skopje, Aug. 5, 1994.

186. *MILS News*, Skopje, Aug. 8, 1994.

187. *MILS News*, Skopje, Aug. 8, 1994.

188. MIC, Skopje, Oct. 3, 1994.

189. *MILS News*, Skopje, Nov. 11, 1994.

190. *MILS News*, Skopje, July 13, 1995.

191. MIC, Skopje, Nov. 9, 1993.

192. *MILS News*, Skopje, Feb. 10, 1994.

193. *MILS News*, Skopje, Feb. 10, 1994.

194. Jim Hoagland, *The Washington Post*, March 30, 1994.

195. Hanna Rosin, "Greek Pique," *The New Republic*, June 13, 1994, pp. 11-12.

196. Jim Hoagland, *The Washington Post*, March 30, 1994.

197. *The New York Times*, April 19, 1994.

198. Michael Radu, "Trouble Looms in Macedonia: Potential for Greek Mischief Greater Than Ever," *Insight*, Jan. 17, 1994.

199. William N. Dunn, "Macedonia: Europe's Finger in the Dike," *The Christian Science Monitor*, Monday, May 9, 1994, p. 19.

200. Dunn, "Macedonia: Europe's Finger in the Dike."

201. Martin Walker, "USA: Mad as Hell Over What They've Done to America," *Guardian*, London, June 25, 1994.

202. *Reuters*, "Spain: Baker Calls for U.S. Leadership in Europe," July 4, 1994.

203. Action Council for Peace in the Balkans, press release, May 20, 1994.

204. *MILS News*, Skopje, May 21, 1994.

205. *MILS News*, Skopje, Aug. 5, 1994.

206. MIC, Skopje, Oct. 5, 1994.

207. MIC, Skopje, Jan. 16, 1995.

208. *The Washington Times*, April 4, 1995.

209. MIC, Skopje, Jan. 13, 1994.

210. MIC, Skopje, March 3, 1994.

211. MIC, Skopje, March 10, 1994.

212. *MILS News*, Skopje, April 13, 1994.

213. MIC, Skopje, April 25, 1994.

214. *MILS News*, Skopje, May 20, 1994.

215. *MILS News*, Skopje, July 20, 1994.

216. *MILS News*, Skopje, June 27, 1994.

217. *MILS News*, Skopje, Aug. 15, 1994.

218. MIC, Skopje, Sept. 7, 1994.

219. *MILS News*, Skopje, Sept. 22, 1994.

220. MIC, Skopje, Sept. 28, 1994.

221. MIC, Skopje, Oct. 10, 1994.

222. *Strategic Forum*, no. 9 (Oct. 1994).

223. MIC, Skopje, Oct. 21, 1994.

224. *MILS News*, Skopje, Oct. 27, 1994.

225. *The Macedonian Times*, Nov. 30, 1994.

226. *Puls*, Skopje, Dec. 2, 1994.

227. MIC, Skopje, Dec. 8, 1994.

228. MIC, Skopje, Dec. 27, 1994.

229. MIC, Skopje, Feb. 15, 1995.

230. *MILS News*, Skopje, Jan. 6, 1995.

231. *MILS News*, Skopje, Feb. 6, 1995.

232. MIC, Skopje, June 12, 1995.

233. *MILS News*, Skopje, May 17, 1995.

234. MIC, Skopje, June 30, 1995.

235. *Puls*, May 26, 1995.

236. MIC, Skopje, June 19, 1995.

237. MIC, Skopje, Oct. 16, 1995.

238. MIC, Skopje, Oct. 3, 1995.

239. ANA, Athens, Oct. 4, 1995.

240. *MILS News*, Skopje, Oct. 27, 1995.

241. *Puls*, Skopje, Oct. 27, 1995.

Index